Human Rights of Women

P9-BZM-000

University of Pennsylvania Press
Pennsylvania Studies in Human Rights
Edited by Bert B. Lockwood

A complete listing of the books in this series
appears at the back of this volume

Human Rights of Women

National and International Perspectives

edited by Rebecca J. Cook

University of Pennsylvania Press

Philadelphia

Publication of this volume was assisted by a grant from the Ford Foundation.

Several of the chapters in this volume were presented in earlier forms as papers at the Consultation on Women's International Human Rights Law, held at the University of Toronto in September 1992 under the auspices of the International Human Rights Programme of the Faculty of Law, University of Toronto.

An earlier version of Chapter 1 was published as Rebecca J. Cook, "Women's International Human Rights Law: The Way Forward," *Thatched Patio* 5(4) (1992): 29–63 and *Hum. Rts. Q.* 15 (1993): 230–61.

An earlier version of Chapter 4 was published as Celina Romany, "Women as *Aliens*: A Feminist Critique of the Public/Private Distinction in International Human Rights Law," *Harv. Hum. Rt. J.* 6 (1993): 87.

An earlier version of Chapter 6 was published as Karen Knop, "Re-Statements: Feminism and State Sovereignty in International Law," *Transnat'l L. & Contemp. Probs* 3 (Fall 1993): 293–344.

Library of Congress Cataloging-in-Publication Data

Human rights of women : national and international perspectives / edited by Rebecca J. Cook.
   p.   cm. — (Pennsylvania studies in human rights)
   Includes bibliographical references and index.
   ISBN 0-8122-3261-5 (cloth). — ISBN 0-8122-1538-9 (pbk)
   1. Women—Legal status, laws, etc.   2. Women's rights.   3. Human rights.
4. Feminism.   I. Cook, Rebecca J.   II. Series.
K644.H86   1994
342'.0878—dc20
[342.2878]   94-20682
                                                                           CIP

Third paperback printing 1995

Contents

Foreword
Sonia Picado Sotela

International human rights law is facing the challenge of being relevant and credible in improving the circumstances in which the vast majority of the world's women live their lives. The blight of many women's lives exposes the shortcomings that have beset international law, both in its origins and in its more modern developments. Classical international law, like the law of nature and nations, paid no attention to women as such; both nature and nations have been understood through the characteristics of men and through the motivations and strategies of men who led the affairs of nations. The twentieth-century development in international law recognizing the duties that states owe their individual citizens has until recent times discounted the private and public vulnerabilities of women.

A significant step toward recognition of the rights of women as such was achieved in 1979 when the United Nations General Assembly adopted the Convention on the Elimination of All Forms of Discrimination Against Women and opened it to ratification by states. For this initiative to be effective, however, states must take the complementary steps of adopting the Convention in their domestic law, of monitoring respect for the Convention by other states, and suffering it to be enforced against them in their domestic courts and before regional and international human rights tribunals. While achievement of the Convention may properly be celebrated by women and by men who value universality of human rights, it is premature to claim that the Convention is universally respected and enforced. Indeed, it is premature to claim that women are generally aware of the rights the Convention recognizes, or that it improves or influences the quality of their lives.

This book explores how the Convention and the supporting provisions and institutions of international human rights law could become an effective instrument in the quest for women's equality, protection, and individual dignity. It addresses the interactions between women and their families, including their domestic victimization by discrimination and violence, but escapes the stereotype of women having significance only within family structures. Further, the book addresses how laws derived from regional human rights conventions and the human rights provisions of national constitutions and legislation contribute to women's equality with men, and the accommodation of laws of international origin in domestic legal systems.

The book addresses multiple and overlapping agendas. It is a book on international law, particularly international human rights law, but it is also a book on feminist studies, since it derives its focus for the application of international human rights law from women's experiences and perceptions. It is a book on family law, but it is also a book on political science that explores how women can invoke legal rights to operate legal and political systems to remedy legal injustices, social inequities, and economic disadvantages from which they suffer. It is a book of third world studies because it includes analysis, commentary, and perceptions of women who live in third world countries and who have their own understanding of contrasts between developed and developing countries. It is a book on jurisprudence and philosophy that includes the rethinking of rights from the perspectives of women. Contributors are familiar with the conventional literature on the legal and philosophical nature of rights, and challenge scholars to make the literature relevant to women's real lives in their different circumstances. Last but not least, it is a book to give added inspiration and new opportunities to activists, including but not limited to legal practitioners, who seek practical means by which to make the world fairer for women and for the children, families, and men who depend on women and women's work both inside and outside their homes.

The book originated in a series of papers that contributors were invited to prepare for a Consultation on Women's International Human Rights Law hosted by the International Human Rights Programme of the Faculty of Law, University of Toronto, Canada in September, 1992, with funding provided by the Ford Foundation. Participants were invited on the basis of their scholarly knowledge of international human rights law, and of their ability to introduce relevant perspectives of women's experiences of living in a variety of national environments. Not everyone invited to participate was able to do so, and there were constraints of both budget and time for the design and conduct of the consultation process. It is not claimed, therefore, that the Consultation and the resulting book include comprehensive coverage of the theme of women's international human rights. For instance, it proved impossible to devote chapters to women and work, to discrimination and greater outrages against refugee women, and to the protection of women's rights within the European human rights systems. The book claims to be neither the first study of the position of women in international human rights law, nor the last that is needed. It aims to achieve a fruitful interaction of international human rights scholars, scholars in feminist legal analysis, and lawyers experienced in the practicalities of the lives of women in different settings and the way the law has tended to conceptualize their significance.

A special focus of this book is to include but also to transcend analysis of women's human rights recognized by international law, in order to address the challenge of legal implementation of rights. Presently, the implementation and enforcement of human rights law are largely dependent on voluntary compliance, moral pressures, and other forms of influence. This book discusses voluntary compliance with human rights law and moral pressures concerning the relief, remedy, and prevention of injustices to women, but it goes further to consider legal instruments that may be applied to compel recalcitrant states to behave according to the standards they claim to respect by virtue of their membership in the community of nations. A challenge is to identify and condemn rogue or maverick states whose misbehavior is self-evident. A more exacting challenge is to confront states that self-confidently invoke traditional, cultural, and religious principles to justify the oppressive ways in which women citizens are treated under their constitutions, laws, and practices.

The Women's Convention in Article 5(a) includes specific undertakings by states parties

To modify the social and cultural patterns of conduct of men and women, with a view to achieving the elimination of prejudices and customary and all other practices which are based on the idea of the inferiority or the superiority of either of the sexes or on stereotyped roles for men and women.

This book faces the challenge of achieving modification of social and cultural patterns of conduct that operate in practice to the comparative disadvantage of women. These patterns of conduct are likely to be defended by influential agencies within states that deny that they disadvantage women, or that assert that the attitude to women reflected in such patterns of conduct is essential to the social, cultural, religious or other character and integrity of their countries. This book explores the extent to which indigenous cultures and religious and other traditions can be preserved compatibly with observance of women's international human rights, and areas in which such observance would enhance the values that cultures and religions promote.

The rights of women are not pursued by this book at the cost of men's rights or of men's interests; women are not in competition with men for a bigger slice of the rights pie. The aim of the book is to make the rights pie larger, mixing in a just portion for women by including the rights they have long been denied. It adds to the total sum of justice, and does not detract from men's portion, that an equal portion be available to women. Men of justice will be satisfied that the rights they enjoy are equally available to their wives, daughters, sisters, and mothers, but the book does not define women by their relation to men. Rather, it addresses women by reference to their distinctive characteristics, their innate capacities, their needs, and their rights, particularly their rights under international law to be free from all forms of discrimination due to their status as women.

Acknowledgments

The genesis of this book lies in the collaboration of participants in the Consultation on Women's International Human Rights that was held at the Faculty of Law, University of Toronto, August 31–September 2, 1992. Each participant contributed significantly, some through authorship of chapters, others by commentary, analysis and challenge of ideas following which authors were able to develop their texts into chapters of this book. The participation of Christina Cerna, Maja Daruwala, Norma Forde, Anja-Riitta Ketokoski, Brigitte Mabandla, Manfred Nowak, Rashida Patel, Emma Playfair, and Lisa Stearns contributed to the success of the Consultation and to the consequent preparation of this book. The gathering of the experts at the Consultation was perhaps unique in its concentration of experience in advancing women's human rights domestically, regionally and internationally. Immense gratitude is owed to each participant.

The Consultation and the resulting publication were supported by the Ford Foundation. With the other participants, I am indebted to June Zeitlin of the Ford Foundation for the initiative she took and sustained throughout the preparation, conduct and aftermath of the Consultation. Invaluable advice and assistance in preparing the book were given by Bert Lockwood, Professor of Law and Director of the Urban Morgan Institute for Human Rights, University of Cincinnati College of Law and Editor of the Pennsylvania Studies in Human Rights, who was also a participant at the Consultation. Grace Severyn, a graduate of the University of Cincinnati College of Law, provided important editing assistance.

I am very grateful for all the support given by and through the Faculty of Law, University of Toronto. Julia McNally, Valerie Oosterveld, and Barbara Roblin, either as students or graduates of the Law Faculty, provided research assistance in preparing the Consultation and this book. In particular, I would like to acknowledge the special contributions of Heather Gamester, who handled all of the travel, accommodation, childcare, and entertainment arrangements of the Consultation and oversaw the preparation of the typescript of the book. She managed all of the details with constant patience and good humor, facilitating Consultation deliberations and the completion of the typescript.

References, research, and other tasks toward completion of the book were provided by Inge Creydt, Marc Labelle, and John Mathiason of the United Nations, Linda Poole of the Organization of American States, Caroline Ravaux of the Council of Europe, and Peter Wilborn of the International Commission of Jurists, to all of whom I am grateful. Finally, I want to express my appreciation to my husband and colleague, Bernard Dickens, for his thoughtful support and patience throughout the process of the Consultation and preparation of this book.

Rebecca J. Cook
September 1993

Part I
Introduction

Chapter 1
Women's International Human Rights Law: The Way Forward

Rebecca J. Cook

International human rights law has not yet been applied effectively to redress the disadvantages and injustices experienced by women by reason only of their being women. In this sense, respect for human rights fails to be "universal." The reasons for this general failure to enforce women's human rights are complex and vary from country to country. They include lack of understanding of the systemic nature of the subordination of women, failure to recognize the need to characterize the subordination of women as a human rights violation, and lack of state practice to condemn discrimination against women. Moreover, there has been an unwillingness by traditional human rights groups to focus on violations of women's rights, and a lack of understanding by women's groups of the potential of international human rights law to vindicate women's rights.

This chapter reports a consultation of lawyers from Africa, the Americas, Asia, Australia, and Europe held at the Faculty of Law, University of Toronto, in August 1992. The participants brought legal theory and practice to bear on the relationship between international human rights and women's rights in order to develop legal strategies to promote and protect women's international human rights. This chapter is *a* report of that consultation, but by no means *the* report. There are as many reports as participants, but the real impact of the event will appear only when the findings of the consultation are brought to bear on the prevention, investigation, and punishment of violations of women's human rights.

The intention is to offer some idea of the multiple perspectives that emerged on the consultation themes:

i to review the progress of women's rights and identify challenges and prospects;

ii to recharacterize internationally protected human rights to accommodate women's experiences of injustice;

iii to guarantee specific human rights of women; and

iv to make international human rights law more effective for women.

Progress, Challenges, and Prospects

Why Rights?

Hilary Charlesworth, of the Faculty of Law, University of Adelaide, opened the consultation by raising a fundamental question:

Do legal rights really offer anything to women? Women's disadvantages are often based on structural injustice and winning a case in court will not change this.

Her answer was that, "Because women in most societies are starting in such a disadvantaged position, rights discourse offers a significant vocabulary to formulate political and social grievances which is recognized by the powerful."[1]

Celina Romany, of the City University of New York Law School, answered the question differently. She said that rights could be far more powerful if women were not limited by the ways in which men talk about rights, and encouraged women to make "rights talk" their own. She explained that rights are defined by who talks about them, the language that is used, and the process of talking about them. She recommended that women, their language and their ways of talking about their experiences of injustice need to make a far greater contribution to the development of international human rights law.[2] Participants agreed that many more women, and women from many diverse backgrounds, should talk about the kind of content that should be added to women's rights. Andrew Byrnes, of the Faculty of Law, University of Hong Kong, proposed that we need to make "a concerted effort to expand the range of participants in that dialogue, and to wrest some of the power of defining and speaking from narrow androcentric models to address issues of central concern to women."

Other participants questioned the validity of the rights discourse. Adetoun Ilumoka, a legal practitioner from Lagos, Nigeria, said that the rights discourse in Africa is not meaningful, explaining that the severity of socioeconomic problems faced by women in countries undergoing structural adjustment may require a basic needs strategy rather than a rights strategy.[3] Radhika Coomaraswamy, of the International Centre for Ethnic Studies in Colombo, Sri Lanka, said that in Asia the rights discourse is weak, in part because it privileges free, independent women, whereas Asian women tend to be attached to their communities, castes, or ethnic groups.

The consultation adopted the working presumption that there should be a relationship between international human rights and women's rights. However, no one lost sight of the limitations of a rights strategy and the fact that its effectiveness would vary from culture to culture. Participants stressed the importance of expanding understanding of the context of women's subordination, especially where oppression is exacerbated by poverty or ethnic status, and agreed that the means chosen to combat discrimination will need to be varied according to its particular contexts. Asma Halim, a legal practitioner from Khartoum, Sudan, observed that, while the nature of subordination and thus the means to combat it may vary, "we must not lose sight of the fact that we are subordinated *because we are women*" and that the goal of eliminating all forms of subordination of women remains universal.

Whose Rights?

In determining whether recharacterization might be effective to protect women's rights internationally, Charlesworth raised a second fundamental question that pervaded discussions at the consultation:

Can women's rights be universal? Put another way, is the idea of women's international human rights, premised as it is on the fact that women worldwide suffer from patriarchy, misconceived? Is the pervasive devaluation of women's lives enough to link women in the effort to add a gender dimension to international human rights?

Charlesworth sketched three feminist approaches that might serve to recharacterize rights in order to make them more universally applicable by better accommodating women's pervasive experiences of injustice:

- Liberal feminism attempts to realize the equal treatment guaranteed by existing law, and thereby discounts intrinsic differences between men and women. A problem with this approach is that it fails to understand the structural imbalance of power between men and women and the systemic nature of discrimination.
- The goal of cultural feminism is to celebrate the differences between masculine and feminine ways of reasoning. This approach

may lead to marginalization of women's rights because presenting them as different from men's needs may induce the response that they are less worthy of resources.

- The purpose of radical feminism is to transform the masculine world where inequality is based on systemic domination and subordination of women by men. This approach is problematic strategically when it requires revolutionary change in a conservative community that is ready at most for evolutionary change.

Participants agreed that these approaches or a mix of them might be useful in recharacterizing international human rights law to be more responsive to the degradation of women.[4] However, they cautioned that feminist recharacterization of law in one type of society cannot be imported wholesale either into other types of societies or into the international human rights system.

The distinction between the public and private sectors of society offers an example of the insights and pitfalls of applying Western feminist theories to other social and legal systems. The distinction, long a target of feminist critiques in Western liberal societies for masking women's oppression, may manifest itself to different effects in other societies, and may illuminate areas of otherwise unobserved subordination. Charlesworth explained that "what is public in one society may well be private in another," but that, whether a matter is considered public or private, it is the women's domain that is consistently devalued.

The public/private distinctions can be perceived in at least two ways. In the first the public sector, where legal and political order exist, is contrasted with the private sector of home and family, to which regulation is deemed inappropriate. Charlesworth noted that this distinction is gendered because women operate in the private sector, where abuses such as domestic violence and degradation are invisible and unregulated by the law. The second is similar to public and private ownership. The public sector is constituted by the state and its agencies, and the private sector is composed of the vast array of nonstate activities.

Manfred Nowak, of the Ludwig Boltzmann Institut für Menschenrechte and the Federal Academy of Public Administration, Vienna, Austria, thought the second distinction is more important to international human rights law because it corresponds to the classical theory of state responsibility for human rights violations. It is the state that has to provide effective protection and remedies against human rights violations. International law of state responsibility requires governments to respect, ensure, and protect women's international human rights; when they fail to do so, sanctions can be enforced. International law doctrine now goes beyond the classical state duty not to interfere with individual human rights, to hold states accountable for not acting positively to ensure rights.[5] Moreover, Nowak explained, international law now obligates states to use due diligence to prevent, investigate, and punish systemic and egregious human rights violations between private actors.[6] Nowak acknowledged that state responsibility for individual abusers applies only at one step removed from their direct wrongdoing, but argued that this limitation follows from the general nature of international law, not from any gender bias.

Charlesworth responded to this argument by wondering whether, had women been more influential in the development of international law, they would have constructed it more readily to reach violations of human dignity that dominate women's lives, such as domestic violence.

How to Legitimize Rights in Different Cultures

A third fundamental question discussed throughout the consultation was

How can universal human rights be legitimized in radically different societies without succumbing to either homogenizing universalism or the paralysis of cultural relativism?

Coomaraswamy analyzed the barriers to "indigenizing" rights in South Asia.[7] She emphasized the need to avoid the "Orientalist trap" of dividing the world into bipolar categories. Those in the West must guard against the idea that the West is progressive on women's rights and the East is barbaric and backward. Those in the East must be equally cautious not to subscribe to the reverse notion that accepts the East/West distinction, but believes that the East is superior, more communal, and less self-centered with no place for an "adversarial" concept of rights. She cited the coexistence of the two traditions in South Asia to illustrate the dangers of oversimplification.

Coomaraswamy started from the presumption that, for human rights to be effective, they have to become a respected part of the culture and traditions of a given society. In South Asia, the institution of law is generally viewed with deep suspicion and often hatred because it is seen as the central instrument employed by colonizing powers to replace indigenous cultural, religious, and social traditions with the mechanisms of the modern Western nation state.

When the law of women's human rights is associated with an impersonal and homogenizing Western state, the rights are discredited. Coomaraswamy proposed that the future of human rights in South Asia does not lie with the state but with the confluence of the interests of the state and movements in civil society. She cautioned that "unless human rights values take root in civil society and unless civil institutions and non-governmental organizations (NGOs) take up the cause, then women's rights as human rights will have no resonance in the social institutions concerned."

She cited the case of Roop Kanwar, a university student who was burned alive on her husband's funeral pyre in Deorala, Rajasthan, as an example of the dissonance between women's rights and ethnic identity, explaining that

Urban centered women's groups as well as groups of women from all over India were horrified and organized a march in Rajasthan. The Rajasthanis retaliated by filling the streets with thousands of their own ethnic group: the right to commit sati, they claimed, was part of their ethnic culture. After months of delay, the police finally arrested Roop Kanwar's father-in-law and five other members of the family for abetment to suicide. Three months later, the Indian Parliament passed a tough law banning sati, even though an old law already existed, as a sign of central government intolerance of these ethnic practices. (p. 49)

In reflecting on the outcome of the case, she observed that

Though the feminist movement had scored a legal victory, the case exemplified the terrible gulf between human rights and women's rights activists, on the one hand, and those who see the status of women as an integral part of their ethnic identity, on the other. . . .
. . . What is the point of all these laws if the people do not believe that putting an eighteen-year-old woman on a funeral pyre and denying her life is not a violation of the most basic fundamental right—the right to life? What is the point of all the Constitutional protection if "ethnic identity" is an acceptable justification for reducing the status of women according to diverse cultural practice? (pp. 49, 50)

Coomaraswamy pointed out that, in contrast to ethnic practices that deny women their basic human rights, some social movements and traditional ideologies have been used to enhance women's status. She suggested that rights discourse will have more resonance, and therefore more effectiveness, to the extent to which it can "plug into many of the dynamic social movements taking place in South Asia." According to Coomaraswamy, Asian women activists argue that "legal strategies to emancipate women need to allow women to touch base with their traditional sources of empowerment."

Abdullahi An-Na'im, a Sudanese lawyer and director of Africa Watch, underscored the importance of cultural legitimacy of international human rights.[8] He explained that if the question of the cultural legitimacy of international standards is not taken seriously, "it is sometimes raised with the intention of undermining international human rights law, or of justifying its violation" (p. 170). It is not enough, he said, to rely on international law obligations to bring national laws, including religious and customary laws, into compliance with international human rights principles. International law, he explained, "is fully consistent with . . . state sovereignty . . . since it simply seeks to ensure that states effectively fulfill legal obligations that they have already assumed under international law" (p. 167).

An-Na'im suggested that one must go beyond this formalistic understanding of international legal obligations in order to seek a deeper consensus and sustainable commitment to women's international human rights.[9] He argued that unless international human rights have sufficient legitimacy within particular cultures and traditions, their implementation will be thwarted, particularly at the domestic level, but also at the regional and international levels. Without such legitimacy, it will be nearly impossible to improve the status of women through the law or other agents of social change.

He suggested stimulating "internal discourse" and "cross cultural dialogue" on the issue of women's legal status and rights. "Internal discourse" among different sectors of society that hold different views on women's status can validate national achievements that improve women's status. Such discourse can explore avenues to challenge and discredit discriminatory practices in ways that are relevant to, and understood and accepted by, the population in question. "Cross-cultural dialogue" between groups that want to improve the status of women in different cultures can enhance the ability of internal actors to understand and address the nature of women's subordination in their own contexts. He cautioned that cross-cultural dialogue should not press internal actors into understanding and addressing challenges in terms of the experiences of other societies. He explained that "the combination of the processes of internal discourse and cross-cultural dialogue will, it is hoped, deepen and broaden universal cultural consensus on the concept and normative content" of women's international right to be free from all forms of discrimination (p. 174).

Some participants questioned the effectiveness of An-Na'im's approach because religions and cultures are often sources of women's oppression. As a result, they thought "going secular" the only option. His response was that in some countries women do not have the secular option because their sole frames of reference or discourse are religious. As evidence of the possibility of religious or cultural reformation, he pointed to the emergence of women's rights organizations within religious frameworks, such as Women Living Under Muslim Laws and Catholics for a Free Choice.

Making International Human Rights Law Gender Conscious

International human rights and the legal instruments that protect them were developed primarily by men in a male-oriented world. They have not been interpreted in a gender-sensitive way that is responsive to women's experiences of injustice. Critical recharacterization of international human rights is needed in order that women's distinctive human rights will not be marginal, and implementation of such rights becomes part of the central agenda of human rights work.

Treaty interpretation is not exclusively limited to treaty terms. A text may also be interpreted in a way that advances its goals in contemporaneous circumstances, even if they were not imaginable when the treaty was drafted. Moreover, interpretations of human rights treaties by human rights committees and by international, regional, and national courts shall take into account "subsequent practice in the application of the treaty which establishes the agreement of the parties regarding its interpretation."[10] As a result, women can develop the content of treaties on human rights through the "subsequent practice" that adds a gender dimension to those rights.

Human rights may be divided into nondiscrimination rights; civil and political rights; and economic, social, and cultural rights. Developing the "subsequent practice" through recharacterization of all three kinds of rights to accommodate the particular nature of women's vulnerabilities to fundamental injustice is required if international human rights law is to be effectively applied to women.

Recharacterizing Nondiscrimination Rights

What constitutes discrimination against women is not a point on which states readily agree. Nonetheless, the legal obligation to eliminate all forms of discrimination against women is a fundamental tenet of international human rights law. Sex is a prohibited ground of discrimination in the Universal Declaration of Human Rights, the International Covenant on Civil and Political Rights (the Political Covenant), the International Covenant on Economic, Social, and Cultural Rights (the Economic Covenant), and the three regional human rights conventions, namely, the European Convention for the Protection of Human Rights and Fundamental Freedoms (the European Convention), the American Convention on Human Rights (the American Convention), and the African Charter on Human and Peoples' Rights (the African Charter).

The Convention on the Elimination of All Forms of Discrimination

Against Women (the Women's Convention) develops the legal norm on nondiscrimination from a women's perspective. This Convention moves from a sex-neutral norm that requires equal treatment of men and women, usually measured by how men are treated, to recognize that the particular nature of discrimination against women merits a legal response. The Women's Convention progresses beyond the earlier human rights conventions by addressing the pervasive and systemic nature of discrimination against women, and identifies the need to confront the social causes of women's inequality by addressing "all forms" of discrimination that women suffer. This Convention is thereby able to address the particular nature of women's disadvantages.

One approach to clarifying what constitutes discrimination against women in international human rights law is through the development of General Comments or General Recommendations by the committees established under the different human rights conventions. For example, the Human Rights Committee, established to monitor state compliance with the Political Covenant, has issued General Comment 18 on nondiscrimination based upon the "similarity and difference" model of discrimination. The General Comment states that "not every differentiation of treatment will constitute discrimination, if the criteria for such differentiation are reasonable and objective and if the aim is to achieve a purpose which is legitimate under the Covenant."[11]

Kathleen Mahoney, of the Faculty of Law, University of Calgary, criticized the "similarity and difference" model of discrimination based on the liberal theory of feminism discussed by Charlesworth.[12] It uses a male standard of equality and renders women copies of their male counterparts. Under this model, women are forced to argue either that they are the same as men and should be treated the same, or that they are different but should be treated as if they were the same, or that they are different and should be accorded special treatment. The model does not allow for any questioning about the ways in which laws, cultures, or religious traditions have constructed and maintained the disadvantage of women, or the extent to which the institutions are male-defined and built on male conceptions of challenges and harms.

The understanding of discrimination against women evolves with insights, perspective, and empirical information on how women are subordinated by different legal, social, and religious traditions. Standards for determining such discrimination must be developed accordingly. As Mahoney explained,

Systemic discrimination or inequality of condition, the most damaging form of discrimination, cannot be addressed via the rule-based sameness of treatment approach. Indeed, the use of this model virtually makes systemic disadvantage invisible. By structuring equality around the male comparator, the assumption is made that equality exists and that from time to time, individuals will be discriminated against. The persistent disadvantage women suffer across the board because of societal biases is obscured. The question then becomes, can [international human rights law] support and deliver substantive equality? (see p. 442)

Mahoney answered that it can, if a test of discrimination is adopted that is based on powerlessness, exclusion, and disadvantage rather than on sameness and difference. A test adopted by the Supreme Court of Canada,[13] for instance, determines discrimination in terms of disadvantage. If a member of a persistently disadvantaged group can show that a law, policy, or behavior continues or worsens that disadvantage, then that law, policy or behavior is discriminatory. She explained that no comparator, male or otherwise, is required. Adoption of the test of "disadvantage," as opposed to the test of "similarity and difference," requires judges to look at women as they are located in the real world in order to determine whether any systemic abuse and deprivation of power that women experience is due to their place in the sexual hierarchy.

Decisions of international and regional human rights tribunals have used the "similarity and difference" test for discrimination,[14] not the "disadvantage" model that can capture the systemic nature of discrimination against women. The "disadvantage" model of discrimination is more consistent with the object and purpose of the Women's Convention in prohibiting all forms of discrimination against women. The Human Rights Committee, established under the Political Covenant, might be encouraged to adopt the "disadvantage" model, replacing General Comment 18 to help clarify what constitutes discrimination against women. The Committee has reflected on, and further developed, other General Comments. The Committee on the Elimination of Discrimination Against Women (CEDAW), established under the Women's Convention, might also be encouraged to develop a General Recommendation that clarifies its intention to use the "disadvantage" test to determine what constitutes discrimination against women.

Recharacterizing Civil and Political Rights

Participants explored ways to recharacterize civil and political rights for women because, as Charlesworth explained,

the primacy traditionally given to civil and political rights by western international lawyers and philosophers is directed toward protection from men within public life and their relationship with government.

Recharacterization of civil and political rights needs to be done in a variety of ways. For example, the right to life is traditionally referred to as the obligation of states to observe due process of law before capital punishment is imposed. But this interpretation ignores the historic reality of women that persists in many regions of the world. Currently, at least 500,000 women die avoidably each year of pregnancy related causes, such as lack of access to basic obstetric care.[15]

Cecilia Medina, of the Faculty of Law, University of Diego Portales, Santiago, Chile, who is also a researcher at the Netherlands Institute of Human Rights, argued that women's rights to liberty and security are severely constrained by their lack of access to contraceptives. For example, in El Salvador lack of available means of contraception causes women to have about twice the number of children they want.

Rhonda Copelon, of the City University of New York Law School, explored ways to recharacterize the prohibition of torture and inhuman and degrading treatment to accommodate gender-based violence.[16] She argued that gender-based violence is comparable to torture, and that its prohibition ought to be, like prohibition of torture, a principle of *jus cogens*:

My thesis is that, when stripped of privatization, sexism, and sentimentalism, gender-based violence—which is brutal, systemic and structural—must be seen as no less grave than other forms of inhumane and subordinating violence, the prohibition of which has been recognized as *jus cogens*, or peremptory norms, by the international community. I focus on the *jus cogens* not to exclude other formulations of gender-based violence, but because, as a normative matter, it embraces the most heinous offenses, precludes exception and binds universally. My argument is not that gender-based violence has attained the status of *jus cogens*, but rather that it should; and that with a revised process, it could.

Nowak pointed out that if violence against women can be characterized as torture, then states would have universal jurisdiction to prosecute perpetrators of violence against women. Copelon's approach is also designed to have the shock effect of making international lawyers think about why gender-specific violations are absent from the *jus cogens* discourse, the symbolic inner sanctum of international legal rules.

Recharacterizing Economic, Social, and Cultural Rights: The Problem of Structural Adjustment

Participants, particularly from Africa, were concerned about how structural adjustment programs (SAPs) of the World Bank and the International Monetary Fund (IMF) are negatively affecting the economic, social, and cultural rights of women.[17] Women, they noted, suffer in a unique and often invisible way. Florence Butegwa, of Women in Law and Development, based in Harare, Zimbabwe, and Akua Kuenyehia, of the Faculty of Law, University of Ghana, described the double injury sustained by women in their countries due to the demands of structural adjustment; injury suffered as citizens of the South and injury suffered as women.[18] Their stories are echoed in the literature on women and structural development.[19] The findings of this literature show that:

a. The total burden of women's work has increased under recessionary conditions. Structural adjustment programs have reduced social expenditures, rather than increasing them to offset these pressures.
b. Employment creation is weak under SAPs, especially for women.
c. SAPs have done little to address institutional gender inequality in the formal and informal sectors of national economies.
d. In agriculture, the concentration of resources on export crops, which has characterized development and worked to women's disadvantage in the past, has been intensified under SAPs.
e. In both agriculture and industry, women have operated relatively small enterprises and have experienced discrimination because of the bias against smaller scale operations manifest in SAPs.

A consensus emerged at the Consultation that human rights have to be rethought to accommodate women's experience of disproportionate disadvantage under structural adjustment programs.

The first step to rethinking human rights with reference to structural adjustment is to recognize the double injury it causes women. Once recognized, this injury can be addressed in a number of fora in the international system.[20] An additional approach is to confront the financial institutions themselves. As international actors, the World Bank and the IMF are bound by international law, including human rights norms[21] and, therefore, are legally obligated to ensure that women share equally with men in the benefits of their loans.

Guaranteeing Specific Human Rights of Women

The Nationality Problem

Bert Lockwood, of the University of Cincinnati College of Law, examined how the Court of Appeal of Botswana in *Attorney General v. Unity Dow*[22] applied international human rights principles to the nationality problem. The decision held unconstitutional the provision of the Botswana Citizenship Act of 1984, whereby a female citizen of Botswana who is married to a foreigner cannot convey citizenship to her children born in wedlock in Botswana, although a male citizen married to a foreigner can convey such citizenship. The Court of Appeal decided that this provision of the Citizenship Act infringed Unity Dow's fundamental rights and freedoms, her liberty of movement, and her right to nondiscrimination. The Chief Judge, noting the obligations of Botswana as a signatory to the Universal Declaration of Human Rights and the Declaration on the Elimination of Discrimination Against Women, and as a state party to the African Charter, observed that

Botswana is a member of the community of civilised States which has undertaken to abide by certain standards of conduct, and, unless it is impossible to do otherwise, it would be wrong for its Courts to interpret its legislation in a manner which conflicts with the international obligations that Botswana has undertaken.[23]

Lockwood explained that women's disability with regard to citizenship is a problem in many countries,[24] underscored by the fact that Article 9 on nationality is one of the most highly reserved articles of the Women's Convention.[25] Women's legal inability to bestow their nationality on their children born of foreign husbands often leaves legitimate children stateless or unable to benefit from attributes of citizenship such as education, health care, and employment. He hoped that this decision might have a positive impact on draft legislation to amend such discriminatory nationality laws, such as is now pending in Egypt[26] and Tunisia. The decision might also have persuasive authority for cases now pending in Bangladesh and in Pakistan, according to Sara Hossain, a legal practitioner from Dhaka, Bangladesh and Rashida Patel, of the Legal Aid Centre in Karachi, Pakistan. It was pointed out that CEDAW, perhaps together with the Children's Committee established under the Convention on the Rights of the Child, might be encouraged to develop a General Recommendation on women's ability to convey nationality to their children, and that it be made an issue during the 1994 International Year of the Family.

Discriminatory Personal Law

In some regions of the world, personal law governs legal relations in all matters regarding marriage, divorce, maintenance, child custody and guardianship, and inheritance, on the basis of religious identity. Christina Cerna, currently on secondment from the Organization of American States to the UN Human Rights Centre in Geneva, was concerned that the persistence of discriminatory personal laws "undermines the universality of international prohibition of discrimination against women."[27]

Kirti Singh, a legal practitioner from New Delhi, explained that the Indian government retains personal law that discriminates against women for reasons of political expediency. The government does not want to interfere with personal matters in the ethnic (usually minority) communities.[28] A case in point is the much discussed *Shah Bano* decision of the Supreme Court of India.[29] A Muslim man who had divorced his wife of thirty years was ordered to pay monthly maintenance pursuant to a criminal law provision on the prevention of destitution. He objected, arguing that the Muslim personal law requiring him only to return her dowry, which he had done, should prevail over the secular criminal law. His argument was unsuccessful in the Supreme Court of India, but the case triggered a reaction that led to the passage of legislation that overturned the Supreme Court judgment. Singh pointed out that the government, despite the protest of women's groups of all ethnic communities, thought it could not afford to alienate the fundamentalist Muslim community, and so "sealed the fate of millions of Muslim women in India."

Halim addressed the potential for using the Political Covenant and the African Charter to challenge discriminatory aspects of the Sudanese Personal Law for Muslims Act (1991).[30] She said that this act rendered the meaning of equality "valueless." For example, it prevents women from contracting their own marriages, gives men unfettered rights to divorce while requiring women to prove in court some sort of specified harm, and prevents women from leaving their homes without the permission of their husbands or guardians. Even if a divorce is granted, a woman may "be returned" to her former husband without her consent within three months of divorce. She explained that interpretations of the Act consistent with modern realities of women's lives are harshly resisted, even though interpretations of other areas of Islamic law reflecting modernization of men's lives are readily accepted. She pointed out that "women are prisoners of the old interpretations of the Qur'an and sunna."

Halim further explained that the challenges of applying the sexual nondiscrimination provisions of the Political Covenant and the African Charter are formidable:

Muslim women are being told that patriarchy is not what is hindering them, but international law as part of western ideas is the real obstacle to women. Women should be liberated from western ideas that are subjecting them to the double burden of domestic and public work. It is argued that there is no need for women to take up the task of liberation. Men will do it for them through the smooth "Islamic" process, if it is kept outside the ambit of secular international law. (see p. 406)

Coomaraswamy explained that personal law is usually maintained as part of the politics of communalism, and within that context Shah Bano, and women like her, have no rights. "All men are created equal, but women are bound by the position relegated to them by the different systems of personal law, laws which govern the most important area of their lives, the family."[31] She pointed out that personal law is the most impervious to change in favor of women's rights:

Here women are divided by community and among themselves about whether a rights discourse is relevant or necessary. Unless we begin to examine law's approach to the family and the private space in greater detail and understand the dynamics more fully with regard to ideological constructions which resist legal change, we will not be able to bring rights home to the family. The task is daunting but necessary. Without equity in the family, there will not be equity in society. . . . The law should protect and privilege that kind of family and not any other. (pp. 55–56)

Customary Property Law

Butegwa addressed the use of the African Charter to redress the disabilities that women face with respect to property under African customary law. In law and in fact, women are denied access to real and personal property, whether it be by discriminatory inheritance, divorce, or customary law.[32] If one dies without a will, which is generally the case in many African countries, the customary law of one's clan is applied to determine who inherits assets. She explained that the customary law heir is normally the deceased's eldest son, which denies women not only the fruits of the land but also the incidents of land tenure such as its availability as collateral security for bank loans. Upon divorce, women's claims to matrimonial property are often rejected.

Butegwa said that the African Charter obligates states parties "to ensure that whatever cultural values and practices are permitted by domestic law must comply with the human rights principle of freedom from discrimination on the basis of sex." She recommended that the issue of women's property rights be addressed carefully and pragmatically at the national, regional, and international levels.

At the national level, she said, most governments are not taking the necessary legislative steps to change laws, practices, and customs with regard to women's property rights. Consequently, states parties are failing in their obligations under the Charter to reform sex discriminatory laws. She observed, moreover, that women's groups working to reform discriminatory laws and practices are dismissed by some governments "as misguided elite women aping Western concepts. This situation is compounded by a general lack of awareness among women of the law and the lack of opportunities for them to meet and discuss their legal status and map out strategies." She pointed out that women's rights discourse must go on at the national level because, until women understand the fact that "some customs are illegal under the laws of the country," the discourse might backfire and little headway on any women's issues will be possible.

With regard to the African Commission on Human and Peoples' Rights, established under the African Charter, Butegwa put it directly: we have "to wake up the Commission." However, she explained that NGOs, women's groups, and the legal profession have "only a cursory knowledge of the African Charter, the Commission, and their relevance and potential in the promotion of women's human rights. It is not surprising, therefore, that the majority has not sought to include the Charter and the Commission in the legal rights awareness programs currently being implemented." As a result, strategies relating to the Charter and the Commission, including improving state reporting on compliance or noncompliance with the Charter's obligations with regard to women, and submitting communications on violations of women's property rights, will be advanced only through considerable effort.

At the international level, Butegwa thought that support is needed from women's rights groups in developed countries to change bilateral and multilateral loan policies. Such women's groups need to lobby their governments to change their aid policies and the loan and grant policies of international institutions such as the World Bank and, for example, the International Fund for Agricultural Development (IFAD), to encourage change in recipient states' laws that discriminate against women's property rights. Donor governments and multilateral funders need to ensure that women have equal access with men to the benefits of their loans. This equity can be very difficult to achieve where women have no land to use as collateral security for loans provided by such institutions as IFAD through recipient governments. CEDAW, perhaps with input from the Food and Agricultural Organization, might want to develop a General Recommendation on women and property. This could set out guidelines for reporting states to specify how they have overcome the general disabilities under their customary law for women to own, inherit, or otherwise acquire land.

Reproductive Rights

María Isabel Plata, of Profamilia, Bogotá, Colombia, explained how women's groups in Colombia used the Women's Convention to promote equality and reproductive health, observing that "the moment we used an international treaty, the government saw that our claims were legitimate and began to take us seriously." The Colombian women's movement lobbied for incorporation of the principles of the Women's Convention into the 1991 Constitution. In particular, the provision of the Women's Convention on the right to decide freely and responsibly the number of one's children is now part of the new Constitution.[33]

Plata explained that the Ministry of Public Health has interpreted the Women's Convention and the 1991 Colombian Constitution to establish a gender perspective in their health policies that considers "the social discrimination of women as an element which contributes to the ill-health of women."[34] A new ministerial resolution orders all health institutions to ensure women the right to decide on all issues that affect their health, their life, and their sexuality,[35] and guarantees rights "to information and orientation to allow the exercise of free, gratifying, responsible sexuality which can not be tied to maternity." The new policy requires provision of a full range of reproductive health services, including infertility services, safe and effective contraception, integrated treatment for incomplete abortion, and treatment for menopausal women. The policy emphasizes the need for special attention to high risk women, such as adolescents and victims of violence.

Plata considered that this new Colombian initiative might provide ideas to other countries that are making serious efforts to comply with the Women's Convention. She recommended that CEDAW consider issuing a General Recommendation clarifying that the terms "women's health" and "family planning programs" encompass the concepts of "reproductive and sexual health" as used in the new Colombian women's health policy. She urged that CEDAW develop this Recommendation as soon as possible, in part to legitimize the Colombian interpretation of the health provisions of the Women's Convention. Moreover, such a Recommendation would explain that in order to comply with the Convention, states need to develop comprehensive reproductive health services that "empower women and not use women as means to limit population growth, save the environment and speed development." She stressed that it is important for CEDAW to issue such a Recommendation before the 1994 Population Conference, because of her concern that the Conference will be an occasion at which international thinking on population may revert to the solely demographic mentality of the 1960s, when women's well-being was sometimes neglected.

Violence Against Women

Joan Fitzpatrick, of the University of Washington School of Law, Seattle, explored a range of strategies to combat all forms of violence against women.[36] Forms of violence include domestic violence (murder, rape, and battery) by husbands or other male partners, genital mutilation, gender-based violence by police and security forces (including torture of detained women), gender-based violence against women during armed conflict, gender-based violence against women refugees and asylum seekers, violence associated with prostitution and pornography, violence in the workplace, including sexual harassment, forced pregnancy, forced abortion, and forced sterilization.

Copelon explained that

> domestic violence against women is systemic and structural, a mechanism of the patriarchal control of women that is built on male superiority and female inferiority, sex-stereotyped roles and expectations, and the economic, social, and political predominance of men and dependency of women. While the legal and cultural embodiments of patriarchal thinking vary among different cultures, there is an astounding convergence of cultures in regard to the basic tenets of patriarchy and the legitimacy, if not necessity, of violence as a mechanism of enforcing that system. (p. 120)

No issue raises the inherent limitation of the gender-neutral approach to equality more acutely than does domestic violence against women. Fitzpatrick pointed out that a "special treatment" approach is needed, as opposed to formal equality, to recognize that women exist in concrete contexts. The need for a multiplicity of approaches has been suggested in the CEDAW Recommendation 19 on Violence Against Women, the Draft Declaration on the Elimination of Violence Against Women, the European Parliament Resolution on Violence Against Women, and the draft Inter-American Convention on the Prevention, Punishment, and Eradication of Violence Against Women, as well as the UN Crime Prevention and Criminal Justice Branch 1993 *Resource Manual on Strategies for Confronting Domestic Violence*. Fitzpatrick stressed that victims of domestic violence exist under pressures that are not felt by other crime victims. Battered women often lack the economic, social, and emotional means to leave their batterers. Not employed outside the home, they have no financial resources on which to fall back. They have been socialized to define themselves primarily through their relationships with men, and cannot face leaving these relationships. This points to the need for "special treatment" in such forms, for instance, as battered women's shelters.

Participants struggled with the question whether domestic violence is better characterized as a violation of the civil and political right to liberty and security, or as a violation of the nondiscrimination right to equal resources for crime control. The former characterization may do more in the long term to integrate women's experiences of injustice into the concepts of international human rights law, but the latter may enjoy greater short-term success precisely because it poses less of a fundamental challenge to patriarchal systems.

Participants stressed the importance of strategies that would enhance international standards of prohibition of violence against women, such as the CEDAW General Recommendation 19, and means that would facilitate the enforcement of standards, such as the Communication procedures before the Commission on the Status of Women and the individual complaint procedure before the Committee Against Torture, established under the Convention Against Torture and Other Cruel, Inhuman, or Degrading Treatment or Punishment.[37] They also explored strategies that would bring the issue of violence against women into the mainstream of human rights work, such as the international effort to put the issue on the agenda of the 1993 International Conference on Human Rights, to be held in Vienna.

Working With What We Have: Making International Human Rights Law More Effective for Women

State Responsibility for Violations of Women's Rights

The international law of state responsibility makes a state legally accountable for breaches of international obligations that are attributable or imputable to the state.[38] In other words, only a state and its agents can commit a human rights violation. Nonstate actors are not generally accountable under international human rights law, but the state may sometimes be held responsible for related human rights violations. Modern development of international human rights law through state adherence to multilateral human rights conventions has enhanced prospects of state accountability, and women may be able to turn these developments to their advantage.

Kenneth Roth, of the U.S.-based Human Rights Watch, explored the feasibility of applying different theories of state accountability developed in other areas of international human rights law to violations of women's human rights. The international human rights movement has used three distinct theories of government accountability: government agency, government complicity through failure to act, and government responsibility for the unequal application of the law. Roth argued that the same theories of government accountability invoked for state complicity in various forms of violence by nonstate actors,[39] should be applied to domestic violence against women.

Comparing the first and second theories, Roth stressed the limits of the theory of government complicity. Whereas the theory of government agency treats an act of private violence as the act of a government agent and therefore requires that such violence be ended outright, the theory of government complicity requires simply that the state not condone private violence. Where a state is doing the bare minimum in combating domestic violence to escape charges of complicity, an unequal application theory allows insistence on greater diligence as a matter of international human rights law. The demand can be made that a state's efforts to combat domestic violence be at least on a par with its efforts to fight comparable forms of violent crime.

As regards the third theory, Roth argued that the nondiscrimination provisions of the Political Covenant can also be used to require that the same level of state resources used to enforce criminal laws against private acts of violence be devoted to crimes against women. That is, crimes against women, under the nondiscrimination theory of accountability, need to receive at least as thorough an investigation and as vigorous a prosecution as crimes against men. Roth explained that "lesser attention constitutes not only a violation of the antidiscrimination provisions of the Covenant but also evidence of the complicity needed to make out a substantive violation."[40]

Some participants thought the nondiscrimination theory of state responsibility a useful first step. The non-enforcement of laws to protect women's rights was consistently discussed as a reason for women's continued subordination. The nondiscrimination theory of accountability might be applied to require governments to stop neglecting their duties with respect to women and actually implement laws to protect women's rights. The theory might also require the domestic criminal justice system and the international human rights system to at least explore the relative lack of enforcement of criminal laws against those who victimize women, for instance through wife-beating.

Participants questioned whether this approach would be sufficient to combat violence against women. It was pointed out that the approach has all the shortcomings of the "similarity and difference" model of discrimination. Halim questioned whether it would be sufficient in the Sudan to require enforcement of a rarely applied law criminalizing female circumcision. Butegwa observed that comparing this form of violence to other forms of criminal violence committed against other social groups might obscure the systemic nature of violence against women. It was generally thought that further work is needed on theories of state responsibility to hold the state accountable for failures of prevention, investigation, and punishment of violations of women's rights.

International Protection

Byrnes explained that the methods of international protection of women's human rights range from recourse to limited international judicial or quasi-judicial processes to the application of broader means of furthering states parties' accountability, such as through reporting requirements.[41] He noted that the application of human rights norms to national laws and practices alleged to violate women's rights has to be approached in a variety of ways. Any one method may be fragile and inadequate, but there are cumulative ways in which, in Romany's words, "women can make rights their own." Available approaches will be examined below from the perspective of different protective bodies that derive their authority from separate human rights treaties or from the UN Charter.

(a) Treaty-based bodies

Byrnes explained that all major human rights treaties provide for a system of reporting. States parties are required to make regular reports to the responsible supervisory bodies on the steps they have taken to implement their obligations and the difficulties they have experienced in doing so. Reports are examined by the relevant treaty bodies in the presence of representatives of the states concerned. All committees receive information informally from NGOs, which they may use in their questioning. The examination process, he points out, can provide an occasion for exerting pressure on states. For members of a supervisory body to be strongly critical of a state or express the view that the state has not discharged its obligations under the treaty, can put pressure on a government, particularly if the proceedings receive international or national publicity.

All human rights treaty bodies, Byrnes explained, have the power to make General Comments or General Recommendations. These detailed comments can be particularly useful for elaborating the specific content of broadly worded treaty guarantees, and may be helpful in domestic, political, or even judicial contexts. But he cautioned that, with the exception of CEDAW, gender plays a relatively minor role in the General Comments of most committees. Nonetheless, they are grateful for, and in need of, expert input from NGOs, and thus this process is available for advancement of women's rights.

Byrnes pointed out that national NGOs, which might be able to exploit the reporting procedure, may know little about it, the appropriate format for submission of material, and how most effectively to lobby members of a committee or to generate publicity. Every government needs to be encouraged to publish treaty reports in the local language, to share them as a matter of course with the relevant NGOs, and even to debate them in the national parliament.

The Human Rights Committee, established under the Political Covenant, has an individual complaint procedure. This procedure is available to individuals in nearly seventy countries that have ratified the Optional Protocol to the Political Covenant. Under this procedure, the Human Rights Committee has decided a case on a woman's right to enjoy her own culture,[42] and a few sexual nondiscrimination cases.[43] From a women's perspective, the jurisprudence developed by this Committee is limited by the adoption of the "similarity and difference" test of discrimination.[44]

The Human Rights Committee is willing to scrutinize allegations of discrimination in violation of rights recognized by, for example, the Economic Covenant and the Women's Convention.[45] This enables women in those countries to bring complaints about violations of their rights of equal entitlement protected by the Economic Covenant and, for example, the Women's Convention, provided that those countries are parties to the latter-mentioned conventions.

The Committee on the Elimination of Discrimination Against Women (CEDAW) monitors states parties' compliance with the Women's Convention.[46] Norma Forde, of the Faculty of Law of the University of the West Indies, Barbados, and a member of CEDAW, noted that the work of CEDAW is far more effective when its members have recourse to sources of information in addition to data contained in reports of states parties. Accordingly, she explained, CEDAW has requested the Division for the Advancement of Women at the UN Secretariat in New York to compile statistics garnered from official UN sources relevant to members' reports. CEDAW has also requested UN specialized agencies to provide it with relevant information and encourages NGOs to send them information particularly on major problems facing women in the reporting countries.

The Committee on the Elimination of Racial Discrimination, established under the International Convention for the Elimination of All Forms of Racial Discrimination (the Race Convention), provides an im-

portant forum for raising issues of discrimination against women belonging to racial minorities.[47] Participants were concerned that women
of minority communities are subject to discrimination and violence as
members of their communities, and additional discrimination and violence as women. Moreover, in Hossain's words "they are further condemned to carry the brunt of resistance to change by conforming to the
discriminatory traditions and customs practiced by their community."

The Committee on Economic, Social, and Cultural Rights (the Economic Committee) monitors states parties' compliance with the Economic Covenant. It has developed some innovative working methods
to enhance its normative functions. They include formally receiving
written submissions from NGOs, holding annual "general discussions"
on certain rights contained in the Economic Covenant and involving
"recognized experts" to provide oral testimony during these discussions.[48] These methods provide significant opportunities to develop a
feminist content to economic, social, and cultural rights.

Important research shows how economic development has exacerbated women's marginalization, despite programmatic initiatives
to integrate women into development.[49] The Economic Committee
might invite "recognized experts" during the annual "general discussions," in order to explain why some of these programs have not been
successful in improving women's actual status, and what implications
these insights might have for the effective application of economic,
social, and cultural rights. Discussions with these experts might result
in a General Comment on how states parties might more effectively
ensure that women enjoy rights protected by the Economic Covenant.

(b) Charter-based bodies

The UN Commission on the Status of Women has the authority to
review communications sent to it by individuals and organizations
in order to identify those that appear to reveal "a consistent pattern of reliably attested injustice and discriminatory practices against
women."[50] The Commission is authorized under this procedure to
examine communications as a source of information only for purposes
of identifying general trends and patterns of violations against women.
The Commission can make general recommendations to ECOSOC on
the action it may wish to take on trends and patterns, but it is not authorized to take any other action.[51] Byrnes suggested that the Commission
should be encouraged to improve this procedure for the purposes of
identifying specific situations in which individuals need redress, or
inequitable country situations, and conducting thorough studies of
them.

The Commission on the Status of Women has contributed to the 1993 International Human Rights Conference, the 1993 International Year for the World's Indigenous People, the 1994 Population and Development Conference, the 1994 International Year of the Family and, for example, the UN Decade of International Law 1990–99. The Commission is planning the 1995 Women's Conference to be held in Beijing, China. It might be encouraged to appoint Working Groups or Special Rapporteurs on such cross-over themes as women's rights and indigenous rights, the impact of structural adjustment on the exercise of women's rights, and ensuring women's rights in the family and in family planning programs. The Working Groups or the Special Rapporteurs could report during these international conferences and years.

The Sub-Commission on the Prevention of Discrimination and Protection of Minorities (the Sub-Commission) has used Working Groups and Special Rapporteurs to address alleged human rights violations where women are particularly vulnerable. The Sub-Commission's Working Group on Contemporary Forms of Slavery has developed a Plan of Action for governments on child prostitution and child pornography and a Plan for the Prevention of Traffic in Persons and the Exploitation of the Prostitution of Others.[52] The Sub-Commission has created a Special Rapporteur on Traditional Practices Affecting the Health of Women and Children.[53]

The Sub-Commission is also considering the role and equal participation of women in development as a sub-issue of the New International Economic Order and the promotion of human rights, and is considering the prevention of discrimination and protection of women as a sub-issue of the program on Promotion, Protection, and Restoration of Human Rights at National, Regional, and International Levels.[54]

The Resolution 1503 procedure requires that the communications before the Sub-Commission reveal a consistent pattern of gross violations of human rights. However, Byrnes concluded that this procedure has made little contribution to addressing issues of sex discrimination or violations of human rights that have a significant gender dimension.

Regional Protection

Regional human rights conventions have been applied only sparingly to violations of women's human rights. There have been five cases concerning the violation of women's human rights before the European Court of Human Rights,[55] and one case before the Inter-American Court of Human Rights.[56] In addition, the European Commission of Human Rights, the Inter-American Commission of Human Rights, and the Court of Justice of the European Communities, established under the Treaty of Rome, have all considered complaints concerning women's legal status.[57] And yet there are many ways at regional levels beyond specifically judicial approaches to enhance the norm of the prohibition of all forms of discrimination against women. Advocacy at the regional level provides opportunities that do not necessarily exist at the international level. Geographic proximity, cultural similarity, and economic interdependence can all facilitate the development and application of human rights standards.[58] Regional systems can provide opportunities to establish legitimacy of women's human rights within the cultures of the region.

According to Anja-Riitta Ketokoski, of the Finnish Ministry for Foreign Affairs and a member of the Committee for the Equality between Women and Men of the Council of Europe, there are many legal and extra-legal ways in which a European heritage is evolving for "parity democracy in decision making." She advised women to concentrate their efforts on the institutions in which they can most meaningfully participate. In the European human rights system, for instance, Ketokoski characterized the Conference on Security and Cooperation in Europe and the European Economic Community as less woman-friendly than the Council of Europe and the Nordic Council of Ministers, where recipes for the protection and promotion of women's rights are exchanged and refined regularly.

Chaloka Beyani, a Zambian research fellow at Wolfson College, Oxford, stressed the importance of using the sexual equality provisions of the African Charter, because most national constitutions in Africa do not include sex as a prohibited ground of discrimination.[59] He explained that the African Charter requires the elimination of all forms of discrimination against women, as stipulated in international declarations and conventions, including the Women's Convention.

He observed that the African Charter obliges the African Commission to draw inspiration from the international law of human rights and international human rights instruments, which enables it to establish a collaborative relationship with CEDAW. Collaboration is appropriate, since some African states are parties to both the African Charter and the Women's Convention. Furthermore, collaboration would facilitate the African Commission in undertaking an investigation into ways and means of protecting women's rights in Africa, which Beyani considered a top priority for the African Commission.

Medina agreed with Beyani that it is important to broaden the basis of comparison. She explained that the Inter-American Commission on Human Rights and the Inter-American Court of Human Rights have the authority to monitor the conduct of states with regard not only to the American Convention but also to all other obligations in the field of human rights, including the Women's Convention.[60] She observed that the Inter-American Commission on Human Rights might be assisted in its task of protecting and promoting the human rights of women if it had working ties with the Inter-American Commission on Women.

The Commission on Women has the power to consult the Inter-American Court on matters concerning the application of human rights treaties to women. The Commission could seek an Advisory Opinion from the Court on the permissibility of reservations to the Women's Convention filed by countries that are members of the Organization of American States. She cautioned, however, that a prerequisite of effective use of the inter-American system for the protection of human rights of women is education and training of women's groups, judges, and lawyers.

Domestic Protection

Domestic protection of women's human rights is usually the first line of defense for women. As Anne Bayefsky, of the Faculty of Law, University of Ottawa, explained, the international machinery for the protection of human rights is subsidiary to the national machinery. A general rule in international law is that domestic remedies (where they exist) have to be exhausted before international or regional tribunals will take up a case. This rule requires the state to afford a prior opportunity to redress alleged violations by its own means and within the framework of its domestic legal system.

Bayefsky noted that there are alternative general theories about the relationship between municipal law and international law, and one has to look to municipal law to determine which theory is embraced by each country:[61]

1. The adoption theory states that international law is part of domestic law automatically, that is without an act of incorporation, except where it conflicts with statutory law, or well-established rules of the Common Law.
2. The transformation theory states that international law is only part of domestic law when it has been incorporated into domestic law.

When human rights treaties are directly adopted into internal law, they may be invoked before and enforced by municipal courts and administrative authorities. Domestic protection of women's rights can be strengthened in states that favor the latter theory by the transformation of international human rights treaties, either in whole or in part, through legislation or presidential decrees.

Hossain explored the possibility of using the Women's Convention to challenge discriminatory aspects of personal laws and further to define the content of the right to sexual nondiscrimination in domestic law.[62] She explained that personal laws "sanction discrimination against women through practices such as polygamy, limited rights to divorce, guardianship and custody." Use of the sexual nondiscrimination provision of the Bangladesh Constitution to challenge discriminatory aspects of personal laws is limited by the fact that the constitutional guarantee extends only to the state and public spheres.

Hossain argued that the Women's Convention requires Bangladesh, as a state party, to eliminate all forms of discrimination against women *by any person* and to ensure equality with respect to *marriage and family relations*. She contended that Bangladeshi reservations to the Women's Convention are impermissible as they are incompatible with the object and purpose of the Convention. Bangladesh is therefore obligated to implement the entire Convention without delay. She considered that

it is imperative to insist upon the incorporation of universally accepted norms of nondiscrimination in every sphere, which prioritize the rights of the individual above those of the traditionally defined community. State sanction of such norms would assist in the process of their legitimization, critical in a situation where traditional and customary notions of women's roles hold sway. Popular legitimization of these principles would provide leverage not only for substantive internal reform of each community's laws but perhaps also for eventual overhaul of the system. (see p. 486)

Common Denominators

Participants at the Consultation focused on the goal of achieving women's equal human rights, and the role that international law could play in achieving this end. They identified certain basic strategies that should be developed in order to equip activists inspired by the ideal of making women's equality a reality. Participants agreed on their common destination, but also concurred that different pathways towards it would have to be followed because they were setting out from different origins. The Consultation was seen as providing ideas for reform that could move from different origins towards the common destination.

Prerequisites to reform included improved education and training in human rights law and processes, provision of legal services for women's empowerment, development of capacities to research facts and publicize findings, and promotion of the feminist presence on human rights committees, courts, and commissions.

Mona Rishmawi, of the International Commission of Jurists in Geneva, thought that training for judges and personnel providing legal services for women was extremely important.[63] She explained that international law in general and international human rights law in particular is usually foreign to judges. Training is important to show judges how this body of law can be used domestically and to make this law more accessible to them. She also recommended legal services and social counseling for women because, without it, women who are economically dependent on their husbands will not have the means to bring cases.

With training on women's international human rights for judges and legal aid for women, Plata suggested it might be possible to file individual communications from several countries of a region with the regional human rights commission, such as the Inter-American Commission on Human Rights on a particular form of women's subordination, such as the nonenforcement of criminal laws against perpetrators of domestic violence.

Most committees, courts, and commissions are composed of men, a fact that may significantly reduce the chances of success of novel claims about the systemic nature of women's subordination. The feminist presence on domestic, regional, and international human rights tribunals has to be increased to ensure that women's concerns are addressed.

One of the themes that emerged from the consultation was that effective application of women's international human rights depends on both vertical and horizontal interactions. Vertical interaction involves both working down and working up. Working down refers to the process that Byrnes called "bringing the international back home," meaning increasing the use of women's international human rights at the domestic level in legal and political contexts. Working up means introducing legal developments favorable to women, such as the *Andrews* decision, and the diversity of women's experiences within different cultures, into international human rights law.

Horizontal interaction refers to the exchange of experiences among regional human rights systems and among national courts or systems of the same region. For example, Beyani believed that the experience gained in the inter-American system is particularly useful for application of the African Charter. Lockwood spoke of the importance of NGOs filing *amicus curiae* briefs in cases that might have important implications for women fighting similar causes in other countries, as was done by the Cincinnati-based Urban Morgan Institute in *Unity Dow*. States do not have to wait for laws and practices to be challenged, or for human rights tribunals to consider alleged violations of rights, before moving to protect women. They can begin by changing their laws and policies that are similar to those of other countries that have been successfully challenged under human rights conventions to which they are party.

Many recommendations made during the consultation depend for effectiveness on the political will of the state. It must be kept in mind that relationships between women and the state vary from country to country, and are evolving. Ketokoski described the Nordic states as increasingly allied with women, whereas Coomaraswamy explained that Asian women are alienated from the state. Brigitte Mabandla, of the Community Law Centre of the University of the Western Cape, South Africa, spoke of the importance of mobilizing women to ensure that their interests are protected by the new South African Constitution. Karen Knop, of the Faculty of Law, University of Toronto, discussed the different approaches that women might take to the institution of the state, including reconstituting state sovereignty so as to enable women to participate directly in the evolution of international law on issues directly and indirectly affecting them.[64]

The consultation showed that among lawyers there must be better interaction in the work of theoreticians and practitioners. Academic lawyers working on the integration of women's human rights into the universal human rights movement must be aware of how theoretical concepts depend for effectiveness on applicability according to the rules of practice and needs of documentation of human rights committees, courts, and commissions. Legal practitioners must recognize that their work will be enriched by awareness of feminist analysis, and the relation of practical goals to the transcending evolution of the human rights movement.

The nature and extent of violations of women's international human rights continue to be cruel and pervasive. In many countries, violations remain not simply unremedied, but unnoticed as discriminatory or as an affront to human dignity. This widespread failure to honor international obligations poses a challenge to the credibility, universality, and justice of international human rights law.

A slightly different version of this chapter also appears in *Hum. Rts. Q.* 15 (1993): 230–61; *Thatched Patio* 5(4) (1992): 29–63. I am grateful to the participants whose insights reflected in their papers and consultation contributions have made this report possible, to Karen Knop for her extensive help in the preparation of this report and to Julia McNally and Valerie Oosterveld for their note taking during the consultation and subsequent research assistance.

Notes

1. Hilary Charlesworth, "What are 'Women's International Human Rights'?" Chapter 3 in this book.

2. Celina Romany, "State Responsibility Goes Private: A Feminist Critique of the Public/Private Distinction in International Human Rights Law," Chapter 4 in this book.

3. Adetoun O. Ilumoka, "African Women's Economic, Social, and Cultural Rights—Toward a Relevant Theory and Practice," Chapter 12 in this book.

4. See generally Charlotte Bunch, "Women's Rights as Human Rights: Toward a Re-Vision of Human Rights," *Hum. Rts. Q.* 12 (1990): 486; Andrew Byrnes, "Women, Feminism, and International Human Rights Law—Methodological Myopia, Fundamental Flaws, or Meaningful Marginalization?" *Austl. Y.B. Int'l L.* 12 (1992): 205; Hilary Charlesworth, Christine Chinkin, and Shelley Wright, "Feminist Approaches to International Law," *Am. J. Int'l L.* 85(4) (1991): 613; Rebecca Cook, "Women's International Human Rights: A Bibliography," *N.Y.U. J. Int'l L. & Pol.* 24 (1992): 857.

5. *Airey v. Ireland*, 32 Eur. Ct. H.R. (ser. A) (1979) (responsible for not having taken the necessary positive steps to ensure a woman's access to courts to secure a separation from her abusive husband); *X & Y v. the Netherlands*, 91 Eur. Ct. H.R. (ser. A) (1985) (responsible for not having enacted appropriate criminal legislation to vindicate the rights of a mentally handicapped girl who had been raped).

6. *Velásquez Rodríguez v. Honduras*, Judgment of 29 July 1988, Inter-Am. C.H.R., OAS/ser. L./V./III.19, doc. 13 (1988) (responsible for not using the organs of state to prevent, investigate, and punish disappearances perpetrated by private actors); *Herrera Rubio v. Colombia*, Comm. No. 161/1983 U.N. Doc. CCPR/C/OP/2, 192 (responsible for failure to take appropriate measures to prevent disappearances and subsequent killings and failure to take measures to remedy violations of denial of liberty and dignity of person).

7. Radhika Coomaraswamy, "To Bellow like a Cow: Women, Ethnicity, and the Discourse of Rights," Chapter 2 in this book.

8. Abdullahi Ahmed An-Na'im, "State Responsibility Under International Human Rights Law to Change Religious and Customary Laws," Chapter 7 in this book.

9. Abdullahi Ahmed An-Na'im, "Islam, Islamic Law, and the Dilemma of Cultural Legitimacy for Universal Human Rights," in *Asian Perspectives on Human Rights*, ed. Claude E. Welch and Virginia Leary (Boulder, CO: Westview Press, 1990), 31.

10. Vienna Convention on the Law of Treaties, May 23, 1969, art. 31 (3)(b), 1155 U.N.T.S. 331, 340.

11. U.N. Doc. CCPR/C/21/Rev.1/Add.1, para. 13 (1989).

12. Kathleen E. Mahoney, "Canadian Approaches to Equality Rights and Gender Equity in the Courts," Chapter 19 in this book.

13. *Andrews v. Law Society of British Columbia* [1989] 1 S.C.R. 143.

14. See generally Anne F. Bayefsky, "The Principle of Equality or Non-Discrimination in International Law," *Hum. Rts. L.J.* 11 (1990): 1.

15. See generally Rebecca Cook, "International Protection of Women's Reproductive Rights," *N.Y.U. J. Int'l L. & Pol.* 24 (1992): 645, 689.

16. Rhonda Copelon, "Intimate Terror: Understanding Domestic Violence as Torture," Chapter 5 in this book.

17. See generally *Report of the Special Rapporteur to the Sub-Commission on Prevention of Discrimination and Protection of Minorities in the Realization of Economic, Social, and Cultural Rights,* U.N. Doc. E/CN.4/Sub.2/1992/16.

18. Akua Kuenyehia, "The Impact of Structural Adjustment Programs on Women's International Human Rights: The Example of Ghana," Chapter 18 in this book.

19. See generally "Bibliography," in Joint Consultative Group on Policy, *Women and Structural Adjustment* (New York: United Nations Population Fund, 1991).

20. For further discussion see sections below on "Treaty-based bodies" and "Charter-based bodies."

21. James C.N. Paul, "International Development Agencies, Human Rights, and Humane Development Projects," *Denv. J. Int'l L. Pol'y* 17 (1988): 67; Katarina Tomaševski, "The World Bank and Human Rights," in *Yearbook of Human Rights in Developing Countries 1989,* ed. Manfred Nowak (Oslo: Norwegian Institute of Human Rights), 75.

22. Court of Appeal of Botswana, Civil Appeal No. 4/91 (unreported 1992).

23. Botswana, note 22 at 54. See Judgment No. 30 of 9 February 1983 of the Italian Constitutional Court (La Legislazione Italiana: 1983, sec. 14, 28–29) declaring a similar Italian law unconstitutional, U.N. Doc. CEDAW/C/5/Add.62 at p. 53 (1989) (Italy).

24. For the disabilities of the women with respect to nationality in Gabon, Burkina Faso, and Rwanda, see U.N. Economic Commission for Africa, *Implementation in Africa of the Convention on the Elimination of All Forms of Discrimination against Women,* E/ECA/CM.13/27 at para. 33 (1987); *Report of the Committee on the Elimination of All Forms of Discrimination Against Women* (Tenth Session), U.N. Doc. A/46/38, 3 April 1991, paras. 131 and 237.

25. Cyprus, Egypt, Korea, Iraq, Jamaica, and Thailand have reserved; Rebecca Cook, "Reservations to the Convention on the Elimination of All Forms of Discrimination Against Women," *Va. J. Int'l L.* 30 (1990): 643, 693, 714.

26. *Egyptian Gazette,* January 30, 1992, explaining that Mamdouh el-Gohari, a member of the People's Assembly, has proposed such a law; Communication Group for the Enhancement of the Status of Women, *Legal Rights of Egyptian Women in Theory and Practice* (Cairo: Communication Group 1992), 33–35.

27. Christina M. Cerna, U.N. Human Rights Centre, Geneva, in an address to the Consultation on Women's International Human Rights held at the Faculty of Law, University of Toronto, August 31–September 2, 1992.

28. Kirti Singh, "Obstacles to Women's Rights in India," Chapter 16 in this book; Kirti Singh, "Women and the Reform of Personal Law," in *The Hindus and Others: The Question of Identity in India,* ed. G. Pandey (London: Penguin, 1993), 177–97.

29. *Mohammad Ahmed Khan v. Shah Bano,* A.I.R. (1985) S.C. 945.

30. Asma Mohamed Abdel Halim, "Challenges to the Application of International Women's Human Rights in the Sudan," Chapter 17 in this book.

31. Rohini Hensman, "Oppression Within Oppression: The Dilemma of Muslim Women in India," *Thatched Patio* 5 (1990): 22.

32. Florence Butegwa, "Using the African Charter on Human and Peoples' Rights to Secure Women's Access to Land in Africa," Chapter 21 in this book; symposium edition on "Realizing the Rights of Women in the Development Processes: Women's Legal Entitlements to Agricultural Development and Financial Assistance," *Third World Legal Stud.* (1991): 45.

33. 1991 Colombian Constitution, art. 42; see generally María Isabel Plata, "Reproductive Rights as Human Rights: The Colombian Case," Chapter 22 in this book.

34. *Salud para la mujer, mujer para la salud* (Health for Women, Women for Health) (Bogotá: Ministry of Public Health, May 1992).

35. Colombian Ministry of Public Health Resolution 1531 of 6 March 1992.

36. See generally Joan Fitzpatrick, "The Use of International Human Rights Norms to Combat Violence Against Women," Chapter 23 in this book.

37. Andrew Byrnes, "The Committee Against Torture," in *The United Nations and Human Rights: A Critical Appraisal,* ed. Philip Alston (Oxford: Oxford University Press, 1992), 509, 519–20.

38. Rebecca J. Cook, "State Accountability Under the Convention on the Elimination of All Forms of Discrimination Against Women," Chapter 9 in this book.

39. Kenneth Roth, "Domestic Violence as an International Human Rights Issue," Chapter 13 in this book; and case listings, note 7.

40. For further exploration of the application of these theories of state responsibility for the violations of women's rights, see Human Rights Watch, *Criminal Injustice: Violence Against Women in Brazil* (New York: Human Rights Watch, 1991); Human Rights Watch, *Double Jeopardy: Police Abuse of Women in Pakistan* (New York: Human Rights Watch, 1992); Human Rights Watch, *Punishing the Victim: Rape and Mistreatment of Asian Maids in Kuwait* (New York: Human Rights Watch, 1992).

41. Andrew Byrnes, "Toward More Effective Enforcement of Women's Human Rights Through the Use of International Human Rights Law and Procedures," Chapter 8 in this book. See also "Procedures for Complaints of Human Rights Violations," in Commonwealth Human Rights Initiative, *Put Our World to Rights: Towards a Commonwealth Human Rights Strategy,* app. IV (London: Commonwealth Secretariat, 1991), 201–27; Hurst Hannum, ed., *Guide to International Human Rights Practice,* 2d ed. (Philadelphia: University of Pennsylvania Press, 1992).

42. *Lovelace v. Canada,* Communication No. 24/197, U.N. Doc. A/36/40 (1981); U.N. Doc. CCPR/C/OP/1 at 83 (1985) (law requiring that only Indian women, but not Indian men, lose their status and rights when they marry a non-Indian man, held to be a denial of their right to enjoy their own culture).

43. *Aumeeruddy-Cziffra et al. v. Mauritius,* Communication No. 35/1978, U.N. Doc. A/36/40 (1981) (law limiting residency status of foreign spouses of Mauritian women but not similarly situated Mauritian men held discriminatory); *Ato del Avellanal v. Perú,* Communication No. 202/1986, U.N. Doc. A/44/40 (1989) (women held to have equality before the courts).

44. For further discussion see the section below on "Recharacterizing Nondiscrimination Rights."

45. *Broeks v. The Netherlands,* Communications No. 172/1984, U.N. GAOR, 42nd Sess., Supp. No. 40, at 139, U.N. Doc. A/42/40 (1987) (same entitlements to social security benefits for women required as similarly situated men); *Zwaan-de Vries v. The Netherlands,* Communication No. 182/1984, U.N. GAOR, 42nd Sess., Supp. No. 40, at 160, U.N. Doc. A/42/40 (1987) (same holding as in *Broeks*); but see *Vos v. The Netherlands,* Communication No. 218/1986, U.N. Doc. A/44/40 at 232 (1989) (unequal disability allowance justified).

46. To obtain copies of the reports, which are available in the official languages of the United Nations (English, French, Spanish, Arabic, Chinese,

and Russian), write to the United Nations Division for the Advancement of Women, DC-2 Building, 12th Floor, 2 United Nations Plaza, New York, NY 10017, U.S.A. See generally the annual report on the CEDAW meetings of the International Women's Rights Action Watch, Humphrey Institute, University of Minnesota, Minneapolis.

47. *Yilmaz-Dogan v. The Netherlands*, Communication No. 1/1984, U.N. Doc. CERD/C36/D/1/1984 (termination from job in a textile factory of a Turkish woman residing in the Netherlands held racially discriminatory).

48. Scott Leckie, "An Overview and Appraisal of the Fifth Session of the U.N. Committee on Economic, Social and Cultural Rights," *Hum. Rts. Q.* 13 (1991): 545, 546.

49. See generally Irene Tinker, ed., *Persistent Inequalities: Women and World Development* (Oxford: Oxford University Press, 1990); Anne Marie Goetz, "Feminism and the Claim to Know: Contradictions in Feminist Approaches to Women and Development," in *Gender and International Relations*, ed. Rebecca Grant and Kathleen Newland (Bloomington: Indiana University Press, 1991), 133–57.

50. E.S.C. Res. 27, U.N. ESCOR, 26 May 1983.

51. See generally Report of the Secretary General, *Monitoring the Implementation of the Nairobi Forward-Looking Strategies for the Advancement of Women: Examining Existing Mechanisms for Communications of the Status of Women*, U.N. Doc. E/CN.6/1991/10, 9 Nov. 1990.

52. See generally *Report of the Working Group on Contemporary Forms of Slavery*, U.N. GAOR, 15th Sess., U.N. Doc. E/CN.4/Sub.2/1990/44.

53. See generally *Report of the Special Rapporteur on Traditional Practices Affecting the Health of Women and Children*, U.N. Doc. E/CN.4/Sub.2/1991/6.

54. See generally U.N. Secretary General, *Annotations to the Provisional Agenda of the Forty-third Session of the Sub-Commission on Prevention of Discrimination and Protection of Minorities*, U.N. Doc. E/CN.4/Sub.2/1991/1/Add. 1, 17 May 1991.

55. See case listings, note 5; *Marckx v. Belgium*, 31 Eur. Ct. H.R. (ser. A) (1979) (law requiring unmarried mothers to register and officially adopt their own child violates privacy and nondiscrimination rights); *Abdulaziz, Cabales & Balkandali v. United Kingdom*, 94 Eur. Ct. H.R. (ser. A) (1985) (law requiring women, but not men, lawfully settled in the United Kingdom to meet certain requirements before their foreign husbands could join them violates privacy and nondiscrimination rights); *Open Door and Dublin Well Woman v. Ireland*, 64/1991/316/387–388, 29 Oct. 1992 (governmental ban on counseling where to find abortions abroad violates rights to impart and receive information); see generally Buquicchio-de Boer, *Sexual Equality in the European Convention on Human Rights: A Survey of Case Law*, Council of Europe, Doc. EG(89) 3 (1989).

56. *Proposed Amendment to the Naturalization Provisions of the Constitution of Costa Rica*, Inter-Am. C.H.R., Advisory Opinion OC-4/84 of January 19, 1984 (Ser. A., No. 4) (1984) (proposed amendment to Costa Rican Constitution distinguishing between foreign men and women marrying Costa Rican citizens held discriminatory); see generally Cecilia Medina, "Women's Rights as Human Rights: Latin American Countries and the Organization of American States (OAS)," in *Women, Feminist Identity, and Society in the 1980s*, ed. Myriam Diaz-Diocaretz and Iris M. Zavala (Amsterdam: John Benjamins, 1985), 63–79.

57. See generally Rebecca Cook, "International Human Rights Law Concerning Women: Case Notes and Comments," *Vand. J. Transnat'l L.* 23 (1990):

779; Sacha Prechal and Noreen Burrows, *Gender Discrimination Law of the European Community* (Brookfield, VT: Dartmouth Publishing, 1990).

58. Burns H. Weston, Robin Ann Lukes, and Kelly Hnatt, "Regional Human Rights Regimes: A Comparison and Appraisal," *Vand. J. Transnat'l L.* 20 (1987): 585, 589–90.

59. Chaloka Beyani, "Toward a More Effective Guarantee of Women's Rights in the African Human Rights System," Chapter 11 in this book.

60. Cecilia Medina, "Toward a More Effective Guarantee of the Enjoyment of Human Rights by Women in the Inter-American System," Chapter 10 in this book.

61. Anne F. Bayefsky, "General Approaches to Domestic Application of Women's International Human Rights Law," Chapter 15 in this book. Information on domestic legislation enacted pursuant to human rights conventions can be found in the reports of states parties submitted to the human rights treaty bodies.

62. Sara Hossain, "Equality in the Home: Women's Rights and Personal Laws in South Asia," Chapter 20 in this book.

63. Mona Rishmawi, "The Developing Approaches of the International Commission of Jurists to Women's Human Rights," Chapter 14 in this book.

64. Karen Knop, "Why Rethinking the Sovereign State Is Important for Women's International Human Rights Law," Chapter 6 in this book.

Part II
Challenges

Chapter 2
To Bellow like a Cow: Women, Ethnicity, and the Discourse of Rights

Radhika Coomaraswamy

"Why have you appeared before this gathering?
Why do you bellow like a cow in labor?
Your time must be near.
Shameless women with no sense of decorum
Bellow in gatherings of respectable men."
—Addressed to Bhola Moiraon Poetess Jogeswari and her
female troupe, nineteenth century

Introduction

In *The Politics of Rights,* Stuart Scheingold writes:

The appeals made by the myth of rights for the support of Americans are rooted in traditional values and closely associated with venerable institutions. The symbolic voice of the myth of rights can, moreover, be easily understood and readily adapted to political discourse. But just how compelling is it? How pervasive and widespread and uniform a grip do legal values have on the minds of Americans?[1]

Implicit in this argument is that, for human rights to be effective, they have to go beyond the normative, textual essence and become a part of the legal culture of a given society. They must strike a responsive chord in the general public consciousness with regard to political and civil issues. This resonance is therefore the clue to whether the "myth of rights" works in a given society to ensure the political and civil rights of all persons.

This chapter argues that in the area of women's rights as human rights there is the least amount of resonance, especially in the countries of South Asia, and that this lack of resonance has prevented the effective implementation of rights.

The barriers to the implementation of human rights are two-fold. First, the lack of proper implementation machinery to make rights real in the lives of women is an obstacle, as is women's lack of awareness of the rights machinery that would empower them. The second and more formidable barrier is the refusal to accept the values in and of themselves: an ideological resistance to human rights for women.

In saying this I do not want to get caught in what is called the "Orientalist trap."[2] It is easy to divide the world into bipolar categories: the west is progressive on women's rights and the east is barbaric and backward. The reverse of this argument from the eastern point of view is to accept the distinction, but to say that the east is superior, more communal, and less self-centered with no place for this "adversarial" concept of rights. I would argue that in South Asia both traditions exist. There are examples of personal laws and women's rights that informed issues such as no-fault divorce and the best interest of the child centuries before the west considered them. The Kandyan laws of the Kandyan Sinhalese are one example.[3]

The Privileged Female Personality

To analyze the barriers posed by culture, custom, and personal laws with regard to women's rights as human rights, it is important to analyze the underlying assumption about the female personality that accompanies any discourse of women's rights especially in documents such as the Convention on the Elimination of All Forms of Discrimination Against Women (the Women's Convention).[4] The personality that is privileged in such documents is the free, independent woman as an individual endowed with rights and rational agency. It is, in fact, the culmination of the enlightenment project, the "rights of man" now being enjoyed by women. This is perhaps exemplified in the most controversial, and therefore the most important, provision of the Women's Convention, Article 16.

Article 16 requires that the states parties on a basis of equality of men and women ensure that women have the same right to choose a spouse freely and to enter into marriage with their free and full consent.[5] It also requires the state to ensure the same personal rights for husband and wife, including the right to choose a family name, a profession, and an occupation.[6]

Though the Women's Convention's emphasis is on the principle of nondiscrimination, and not on the principle of empowerment,[7] there is the assumption that it privileges the free, independent, and empowered woman. The only female differences accepted by the Women's Convention relate to a woman's condition of maternity in the section on labor law[8] and with regard to special rights related to the redressing of historical grievances.[9] The highlighting of these differences is only to ensure that the state take necessary measures to ensure that a woman is given the opportunity to develop her individual identity, rooted in an enlightenment view of the human personality, a personality without fetters or community context.

I am in agreement with the enlightenment view of the human personality. But it would be wrong to assume that the values contained in the Universal Declaration of Human Rights are truly universal. Such an assumption would make more than half the world the subject of ridicule. However, to work toward this enlightenment ideal, it is important to expose the ideologies of power that sustain counter-ideologies which view women as inferior. It is also important to learn how Asian societies may in fact further the rights of women even beyond those contained in international conventions—those rights which are attached to a woman in the context of her class, her caste, and her ethnic group.

The Duality in Modern Law

For the greater part of the non-western world, the approach to women is couched in ambiguity. The Sri Lankan Constitution inspired by liberal, socialist norms is one such example. It states after a general nondiscrimination clause that includes sex:

Nothing in this Article shall prevent special provision being made by law, subordinate legislation or executive action for the advancement of women, children and disabled persons.[10]

On the one hand, the drafters argue that this formulation is to allow room for affirmative action on behalf of women, but the juxtaposition of women, children, and the mentally retarded is an extremely interesting feature. It is especially so if we compare it to Article 4 of the Women's Convention:

Adoption by States Parties of temporary special measures aimed at accelerating de facto equality between men and women shall not be considered discriminatory.[11]

The first formulation as expressed in the Sri Lankan Constitution does not accept responsibility for historical wrong while the second implicitly does. The reason for this lies also in the fact that Sri Lanka is a Buddhist society; many of its leading scholars feel that there was no traditional discrimination against women and that discrimination is a colonial legacy. This line of thinking is dominant—discrimination originated with colonialism.[12]

Second, the Sri Lankan Constitution, in juxtaposing women with children and the disabled accentuates the duality present in all laws with regard to women. On the one hand, there is nondiscrimination and an assertion of women's equality with men. On the other hand, there is the belief that woman is vulnerable and needs protection. In this paternalistic project, women, along with children and the mentally disabled, are denied agency—the right to protect themselves.

The special protection provision on behalf of women is also defended on the ground that the reality of working conditions in a developing country often puts a worker's health at risk. That proposition is indisputable. But the argument of nondiscrimination requires that men also be protected from the terrible working conditions that may impair health. Equality in this worldview is only present to help women, it is not reciprocal. This line of thinking is similar to the cases on social security that came before the U.S. courts in the early 1970s, where men as widowers, husbands, and dependents claimed social security benefits to which they felt entitled.[13]

The Anthropological Reality: Ideological Barriers

The Sri Lankan Constitution is a modern document drawn from liberal and socialist inspiration. In some ways the issues it raises are easily identifiable and are within the framework of discourse that characterizes legal thinking with regard to women's rights as fundamental rights. The barriers, though real, are thought out and solutions of various inclinations have been put forward. It is a modern problem in the realm of world history and rights discourse. While the so-called modern Constitution reflects this duality between freedom and vulnerability, the situation becomes still more complicated if one deals with what is often called the "anthropological reality."

The "extra-legal" factors that are barriers to the consideration of women's rights as human rights in South Asia are rooted in ideological aspects, especially as they relate to the tension between the law and civil society, as well as within the legal system itself. Let us begin with the former.

Law and Civil Society

Ashis Nandy, an influential Indian scholar, analyzes the roots of the modern Indian crisis in the disjunction between the traditions of Indian civil society and the colonial inheritance of a modern nation-state run on Weberian lines, with bureaucracy and the market being the central organizational features. The law is the central instrument in this colonial process that aims at erasing tradition and plurality, and restructuring civil society along modern lines. The law and the state are the special targets of hatred and the rights discourse is seen as a manifestation of this impersonal, homogenizing, activist state. Judicial activism is anathema to scholars such as Nandy.

Nandy is one of the most influential scholars in South Asia. His challenge to rights discourse is the best articulated response to modern statehood which, through the use of law, attempts to ensure equality. It is important to examine his argument to recognize the type of ideological barriers that we face in South Asia when we talk about women's rights as human rights. The speeches and pamphlets of religious and ethnic dignitaries are self-evident in their rejection of the west, including rights, in what may be considered the Orientalist encounter. But Nandy is a more sophisticated, and perhaps a more enticing, articulator of the rejection of the concept of an activist state intervening to impose a model of equality based on the values of the Universal Declaration of Human Rights.

In "The Making and Unmaking of Political Culture,"[14] he argues that India has a measure of cultural autonomy from western values and institutions and that this autonomy persists despite the best efforts of the government. He argues that in the worldview of traditional Indian culture politics was considered the Machiavellian art of the possible. It occupied only a very limited sphere, that of providing security to the population. Civil society was the arena for struggle and conflict in traditional India, and it was ruled by precepts of *dharma* and ethics. Tolerance, he claims, was an aspect of everyday life. In the hierarchy of power, power over self was valued above state power, which was the least respected and the most brutal. Nandy's argument is supported by Deepak Lal's two-volume work, *The Hindu Equilibrium.*[15]

In this view of the dichotomy between civil society and the state, the root of all evil is located at the colonial encounter where the Weberian concept of state was transferred to Indian soil. The competition among political parties, the struggle for state resources, and the supremacy of state power are what Nandy points to as the main reasons for what Atul Kohli calls "the crisis of governability."[16]

The implications of this scheme of analysis for human rights are not very clear. Nandy is not opposed to the substance of human rights, which he feels is at the root of popular culture, and the humanistic face of civil society. However, he is totally opposed to the mechanism employed for its enforcement—the law and the paternalistic state. He argues instead for strengthening human rights values in civil society.

Nandy's point of view has been criticized as a romanticized view of the Indian past and of Indian popular culture. The rigors of the caste system or sex-based oppression cannot all be laid at the doorstep of colonial India. Many practices in Indian civil society shock the conscience and cannot be willed away as an aberration. And yet there is a voice there that should also be heard.

If one looks at the Women's Convention and other international documents of human rights, every article begins with the word "states parties" and proceeds to unfold the obligation imposed upon the state. As states are the foundation of the international order, this is inescapable. However, if the state is entrusted with the responsibility of ensuring women's rights, if it is always viewed as active and paternalistic in a benign manner, then this does pose serious questions. The nation-state in the third world does not carry this "Scandinavian aura." In addition, there is a major problem of implementation in what Kohli calls the redistribution of poverty.[17] Nandy is correct in one sense, that unless these human rights values take root in civil society and unless civil institutions and non-governmental organizations (NGOs) take up the cause, then women's rights as human rights will have no resonance in the social institutions concerned.

There are situations, of course, where state action or inaction with regard to a particular community galvanizes an awareness of human rights as part of the struggle of elements within society. The Chipko movement in India is one such example. Women protected their livelihood by wrapping themselves around trees when the bulldozers, which were part of a larger development project, came into their areas.[18] In Sri Lanka ethnic and civil violence has galvanized groups into action from all strata of society and has in itself instilled values of the right to life and freedom from arbitrary arrest. Lived experience is the best fermenting ground for human rights awareness and action, including the rights of women. In that sense Nandy is correct. The future of human rights in the South Asian region does not lie with states parties but with the movements in civil society.

Where Nandy is wrong is that the law is not only an empty shell but also a catalyst for mobilization. Even if the future lies in civil society, there have to be standards by which one can hold individuals and states accountable. In addition, in some rare instances, the courts are also galvanized into action. In such a context this artificial separation into civil society where the popular will resides, and the state where the legal and bureaucratic will resides, may create more problems in the realization of women's rights. It is only a combination of the two, coming together at a particular historical moment that results in change, creativity, and social action. The first is only limited to mobilization and awareness, the second to articulation and implementation. Of course, after enactment, forces in civil society have to act as watchdogs to ensure that the rights guaranteed are protected. So Nandy's point is well taken: civil society is necessary for creating the conditions for law to be relevant. It is also useful in ensuring that law is enforced. But, at the same time, it has to be recognized that without law, any human rights activist will only be tilting at windmills.

While discussing issues of civil society, it may be important to reiterate here that the essentialist view that western civil society and law empowers women while the eastern only subordinates them is not strictly correct. There are instances where traditional laws have been more progressive than modern legislation and the colonial encounter actually robbed women of pre-existing rights. A case in point is the Kandyan law of the Sinhalese, where standards such as no-fault divorce and best interests of the child and even polyandry were recognized in the Kandyan areas of Sri Lanka, and still have some legitimacy under the modern system of law, although, of course, the practice of polyandry faded with the importation of western values.

In addition, the colonial encounter forced reinterpretation of law according to legal norms prevalent in the west. The Thesawalamai of the Sri Lankan Tamils had notions of community property akin to that of the Roman Dutch law, but Dutch drafters interpreted the notion of community property according to their law before the nineteenth-century reforms with regard to married women's property. They imposed on Tamil women the denial of the right of alienation of property without their husband's consent, with no reciprocal duty. Today, married Dutch women can freely buy and sell property acquired in their name, but married Tamil women, subject to this archaic law and its medieval interpretation, cannot do so and do not enjoy the rights given by the Married Women's Property Ordinance of the nineteenth century. And since Sri Lankan Tamil women are a minority, they have no access to change the law, which, for all purposes, may govern them until the end of time, regardless of the change in circumstances or the practices of the community.

Law and Other Ideologies of Empowerment

Since in the final analysis rights are about empowerment, what many South Asians argue is that the traditional roots of empowerment in South Asian societies are denied in rights discourse. The legal strategies that accompany rights discourse aim at an adversarial contest in the courts between the victim and the state. However, it is argued that women's empowerment in these traditional societies has manifested itself not through rights ideology but through family ideology. There have been in South Asia recently a spate of writings about "Mother, Mother-Community, and Mother-Politics."[19]

South Asia has the greatest concentration of women heads of state. India, Pakistan, Sri Lanka, and Bangladesh have all experienced women heads of state. There is ideological acceptance of women in the public realm, but this is because these women have appropriated the discourse of motherhood. Anthropologists have also noted a major rise in mother-goddess worship.[20] Of course, the glorification of woman as mother means the denigration of unmarried women, widows, childless women, and divorced women. And yet this ideology is so powerful that the present Tamil Nadu Chief Minister Jayalalitha has appropriated motherhood as a symbol even though she is neither married nor a mother. She is called the "Avenging Mother" from the context of being a protector of the poor and underprivileged.

Women activists argue that legal strategies do not allow women to touch base with their traditional sources of empowerment. In Sri Lanka the ideology of motherhood has been appropriated for political action, symbolizing the widows and mothers who have lost their husbands and children in the recent violence. The Mothers for Peace or the Mothers of the Disappeared, precisely because of their appropriation of the mother ideology, have found a great deal of political maneuverability which even politicians, caught within the same ideological construct, are hard pressed to overcome.[21]

There has been a lot of criticism about this type of strategy which uses indigenous symbols because of the other side of the same process. If one accepts mother ideology, how do we privilege the voices of the unmarried and widows? The strategy appears to divide the female community with no real, concrete, political goal save that of agitation. But what is significant is that rights discourse, because of its construction and its style of implementation, is not plugging into many of the dynamic social movements taking place in South Asia. Perhaps one should accept that one is the realm of politics, the other the realm of law. Either way, it is important to recognize that there is an important division within the sphere of social action.

Whose Equality?

Before we move on to a discussion of the law as a strategy for the attainment of women's rights through human rights, it seems important to consider for a moment the discourse of equality. Often at the same conference the word equality is used in diametrically opposite constructions. Even international documents vary. Under the Women's Convention equality is nondiscrimination—a constant measure of men against women. In other contexts equality is access to empowerment as individuals, not as a measurement of the final end that men versus women actually reaches. In some cultures, equality retains notions of separate spheres, the public and the private and separate but equal doctrines prevail, justified by the uniqueness of the maternal function.

In socialist societies equality carries with it the responsibility of the state to socialize maternity and maternal functions so as to allow a woman to work and fulfill her public life. To many others equality is an ideological disposition, rooted in attitudes and psychological make-up which can only be removed through strategies drawn from psychology and post-structuralism. For many others, equality of women is completely dependent on their class, caste, or ethnic group—if these attain equality, then women in these groups will also achieve equality. For feminists, of course, equality is the other side of patriarchy. Since every aspect of life seems to be infected by the gender bias and classification, equality will only be achieved if it is linked to social transformation of a very radical sort.

Given these diverse conceptions of equality, the law in many of these societies as well as at the international level has taken the easy way out. It is only in areas where discrimination can be factually ascertained through empirical data and actual case studies that law is relevant to the question of female equality. It is therefore not unusual that non-discrimination remains the model legislation in all parts of the world when it comes to the equality of women. Women's rights couched in this limited human rights discourse are also confined to concepts of equality that are linked to the structure of the law and its relationship with the state in any particular society. In addition, in our part of the world, there is very little autonomy that law enjoys vis-à-vis the state and politics. Human rights are then confined to this post-colonial sector of the law, legislation, the state, the bureaucracy, and political party mobilization. This is the clue to its success as well as its failure.

Opportunities and Innovations

This is not to say that interesting innovations cannot take women's rights beyond nondiscrimination in certain constitutional contexts. Since the Indian Constitution recognizes the right to life and dignity, in a series of cases the Indian courts dealt with situations that were clearly not issues of measuring men against women but rooted in life and dignity. The living conditions of the women of Agra Remand was one such case.[22] There have been others dealing for instance with women under trial, women prisoners, and women construction workers.[23] In these contexts the principles contained in the Indian Constitution permitted a move away from simple nondiscrimination—or the redistribution of poverty as it is sometimes called in third world societies—to a more empowering stance focusing on the clauses relating to human dignity. Unfortunately many countries do not have these provisions or judges willing to interpret them in a holistic light.

Barriers: Family and Personal Law

This chapter is not about opportunities but about barriers. The issues of women, ethnicity, and rights discourse eventually come to a head in the area of family law or personal law. Labor law and other forms of economic and labor legislation have a certain similar standard, modeled on ILO recommendations and directing themselves to the urban labor force. In this context the vast majority of women (87 percent of the Sri Lankan women workers)[24] work in the agricultural sector and are unprotected by the law. The barriers relating to their rights are in the urban labor bias of labor legislation. The criminal law is, of course, the security safety net of any society, and though there are many issues to raise with regard to women and violence, issues that are not directly addressed in the Women's Convention, the provisions are generally similar and have a certain uniform structure.

It is in family law, however, that completely different and plural standards and constructions exist of how we must conduct our personal and social life. It is, in fact, the litmus test in any society with regard to legal norms and the status of women. It is also the area where the law, ethnicity, and ideology with regard to the rights of women merge to become a powerful ideological force. Before we come to any conclusions about the barriers that exist about women in this area, let us look at four case studies: (1) sati in India; (2) the Hudood Ordinance in Pakistan; (3) the recent attempts at divorce reforms in Sri Lanka; and (4) the well-known *Shah Bano* case in India.

Roop Kanwar: The Sati Case

On September 4, 1987, in Deorala, Rajasthan, Roop Kanwar was burned alive on her husband's funeral pyre. She was an eighteen-year-old university student, and her husband was an unemployed university graduate when he died. Her shrine became a place of pilgrimage. Many believed she was a goddess and that offerings to her shrine would cure them of cancer, the illness that took the life of her husband. There are conflicting versions of her state of mind before her death. Some have argued that she was willing to die, others that she was coerced, still others that she was unsure but in the end succumbed to family pressure.[25]

The newspapers carrying the story a week later kindled a huge controversy. Urban-centered women's groups as well as groups of women from throughout India were horrified and organized a march in Rajasthan. The Rajasthanis retaliated by filling the streets with thousands of their own ethnic group: the right to commit sati, they claimed, was part of their ethnic culture. After months of delay the police finally arrested Roop Kanwar's father-in-law and five other members of the family for abetment to suicide. Three months later the Indian Parliament passed a tough law banning sati, even though an old law already existed, as a sign of central government intolerance of these ethnic practices declared by Rajiv Gandhi to be "utterly reprehensible and barbaric."

Though the feminist movement had scored a legal victory, the case exemplified the terrible gulf between human rights and women's rights activists, on the one hand, and those who see the status of women as an integral part of their ethnic identity, on the other. A leading Hindi journal pointed an accusing finger at secular, western-educated intellectuals, arguing that only godless people who did not believe in reincarnation would denigrate Roop's brave act.[26]

The debate over sati and Roop raged for weeks in the newspapers. There were those who argued that if it was voluntary it was all right. Suicide is a time-honored Rajasthani practice and should be accepted. It was cultural discrimination to prevent those who really wished to commit sati from doing so. There were others, such as Nandy, who argued that, although sati was a terrible affair, it was no business of the state. The onus must lie with the people and communities of Rajasthan; they must be the ones to outlaw the practice, not the central government. There were women's groups that felt that sati was so offensive that if a woman died of burns in a public place the burden of proof, as in Indian penal provisions on custodial rape, should shift to the family to prove that sati did not take place. Human rights activists, many at the forefront of the struggle against arbitrary arrest and detention, called for the imposition of the death penalty on those who aid and abet sati. The international struggle against the death penalty was forgotten in the heat of the moment.

Roop Kanwar's case sent the human rights community of India into deep crisis. First, Rajput defiance and Hindi-language newspapers pointed to how human rights consciousness was not an Indian norm; it was increasingly attributed to the "urban Western intelligentsia." This marginalization is purposeful, but, given the fact that many of the leading activists are Delhi based, it carries a measure of credibility and supports the counter belief that these human rights people are out to denigrate national culture. Spectators in Rajasthan during those days saw the people as joyous, celebrating a great event and a courageous act: they did not see anything wrong. This realization alone was terrifying to most feminists working in the twentieth century. Ironically, although the state came down strongly on the side of the women activists there was a sense that the battle was lost. Everywhere there were echoes of Nandy's initial analysis. What is the point of all these laws if the people do not believe that putting an eighteen-year-old woman on a funeral pyre and denying her life is not a violation of the most basic fundamental right—the right to life? What is the point of all the Constitutional protection if "ethnic identity" is an acceptable justification for reducing the status of women according to diverse cultural practice? As one activist said in conversation, "something died in the Indian women's movement with Roop Kanwar; the innocence of believing that what shocks your conscience will also shock the world."[27]

The Case of Safia Bibi: The Hudood Ordinance

The second case in point is the celebrated Pakistani case of Safia Bibi. Safia was a blind girl who alleged that she was raped. She was still a minor so her father filed a complaint of rape two days before she delivered the child supposedly born of this union. Her parents claimed that Safia had told them of the rape, but that fear and humiliation had kept them silent. The alleged rapist retorted that the blind girl was of loose virtue.

Under the newly promulgated Hudood Ordinance, under the Offences of Zina Ordinance,[28] Safia and victims of rape faced a major dilemma. If Safia alleged rape and failed to prove it (rape conviction requires four male witnesses), then she could be sent to jail for "adultery" if she was married and "fornication" if she was single. This is precisely what happened. The Sessions Court found Safia in violation of the Zina Ordinance and sentenced her, despite her blindness, to three years rigorous imprisonment. There was a national and an international outcry. The Federal Shariat Court set aside the judgment on technical grounds. However the alleged rapist did not spend a day in jail because of insufficient evidence.[29]

Safia Bibi's case was another crisis for the women's movement in South Asia. It was, without a doubt, the mobilization of women's groups in Pakistan along with their international network, that exerted sufficient pressure on the judges to revise the judgment.

Safia Bibi raises a very different set of issues from those raised by Roop Kanwar. In the Kanwar case, practices in civil society that were against women suddenly re-emerged in the context of new power and class struggles.[30] In the case of Safia Bibi, civil society had become accustomed to certain colonial norms with regard to criminal and civil procedures. The state, in its infinite wisdom and under martial law, introduced laws that had not been applied in Pakistan for centuries, based on its own interpretation of the Qur'an. This act of state took place after Pakistan had joined the United Nations and was thereby bound by the Universal Declaration of Human Rights. The spirit of the Hudood Ordinance, in the section on Zina and even with regard to criminal procedure in certain types of moral offenses, was clearly contrary to the Universal Declaration. In this case, the state flouted international norms so as to articulate religious fundamentalist ideals when there was no pressure from below for their promulgation. This manipulative use of religion and religious codes to defy international norms is a new manifestation of the post-colonial nation-state—a trend that may increase in the near future. The only option against this type of activity is not the legal system, which has become perverted by political will, but political mobilization from within and international support from without. The Safia Bibi case is an indication that such international efforts may succeed in some instances.[31]

No-Fault Divorce Laws: Sri Lanka

In 1991 a Committee set up to look into reform with regard to the divorce laws of Sri Lanka came up with the following recommendations:

(a) The establishment of family courts.
(b) A non-adversarial approach to marriage break-up by adopting the theory of marital breakdown.
(c) A move away from fault-based divorce to consensual divorce after two years judicial separation and/or five years separation as evidence of marital breakdown.
(d) Introducing standards with regard to the best interest of the child as the grounds for custody rather than the concept of a natural guardian—in Sri Lanka under Roman Dutch inheritance the natural guardian is the father.[32]

The Committee's recommendations were far-reaching in terms of Sri Lankan law which was still fault-based and adversarial with concepts of natural guardian, but the recommendations were well within the trend of divorce reforms sweeping most of the legal world except the Islamic countries. The reaction to the reforms was vociferously negative even from an organization such as the Sri Lanka Women Lawyers' Association. They argued vehemently for maintaining the old system with a few minor changes, their argument being that the present divorce reforms as suggested by the Committee threatened the family unit and therefore went against the interests of women.

The case law of the country had already set a precedent when a Supreme Court judgment stated that even a guilty man could move for divorce after seven years separation, thus allowing room for the introduction of no-fault divorce.[33] But this was unacceptable to the women lawyers who challenged the efficacy of the judgment.

The consensus was so openly against the proposed reforms that they were not adopted. The main furor against the reforms was that no-fault divorce went against the interest of the family and especially the wife. Women were in the forefront in challenging the Committee, which comprised leading women academics and professionals.

This crisis among women and their perceptions concerning family and divorce raises some extremely interesting questions. The Women's Convention, to which Sri Lanka is a state party, clearly privileges an independent free woman, but in the case of Sri Lanka the ideology of the family remains supreme. It is the belief that the protection of a woman lies in the protection of the family. Ironically, however, the data show an increasing number of female-headed households and the female as the primary earner, whether on the plantations, in the free trade zones, or as a migrant worker. This gap between myth and reality is the ideological construction, the barrier toward formulating laws that will protect women and children at the margins, margins that are increasingly becoming mainstream.[34]

While the Indian and Pakistani cases show us the dilemma generated by the tension between civil society and the law, in this case the whole struggle has been within the framework of the law—the preference for standards that were set in the late nineteenth century over modern day formulations. These divorce laws, of course, do not affect the personal laws of the minorities but only the general population. Rights discourse with its notion of the empowered individual comes up against communitarian notions of the family: an ideological force far stronger than rights discourse and perhaps the most formidable obstacle women's rights activists face. In fact, it is only recently that Sri Lankan scholars could even talk about domestic violence without being considered family wreckers. So even in a context where colonial legal norms prevail and have been indigenized, where rights discourse would be the natural outgrowth of these systems, the ideological barrier of the sanctity of the family unit will not allow reform in these areas even if, in the long run, it would empower women and give them an equal stake as individuals.

The Shah Bano Case: India

The final case study is the celebrated Indian case of Shah Bano. In 1975 Shah Bano's husband made her leave his home after over forty years of marriage. Initially he paid her a small maintenance, but then that stopped. In 1978 Shah Bano filed a prevention of destitution provision under Section 125 of the Criminal Procedure Code for maintenance of Rs. 500 a month (her husband was a lawyer with a five-figure income). While her application was pending, her husband pronounced *Talak* on her and divorced her, returning the *mehr*, the money she brought as a dowry (Rs. 3,000). He then refused to pay maintenance. The magistrate, under the Criminal Code, ordered him to pay Rs. 25, the High Court raised the payment to Rs. 179.20. The husband appealed to the Supreme Court. His argument was simple. He was a Muslim and his marriage was governed by Muslim personal law. Under that law there is no duty of maintenance, only the duty of returning the *mehr*. The personal law, he declared, was superior to the Criminal Procedure Code in this respect.

Ten years from the year the case began, the Supreme Court dismissed the husband's appeal saying that the provision against destitution did not conflict with Muslim rules of maintenance. If the wife cannot maintain herself within the three-month period of *Iddat* (initial separation before divorce), then she can have recourse to the criminal procedure.[35]

The most controversial case of the decade, it points to the enormous problems and dilemmas that South Asian nations face when they promote women's rights as human rights. In this case it would be Article 16 of the Women's Convention that would be relevant, the Article to which India made reservations when it signed in 1980. Therefore, at the time, India was not internationally bound. In 1993, it ratified the Convention without reservations and is now bound by the entire Convention.

The forces taking sides with regard to this confrontation were:

(a) *For Shah Bano:* Women's groups, Hindu fundamentalists who wished to rid India of Muslim law, and a very few moderate Muslims.

(b) *Against Shah Bano:* The Muslim community and, in the end, the Indian state, when Rajiv Gandhi moved to appease the minority community by passing legislation to override the Supreme Court

judgment. Today destitute Muslim women do not have the right
to go to court under the penal law.

The problem of Shah Bano was compounded by the fact that she was
a minority woman in a country with a hostile majority where communal prejudices run deep and are volatile and explosive. Her community
considered her a traitor. She also lived in a country that, like most
others in South Asia, accepted a formal framework of law which stated
in effect: "All men are equal, but women are bound by the position
relegated to them by the different systems of personal law, laws which
govern the most important area of their lives, the family." In 1984 Rajiv
Gandhi made it clear that personal law was superior to any provision in
the Criminal Code—it is privileged over all other legal provisions that
may have some bearing on the provisions of personal law.

In Shah Bano's case the state stepped in to protect the rights of the
minority community at the expense of women; a state that, in other
contexts, might not think it wrong to fan the flames of communalism
when it comes to other issues, especially in Kashmir. So, as Hensman
puts it, the triple oppression of Shah Bano is clearly demonstrated: She
suffers as a woman, she suffers as a Muslim, and in this particular
context, she suffers as a Muslim woman who wants to assert a different
voice in her community.[36] She was indeed the subaltern voice that
suddenly found itself in a court of law.

Initially Shah Bano received a great deal of support, not least of
which came from the Supreme Court of the land. However, some of
the Court's interpretation of the Qur'an angered many Muslims who
accused it of being wrong and insensitive.[37] The support she received
from Hindu fundamentalists was also terrifying. The leader of one of
the Hindu movements said in anger that one country must have one
law. Of course he meant a law acceptable to the majority—Hindus.[38]

Women's groups supported Shah Bano vociferously, but their discourse of rights and equality was muffled by the voices of communalism on both sides. Trapped in the middle, especially when riots ensued,
their voice was naturally weakened. When a delegation went to see
Rajiv Gandhi, then Prime Minister, he sympathized but added: "How
many women can you get on the streets to defend the Supreme Court
judgment and stop the rioting?" So it was, in the end, a question of
numbers and of violence, fear and terror, the very factors that are least
conducive to a rights regime.

In the end Shah Bano had no rights. She became a metaphor in the
political discourse of communalism which has shaped the violent history of post-colonial South Asia.

Conclusion

Shah Bano's case, and the others mentioned earlier, are indicative of the many problems that translate into barriers for implementing women's rights as human rights in the South Asian region:

(a) Rights discourse is a weak discourse, secondary to other legal discourses, especially when it comes to women and family relations.

(b) The values of rights discourse as it relates to women are not part of the popular consciousness, and, in fact, in some contexts, the reverse may persist in the practices of civil society.

(c) The post-colonial South Asian state has played a very arbitrary and ad hoc role depending on its composition and priorities, siding with different parties, different discourses, depending on the political exigencies and the numbers game. While the state may intervene to stop sati, it will refrain from giving a Muslim woman maintenance. While it encourages modern commerce, usury and banking, it will invoke laws that impose extreme penalties with regard to issues of rape, adultery and fornication. It has mastered the art of cultivated hypocrisy with regard to women.

(d) Even if the conditions exist with regard to rights discourse, the Sri Lankan case shows clearly that even among women certain ideologies are far more powerful than that of individual rights. The sanctity of the family moves women more than the freedom and, perhaps, the responsibility that empowerment is supposed to bring.

In the late nineteenth century a renowned North Indian poet charged a poetess with "bellowing like a cow," denying decorum, and invading male public space. Ironically, with regard to the law at least, the public space, often governed by recent thinking in the law, grants equal access to women in most South Asian societies. In Sri Lanka, the most progressive of the South Asian societies, women comprise 50 percent of the medical faculty; 50 percent of the law faculty and more than 50 percent of the arts faculty at the university. Women are joining the urban labor force at an ever-increasing rate. Laws are also being drafted to assist women in the rural areas, women who for centuries have worked in the fields without protection.

It is, however, the private sphere, a distinction that came to us with a colonial inheritance of personal laws, that is the most impervious to change with regard to women's rights. Here women are divided not only by community but among themselves about whether a rights discourse is relevant or necessary. Unless we begin to examine the law's approach to the family and to private space in greater detail, and understand the dynamics more fully with regard to ideological constructions that resist legal change, we will not be able to bring rights home to the family. The task is daunting but necessary. Without equity in the family, it is argued, there will not be equity in society. Without mutual respect in the family, we can be sure that there will be no respect for the rights of others in society. As has often been repeated, the family should not be defined in a formalistic, nuclear construction as a husband, wife, and children. The family is the place where individuals learn to care, to trust, and to nurture each other. The law should protect and privilege that kind of family and no other.

Notes

1. See Stuart A. Scheingold, *The Politics of Rights* (New Haven, CT: Yale University Press, 1974), 62.

2. Ronald B. Inden, *Imagining India* (Oxford: Basil Blackwell, 1990).

3. Savitri Goonesekere, *Sri Lanka Law on Parent and Child* (Colombo: Gunasena, 1987). See sections on Kandyan Law.

4. Convention on the Elimination of All Forms of Discrimination Against Women, G.A. Res. 34/180, U.N. GAOR, 34th Sess., Supp. No. 46 at 193, U.N. Doc. A/34/46 (1979), adopted 3 September 1981. Hereinafter cited as the Women's Convention.

5. Women's Convention, art. 16(1)(b).

6. Women's Convention, art. 16(1)(g).

7. Women's Convention, art. 1.

8. Women's Convention, arts. 11, 12.

9. Women's Convention, art. 4.

10. Constitution of the Democratic Socialist Republic of Sri Lanka, art. 12(4), 1978.

11. Women's Convention, art. 4.

12. See generally Sri Lanka Foundation Institute, *Human Rights and Religions in Sri Lanka* (Colombo: SLFI, 1988), on Buddhism. See Joanna Liddle and Rama Joshi, *Daughters of Independence* (London: Zed Books, 1986), for the colonial encounter and women.

13. See Kenneth Davidson, Ruth B. Ginsburg, and Herma H. Kay, eds., *Sex-Based Discrimination* (St. Paul, MN: West Publishing, 1974), 35, "Men as Victims."

14. Ashis Nandy, "The Making and Unmaking of Political Cultures in India," in *At the Edge of Psychology*, ed. Ashis Nandy (New Delhi: Oxford University Press, 1980), 47.

15. See Deepak Lal, *The Hindu Equilibrium* (Oxford: Clarendon Press, 1988).

16. Atul Kohli, *Democracy and Discontent* (Cambridge: Cambridge University Press, 1991).

17. Kohli, *Democracy and Discontent*, note 16 at 303.

18. Elisabeth Bumiller, *May You Be the Mother of a Hundred Sons* (New York: Fawcett Columbine, 1990), 133.

19. C.S. Lakshmi, *Mother, Mother-Community, and Mother Politics in Tamil Nadu* (New Delhi: EPW, 1990).

20. Lakshmi, *Mother, Mother-Community,* note 19 at 73.

21. Sunila Abeyesekera, "The Subversion of Motherhood," presentation to ICES, Colombo, August 1992.

22. *Dr. Upendra Baxi v. State of Bihar,* W.P. 5943 of 1980.

23. See generally Upendra Baxi, "Taking Suffering Seriously," in *The Judiciary in Plural Societies,* ed. N. Tiruchelvam and Radhika Coomaraswamy (London: Frances Pinter, 1987).

24. Department of Labour, *Employment Survey* (Sri Lanka, 1981).

25. See Bumiller, *May You Be the Mother,* note 18 at 62 for first-hand account.

26. Bumiller, *May You Be the Mother,* note 18 at 72.

27. Kamla Bhasin in conversation, August 1990.

28. The Hudood Laws, promulgated 1979; enforced 1980. See also Asma Jahangir and Hina Jilani, *The Hudood Ordinances: A Divine Sanction?* (Lahore: Rhotas, 1990), pp. 23, 85–130.

29. Jahangir and Jilani, *The Hudood Ordinances,* note 28 at 88–89.

30. Ashis Nandy, "Sati: A Nineteenth Century Tale of Woman, Violence and Protest," *At the Edge of Psychology,* ed. Nandy, note 14 at 1.

31. See Jahangir and Jilani, *The Hudood Ordinances,* note 28 at 88.

32. *Report of the Divorce Reforms Committee,* Ministry of Justice, Colombo, 1992.

33. *Muthuranee v. Thuraisingham* 1 N.L.R. (1984), p. 381, Colombo, Sri Lanka.

34. See generally Carla Risseauw, *The Fish Don't Talk About the Water* (Leiden: Brill, 1988), for the type of power women have in the informal sector.

35. Rohini Hensman, "Oppression Within Oppression: The Dilemma of Muslim Women in India," *Thatched Patio* (1990): 22.

36. Hensman, "Oppression," note 35 at 22.

37. Hensman, "Oppression," note 35 at 24.

38. Hensman, "Oppression," note 35 at 26.

Chapter 3
What are "Women's International Human Rights"?

Hilary Charlesworth

Introduction

What does a category of women's international human rights mean and what are its implications? This chapter considers these questions, arguing that the development of women's international human rights has the potential to transform human rights law generally.

Human rights law challenges the traditional scope of international law. It gives individuals and groups, otherwise without access to the international legal system, the possibility of making international legal claims and thus expands the state-centered discourse of international law. International human rights law is a product of the post–World War II order. The United Nations Charter recognized in principle the centrality of the importance of the protection of human rights,[1] and a great range of both general and specific international instruments have since given definition and texture to this commitment.[2]

The development of human rights law is often, if controversially, described in terms of "generations": the "first" generation of rights covers civil and political rights, still regarded by many Western commentators as the paradigm against which all newer claims of rights must be measured (indeed some assert that civil and political rights are the only possible form of international human rights);[3] the "second" generation of rights means economic, social, and cultural rights; and the "third," most recently defined, generation encompasses group or peoples' rights. The generational metaphor is controversial because it implies a hierarchy in the development of human rights within the United Nations system. Western states, once the dominant players in the international community, have typically regarded civil and political rights as the most crucial for international protection. Socialist and developing states have usually been the strongest supporters of economic, social, and cultural rights. And group or peoples rights have been the particular concern of many of the developing nations which have more recently joined the international community. From a woman's perspective, however, the definition and development of the three generations of rights have much in common: they are built on typically male life experiences and in their current form do not respond to the most pressing risks women face.

While there have been lively debates about the relationship between the generations of rights and the best methods of implementing human rights law, there has been a general reluctance to question the basis or value of the international human rights system itself. Analyses of the foundations and scope of international human rights law frequently lapse into heroic or mystical language: it is almost as if this branch of international law were both too valuable and too fragile to sustain critique. The development of women's international human rights challenges this reluctance to examine the basis of human rights law.

How is the term "women's international human rights" to be understood?[4] At one level it can be taken to refer simply to those international instruments that deal specifically with women.[5] Most of them are elaborations of the norm of formal nondiscrimination, providing that, in particular or general contexts, women should be treated the same as men.[6] While this development in international law has been valuable, it has not been adequate to address the subordination of women worldwide. Apart from the limited promise of formal equality, discussed below, the creation of a specialized branch of human rights law has allowed its marginalization: "mainstream" human rights bodies have tended to ignore the application of human rights norms to women.[7] Moreover, the structure and institutions of women's international human rights law are more fragile than their apparently more generally applicable counterparts: international instruments dealing with women have weaker implementation obligations and procedures;[8] the institutions designed to draft and monitor them are under-resourced and their roles often circumscribed compared to other human rights bodies;[9] the widespread practice of states in making reservations to fundamental provisions in the instruments is apparently tolerated;[10] as is the failure of states generally to fulfill their obligations under the instruments.[11]

My concern here is to argue for the development of a notion of women's international human rights law in a more general sense. How can women be taken seriously across the entire spectrum of human rights? Some might respond that the very notion of human rights implies universal application and that the term "women's human rights" is a distracting redundancy. But the development of international human rights law generally has been partial and androcentric, privileging a masculine worldview. Non-governmental organizations have recently begun to document abuse of women that falls within the traditional scope of human rights law.[12] But the very structure of this law has been built on the silence of women. The fundamental problem women face worldwide is not discriminatory treatment compared with men, although this is a manifestation of the larger problem. Women are in an inferior position because they have no real power in either the public or private worlds, and international human rights law, like most economic, social, cultural, and legal constructs, reinforces this powerlessness. As Noreen Burrows writes: "For most women, what it is to be human is to work long hours in agriculture or the home, to receive little or no remuneration, and to be faced with political and legal processes which ignore their contribution to society and accord no recognition of their particular needs."[13] A more fundamental treatment of the skewed nature of the international human rights system would redefine the boundaries of the traditional human rights canon, rather than tinkering with the limited existing model of nondiscrimination.

Before developing this argument, I want to consider two important objections to my project. The first is that the pursuit of rights is a flawed feminist strategy, the second that developing a generally applicable women's international human rights law depends on a monolithic, essentialized view of women that cannot take into account the great differences among women worldwide.

Feminist Critiques of Rights

A number of feminist scholars have argued, in the context of national laws, that campaigns for women's legal rights are at best a waste of energy and at worst positively detrimental to women.

The critique, developed also by the Critical Legal Studies movement, has several aspects. One is the claim that statements of rights are indeterminate and thus highly manipulable both in a technical and a more basic sense. Recourse to the language of rights may give a rhetorical flourish to an argument, but provides only an ephemeral polemic advantage, often obscuring the need for political and social change.[14] To assert a legal right, some Critical scholars argue, is to mischaracterize our social experience and to assume the inevitability of social antagonism by affirming that social power rests in the state and not in the people who compose it.[15] The individualism promoted by traditional understandings of rights limits their possibilities by ignoring "the relational nature of social life."[16] Talk of rights is said to make contingent social structures seem permanent and to undermine the possibility of their radical transformation: the only consistent function of rights has been to protect the most privileged groups in society.[17]

Feminists have argued that, while the formulation of equal rights may be useful as a first step toward the improvement of the position of women, a continuing focus on the acquisition of rights may not be beneficial: women's experiences and concerns are not easily translated into the narrow, individualistic language of rights;[18] rights discourse overly simplifies complex power relations and their promise may be thwarted by structural inequalities of power;[19] the balancing of "competing" rights by decision-making bodies often reduces women's power;[20] and particular rights, such as the right to freedom of religion or the protection of the family, can in fact justify the oppression of women.[21] Feminists have examined the interpretation of rights apparently designed to benefit women by national tribunals and pointed to their typically androcentric construction.[22]

Feminist critiques of rights are remarkably rare in the literature on international women's rights.[23] Most commentators assume that the quest for rights for women is an important and useful strategy internationally. But is this task worth the energy that must be expended on it? Are we simply creating new sites for the subtle oppression of women?

While the acquisition of rights is by no means the only solution for the worldwide domination of women by men, it is an important tactic in the international arena. Because women in most societies operate from such a disadvantaged position, rights discourse offers a recognized vocabulary to frame political and social wrongs. Martha Minow has described the problems in denying rights discourse to traditionally dominated groups: "I worry about criticizing rights and legal language just when they have become available to people who had previously lacked access to them. I worry about those who have, telling those who do not, 'you do not need it, you should not want it.' "[24] So, too, Patricia Williams has pointed out that, for African Americans, talk of rights has been a constant source of hope: " 'Rights' feels so new in the mouths of most black people. It is still so deliciously empowering to say. It is a sign for and a gift of selfhood that is very hard to contemplate restructuring . . . at this point in history. It is the magic wand of visibility and invisibility, of inclusion and exclusion, of power and no power."[25] The empowering function of rights discourse for women, particularly in the international sphere where we are still almost completely invisible, is a crucial aspect of its value.

Rights discourse also offers a focus for international feminism which can translate into action if responses to women's claims are inadequate. It affirms "a community dedicated to invigorating words with a power to restrain, so that even the powerless can appeal to those words."[26] In discussing the experience of African Americans with the United States constitutional guarantees of rights, Patricia Williams remarks that "the problem with rights discourse is not that the discourse is itself constricting but that it exists in a constricted referential universe."[27] This observation is particularly apt with respect to women's international human rights law, which operates within the narrow referential universe of the international legal order. The need to develop a feminist rights discourse so that it acknowledges gendered disparities of power, rather than assuming all people are equal in relation to all rights, is crucial. The challenge is then to invest a rights vocabulary with meanings that undermine the current skewed distribution of economic, social, and political power.[28] In non-western societies this task may be particularly complex. For example, as Radhika Coomaraswamy points out, in the South Asian region "rights discourse is a weak discourse," particularly in the context of women and family relations.[29]

First and Third World Feminisms

A conceptual problem for all feminist analysis is that of essentialism: assuming that all women have similar attributes and experiences and ignoring the impact of other variables such as race, class, wealth, and sexual preference on the position of women.[30] This issue is particularly acute in international law, which, by definition, is concerned with transnational standards, applicable in a vast range of circumstances. Is it ever possible to speak meaningfully of women's voices in an international framework? Some feminists of color and from developing nations have questioned attempts to universalize a particular understanding of feminism, charging white, western feminists with inappropriately assuming that their concerns are shared worldwide. "Have we got a theory for you!"—the title of such a critique of western feminists—sums up the concern of a new, feminist brand of colonialism.[31] But patriarchy and the devaluing of women, although manifested differently within different societies, are almost universal. As Peggy Antrobus, Director of Women and Development at the University of the West Indies, told the 1991 Women and Environment consultation in Florida,

although we are divided by race, class, culture and geography, our hope lies in our commonalities. All women's unremunerated household work is exploited, we all have conflicts in our multiple roles, our sexuality is exploited by men, media and the economy, we struggle for survival and dignity, and, rich or poor, we are vulnerable to violence. We share our "otherness," our exclusion from decision making at all levels.[32]

Since the very basis of feminist theory is the experience of women, there will inevitably be tension between universal theories and local experience in any feminist account of international law. Differences of class, race, and nationality will lead to differing power relationships among women. But while no monolithic "women's point of view" can be assumed,[33] it is also important to acknowledge commonalities across cultures.

Women and International Human Rights Law

Why has the androcentric nature of human rights law only recently begun to be analyzed? One reason must be simply that, as in all areas of international law, women have been almost entirely excluded from the important human rights fora where standards are defined, monitored, and implemented.[34] Only recently have non-governmental organizations in the human rights area begun to acknowledge the particular disadvantages faced by women. There have been, then, few effective channels to carry women's voices, interests, and concerns into the mainstream human rights law-making arena, and women have remained in a sidelined, specialized international sphere. Another reason may be that the comparatively radical, and vulnerable, nature of human rights law within the international legal order has protected it from internal critique. Those concerned with the protection of human rights in general may well be reluctant to challenge the form of human rights law at a fundamental level, fearing that such a critique may be used to reduce the hard-fought-for advances in the area. A third reason may be the retarded impact that feminist theories have had on the study of legal systems generally, and international law in particular.

Feminist scholars have noted distinct, if overlapping, phases in the study of the relationship between women and western national legal systems generally.[35] And there are parallels in the attempt to take women seriously in the international human rights system. An initial stage of feminist critique of law is often associated with "liberal" feminism. It identifies sexual equality with equal treatment, rejecting any notion that the law should tolerate or recognize intrinsic differences between women and men.[36] The strategy adopted by liberal feminists is to require the law to fulfill the liberal claims for its objectivity and principled basis. They have worked for reform of the law, dismantling legal barriers to women being treated like men in the public sphere. The assumption is that the disadvantages suffered by women can be compartmentalized and redressed by a simple requirement of equal treatment. This approach adopts the vocabulary, epistemology, and political theory of the law as it currently operates.

Such an approach characterizes much of the existing women's international human rights law.[37] The rationale of, for example, the United Nations Convention on the Political Rights of Women of 1953,[38] the United Nations Convention on the Nationality of Married Women of 1957,[39] the UNESCO Convention on Discrimination in Education of 1960,[40] and the norm of nondiscrimination contained in both the Human Rights Covenants[41] is to place women in the same position as men in the public sphere. The activities of the Commission on the Status of Women generally have also been informed by such an approach.[42] Thus the international prohibition on sex discrimination promises equality to women who attempt to conform to a male model, and offers little to those who do not. The problem with such an approach, as Nicola Lacey has observed in the context of national discrimination laws, is that it is "inadequate to criticize and transform a world in which the distribution of goods is structured along gender lines."[43] It assumes "a world of autonomous individuals starting a race or making free choices [which] has no cutting edge against the fact that men and women are simply running different races."[44] The language of "equal rights" and "equal opportunities" tacitly reinforces the basic organization of society.[45] The promise of equality as "sameness" as men only gives women access to a world already constituted.[46]

The comparatively broad definition of discrimination contained in the UN Convention on the Elimination of All Forms of Discrimination Against Women,[47] which covers both equality of opportunity (formal equality) and equality of outcome (de facto equality), is nevertheless based on the same limited approach. The measure of equality in Article 1 is still a male one. And the discrimination it prohibits is confined to accepted human rights and fundamental freedoms. If these rights and freedoms can be shown to be defined in a gendered way, access to them will be unlikely to promote any real form of equality. The Convention's sanction of affirmative action programs in Article 4 similarly assumes that these measures will be temporary techniques to allow women eventually to perform exactly like men. The male-centered view of equality is tacitly reinforced by the Convention's focus on public life, the economy, the law, education, and its very limited recognition that oppression within the private sphere, that of the domestic and family worlds, contributes to women's inequality.[48] The 1992 General Recommendation of the Committee on the Elimination of Discrimination Against Women, describing gender-based violence as a form of discrimination against women,[49] underlines the significance of the private sphere as a site for the oppression of women.

The discrimination approach of the Women's Convention was translated directly, and Noreen Burrows suggests, too hurriedly, from the

1966 Convention on the Elimination of All Forms of Racial Discrimination.[50] Little attention seems to have been given to whether this was an appropriate model, given the problems women face worldwide. Indeed, one of the obstacles faced by women in the area of international law is the general consensus at the state level that oppression on the basis of race is considerably more serious than oppression on the basis of gender.[51] This perhaps explains why the Women's Convention contains much weaker implementation mechanisms than the Race Convention.[52]

Another strand in legal feminism is the counterpart of approaches in other disciplines that have described, for example, a feminist theology[53] or a women's literature.[54] The essence of this approach, sometimes termed "cultural feminism," is the identification of a distinctive "woman's voice" in the legal context and a reevaluation of the contribution it can make to legal doctrine. The work of the child psychologist Carol Gilligan has had a particular influence in the development of this form of feminist jurisprudence.[55] Gilligan notes the disparity between women's experience and the representation of human development contained in the psychological literature. The usual interpretation of this phenomenon was that it indicated problems in women's psychological development. Gilligan turns this analysis on its head by arguing that the failure of women to fit existing models of human growth suggested a limitation in the notion of the human condition. The hypothesis drawn from Gilligan's research by feminist legal scholars in the context of national legal systems is that, just as traditional psychological theories have privileged a male perspective and marginalized women's voices, so, too, law privileges a male view of the universe. Many feminists have pointed out that law is part of the structure of male domination. Its hierarchical organization, its adversarial format, and its aim of the abstract resolution of competing rights make the law an intensely patriarchal institution. Law represents a very limited aspect of human experience. The language and imagery of the law underscore its maleness: it lays claim to rationality, objectivity, and abstraction, characteristics traditionally associated with men, and is defined in contrast to emotion, subjectivity, and contextualized thinking, the province of women.[56]

Celebrating the differences between feminine and masculine modes of reasoning in legal systems is not without problems.[57] But the value of cultural feminist approaches is that they highlight the almost comprehensive exclusion of women's experiences from the development of the law, and challenge its claim of neutrality and objectivity. There is a parallel in the approach of cultural feminists to national legal systems and that of scholars and activists in the area of international human rights law who attempted to develop a category of specific women's rights. (I should note that the international parallel with the project of cultural feminists is not precise. The international legal system is certainly less dependent on adversarial modes of dispute resolution than are those of the west, and in this sense less tied to patriarchal, competitive paradigms of justice.[58] But what is striking is that even in an apparently more open and flexible system, women and their experiences are still quite comprehensively excluded.)

Noreen Burrows, for example, sees the definition of women's rights as the means to move beyond the limitations of the nondiscrimination focus on women's international human rights law. She identifies rights associated with reproductive choice and childbirth as central to the category of international women's rights.[59] Other potential women's rights include the right to a minimum wage for work within the home or in subsistence farming, and the right to literacy: all rights that address particular disadvantages women face. This approach would allow the international vocabulary of rights to be employed in the private sphere, and thus responds more accurately to the reality of most women's lives than does the liberal feminist strategy of prohibiting discrimination in the public sphere. A possible disadvantage is that the formulation of women-specific rights could lead to their marginalization within the human rights system. Laura Reanda has described the strategic dilemma with respect to international legal structures and women well: the price of the creation of separate institutional mechanisms and special measures dealing with women within the United Nations system has typically been the creation of a "women's ghetto," given less power, fewer resources, and a lower priority than "mainstream" human rights bodies. On the other hand, the attempt to improve the position of women through more generally applicable measures has allowed women's concerns to be submerged by what are regarded as more "global" issues.[60]

A third strategy to redress the subordinate position of women developed in feminist jurisprudence is to understand it as the product of domination of women by men: inequality as sexual in nature. Catharine MacKinnon has been the most consistent exponent of this approach. She argues that the common failing of theories associating equality with equal treatment or with different treatment is that they implicitly accept a male yardstick: women are either the same as or different from a male norm.[61] MacKinnon views social relations between women and men as organized so "that men may dominate and women must submit."[62] The law, she says, keeps women "out and down"[63] by preserving a hierarchical system based on gender. MacKinnon describes an alternative legal analysis of inequality for which the central question always is "whether the policy or practice in question integrally contributes to the maintenance of an underclass or a deprived position because of gender status." The law should support freedom from systematic subordination because of sex rather than freedom to be treated without regard to sex.

MacKinnon's approach is not always easily applied because many of the relationships of subordination sanctioned by the law are so deeply engrained that they appear quite natural. It involves looking "for that which we have been trained not to see . . . [identifying] the invisible."[64] If the issue of inequality is redescribed as one of domination and subordination, sex discrimination laws simply promising equal treatment appear of limited utility. Catharine MacKinnon has worked rather for an expansion of the ambit of the law to cover traditionally legally unrecognized harms of particular concern to women such as sexual harassment[65] and pornography.[66] She argues that the feminist project in law is to legitimize the real injuries women suffer in order to make them unacceptable.[67] In this way gender relations can be, slowly, transformed.[68] Using MacKinnon's analysis, other feminist lawyers have described discrimination in institutions, such as the workplace, where practices are more compatible with culturally defined male life patterns than female ones. Christine Littleton, for example, has proposed defining the goal of equality as "acceptance" so that institutions could be required to react to gender differences by restructuring to fit women and their life patterns.[69]

How might the "radical" strand in feminist jurisprudence be translated into the context of international human rights law? It suggests the value of transforming the masculine world of rights, masquerading as "human," by extending it to include protection against all forms of subordination on the basis of gender. We need to identify policies and practices that contribute to women's inferior position in different societies and insist that the structure of human rights law offer protection against them.

Do the three strands of feminist jurisprudence sketched here share the problem of conceding too much authority to law, whether national or international? They may encourage a reconsideration of the values informing the law, but nevertheless all accord it considerable power, preserving its place in the hierarchy of male structures.[70] Carol Smart and others have also questioned whether the construction of Grand Feminist Theory really is useful in achieving equality between the sexes, arguing that such endeavors do not capture the contextualized and partial nature of our knowledge.[71] Moreover, if we get the legal theory correct, will legal practice follow? The best-intentioned laws can be thwarted in practice if their interpreters do not appreciate why and how the prohibited behavior contributes to the subordination of women. Smart argues that we should avoid general, abstract theories and focus instead on the realities of women's lives, studying the inconsistencies and contradictions in legal regulation:[72] the law does not operate in a monolithic way to oppress women and advantage men. She supports action at the micro-political level rather than the slippery path of legal reform. It is better, Smart has said, to be a feminist journalist than a feminist lawyer.[73]

The international struggle against the oppression of women must use all the approaches outlined above because inequality has both overt and subtle forms. The model of nondiscrimination can change the formal language of power and offer particular individuals limited remedies against inequality. Attempting to balance the thoroughly gendered nature of the international human rights system by defining a category of women's rights can alter a monolithic conception of inequality. And understanding the relations of power and subordination endorsed by the law can suggest methods of reform that will not fall into the same trap. At the same time, it is necessary to remain realistic and somewhat skeptical about the importance of any law, national or international, in achieving social change.

Transforming "Men's" Rights Law

A truly human rights law will only be possible when the limitations of the current international system are understood. I want now to explain and develop the claim made earlier that what is presently referred to as international human rights law is thoroughly gendered, using examples from each "generation" of rights. Despite their apparently different philosophical bases, the three generations are remarkably similar from a woman's perspective.

It is worth noting to begin with that, with the exception of the Convention on the Rights of the Child,[74] all "general" human rights instruments refer only to men. The importance of language in constructing and reinforcing the subordination of women has been much analyzed by feminist scholars,[75] and the consistently masculine vocabulary of human rights law operates at both a direct and subtle level to exclude women. More basically, all international human rights law rests on and reinforces a distinction between public and private worlds, and this distinction operates to muffle, and often completely silence, the voices of women.

Analysis of the distinction between public and private spheres has been a recurring theme in feminist scholarship.[76] The dichotomy is central to liberalism—the dominant political, and legal, philosophy of the west.[77] It assumes a public sphere of rationality, order, and political authority in which political and legal activity take place, and a private, "subjective" sphere in which regulation is not appropriate. Domestic, family life is typically regarded as the center of the private world.[78] A passage from the 1957 British Government's Wolfenden Committee's Report on Homosexual Offences and Prostitution illustrates this well: "there must remain a realm of private morality and immorality, which is, in brief and crude terms, not the law's business."[79]

As described by liberal theorists, the distinction between public and private realms operates generally and neutrally with respect to individuals. However, in western society women are relegated to the private sphere of home, hearth, and family. The public sphere of workplace, law, economics, politics, intellectual and cultural life is regarded as the province of men. This phenomenon is explained as a matter of nature, convenience, or individual choice. One feminist response to these claims is that the public/private distinction in fact operates both to obscure and to legitimate men's domination of women. The public/private dichotomy is gendered: it is a "metaphor for the social patterning of gender, a description of sociological practice, and a category grounded in experience."[80] It is also a normative distinction, because greater significance and power attaches to the public, male world. The assignment of women to the domestic sphere entrenches their inequality with men, for women are regarded as dependent on men for subsistence. Moreover the privacy of domestic life makes women's concerns invisible and ensures preservation of the status quo.

Some feminist scholars have cautioned against general explanations of the universally observed[81] domination of women by men. Particular cultural and social contexts, they argue, must be taken into account and "universal" analytic categories such as the public/private distinction run the risk of simply being shorthand for biological explanations of women's subordination.[82]

The anthropologist Maila Stivens, for example, points out that it is very difficult to define the private domain in agrarian societies in Southeast Asia. She observes the complete gendering of all levels of social life right across the traditional public/private division and argues that we should expand our notion of politics rather than analyze all societies within the confines of a particular western construct of the public/private distinction.[83]

But the distinction remains western only if the content of each sphere is defined by western experience, if women are regarded as always opposed to men in the same ways in all contexts and societies: for example if women's social inferiority is universally attributed to their role in bearing and raising children.[84] What is important to observe universally is that it is not the activity which characterizes the public and the private, but rather the actor:[85] that is, women's subordination to men is mediated through the public/private dichotomy. What is "public" in one society may well be "private" in another, but women's activities are consistently devalued by being construed as private. In any event, the western "version" of the public/private dichotomy lies at the heart of public international law, a discipline still largely informed by western values and structures. In this sense, international law is a medium for the ideology of the distinction to be exported from the developed to the developing world: it thus replicates the "reforms" imposed by many colonial administrators which often weakened the position of women in colonial societies.[86]

Feminist concern with the public/private dichotomy in western legal thought has two different aspects: the way that the law has been used to exclude women from the public sphere—from professions, from the marketplace, from the vote;[87] and a more basic form of the dichotomy, between what is considered the business of law and what is left unregulated. Analyzing the distinction in this latter sense can be particularly useful in the area of international human rights law.

Why is lack of regulation of particular areas of social life significant for women? Some feminist jurists argue that "law's absence devalues women and their functions: women are simply not important enough to merit legal regulation."[88] But it is important to also recognize that a deliberate policy of non-intervention by the state does not signify non-control or neutrality.[89] Thus lack of regulation of rape in marriage supports and legitimates the power of husbands over wives. Further, regulation of areas such as employment, taxation, social security, and crime have significant, if indirect, impact on the private sphere and reinforce a particular sort of family unit—a nuclear family in which there is a division of labor between men and women.[90] Lack of direct state intervention in the name of protection of privacy can thus disguise the inequality and domination exercised in the private sphere.[91] In western domestic legal systems, the distinction drawn between public and private supports the sexual violence on which patriarchy is based: it creates a "space into which the law's ordinary protection against violence will not be allowed to penetrate."[92] The most pervasive harm against women tends to occur right within the inner sanctum of the private realm, within the family.

Like national legal systems, international law is constructed within a "public" world, although national and international "public" spheres are often differently defined. International law operates in the most public of all public worlds, that of nation states. Thus the United Nations Charter makes the (public) province of international law distinct from the (private) sphere of domestic jurisdiction;[93] the acquisition of statehood or international personality confers "public" status on an entity with consequences, for example, for jurisdiction, representation, and ownership; the law of state responsibility sorts out (public) actions for which the state is accountable from those "private" ones for which it does not have to answer internationally. The development of human rights law has altered one set of boundaries between public and private in international law to allow the law to address violations of designated individual and group rights. This development, however, has not challenged the much deeper public/private dichotomy based on gender: rights are defined by the criterion of what men fear will happen to them. As in domestic law, the non-regulation of the private sphere internationally legitimates self-regulation, which translates inevitably into male dominance.[94]

First Generation Rights

The very epithet "civil and political" to describe those rights that make up the traditional "first" generation of international human rights law suggests the defining nature of a public/private dichotomy in their content. These are rights that the individual can assert against the state: the public world of the state must allow the private individual protection and freedom in particular areas. The primacy traditionally given to civil and political rights by western international lawyers and philosophers is directed toward protection for men within public life, their relationship with government. But these are not the harms from which women most need protection.

The operation of a public/private distinction at a gendered level is most clear in the definition of civil and political rights, particularly those concerned with protection of the individual from violence: the construction of these norms obscures the most pervasive harms done to women.[95] One example of this is the "most important of all human rights,"[96] the right to life set out in Article 6 of the Civil and Political Covenant[97] and forming part of customary international law.[98] The right is concerned with the arbitrary deprivation of life through public action.[99] But protection from arbitrary deprivation of life or liberty through public actions, important as it is, does not address how being a woman is in itself life-threatening and the special ways in which women need legal protection to be able to enjoy their right to life.

From conception to old age, womanhood is full of risks: of abortion and infanticide because of the social and economic pressure to have sons in some cultures; of malnutrition because of social practices of giving men and boys priority with respect to food; of less access to health care than men; of endemic violence against women in all states.[100] Although the empirical evidence of violence against women is overwhelming and undisputed,[101] it has not been adequately reflected in the development of international law. The great level of documented violence against women around the world is unaddressed by the international legal notion of the right to life because that legal system is focused on "public" actions by the state.

A similar myopia can be detected also in the international prohibition on torture.[102] A central feature of the international legal definition of torture is that it takes place in the public realm: it must be "inflicted by or at the instigation of or with the consent or acquiescence of a public official or other person acting in an official capacity."[103] Although many women are victims of torture in this "public" sense,[104] by far the greatest violence against women occurs in the "private" nongovernmental sphere.

The pioneering work of the Women's Rights Project of Americas Watch (WRP) on violence against women in Brazil[105] underlines how arbitrary the distinction between "public" and "private" action is in the context of violence against women. The WRP documented a structure of discriminatory non-prosecution, and indeed sometimes overt acceptance, of three significant forms of violence against women: wife-murder, battery, and rape. With respect to wife-murder, the defense of "honor" in the murder of an allegedly unfaithful wife was successful in some regions in 80 percent of cases in which it was invoked and in other cases operated to reduce sentences significantly.[106] Husband-murder, by contrast, was treated considerably more seriously.[107] Although over 70 percent of reported cases of violence against women in Brazil take place in the home (compared to 10 percent for men), domestic violence has typically been treated either as a matter outside the criminal justice system, or more recently as a minor, peripheral problem.[108] The WRP also reported the common non-prosecution and non-punishment of rape in Brazil, and the difficulties created for rape victims in proving their case.[109]

One reason for the wide scale toleration of violence against women in Brazil was the explicitly and implicitly held view that it was a "private" matter, not within the proper scope of the criminal justice system. The public/private distinction operates here at an international legal level as well in the context of attributing state responsibility: can a state be held accountable in international law for the actions of private individuals given that the traditional international legal rules confine state responsibility to activities by, or at the instigation of, its public officials?[110] The WRP Brazil report pointed to the discriminatory pattern of state responses to crimes of violence based on the gender of the

victims, and founded Brazil's international responsibility on its violation of the international norm of nondiscrimination.[111]

However, if violence against women is understood, not just as aberrant behavior, but as part of the structure of the universal subordination of women, it can never be considered a purely "private" issue.
Charlotte Bunch has pointed out that such violence is caused by "the
structural relationships of power, domination and privilege between
men and women in society. Violence against women is central to maintaining those political relations at home, at work and in all public
spheres."[112] These structures are supported by the patriarchal hierarchy of the nation-state. To Catharine MacKinnon's proposed test of
"whether a policy or practice . . . integrally contributes to the maintenance of an underclass or a deprived position because of gender status"
the answer in this context must be a resounding yes. The maintenance
of a legal and social system in which violence or discrimination against
women is endemic and where such action is trivialized or discounted
should therefore engage state responsibility. Rethinking the traditional
notions of state responsibility is a vital project in women's human rights
law. In 1992, the Commission on the Status of Women adopted a Draft
Declaration on Violence Against Women.[113] This is a valuable development in women's international human rights law because it makes
violence against women an international issue. The Draft Declaration,
however, also illustrates a consistent problem in this field. Apart from a
preambular statement, the Declaration does not clearly present violence against women as a general human rights concern: it appears as a
discrete and special issue rather than an abuse of, for example, the
right to life or equality. If the relevance of the Declaration to the
interpretation of "general" human rights were made more explicit, it
may more strongly influence the mainstream human rights bodies and
encourage them to view violence against women as within their mandate and not just the province of the specialized women's institutions.

Apart from the right to life and freedom from torture, other rights
in the traditional civil and political catalogue also have been interpreted in a way that offers very little freedom or protection to women.
The right to liberty and security of the person in Article 9 of the Civil
and Political Covenant, for example, operates only in the context of
direct action by the state. It does not address the fear of sexual violence,
which is a defining feature of women's lives.[114] The right to freedom of
expression has been defined in some national contexts as including the
right to make, distribute and use pornography, which contributes directly to the level of violence against women.[115] And the right to
privacy can be interpreted as protecting from scrutiny the major sites
for the oppression of women: home and family.

Second Generation Rights

"Second" generation rights, economic, social, and cultural rights, might be thought by their very nature to transcend the public/private dichotomy and thus offer more to women's lives. Certainly, the fact that these rights do not neatly fit the "individual versus state" paradigm has contributed to their more controversial status and to weaker methods of implementation at international law. But the definition of these rights as set out in the Covenant on Economic, Social, and Cultural Rights indicates the tenacity of a gendered public/private distinction in human rights law. The Covenant creates a public sphere by assuming that all effective power rests with the state. But, as Shelley Wright has pointed out, "For most women, most of the time, indirect subjection to the State will always be mediated through direct subjection to individual men or groups of men."[116] The Covenant, then, does not touch on the economic, social, and cultural context in which most women live. For example, the definition of the right to just and favorable conditions of work in Article 7 is confined to work in the public sphere. Marilyn Waring has documented the tremendous amount of economic activity by women all over the world which is rendered invisible precisely because it is performed by women without pay and considered within the private, domestic sphere.[117] Article 7's guarantee to women of "conditions of work not inferior to those enjoyed by men, with equal pay for equal work" thus sounds rather hollow in light of the international myopia with respect to the extent and economic value of women's work. The right to food, set out in Article 11 of the Covenant, is even more clearly relevant to the private, domestic sphere and yet has been elaborated in a way that offers little to women.[118]

Moreover, the notion of cultural, and religious, rights can often reinforce a distinction between public and private worlds that operates to the disadvantage of women: culture and religion can be seen as spheres protected from legal regulation even though they allow oppression of women by men. While the right to gender equality on the one hand, and religious and cultural rights on the other can be reconciled by limiting the latter,[119] in political practice cultural and religious freedom are accorded a much higher priority nationally and internationally.[120]

The international community does not yet recognize the fundamental gender inequity perpetuated by the current interpretations of economic, social, and cultural rights. For example, in his final (1992) report, the Sub-Commission on Prevention of Discrimination and Protection of Minorities Special Rapporteur on the Realization of Economic, Social, and Cultural Rights, Danilo Turk, discussed barriers to the observance of these rights.[121] He identified problems ranging from structural adjustment policies, to income distribution and deficient political will but did not deal at all with the more basic issue of the relevance of these rights to women, half the world's population. Failing to take gender into account means that economic, social, and cultural rights will offer very little to women.[122]

Third Generation Rights

"Third" generation rights cover collective or group rights. They have been championed within the United Nations by developing nations in particular and they have been only cautiously accepted by the mainstream international human rights community because of their challenge to the western, liberal model of individual rights invocable against the sovereign. The philosophical basis of group rights rests on a primary commitment to the welfare of the community over and above the interests of particular individuals. From one point of view, it might seem that such rights would be of particular promise to women, whose lives typically have the quality of connectedness with others, centering more around the family, the group, and the community than the individual. The theoretical and practical development of third generation rights has, however, delivered very little to women. The right to development, for example, is both defined and implemented internationally to support male economic dominance.[123] So, too, the right to self-determination, allowing "all peoples" to "freely determine their political status and freely pursue their economic, social and cultural development" has been invoked, and supported, recently in a number of contexts to allow the oppression of women. The complex and often contradictory position of women in nationalist movements and in the decolonization process has been well documented.[124] As Halliday has observed, "nationalist movements subordinate women in a particular definition of their role and place in society, [and] enforce conformity to values that are often male-defined."[125] However, the oppression of women within groups claiming the right of self-determination has never been considered relevant to their validity or to the form self-determination should take:[126] in this sense the right is relevant only in the most public of contexts: male political life. The right to self-determination attaches to "peoples," entities defined ethnically or culturally, even if half the persons constituting the people have little or no power in that community.[127]

By failing to take the phenomenon of male domination of women in both the public and private worlds into account, the right to self-determination and the very notion of statehood can in fact reinforce oppression against women through its complicity in systemic male oppression and violence. An example of this is the strong United States support for the Afghani resistance movement after the 1979 Soviet invasion without any apparent concern for the very low status of women within traditional Afghan society.[128] And the victory of the Mujahadeen was accompanied by the withdrawal of social and educational possibilities for women.[129] Another example is the immediate and powerful United Nations response after Iraq's 1990 invasion of Kuwait, justified in part in the name of the self-determination of the Kuwaiti people. None of the plans for the liberation or reconstruction of Kuwait were concerned with that state's denial of political rights to women. Although some international pressure was brought to bear on the Kuwaiti government during and after the invasion to institute a more democratic system, the concern did not focus on the political repression of women and was, in any event, quickly dropped. The achievement of self-determination in Kuwait has benefited only an elite cadre of men, those permitted to participate in government and public life. It has had indeed a negative impact on women in the private sphere: a recent Middle East Watch report documents the widespread physical and sexual abuse of Asian women domestic workers in Kuwait since its liberation and the Kuwaiti government's frustration of attempts for legal redress.[130]

Conclusion

How can international human rights law tackle the oppressed position of women worldwide? Women's international human rights must be developed on a number of fronts. Certainly the relevance of the traditional canon of human rights to women is important to document. The instruments and institutions of the "first wave" of international law with respect to women must also be supported and strengthened. The potential of an individual complaints procedure under the Women's Convention, for example, should be seriously explored. At the same time, rights that focus on harms sustained by women in particular need to be identified and developed, challenging the public/private distinction by bringing rights discourse into the private sphere. But, most fundamental and important, we must work to ensure that women's voices find a public audience, to reorient the boundaries of mainstream human rights law so that it incorporates an understanding of the world from the perspective of the socially subjugated.[131] One way forward in international human rights law is to challenge the gendered dichotomy of public and private worlds.

Notes

1. U.N. Charter, arts. 1, 55 and 56.
2. A useful guide to the development of international human rights law is Theodor Meron, ed., *Human Rights in International Law* (Oxford: Clarendon Press: 1984).
3. E.g., Maurice Cranston, "Are There Any Human Rights?" *Daedalus* 112 (1983): 1.
4. A number of scholars have discussed the distinction sometimes drawn between "women's rights"—women-specific rights, such as the right to reproductive freedom—and "women's human rights"—general human rights norms applicable to women in particular contexts. See, e.g., Andrew Byrnes, "Women, Feminism and International Human Rights Law—Methodological Myopia, Fundamental Flaws or Meaningful Marginalization? Some Current Issues," *Austl. Y.B. Int'l L.* 12 (1992) 205, 215; Noreen Burrows, "International Law and Human Rights: The Case of Women's Rights" in *Human Rights: From Rhetoric to Reality,* ed. T. Campbell et al. (New York: Basil Blackwell, 1986), 8; Charlotte Bunch, "Women's Rights as Human Rights: Toward a Re-Vision of Human Rights," *Hum. Rts. Q.* 12 (1990): 486; Frances Hosken, "Towards a Definition of Women's Human Rights," *Hum. Rts. Q.* 3 (1981): 1. In this paper, I generally use the term "women's international human rights" to refer to both categories of rights.
5. For a useful overview of these instruments, see Rebecca Cook, "Sectors of International Cooperation through Law and Legal Process: Women," in *The United Nations and the International Legal Order,* ed. Oscar Schachter and Chris Joyner (Cambridge: Grotius Press, forthcoming, 1994). See also M. Halberstam and E. De Feis, *Women's Legal Rights: International Covenants as an Alternative to ERA?* (Dobbs Ferry, NY: Transnational Publishers, 1987), 18–33.
6. See Natalie K. Hevener, "An Analysis of Gender-Based Treaty Law: Contemporary Developments in Historical Perspective," *Hum. Rts. Q.* 8 (1986): 70, for a classification of these instruments into "protective," "corrective," and "nondiscriminatory" categories.
7. Byrnes, "Women, Feminism," note 4 at 216–23.
8. See Burrows, "The Case of Women's Rights," note 4 at 93–95; Theodor Meron, "Enhancing the Effectiveness of the Prohibition of Discrimination Against Women," *Am. J. Int'l L.* 84 (1990): 213. Indeed, Laura Reanda has observed that the reluctance of states to endow the Commission on the Status of Women with monitoring and review powers is "rooted in a deeply held view that the condition of women, embedded as it is in cultural and social traditions, does not lend itself to fact-finding mechanisms and complaints procedures such as those developed in the human rights sphere." Reanda, "The Commission on the Status of Women," in *The United Nations and Human Rights: A Critical Appraisal,* ed. Philip Alston (Oxford: Oxford University Press, 1992), 274.
9. Laura Reanda provides detailed evidence of this in the context of the Commission on the Status of Women: Reanda, "Status of Women," note 8 at 265.
10. See e.g., Belinda Clark, "The Vienna Convention Reservations Regime and the Convention on Discrimination Against Women" *Am. J. Int'l L.* 85 (1991): 281; Rebecca Cook, "Reservations to the Convention on the Elimination of All Forms of Discrimination Against Women," *Va. J. Int'l L.* 3 (1990): 643.

11. Cook, *Sectors of International Cooperation*, note 5 at 24.

12. E.g., Amnesty International, *Women in the Front Line: Human Rights Violations Against Women* (New York: Amnesty International, 1991).

13. Burrows, "International Law and Human Rights," note 4 at 82.

14. Mark Tushnet, "An Essay on Rights," *Tex. L. Rev.* 62 (1984): 1363, 1371–72.

15. See Peter Gabel and Paul Harris, "Building Power and Breaking Images: Critical Legal Theory and the Practice of Law," *N.Y. Rev. L. & Soc. Change* 11 (1982–83): 369, 375–76.

16. Mark Tushnet, "Rights: An Essay in Informal Political Theory," *Pol. & Soc'y* 17 (1989): 403, 410. This aspect of the critique of rights echoes reservations about individual rights held in some non-Western cultures. As Radhika Coomaraswamy notes in "To Bellow like a Cow: Women, Ethnicity, and the Discourse of Rights," Chapter 2 in this book, the notion of adversarial rights held against the state can be interpreted, not as a symbol of civilization and progress but as a sign of a malfunctioning community.

17. D. Kairys, "Freedom of Speech," in *The Politics of Law*, ed. D. Kairys (New York: Pantheon Books, 1982), 140–41.

18. See generally Robin West, "Feminism, Critical Social Theory, and Law," *U. Chi. Legal F.* 1989 (1989): 59.

19. E. Gross, "What is Feminist Theory?" in *Feminist Challenges: Social and Political Theory*, ed. Carol Pateman and Elizabeth Gross (Sydney: Allen and Unwin, 1986), 190, 192; Carol Smart, *Feminism and the Power of Law* (New York: Routledge, 1989), 138–44.

20. Smart, *Feminism*, note 19 at 145.

21. Hilary Charlesworth, Christine Chinkin, and Shelley Wright, "Feminist Approaches to International Law," *Am. J. Int'l L.* 85 (1991): 613, 635–38; Donna E. Arzt, "The Application of International Human Rights Law in Islamic States," *Hum. Rts. Q.* 12 (1990): 202, 203; Helen B. Holmes, "A Feminist Analysis of the Universal Declaration of Human Rights," in *Beyond Domination: New Perspectives on Women and Philosophy*, ed. Carol C. Gould (Totowa, NJ: Rowman and Allenheld, 1983), 250, 252–55.

22. Canadian feminists have made a distinctive contribution to this critique in their analysis of judicial interpretation of the Canadian Charter of Rights and Freedoms. See, e.g., Elizabeth A. Sheehy, "Feminist Argumentation Before the Supreme Court of Canada in *R. v. Seaboyer; R. v. Gayme:* The Sound of One Hand Clapping," *Melb. U. L. Rev.* 18 (1991): 450; Judy Fudge, "The Effect of Entrenching a Bill of Rights upon Political Discourse: Feminist Demands and Sexual Violence in Canada," *Int'l J. Soc. L.* 17 (1989): 445. See also, in the United States context, Frances Olsen, "Statutory Rape: A Feminist Critique of Rights Analysis," *Tex. L. Rev.* 63 (1984): 387.

23. See Karen Engle, "International Human Rights and Feminism: When Discourses Meet," *Mich. J. Int'l L.* 13 (1992): 517.

24. Martha Minow, "Interpreting Rights: An Essay for Robert Cover," *Yale L.J.* 96 (1987): 1860, 1910.

25. Patricia J. Williams, "Alchemical Notes: Reconstructing Ideals from Deconstructed Rights," *Harv. C.R.-C.L. Rev.* 22 (1987): 401, 431.

26. Minow, "Interpreting Rights," note 24 at 1881.

27. Patricia J. Williams, *The Alchemy of Race and Rights* (Cambridge, MA: Harvard University Press, 1991), 159.

28. Minow, "Interpreting Rights," note 24 at 1910.

29. Coomaraswamy, "To Bellow like a Cow," note 16 at 55.

30. See generally Elizabeth Spelman, *Inessential Woman: Problems of Exclusion in Feminist Thought* (Boston: Beacon Press, 1988). See also Angela P. Harris, "Race and Essentialism in Feminist Legal Theory," *Stan. L. Rev.* 42 (1990): 580.

31. For a fuller discussion of this issue see Charlesworth, Chinkin, and Wright, "Feminist Approaches," note 21 at 618–21.

32. See, also, Birgit Brock-Utne, "Women and Third World Countries—What Do We Have in Common?" *Women's Stud. Int'l F.* 12 (1989): 495, 500.

33. See Deborah L. Rhode, "The 'No-Problem' Problem: Feminist Challenges and Cultural Change," *Yale L.J.* 100 (1991): 1731, 1790.

34. See the 1991 figures set out in Charlesworth, Chinkin, and Wright, "Feminist Approaches," note 21 at 624, n. 67. In her recent study of the Commission of the Status of Women, Laura Reanda notes a particular problem of its largely female composition: women representatives of states typically enjoy less support from home governments than do men. Reanda, "Status of Women," note 8 at 269.

35. E.g., Frances Olsen, "Feminism and Critical Legal Theory: An American Perspective," *Int'l J. Soc. L.* 18 (1990): 199.

36. E.g., Wendy W. Williams, "Equality's Riddle: Pregnancy and the Equal Treatment—Special Treatment Debate," *N.Y.U. Rev. L. & Soc. Change* 13 (1985): 325.

37. The major exceptions to the formal equality model are those older ILO conventions which were apparently designed to protect women workers. For example, the Convention Concerning Night Work of Women Employed in Industry (Revised) No. 89 (81 U.N.T.S. 147 (1948)) generally prohibits the employment of women at night.

38. 193 U.N.T.S. 135 (1953).

39. 309 U.N.T.S. 65 (1957).

40. 429 U.N.T.S. 93 (1960).

41. International Covenant on Economic, Social, and Cultural Rights, Dec. 16, 1966, 993 U.N.T.S. 3; International Covenant on Civil and Political Rights, Dec. 16, 1966, 999 U.N.T.S. 171.

42. Reanda, "Status of Women," note 8 passim; Burrows, "International Law and Human Rights," note 4 at 87–88.

43. Nicola Lacey, "Legislation Against Sex Discrimination: Questions from a Feminist Perspective," *J. L. & Soc.* 14 (1987): 411, 415.

44. Lacey, "Legislation," note 43 at 420.

45. D. Polan, "Toward a Theory of Law and Patriarchy," in *Politics of Law*, ed. Kairys, note 17 at 294, 300. See also Patricia A. Cain, "Feminism and the Limits of Equality," *Ga. L. Rev.* 24 (1990): 85.

46. Clare Dalton, "Where We Stand: Observations on the Situation of Feminist Legal Thought," *Berkeley Women's L.J.* 3 (1987–88): 1, 5.

47. March 1, 1980, 19 I.L.M. 33 (1980). Article 1 defines "discrimination against women" as

any distinction, exclusion or restriction made on the basis of sex which has the effect or purpose of impairing or nullifying the recognition, enjoyment or exercise by women, irrespective of their marital status, on a basis of equality of men and women, of human rights and fundamental freedoms in the political, economic, social, cultural, civil or any other field.

48. Preamble, art. 5.

49. U.N. Doc. CEDAW/C/1992/L.1/Add.15.

50. Reanda, "Status of Women," note 8 at 286; Burrows, "International Law and Human Rights," note 4 at 86–88.

51. This approach is well illustrated by the comment of an Indian delegate at the 1985 Copenhagen UN Mid-Decade for Women Conference that, since he had experienced colonialism, he knew that it could not be equated with sexism. Quoted in Charlotte Bunch, *Passionate Politics* (New York: St. Martin's Press, 1987), 297.

52. In the context of the Commission on the Status of Women, Reanda observes that ultimately unsuccessful proposals to allow the Commission to review complaints and to receive information from non-governmental organizations were strongly opposed by socialist and developing nations on the grounds that "violations of women's rights could not be placed on the same footing as under repressive and racist regimes" (Reanda, "Status of Women," note 8 at 288).

53. E.g., Rosemary Radford Ruether, *Sexism and God Talk: Toward A Feminist Theology* (Boston: Beacon Press, 1983).

54. E.g., Elaine Showalter, *A Literature of Their Own: British Novelists from Brontë to Lessing* (Princeton, NJ: Princeton University Press, 1977).

55. Carol Gilligan, *In a Different Voice: Psychological Theory and Women's Development* (Cambridge, MA: Harvard University Press, 1982).

56. Olsen, "Critical Legal Theory," note 35 at 199. Compare the approach of Katherine Bartlett, who argues that there is no sharp dichotomy between abstract and contextualized reasoning in either legal or feminist method ("Feminist Legal Methods," *Harv. L. Rev.* 103 (1990): 829, 856–88).

57. Indeed, Gilligan's work has been referred to as a potential "Uncle Tom's Cabin" for feminist legal theory (Anne Scales, "The Emergence of Feminist Jurisprudence: An Essay," *Yale L.J.* 95 (1986): 1373, 1381). It also begs the question of the cause of the difference between gendered modes of reasoning. Catharine MacKinnon has questioned the authenticity of the feminine voice documented by Carol Gilligan. The "feminine," she argues, is defined by a patriarchal culture: "For women to affirm difference, when difference means dominance, as it does with gender, means to affirm the qualities and characteristics of powerlessness. . . . [W]hen you are powerless, you don't just speak differently. A lot, you don't speak." "Take your foot off our necks," MacKinnon says, "then we will hear in what tongue women speak." Catharine MacKinnon, *Feminism Unmodified: Discourses on Life and Law* (Cambridge, MA: Harvard University Press, 1987), 45.

58. Compare Lynne N. Henderson, "Legality and Empathy," *Mich. L. Rev.* 85 (1987): 1574.

59. Burrows, "International Law and Human Rights," note 4 at 85. See also Sheila McLean, "The Right to Reproduce," in *Rhetoric to Reality*, ed. Campbell, note 4 at 99.

60. Reanda, "Status of Women," note 8 at 267.

61. MacKinnon, *Feminism Unmodified*, note 57 at 34. See also Lacey, "Feminist Perspective," note 43 at 417.

62. MacKinnon, *Feminism Unmodified*, note 57 at 3.

63. MacKinnon, *Feminism Unmodified*, note 57 at 205.

64. Scales, "Feminist Jurisprudence," note 57 at 1393.

65. Catharine MacKinnon, *Sexual Harassment of Working Women* (New Haven, CT: Yale University Press, 1979).

66. MacKinnon, *Feminism Unmodified*, note 57 at 127–213.

67. MacKinnon, *Feminism Unmodified*, note 57 at 104.

68. Critics have sometimes questioned how MacKinnon can identify an authentic women's voice in a world she describes as utterly dominated by men. See, e.g., Smart, *Feminism*, note 19 at 75–77.

69. Christine A. Littleton, "Equality and Feminist Legal Theory," *U. Pitt. L. Rev.* 48 (1987): 1043, 1052. Similarly, Riki Holtmaat describes a feminist "other law" that systematically takes women's needs into account: "The Power of Legal Concepts: The Development of a Feminist Theory of Law," *Int'l J. Soc. L.* 17 (1989): 481, 492–94.

70. Smart, *Feminism*, note 19 at 81, 88–89.

71. Smart, *Feminism*, note 19 at 70–72; Bartlett, "Feminist Legal Methods," note 56 at 872–77.

72. Smart, *Power of Law*, note 19 at 68–69.

73. Carol Smart, "Feminist Jurisprudence" (talk at La Trobe University, Melbourne, Australia, 2 December 1987). In a review of Catharine MacKinnon's *Feminism Unmodified*, Frances Olsen defends MacKinnon's "grand theory" as analytically useful and politically mobilizing, even if over-simplified: "Feminist Theory in Grand Style," *Colum. L. Rev.* 89 (1989): 1147.

74. 20 Nov. 1989.

75. See, e.g., Dale Spender, *Man Made Language* (Boston: Routledge and Kegan Paul, 1980).

76. This discussion draws on Hilary Charlesworth, "The Public/Private Distinction and the Right to Development in International Law," *Austl. Y.B. Int'l L.* 12 (1992): 190; See also Byrnes, "Women, Feminism," note 4; Shelley Wright, "Economic Rights and Social Justice: A Feminist Analysis of Some Human Rights Conventions," *Austl. Y.B. Int'l L.* 12 (1992): 242.

77. For a historical account of this distinction in western thought, see Jean B. Elshtain, *Public Man, Private Women* (Princeton, NJ: Princeton University Press, 1981).

78. The distinction between public and private spheres is drawn by theorists in a variety of ways. For example, it can refer to the distinction between politics and economic and social life or between state and society. Carol Pateman discusses some of the complexities of the distinction in "Feminist Critiques of the Public/Private Dichotomy," in *Public and Private in Social Life,* ed. Stanley I. Benn and Gerald F. Gaus (New York: St. Martin's Press, 1983), 281, 285.

79. (1957) para. 61, quoted in Kathleen O'Donovan, *Sexual Divisions in Law* (London: Weidenfeld and Nicolson, 1986), 8–9.

80. Eva Garmanikow and J. Purvis, "Introduction," in *The Public and the Private,* ed. Eva Garmanikow et al. (New York: St. Martin's Press, 1983), 1, 5.

81. Janet H. Momsen and Janet G. Townsend, *Geography of Gender in the Third World* (Albany: State University of New York Press, 1987), 28: "in the history and geography of humanity, women's subordination is omnipresent. . . . The forms of subordination differ greatly, but, all over the world, women's work tends to be defined as of less value than men's and women tend to have far less access to all forms of social, economic and political power." See, also Michelle Zimbalist Rosaldo, "Women, Culture and Society: A Theoretical Overview," in

Women, Culture, and Society, ed. Michelle Zimbalist Rosaldo and Louise Lamphere (Stanford, CA: Stanford University Press, 1974), 19.

82. Henrietta L. Moore, *Feminism and Anthropology* (Minneapolis: University of Minnesota Press, 1988), 25–28; Hester Eisenstein, *Contemporary Feminist Thought* (Sydney: Unwin, 1983), 2–26; Michelle Zimbalist Rosaldo, "The Use and Abuse of Anthropology: Reflections on Feminism and Cross-cultural Understanding," *Signs* 5 (1980): 389.

83. Maila Stivens, "Why Gender Matters in Southeast Asian Politics," *Asian Stud. Rev.* (1989): 4, 7.

84. L. Imray and A. Middleton, "Public and Private: Marking the Boundaries," in *Public and Private,* ed. Garmanikow et al., note 80 at 12, 13–14.

85. Imray and Middleton, "Boundaries," note 84 at 16; P. Thomas and A. Skeat, "Gender in Third World Development Studies: An Overview of an Underview," *Aust. Geog. Stud.* 28 (1991): 5, 9. See also Moore, *Feminism and Anthropology,* note 82 at 54–59.

86. See Moore, *Feminism and Anthropology,* note 82 at 44.

87. See, e.g., Polan, "Toward a Theory of Law and Patriarchy," note 45 at 294, 298; Nadine Taub and Elizabeth M. Schneider, "Perspectives on Women's Subordination and the Role of Law," in *Politics of Law,* ed. Kairys, note 17 at 117, 118–20.

88. Taub and Schneider, "Perspectives," note 87 at 122.

89. O'Donovan, *Sexual Divisions,* note 79 at 7.

90. O'Donovan, *Sexual Divisions,* note 79 at 14–15. See also Margaret Thornton, "Feminist Jurisprudence: Illusion or Reality?" *Aust. J. L. & Soc.* 3 (1986): 5, 6.

91. See O'Donovan, *Sexual Divisions,* note 79 at 12; Taub and Schneider, "Perspectives," note 87 at 121–22; Thornton, "Feminist Jurisprudence," note 90 at 8.

92. West, "Critical Social Theory," note 18 at 65.

93. UN Charter, art. 2(7).

94. M. Thornton, "Feminism and the Contradictions of Law Reform," *Int'l J. Soc. L.* 19 (1991): 453.

95. The following discussion is drawn from Hilary Charlesworth and Christine Chinkin, "The Gender of *Jus Cogens,*" *Hum. Rts. Q.* 15 (1993): 63–76.

96. Yoram Dinstein, "The Right to Life, Physical Integrity, and Liberty," in *The International Bill of Rights: The Covenant on Civil and Political Rights,* ed. Louis Henkin (New York: Columbia University Press, 1981), 114.

97. See also Universal Declaration on Human Rights, art. 3 (10 Dec. 1948) G.A. Res. 217 A (III); European Convention for the Protection of Human Rights and Fundamental Freedoms, art. 2 (1950) 213 U.N.T.S. 221.

98. Dinstein, "Right to Life," note 96 at 115.

99. There is debate among various commentators as to how narrowly the right should be construed. Fawcett has suggested that the right to life entails protection only from the acts of government agents. James Fawcett, *The Application of the European Convention on Human Rights* (Oxford: Clarendon Press, 1969), 30–31. Dinstein notes that it may be argued under Article 6 that "the state must at least exercise due diligence to prevent the intentional deprivation of the life of one individual by another." He seems, however, to confine the obligation to take active precautions against loss of life only in cases of riots, mob action, or incitement against minority groups (Dinstein, "Right to Life," note 96 at 119). Ramcharan argues for a still wider interpretation of the right

to life, "plac[ing] a duty on the part of each government to pursue policies which are designed to ensure access to the means of survival for every individual within its country." Bertie G. Ramcharan, "The Concept and Dimensions of the Right to Life," in *The Right to Life in International Law,* ed. B.G. Ramcharan (Boston, Dordrecht: Martinus Nijhoff, 1985), 1, 6. The examples of major modern threats to the right to life offered by Ramcharan, however, do not encompass violence outside the "public" sphere (7–8).

100. Charlesworth and Chinkin, "Jus Cogens," note 95. On violence against women see also the excellent collection of essays in Margaret Schuler, ed., *Freedom from Violence: Women's Strategies from Around the World* (New York: Unifem, 1992).

101. See United Nations, *Violence Against Women in the Family* (New York: United Nations, 1989).

102. A more detailed analysis of the international law prohibition on torture from a feminist perspective is contained in Charlesworth, Chinkin, and Wright, "Feminist Approaches," note 21 at 628–29.

103. United Nations Convention Against Torture and Other Cruel, Inhuman or Degrading Treatment or Punishment, art. 1(1), G.A. Res. 39/46 (Dec. 10, 1984), draft reprinted in 23 I.L.M. 1027 (1984), substantive changes noted in 24 I.L.M. 535 (1985).

104. See, e.g., Amnesty International, *Women in the Front Line: Human Rights Violations Against Women* (New York: Amnesty International, 1991).

105. Americas Watch, *Criminal Injustice: Violence Against Women in Brazil* (Americas Watch, 1991).

106. Americas Watch, *Injustice,* note 105 at 4.

107. Americas Watch, *Injustice,* note 105 at 35.

108. Americas Watch, *Injustice,* note 105 at 43–49.

109. Americas Watch, *Injustice,* note 105 at 54–55.

110. See generally Gordon Christenson, "Attributing Acts of Omission to the State," *Mich. J. Int'l L.* 12 (1991): 312.

111. See Dorothy Thomas and Michele Beasley, "Domestic Violence as a Human Rights Issue," *Hum. Rts. Q.* 15 (1993): 36, for a helpful discussion of the conceptual problems in preparing the report.

112. Bunch, "Re-vision of Human Rights," note 4 at 491. See also United Nations, *Violence Against Women,* note 101 at 30.

113. U.N. Doc. E/CN.6/WG.2/1992/L.3.

114. West, "Feminism," note 18 at 63.

115. See MacKinnon, *Feminism Unmodified,* note 57 at 163–97.

116. Wright, "Feminist Analysis," note 76 at 249.

117. Marilyn Waring, *If Women Counted: A New Feminist Economics* (San Francisco: Harper and Row, 1988).

118. See Christine Chinkin and Shelley Wright, "The Hunger Trap: Women, Food and Development," *Mich. J. Int'l L.* 14 (1993): 262.

119. See Donna J. Sullivan, "Gender Equality and Religious Freedom: Toward a Framework for Conflict Resolution," *N.Y.J. Int'l L. & Pol.* 24 (1992): 795.

120. Radhika Coomaraswamy, "To Bellow like a Cow: Women, Ethnicity, and the Discourse of Rights," Chapter 2 in this book, for excellent examples.

121. U.N. Doc. E/CN.4/Sub.2/1992/16.

122. The Committee on Economic, Social, and Cultural Rights, which monitors the Covenant on Economic, Social, and Cultural Rights, has shown more signs of taking women seriously than other expert committees in the United

Nations human rights system. For example, in its General Comment on the right to adequate housing in Article 11(1) of the Covenant, the Committee specifically notes the need for the right to apply to female-headed households. General Comment 4, reprinted in U.N. Doc. E/1992/23.

123. This argument is more fully pursued in Charlesworth, "Public/Private," note 76.

124. E.g., Kumari Jayawardena, *Feminism and Nationalism in the Third World* (London: Zed Books, 1986).

125. H. Halliday, "Hidden from International Relations: Women and the International Arena," *Millennium* 17 (1988): 419, 424.

126. See Christine Chinkin, "Gendered Perspective to the International Use of Force," *Austl. Y.B. Int'l L.* 12 (1992): 279; Charlesworth, Chinkin, and Wright, "Feminist Approaches," note 21 at 642–43.

127. See Chinkin, "Gendered Perspective," note 126.

128. See Charlesworth, Chinkin, and Wright, "Feminist Approaches," note 21 at 642–43.

129. "Rebels Revive the Law of the Veil," *The Age* (Melbourne), 6 May 1992.

130. Middle East Watch, *Punishing the Victim: Rape and Mistreatment of Asian Maids in Kuwait* (New York: Middle East Watch, 1992).

131. See Sarah Brown, "Feminism, International Theory, and International Relations of Gender Inequality, *Millennium* 17 (1988): 461, 472, arguing that this is the central task of feminist theory in international relations.

Chapter 4
State Responsibility Goes Private: A Feminist Critique of the Public/Private Distinction in International Human Rights Law

Celina Romany

Introduction

Human rights discourse is a powerful tool within international law to condemn those state acts and omissions that infringe core and basic notions of civility and citizenship. "To assert that a particular social claim is a human right is to vest it emotionally and morally with an especially high order of legitimacy."[1] Violence is an egregious form of such an infringement of the core and basic notions of civility and citizenship. Violence assaults life, dignity, and personal integrity. It transgresses basic norms of peaceful coexistence.

Women are everyday subjects of a system of familial terror that includes diverse modalities of violence. Yet the human rights discourse of protection has not been available to women. Women are the paradigmatic alien subjects of international law. To be an alien is to be *another,* to be an *outsider.* Women are *aliens* within their states, *aliens* within an international exclusive club that constitutes international society.

This chapter is an indictment of the human rights discourse, in the hope that this discourse will become responsive to the most basic rights of women.[2] It condemns a human rights framework that construes the civil and political rights of individuals as belonging to public life while neglecting to protect the infringements of those rights in the private sphere of familial relationships. It condemns such a framework for not making the state accountable even for those violations that are the result of a systematic failure on the part of the state to institute the political and legal protections necessary to ensure the basic rights of life, integrity, and dignity of women.

Part I elaborates a critical approach to the international law framework where human rights are inserted. By revealing the genealogy of the structural foundations of international law, I hope to expose how international law, as a site of open conflict among social arrangements, provides a discursive space that can include the guarantees of freedom and dignity for women through the reconceptualization of civil and political human rights.

Part II deals with a discussion of the contours of such a reconceptualization in the context of norms of state responsibility for human rights violations. This part first addresses the contradictions inherent in a human rights discourse that promotes liberal values of freedom and dignity. Special attention is given to how patriarchal values coupled with a construction of the state along the lines of a public/private distinction obstruct women's attainment of liberal values, thereby leaving the promises of liberal humanism unfulfilled.

Part II then exposes the ravages of patriarchy in the context of violence in the private sphere. The discussion focuses upon how constructions of the "private" family serve to perpetuate a hierarchical order of family relations implemented through coercion and force. This Part closes with a discussion of how a critique of a rights discourse should not be applied wholesale in the women's human rights context. In positing the idea of a reconceptualization of current human rights law, I argue for the need to resist legal discourse's recruitment of competing rights claims such as the right to privacy in an attempt to perpetuate the privatization of women's subordination.

Part III applies the critique of the human rights discourse's adoption of the public/private distinction to international law's principles of state responsibility. By inserting itself into the cross-fertilization that exists between notions of state responsibility to aliens and state responsibility for human rights violations, this critique serves as the foundation for arguing that the state is in complicity with private actors who infringe upon the human rights of women to be free from violence. The state's complicity is established by showing how its systematic failure to prevent and punish "private" acts of violence represents the existence of a parallel state with its own system of justice. The case of wife murders in Brazil is examined in this framework of complicity. Part III also contains a discussion of how state responsibility is implicated by the failure of the state to prevent and punish violence in violation of its affirmative duty to enforce its human rights obligations in a nondiscriminatory manner.

Part IV discusses the need to problematize feminist accounts in light of cultural diversity. In Part IV, I argue for a methodology of discussion and dialogue that can adequately factor in the diverse ways in which patriarchy is manifested without succumbing to a relativist paralysis that perpetuates women's common experiences of subordination throughout the globe.

Part V advocates for a reconstruction of the human rights framework with due emphasis on the need to incorporate economic and social rights in the reconceptualization of women's civil and political rights in tandem with the recognition that violence against women is inserted within a structure of social and economic subordination.

I. A Genealogy of the Structural Identity of International Human Rights Law

International Law

The structure of international relations is informed by the construction of the liberal state. This structure presupposes the will of its subjects in instituting the legal order without reference to a natural normative order while simultaneously binding itself to the legal order as constituted.[3] Thus international law adopts the social contract discourse of the liberal state, and its values as well. Within international law, states are the individuals in a "position of equality, freedom and independence towards each other."[4] International society can thus be viewed as a blown-up liberal state that legislates in accordance with liberal humanistic values and that accepts as part of such a contract those values that refer to the essential dignity and freedom of human beings.

The "Liberal" Character of Human Rights Law

Liberalism constructs a social and political order that aims to emancipate the individual from the oppression of political formulations that reinforce hierarchical forms of human association. Yet in such emancipatory formulations patriarchy still remains a strong remnant. The presence of patriarchy serves to expose the gap between liberal concepts and their actual realization. By exposing liberal society's artificial character, a critique of liberal society can narrow the gap between its aspirations and their realization.

In unveiling the genealogy of liberalism and its extrapolation to the construction of the human rights field within international law, male supremacy must be exposed. This is essential in advancing a feminist critique that recognizes the emancipatory potential of liberalism, in the hope of pushing liberalism's main political tenets to their conclusions.

The Liberal Framework in International Human Rights Law

Law is a paradigmatic site of power; in claiming autonomy from the political framework, law gives legitimacy to the social constructions of that framework. In international human rights law the links between law and politics are more blurred than in other fields since raising questions of human rights "touches on the very foundations of a regime, on its sources and exercises of power."[5] Nonetheless, the appearance of autonomy in law is maintained by a methodological framework called "legal reasoning," which purports to derive objective rules and principles. Feminist critiques of law have thus centered on how legal discourse has served to silence voices of experience through its expertise in ordering and organization.[6]

A feminist reading of such an objective script centers on twin pillarplots—objectivism and formalism—with the hope of destabilizing frozen versions of social life and human association that exclude women's experience. In critiquing the formalism[7] and objectivism[8] inherent in human rights legal thought, feminist theory engages in a deconstructive and reconstructive critique.

The implication of international human rights law with masculinity does not amount to saying that "all law is man made." Rather it reveals "an understanding of how the constitution of law and the constitution of masculinity may overlap and share mutual resonances."[9] Thus, in approaching international human rights law, a feminist perspective assumes law as a "site of struggle." While a feminist perspective does not hold the "key to unlock [the] patriarchy," law does provide the "forum for articulating alternative visions and accounts."[10]

A Sketch of a Feminist Critical Historical Assessment

A feminist approach would incorporate a critical political-historical assessment of both the emergence and hierarchization of human rights, it would reveal that the historical moment for the recognition of women's political and civil rights in a way that liberates them from their social and economic subordination is past due. In such a historicization of human rights, a feminist critique can demonstrate how the emergence of human rights derives legitimacy from sources and process doctrines that embrace political and moral choices played out through historically-specific conceptions of justice, equality, and dignity. The critique can show how core concepts of human rights law such as the dignity and personal integrity of human beings bear the imprint of the historical struggles of groups and individuals who bring about changes in the discursive and non-discursive conditions that ultimately realign structures of power, and thus generate legitimate legal rules. Such engagement with political and moral choices can show, for example, how from the French Revolution onward principles of liberal humanism have undergone substantial transformation giving birth to revised conceptions of freedom and dignity. It can show how the so-called generation of international human rights gave legal legitimacy to such reinterpretations, giving voice to those individuals who viewed the liberal structure and its legal system as failing to transform their needs into rights. As Professor George Abi-Saab notes:[11]

In reality law does not come out of social nothingness—nor does it come into being with a big-bang. In most cases it is a progressive and imprescriptible growth over a large gray zone separating emerging social values from the well-established legal rule—a zone which is very difficult (and sometimes even impossible) to divide a posteriori between the two.

The so-called first generation of human rights emerges from contemporaneous interpretations of those needs in search of transformation. The experience still had a fresh recollection of the atrocities of totalitarianism and deemed as a paramount concern the separation of state and the individual, in tandem with such initial liberal conceptions of freedom as a negative set of rights.[12] This negative characterization of rights gave way to the emergence of more positive obligations on the part of the state fueled by the experience of exploitation which arose from the abuses of that first generation. The coexistence of first generation rights with economic and racial forms of exploitation and colonization paved the way for a so-called second generation of rights that addressed the social and economic structural conditions essential for the development of that first generation.[13] The second generation underscored the inconsistencies within principles of justice and dignity alongside forms of political, racial, and economic exploitation such as those exhibited by colonialist regimes that denied basic rights of self-determination.[14] I use the term *second generation* as a helpful historical characterization tool, and in no way adopt the "supercession" model. Rather, this paper's central argument is that the first generation still needs to be collapsed with the second in an effort to grant women's political and civil rights.

A feminist critical historical review of those norms considered as *jus cogens,* for example, which get universal acclaim by virtue of their protection of interests which are not limited to a particular state or group of states, but which belong to the community as a whole[15] must ask why women's issues do not belong to the international community and merely belong to individual states, or to treaty law. A feminist critique must ask why white supremacy belongs to such "community" and male supremacy belongs to the individual state, why gender issues are deemed private within international society.[16]

Eleanor Roosevelt clearly saw the insertion of human rights within the realm of the civil, the political, the economic, and the social and thus clearly foresaw the correct characterization of women's political and civil rights:

Where after all, do universal human rights begin? In small places, close to home—so close and so small that they cannot be seen on any map of the world. Yet they *are* the world of the individual person: the neighborhood he lives in; the school or college he attends; the factory, farms or office where he works. Such are the places where every man, woman or child seeks equal justice, equal opportunity, equal dignity, without discrimination. Unless these rights have meaning there, they have little meaning anywhere.[17]

The destabilization of the legitimacy foundations embedded in sources and process doctrines of international human rights law can, through a historical feminist assessment, advance such a destabiliza-tion agenda. Women's struggle for dignity, justice, and equality still needs to capture the attention of those legislators and adjudicators whose blinders do not allow them to see that women's civil and political rights in the private sphere are systematically abused as part of a global structure of gender subordination.

II. "Expanding and Enlarging" Principles and Doctrines of International Human Rights Law

Adapting the Critique of Rights to the International Law Framework

A critique of the rights discourse has to be historicized. Rights have historically played a significant role in the eradication of legal privilege. At the current historical juncture the challenge awaiting a feminist critique is to oversee that the discourse of rights learns to walk on its own in the human rights field as applied to women. To argue that such a discourse has "run its course" is to lose sight of the relationship between rights and historical stages.

At a formal level, women do not even have an entrance pass to main-stream human rights law. The public/private distinction continues to be a manifestation of legal privilege that dispenses licenses along gen-der lines. Thus, without discarding altogether the value of critiques which bring rights discourse limitations to the surface, the task of a feminist understanding of human rights law is to situate those critiques within "the political climate," to recognize their "defensive character"[18] and allow them to exist not as definitive rigid artifacts, but as instruments that in eradicating legal privilege draw boundaries and instill fairness in the organization of social relations.

In advocating for a rights discourse in human rights law there is a clear historical understanding of the current position of women within such a legal framework. This would be the net result of the reordering of the current allocation of power embedded in the public/private distinction. The woman who demands her human rights "is not a supplicant or a seeker of charity, but a person with dignity demanding a just outcome according to widely accepted criteria of fairness."[19]

The "Substantive" Law of State Responsibility

The requirement of state action as a threshold justiciability question in the context of human rights owes its genesis to the demarcation of spheres between the state and the individual. Such a demarcation is paradigmatic of a social organization founded upon the mythical story of the social contract and crystallized by the emergence of the nation state, via sovereignty theories of the sixteenth and seventeenth centuries.[20]

International law and in particular the human rights field becomes a crucial medium through which underlying liberal values get shaped, advanced, and refined. A feminist reconceptualization of human rights law therefore grapples with such core narratives underlying the individual and the state and, in doing so, exposes from a gender perspective their inconsistencies and exclusions. A key component of such an exposure is the critique of the story of the social contract, that narrative based on natural freedom and agreement, which stems from a conception of the self deemed autonomous and free and which immunizes the state from implication in the genesis of a system of gender subordination. Such a reconceptualization reveals the gender bias of those social relations upon which the state is constituted; such a critique "casts shadow on the ability of the western tradition to give an accurate picture of human relations."[21]

The natural social contract story has not been immune from revisions brought about by historical forces. Yet its concept of the negative state that guarantees individual freedom has been deeply entrenched. After experiencing some erosion with the advent of social institutions promoting the public interest (brought about by twentieth-century progressivism), the public/private distinction regained hegemony as a defense against totalitarianism after World War II.[22] The reaction to the spread of totalitarianism made progressive forces capitulate to the argument that "any substantive conception of the public interest was simply a first step on the road to totalitarianism."[23] The neutrality of the state was re-covered as the story of a state defined as the "sum of the vectors of private conflict."[24]

The liberal foundations of state action requirements in the human rights field need to undergo both external and internal critiques that expose its ideological character. The external critique, by exposing the ideological values in conflict, reveals the flaws inherent in a system of state responsibility built upon the liberal public/private distinction. At the same time this critique fuels an incremental approach upon which an internal critique can be elaborated.

A Deconstruction of the Public/Private Distinction

A critical assessment of the public/private distinction centers on the role of legal discourse as mirroring forms of "systematized symbolic interaction."[25] Legal discourse "informs our beliefs about how people learn about and treat themselves and others."[26] In the public/private distinction context, legal discourse reveals a series of "ways of thinking about public and private" as being in constant flux and capable of undergoing revision and reformulation.[27]

A critical evaluation of the public/private distinction also enables us to expose the repressive character of legal formulations, inasmuch as it underscores the role of law in obstructing "aspirations for alternative social arrangements by predisposing us to regard comprehensive alternatives to the established order as absurd."[28] This evaluation unveils the diverse layers of coercion embedded in legal discourse and aims at rehabilitating *reflection* as a category of valid knowledge that enables individuals to assess their true interests and compare them with those that are deemed objective.

(i) A critical feminist assessment. Modern patriarchy's history is an integral part of the story of an original contract. This contract has been the legitimation pillar of state and civil law and the cornerstone of modern civil government. The original contract is a story that has repressed the existence of a sexual contract.[29]

Deconstructing through a feminist lens the classical texts that legitimate modern civil government is an essential task in an external critique. A feminist critique of such an emancipation story needs to carefully draw lines between form and substance since such a story obscures patriarchy.[30] A feminist critique needs to challenge how "the classic contract theorists began from premises that rendered illegitimate any claim to political right that appealed to nature, and then went on to construct the difference between men and women as the difference between natural freedom and natural subjection."[31] Sexual difference and sexual relations in the private sphere, therefore, have to be considered paradigmatically non-political, peripheral to political theory if there is to be any consistency behind a public/private divide that injects a caste system into a liberal framework.[32] Seizing the paradox of a contract that constructs political rights on the basis of equality while separating spheres on the basis of a "natural" division which is in effect a conception of freedom and subjection, is at the forefront of a feminist critique.[33]

The liberal state is thus "male jurisprudentially," a state that adopts "the standpoint of male power in the relation between law and society."[34] The blown-up liberal state of international society, like its model, supplanted feudalism with democratic revolutionary struggles but nonetheless left women's human rights in the obscurity of medieval times.[35]

The role of the liberal state in the structuring and maintenance of gender relations of subordination and dominance remains hidden. Unlike structures of dominance and political inequalities among men, men's forms of dominance over women are "accomplished socially as well as economically, prior to the operation of law, without express state acts, often in intimate contexts, as everyday life."[36] The state's role in gender hierarchy remains unacknowledged. Thus critical questions regarding the role of the state in embodying and serving male interests "in its form, dynamics, relation to society and specific policies," regarding its construction "upon the subordination of women" and the ways through which "male power becomes state power, need to be explicitly formulated."[37] The consent of women to these forms of social and political organization is an assumption that also remains undisturbed.

Negative conceptions of freedom in the liberal state also hide women's subordination. The "invocation of the superiority of negative freedom . . . the right to be left to do or be what [he] is able to do or be, without interference from other persons" reinforces the status quo of women's social subordination.

The categories of equality are elaborated on abstract and formalistic conceptualizations of gender relations, which do not deal with oppressive conditions in the real world. The dispensation of fairness in the human rights world is modeled after the abstract construction of women imposed upon them by the forefathers, the architects of the theoretical narratives, the main actors in those revolutionary struggles that aimed to democratize and restore respect for the inner worth and dignity of human beings. These forefathers, with a few exceptions, saw the world through the lens of privileged patriarchy, an angle hard to relinquish.

To the extent that the state is viewed as genderless, as not implicated in the construction of gender subordination, state responsibility for the

systemic perpetuation of such subordination in the realm of civil society will not be acknowledged. Therein lies the need to confront the
gender stratification embedded in the liberal state.

Susan Okin, in her critique of justice, provides a useful framework
for the critique of the public/private dichotomy within human rights
law. Such a division of spheres, by ignoring the political character of
power unequally distributed in family life, does not recognize the
political nature of the so-called private life. Such a division of spheres
clouds the fact that the domestic arena is itself created by the political
realm where the state reserves the right to choose intervention. This
division of spheres sidesteps the unit where our selves become gendered; it obscures the psychological and practical barriers that the
social division of labor imposes upon women.[38] As Okin notes,

once we admit the idea that significant differences between women and men
are created by the existing division of labor within the family, it becomes
increasingly obvious just how political an institution the family is.[39]

Similarities between the structural components of the family and the
state illustrate the arbitrariness inherent in the demarcation of social
spheres. The blurring of institutional lines between the family and the
state is less pronounced than those between the market and the family.[40] Both the family and the state are units of government within
which actors play fiduciary roles while the market is deemed pre-
political. Both the family and the state lack the relative space of freedom from rules, which the market enjoys, since the family and the
state's decisions are informed by "overarching ideals."[41] Both the family and the state share similar discourses whereby political philosophy
refers to family ideals while family theorists allude to political ideals,
sharing an arsenal of linguistic imagery when describing the market as
a cornerstone of consent.[42] Finally, the "world of work" also lumps
together the world of politics, religion, and sexuality in its categorization of social spheres.[43]

The dichotomization of the public and the private sphere cripples
women's citizenship. It inhibits the authoritative speech and dialogue
that derives from self-determination and thus impairs the successful
participation of women in democratic life. It has been explained that:
"Democracy is the political way of allocating power . . . what counts is
argument among the citizens. Democracy puts a premium on speech,
persuasion, rhetorical skill. Ideally the citizen who makes the most
persuasive argument . . . gets his way."[44]

(ii) *"Private" terror in the patriarchal family.* Family, through canoniza-
tion, becomes the refuge for the flourishing of those spheres of privacy
and freedom that lie at the core of the non-political foundations of the

liberal state. At the root of the enshrinement of family in conventional human rights law within the blown-up liberal state of international society lies a convergence of narratives which legitimates a hierarchical ordering of intimate relations; this convergence is hidden from the refuge narrative claims that the family as a social unit is beyond the purview of the state. Love and intimacy become guards in the borders that place the family unit "beyond justice."[45] Thus, beyond justice is the distribution of key crucial social goods, of rights and responsibilities.[46]

Women lose their individuality and are represented in society through the male-headed family unit. An indivisibility image runs through the liberal script and perpetuates women's subordination under the fiction of coverture.[47] This fiction assures that property rights remain in the hands of the male ruler. This coverture expands property to "cover" the female member's body as well as her children. This fiction, through history, has stood in the way of women's claims for basic rights and remains codified with universal standing in the blown-up liberal state of international society. It is this fiction that allows women to be isolated in the private sphere and that has historically contributed to the general condoning of abuse of women within the privacy of the family.

As Linda Gordon has documented, the combined efforts of early feminist activists and "enlightened helping professionals" contributed to adequately naming violence against women as a public crime. Women abuse moved beyond that incorrect characterization of being "a mere emotional expression of annoyance or a symbolic display of power, the result of an individual man's need to demonstrate masculinity."[48] Battered women's formulations of violence have surfaced how beatings "kept women from leaving, kept them providing sexual, housework and child care services as male entitlement";[49] how it is now "taken for granted that gender inequality, economic dependence of women and the dual labor market all contribute to creating a structural context in which women's options have been severely curtailed."[50]

The history of patriarchal subordination is amply documented. Women's legal, economic, and social dependency has made them historically subordinated and especially vulnerable to male aggression. In both Greek and Roman societies, men had the right to beat and kill women. Christian, Jewish, and Muslim religions encouraged and tolerated wife-beating during medieval times; women were special targets of the Holy Inquisition; witch hunts in Europe, England, and colonial America became the punishment for "deviancy" in women. The eighteenth and nineteenth centuries carried over family laws allowing men's rights to abuse. Napoleon's legislation characterized women as "lifelong, irresponsible minors." As Nanette Davis points out, five themes emerge from these historical accounts: (1) men were considered to own their wives; (2) as owner, the man assumed legal and social responsibility for his wife's actions; (3) women were expected to obey their husbands, and to conform to the gender-specific norm of self-denial; (4) men had complete authority over their wives in domestic, legal, economic and social matters, and (5) the woman's place was in the home.[51]

III. Making Norms and Principles of State Responsibility Responsive to Violations of the Human Rights of Women

State responsibility, a *terra incognita* for human rights lawyers,[52] is central to an expansive interpretation of human rights law that seeks to encompass women's rights. For human rights law to be meaningful, it must incorporate and inform principles of state responsibility. State responsibility norms for the protection of aliens provide fertile ground for expanding state responsibility in human rights law.

Human Rights and Norms of State Responsibility

State responsibility norms do not address the extent of state substantive obligations.[53] To avoid deadlock over defining such obligations, the drafters of the International Law Commission chose to codify general principles of state responsibility for so-called wrongful acts of states. The Commission envisaged "a single regime of responsibility for any wrongful act of state, irrespective of the sources of the obligation that has been violated."[54]

By recognizing the individual as an active subject of international law, human rights discourse significantly alters state responsibility norms, necessitating a reconceptualization. Because the end results of the cross-fertilization of these two frameworks is far from crystallized, a feminist critique can effectively insert itself into the process.

The Third Restatement of International Law acknowledges the cross-fertilization in order to bring the "authority of a traditional and long-standing body of law to the emerging, dynamic law of human rights."[55] It explains that "the difference in history and in jurisprudential origins between the old law of responsibility for injury to aliens and the new law of human rights should not conceal their essential affinity and their increasing convergence."[56]

The Restatement's expansive interpretation of the protections owed to aliens goes beyond those traditionally afforded to nationals to cover personal rights, supporting the claim that women, as aliens, deserve broader protections. The exact contours of these personal rights are not identified in the Restatement. A comment to Section 711 notes that the personal rights clause includes "injuries that are not commonly recognized as violations of human rights but for which a state is nonetheless responsible under international law when the victim is a foreign national."[57] Thus personal rights include those human rights that do not rise to the level of *jus cogens*. The latter, itemized in Section 702, refer to the most egregious type of violations. As Stephen Ramsey notes,

This would seem to indicate that activities that do not rise to the level of human rights violations as defined in the static definitions of human rights protected by Section 702 may infringe cognizable rights of aliens. Under this formulation aliens are protected from human rights violations not identified in section 702 even if there is no pattern of violations and even if the violation is not gross. Thus, the law of state responsibility is used—particularly the concept of personal rights—*to allow the dynamic expansion of the human rights of aliens.* (emphasis added)[58]

The Restatement's failure to define personal rights is arguably intentional, "allow[ing] progressive development of an expansive definition."[59] The Restatement's comments, however, characterize personal rights in a manner particularly relevant to cases where states fail to protect women's rights to be free from violence. Comment (e) of Section 702 extends personal rights to include activities "whose recognition as human rights is uncertain," such as the failure "to provide reasonable police protection, injuries caused by private violence encouraged by government officials, failure to provide adequate remedies for injury to person or property, and certain types of undefined reasonable discrimination between aliens and nationals."[60]

Comments to Section 711 of the Restatement state how "injur[ies] to alien[s] for which a state is responsible under this chapter ha[ve] sometimes been characterized as 'a denial of justice,' . . . commonly used to refer to denial of access to courts or denial of procedural fairness and due process," and that "most injuries that in the past would have been characterized as denials of justice are now subsumed as human rights violation under clause (a)."[61]

Any theory of state responsibility must be premised upon the principle that the beneficiaries of human rights protections are individuals, "those for whose benefit the law assigns all rights and duties . . . the peoples of the world."[62] State responsibility should be premised upon the principle that "The wrongful act of a state is the wrongful act of one set of human beings in relation to another set of human beings."[63]

Although principles of state responsibility can acquire rigid qualities in tune with the increasing bureaucratization of United Nations structures,[64] there is evidence of greater dynamism in its codification history. Contextualization, as a legal artifact for "inclusion," has been deployed in this history. The participation of Latin American actors in the codification of state responsibility problematized limited constructions and advocated instead for expansive readings. The First Report drafted by the International Law Commission in 1953 endorsed a "principles" approach to state responsibility that laid out the rules and principles of international law applicable to "all kinds of unlawful acts." Although not receiving final approval, the draft included a non-western conception of state responsibility in which individuals functioned as subjects and were entitled to pursue claims directly.[65]

Building a corpus of international customary law will accelerate the recognition of violence against women as encompassing so-called traditional human rights as well as the corresponding norms of state responsibility.[66] The First Conference of European Ministers on Physical and Sexual Violence Against Women held on 14 November 1991 concluded that "every form of physical and sexual violence is a traumatic experience for the victim, that affects several aspects of the quality of the woman's future life, human rights as well as the woman's dignity and integrity" and recommended concrete measures in terms of legislation, law enforcement, prevention, and social services.[67] The draft Inter-American Convention on the Prevention, Punishment, and Eradication of Violence Against Women, which is currently pending before the Organization of American States, provides that the women's right to be free from violence includes: "a—the right to life, b—the right to physical, mental and moral integrity, c—the right to sexual non-discrimination, d—the right to privacy, e—the right to equal protection under the law, f—the right to judicial protection."[68] This draft Convention requires a state to

include in its domestic legislation penal and civil sanctions to punish and redress the wrongs caused to women and adopt appropriate administrative measures as necessary; to take all appropriate measures, including legislative measures, to modify or abolish existing laws, regulations, customs and practices which constitute discrimination against women with respect to the punishment of the aggressor and the protection of the victim; provide just and effective legal remedies to women subjected to violence; . . . the development of curricular and extracurricular programs . . . to counteract prejudices and customs and all other practices which are based on the idea of the inferiority or superiority of either of the sexes or on stereotyped roles for men and women.[69]

Drawing from these principles of state responsibility, I contend that when women's human rights are infringed by private actors in the context of male violence against women, such acts are attributable to the state. To be effective, the norms of attribution that establish state responsibility must be expanded by filtering them through a contextual framework. The failure of states to consistently respect the rights of women subjected to violence in the "private" sphere is one area where such filtering would dramatically expand state responsibility for "private" harms.

States can be held responsible for systematic "private" male violence against women via two routes. First by systematically failing to provide protection for women from "private" actors who deprive women of their rights to life, liberty, and security, the state becomes complicit in the violation. In effect, the state creates a parallel government in which women's rights are systematically denied. The state thus functions as an accomplice to the actual human rights violations and can be held responsible for them. Second, the state can be responsible for failing to fulfill its obligation to prevent and punish violence against women in a nondiscriminatory fashion, a failure denying women the equal protection of the law.

State Complicity

Violence against women denies women their fundamental humanity, their freedom to be, as women.[70] This freedom need not be earned—it is an entitlement of all human beings, male and female.

Violence against women also maintains patriarchy. To focus on gender equality solely in the public realm amounts to accepting the "view that the civil realm and the individual are uncontaminated by patriarchal subordination."[71] Under such an impoverished conception, patriarchy constitutes merely a private familial problem, and the only state duty is to treat women and men equally in the public sphere.

International law has not escaped this impoverished view. Women's issues are invariably characterized in terms of equality and nondiscrimination, concepts that can only partially explain gender subordination and that often trap women's rights within legal confines that do not adequately capture the nature of such subordination.[72]

(a) State complicity in the deprivation of life, liberty, security, and the right to be free from torture, cruel, degrading, and inhuman treatment

States are responsible for the failure to respect, whether through acts or omission, women's human rights to life, liberty, and the security of person.[73] Women have the right to not be arbitrarily deprived of their lives.[74] The Draft Code of State Responsibility provides that the conduct of an individual or group not acting on behalf of the state is not to be considered an act of the state.[75] However, failure on the part of the state to carry out an international obligation, can be attributed to the state by virtue of complicity. The Convention Against Torture and Other Cruel, Inhuman and Degrading Treatment or Punishment, 1987, applies to acts "inflicted by or at the instigation of or with the consent or acquiescence of a public official or other person acting in an official capacity."

State complicity in "private" violations against women is not established by random incidents of non-punishment of violence against women, nor by merely equating approval of a particular crime with complicity in the crime, nor by arguing that non-punishment of a particular murderer amounts to complicity in the murder, nor by reliance on theories of derivative or remote liability or attenuated forms of responsibility. Complicity depends upon the verifiable existence of a parallel state with its own system of justice; a state that systematically deprives women of their human rights; a state that is designed, promoted, and maintained by official state acts; a state sanctioned by the official state, which "protects male power through embodying and ensuring existing male control over women at every level—cushioning, qualifying, or de jure appearing to prohibit its excesses when necessary to its normalization."[76]

Pervasive violence against women exemplifies the official/parallel regime. It is the acts of violence and domination in the parallel state that allow the official public sphere to maintain its patriarchal underpinnings while keeping its hands relatively clean. Violence against women is a political act; its message is domination: "Stay in your place or be afraid."[77] Women's basic human rights are violated in global and systematic ways, and the sexist narrative informing a private/public distinction kills.[78]

A United Nations report on violence against women has clearly documented its global nature and, through the exploration of the intersection of its social, cultural, and economic components, the report indicts states for their complicity in perpetuating its invisibility and privatization.[79] The report exposes how privatization works to the perpetrator's advantage and that the acts are "tacitly adopted by public authorities, such as doctors, social workers, the police, the legal profession and the judiciary, who join in a conspiracy of silence and in some ways almost approve of the man's behavior."[80] As Lori Heise says, violence against women is not random violence, the "risk factor is being female."[81]

There are several concrete ways that state action (or inaction) amounts to complicity. State failure to arrest, prosecute, and imprison perpetrators of violence against women can be interpreted as acquiescence in (or ratification of) the private actor's conduct.[82] State failure to prevent crimes of violence against women can also be viewed as a conspiracy between the private actor and the state law enforcement agencies, thus rendering the state complicit. This tacit agreement in the continuing violence can also be characterized as a "policy" or "custom" of the state.[83]

(b) The failure to ensure and respect the free and full exercise of human rights as a form of complicity—Velásquez Rodríguez

The decision by the Inter-American Court of Human Rights in *Velásquez Rodríguez v. Honduras*[84] can be read to establish a principle of complicity in (and therefore state responsibility for) state failure to implement its human rights obligations. The Court held that, under Article 1(1) of the American Convention, requiring the state to "ensure . . . the free and full exercise of . . . rights and freedoms," the Honduran government was responsible for politically motivated disappearances not overtly carried out by government officials. The court articulated a doctrine of state responsibility encompassing acts or omissions by the state, deriving its normative foundations from an affirmative state duty to implement its human rights obligations.[85] In giving life to Article 1, the court applied a functionalist approach to human rights law, which moved away from a formalist interpretation of the convention and thus underscored the centrality of "effectiveness" as a substantive analytical component.

The Court in *Velásquez Rodríguez* examined the nature of the Honduran government's omissions and, in a contextualized analysis which considered the rampant nature of political persecution, expanded the parameters of state responsibility. The court rejected the Honduran government's arguments that it was not responsible for the disappearances, holding that the kidnappings of Manfredo Velásquez Rodríguez and others were carried out by military personnel, the police, or persons acting under their guidance.[86] In a critical move, the court further held that the government was responsible even if the disappearance was not carried out by an agent acting under color of public authority, because the state's apparatus failed to prevent the disappearances or to punish those responsible.[87] The court concluded that since Honduran officials either carried out or acquiesced in the kidnappings, the government was liable for failing to guarantee Velásquez Rodríguez his human rights.[88]

The Court in *Velásquez Rodríguez* held that the state violated its duty under the Convention "to organize the governmental apparatus and in general, all of the structures throughout which public power is exercised" to ensure the full and free exercise of all rights contained therein.[89] The state's duty requires it to make a good faith effort to investigate and prosecute those who violate the Convention and must provide compensation for injuries sustained.[90] In sum, the Court held the Honduran government complicit in the pattern of disappearances for creating a climate in which such violations could occur.

Contextualization was crucial to the *Velásquez Rodríguez* decision. By applying the American Convention in recognition of the prevalent social conditions, the Court took significant steps toward transforming human rights law. This move demonstrates how the empirical reality of women's subordination (and its concomitant tacit state approval) can be factored into the analysis of state responsibility for "private" sphere violence.

Contextualization is crucial to understanding the nature of state responsibility for the violation of women's human rights. The systematic exclusion of women by international law structures becomes a normative link in bridging the gap between norms of state responsibility for redressing injury to aliens and human rights violations. The exclusion of women from formulating norms that encompass the private sphere, that area of life in which their most basic rights are systematically violated, makes them the paradigmatic *alien*—the outsider, the foreigner, the stateless subject. Just as state responsibility to protect foreign nationals is triggered regardless of what actor causes the harm, the situs of the injury in the private or public sphere should not be relevant to the state responsibility equation. In adjudicating women's human rights claims, courts must recognize the emancipatory potential of the law, must look to context to articulate meaning beyond formalist traps, must adopt effectiveness as the meaningful standard for human rights protection, and must acknowledge women's status as stateless *aliens*.

The rationale undergirding *Velásquez Rodríguez* provides the mechanism for holding states responsible for failing to prevent and punish violence against women in this informed way. I will examine the case of wife-murder in Brazil to illustrate.

(c) An illustrative case of state complicity: wife-murders in Brazil and the defense of honor

The failure to prevent and punish the murder of women by their husbands and lovers in Brazil is a tragic example of state complicity in and responsibility for human rights violations. As we examine this tragedy, we must keep in mind that the duty imposed on the state to prevent and punish should be one of due diligence. Due diligence requires the existence of "reasonable measures of prevention that a well administered government could be expected to exercise under similar circumstances."[91]

The main script could go like this: she does not fulfill her responsibilities as wife and mother, she oversteps the boundaries of chattelhood.[92]

Act I. She is suspected of having an extramarital affair, since she is spending too much time outside her sweet home. She is found sitting on the couch of sweet home with an electrician whom *He* believes is her lover. *He* becomes enraged and shoots them both. She is instantly killed. The electrician, although wounded seriously, survives. In an adjacent room *He* tells her mother that *He* has cleansed his honor.

Act II. He is on trial. The defense convinces the jury that *He* was a good and honest worker, a dedicated father and husband, while she was unfaithful and did not fulfill her responsibilities as a housewife and mother. The judge cites family experts who state that: "when a man violates the conjugal loyalty he does that by futile desire. That doesn't destroy the love of the woman, or the fundament of conjugal society. The woman's adultery, on the contrary, affects the family's internal order, compromising the stability of the conjugal life. The woman's adultery is more serious, not only for the scandal it causes, but also because it hurts the moral values and the law more deeply. There is the danger of her introducing strange children to her home."

The electrician testifies that he had been called to the house by the husband. *He* is acquitted on the basis of the legitimate defense of honor.[93]

At least 400 women were murdered by their husbands or lovers in the Penambuco state of Brazil between 1987 and 1989; overall, 70 percent of reported incidents of violence against women occurred in "private" homes, almost all of them committed by a husband or lover.[94] In the face of this pervasive violence, the Brazilian criminal system sanctions defenses that either reduce the punishment for such violence or absolve perpetrators altogether. The most pernicious such defense is the "defense of honor," which absolves wife-murderers who can prove that they acted spontaneously in legitimate self-defense against an imminent aggression against their honor. Honor is broadly defined to include perceived adulterous conduct—any activity by the woman outside of the conjugal norm is deemed an attack on the man himself legitimating violent response.

Passion or intent to kill are not essential to the success of the honor defense—a showing of the woman's dishonorable conduct within the conjugal relationship suffices. The honor defense is also not easily defeated—neither a mistake in belief by the man, nor the fact that the victim was attempting to extricate herself from an abusive relationship matters.

Although the Brazilian Superior Tribunal of Justice (the highest court of appeals) overturned an acquittal based on the honor defense, clearly holding the defense invalid, honor defense continues to be successfully invoked.[95] In the Brazilian interior, the honor defense is successful in approximately 80 percent of the wife-murder cases.

In addition to the honor defense, the Brazilian criminal justice system works in other ways, both de jure and de facto, to deprive women of their human rights. For example, courts mitigate the sentences of wife-murderers via the "violent emotion" exception, which holds that where the defendant acted with "violent emotion" following "unjust provocation" by the victim, such killing is a privileged homicide, carrying a prison sentence of one to six years rather than the twelve to thirty years for intentional homicide.[96]

At trial, the victim's behavior—her violation of the codes of subordination within the family—is given paramount attention, while evidence of the defendant's intent is routinely ignored. Even in the absence of "unjust provocation," the "violent emotion" mitigation is often allowed despite evidence that the murder was premeditated. Consequently, wife-murderers who should receive a minimum sentence of twelve years sometimes serve as little as eighteen months.[97]

Bail and sentencing evidence the same systematic gendered treatment. With few exceptions, wife-murderers are routinely allowed bail, with most of those subsequently convicted never spending a day in jail awaiting trial. Convicted wife-murderers are also given preferential sentencing and early release.[98]

Gender-biased treatment of women also pre-dates the courtroom experience. Law enforcement, a key component of the state's duty to ensure respect for human rights, is pervasively neglectful of women.[99] Both police and prosecutors systematically charge wife-murderers with lesser crimes, and police rarely investigate such crimes fully.[100] In addition, the *delegacias,* special women's police stations set up to deal with domestic violence, are excluded from investigating homicides. The *delegacias,* created by the Brazilian women's movement, confront many obstacles in pursuing their objectives. Women *delegadas* are treated discriminatorily within the police stations and lack the training and resources to deal adequately with domestic violence. Moreover, since the *delegacias* lack proper funding for adequate training and resources, they are often unable to deal competently with domestic violence, or even recognize it as a crime. Some of the *delegacias* have become nothing more than props that make the state look as though it is making an effort toward preventing domestic violence when in fact it is doing nothing at all.[101]

Through its law enforcement and judicial practices, the State of

Brazil has failed to investigate, prosecute, and punish wife-murderers, and has taken no steps to remedy the situation. By these actions and inactions, Brazil is in complicity with gross and systematic violations of women's human rights. Gross and systematic violations of human rights are "those violations, instrumental to the achievement of government policies, perpetrated in such a quantity and in such a manner as to create a situation in which the rights to life, to personal integrity or to personal liberty of the population as a whole or of one or more sectors of the population of a country are continuously infringed or threatened."[102] The state has therefore breached its duty, under a standard of due diligence, to ensure the free and full exercise of the rights recognized by the American Convention.

The watershed significance of *Velásquez Rodríguez* to human rights jurisprudence is illustrated by the Brazilian case. The court in *Velásquez Rodríguez* created precedent for protecting human rights where states are not necessarily active actors. Significant to the decision was evidence that the systematic and selective practices of disappearances involved the state, directly or indirectly. Brazil's complicity with wife-murderers is equally demonstrable. The multifaceted actions and inactions by the state constitute acquiescence in the continuing rampant violence against women. The behavior of the police, prosecutors, judges, and legislators is action undertaken by agents acting under color of law and constitutes direct complicity in the denial of Brazilian women's rights. Through this complicity, and by its failure to exercise due diligence in preventing such violations, the government of Brazil is directly responsible for violating the rights of Brazilian women.

State Responsibility for Its Failure to Prevent and Punish Violence Against Women in a Nondiscriminatory Fashion—Equal Protection

The behavior of the Brazilian government also constitutes a failure to ensure and respect women's human rights violations in a nondiscriminatory manner as required by international law. The American Convention requires that human rights be ensured "without any discrimination for reasons of race, color, sex, origin, economic status, birth or any other social condition,"[103] and provides that "all persons are equal before the law . . . [and] are entitled, without discrimination, to equal protection of the law."[104]

One aspect of genuine protection for human rights is effective access of the victim to a legal system capable of fully and fairly redressing the harm in a nondiscriminatory way.[105] Brazil's failure to provide vigorous and nondiscriminatory law enforcement and judicial redress in cases of wife-murder, as detailed above, clearly violates this duty and constitutes denial of Brazilian women's rights to equal protection of the laws as required under international law.

International law also obligates states to eliminate discrimination against women in the enjoyment and exercise of human rights and fundamental freedoms.[106] This obligation extends to rights of personal integrity protected under the various international human rights instruments.[107] The Women's Convention further provides that states parties shall "take all appropriate measures, including legislation, to ensure the full development and advancement of women, for the purpose of guaranteeing them the exercise and enjoyment of human rights and fundamental freedoms on a basis of equality with men."[108] Importantly, the Women's Convention reaches interference by private individuals with the exercise and enjoyment of rights by other citizens. Article 2 (a) requires states to eliminate discrimination by "any person, organization or enterprise." Article 5(a) seeks to eliminate "prejudices and customary and all other practices which are based on the idea of the inferiority or the superiority of either of the sexes or on stereo-typed roles for men and women."

IV. The Anti-Essentialist Feminist Critique

A feminist critique of human rights law needs to engage in a dialogue which forces the anti-subordination thrust of feminism through the filter of cultural diversity. Such dialogue would address how the construction of the civil and political character of human rights stems from a patriarchal construction of the public and private spheres, and vice versa. Such a dialogue would be informed by the need to transcend any relativistic paralysis since in "a world of radical inequality, relativist resignation reinforces the status quo."[109] This premise is in tune with my desire to make the feminist critique in this article politically translatable. As Ann Marie Goetz notes, since "the field is defined by an urgent political project and not by a method or stance,"[110] we cannot succumb to paralysis, "we cannot replace the question what must be done with who I am or with the retreating statement: I cannot claim to know and so I can do nothing."[111]

It is particularly important to avoid a feminist approach that glorifies feminine values without a clear structural social content that reflects how structures of power construct gender differences. Such glorification could be fatal to a critique of the public/private dichotomy, which aspires to unmask the state's recruitment of culture in the creation of gender subordination, in the devaluation of women.

"Protocols of persuasion"[112] would be established through such dialogues which could examine the value of "embodied objectivity" in identifying our common denominators in a multicultural international society. Embodied objectivity claims the impossibility of reaching abstract objectivity; it views objectivity as embodied, as representing "a partial knowing in which the knower consciously takes responsibility for her claims and her enabling practices" and "opens itself up to continual testing in relation to other knowing positions."[113] Embodied objectivity originates in notions of constructed identities, and how such constructions by virtue of their artificial character are subject to constant revisions. It views participants in a dialogue as both "agents and participants in the production of knowledge."[114] "Embodied objectivity" would require that women engage in a dialogue where the intersections between patriarchy and other sites of oppression, such as class, ethnicity, and race, come to the fore; where each claim to knowledge is open to revision.

To isolate the cultural component from the workings of patriarchy is akin to walking (blindfolded) along the tightrope of cultural traditions. Two of the crucial questions that demand dialogic interaction among women are how much authority is given to tradition, and how much in doing so is the challenge to the hegemony of male values surrendered. Such dialogic interaction should enable diverse women to discover how "different forms of collective and private appropriation" of women do not intrinsically exclude their constitution as "one system of appropriation,"[115] a reality best exemplified by male violence against women.[116]

V. Transcending the Rights Versus Goals Dichotomy: Interpreting Women's Political and Civil Rights Within a Social and Economic Framework

A feminist critique of human rights discourse has to grapple with the current dichotomization of political/civil rights and economic/social rights, which characterizes the latter not as entitlements but as mere aspirations. In doing so, a feminist critique must underscore the social structural framework's role in the construction of gender subordination.

The theory that social and economic rights are purely aspirational relies on both legal and non-legal arguments. On the non-legal side is the limited availability of resources, championed as a pragmatic consideration that precludes conceiving economic and social rights as rights to be guaranteed. This reality is translated onto the legal side through the absence of a "respect and ensure" clause in the Covenant on Economic and Social Rights which declares that a state party "undertakes to take steps . . . to the maximum of its available resources, with a view to achieving progressively the full realization of the rights recognized in the present Covenant by all appropriate means."[117]

The global imbalance between the developed and underdeveloped nations must be accounted for in any human rights discourse that purports to guarantee basic citizenship rights. Important as this imbalance is for a meaningful conception of human rights, for women the reality of social and economic underdevelopment transcends the north/south axis. Male supremacy institutes a system of subordination that becomes the organizing principle in the economic and social distribution of resources, and that compounds the subordinated position of women across the globe. Through the workings of such supremacy, women lie at the bottom of the economic and social ladder, a position that attains legitimacy in the concrete ways that cultural and social attitudes characterize gender differences. This reality is buttressed by the socially constructed dependency of women on men, by their socialization that attaches their self-esteem to men, by their underpaid labor, by their lack of education, and by the commodification of their sexuality.

In order minimally to comply with women's civil and political rights, in order to ensure the minimum rights of citizenship, the dichotomy that exists in the current human rights discourse needs to be transcended. Thus, in ensuring women's civil and political rights, the state must be held to an affirmative duty to ensure the eradication of those social and economic conditions that maintain and perpetuate subordination.[118]

The Women's Convention recognizes the inextricability of subordination and the economic and social structures that generate and perpetuate it. Article 3 mandates an affirmative state obligation to "take all appropriate measures, including legislation, to ensure the full development and advancement of women, for the purpose of guaranteeing them the exercise and enjoyment of human rights and fundamental freedoms on a basis of equality with men."[119]

Violence against women fits on a continuum of subordination that deeply affects women's ability to develop as citizens. Women are deprived of participation since they "cannot lend [their] labor or creative ideas fully when [they] are burdened with the physical and psychological scars of violence."[120]

The Draft Inter-American Convention on the Prevention, Punishment and Eradication of Violence Against Women acknowledges the link between subordination and economic and social structures, providing that "the right of every woman to be free from violence can only be achieved if conditions are created whereby women and men equally enjoy and exercise the human rights enunciated in the international and regional legal instruments."[121] Recognition of the link is also present in the historical development of human rights.[122]

The development of human rights, as seen through these examples, clearly contemplates the incorporation of the social and economic framework in, at the very least, a quasi-conditional manner. Yet in none of these approaches do we see any reference to the higher burden underdevelopment poses for women or the centrality of women to meaningful development.[123]

I contend that the right to be free from violence is a lowest common denominator that must inform a dialogue about the links existing between violence and social and economic development.[124] In this article I have limited myself to arguing for a reconceptualization of civil and political rights in a manner that encompasses women's right to be free from violence as a right with political, economic, and social dimensions. Those models of development that will facilitate the attainment of the reconceptualized civil and political rights of women also need to emerge from a dialogic framework that incorporates the different ways that gender subordination is experienced in different cultures.

Toward a Dialogic Framework

To conceive of international legal argument as a dialogic framework[125] would create a significant methodological and substantive tool for subjecting frozen versions of international law to a substantial dose of deviation. A dialogue that incorporates a feminist understanding of social arrangements and legal argument as part of a critique of international law and the human rights field would help to undo its repressive component and enable law's transformative potential to run its course.

The patriarchal narrative that separates the economic and social framework from the political and the civil generates a story of "civility" and citizenship that neglects the socioeconomic structures in which women's subordination occurs. It informs the public and private demarcation of social spheres. It creates a coerced exile of the experiences of women in the rights framework. This narrative must be the subject of a reconstituted dialogue that highlights the ideological nature of such constructions and that creates conditions for a reasoned construction of alternatives.

Women as aliens within such a system must enter a dialogue that shies away from the one-dimensionality that currently infects the human rights discourse. Domination is "a state of being" that goes beyond material conditions of subordination; women are also stripped of the "psychic, linguistic and textual vehicles of resistance."[126] International society is one of enveloping silence where actors who mirror masculine world views operate unhindered by the need to provide discursive justifications of their authority and who do not disclose to the "citizens-readers" (through the mystification of legal discourse) the exclusionary nature of the master script.

The legitimation of human rights discourse must therefore rest on the renunciation of the hegemonic communicative competence held by a few. Ideal speech situations which create the conditions for transformation require that actors-participants enjoy more or less equal chances to participate effectively in norm constituting dialogues. Such conditions enable women to recapture control of their lives. Law as a site of struggle becomes debureaucratized and deinsulated from the barriers of expertise. Communicative competence for the *alien* woman requires a rejection of a language of silence that only a few can master; it requires renewed political speaking.[127] Such renewed dialogue gives *all* participants "mobilizing" insights that depose the "structured silence" enthroned by ideological constructions perpetuated by the praxis of historical elites.[128]

I thank the Ford Foundation and the Schell International Human Rights Program at Yale Law School for their generous support to this project. I am especially grateful to Michael Deutsch for his valuable insights and my colleague Rhonda Copelon for our valuable discussions on this subject.

Notes

1. Richard Bilder, "Rethinking International Human Rights Law; Some Basic Questions," *Wis. L. Rev.* 1969 (1969): 171.

2. For a longer version of this paper see Celina Romany, "Women as *Aliens:* A Feminist Critique of the Public/Private Distinction in International Human Rights Law," *Harv. Hum. Rts. J.* 6 (1993): 87.

3. Martti Koskenniemi, *From Apology to Utopia: The Structure of International Legal Argument* (Helsinki: Lakimiesliiton Kustannus, 1989), 6.

4. Modern liberals such as Rawls view interstate justice as a hypothetical contract between states, "the principles which states would choose in such situation—behind a veil of ignorance of their own and others' particular interests, capabilities, wants, etc.—would be familiar and would essentially see equality and independence." Quoted in Koskenniemi, *From Apology to Utopia,* note 3 at 71.

5. Stanley Hoffman, "The Hell of Good Intentions," *Foreign Policy* 29 (1977–78): 3, cited in Oscar Schachter, *International Law in Theory and in Practice* (Dordrecht: Martinus Nijhoff, 1991), 345.

6. Carol Smart, *Feminism and the Power of Law* (New York: Routledge, 1989), 9, 11.

7. Formalism is the "search for a method of deduction from a gapless system of rules," which contrasts methods of legal justification with disputes as to the reorganization of social life—termed ideological or philosophical. Roberto M. Unger, *The Critical Legal Studies Movement* (Cambridge, MA: Harvard University Press, 1986).

8. Objectivism is the belief that authority within legal instruments "embod[ies] and sustain[s] a defensible scheme of human association. . . . an intelligible moral order" (Unger, note 7 at 2).

9. Smart, *Power of Law,* note 6 at 86.

10. Smart, *Power of Law,* note 6 at 88.

11. Smart, *Power of Law,* note 6.

12. Stephen Marks, "Emerging Human Rights: A New Generation for the 1980s," in *International Law: A Contemporary Perspective,* ed. Richard Falk, Friedrich Kratochwil, and Saul Mendlovitz (Boulder, CO: Westview Press, 1985), 503.

13. Marks, "Emerging Human Rights," note 12 at 504.

14. Declaration on Granting of Independence to Colonial Countries and Peoples of 1960; Proclamation of Teheran, 1968.

15. Schachter, *International Law,* note 5 at 343.

16. Karen Engle, "International Human Rights and Feminism: When Discourses Meet," 13 *Mich. J. Int'l L.* 13 (1992): 517.

17. Remarks made by Eleanor Roosevelt at a ceremony at the United Nations, New York, March 27, 1958, in Phillips, *You In Human Rights* 2 (1967) quoted in Bilder, *Rethinking,* note 1 at 178.

18. Smart, *Power of Law,* note 6 at 158.

19. Smart, *Power of Law,* note 6 at 152.

20. Morton Horwitz, "The History of the Public/Private Distinction" *U. Penn. L. R.* 130 (1982): 1423.

21. Rebecca Grant, "The Sources of Gender Bias in International Relations Theory," in *Gender and International Relations,* ed. Rebecca Grant and Kathleen Newland (Bloomington: Indiana University Press, 1991), 14.

22. Horwitz, "History of the Public/Private Distinction," note 20 at 1427.

23. Horwitz, "History of the Public/Private Distinction," note 20.

24. Horwitz, "History of the Public/Private Distinction," note 20.

25. Karl Klare, "The Public/Private Distinction in Labor Law," *U. Penn. L. Rev.* 130 (1982): 1358.

26. Klare, "Public/Private," note 25.

27. Klare, "Public/Private," note 25 at 1361.

28. Klare, "Public/Private," note 25.

29. Klare, "Public/Private," note 25.

30. Carol Pateman, *The Sexual Contract* (Cambridge, MA: Polity, 1988), 1.

31. Pateman, *Sexual Contract,* note 30 at 222.

32. Pateman, *Sexual Contract,* note 30 at 221.

33. Pateman, *Sexual Contract,* note 30 at 223.

34. Catharine MacKinnon, *Towards a Feminist Theory of the State* (Cambridge, MA: Harvard University Press, 1989), 163.

35. MacKinnon, *Towards a Feminist Theory,* note 34 at 164.

36. MacKinnon, *Towards a Feminist Theory,* note 34 at 161.

37. MacKinnon, *Towards a Feminist Theory,* note 34.

38. Susan M. Okin, *Justice, Gender, and the Family* (New York: Basic Books, 1989), 115.

39. Okin, *Justice, Gender,* note 38 at 132.

40. Duncan Kennedy, "The Stages of the Decline of the Public/Private Distinction," *U. Penn. L. Rev.* 130 (1982): 1349 at 1356.

41. Kennedy, "Stages of Decline," note 40 at 1355, citing Fran Olsen.

42. Kennedy, "Stages of Decline," note 40 at 1356.

43. Kennedy, "Stages of Decline," note 40.

44. Michael Waller cited in Okin, *Justice, Gender,* note 38 at 132.

45. Okin, *Justice, Gender,* note 38 at 26–27.

46. Okin, *Justice, Gender,* note 38 at 114.

47. Okin, *Justice, Gender,* note 38 at 30.

48. Nanette Davis, "Battered Women: Implications for Social Control," *Cont. Crises* 12 (1988): 345 at 349, citing Linda Gordon, *Heroes of Their Own Lives: The Politics and History of Family Violence* (New York: Viking Press, 1988), 152.

49. Davis, "Battered Women," note 48 at 349.

50. Davis, "Battered Women," note 48 at 350.

51. Davis, "Battered Women," note 48 at 348.

52. Theodor Meron, "State Responsibility for Violations of Human Rights," *Proc. Am. Soc. Int'l L.* 83 (1989): 372.

53. Richard Lillich, "Recent Developments in State Responsibility," *Proc. Am. Soc. Int'l L.* 83 (1989): 226.

54. Lillich, "Recent Developments," note 53.

55. Stephen Ramsey, "State Responsibility Under the Restatement," in *Recent Developments in State Responsibility: A Panel, Proc. Am. Soc. Int'l L.* 83 (1989): 232 at 234.

56. Ramsey, "State Responsibility," note 55 at 233.

57. Ramsey, "State Responsibility," note 55.

58. Ramsey, "State Responsibility," note 55.

59. Ramsey, "State Responsibility," note 55.

60. Ramsey, "State Responsibility," note 55.

61. Ramsey, "State Responsibility," note 55.

62. Philip Allott, "State Responsibility and the Unmaking of International Law," *Harv. Int'l L.J.* 29 (1988): 1, 14.

63. Allott, "The Unmaking," note 62 at 14.

64. Allott, "The Unmaking," note 62 at 9–10.

65. Allott, "The Unmaking," note 62 at 4–5. See also Lillich, "Recent Developments," note 53 at 224.

66. See Recommendation No. R (90)2 of the Committee of Ministers to Member States on Social Measures Concerning Violence Within the Family (adopted on January 15, 1990); the resolutions and recommendations of the Colloquy on Violence Within the Family: Measures in the Social Field, Council of Europe, November 25–27, 1987; and European Committee for Equality Between Women and Men, Sexual Violence Against Women: Contribution to a Strategy for Countering Various Forms of Such Violence in the Council of Europe Member States, Strasbourg. 1991. An Expert Group Meeting on Violence Against Women, in Vienna, November 11–15, 1991, urged member states to adopt legislation prohibiting violence against women and to take all appropriate measures to protect women from all forms of physical and mental violence. U.N. Doc. EGM/VAW/1991/1.

67. Final Declaration of the First Conference of European Ministers on Physical and Sexual Violence against Women, March 15, 1991.

68. OEA/Serv. L. 11.7.4, CIM doc. 1/91.

69. OEA/Serv. L. 11.7.4, CIM doc. 1/91.

70. Pateman, *Sexual Contract,* note 30 at 231.

71. Pateman, *Sexual Contract,* note 30 at 17.

72. See generally Noreen Burrows, "International Law and Human Rights: The Case of Women's Rights" in *Human Rights: From Rhetoric to Reality,* ed. Tony Campbell et al. (Oxford: Basil Blackwell, 1986) at 83. See Sarah C. Zearfoss, Note, "The Convention for the Elimination of All Forms of Discrimination Against Women: Radical, or Reasonable or Reactionary," *Mich. J. Int'l L.* 12 (1991): 903.

73. American Convention, art. 1.

74. American Convention, art. 4.

75. 2 *Y.B. Int'l L. Comm'n,* Part II (1980) at 31.

76. MacKinnon, *Towards A Feminist Theory,* note 34 at 167.

77. Charlotte Bunch, "Women's Rights as Human Rights: Toward a Re-Vision of Human Rights," *Hum. Rts. Q.* 12 (1990): 486 at 491.

78. Bunch, "Re-Vision," note 77 at 492.

79. *United Nations Report on Violence Against Women in the Family* (New York: United Nations, 1989), 105. See also Diane Russell and Nicole Van de Ven, eds. *Crimes Against Women: The Proceedings of the International Tribunal* (East Palo Alto, CA: Frog in the Well, 1984).

80. Russell and Van de Ven, *Crimes Against Women,* note 79.

81. Lori Heise, "International Dimensions of Violence Against Women," *Response* 12 (1989): 13.

82. See *NAACP v. Clairborne,* 458 U.S. 886 (1972) (one who has knowledge of unlawful or tortuous activity and ratifies such action is liable for that conduct).

83. *Monell v. Dept. of Social Services,* 436 U.S. 658 (1978) and *Watson v. City of Kansas,* 857 F. 2d 690 (10th Cir 1988) (an unwritten municipal policy or custom responding differently to victims of domestic violence than to other assault cases renders the municipality liable for the harm caused by the domestic violence).

84. 28 I.L.M. 294 (1989) Hereinafter referred to as *Velásquez Rodríguez.*

85. *Velásquez Rodríguez,* note 84 at 328.

86. *Velásquez Rodríguez,* note 84 at 327.

87. *Velásquez Rodríguez,* note 84 at 329.

88. *Velásquez Rodríguez,* note 84 at 323.

89. *Velásquez Rodríguez,* note 84 at 323.

90. *Velásquez Rodríguez,* note 84 at 328.

91. Draft Convention on the International Responsibility of States for Injuries to Aliens (Harvard Draft), arts. 1391 and 1392, reprinted in Francisco V. Garcia Amador, Louis B. Sohn and R. R. Baxter, *Recent Codification of the Law of State Responsibility for Injuries to Aliens* (Dobbs Ferry, NY: Oceana Publications, 1974), 24, 27; Ian Brownlie, *The System of the Law of Nations: State Responsibility* (Oxford: Clarendon Press, 1983), 162; *Responsibility of States for Damage Caused in Their Territory to the Person or Party of Foreigners,* League of Nations Doc. C.75M.69., 1929 V (1929) at 67; Dinah Shelton, "Private Violence, Public Wrongs, and the Responsibilities of the States," *Fordham Int'l L.J.* 13 (1989–1990): 1 at 22.

92. Human Rights Watch, *Criminal Injustice: Violence Against Women in Brazil* (New York: Human Rights Watch, 1991); *Quando a vitima e mulher* (When the Victim is a Woman) National Council on the Rights of Women, Brazil).

93. Human Rights Watch, *Criminal Injustice,* note 92 at 22–23.

94. The Brazil wife-murder data rely heavily on Human Rights Watch, *Criminal Injustice,* note 92 at 14–17, and interviews with Jacqueline Pitanguy, former head of the National Council for Women's Rights (1991).

95. *João Lopes* case, Decision of the Tribunal Superior de Justica, 11 March 1991 ("adultery does not place the husband in a state of self-defense as contemplated by the Penal Code . . . honor is a personal attribute which is the property of each spouse. . . . There is no offense to the husband's honor by the wife's adultery. There is no such conjugal honor." Human Rights Watch, *Criminal Injustice,* note 92 at 19).

96. Art. 28, Código de Processo Penal (C.P.P.) (Braz.); Human Rights Watch, *Criminal Injustice,* note 92 at 22.

97. Art. 28, note 96.

98. Art. 28, note 96 at 27–29.

99. Art. 28, note 96 at 33–38.

100. Human Rights Watch, *Criminal Injustice,* note 92 at 43–49.

101. Human Rights Watch, *Criminal Injustice,* note 92 at 36, and interviews with delegadas in São Paulo, August 1990.

102. Cecilia Medina, *The Battle of Human Rights: Gross, Systematic Violations and the Inter-American System* (Dordrecht: Martinus Nijhoff, 1988), 16.

103. Art. 1.

104. Art. 24.

105. American Convention, art. 25.

106. Women's Convention, art. 2.

107. For example, Articles 3, 4, and 5 in the Universal Declaration of Human Rights, Articles 7, 8, and 9 of the International Covenant on Civil and Political Rights, and the Convention Against Torture and Other Cruel, Inhuman or Degrading Treatment or Punishment. Donna Sullivan, "Violence Against Women: The Legal Framework," in *Combatting Violence Against Women,* Report by the International League for Human Rights (New York: International League for Human Rights, 1993), 55.

108. Women's Convention, art 3.

109. Robert O. Keohane, "International Theory and Contributions of a Feminist Standpoint" in *Gender and International Relations,* ed. Grant and Newland, note 21 at 47, citing Mary Hawkesworth, "Knowers, Knowing, Known: Feminist Theory and Claims of Truth," *Signs* 14 (1989): 554.

110. Anne Marie Goetz, "Feminism and the Claim to Know: Contradictions in Feminist Approaches to Women," in *Gender and International Relations,* ed. Grant and Newland, note 21 at 147.

111. Goetz, "Claim to Know," note 110 at 134.

112. Nancy Fraser, "Rethinking the Public Sphere," *Social Text* 25/26 (1990): 56 at 69.

113. Goetz, "Claim to Know," note 110 at 151.

114. Goetz, "Claim to Know," note 110 at 152.

115. Sylvia Walby, *Theorizing Patriarchy* (Oxford: Basil Blackwell, 1990), 174.

116. See generally Melissa Spatz, "A Lesser Crime: A Comparative Study of Legal Defenses for Men Who Kill Their Wives," *Colum. J. L. & Soc. Prob.* 24 (1991): 597.

117. Art. 2.

118. Patricia Williams, "Alchemical Notes: Reconstructing Ideals from Deconstructed Rights," *Harv. C.R.-C.L. L. Rev.* 22 (1989): 401, 417.

119. Art. 3.

120. Heise, "International Dimensions," note 81.

121. Draft Inter-American Convention on Violence, O.A.S. Doc. OEA/Ser.L./II.7.4, CIM/Doc.1/91.

122. G.A. Res. 543 (VI) advocated for the codification of economic, social, civil, and political rights. Imre Szabo, "Historical Foundations of Human Rights," in *The International Dimensions of Human Rights,* vol. 1, ed. Karel Vasak (Westport, CT: Greenwood Press, 1982), 29. See, also, Theo van Boven, "Distinguishing Criteria of Human Rights," in *International Dimensions,* ed. Vasak, note 122 at 51.

123. Hilary Charlesworth, Christine Chinkin, and Shelley Wright, "Feminist Approaches to International Law," *Am. J. Int'l L.* 85 (1991): 639.

124. See Goetz, "Claim to Know," note 110 at 138–39 for a discussion of the different approaches to women's issues within the development framework.

125. Jurgen Habermas, *The Theory of Communicative Action* (Boston: Beacon Press, 1981).

126. Ben Agger, *A Critical Theory of Public Life: Knowledge, Discourse, and Politics in an Age of Decline* (New York: Falmer Press, 1991), 164.

127. Agger, *Critical Theory,* note 126.

128. Agger, *Critical Theory,* note 126 at 167.

Chapter 5
Intimate Terror: Understanding Domestic Violence as Torture

Rhonda Copelon

> To punish disobedience and discipline liberty, family tradition perpetuates a culture of terror that humiliates women, teaches children to lie, and spreads the plague of fear. Human rights should begin at home.
> —Eduardo Galeano, *The Book of Embraces* (1989), 143

Introduction

The abuse of women by their male partners is among the most common and dangerous forms of gender-based violence.[1] Its victims exceed those of the most brutal dictatorships. As a result of the global mobilization of women, and international attention to certain ongoing atrocities, both official and private violence against women have begun to be recognized as a human rights concern. Nonetheless, intimate violence remains on the margin: it is still considered different, less severe, and less deserving of international condemnation and sanction than officially inflicted violence.[2]

There are essentially two major obstacles to the treatment of intimate violence as a human rights violation. One is the role of the public/private dichotomy in international law that my colleague and collaborator Celina Romany has so ably deconstructed in the preceding chapter. The second, which is the focus of this piece, is the fact that intimate violence—with the exception of some of its more sensationalized and culture-specific examples—tends not to be viewed as violence. Seen as "personal," "private," a "domestic" or a "family matter," its goals and consequences are obscured, and its use justified as chastisement or discipline. But when stripped of privatization, sexism, and sentimentalism, gender-based violence is no less grave than other forms of inhumane and subordinating official violence, which have been prohibited by treaty and customary law and recognized by the international community as *jus cogens,* or peremptory norms that bind universally and can never be violated.

To elucidate the egregiousness of gender-based violence, I have chosen to compare official torture with commonplace domestic violence against women partners. On the one hand, torture, which has been elaborated through treaties and recognized as *jus cogens,* illustrates what renders violence exceptional and heinous.[3] On the other hand, domestic violence which includes battering, rape and sexual abuse, appears through a conventional human rights lens as a "hard case," while from women's experience it is an obvious one.

Thus Part I examines what makes violence egregious, through analyzing the characteristics of domestic violence in light of the international legal understanding of what constitutes torture and its near relative, cruel, inhuman, and degrading treatment. My conclusion is that the process, purposes, and consequences are startlingly similar and that the fact that domestic violence is privately, as opposed to officially, inflicted does not diminish its atrociousness nor the need for international sanction. Part II sketches some of the implications of this comparison: the possibility of understanding domestic violence as a form of torture and sanctioning it as such under the relevant conventions; the necessity of recognizing domestic violence against women as an independent violation of human rights as well as *jus cogens,* as among the most heinous human rights violations.

Several caveats before I begin. Official torture and domestic violence are not the same; each is unique in its egregiousness. The purpose of comparison is to elucidate commonalities as well as sex-specific differences and to tread a course between two kinds of essentialism. One sees torture as having a fixed set of characteristics, unaffected by differences in context that may be political, social, economic, and cultural as well as gendered. The other, feminist, essentialism posits a "woman's perspective" without regard to different racial, class, cultural, and sexual positions that transform gender and define differences among women.[4] This discussion of both torture and gender-based violence is largely drawn from western sources that dominate the literature. While this underscores a fact central to feminist international work— that gender-based violence is not a phenomenon that obeys the north/ south axis nor is it peculiar to traditionalist societies—it also limits the cultural relevance and specificity of the description and analysis of domestic violence as well as eschews the different strategic issues involved in reconceptualizing intimate violence as torture.[5] It is intended to suggest a methodology that can be applied to domestic violence against women in different cultural settings as well as to different forms of violence against women and, thereby, open a dialogue on commonalities and differences.

I. Domestic Violence Through the Lens of Torture

One Woman's Story

During that first year together, Molly and Jim moved three times and Molly's life became more isolated. He wouldn't let Molly go outside unless he was there and he forbade her to open the blinds or talk to the neighbors.

One night in a bar, Jim told Molly to put money in the jukebox. When the bartender said something to Molly, Jim picked him up off the floor and accused him of having an affair with his wife, threatening to kill him. In the van, Jim knotted one hand in Molly's hair and pounded her head against the dashboard. A police cruiser finally pulled them over and Jim was jailed for drunkenness. Molly considered leaving Jim. But he already talked as though something terrible would happen if she left. On top of that, she thought she was pregnant. Where could she go with no money and no car? Besides, she loved Jim and hoped he would change; she saw alcohol as his main problem.

By the next year, the physical abuse was occurring once a month. Jim would hit Molly with his fist for no reason, then tell her to get up and sometimes knock her down again and go on until she couldn't get up again. At first, Jim said he was sorry and occasionally brought Molly gifts, although he still blamed the violence on something she had done or forgotten to do. In June, he hit Molly in the head and she fell and later miscarried. Her dreams of improvement were shattered. Molly stayed because Jim said he would kill her family if she left, and she believed him. She never left the house if she thought he might come home. She began having constant headaches and dizziness, and was living on Empirin III. She knew she ought to do something, but it was enough just to get through the day.

By 1982, Jim was drinking more heavily. He would accuse Molly of having affairs and then begin hitting her. He insisted on having sex nearly every night, and this frequently involved violence as well. Molly always had bruises, teeth marks, and abrasions. Jim also required sex after beatings, which was especially painful when Molly was injured. She began to welcome unconsciousness as a refuge. Molly simply lived in fear of Jim's rage and tried to avoid things that might set him off. But there was nothing she could do.

Molly gave birth to a son in August. Jim found the baby annoying and would spank him in irritation. He added the baby to his list of warnings against her departure. Sometimes he threatened her with the revolver he kept in the pickup—holding it to her head and saying that he didn't love her, that she wasn't good enough for him. Jim began dating and would tell Molly about the women—young, beautiful, no stretch marks, no kids. He said he abused her sexually because of her age; she wasn't a virgin any more and she deserved it. Molly started making plans to escape. She persuaded Jim to let her take in ironing, and began hiding some of her earnings under the sink.

By 1983 Molly was severely depressed. Jim was no longer working and refused to let Molly work. Her ironing money had been spent for food and Jim had sold most of the things Molly owned before they got married, including the special things she had kept from her family. Molly almost never talked anymore, except to her son. Jim said he'd see to it that she never managed to leave with the baby. He would take the rifle down from the wall when she was quiet for too long, and Molly would try to perk up and seem more cheerful. She promised herself they would get away when Kevin was a little older.

One day Jim came home and caught Molly in the backyard talking to a neighbor woman. He began hitting Molly with his fists, throwing her against cabinets and appliances, knocking her to the floor, pulling her up, and hitting her again. He threw everything in the kitchen that was movable, saying over and over, "I can't trust you." Then Jim dragged Molly into the living room and demanded that she take off all her clothes. He burned them together with her clothes from the closet, saying she wouldn't be needing them if she was going to be a whore. He yelled and yelled at her about being outside, screaming, biting, pinching, pulling hair, kicking her in the legs and back. Molly held her breath and prayed it would be over soon. This time she thought she might die. After about an hour, Jim seemed to wear out. Molly pulled herself to the bathroom and tried to stop shaking. But Jim burst in and accused her of trying to hide something, saying this proved she had been unfaithful. He pushed her forward over the sink and raped her anally, pounding her head against the mirror as he did so. Molly started throwing up, but he continued. Then he grabbed the scissors and began shearing off Molly's long dark beautiful hair, scraping her scalp with the blades, ripping out handfuls, shaking her violently, saying, "How do you like how you look now? No one will look at you now, will they? No one will ever want you now!" She had never been in so much pain. The next day, Jim told Molly she was never to go outside the house again, for any reason. Molly was bleeding, throwing up, badly bruised, and unable to walk, but Jim seemed unconcerned with any of her injuries. He warned her that she would "lose" Kevin if she ever did anything else to disobey him. After this, Jim stayed around the house more and frequently checked on Molly if he was away. Molly felt ill for months. She moved slowly and just tried to take care of Kevin.

Jim wrecked his truck, injured himself, ruined his business and blamed Molly. He kept her awake until early morning while he raged, and threw bottles of beer at her or poured hot coffee over her if she fell asleep. Sexual abuse occurred almost nightly. Molly's bite marks and cuts became permanent scars. When he had been drinking, sex would go on for hours because he couldn't climax. Jim would blame Molly for that, grinding his teeth, banging her head against the headboard and choking her. He also threatened her or traced on her with a fillet knife during sex. Sometimes he would kick her across the room. She would just concentrate on her breathing and wait for it to be over. Jim said she wasn't feeling enough pain and hit her harder, but Molly remained silent, thinking, "He might have my body, but I'll try not to let him have my mind." Still, she stayed—exhausted, ill, not knowing where to go. She kept telling herself, "If I could just get some more sleep; if I could make myself eat again, get my strength back." Jim was so wild now, she did not think she could get away with the baby without someone getting killed.[6]

A Gendered System of Terror

Domestic violence is not gender-neutral. While in heterosexual relationships women sometimes fight back and in exceptional cases men are injured or killed, severe, repeated domestic violence is overwhelmingly initiated by men and inflicted on women. Nor is this violence isolated, random, or explicable by the abnormal characteristics of the abuser or victim or by dysfunction in the family. In developed and developing societies, studies indicate that between 20 percent and 67 percent of women have experienced violence in intimate heterosexual relationships. The very prevalence of wife-battering unmasks the prevailing concepts of normalcy and functionality.[7] While many theories have been advanced to explain this violence, gender inequality is key. For example, the UN Report, *Violence Against Women in the Family*, concludes its analysis of the literature with the statement that

there is no simple explanation for violence against women in the home. Certainly, any explanation must go beyond the individual characteristics of the man, the woman and the family and look to the structure of relationships and the role of society in underpinning that structure. In the end analysis, it is perhaps best to conclude that violence against wives is a function of the belief, fostered in all cultures, that men are superior and that the women they live with are their possessions or chattels that they can treat as they wish and as they consider appropriate.[8]

Indeed, domestic violence against women is systemic and structural, a mechanism of patriarchal control of women that is built on male superiority and female inferiority, sex-stereotyped roles and expectations, and economic, social, and political predominance of men and dependency of women. While the legal and cultural embodiments of patriarchal thinking vary among different cultures, there is an astounding convergence in regard to the basic tenets of patriarchy and the legitimacy, if not necessity, of violence as a mechanism of enforcing that system. Violence is encouraged by and perpetuates women's dependence and her dehumanization as "other," a servant, and a form of property. It is also necessary to preserve overbearing male entitlement and unbearable female constraint. The imperfection of—or necessary tension in the system—is reflected in the ever-present potential and fact that women will defy this destiny. Jealousy is a common theme in violent scenarios. Women are to be feared because they are sexually voracious, tricksters, sorceresses, and lesbians. Women's capacity and power triggers attack—whether it be pregnancy, mothering, beauty, or the offer of intimacy; competence at wage-earning work, social relations, or household management; or actual "rebellions" small and large. Through violence men seek both to deny and destroy the power of women. Through violence men seek and confirm the devaluation and dehumanization of women.[9]

In spite of the modernization of life, the basic patriarchal dynamic continues to express and replicate itself through violence in the private sphere. Indeed, the fact that most studies of domestic violence come from western societies—mainly the United Kingdom and the United States—where the traditional patriarchal arrangements are thought to have been most challenged by shifting economic, social, political, and ideological conditions, attests to the extraordinary durability of patriarchy as well as to the importance of redressing gender-based violence in a multi-faceted way.[10]

The Elements of Torture as Applied to Domestic Violence

Although widely practiced, torture is universally condemned as one of the most heinous forms of violence and, therefore, provides a framework against which to examine the gravity of domestic violence. Over the centuries, torture evolved in the West from a quasi-judicial or judicial method of eliciting or testing truth into a weapon of terror.[11] The terroristic use of torture common today was born in the Inquisition and reached its apogee in the European witch-hunt of the sixteenth and seventeenth centuries.[12] Subsequently revulsion against royal authority and the humanitarian impulses of the Enlightenment led to condemnation of torture at the same time as changes in criminal procedure and new forms of punishment and social control gave the state more penetrating control over people's lives and appeared to render torture superfluous.[13] Torture did not die out, however, but re-emerged as a tool of colonial powers, and unregulated, low visibility police practice in the United States; and a tool of nationalism, fascism, and Stalinism. In Nazi Germany, torture was industrialized, reaching unprecedented levels of sophistication and horror.[14]

Revulsion against Nazi atrocities led to the prohibition of torture and cruel, inhuman, and degrading treatment in the Universal Declaration of Human Rights, the International Covenant on Civil and Political Rights (ICCPR) and the Geneva Conventions. The resurgence of torture in recent decades, together with the campaign against torture spearheaded by Amnesty International and other human rights groups around the world, has led to the adoption of increasingly detailed and binding instruments prohibiting torture and cruel, inhuman, and degrading treatment on both international and regional levels, as well as their elaboration by investigatory and adjudicatory bodies.[15]

Where torture is defined in the binding instruments,[16] it generally involves four critical elements: (1) severe physical and/or mental pain and suffering; (2) intentionally inflicted; (3) for specified purposes; (4) with some form of official involvement, whether active or passive. As to each of these elements, this section will compare the evolving understanding of torture with domestic violence against women partners.

Severe Physical and/or Mental Pain and Suffering

The classic notion of torture in western history and imagination focuses on gross physical invasion of the body. Derived from the Latin *tortura,* it means "twisting," "wreathing," and "torment."[17] But, to treat physical brutality as a sine qua non of torture obscures the essential goals of modern official torture—the breaking of the will and the spread of terror. It obscures the relationship between acts of violence and the context of torture, between physical pain, and mental stress, and between mental integrity and human dignity. And it ignores that abuse of the body is humiliating as well as searing, and that the body is abused and controlled not only for obscene sadistic reasons but ultimately as a pathway to the mind and spirit. Elaine Scarry, in her profound study of the torture process, emphasizes the "world-destroying" aspect of severe physical pain, the destruction of the mental and physical worlds outside the body, the conversion of the mind into the body as pain.[18]

Conversely, Amnesty International emphasizes that the subtler psychological methods of torture render distinctions between the physical and mental illusory.[19] Thus, while it is possible to identify both physical and psychological methods of torture and their analogues in the context of domestic violence, it is critical to recognize the impossibility of segregating them in terms of either goals or effects in practice.

The Physical Component

According to Amnesty International, the infliction of physical pain is common in the practice of official torture. Some methods are ancient— the falanga, the thumbscrew, pulling out of fingernails, and near-drowning submersion in foul water. With the exception of electro-shock, however, the most common forms of physical torture involve no special equipment. They include beating and kicking and the infliction of pain with objects such as canes, knives, and cigarettes.[20] For women, sexual abuse, rape, and the forcing of instruments or animals into the vagina are common, as well as among the most devastating, forms of torture. Sexual violence in the form of forced undressing, pawing, threats of rape, or being forced to perform sexual acts is also common.[21] In other words, torture is very frequently inflicted through means available in everyday life; the commonplace, innocuous, or benign transformed into a weapon of brutality.

Like torture, domestic violence commonly involves some form of, usually escalating, physical brutality. The methods of intimate violence resemble the common methods of torture, and include beating with hands or objects, biting, spitting, punching, kicking, slashing, stabbing, strangling, scalding, burning and attempted drowning. The consequences include physical and mental pain and suffering, disfigurement, temporary and permanent disabilities, miscarriage, maiming, and death.[22] Rape and sexual abuse are likewise common concomitants of battering.[23] Sexual abuse takes many forms, including "the insertion of objects into the woman's vagina, forced anal and oral sex, bondage, forced sex with others, and sex with animals." Some women are threatened with mutilation of their breasts or genitals and suffer permanent disfigurement. As in the story of Molly and Jim, rape and sexual abuse may be prolonged for hours, interspersed with escalating battering as the man fails to climax. Domestic violence also causes women to fear for their lives and with good reason. It is a leading cause of death among women.[24]

The Psychological Component

The psychological component of torture consists of the anguish, humiliation, debilitation, and fear caused by physical brutality, rape, and sexual abuse; by threats of such brutalities and death; and by methods of sensory deprivation, stress, and manipulation designed to break the will of the tortured. The inseparability of physical and mental tortures is illustrated by the fact that in both domestic and official contexts, rape and sexual abuse, which may do less physical damage than beatings, are often experienced by women as the gravest violation.[25]

Among the most insidious forms of torture are those that do not involve overt brutality. Anguish and disintegration of the self can be accomplished through methods that passively as well as actively attack the body. Such hybrid techniques include forcing prisoners to assume positions such as wall-standing for prolonged periods thereby causing agonizing pain without directly administering it. Not only do these methods leave no marks, but they create in the prisoner the bizarre sense that the pain is self-induced. Sensory deprivation techniques, which create anxiety and disorientation, include exposure to loud, continuous noises, hooding, alternating with blinding light, sleep deprivation, starvation, and dehydration. Control of bodily functions and, with women trained in modesty and degraded as sex objects, forced and observed nudity are intended not only to terrify but also to humiliate and destroy all sense of autonomy.[26]

Some methods rely wholly on the psychological. Fear is instilled through threats to kill, mutilate, or torture the person, or her family members or friends. Torturers stage mock executions and force people to listen to the screams of others being tortured. With women, threats to abuse their children or abuse the women in front of their children, as well as observing or hearing the rape of other women, are especially potent. Torturers also use yet more subtle methods to break the prisoner's will: isolation, arbitrary and unpredictable punishments, intermittent rewards, and the alternation of active and passive brutality with kindness in order to undermine the prisoner's morale-sustaining hatred of the torturers and convert the torturer into savior.[27] All these methods, designed to exhaust endurance and manipulate dependency, underscore the significance of the psychological in torture—that torture is a context and process of domination and not simply or necessarily a set of brutal acts.

Amnesty International has devoted considerable attention to the centrality of psychological stress and manipulation as methods of torture, based on the theories of A.D. Biderman who showed that compliance among POWs resulted from a combination of techniques designed to induce dependency, debility, and dread and thereby break the personality.[28]

Drawing on Biderman's theory to explain the dynamics of battering, psychologists and advocates for battered women have also analogized the condition of POWs to that of battered women.[29] Batterers manipulate and create stress much the same way as official torturers. As the story of Molly and Jim illustrates, women are isolated from family, friends, and others. They are subjected to verbal insult, sexual denigration, and abuse. Their lives and that of their loved ones are threatened, and they are made to fear the loss of their children. At the same time, at least early in the battering cycle, they are occasionally showered with apologies, promises, and kindness. The possibility of explosion over the smallest domestic detail, however, places battered women in a condition of severe and unremitting dread. For some women, the psychological terror is the worst part. Indeed, it can be so great that women will precipitate battering as opposed to enduring the fear.

The suffering caused to women as a consequence of living in a battering relationship is profound. Lenore Walker describes a cycle of battering that begins with limited physical violence followed by remorse and intensive caretaking (occasional indulgence), which is followed, in turn, by escalating violence and less remorse or "compensatory time." The process of battering—whether physical or psychological or both, often produces anxiety, depression, and sleeplessness. It can produce extreme states of dependency, debility, and dread as well as the same intense symptoms that comprise the post-traumatic stress disorders experienced by victims of official violence as well as by victims of rape.[30]

There is, however, an important debate about whether battering succeeds in its goal to debilitate women. Drawing on Seligman's studies of dogs, who, subjected to shock, remained passive and did not leave even when the cage was open, Lenore Walker applied the concept of "learned helplessness" to explain the effects of battering. She described a state of depression, anxiety, and passivity and originally hypothesized that women are passive and feel helpless to leave as a result of blaming themselves for the violence.[31] While the term "learned helplessness" describes the apparent condition of many battered women, just as it does that of many abused prisoners, more recently, scholars and advocates of battered women have demonstrated that it obscures the degree to which both prisoners and battered women are concretely precluded from, or actively struggling to, change or survive their condition.[32] Likewise, the term "battered woman syndrome," although intended as a description, communicates disability and abnormality. These terms are also biased, often on race and class grounds, against women who do not appear helpless, and they fail to explain why some women kill their batterers.[33]

Disputing the stereotype of passivity, weakness, dysfunction, and loss of agency implied by the term "helplessness," scholars thus stress the concrete constraints against leaving. Women lack economic means and support systems to find shelter and provide for themselves and their children. Fearing pursuit, they may need to find clandestine shelter or move miles away and assume new identities. This is frightening for them and their children. Edward Gondolf and Ellen Fisher emphasize the desire and heroic strength of battered women to survive. They assert that as violence escalates and self-blame recedes, battered women increase their efforts to get help, despite fear, danger, depression, low self-esteem, guilt, or economic constraints. The authors ascribe these women's failures to obtain help largely to the inadequacy of community response and resources.

Others underscore the fact that battered women realistically fear that leaving will precipitate deadly rage. Martha Mahoney identifies this as "separation assault": that "at the moment of separation or attempted separation—for many women, the first encounter with the authority of law—the batterer's quest for control often becomes most acutely violent and potentially lethal."[34] Finally, Julie Blackmun suggests that violence and terror do not destroy women's agency but, together with profound social and economic constraints, narrow the cognitive frame in which that agency is, often heroically, exercised: "the societally based limitations of patriarchy, the psychological decrements in self-esteem, the high intensity of violent interactions and the fear-induced restrictions on an individual's ability to think in complex terms—contribute to the dearth of real and perceived alternatives available to chronic victims of wife abuse."[35]

The comparison between survivors of official torture and imprisonment and battered women makes clear that submission is not a particularity of women's pathology, but rather a consequence of terroristic efforts at domination.[36] Just as we do not excuse torture that fails to accomplish the complete submission of the victim, so there is no need for battering to result in complete surrender to violate international law. The practitioners of terror should not be exonerated because women, like prisoners of war and dictatorships, are capable of heroic efforts to endure and survive.

The International Legal Standards

The evolving definition of torture in the international instruments reflects increasing recognition of the inseparability of the physical and mental in torture as well as the sufficiency of psychological abuse, standing alone.[37] The UN Torture Convention, defines torture as including mental as well as physical suffering and softens the distinction between torture and ill-treatment.[38] Burgers and Danelius include in the category of mental torture, threats of death or reprisal against the subject or family, witnessing the execution or torture of other detainees or family members, or deprivation of food, water, or sleep, or prolonged isolation, or darkness—all of which induce extreme suffering. The Human Rights Committee, ruling on several cases under the Optional Protocol to the ICCPR has treated threats of death or grave physical harm as torture.[39] The Inter-American Convention, drafted in light of gross dictatorial violence in many Latin American countries goes further; it emphasizes the sufficiency of the psychological component of torture by explicitly encompassing debilitating mind-control methods that are not experienced as pain or suffering. In addition, the Human Rights Committee has commented that "It may not be necessary to draw sharp distinctions between the various prohibited forms of treatment or punishment."[40] In practice, it has only occasionally segregated the prohibitions on torture and ill-treatment and never with sufficient specificity from which to discern a coherent distinction.[41]

Nonetheless, there are some problems on the lower end of the spectrum. The European Commission has distinguished a few slaps from cruel, inhuman, and degrading treatment, because such treatment tends to be well-tolerated or expected.[42] The Human Rights Committee has treated debilitating conditions of confinement such as "arbitrary sanctions . . . continually applied for the purpose of generating moments of hope followed by frustration . . . aimed at destroying the detainees' physical and psychological balance . . . [keeping them] in a state of anxiety, uncertainty and tension . . . [and forbidding expression] of any feeling of friendship or solidarity"[43] not as cruel, inhuman, and degrading treatment under Article 7 but as "inhuman" treatment under Article 10(1) of the ICCPR. Rodley concludes, however, that the lower threshold reflects disagreement within the Committee which "has offered no reasoned argument for its choice."[44]

For the purposes of treating typical domestic violence against women partners as torture, the frequency of physical brutality and the severity of psychological abuse are generally dispositive. Moreover, while it is important to counter the tendency to trivialize domestic violence, there is no doubt that many less severe forms qualify as cruel, inhuman, and degrading treatment. Beyond that, what qualifies as torture lies not in the quality of the experience, but in the relative degree to which society recognizes both physical and psychological brutality and suffering in the two contexts. That recognition is complicated by gender. On the one hand, the physical brutality of domestic violence inflicted on women is denied—batterers don't see it, hospitals don't identify it, and women try to hide it. On the other, the gravity of subtler forms of psychological torture, including stress-producing and debilitating measures, may be denied, even in the context of torture in part because of its association with the "feminine"—its methods are invisible and familiar; the vulnerability it creates, fearsome and contemptible. While some argue that the analogy to domestic violence dilutes the concept of torture, it is more likely that the global women's movement against violence will hasten the achievement of greater consonance between the international legal standards of torture and the suffering it intends and inflicts.

Intentionality

To constitute torture, pain must be intentionally inflicted against the will of the victim. This distinguishes torture from accidents or disease as well as from situations where pain is accepted in the hope of attaining some greater good. The intentional infliction of excruciating pain and suffering for its own sake, whatever the subjective state of mind or goal of the torturer, mocks all pretense of civilization and thereby demands the most severe condemnation.

The intent required is simply the general intent to do the act that clearly or foreseeably causes terrible suffering. The drafters rejected the view that torture be "deliberately and maliciously" inflicted.[45] Milgram's famous experiments with authority, as well as the training and practices of torturers, reveal that torturers are trained to deny the humanity of the victim, to follow orders, rationalize their actions, and use a variety of mechanisms to distance themselves from the fact that they are inflicting terrible pain.[46] Having studied the training of the Greek military torturers, Dr. Mika Haritos-Fatouros concludes that "to believe that only sadists can perform such violent acts is a fallacy and a comfortable rationalization to ease our liberal sensibilities."[47] Likewise, Hannah Arendt emphasizes the banality of evil, noting that the Nazis sought to eliminate from the elite corps those who derived pleasure from what they did.[48]

By contrast, it is commonly argued that most men who abuse their wives or women partners do not act purposively, but impulsively. From a legal perspective, this claimed loss of control does not exonerate violent acts as a general matter. Short of proof of insanity or mistake, the act is intentional and, therefore, culpable. In Anglo-American jurisprudence, heat of passion or rage may reduce murder to manslaughter and mitigate the penalty, but it does not exonerate the offender. Gender discrimination enters, however, when disproportionately light sentences are imposed on men who kill or abuse women partners.[49] In some systems a "defense of honor"—recognized by law or custom—allows the husband's jealousy or rage over the real or imagined offenses by the wife to excuse even homicide. This defense, available only to men, licenses not only impulsive behavior, but deliberate vengeance.[50] So does the marital rape exception—an implicit defense of honor—still the law in most countries.[51]

Moreover, the claim that domestic violence is the product of loss of impulse control has been severely criticized in light of the dynamics of battering. "Battering, whether or not it is premeditated, is purposeful behavior"[52] and "should be seen as an attempt to bring about a desired state of affairs."[53] Battered women report that men often plan their attack. Men who beat women partners commonly exhibit excellent impulse control in other contexts; their major or only targets are woman partners or children, pets, and inanimate objects. The contention that alcohol causes violence also ignores the fact that many men get drunk without beating their wives and that men often beat their wives without being drunk. To the extent that alcohol facilitates male violence, it is an important factor in the effort to reduce battering, but it is not the cause.[54] Finally, professions of remorse from the batterer earn ill-placed sympathy. He does not perceive his violence as un-justified.[55] Often a tactic for preventing his wife from leaving, remorse is inherently suspect where, despite pleas for forgiveness, the violence cycle is repeated.

Conversely, the notion that the torturer always acts under control, according to protocol or orders, ignores the fact that they engage in both programmed and spontaneous brutal and sadistic behavior. Tor-turers have also been reported to abuse alcohol and drugs in the course of their "duties." Some, like batterers, may experience tremendous guilt over what they have done, while others have become inured to the damage they inflict.[56] But none of this, nor the claim to be acting under orders, exonerates the torturer under international law.

Thus in the contexts of both official torture and domestic battering, individual malice is not necessary and loss of control is not exculpatory. To focus on the intent of the perpetrator obscures the severity of the suffering threatened or inflicted, forgiving the perpetrator rather than recognizing the victim. Indeed the contention that battering is simply an impulsive letting-off-steam is an aspect of the depoliticization of domestic violence against women. This view treats battering as an individual problem of personal or family dynamics and obscures the underlying and purposive gender dynamic of domination and subor-dination. The human rights focus must be on the perpetrator's ac-countability in order to counter the traditional complicity of law and custom in giving license to violent "impulses" against women.

Prohibited Purposes

Not all deliberately inflicted severe violence amounts to a human rights violation or warrants the label "heinous." Purpose plays a role. The UN and Inter-American conventions prohibit the use of torture for otherwise legitimate purposes such as the obtaining of information or punishment, as well as for clearly illegitimate purposes such as intim-idation, personal punishment, the obliteration or diminution of the personality, or discrimination. In the international decisions on torture the element of purpose has not occasioned much attention. Nor should it. For the state deliberately to employ or permit torture is, by defini-tion, an abuse of power and an offense against human dignity.

Nevertheless, the element of purpose—so long as it is understood not as requiring a showing of specific or conscious intent, but only as identifying the goals or functions of violence at issue—helps to elucidate the evil of torture. It underscores the principle of non-derogability—that even where the ends may be legitimate—obtaining information or judicially sanctioned punishment—the use of torture is not. It also emphasizes the psychological aspects of torture. Where the methods of torture involve infliction of extreme physical pain, there is no need to separately identify purpose; but where the methods are psychological, an understanding that the goal is, for example, the destruction of human dignity may be critical to understanding the mistreatment as torture. Finally, the enumerated purposes illuminate the political and social evil of torture as a means of suppressing a group or whole society.

The delineation of prohibited purposes likewise elucidates why privately inflicted gender-based violence is egregious. Isolated, random, albeit deliberate, brutality is a subject for law enforcement, but not necessarily for the international community. Gender-based violence is different. It should be recognized as an international human rights violation because it violates the human rights of women as persons to integrity, security, and dignity, and also because it constitutes discrimination against women as a group in that its purpose is to maintain both the individual woman and women as a class in an inferior, subordinated position. It is thus illuminating to examine the degree to which the purposes that render torture heinous apply to the phenomenon of domestic violence.

To Elicit Information

The most common response to the analogy between torture and domestic violence is the contention that torture is different because its purpose is to elicit information. This distinction, which harks back to the original nature of torture, ignores the contemporary understanding of torture as an engine of terror. It misapprehends the function of interrogation in torture as well as its place in domestic violence. It may also reflect a gender-biased identification with the victims of state torture as opposed to domestic violence—the torture victim resisting the giving of information is heroic, whereas the battered woman somehow deserves it.

The practice of torture negates the contention that the search for information is an integral and defining aspect of torture. The idea of the ancient Greeks that torture would elicit the truth from the body of a slave fell into early desuetude, as did the use of torture as a mechanism of judicial process. Not only is violence the antithesis of a truth-eliciting device, but false information and accusation have also been, since the witch hunts, the torturer's trade. The historian Edward Peters writes:

"It is not primarily the victim's information, but the victim, that torture needs to win—or reduce to powerlessness."[57]

That truth is a foil for other motives does not, however, diminish the significance of the interrogation as a method of torture. Elaine Scarry argues that the pain of torture is almost always accompanied by the "Question." The interrogation—consisting of questions, statements, insults, and orders—is "internal to the structure of torture, exists there because of its intimate connections to and interactions with physical pain."[58] The interrogation—trivial, meaningless, or irrational as its content may be—is essential to the torturer's self-justification and a tool in the destruction of the victim. The confession—true or false—demonstrates the supremacy of the torturer. The victim is mortified, ashamed at her weakness and agonized at the prospect that she has put others at risk. The interrogation is thus primarily a means, not an end.

Just as torture seems to be in pursuit of confession or information, domestic violence seems not to be. But this, too, is a misconception. Like torture, domestic violence is both physical and verbal. Whether precipitated by rage, jealousy, or a real or feared loss of control, domestic violence has its own interrogation—questions, accusations, insults, and orders: Where were you today? Who were you with? Who visited you? What do you mean you want to go out to work? Why is the coffee cold? the house a mess? this item moved? You're dumb, ugly, old; or Jim's question to Molly: "How do you like how you look now?"

The goal of the domestic interrogation is not truth or information, but dread, humiliation and submission. What the confession is to torture, the explanation, the accounting-for-oneself, the apology, the begging is to domestic violence. In both contexts, the victim/survivor seeks to stop or avert the pain, to protect others from harm, and to pacify the aggressor. In the context of official torture, the confession, even if false, has a greater likelihood of endangering others, while with domestic violence, confession and apology may more often be designed to protect others, particularly children. The victim's anguish is likely to be more extreme where the confession does or is believed to risk the safety of another, but for the aggressor confession is proof of submission. Interrogation is not a necessary element of violence against women, but it is a common one, and its purpose, as in torture, is not truth but power.[59]

To Punish

The impermissibility of torture as a form of punishment does not require extended discussion. But torture is also itself an extra-legal form of punishment. The Inter-American Torture Convention appears to stress this by prohibiting torture as a "means of . . . personal punishment." Military governments operating under exceptional powers or self-declared states of emergency bypass the civilian prosecutorial system, dispensing with due process such as notice of the charges, confrontation, a presumption of innocence, or an impartial tribunal. Torture thus constitutes an alternative system of punishment, unaccountable to the existing system of justice. Though an official system in the sense that it is carried out by and at the instigation of state officials, it is neither authorized nor regulated by law; individual torturers may be reined in by superiors or given license to indulge their cruelty or whim. Torture is used openly to intimidate the population at the same time that it is officially denied.[60]

Gender-based violence resembles the military's extra-legal use of torture in a number of respects. Violence against women in the home operates as an alternative system of social control unaccountable to the formal legal system—a system of "personal punishment." Alda Facio and Rosalia Camacho critique criminology from a feminist perspective for examining only the official and public sphere forms of punishment and social control rather than those that are unofficial and pervade the private sphere and the lives of women.[61] With Celina Romany, I would describe the power structure operative in the domestic sphere as a "parallel state," which operates on an informal customary system of social control with the explicit or implicit permission of the formal state. At the same time, it interacts with the state, constantly bolstering the formal impunity given to gender aggression.[62]

In the case of intimate violence, patriarchal ideology and conditions, rather than a distinct, consciously coordinated military establishment, confer upon men the sense of entitlement, if not the duty, to chastise their wives. Wife-beating is, therefore, not an individual, isolated, or aberrant act, but a social license, a duty or sign of masculinity, deeply engrained in culture, widely practiced, denied, and completely or largely immune from legal sanction. It is inflicted on women in the position of wives for their failure to properly carry out their role, for their failure to produce, serve, or be properly subservient. As Dobash and Dobash write:

Being too talkative or too quiet, too sexual or not sexual enough, too frugal or too extravagant, too often pregnant or not frequently enough all seem to be provocative. The only pattern discernible in these lists is that the behavior, whatever it might be, represents some form of failure or refusal on the part of the woman to comply with or support her husband's wishes and authority.[63]

Given the tendency to blame the victim, it is perhaps dangerous to speak of provocation. But not to do so ignores the political nature of gender-based violence—the illegitimacy of the batterer's expectations and the dissidence expressed in the woman's refusal or inability to comply.[64]

In sum, intimate violence is a systemic form of punishment that bypasses all the procedural guarantees of due process. Indeed, with the "home as his castle," the domestic aggressor may operate with even fewer external constraints than the official torturer. Absent cultural condemnation, effective community intervention, and access to responsive law enforcement, there is no internal or external system of review and denunciation, whether formal or informal.

To Intimidate

Torture seeks to intimidate on three levels: the individual victim, the group with which the victim is identified and, ultimately, the entire society.[65] The horror of the experience of torture is calculated to deter that person from oppositional activities or any association with those viewed as at risk; it creates dread that even innocuous actions will be interpreted as oppositional; and it often forces a person into exile.

On the collective level, torture operates to spread fear among those who identify with the targets of torture. It is designed then to sap the strength of potential opposition movements; to subordinate classes to the ruling authority; to facilitate economic exploitation through terror. The climate of fear intended by torture may be confined to the targeted subgroups or it may envelop an entire society, where the regime seeks its enemies among the elite as well as the less privileged. The selection of targets may appear politically motivated or completely irrational. The fact that there is no way to insulate oneself heightens the terror and engenders the pacification it seeks.[66]

Domestic violence is also designed to intimidate both the individual woman who is the target and all women as a class. On the individual level, the goal of domestic violence is to "domesticate" her; to terrify her into obedience; to prevent or deter her assertion of difference or autonomy. The possibility that violence may erupt in response to certain actions of her own leads her to try to avoid "precipitating" conduct. But beyond that, the fact that the violence may erupt at any time and for any reason creates in the woman an ubiquitous anxiety and dread, a complex game of placation, endurance, and survival.

Domestic violence undermines not only women's security at home, but also their possibilities for independence, the exercise of human rights, and self-development. The United Nations Development Fund for Women (UNIFEM) recognizes "violence as a form of control that limits their ability to pursue options in almost every area of life from the home to schools, workplaces, and most public spaces . . . [and as a] . . . direct obstacle to women's participation in development projects."[67] The central role of violence as an obstacle to women's rights and development has been acknowledged in the Forward-Looking Strategies for the Advancement of Women, and recently reiterated by the Committee for the Elimination of Discrimination Against Women (CEDAW), as well as in proposed instruments on violence against women.[68] Threats of violence are every bit as effective as acts of violence in "making women act as their own jailors."[69] Violence thus perpetuates the economic, social, and psychological dependency which, in turn, contributes to women's vulnerability to violence.

For Any Reason Based on Discrimination of Any Kind

To correct the silence in the Convention to Eliminate All Forms of Discrimination Against Women on the question of violence, CEDAW recently adopted the following interpretative recommendations to clarify that "violence against women is a form of discrimination."[70]

The UN Draft Violence Declaration likewise emphasizes violence as "the essential and ultimate social mechanism by which women are forced into a subordinate position as compared to men."[71] It should be noted that to recognize violence as a form of discrimination is more far reaching than the argument that violence affects women disproportionately or that laws against it are not enforced to the same extent as are those that govern violence against men. As an obstacle to and engine of inequality, gender-based violence is itself discrimination that requires positive measures regardless of whether violence against men is similarly redressed.

To Obliterate the Personality and/or Diminish Capacities

The Inter-American Torture Convention to Prevent and Punish Torture also defines torture as "the use of methods upon a person intended to obliterate the personality of the victim or to diminish his [her] physical or mental capacities, even if they do not cause pain or mental anguish." As such, this Convention emphasizes the psychological dimension of torture and would encompass the use, for example, of psychotropic drugs, which cause severe disorientation and loss of self without causing suffering. Although the UN Convention did not adopt similar language, it would appear to encompass these purposes so long as there is some severe physical and mental suffering.[72]

The purpose of obliterating the personality captures the ultimate horror of both torture and domestic violence as an assault on human dignity. While severe pain is world-destroying, when pain passes, the person usually regains the "self." Torture—both intimate and of-ficial—seeks more than temporal pain. It seeks to reduce a person to passivity and submission, to destroy self-esteem, confidence in life, and the capacity for resistance. It involves degradation, humiliation, terror, and shame which outlast the pain and work on the personality, the sense of wholeness, and self-worth. The intent need not be wholly to destroy the person: the Inter-American Convention would prohibit violence whose purpose is to "diminish" the person's physical or mental capacities as well. Clearly the psychological as well as physical effects of domestic violence meet this standard.

State Versus Intimate Terror

Finally, it is necessary to explore whether the sheer fact that violence is privately versus publicly inflicted so qualitatively alters the character of the violence as to deprive it of the enormity of torture or cruel, inhu-man, and degrading treatment. As we have seen, official involvement is not a distinction that affects the intensity or impact of gender-based violence. Given the pervasiveness and damage inflicted by gender-based violence, particularly in the home, it cannot be argued that the frequency or scope of official torture is greater. There are, however, three possible grounds of distinction, all of which fail under inspection. First, it is argued that official torture is distinct because it precludes redress through the state; second, that official violence presumes that the victim is in custody whereas victims of private violence are not; and third, that state brutality is worse than the cruelty of an intimate. Beyond these is the argument that to use the term "torture" to refer to individual rather than official cruelty threatens to dilute its meaning.

The Lack of State Redress

Burgers and Danelius explain the limitation of the UN Torture Con-vention to state actors on the ground that where the state is the violator, the victim will not be able to rely on domestic law enforcement for redress.[73] This explanation of the state action requirement does not address the egregiousness of the conduct constituting torture, but rather the necessity of international human rights intervention to pre-vent impunity.

The fact that gender violence is the consequence of as well as con-stitutive of an informal parallel state likewise leaves women without redress. Domestic sanctions are frequently lacking or under-enforced. The resulting impunity legitimizes the domination of the husband; it deprives the woman subjected to violence of the possibility of effective protection or escape through the system of justice; and it denies her vindication, public recognition that she is the one who is deeply and horribly wronged. Notwithstanding debate about the nature and sufficiency of a criminal justice response to domestic violence,[74] international condemnation and intervention are required to dismantle this parallel state.

Custody and Captivity

Dominion over the victim is critical to the ability to inflict terrible violence and to its potential to degrade a person and her will. The experience of isolation from help, of not being able to escape, of being at the mercy of a malevolent, and overpowering, force is key to the effectiveness of the torturer. Imprisonment in police or military custody is the paradigm. But dominion does not require walls or custody in the traditional sense. Custody exists where a person does not consider herself free to leave or resist. Interpreting the UN Torture Convention in light of the travaux, Burgers and Danelius suggest that the victims "must be understood to be persons who are deprived of their liberty or who are at least under the factual power or control of the person inflicting the pain and suffering."[75]

The same processes used to break the will of political prisoners and prisoners-of-war are used by domestic aggressors to render battered women—despite their apparent freedom to leave—captive.[76] Despite the lack of formal training and the presence of individual variation, the coercive measures used in the home not only resemble those of other batterers but also those of official captors. Like the captor, the batterer creates a constant state of fear, through threats against family, friends, and particularly children, and through unpredictable violence often to enforce petty rules. Through scrutiny and control of her body—forced nakedness, sexual abuse and rape, control over food, sleep, and bodily functions—captors and batterers aim to destroy women's sense of autonomy and dignity. Judith Herman writes that the goal of the perpetrator is to prove that "resistance is futile, and that her life depends upon winning his indulgence through absolute compliance, [as well as] . . . to instill in his victim not only fear of death but also gratitude for being allowed to live."[77]

Dependency is also encouraged through isolating the victim, destroying possessions that reflect attachment to others, and showing intermittent kindness. Where political prisoners share their torments with peers, they frequently bond with one another as a critical means of survival; where there is no peer, they are likely to bond with and idealize their captors and take their side, a phenomenon described as the Stockholm Syndrome.[78] In the domestic context, the woman is gradually isolated from all potential sources of help and silenced by threats or shame into not admitting her plight to others. Isolation interacts in both contexts with indulgence, encouraging the victim to look to the captor for solace, creating delusions about the specialness of the person or their relationship, and negating her will to resist or question.

Moreover, the victim of intimate violence is likely to be far more vulnerable to manipulation than the political prisoner whose captivity begins in force not consent and whose resistance will be buoyed by ideological commitments and hatred of the captor rather than undermined by love, empathy, and a sense of womanly duty. "Since most women derive pride and self-esteem from their capacity to sustain relationships, the batterer is often able to entrap his victim by appealing to her most cherished values. It is not surprising, therefore, that battered women are often persuaded to return after trying to flee from their abusers."[79]

The final stage in the process of obtaining control, which Herman calls "total surrender," and Amnesty, "chronic stress,"[80] is the result of requiring the victim to do things that violate her own principles or loyalty and engender in her a sense of self-loathing. With political prisoners, it may involve watching a family member or colleague be tortured or killed, breaking under interrogation, or sexual degradation. In the home, it often involves sexual humiliation or complicity in the batterer's abuse of the children.

Surrender involves two stages: first, draining oneself of emotion and resistance as a means of survival, and, second, giving up the will to live. These are not necessarily stable states, and they alternate with renewed will to survive. In regard to the first, Molly's effort to go numb under attack, to concentrate on her breathing and dissociate from her body compares with Timerman's reaction during torture: "becoming a vegetable, casting aside all logical emotions and sensations—fear, hatred, vengeance—for any emotion or sensation meant wasting useless energy."[81] Giving up the will to live is not the same as becoming suicidal, which is a form of resistance; it is rather total passivity, or robot-like functioning—that is, living dead.

Many battered women do not remain in the relationship through to the stage of total surrender. Nor is surrender the prerequisite of psychological or social captivity. Captivity exists along a spectrum that includes the period when the woman is fearfully but actively trying to save the relationship, the period when she is fearfully but actively trying to avert greater danger or escape, and the point (reached in some cases) when her hope or resistance is intermittently or totally broken.

It is important to recognize that captivity is a complex process that most often involves—for prisoners as well as battered women—highly constricted but active coping strategies which are often invisible or trivialized. This permits acknowledgment of the imprisoning effects of domestic violence without demanding total annihilation of the will or personality of the battered woman. It also elucidates the fallacy of limiting captivity to official custody. Is the power of the abusive husband less total or awful than that of the occupying military officer? What makes both men dangerous is their assumption of the right to exercise dominion over a woman. The fact that one is backed directly by the official state and the other indirectly by patriarchal custom enjoying the complicity or acquiescence of the state, does not mitigate the experience of the woman. If anything, it heightens her vulnerability.

The Factor of Intimacy

The next question is whether there is something less terrible for the victim or for the social fabric when the violence is inflicted by an intimate rather than an official. The fact that intimate violence involves a breach of trust cannot be underestimated. The torturer knows this well. Small kindnesses—asking about the victim's family, occasional indulgences—evoke the desire to trust and are among the most effective psychological tools. Scarry points out as well that torturers use domestic props—refrigerators, bathtubs, soft-drink bottles—as weapons in order to disorient the victim. Thereby, "the domestic act of protecting becomes an act of hurting."[82] The shock of being beaten by a partner as opposed to a jailor can be more numbing and world-destroying. Rape by husbands is experienced as more devastating and longer lasting than rape by strangers. And, ultimately, resistance to emotional dependency and the most profound trauma is more complicated for the battered woman than for the hostage, as she is courted rather than kidnapped into violence. She must, in Herman's words, "unlearn love and trust, hope and self-blame."[83]

The impact of gender-based versus official violence on the social fabric is incomparable only so long as the parallel state of patriarchy, the harm it perpetrates, and the violence it engenders remains invisible, sentimentalized, and legitimized. Gender-based violence in the home is profoundly traumatizing for both victims and observers; it shapes (fortunately sometimes by negative example) ideas about the gender hierarchy, about male dominance and female submission; and it helps to prepare people and a society for the use of official violence. Efforts to assess the impact on children and the people they become as a result of having observed their father battering their mother or their mother being beaten do not show clear-cut correlations. But the data suggest that such experience does play a role—albeit a complex one—in the formation of adult personality and in the perpetuation of discrimination and violence in families and society.[84]

The "Dilution" Argument

The remaining arguments for recognizing as torture only violence that is state-inflicted are rather circular. Historian Edward Peters argues that "Torture is torment inflicted by a public authority for ostensibly public purposes"[85] and that the failure to insist on state involvement risks the dilution of torture to encompass all brutality. Peters assumes, without discussion, the incomparability of official torture and wife-beating, describing their equation as among the "sentimental" uses of the term torture.[86]

Peter's approach illustrates the way the public/private dichotomy privileges the political and renders trivial the private. The impunity that results is intolerable for many reasons, not the least of which is that the sentimentalization of domestic violence enhances its terrible impact on women by depriving them of one of the key mechanisms of defense, healing, and survival—the identification and condemnation of clearly wrongful authority.

Indeed, once the gravity and comparability of intimate violence is acknowledged, the problem is not that the meaning of torture is diluted but that the practice of torture is pervasive. Recognition of gender-based violence as torture and cruel, inhuman, and degrading treatment is problematic because it reveals the banality of evil and the enormity of the suffering that society has accepted and must confront. As Primo Levi, a Holocaust survivor, wrote of the experience of captivity and dehumanization:

We have learnt that our personality is fragile, that it is in much more danger than our life; and the old wise ones, instead of warning us 'remember you must die,' would have done much better to remind us of this greater danger that threatens us. If from inside the Lager, a message could have seeped out to free men, it would have been this: take care not to suffer in your own homes what is inflicted on us here.[87]

II. Consequences for International Law of Understanding Domestic Violence as Torture

The primary goal of this chapter is to challenge the assumption that intimate violence is a less severe and terrible form of violence than that perpetrated by the state. If I have been successful, then it is necessary to suggest the potential consequences for international law. This section will examine three: (1) inclusion of domestic violence within the framework of the instruments prohibiting torture and cruel, inhuman and degrading treatment; (2) recognition of gender-based violence as an independent violation of international human rights; and (3) recognition of gender-based violence, along with torture, as *jus cogens* as a violation of customary international norms having peremptory status.[88]

Domestic Violence as Torture and III-Treatment

As we have seen, direct official involvement is not an inherent or necessary characteristic of violence having the dimension of torture. The binding instruments—the ICCPR, the UN Torture Convention and the Inter-American Torture Convention—reflect somewhat different approaches to the question of state responsibility, yet all should be interpreted to hold states accountable for failure to condemn and effectively enforce sanctions against domestic violence.[89] Where universal criminal jurisdiction is provided, it should be interpreted to apply directly to the private actor as well.

The ICCPR

Article 7 of the ICCPR announces simply the "right not to be subjected to torture and cruel, inhuman or degrading treatment or punishment." This prohibition is framed as a positive freedom, exactly as the prohibition against slavery and servitude, which has always applied directly to private conduct.[90] Article 2 requires states parties to "respect and ensure" the rights protected by the Convention "without distinction . . . such as . . . sex" and to adopt legislative remedies and other measures, including effective remedies before appropriate tribunals "to give effect" to these rights. Thus it seems entirely appropriate for the Special Rapporteur on Torture and the Human Rights Committee to consider complaints of state failure to fulfill their obligation to ensure the freedom from domestic torture where it is not effectively investigated and prosecuted. The decision of the Inter-American Court of Human Rights in the *Velásquez Rodríguez* case exemplifies this approach. There the Court interpreted the "respect and ensure" language in the American Convention, paralleling that of the ICCPR, to hold Honduras responsible, not only for active complicity in the operations of the death squads, but also for its failure to investigate and prosecute violations, assuming that they were, as claimed, carried out by entirely private paramilitary groups. The Court reasoned:

The state is obligated to investigate every situation involving a violation of the rights protected by the Convention. If the state apparatus acts in such a way that the violation goes unpunished, and the victim's full enjoyment of such rights is not restored as soon as possible, the state has failed to comply with its duty to ensure the free and full exercise of those rights to the persons within its jurisdiction. The same is true when the state allows private persons or groups to act freely and with impunity to the detriment of rights recognized by the Convention.[91]

Domestic violence creates a terror for women living in its shadow that is no less terrible than that perpetrated by the independent death squads. The absence of effective state response—the impunity—should likewise be a basis for state accountability.

The UN Torture Convention

The UN Convention is more specific about state responsibility. Compromising between those who wanted to include privately inflicted torture and those who felt that domestic law enforcement should take care of those cases, the drafters of the Convention included private acts of torture or ill-treatment when carried out with the "consent or acquiescence of a public official."[92] Clearly, laws and customs, like marital rape exceptions or the defense of honor, that exempt domestic aggressors from sanction reflect the active encouragement and consent of the state as well as formal discrimination. The same is true of sex-discriminatory state law enforcement practices which implicitly condone or minimize the seriousness of gender-based violence.

If the purpose of the "consent or acquiescence" language was to cover situations where the state machinery does not work, or in Rodley's terms, where government "turns a blind eye to [their] atrocities,"[93] then gender-based violence is a case in point. Byrnes notes that the broader view of the concept of acquiescence encompasses "private violations against women to which the State has not responded adequately in a preventive or punitive way."[94] Moreover, the provisions for universal criminal jurisdiction and for compensation should apply against any private person who commits torture/domestic violence "at the instigation of" or "with the consent or acquiescence of" an official.[95]

The Inter-American Convention Against Torture

The framers of the Inter-American Convention were perhaps most divided over whether to require official involvement up until the last moment.[96] Thus Article 3 names those guilty of the crime of torture separately from the definition in Article 2. They include any official who "orders, instigates or induces the use of torture, or who directly commits it or who, being able to prevent it, fails to do so," as well as a private person who is "instigated" by a public official to do any of the above. Under this standard, the failure to train police officials in effective domestic violence intervention, the failure of the police to respond to a battered woman's call for help, of the courts to provide a mechanism for and issue protective orders in appropriate cases, and of prosecutors to effectively investigate and prosecute could all qualify as failures to prevent this violence.[97] Universal criminal jurisdiction and the right to compensation should apply as well to batterers who acted under "orders" or "at the instigation" of a public official as well as where state officials failed to prevent the assault.

Were domestic violence to be treated as torture under the UN and Inter-American Torture Convention, states would be obliged to take legal and other measures to prevent it through training, investigation, and prosecution or extradition of all offenders. Under these provisions, victims of domestic violence would not lose the possibility of redress if the aggressor were to leave the country where the violence was committed. They would also be entitled to protection against retaliation and to fair and adequate compensation including that needed for rehabilitation.[98] Finally, the Convention would also prevent expulsion, return (*refoulement*) or extradition of a woman to another state "where there are substantial grounds for believing that [s]he would be in danger of being subjected to torture [or gender-based violence]."[99]

The distinction between torture and cruel, inhuman and degrading treatment or punishment, however, affects the scope of obligations and remedies under the UN Torture Convention, however, and to a lesser extent under the Inter-American Convention.[100]

Thus the recognition of domestic and other forms of gender-based violence as torture and, to a lesser extent, as cruel, inhuman, and degrading treatment, would trigger a substantial range of state responsibilities and potential individual responsibilities under the Conventions. But, given the tendency to minimize domestic violence, the suggested distinction of degree between torture and ill-treatment could present problems for women seeking the full scope of remedies. Moreover, the remedies provided in the Torture Conventions are not adequately tailored to the problem of domestic violence, as discussed in the next section.

Domestic Violence as an Independent Human Rights Violation

A feminist reconceptualization of human rights must grapple with the tension between mainstreaming women's concerns and emphasizing their separate sex-specific character.[101] While recognition of gender-based violence as torture and ill-treatment is critical and deserved, it is also essential explicitly to recognize gender-based violence as an independent human rights violation given both its historic invisibility and trivialization and its particular character and effects. The CEDAW Recommendation No. 19 on Violence Against Women opened the way; approval of instruments such as the 1993 UN Declaration Against Violence Against Women and, even more significantly, the proposed Inter-American Convention on the Prevention, Punishment, and Eradication of Violence Against Women, which contains enforcement mechanisms, are critical steps.[102]

As an independent violation, the distinction between torture and ill-treatment—however it should evolve in international jurisprudence—would be irrelevant. Distinctions as to severity or type of abuse would be tailored to both the purposes and women's experience of the gender-based violence at issue. Gender-based violence as an independent violation would also encompass directly and unequivocally harms inflicted in the private sphere. This eliminates the need to prove official instigation, acquiescence, consent, or specific failure to prevent the violence.

The dilemma of mainstreaming is illustrated by the inadequacy of the Torture Convention remedies when applied to domestic and other forms of gender-based violence. With official torture, for example, the state has the power to control whether torture occurs. Whereas gender-based violence cannot be stopped by a change of regime, or even by vigorous enforcement of formal sanctions, or implementation of preventive policies such as training and supervision of police. Although impunity contributes to the pervasiveness of gender-based violence, state responsibility to prevent and eliminate it must be more far-reaching.[103]

The proposed instruments on gender violence call upon states to address the cultural acceptance of gender-based violence as well as economic dependency and the political, social, and cultural disentitlement that render women vulnerable to violence and encumber their capacity to escape it. This requires not only vigorous enforcement of nondiscrimination laws, but also, as the Women's Convention recognizes, positive measures that alleviate and assist women to overcome the effects of discrimination.

The approval of these proposed international instruments tailored to gender-based violence is for all these reasons a high priority. It is particularly important that this be secured by conventions that contain international mechanisms of accountability, such as the Inter-American Draft. Recognition of the gravity of private gender-violence might well lead the international community to take such real, and not simply rhetorical, steps.

Ultimately gender-based violence should be recognized as *jus cogens,* as among the values of supreme, overriding, and fundamental importance to the international community. As Hilary Charlesworth and Christine Chinkin write, "the concept of the *jus cogens* is not a properly universal one: its development has privileged the experiences of men over those of women and it has provided a protection to men that is not accorded to women."[104]

Understanding the reality, the harm, and the illegitimacy of gender-based intimate terror is essential to developing consensus against it as well as the sense of outrage that propels recognition of a new *jus cogens* norm, even, as with torture, in the presence of widespread violations.

Given, however, that virtually every society is built upon some form of brutality and degradation of women, and that women are largely excluded from equal political participation, the state-centric nature of international law-making is extremely problematic and requires extended treatment. Most immediately, it is essential to increase the voice of women's non-governmental organizations (NGOs) in the international law-making processes through enhanced participation in official delegations, closer interaction with international organizations, and gender parity in employment at all governmental and intergovernmental levels. This might democratize somewhat the state's role as exclusive arbiter of fundamental human rights.

Conclusion

The primary goal of this chapter is to contribute to a feminist reconceptualization of human rights by examining the egregiousness of one of the most prevalent and privatized forms of gender violence and its striking parallels with one of the most heinous human rights violations. It calls upon the international human rights community to recognize its responsibility to address the exercise of brutal domination in the private sphere and to take measures to end the formal and informal impunity such violence heretofore has enjoyed.

It is also my hope that understanding domestic violence as torture will contribute to a new perspective on domestic battering and a new respect for the women who are both victims and survivors. The comparison with torture highlights the often invisible strengths of battered women as survivors as well as the cruel absurdity of the common tendency to "blame the victim" of domestic violence—for provoking violence, for failing to satisfy her violent partner, for falling apart, for failing to leave. By contrast, torture is never deserved or excused.

Understanding domestic violence through the lens of torture should contribute to shifting the burden of responsibility from victim to perpetrator. This is a crucial step not only in doing justice to battered women, but also in recognizing that the roots of this violence lie in the structural inequality and subordination of women.

As the horrifying parallels between torture and domestic violence are explored, perhaps the insistence that "human rights should begin at home" will take on a new urgency. Gender violence illustrates paradigmatically the impossibility of imagining democracy or peace without addressing inequality and oppression on every level, from the official to the intimate. It underscores the central positive role of feminist reconceptualizations to the universalization and non-divisibility of human rights as well as to the profoundly needed social transformation from dominion to participation.

I want to thank: Bernice Cohn, Dorothy Matthew, Maureen McCafferty, Laurie Beck, Marissa Steffers and Harlene Katzman for their help; Alda Facio, Joan Fitzpatrick, Jonathan Lipson, Rosalind Petchesky, and Donna Sullivan for their comments on drafts, and, most especially, all the people who share their experience and/or reflections on official as well as domestic violence.

This chapter is part of a joint project toward a feminist reconceptualization of human rights undertaken with Celina Romany. I acknowledge the support of the Ford Foundation as well as the Programa de Mujeres of the Inter-American Institute of Human Rights and the Program Mujer y Justicia of the United Nations Latin American Institute on the Prevention of Crime and the Treatment of Delinquency (ILANUD) both in San José, Costa Rica.

Notes

1. Gender-based violence encompasses forms of violence that perpetuate and exploit the dichotomy between women and men in order to assure the subordination and inferiority of women and everything associated with the feminine. Although women are overwhelmingly the victims—and violence against women is the focus here—gender-based violence can be inflicted upon men as well as in the rape of male prisoners to humiliate them through "feminization," or violence against men because they are or appear to be gay or feminine.

For a view of the scope and universality of gender-based violence against women, see, for example, UN Center for Social Development and Humanitarian Affairs, *Violence Against Women in the Family*, U.N. Sales No. E.89.IV.5 (New York: United Nations, 1989) (hereinafter *U.N. Report*); Charlotte Bunch, "Women's Rights as Human Rights: Towards a Re-Vision of Human Rights," *Hum. Rts. Q.* 12 (1990): 12 at 486; Lori Heise, "International Dimensions of Violence Against Women," *Response* 12 (1989): 13; Margaret Schuler, ed.,

Freedom from Violence: Women's Strategies Around the World (New York: UNIFEM, 1992); Ximena Bunster and Regina Rodríquez, eds., *La mujer ausente* (The Absent Woman), Ediciones de las Mujeres 15 (Santiago: Isis Internacional, 1991); Yori Matsui, *Women's Asia* (London: Zed Books, 1989).

2. See, e.g., Report of the Drafting Committee. Addendum. Outcome of the World Conference on Human Rights, U.N. Doc. A/Conf. 157/PC/Add. 1 (June 24, 1993) (Vienna Declaration); Pamela Goldberg and Nancy Kelly, "International Human Rights and Violence Against Women," *Harv. Hum. Rts. J.* 6 (Spring 1993): 195; Rhonda Copelon, "Surfacing Gender: Reconceptualizing Crimes Against Women in the Time of War," in *Mass Rape*, ed. Alexandra Stiglmayer (Lincoln: University of Nebraska Press, 1994).

3. Exploration of the analogy between domestic violence and slave-like practices or involuntary servitude under international law would also be appropriate. See, e.g., Joyce McConnell, "Beyond Metaphor: Battered Women, Involuntary Servitude and the Thirteenth Amendment," *Yale J. L. & Feminism* 4 (1992): 207. Conversely, domestic violence of lesser severity is comparable to cruel, inhuman, and degrading treatment that encompasses less severe forms of official violence.

4. See, e.g., Elizabeth V. Spellman, *Inessential Woman: Problems of Exclusion in Feminist Thought* (Boston: Beacon Press, 1988).

5. See Radhika Coomaraswamy, "To Bellow like a Cow: Woman, Ethnicity, and the Discourse of Rights," Chapter 2 in this book.

6. This story is excerpted from Angela Browne, *When Battered Women Kill* (New York: Free Press, 1987), 56–58, 90–93. The story, involving a U.S. working-class couple struggling economically, reflects dynamics and patterns that are not limited to the class context. Browne compared cases that ended in lethal violence to cases which did not. In her view, the progression defined as "typical violence" is typical of both types of cases. The conduct described as "outer limits" also occur in both, but in the lethal cases, the intensity and frequency of violence is heightened—more of the severe attacks happen more often (conversation with Angela Browne, November 1993). Eight months later, the violence became so extreme that Molly killed Jim (131–33).

7. See, e.g., *U.N. Report,* note 1 at 14–33; Susan Schechter, *Women and Male Violence* (Boston: South End Press, 1982); R. Emerson Dobash and R. Dobash, *Violence Against Wives: A Case Against Patriarchy* (London: Open Books, 1980).

The incidence of battering in lesbian relationships cautions, however, against biological as well as gender essentialism. It defies stereotypical assumptions transposed from heterosexual relationships, such as that lesbian violence is inflicted by the "butch" partner on the "femme." While it may be that there are some shared causes, the profound difference in social context and the impact of patriarchal ideology must be explored. See, e.g., Ruthann Robson, "Lavender Bruises: Intra-Lesbian Violence, Law and Lesbian Legal Theory," *Golden Gate Law Review* 20 (Fall 1990): 567–91. This does not mean that this violence should be treated differently by domestic or international legal systems.

8. *U.N. Report,* note 1 at 33.

9. See authorities cited in note 1. Compare Ervin Staub, "The Psychology and Culture of Torture and Torturers," in *Psychology and Torture*, ed. Peter Suedfeld (New York: Hemisphere Publishing, 1990), 49–72.

10. *U.N. Report,* note 1 at 32.

11. See Paige Du Bois, *Torture and Truth* (New York: Routledge, 1991);

Edward Peters, *Torture* (New York: Basil Blackwell, 1985); Malise Ruthven, *Torture: The Grand Conspiracy* (London: Wiedenfeld and Nicolson, 1978).

12. The witch hunts reflected on a macro-level the contempt for and fear of the power of women that is still individualized in the battering context. See Heinrich Institoris and Jakob Sprenger, *Malleus Maleficarum* (The Hammer of Witches), trans. Montague Summers (London: J. Rodker, 1928); Joseph Klaits, *Servants of Satan: The Age of the Witch Hunts* (Bloomington: Indiana University Press, 1985); Carol F. Karlsen, *The Devil in the Shape of a Woman: Witchcraft in Colonial New England* (New York: Norton, 1987).

13. See, e.g., John H. Langbein, *Torture and the Law of Proof: Europe and England in the Ancien Régime* (Chicago: University of Chicago Press, 1976); Michel Foucault, *Discipline and Punishment: The Birth of the Prison* (New York: Vintage Books, 1979); Peters, *Torture*, note 11.

14. Peters, *Torture*, note 11.

15. See J. Herman Burgers and Hans Danelius, *The United Nations Convention Against Torture—A Handbook on the Convention Against Torture and Other Cruel, Inhuman or Degrading Treatment or Punishment* (Boston: Martinus Nijhoff, 1988) (appendix contains instruments respecting torture); Nigel Rodley, *The Treatment of Prisoners Under International Law* (Oxford: Clarendon Press, 1987); Andrew Byrnes, "The Committee Against Torture," in *The United Nations and Human Rights: A Critical Appraisal,* ed. Philip Alston (Oxford: Clarendon Press, 1992), 509. For the general prohibitions on torture, the Universal Declaration, ICCPR and Geneva Conventions, see U.N. Center for Human Rights, *Human Rights: A Compilation of International Instruments,* part 2. vol. 2 (New York: United Nations, 1993), 1, 20, 799, 862, 930.

16. Art. 1 of the UN Torture Convention defines torture as

any act by which severe pain or suffering, whether physical or mental is intentionally inflicted on a person for such purposes as obtaining from him or a third person information or a confession, punishing him for an act that he or a third person has committed or is suspected of having committed, or intimidating or coercing him or a third person, or for any reason based on discrimination of any kind, when such pain or suffering is inflicted by or at the instigation of or with the consent or acquiescence of a public official or other person acting in an official capacity. It does not include pain or suffering arising only from, inherent in or incidental to lawful sanctions.

Art. 2 of the Inter-American Torture Convention to Prevent and Punish Torture defined torture as

any act intentionally performed whereby physical or mental pain or suffering is inflicted on a person for purposes of criminal investigation, as a means of intimidation, as personal punishment, as a preventive measure, as a penalty, or for any other purpose. Torture shall also be understood to be the use of methods upon a person intended to obliterate the personality of the victim or to diminish his physical or mental capacities, even if they do not cause physical pain or mental anguish.

With respect to the element of official involvement, art. 3(a) applies the crime of torture to an official who "instigates or induces the use of torture, . . . directly commits it or who, being able to prevent it, fails to do so." Art. 3(b) applies it to private persons "who at the instigation of a[n] official . . . orders, instigates or induces, . . . directly commits it or is accomplice thereto." Conventions reprinted in Burgers and Danelius, *Handbook,* note 15.

17. *Oxford English Dictionary* (Oxford: Clarendon Press, 1933).

18. Elaine Scarry, *The Body in Pain: The Making and Unmaking of the World* (New York: Oxford University Press, 1985), 29.

19. Amnesty International, *Report on Torture* (New York: Farrar, Straus and Giroux, 1974) 39–40.

20. Burgers and Danelius, *Handbook,* note 15 at 117. As a general matter, Burgers and Danelius's interpretations carry significant weight since Burgers was Chair-Rapporteur of the working groups established by the U.N. Commission on Human Rights to draft the Torture Convention from 1982 to 1984; Danelius, the Swedish representative, participated in all the sessions (vi). See also Peters, *Torture,* note 11 at 170–71; Rodley, *Treatment of Prisoners,* note 15 at 73.

21. Ximena Bunster-Burotto, "Surviving Beyond Fear: Women and Torture in Latin America," in *Women and Change in Latin America,* ed. June Nash and Helen Safa (Boston: Bergen and Garvey, 1986), 297–325; Ximena Fornazzari and M. Freire, "Women as Victims of Torture," *Acta Psych. Scand.* 82 (1990): 257–60; F. Allodi and S. Stiasny, "Women as Torture Victims," *Canadian J. Psych.* 35 (March 1990): 144–48; Inge Lunde and Jorge Ortmann, "Prevalence and Sequelae of Sexual Torture," *The Lancet* 336 (Aug. 1990): 289–91; Mia Groenenberg, "The Treatment of Mental Problems of Female Refugees," paper presented at Third International Conference: Health, Political Repression and Human Rights, Santiago, 1991.

22. *U.N. Report,* note 1 at 13, and J. J. Gayford, "Aetiology of Wife Beating," *Medicine, Science, and the Law* 19 (1979): 19, 21–22, noting that studies from the U.S., Kenya, Chile, and Kuwait confirm the typicality of these injuries.

23. From in-depth interviews of 42 women who ultimately killed their batterers, compared with a sample of battered women who did not, psychologist Angela Browne reports that 76 percent (vs. 59 percent in the non-homicide group) reported being raped, with nearly 40 percent (vs. 13 percent) reporting that it occurred "often." See generally Browne, *When Battered Women Kill,* note 6 at 95–101; Irene Frieze, "Investigating the Causes and Consequences of Marital Rape," *Signs* 8 (1983): 532–53; David Finkelhor and Kersti Yllo, *License to Rape: Sexual Abuse of Wives* (New York: Holt, Rinehart, and Winston, 1985); Diana E. Russell, *Rape in Marriage* (New York: Macmillan, 1982); *U.N. Report* note 1 at 13.

24. Russell, *Rape in Marriage,* note 23 at 21–22.

25. Bunster-Burotto, "Surviving Beyond Fear," note 21 at 307–8; Browne, *Battered Women,* note 6 at 95, 97, 101. See citations, note 21.

26. Rodley, *Treatment of Prisoners,* note 15 at 83–86. See also *Ireland v. United Kingdom,* 25 Eur. Ct. H. R. (ser. A) (1978); Bunster-Burrotto, "Surviving Beyond Fear," note 21; and Lunde and Ortmann, "Sequelae," note 21 at 289; Recently the connection between the traumatization of prisoners through torture and detention with that of battered women in intimate contexts has been most fully elaborated by psychologist Judith Lewis Herman, *Trauma and Recovery* (New York: Basic Books, 1992).

27. Herman, *Trauma and Recovery,* note 26; Amnesty International, *Report on Torture,* note 19 at 49.

28. Among the tactics Biderman identifies are isolation, monopolization of perception, induced debility through insults and humiliations, threats, occasional indulgence or kindness, demonstrations of omnipotence, degradation, and enforcing trivial demands. Amnesty International, *Report on Torture*, note 27 at 49, 52.

29. See, e.g., Herman, *Trauma and Recovery*, note 26; Lenore E. Walker, *The Battered Woman* (New York: Harper and Row, 1979), 55–70; Russell, *Rape in Marriage*, note 23; Mary Romero, "A Comparison Between Strategies Used on Prisoners of War and Battered Wives," *Sex Roles* 13 (1985): 537–45.

30. See also Walker, *Battered Woman*, note 29 at 55–70; *U.N. Report*, note 1 at 22; Herman, *Trauma and Recovery*, note 26 at 90–91.

31. Walker, *Battered Woman*, note 29 at 33, 42–55. Later Walker recognized that the battered woman is not necessarily completely passive, but may be coping or taking defensive activities within a very narrow frame.

32. See, e.g., Herman, *Trauma and Recovery*, note 26 at 90–91; Browne, *Battered Women*, note 6; Edward Gondolf and Ellen Fisher, *Battered Women as Survivors: An Alternative to Treating Learned Helplessness* (Lexington, MA: Lexington Books, 1988); Walker, *Battered Woman*, note 29 at 35; Martha Mahoney, "Legal Images of Battered Women: Redefining the Issue of Separation," *Mich. L. Rev.* 90 (1991) 1, 55; Julie Blackmun, *Intimate Violence: A Study of Injustice* (New York: Columbia University Press, 1989), 75–76, 132.

33. See Elizabeth M. Schneider, "Describing and Changing: Women's Self-Defense Work and the Problem of Expert Testimony on Battering," *Women's Rts. L. Rep.* 9 (1986): 195; Lenore Walker, "A Response to Elizabeth Schneider's Describing and Changing," *Women's Rts. L. Rep.* 9 (1986): 223–25.

34. Mahoney, "Legal Images," note 32 at 5–6.

35. Blackmun, *Intimate Violence*, note 32 at 75–76. See also Herman, *Trauma and Recovery*, note 26 at 91.

36. See, e.g., Herman, *Trauma and Recovery*, note 26 at 91; Jacobo Timerman, *Prisoner Without a Name, Cell Without a Number*, trans. T. Talbot (New York: Vintage Books, 1988).

37. The European Court of Human Rights had introduced a mind/body distinction in its 1978 ruling that five sensory deprivation techniques constituted ill-treatment but not torture. Its decision, however, has been widely criticized and increasingly repudiated. *Ireland v. United Kingdom*, note 26, reversing *Ireland v. United Kingdom*, 19 Y.B. Eur. Conv. H. R. 792 (1976); see Rodley, *Prisoners*, note 15 at 83–86.

38. Burgers and Danelius, *Handbook*, note 15 at 117–18; Rodley, *Prisoners*, note 15 at 89.

39. Burgers and Danelius, *Handbook*, note 15 at 117. See also, Peters, *Torture*, note 11, at 171; Rodley, *Prisoners*, note 15 at 82.

40. *Report of the Human Rights Committee*, U.N. GAOR, 37th Sess., Supp. no. 40 (1982), Annex V, general comment 7(16), para. 2.

41. Rodley, *Prisoners*, note 15 at 80–88.

42. Rodley, *Prisoners*, note 15 at 92–93.

43. *Estrella v. Uruguay*, (74/1980) Report of the Human Rights Committee, U.N. GAOR, 38th Sess., Supp. no. 40 (1983), Annex XII, para. 1.12.

44. In most but not all cases, allegations of overcrowding and prolonged solitary confinement are present when Article 7 violations are found. See Rodley, *Prisoners*, note 15 at 226–29.

45. Burgers and Danelius, *Handbook*, note 15 at 41.

46. See Stanley Milgram, "Some Conditions of Obedience and Disobedience to Authority," *Hum. Rel.* 18 (1965): 57–74, discussed in Amnesty International, *Report on Torture,* note 19 at 63–68. On the training of torturers, see Amnesty International, *Torture in Greece: The First Torturers' Trial, 1975* (New York: Amnesty International Publications, 1977); Mika Haritos-Fatouros, "The Official Torturer: A Learning Model for Obedience to the Authority of Violence," *J. App. Soc. Psychology* 18 (1988): 1107–120; Janice T. Gibson, "Training People to Inflict Pain," *J. Humanistic Psychology 31* (1991): 72–87.

47. Haritos-Fatouros, "The Official Torturer," note 46 at 1119.

48. Hannah Arendt, *Eichmann in Jerusalem: A Report on the Banality of Evil,* 2d ed. (New York: Penguin Books, 1964), 93.

49. See, e.g. *U.N. Report,* note 1 at 68; Melissa Spatz, "A Lesser Crime: A Comparative Study of Legal Defense for Men Who Kill," *Colum. J. L. & Soc. Probs.* 24 (1991): 597.

50. For a discussion of the defense of "honor" in Brazil, see Women's Rights Project and Americas Watch, *Criminal Injustice: Violence Against Women in Brazil* (New York: Human Rights Watch, 1991), 20–26; on the concept of "honor" in Pakistan, see Simorgh Collective and Shazreh Hussein, *Rape in Pakistan* (Lahore: Simorgh Women's Resource and Publication Center, 1990), 26.

51. *U.N. Report,* note 1 at 67 n. 88.

52. Schechter, *Women and Male Violence,* note 7 at 17.

53. Dobash and Dobash, *Violence Against Wives,* note 7 at 24.

54. *U.N. Report,* note 1 at 26.

55. James Ptacek, "Why Do Men Batter Their Wives?" in *Feminist Perspectives on Wife Abuse,* ed. Kersti Yilo and Michele Bograd (Newbury Park, CA: Sage Publications, 1988), 133–45.

56. See, e.g., Amnesty International, *Torture in Greece,* note 46 at 41; Amnesty International, *Report on Torture,* note 19 at 63–68.

57. See also Peters, *Torture,* note 11 at 164, 11–74; Du Bois, *Torture and Truth,* note 11 at 62–66; Amnesty International, *Torture in the Eighties* (London: Amnesty International Publications, 1984), 19–21; Klaits, *Servants of Satan,* note 12.

58. Scarry, *Body in Pain,* note 18 at 29, 28–38.

59. See, e.g., Schechter, *Women and Male Violence,* note 7 at 17; Herman, *Trauma and Recovery,* note 26 at 80.

60. See, e.g., Amnesty International, *Report on Torture,* note 19; *Nunca Más: Report of the Argentine National Commission on the Disappeared* (New York: Farrar Straus and Giroux, 1986). Laurence Weschler, *A Miracle, A Universe: Settling Accounts with Torturers* (New York: Pantheon, 1990). See also *Filártiga v. Peña,* 630 F.2d 876 (2d Cir. 1980).

61. "In Search of the 'Lost' Women: A Critique of Criminology: An Approximation," 20–21, paper prepared by the United Nations Latin American Institute for the Prevention of Crime and Treatment of Delinquents, Women and Penal Justice Project, San José, Costa Rica, April 1992 (on file with author).

62. Celina Romany, "State Responsibility Goes Private: A Feminist Critique of the Public/Private Distinction in International Human Rights Law," Chapter 4 in this book. Alda Facio stressed the constant interaction between formal impunity and the parallel system (conversation with author, February, 1993).

63. Dobash and Dobash, *Violence Against Wives,* note 7, at 135.

64. Dobash and Dobash, *Violence Against Wives,* note 7 at 136–137; *U.N. Report,* note 1 at 28; see also Ptacek, "Why Do Men Batter," note 55 at 142–45.

65. See, e.g., Amnesty International, *Report On Torture,* note 19 at 69.

66. See, e.g., Elizabeth Lira and Maria Isabel Castillo, *Psicologia de la Amenaza Politica y del Miedo* (Psychology of Political Terror and Fear) (Santiago: Ediciones Chile-America-CESOC, 1991); Henry Shue, "Torture," *Phil. & Pub. Aff.*, 7 (1978): 124, 133 n.11.

67. Roxanna Carrillo, *Battered Dreams: Violence Against Women as an Obstacle to Development* (New York: United Nations Development Fund for Women, 1992).

68. *Report of the World Conference to Review and Appraise the Achievements of the United Nations Decade for Women: Equality, Development and Peace, Nairobi, Kenya, 15–26 July 1985*, U.N. Doc. A/CONF.116/28/Rev.1; CEDAW, General Recommendation No. 19 (11th Sess., 1992) Violence Against Women, U.N. Doc. CEDAW/C/1992/L.1/Add.15 (29 Jan. 1992); Draft Declaration on the Elimination of Violence Against Women, U.N. Economic and Social Council, Commission on the Status of Women, Working Group on Violence Against Women, Adoption of the Report of the Working Group, U.N. Doc. E/CN.6/WG.2/1992/L.3, Annex I (1992) (hereinafter U.N. Violence Declaration); Inter-American Commission of Women, *Report on the Results of the Meeting of Experts to Consider the Viability of an Inter-American Convention on Women and Violence*, Sept. 27, 1991, OEA/Ser.L/II.7.4, CIM/doc.1/91 (hereinafter Inter-American Violence Convention).

69. Carillo, *Battered Dreams*, note 67 at 13, citing Christine Bradley, "Wife Beating in PNG—Is It A Problem?" *Papau N.G. Med. J.* (Sept. 1988).

70. CEDAW Recommendation, note 68, para. 15 at 4.

71. CEDAW Recommendation, note 68, preamble.

72. Burgers and Danelius, *Handbook*, note 15 at 42, 45 and 118.

73. Burgers and Danelius, *Handbook*, note 15 at 119–20.

74. See, e.g., *U.N. Report* note 1 at 51–55, 75–80.

75. Burgers and Danelius, *Handbook*, note 15 at 120.

76. Compare Amnesty International, *Report on Torture*, note 19, at 39–69, with Herman, *Trauma and Recovery*, note 26, at 74–95; Walker, *Battered Woman*, note 29; Romero, "Prisoners of War," note 29.

77. Herman, *Trauma and Recovery*, note 26 at 77.

78. Herman, *Trauma and Recovery*, note 26 at 82; see also Amnesty International, *Report on Torture*, note 19; Dee L. R. Graham, Edna Rawlings, and Nelly Rimini, "Survivors of Terror: Battered Women, Hostages, and the Stockholm Syndrome" in *Feminist Perspectives on Wife Abuse*, ed. Yilo and Bograd, note 55 at 217–33.

79. Herman, *Trauma and Recovery*, note 26 at 82–83.

80. Herman, *Trauma and Recovery*, note 26 at 83–86; Amnesty International, *Report on Torture*, note 19 at 50.

81. Timerman, *Prisoner*, note 36 at 35.

82. Scarry, *Body in Pain*, note 18 at 41.

83. Herman, *Trauma and Recovery*, note 26 at 82. See citations, note 26.

84. *U.N. Report*, note 1 at 23–24, 27–28.

85. Peters, *Torture*, note 11 at 3–4.

86. Peters, *Torture*, note 11 at 154.

87. Primo Levi, *Survival in Auschwitz: The Nazi Assault on Humanity*, 1958, trans. Stuart Woolf (New York: Collier, 1961), 49, cited in Herman, *Trauma and Recovery*, note 26 at 95.

88. Other vehicles for recognizing violence against women as a human rights violation are discussed in Joan Fitzpatrick, "The Use of International Human Rights Norms to Combat Violence Against Women," Chapter 23 in this book.

89. See Byrnes, "Committee Against Torture," note 15 at 513. For a broader discussion of the principle of state responsibility and its application to private gender-based violence, see Romany, "State Responsibility Goes Private," note 62; and Rebecca Cook, "State Accountability Under the Convention on the Elimination of All Forms of Discrimination Against Women," Chapter 9 in this book.

90. Compare ICCPR, Art. 8, note 15. See Sherif Bassionni, "Enslavement as an International Crime," *N.Y.U. J. Int'l L. & Pol.* 23 (Winter 1991): 445–517.

91. *Velázquez-Rodríguez,* 28 I.L.M. 294 (1989). See Romany, "State Responsibility Goes Private," note 62.

92. Burgers and Danelius, *Handbook,* note 15 at 119–20.

93. Rodley, *Treatment of Prisoners,* note 15 at 91; See also Byrnes, "Committee Against Torture," note 15 at 518; and Peters, *Torture,* note 11 at 3 ("Torture is thus something that a public authority does or condones").

94. Byrnes, "Committee Against Torture," note 15 at 520.

95. U.N. Torture Convention, note 15, arts. 14, 19–22.

96. See, e.g., *Report of the Committee on Judicial and Political Affairs on the Study of Alternatives to the Articles of the Draft Inter-American Convention to Prevent and Punish Torture,* OEA/Ser.P/AG/doc. 1962/85 (November 7, 1985), 14–15.

97. Inter-American Torture Convention, note 15, arts. 6 and 7.

98. Inter-American Torture Convention, arts. 4–14.

99. Inter-American Torture Convention, arts. 3(1) and (2). Contrast Convention Relating to the Status of Refugees, opened for signature July 28, 1951, 19 U.S.T. 6259, 189 U.N.T.S. 150 (1954). See Fitzpatrick, "Norms to Combat Violence," note 88; Goldberg and Kelly, "International Human Rights," note 2 (discussing recent developments and new theories for recognizing gender-based prosecution as a basis for asylum).

100. UN Torture Convention, note 15, arts. 16, 20–22; Inter-American Torture Convention, note 15, arts. 8, 9.

101. See, e.g., Hilary Charlesworth, "What Are Women's International Human Rights?" Chapter 3 in this book; Bunch, "A Re-Vision," note 1.

102. CEDAW *Recommendation,* note 68; U.N. Violence Declaration, note 68; Inter-American Violence Convention, note 68.

103. See, e.g., Coomaraswamy, "To Bellow like a Cow,"note 5; Sharon Hom, "Female Infanticide in China: The Human Rights Specter and Thoughts Towards (An)other Vision," *Colum. Hum. Rts. L. Rev.* 23 (1992): 249.

104. Hilary Charlesworth and Christine Chinkin, "The Gender of *Jus Cogens,*" *Hum. Rts. Q.* 15 (February 1993): 61, 65.

Chapter 6
Why Rethinking the Sovereign State is Important for Women's International Human Rights Law

Karen Knop

Introduction

This chapter argues for a re-examination of the relationship between international law and women's international human rights law, more specifically, the relationship between the current conceptualization of state sovereignty in international law and the participation of women in the creation of women's international human rights law.

International law structures women's international human rights law, yet, for reasons ranging from lack of knowledge to realism to the rejection of authority as antithetical to feminist perspectives, women are only beginning to explore these underlying structures.[1] This chapter focuses on two fundamental aspects of contemporary international law: (1) its statism and (2) the centrality of the sovereign state in the international legal system.

By statism, I mean the view of international law that regards state sovereignty as a function of political power, rather than justice; as the acknowledgment of political control by a government over a people and territory, rather than the judgment that a government justly represents the people. While the centrality of the sovereign state in international law is related to statism, it is not the same thing. The centrality of the sovereign state reflects the understanding that despite the growing cast of characters on the international scene, the state continues to be the only actor in international law that really matters, that is, the actor that plays the decisive role in making, interpreting, and enforcing international law.

By and large, mainstream international human rights discourse on women's rights has internalized the logic of state sovereignty. Mainstream discourse characterizes both progress and challenges for international human rights in terms of the limitation of state sovereignty: like Gulliver tied down by the Lilliputians, state sovereignty is to be limited by a multitude of international human rights norms. Yet the positivist would reply that these norms do not fundamentally change state sovereignty because states consent to be bound by them. Even the acceptance of women's right of nondiscrimination[2] or the right to be free from gender-based violence[3] as *jus cogens* would not ultimately alter state sovereignty, since article 53 of the Vienna Convention on the Law of Treaties defines a peremptory norm as "a norm *accepted and recognized* by the international community as a whole as a norm from which no derogation is permitted" (emphasis added).[4]

In this chapter, I ask whether the system of sovereign states that undergirds women's international human rights law is problematic for feminist political and legal change. This is both a theoretical question (what do feminist theories have to say about state sovereignty?) and a practical question (what difference would rethinking state sovereignty make in concrete terms?). As space does not permit a discussion of the former,[5] I confine my remarks to the latter.[6] I attempt to show through a series of examples what altering either the statist assumption or the assumption of the sovereign state as central to international law-making might mean for women's participation in the creation of women-conscious international human rights norms.

The aim here, then, is not to argue for a particular feminist theory of the state or the absence thereof.[7] Indeed, there is an argument that understanding cultural differences between women should encompass different views of the state, and its domestic and international roles in the advancement of women's rights. The aim is to persuade those active in women's international human rights law that alternative visions of state sovereignty are a vital necessity.

Alternatives to Statism

The best-known formulation of the criteria for statehood in international law, that of the Montevideo Convention on Rights and Duties of States,[8] requires (a) a permanent population, (b) a defined territory, (c) a government, and (d) the capacity to enter into relations with other states. The essence of this formula is the requirement of effective government: an effective government, by definition, is effective with respect to an ascertainable population and territory, and therefore capable of entering into relations with other states.[9]

Thus defined, statehood in no way depends on whether the state

observes human rights, including women's rights; or whether it represents the population, judging by liberal, feminist, or other criteria of
representation. A regime that grossly violates women's rights can be
recognized as a state and can participate in the creation of international
law.

This part of the chapter give examples of alternative conceptions of
statehood, as seen through the lenses of recognition and participation
in international law.

Recognition

Recent American and European Community (E.C.) guidelines on recognition of new states in Eastern Europe and the Soviet Union evidence a new willingness to condition recognition on respect for individual and minority rights. While the recognition criteria listed by both
the United States and the European Community are broad enough to
encompass respect for women's rights, it was minority rights that came
under particular scrutiny in the application of the guidelines. Nevertheless, these guidelines indicate the potential to base recognition of
the very emergence of the state on respect for women's rights.

The five principles intended to govern American recognition of the
Soviet and Yugoslav republics, as summarized by Deputy Assistant
Secretary of State Ralph Johnson in October 1991, include

- Safeguarding of human rights, based on full respect for the individual and including equal treatment of minorities; and
- Respect for international law and obligations, especially adherence
  to the Helsinki Final Act and the Charter of Paris.[10]

The E.C. Guidelines on the Recognition of New States in Eastern
Europe and in the Soviet Union, adopted on December 16, 1991,
require, among other things,

- respect for the provisions of the Charter of the United Nations and
  the commitments subscribed to in the Final Act of Helsinki and in
  the Charter of Paris, especially with regard to the rule of law, democracy and human rights;
- guarantees for the rights of ethnic and national groups and minorities in accordance with the commitments subscribed to in the
  framework of the CSCE.[11]

An E.C. statement on recognition of the Yugoslav republics, adopted
the same day as the more general Guidelines, reiterates the Commu-

nity's concern for human rights in war-torn Yugoslavia. That statement provides that Yugoslav republics wishing to be recognized as independent states were by December 23, 1991 to state, among other things, whether

- they accept the commitments contained in the above-mentioned guidelines;
- they accept the provisions laid down in the draft Convention—especially those in Chapter II on human rights and rights of national or other ethnic groups—under consideration by the Conference on Yugoslavia.[12]

Participation

Critics of statism in international law tend to argue that only a state that represents the people is legitimate and should be entitled to participate in the creation of international law.[13] Critics differ, however, on what constitutes representation, both domestically and internationally.

For a Kantian such as Fernando Tesón, only a state that respects human rights, and the principle of democratic representation, is legitimate and therefore entitled to represent its citizens internationally.[14] According to Tesón's Kantian theory of international law, while an illegitimate state should retain some rights, it should not benefit from the rights conferred by membership in the alliance of legitimate, that is, liberal democratic, states.[15] He would undoubtedly argue, though, that so long as a state respects the principle of equality, which for women means nondiscrimination and equal opportunity, it is not unrepresentative simply because there are few or no women in the government or the diplomatic service.

In contrast, feminists may regard "parity democracy" between men and women in domestic and international decision making as the goal of representation[16] and, hence, some type of affirmative action, such as quotas, as necessary. As the case of the International Labour Organisation suggests, however, how representation reconciles feminist principles with the purposes of a particular international organization may not be easily resolved. Article 3 of the ILO Constitution reads in part:

3(1) The meetings of the General Conference of representatives of the Members shall be held . . . at least once in every year. It shall be composed of four representatives of each of the Members, of whom two shall be *Government* delegates and the two others shall be delegates representing respectively the *employers* and the *workpeople* of each of the Members.

(2) Each delegate may be accompanied by advisers, who shall not exceed two in number for each item on the agenda of the meeting. *When questions specially*

affecting women are to be considered by the Conference, one at least of the advisers should be a woman.

(6) Advisers shall not speak except on a request made by the delegate whom they accompany and by the special authorisation of the President of the Conference, and may not vote. (emphasis added)[17]

The annual Manual for the Conference expands as follows:

The questions considered at the ILC and other ILO meetings nowadays are of equal relevance to women and men . . . as early as 1975, at its 60th Session, the Conference asked in a resolution that women be appointed to delegations on the same basis and by the same standards as men.[18]

Should women strive to be equally represented within each of the three groups (government, employers, and workpeople) that compose the member-state delegations to the International Labour Conference, or should the tripartite composition of the member-state delegations be changed to quadripartite for some or all agenda items by adding representatives of women to the representatives of government, employers, and workpeople? This question engages the ongoing Marxist-feminist debate on the relative importance of class and gender.[19]

Alternatives to the Centrality of the State

The first part of this chapter examined how women might work *through the state* in international law and hence women's international human rights law. Without questioning the centrality of the state to international law, it discussed, as an alternative to statism, how the state's legitimacy might be linked to its respect for women's rights and women's participation in the domestic and international decision-making processes of the state.

This part of the chapter shows that by rejecting the centrality of the state, women can work *through the non-state groups and networks* that make up international civil society to influence the development, interpretation, and implementation of international law by states. Alternatively—and more radically—it suggests that women can break down the monolith of the sovereign state to *represent their interests directly* in international law where the state would traditionally represent women's interests.

Why might it be important for women to reject—or, at least, not to assume—the centrality of the state? Perhaps the most obvious reason is that women's interests and concerns are not defined exclusively, or in many cases even significantly, by state borders; they are shaped by gender, sexuality, culture, and other factors. The fact of common citizenship does not mean that women and men of the same state think similarly or are affected similarly by international issues on which their state takes a position. At the same time, women may feel themselves members of a group based on gender, or gender in combination with factors such as religion or ethnicity, that extends beyond their state. So long as states are the primary international actors, however, women's voices can be heard only through the medium of the state, and alliances between groups of women in different states depend on alliances between their respective states.

International Civil Society

Richard Falk hypothesizes the development of an "international civil society," within which groups would form to take normative initiatives without state authorization, as exemplified by the MacBride Commission to assess Israel's conduct in the 1982 Lebanon War and the Permanent People's Tribunal established by the 1976 Algiers Declaration of the Rights of Peoples.[20] The Global Tribunal on Violations of Women's Human Rights held at the 1993 World Conference on Human Rights in Vienna, a non-governmental tribunal that heard women from many different states testify about their experiences of oppression and violence against women, may be seen as another such initiative.[21] In the post-Cold War international legal order, non-governmental organizations, a constituent part of the international civil society Falk describes, may assume greater importance.[22] Seeing this general development as a chance for women's voices to be heard, some authors argue that non-governmental organizations could even be granted some status in certain law-making activities.[23]

From the perspective of some Western feminists, the fluid and unconstricted nature of this emerging international civil society may make it the optimal site for the cross-cultural feminist coalition politics advocated by Anne Marie Goetz[24] that "struggles to eliminate the elements of centre, unity and totality that organize structures into hierarchical oppositions" and "allows for the fact that women experience simultaneously many oppressions and must engage in a multitude of struggles that conflict and supplement each other."[25]

The construct of international civil society may also respond to the concern of some non-western feminists that the state is neither a possible nor an appropriate arena for change. While Finnish diplomat Anja-Riitta Ketokoski regards the Nordic states as allies of women,[26] Sri Lankan scholar Radhika Coomaraswamy writes:

if the state is entrusted with the responsibility of ensuring women's rights, if it is always viewed as active and paternalistic in a benign manner, then this does pose serious questions. The nation-state in the third world does not carry this "Scandinavian aura."[27]

Coomaraswamy concludes that the future of women's human rights in the South Asian region does not lie with states but with movements in civil society.[28] She attributes social change to the coming together of civil society and the state at particular historical moments. The role of civil society, Coomaraswamy argues, is that of mobilization and raising awareness, while that of the state is articulation and implementation.[29]

Ultimately, international civil society is a creature both liberated and enslaved by its marginality. Its existence at the edges of the system of states frees this mix of non-governmental organizations, unofficial groups of experts, and other initiatives from the calculus of self-interest that often dictates the position of states, and enables it to be more responsive to women's aspirations and more creative in developing proposals for change. At the same time, Sudanese scholar Abdullahi Ahmed An-Na'im has commented that relations in international civil society tend to reflect the power imbalance in the system of states.[30] Moreover, the participation of international civil society in the development of international human rights norms relies on the hope that some form of meaningful public debate is possible under the conditions of the late twentieth-century international order.[31]

Breaking down the State

Perhaps the most radical claim that women could make, short of calling for the abolition of the system of sovereign states altogether, is that women are entitled to recognition as limited subjects of international law with the right to participate directly in the formulation of international and regional norms of particular concern to them and the right of direct recourse to global and regional mechanisms designed to protect their rights. In other words, women should have the right to draft conventions on women's rights and to bring cases about women's rights to the appropriate international body. This type of demand for direct participation in the international legal process is based on the idea that the state neither represents nor is structurally capable of representing women's interests on some or all international issues.

Although women have yet to make this claim, indigenous peoples have been conducting a campaign to be recognized as subjects of international law against the backdrop of the conclusion of the 1989 ILO Convention No. 169 Concerning Indigenous and Tribal Peoples[32] and the drafting of a UN declaration on the rights of indigenous peoples,[33] each process with its own institutional limitations on the participation of indigenous groups.

The most far-reaching proposals for indigenous peoples favor the recognition of all indigenous peoples as "subjects of international law competent to represent their interests in the international arena."[34] Other possibilities include "the right to address international organs directly, to receive economic or development assistance from international institutions unmediated by the state, to request international conciliation for the resolution of disputes, or to bring certain matters before the International Court of Justice."[35] The capacity to form networks of solidarity is also mentioned.[36]

Greenland furnishes a concrete example of how the direct participation of a non-state actor in international and regional law-making processes was balanced against the participation of the state itself. While Greenland itself is not a subject of international law, it has certain qualified statutory rights of participation in international law under the 1978 Greenland Home Rule Act.[37] For instance, section 16(3) provides:

> Where matters of particular interest to Greenland are at issue, the central authorities may on a request by the home rule authorities authorize them to negotiate directly, with the cooperation of the Foreign Service, provided such negotiation is not considered incompatible with the unity of the Realm.

It is also noteworthy that Greenland "left" the European Community in 1985 in the sense that the geographical application of the E.C. treaties to Denmark was subsequently restricted so as to exclude Greenland, and Denmark on behalf of Greenland negotiated an association agreement with the E.C.[38]

Conclusion

International legal scholars and activists working in the area of women's international human rights require what Richard Falk has described as "a special sort of creativity that blends thought and imagination without neglecting to understand obstacles to change."[39]

This chapter has argued that not even the system of sovereign states, the underlying structure of women's international human rights law, should be immune from such creative examination. It has shown by example that altering either the statist assumption of international law or the assumption of the centrality of the state in international law-making is of concrete relevance for states' observance of women's international human rights and, more important, for women's participation in the creation of those rights.

The lingering question may be why should we—faced with such urgent women's international human rights projects—engage in this utopian exercise? Perhaps the most compelling reason for those realists who ask is that international law and the world order are (once again) seen to be in a transitional period, what has been dubbed a "Grotian moment."[40] As this transition is at once imagined and real, conceived and perceived, gender-conscious international lawyers have an opportunity to shape both imagination and reality.

A longer version of this chapter appears as "Re/Statements: Feminism and State Sovereignty in International Law," *Transnat'l L. & Contemp. Probs* 3 (1993): 293–344.

Notes

1. The groundbreaking article in this regard is Hilary Charlesworth, Christine Chinkin, and Shelley Wright, "Feminist Approaches to International Law," *Am. J. Int'l L.* 85 (1991): 613.

2. See Cecilia Medina, "Toward a More Effective Guarantee of the Enjoyment of Human Rights by Women in the Inter-American System," Chapter 10 in this book.

3. See Rhonda Copelon, "Intimate Terror: Understanding Domestic Violence as Torture," Chapter 5 in this book.

4. Vienna Convention on the Law of Treaties, May 23, 1969, 1155 U.N.T.S. 331.

5. See generally Karen Knop, "Re/Statements: Feminism and State Sovereignty in International Law," *Transnat'l L. & Contemp. Probs* 3 (1993), 293–344.

6. A related question is asked by D. M. McRae, Notes for Presentation to Department of Justice Seminar 20–23 (Sept. 14, 1992, on file with the author).

7. Catharine MacKinnon writes, "Feminism has no theory of the state." Catharine A. MacKinnon, *Toward a Feminist Theory of the State* (Cambridge, MA: Harvard University Press, 1989), 157. Nor, despite the promise of the book's title, is MacKinnon successful in developing her own feminist theory of the state. See Drucilla Cornell, "Sexual Difference, the Feminine, and Equivalency: A Critique of MacKinnon's *Toward a Feminist Theory of the State*" (Book Review), *Yale L.J.* 100 (1991): 2247; Denise G. Réaume, "The Social Construction of Women and the Possibility of Change: Unmodified Feminism Revisited" (Book Review), *Can. J. Women & L.* 5 (1992): 463.

8. Montevideo Convention on Rights and Duties of States, Dec. 26, 1933, 49 Stat. 3097, T.S. No. 881, 165 L.N.T.S. 19, art. 1.

9. See James Crawford, *The Creation of States* (Oxford: Clarendon Press, 1979), 42.

10. "Yugoslavia: Trying to End the Violence," *For. Pol'y Bull.* 2 (Nov.–Dec. 1991): 39, 42 (testimony of Ralph Johnson, Deputy Assistant Secretary of State for European and Canadian Affairs, Oct. 17, 1991). See also "The New

Situation in the Soviet Union and the Republics," *For. Pol'y Bull.* 2 (Sept.–Oct. 1991): 39, 44 (statement of Robert B. Zoellick, Under Secretary of State for Economic and Agricultural Affairs and Counselor, Oct. 2, 1991).

11. 31 I.L.M. 1486, 1487 (1992).

12. 31 I.L.M. 1485, 1486 (1992).

13. Along these lines, see, e.g., Gregory H. Fox, "The Right to Political Participation in International Law," *Yale J. Int'l L.* 17 (1992): 539; Thomas M. Franck, "The Emerging Right to Democratic Governance," *Am. J. Int'l L.* 86 (1992): 46; McRae, "Justice Seminar," note 6 at 22; Fernando R. Tesón, "The Kantian Theory of International Law," *Colum. L. Rev.* 92 (1992): 53.

14. Tesón, "Kantian Theory," note 13 at 69–70.

15. Tesón, "Kantian Theory," note 13 at 89.

16. Anja-Riitta Ketokoski, "Toward a More Effective Application of Women's Rights in the European System," paper presented at the Consultation on Women's International Human Rights, Toronto, Sept. 2, 1992 (on file with the author).

17. Constitution of the International Labour Organisation and Standing Orders of the International Labour Conference (Geneva: International Labour Office, May 1989).

18. Quoted in Hilkka Pietilä and Ingrid Eide, "United Nations and the Advancement of Women: The Role of the Nordic Countries to Promote Efforts by the UN System for the Advancement of Women," *Nordic U.N. Project Report* 16 (1990): Annex 3 at 2.

19. For an overview of the debate, see Marianne Hester, *Lewd Women and Wicked Witches: A Study of the Dynamics of Male Domination* (London: Routledge, 1992), chaps. 2–3.

20. Richard Falk, "The Rights of Peoples (in Particular Indigenous Peoples)," in *The Rights of Peoples,* ed. James Crawford (Oxford: Clarendon Press, 1988), 17, 27–31. See also Richard Falk, "Keeping Nuremberg Alive," in *International Law: A Contemporary Perspective,* ed. Richard Falk, Friedrich Kratochwil, and Saul H. Mendlovitz (Boulder, CO: Westview Press, 1985), 494.

21. Information on the Global Tribunal on Violations of Women's Human Rights may be obtained from the Center for Women's Global Leadership at the State University of New Jersey, Rutgers, Douglass College, 27 Clifton Avenue, New Brunswick, NJ 08903; FAX (908) 932–1180. For an account of an earlier international tribunal on crimes against women, see Diana E. H. Russell and Nicole Van de Ven, eds., *Crimes Against Women: Proceedings of the International Tribunal* (East Palo Alto, CA: Frog in the Well, 1984).

22. See, e.g., Rachel J. Brett, "NGOs and the Human Dimension of the CSCE," *Bull.* (CSCE Office for Democratic Institutions and Human Rights) 1 (1992–93): 1 (increasing role of NGOs in the CSCE process); James Rusk, "Top UN Post Was a Shocker," *Globe and Mail,* April 21, 1993: at A3, col.1, 2–3 (Elizabeth Dowdeswell, UN Undersecretary-General and Executive Director of UNEP and Habitat, on entrenchment in the U.N. system of NGO involvement in the preparation for a U.N. conference and in the conference itself); Danilo Türk, *The Realization of Economic, Social, and Cultural Rights,* U.N. Doc. E/CN.4/Sub.2/1992/16, paras. 244–46 (recommendations of Special Rapporteur Danilo Türk on the role of NGOs in the realization of economic, social, and cultural rights through the UN system).

23. Christine Chinkin, "A Gendered Perspective to the International Use of Force," *Austl. Y.B. Int'l L.* 12 (1992): 279, 292; Isabelle R. Gunning, "Moderniz-

ing Customary International Law: The Challenge of Human Rights," *Va. J. Int'l L.* 31 (1991): 211, 220–22, 227–34; McRae, "Justice Seminar," note 6 at 23.

24. Anne Marie Goetz, "Feminism and the Claim to Know: Contradictions in Feminist Approaches to Women in Development," in *Gender and International Relations*, ed. Rebecca Grant and Kathleen Newland (Bloomington: Indiana University Press, 1991).

25. Goetz, "Feminism and the Claim to Know," note 24 at 151–52.

26. Ketokoski, "Toward a More Effective Application," note 16 at 14–15. On the Norwegian experiment in the feminization of political power, see Hege Skjeie, *The Feminization of Power: Norway's Political Experiment (1986–)* (Oslo: Institute for Social Research, 1988), Report 88: 8.

27. Radhika Coomaraswamy, "To Bellow like a Cow: Women, Ethnicity and the Discourse of Rights," Chapter 2 in this book at 44.

28. See also Abdullahi Ahmed An-Na'im, "State Responsibility Under International Human Rights Law to Change Religious and Customary Laws," Chapter 7 in this book.

29. Coomaraswamy, "To Bellow like a Cow," note 27 at 45.

30. Discussion, Consultation on Women's International Human Rights, Toronto (Sept. 1, 1992).

31. See J. A. Carty, "Changing Models of the International System," in *Perestroika and International Law*, ed. W.E. Butler (Dordrecht: Martinus Nijhoff, 1990), 13.

32. Convention (No. 169) Concerning Indigenous and Tribal Peoples in Independent Countries, in *International Labour Conventions and Recommendations, 1919–1991* (Geneva: International Labour Organisation, 1992) 2: 1436.

33. Most recently, see Draft Declaration on the Rights of Indigenous Peoples, U.N. Doc. E/CN.4/Sub.2/1993/26 (June 8, 1993) (first reading as revised by Chairperson-Rapporteur, Erica-Irene Daes) (hereinafter 1993 Draft Declaration). See also Erica-Irene A. Daes, Explanatory Note Concerning the Draft Declaration on the Rights of Indigenous Peoples, U.N. Doc. E/CN.4/Sub.2/1993/26/Add.1 (July 19, 1993). Cf. *Report of the Working Group on Indigenous Populations on its Tenth Session*, U.N. Doc. E/CN.4/Sub.2/1992/33 (Aug. 20, 1992) Annex I (first reading) (hereinafter 1992 Draft Declaration).

34. Maivân Clech Lâm, "Making Room for Peoples at the United Nations: Thoughts Provoked by Indigenous Claims to Self-Determination," *Cornell Int'l L. J.* 25 (1992): 603, 621.

35. Howard R. Berman, "Are Indigenous Populations Entitled to International Juridical Personality?" Panel Presentation, *Proc. Am. Soc'y Int'l L.* 79 (1985): 190, 192. See 1993 Draft Declaration, note 33 at operative paras. 17, 26, 34, 36–39; Daes, Explanatory Note, note 33 at para. 39; 1992 Draft Declaration note 33 at operative paras. 18, 26, 31–32.

36. E.g., Falk, "The Rights of Peoples," note 20 at 35. Cf. Principle 10, *Principles and Elements of Self-Government* adopted by Inuit delegates in Alaska 1986, reprinted in U.N. Doc. HR/NUUK/1991/SEM.1/BP.10 (Sept. 25, 1991); 1993 Draft Declaration, note 33 at operative para. 33.

37. Reprinted in U.N. Doc. HR/NUUK/1991/SEM.1/BP.6 (Sept. 20, 1991).

38. Lars Adam Rehof, Effective Means of Planning for and Implementing Autonomy, Including Negotiated Constitutional Arrangements and Involving Both Territorial and Personal Autonomy, in U.N. Doc. E/CN.4/1992/42/Add.1 at 87, 107, n.32 and accompanying text.

39. Richard Falk, *The End of World Order* (New York: Holmes and Meier, 1983), 25.

40. *International Law.* ed. Folk et al., note 20 at 7, quoted recently by Stephen Toope, "Report of the Conference Rapporteur," in *State Sovereignity: The Challange of a Changing World,* Proceedings of the XXI Annual Conference of the Canadian Council on International Law (Ottawa: the Council, 1992), 294.

Part III
International and
Regional Approaches

Chapter 7
State Responsibility Under International Human Rights Law to Change Religious and Customary Laws

Abdullahi Ahmed An-Na'im

Introduction

States are responsible for bringing their domestic law and practice into conformity with their obligations under international law to protect and promote human rights. This responsibility applies not only to laws enacted by formal legislative organs of the state but also to those attributed to religious and customary sources or sanction, regardless of the manner of their "enactment" or articulation and/or implementation.[1] In other words, every state has the responsibility to remove any inconsistency between international human rights law binding on it, on the one hand, and religious and customary laws operating within the territory of that state, on the other. This responsibility is fully consistent with the principle of state sovereignty in international law, since it does not purport to force any state to assume legal obligations against its will. It simply seeks to ensure that states effectively fulfill legal obligations they have already assumed under international law.

These obligations could be based, in general terms, on customary international law, and on the Charter of the United Nations in relation to all its member states. But since neither international custom nor the UN Charter is adequate or specific enough,[2] the existence of an international obligation to respect and protect particular human rights, and the consequent obligation to change domestic laws, can be problematic in the absence of specific treaty provisions. Moreover, there are questions about the circumstances and context of the implementation of that obligation. In view of space limitations, I will focus in this chapter on issues raised by the realistic circumstances of implementation in countries where practices attributed to religious and customary laws are most likely to violate the international human rights of women. This choice of emphasis is supported by the fact that, to my knowledge, this set of issues has not received sufficient attention in available literature. But I will begin by briefly highlighting some questions relating to the sources and nature of the obligation.

The principle that states are responsible for changing domestic laws in order to bring them into conformity with international human rights law could simply be based on the notion that the state is bound to do so by international custom or treaties. However, it may not be sufficient to rely on a formalistic understanding of this notion, especially in relation to the international human rights of women. The argument that this obligation can be founded on customary international law may be somewhat controversial and strained in relation to the human rights of women. Customary international law, in general, is notoriously vague and difficult to prove.[3] Moreover, it would probably be difficult to establish a principle of customary international law prohibiting all forms of discrimination on grounds of gender. The restrictive formulations suggested by the few authors who support the existence of such a principle in customary international law clearly show that its scope and implications would be problematic and controversial.[4]

The rationale of binding agreements would, of course, apply when the state is party to a relevant treaty. For example, Articles 2(f) and 5(a) of the International Convention for the Elimination of all Forms of Discrimination Against Women (the Women's Convention) require states parties to implement "appropriate measures" to eliminate discrimination against women in customary practices.[5] However, this rationale would not be applicable where the state has not ratified relevant treaties or has entered reservations that exclude the obligation to change religious or customary laws. For example, Egypt ratified the Women's Convention, but entered a reservation on, inter alia, Article 16, concerning equality between men and women in all matters relating to marriage and family relations, which are governed in Egypt by Islamic Shari'a law.[6]

Even where a state is party to an appropriate treaty and has not entered a reservation with regard to a particular human right, it should not be assumed that the application of the notion of binding treaties to the obligation to change religious and customary laws will be a simple or straightforward matter. First, an effort to identify or define the exact extent and nature of the obligations of states parties to a treaty will probably face some problems of interpretation and operation of the provisions of the treaty in question.[7]

Second, there are serious questions about who is going to raise the issue of the state's failure to comply with its treaty obligations, where, and how? For example, it is probably true that Egypt's reservations on the Women's Convention are inadmissible under the law of treaties.[8] But who is going to raise the issue, where, and how? Unlike commercial and other treaties where the states parties would usually have the motivation and resources to raise and pursue the issue of failure to comply in appropriate fora, state self-interest is normally lacking in relation to human rights treaties. Although there are some enforcement mechanisms for human rights treaties,[9] this aspect of international law remains extremely underdeveloped and largely dependent on the activities of underfunded and overworked non-governmental and voluntary organizations.

In light of these considerations, the nature of international law in general,[10] and its dependence on largely voluntary compliance and cooperation of sovereign states in the field of human rights in particular,[11] I suggest that it is better to seek deeper consensus and sustainable commitment to the human right in question in order to support its implementation in practice, including efforts to change religious and customary laws accordingly. This can and should be done, I believe, in addition to invoking the notion of binding international custom or agreement whenever and to the extent possible, and in support of that notion itself.

It is also important, I suggest, to understand the nature and dynamics of the behavior of governments as political entities, acting within the context of specific political, economic, and social conditions, and also the nature and dynamics of power relations prevailing in the particular country. No government can afford to disregard the politically articulated wishes or positions of powerful groups or segments of its population who might want to maintain religious and customary laws. This will be true, I suggest, of even the most authoritarian or undemocratic governments, in the unlikely event of their being "interested" in effecting such change.

Although it is obvious that the responsibility to change domestic laws must apply to religious and customary law, the implementation of this principle can be problematic in many parts of the world. In practice, a state's willingness or ability to influence practices based on religious and customary laws depends on many factors, any of which could cause difficulty in situations where domestic religious and customary laws are likely to be in conflict with internationally recognized standards of human rights.

Take the example of customary land tenure practices favoring males or the practice of female genital mutilation in some African countries.[12] There is first the question whether these practices do in fact violate the international human rights obligations of the particular state. In other words, is the state required or obliged to eradicate these practices not only as a matter of good or just domestic policy, but also by reason of international human rights law? The latter proposition presupposes that the practices in question violate specific human rights that are binding on the state as a matter of international law.

Assuming the existence of an international human rights obligation to eradicate these practices, there may still be some problems of implementation. A government may not be sufficiently motivated to engage in land tenure reform unless, for example, there are clear fiscal or other incentives to do so. Similarly, not all governments are particularly concerned with the serious health and psychological consequences of female genital mutilation. Even if there is the political will to act, it may not be easy for a government to influence the socio-cultural roots of these practices. As explained below, this task is complicated by the nature of these practices and the inaccessibility of their manifestation or incidence. Moreover, in practice, governments do not necessarily speak with one voice or act with a unified will. Policies adopted at higher political or administrative levels can be frustrated by hostile or uncooperative bureaucrats, officials, or local actors.

In recognizing and appreciating these and other difficulties of changing religious and customary laws in order to bring them into conformity with international human rights law, I am not arguing for relieving the state of its obligation to effect such change. I would personally support the establishment of this obligation as a matter of international human rights law when that is not already the case, and support its effective implementation where it exists. It is precisely because of this commitment that I would argue for developing a realistic understanding of the problems involved in the application of this principle with a view to overcoming them. In the rest of this chapter, I will try to explore some facets of the required change process, and suggest guidelines for its achievement.

To place the objectives of this chapter in context, however, I wish to address the question of the universal cultural legitimacy of internationally recognized standards of human rights. That is to say, to what extent are these standards accepted as legitimate and binding in all the major cultural traditions of the world? This question must be taken seriously precisely because it is sometimes raised with the intention of undermining international human rights law, or of justifying its violation. Those who raise the issue of universality in the context of a given culture do so because they anticipate that the argument has strong appeal or apparent validity to the constituencies they address. Therefore the best course of action for proponents of international human rights standards is to address these questions rather than ignore them.

The Universal Cultural Legitimacy of Human Rights

The following brief discussion of the cultural legitimacy of human rights is premised on a view of culture as a primary source of normative systems, and as the context within which such norms are interpreted and implemented. In this light, it is reasonable to assume that the prospects for practical implementation of a given regime of human rights as a normative system are related to the degree of its legitimacy in the context of the culture(s) where it is supposed to be interpreted and implemented in practice. Otherwise, how can a people be expected to accept and effectively implement a system that they believe to be inconsistent with their own cultural values and institutions? Since the present system of internationally recognized standards of human rights is supposed to apply throughout the world, it should be accepted as legitimate in all the major cultural traditions of the world.[13]

In my view, this premise is beyond dispute because I am unable to conceive of coercing people into implementing a human rights system they do not accept as legitimate. What might be at issue, I suggest, are two questions that follow from this premise. First, are the present internationally recognized standards of human rights, or aspects thereof, in fact culturally legitimate on a universal level? If, or to the extent that, this is not the case, what is to be done about the lack of cultural legitimacy in any given situation?

The argument against the universal cultural legitimacy of the present internationally recognized standards of human rights in general is often made on the ground that the basic conception and major principles expressed in these standards emerged from western philosophical and political developments. This may well be true as a matter of historical fact.[14] Moreover, it may also be true that the predominance of western assumptions and conceptions of human rights was reinforced by such factors as the nature and context of the drafting process, the limitations of studies purporting to cover a variety of cultural perspectives on the subject and the quality of representation of non-western points of view.[15]

It must also be emphasized here that the history and development of the present internationally recognized standards of human rights can also give rise to other concerns. Given the male bias of all cultures, western and non-western, to varying degrees, there is good reason for concern about the lack of representation of feminist perspectives in the present formulations of internationally recognized human rights standards. Although I am not competent to address the substance and implications of this concern, I believe that it is at least as important as, and often overlaps with, the question of cultural legitimacy as such.

But raising these concerns in general terms, from either a cultural or feminist perspective, cannot justify a blanket condemnation and rejection of all international human rights standards, or even of a particular one, without very careful inquiry and substantiation of the alleged objections. It is true that, at least in the interest of further refinement and elaboration, the opportunity to challenge any present international human right should remain open. Otherwise, the international human rights movement will be condemned to its present state or course of development, without allowing for future needs and opportunities for change or modification. From this perspective, a culturally based (or feminist-based) challenge should be investigated in good faith. However, the case against any specific international human right must be extremely strong in order to justify discarding or reformulating the right in question.

The reasons for requiring a very high standard of proof from those who mount a challenge to an internationally recognized human right include the following. First, there is already significant consensus on internationally recognized human rights through the very deliberate and settled process by which they were articulated and adopted over the course of several decades, as well as the wide ratification of most international treaties on the subject. Second, however one may feel that these rights, or aspects thereof, are inadequate, they do provide a level of protection. Even those who object to these rights in their present formulation need the protection afforded by them in making their case. Third, if the right is set aside, or its present formulation changed, too lightly or prematurely, there is the risk of failing to achieve even the level or type of human right one is objecting to.

Furthermore, and in relation to culturally based challenges in particular, I wish to recall and explain some aspects of the politics of culture referred to earlier. In addressing these questions, it should first be emphasized that the cultural legitimacy or illegitimacy of any thing or matter is necessarily problematic in that it can only be considered within the framework of a number of vague and contestable variables. To claim that something is culturally legitimate or illegitimate presupposes a settled and well-defined set of standards and a fair and consistent process by which those standards are applied. Both aspects, I would add, should themselves be culturally legitimate. Many difficult and inherently political questions are raised by this scenario. Which standards of cultural legitimacy should apply? Who selects them and how? What about alternative or competing standards of cultural legitimacy? What is the nature and dynamics of power relations among the holders of various views or positions, and how are their interests affected by the issues in question? Who adjudicates the process of selecting applicable standards and ensures the fairness and consistency of their application in practice?

Although it is not possible to resolve any of these questions and concerns here, I suggest that responses to the question of the cultural legitimacy of the international human rights of women, and what can be done about such claims, should be cast against the background of the problematic nature of what might be called the politics of culture. The politics of culture, in turn, should be seen in light of what I call the ambivalence and contestability of cultural norms and institutions, which permits a variety of interpretations and practices. Since culture needs to respond to different and competing individual and collective needs and aspirations, it tends to combine stability and continuous change, offer its adherents a range of options, and seek to accommodate varying responses to its norms.[16] These features reflect the fact that culture is constantly contested in a political struggle between those who wish to legitimize their power and privilege and those who need to challenge the status quo in order to redress grievances, realize their human dignity, and protect their well-being. Cultural symbols and processes are constantly used in this struggle at the local, national, or international levels. Therefore human rights advocates need to understand the process of cultural legitimacy and change, and utilize that process effectively in their efforts to enhance the implementation and enforcement of human rights standards throughout the world.

In light of the preceding remarks and reservations, I now turn to the question of universal cultural legitimacy of human rights. It is neither possible, nor desirable in my view, for an international system of human rights standards to be culturally neutral. However, the claim of such an international system to universal cultural legitimacy can only be based on a moral and political "overlapping consensus" among the major cultural traditions of the world.[17] In order to engage all cultural traditions in the process of promoting and sustaining such global consensus, the relationship between local culture and international human rights standards should be perceived as a genuinely reciprocal global collaborative effort.

Rather than an "all-or-nothing" approach to the relationship between local culture and international human rights standards, I would recommend the intermediatory approach suggested by Richard Falk, who argues that without mediating international human rights through the web of cultural circumstances, it will be impossible for human rights norms and practice to take deep hold in non-Western societies except to the partial, and often distorting, degree that these societies—or, more likely, their governing elites—have been to some extent Westernized. At the same time, without cultural practices and traditions being tested against the norms of international human rights, there will be a regressive disposition toward the retention of cruel, brutal, and exploitative aspects of religious and cultural tradition.[18]

Thus the process of promoting and sustaining global cross-cultural legitimacy for an international system of human rights can work in the following manner.[19] Since we already have an international system of human rights law and institutions, the process should seek to legitimize and anchor the norms of this established system within, and between, the various cultural traditions of the world. In other words, the norms of the international system should be validated in terms of the values and institutions of each culture, and also in terms of shared or similar values and institutions of all cultures. This can be achieved, I suggest, through what I call "internal discourse" within the framework of each culture, and "cross-cultural dialogue" among the various cultural traditions of the world.

I believe that it is of vital importance that internal discourse should be undertaken within each and every cultural tradition for at least two main reasons. First, internal validation is necessary in all cultural traditions for one aspect or another of the present international human rights system. It might be necessary for civil and political rights in one culture, economic and social rights in another, the rights of women or minorities in a third, and so forth. Second, for such discourse within one culture to be viable and effective, its participants should be able to point to similar discourse which is going on in the context of other cultures.

A parallel process of cross-cultural dialogue is also important for two main reasons. First, from a methodological point of view, all participants in their respective internal discourses can draw on each other's experiences and achievements. Second, cross-cultural dialogue will enhance understanding of, and commitment to, the values and norms of human dignity shared by all human cultures, thereby providing a common moral and political foundation for international human rights standards. In this way, the combination of the processes of internal discourse and cross-cultural dialogue will, it is hoped, deepen and broaden universal cultural consensus on the concept and normative content of international human rights.

It should be emphasized, however, that the proposed approach is methodological and not substantive: it prescribes a methodology of internal discourse and cross-cultural dialogue on reciprocal, dynamic, and sensitive terms, but it does not otherwise anticipate or restrict the arguments to be used, or the manner in which discourse(s) and dialogue(s) are to be conducted in each situation. It would therefore be possible to consider and analyze experiences in various cultural or country-specific contexts as a means of informing and promoting more constructive discourse and dialogue.[20]

In the next section, I highlight some issues relevant to the application of this approach to the responsibility of states to change religious and customary laws that violate internationally recognized standards of human rights. As I indicate at the end of that section, the proposed approach might also help resolve conflicts between national fundamental or human rights standards, on the one hand, and communal (religious, customary, or traditional) standards within a nation state, on the other. The last section is devoted to a brief illustration of a possible application of this approach to changing Islamic religious laws in relation to the international human rights of women.

Changing Religious and Customary Laws

It is true, from a legal point of view, that international law can only address states with due regard for their sovereignty, and that it does not have the authority, concepts, or mechanisms for achieving compliance with its norms except through the agency of the state in question. This does not mean, however, that nothing can be done to encourage and support states in their efforts to comply with international human rights law. In this light, it would be useful to explore possible strategies for changing religious and customary laws in order to bring them into conformity with international human rights law. Integral to this inquiry is the question of how such strategies may be employed by internal actors, and how external support and assistance can be rendered without undermining the integrity and efficacy of the process as a whole. It is necessary for both aspects of the process to be grounded in a clear understanding of the nature and operation of religious and customary laws in relation to what the state can realistically be expected to do. Although it is not possible to present here a comprehensive treatment of this matter, some tentative remarks might be helpful.

On the Nature and Operation of Religious and Customary Law

The authority of religious and customary laws is commonly perceived to derive from either the people's religious beliefs or their communal practice from time immemorial. That is to say, the common perception is that the validity of religious laws is ensured by divine sanction, while the utility of customary laws is assumed to have been proven through long experience. Since the two sources of authority overlap, they can be invoked interchangeably or in combination. In the case of Islamic societies, for example, local custom is assumed to be sanctioned by divine authority, provided that such custom does not contradict the explicit dictates of religious law, commonly known as "Shari'a." The validity of religious law, on the other hand, is believed to be vindicated by practical experience, as well as being supported by divine sanction. To the extent that traditional religions still prevail in some parts of Africa, it may be difficult to distinguish between divine sanction and communal authority.[21]

This common perception of the authority of religious and customary laws is founded on a complex web of economic, social and political factors, and tends to reflect existing power relations within the community. The perception is also maintained and promoted through processes of individual socialization and communal identification. While it is useful to understand its basis and dynamics, it may not be necessary or desirable to challenge or repudiate the perception itself in order to change the religious and customary laws it legitimizes. It is important to remember that the objective is to bring religious and customary laws into conformity with international human rights law, not to extinguish religious and customary laws themselves or transform their jurisprudential character. In any case, whether, to what extent, and how indigenous perceptions about religious and customary laws should and can be challenged, changed, or modified should be left to the process of internal discourse indicated earlier. An external effort to impose change would probably be perceived as an exercise in cultural imperialism, and rejected as such.

It should also be emphasized that religious and customary laws can, and usually are, implemented independently of the structures and mechanisms of the state. The state might try to regulate the operation of these laws, for example, by providing for procedural safeguards to be enforced by administrative organs or tribunals. But it can neither immediately eradicate the practice of these laws altogether, nor transform their nature and content, at least not without engaging in massive oppression and intimidation of the particular population over a long period of time. Even if the state were able and willing to maintain such a program as a high priority in its domestic policies, such policy or practice would be totally unacceptable from a human rights point of view.

An effort to change religious and customary laws in accordance with international human rights law should seek to persuade people of the validity and utility of the change. Such persuasion must, of course, be grounded in a complete and realistic understanding of the rationale or authority of these laws, and of the way they operate in practice. For example, customary land tenure practices that assign ownership or possession of land to men rather than women might be apparently justified or rationalized on the ground that only men can cultivate or otherwise use the land in order to support their families. Beyond that apparent rationale, however, such practices will probably also rely on assumptions about the competence and "proper" roles of men and women in society. This type of underlying rationale can be strong enough to override or negate efforts by the state to change or regulate customary land tenure practices.

For instance, the state may introduce a different land distribution scheme in order to give women their share, and seek to enforce this through an official land registration system. Nevertheless, previous customary land tenure practices may persist "off the record," with the apparent acquiescence of the women who are supposed to benefit from the enforcement of the new system. An effort to change this aspect of customary law must take into account and address not only apparent economic and sociological factors or justifications, but also the circumstances and underlying rationales that might cause the practice to continue despite attempts at legal regulation or change by the state.

Similarly, one or more justifications may be given for the practice of female genital mutilation. A more sophisticated inquiry, however, may reveal other rationales or underlying assumptions, for example, about male/female sexuality and roles, power relations, and economic and political interests. Moreover, this practice can be attributed to customary sanction, but not to customary law in a jurisprudential sense. The customary sanction in this case is not enforced in any judicial or public setting. Rather the sanction operates through the socialization or conditioning of women in order to induce them to "consent" to such mutilation being inflicted on their young daughters. Again, customary sanction for this practice may be strong enough to override state efforts to eradicate it, even through the imposition of criminal punishment, as in the Sudan, where the practice has been a criminal offense punishable by up to two years of imprisonment since 1946.[22] An effort to eradicate genital mutilation must take into account and address not only every and all types of justifications, but also the cultural circumstances and underlying rationales that might cause the practice to continue in the particular community.

Toward Coherent Strategies for Change

In view of these factors, it is clear that the only viable and acceptable way of changing religious and customary laws is by transforming popular beliefs and attitudes, and thereby changing common practice. This can be done through a comprehensive and intensive program of formal and informal education, supported by social services and other administrative measures, in order to change people's attitudes about the necessity or desirability of continuing a particular religious or customary practice. To achieve its objective, the program must not only discredit the religious or customary law or practice in question, but also provide a viable and legitimate alternative view of the matter. Such an alternative view of an existing practice can be either the simple discontinuation of the practice in question or the substitution of another.

Since the original practice derives its authority from religious or customary sanction, an effort to discredit it (and to substitute another where appropriate) must draw its authority from the same source on which the original practice was founded. This effort must also be presented through a reasoning or rationale intelligible to the affected population. For example, efforts to change customary land tenure practices must seek to challenge and discredit whatever economical, sociological, or other rationale is perceived by the population at large to support or justify those practices. Such efforts must also seek to challenge and discredit the original practice in ways that are relevant to, and understood and accepted by, the population in question.

It is difficult to envision the application of the proposed approach in abstract terms, without reference to the nature and operation of a specific religious or customary law system in the context of a particular society. Generally speaking, however, it is possible to identify some internal requirements for a successful process of changing religious and customary laws to ensure their compliance with international human rights law. In an ideal scenario, there are two levels of requirements that need to be satisfied. First, the state in question must be legally bound by the relevant principle of international human rights law. It should also have committed itself to effectively discharging its responsibility to bring domestic religious and customary laws into conformity with the requirements of international human rights law. Second, there is a need for broadly based political support for the official commitment of the state. Moreover, a strongly motivated and well-informed local constituency, willing and able to engage in organized action, is needed to mobilize political support and press for the implementation of policies and strategies for change.

However, these ideal requirements are neither likely to be immediately and fully realized all at once, nor to be completely lacking when the issue of changing religious or customary law arises in a given situation. In all probability, there would be some level of official obligation and commitment to change, some degree of broad political support, and some sort of constituency willing to work for it. Otherwise the issue would not have arisen in the first place. If there is no political support for, or official commitment to, changing religious or customary laws in order to ensure their conformity with international human rights law, then the question will not arise at all in the particular country.

Moreover, a dynamic relationship exists between and within each level of requirement. A highly motivated and capable constituency, for instance, can cultivate popular political support for change, and pressure the state into ratifying the relevant treaty or into increasing or effectuating its commitment to implement change in accordance with international human rights law. Conversely, the existence of an official commitment can encourage the growth of an active local constituency, or facilitate the development of broadly based political support for change. This dynamic is part of the process of internal discourse whereby the proponents of an internationally recognized human right seek to justify and legitimize that right in terms of their own culture, as explained above.

In addition to these internal aspects, there is also the external dimension of the process of changing religious or customary laws. External actors can support and influence the process of internal discourse through cross-cultural dialogue, as explained above. However, it is crucial that external support and influence be provided in ways that enhance, rather than undermine, the integrity and efficacy of the internal discourse. The process of cultural legitimation will be undermined, if not totally repudiated, by even the appearance of imposition of extra-cultural values and norms. External actors should support and encourage indigenous actors who are engaging in internal discourse to legitimize and effectuate a particular human right. However, external actors must not, in any way, attempt or appear to dictate the terms of internal discourse or pre-empt its conclusions. Possible ways and means of external support include international action to protect the freedoms of speech and assembly of internal actors, the exchange of insights and experiences about the concept of the particular human right and the sociopolitical context of its implementation, and assistance in developing and implementing campaign strategies.

The need for cultural sensitivity and discretion in providing external support is underscored by the fact that those acting as internal agents of change are liable to be regarded by local religious or political forces as subversive elements acting on behalf of the imperial interests of alien powers and cultures. This may appear obvious and elementary in such a political struggle, where the internal "guardians" of tradition and the status quo would want to seize on every opportunity and pretext in their efforts to undermine the credibility of the proponents of changing religious or customary laws. However, the subtle dangers of ethnocentricity and bias should not be underestimated in this connection. Cross-cultural dialogue should enhance the ability of internal actors to understand and address the nature and operation of cultural and political factors in their own context, not to press them into understanding and addressing these factors in terms of the experience of other societies.

As indicated above, the proposed approach might contribute to resolving conflicts between national fundamental or human rights standards, on the one hand, and communal (religious, customary, or traditional) standards within a nation state, on the other. The *Lovelace* case in Canada[23] and the *Shah Bano Begum* case in India[24] reflect such situations of conflict within a single nation state. Similar issues may arise in many other settings. Although each situation should be discussed in its own context, I believe that such situations raise the same basic set of dilemmas.

For instance, the dilemma confronting national policy-makers would be how to respect and protect the integrity (and independence, where relevant) of the community in question without allowing or tolerating violation of fundamental or human rights norms that are binding on the state as a matter of constitutional or international law. Such a dilemma would be particularly acute where the integrity and independence of the community in question is also dictated by constitutional or political imperatives.[25]

At a personal level such situations face women, for example, with a difficult choice between enduring inequality and discrimination in order to enjoy many vital benefits of membership in their own communities, or abandoning all that by opting-out of the community in order to enjoy equality and freedom from discrimination within the wider state society. I suspect that the dilemma would be even more cruel and traumatic for women who are aware of the choice, and are capable of exercising the right to opt out, than for those who are not so aware. On the one hand, they are likely to be castigated or harassed within the community because of their attitudes and life-style, thereby diminishing the benefits of belonging to the community. They would also be aware, on the other hand, of the limitations or inadequacy of equality and nondiscrimination promised by the wider society, especially to women of their status and background.

Such dilemmas would be resolved, I suggest, by transforming the internal communal (religious, customary, or traditional) standards relating to the status and rights of women and bringing them into conformity with the norms of equality and nondiscrimination prevailing in the wider state society through the processes of internal discourse and cross-cultural dialogue described above. In the absence of a better alternative, I would suggest that this approach should be tried by both official agencies and private actors as a way of resolving conflicts between national and communal standards. Although space does not permit further elaboration, it bears repeating that the proposed approach is methodological and not substantive. Full consideration can therefore be given to insights gained from other experiences of discourse and dialogue in adjusting and adapting the proposed approach to the circumstances and context of each case.

Islamic Religious Laws and the Rights of Women

In light of the above remarks about developing general strategies for changing religious and customary laws, I wish now to illustrate how the process might operate in relation to changing Islamic Shari'a laws in particular. It is not possible here either to explain the nature and development of Shari'a, or to discuss the many human rights problems raised by its application in the modern context.[26] In this brief section, I will present a theoretical discussion of the process of changing Shari'a family law, which, in my view, violates the human rights of Muslim women in even the most "secularized" Islamic societies.[27] This branch of Shari'a is enforced as the official law of the great majority of predominantly Muslim countries today, and even in some non-Muslim countries, like India as noted earlier,[28] where Muslims are a minority. Moreover, the underlying assumptions and norms of this branch of Shari'a have a negative impact on the human rights of women in broader sociopolitical terms.

The basic problem can be outlined as follows. Shari'a family law is fundamentally premised on the notion of male guardianship over women (*qawama*), and is consequently characterized by many features of inequality between men and women in marriage, divorce, and related matters. Thus, for example, as a general rule, a man may take up to four wives, and divorce any of them at will, and without having to show cause or account to any judicial or other authority for his decision. In contrast, a woman can only be married to one man at a time, and is not entitled to obtain a divorce except through a judicial ruling on a few specific grounds.[29] Although there are differences between and within the major schools of Islamic jurisprudence, as applied by the judicial systems of various countries, the above-mentioned premise and characterization are true of all situations where Shari'a family law is enforced today.

The notion of male guardianship has serious implications for the marriage relationship as a whole, and for the economic and social rights of married women. According to most jurists, a husband is entitled to the obedience of his wife, and can prevent her from taking employment, if he wishes. A wife who is disobedient to her husband (*nashid*) is not entitled to maintenance. Consequently, a woman can be forced to submit to her husband's will when she cannot obtain his consent in order to be able to work and thereby support herself, receive maintenance from him, or obtain a divorce. In some jurisdictions, a wife who leaves the matrimonial home can be physically forced to return through the execution of a judicial "obedience decree." Moreover, as noted earlier, this and other features of Shari'a family law have serious political and social consequences for women, in that their freedom to engage in activities outside the home is inhibited by the legal control men are entitled to exercise over their female "wards." These aspects of Shari'a also reinforce and sanction the socialization of women, who are conditioned, from early childhood, into submission, learned helplessness and dependency.

It is obvious that these principles of Shari'a family law violate the fundamental human right of nondiscrimination on grounds of gender. In some situations, these principles are used to justify cruel, inhuman, or degrading treatment. Most Islamic states are parties to international treaties that provide for a wide range of human rights that are violated by Shari'a personal law applied by the official courts of the same countries. A few Islamic states are even parties to the 1979 International Convention on the Elimination of All Forms of Discrimination Against Women, which is clearly violated by all these aspects of Shari'a family law. In other words, it is not difficult to establish the responsibility of many Islamic states to change these aspects of religious law in accordance with their obligations under international human rights law. The question is how to effect such change in practice. I will first address this question from an Islamic jurisprudential point of view, and then consider the role of internal and external actors in the process of change.

Two fundamental points to note about the jurisprudential question are (1) that Shari'a was constructed by early (male) Muslim jurists, and (2) that they acted in accordance with their historical context.[30] Whether through the selection and interpretation of the relevant texts of the Qur'an and Sunna (traditions of the Prophet), or through the application of such techniques as consensus (*ijma'*) and analogy (*qiyas*), the founding jurists of Shari'a constructed what they believed to be an appropriate legal and ethical system for their communities in very local terms. Clearly, the jurists were not engaged in the construction of a "divine and eternal" Shari'a, as claimed by many Muslims today. In fact, the most authoritative jurists expressed their views as individual theoretical derivations and cautioned against codifying or implementing them as the only valid version of Shari'a. Given this state of affairs, it is perfectly legitimate, indeed imperative in my view, for modern Muslim jurists and scholars to construct an Islamic legal and ethical system that is appropriate for the present historical context of Islamic societies.

In constructing Shari'a, the early Muslim jurists emphasized certain texts of the Qur'an and Sunna as relevant and applicable to the issue at hand, and de-emphasized or excluded others. This process was taken by the majority of succeeding generations of jurists to mean that the de-emphasized texts were repealed or abrogated (*nusikhat*) for legal purposes, though they remain part of the tradition in other respects. Moreover, the technical rules employed by the early jurists in constructing their visions of Shari'a, known as "the science of foundations of jurisprudence" (*ʿilm usul al-fiqh*), were entrenched by subsequent generations of Muslims as the only valid way of deriving principles and rules of Shari'a. Given the fact that both aspects of this process were the work of the early Muslim jurists, it is obvious that they are open to question and reformulation by contemporary Muslims.

In light of these considerations, Ustadh Mahmoud Mohamed Taha, the late Sudanese Muslim reformer, developed a coherent methodology for what he called "the evolution of Islamic legislation," that is, the reconstruction and reformulation of the constitutional and legal aspects of Shari'a.[31] Through the application of this methodology it is possible, indeed imperative, he argued, to abolish the principle of male guardianship over females, and to remove every feature of inequality of women or discrimination against them, as a matter of Islamic law. This theological and jurisprudential framework will, in my view, achieve complete consistency between Shari'a religious laws and international human rights law. Taha's methodology of Islamic law reform is readily available now and is, I believe, fully substantiated in Islamic terms. The remaining issue is how to implement this methodology in order to transform the principles and rules of Shari'a in concrete practical terms.

As indicated earlier, this is the role of internal discourse, as supported by cross-cultural dialogue. It is up to Muslim women and men to engage in a political struggle to propagate and implement reform of Islamic law (whether on the basis of Taha's methodology or another adequate Islamic alternative to it) in their own communities and countries. These internal actors may indeed receive external support and assistance, but only in accordance with the guidelines emphasized above. This is particularly important in view of the recent and current experience of Muslim peoples with western colonialism and domination. Islamic human rights advocates in general are already suspected of subverting their own cultures and traditions in favor of western values and institutions. It is therefore imperative that both the internal actors and their external supporters should avoid acting in a way that might be used as a pretext for undermining the credibility and legitimacy of the process of changing Shari'a laws.

I am not underestimating the difficulty and complexity of the task. Speaking from personal experience, I can say that prevailing conditions of political repression and social authoritarianism are hardly conducive to human rights organization and activism. Moreover, human rights advocates in Islamic countries are few and disorganized, their resources and experience are limited, and the demands on their time and energy are many and complex. Nevertheless there is no substitute for internal discourse for transforming attitudes and perceptions about the nature and implications of Shari'a, and for achieving the necessary legal reform and change. It is primarily the task of internal actors, supported and encouraged by external allies, to promote and sustain the necessary degree of official commitment and popular political support for a program for changing Shari'a laws.

Finally, I should indicate that while Taha's methodology has its limitations,[32] I believe that it can at least be useful as an initial framework for an internal discourse, which can then continue to seek other Islamic reform methodologies to supplement or replace it. I also believe it is important to note that international human rights law itself is not immune to critical examination and reformulation.[33] Unless human rights advocates in all parts of the world are open to this possibility, it would be unrealistic to expect Muslims to be open to critical examination of their religious law.

Conclusion

It is not possible accurately to evaluate the potential of the approach to changing religious and customary laws presented here until it is applied to specific situations of conflict and tension between such laws and international human rights law. However, judging by my knowledge of the possibilities for Islamic law reform, I envision a far-reaching potential for the proposed approach in relation to other systems of religious and customary law. I find this approach useful not only for maximizing the possibilities of resolution within the existing framework of a religious or customary law system, but also for expanding or transforming that framework itself. This is what I would regard as a proper or legitimate internal (within the culture or tradition) challenge and change of a people's perceptions about the nature and implications of their religious beliefs or long-standing communal practice. However, one must expect strong and sustained opposition or resistance from those whose vested interests are threatened by any change in the status quo.

As indicated at the end of the last section, a given reform methodology might not succeed in achieving the required reform of one or more aspects of a system of religious or customary law. In such a case, I suggest, that would be a failure of the particular methodology, and not necessarily of the internal discourse/cross-cultural dialogue approach as a whole. Other methodologies can and must be found by the people themselves, through internal discourse, supported by cross-cultural dialogue.

I am grateful to Tore Lindholm and Shelley Cooper-Stephenson for their very helpful comments and suggestions on an earlier draft of this paper.

Notes

1. As explained below, religious and customary laws come in a wide variety of forms and operate in many different ways. It might, therefore, be inappropriate or misleading to describe all of them as "law" in a coherent jurisprudential sense. They are referred to here as "laws" in the plural because there is usually more than one religious or customary law "systems" in a country, and also in order to distinguish them from the formal or official state law.

2. Some of the problems of custom as a source of international human rights standards are highlighted below. Arts. 1.3, 55, and 56 of the United Nations Charter impose an obligation of respect for, and observance of, "human rights and fundamental freedoms." But since that treaty does not define this clause, it is necessary to find another source for any particular or specific human right that states parties to the UN Charter are obliged to respect and protect.

3. For a brief review of the requirements and qualifications of custom as a source of international law, see Ian Brownlie, *Principles of Public International Law*, 3rd ed. (Oxford: Clarendon Press, 1979), 4–12.

4. See, for example, Louis Henkin et al., eds., *International Law: Cases and Materials* (St. Paul, MN: West Publishing, 1987), 998; and David J. Harris, *Cases and Materials on International Law*, 4th ed. (London: Sweet & Maxwell, 1991), 696. Cf. Isabelle R. Gunning, "Modernizing Customary International Law and the Challenge of Human Rights," *Va. J. Int'l L.* 31 (1991): 301–42.

5. G.A. Res. 34/180 U.N. GAOR, 34th Sess., Supp. No. 46, at 193, U.N. Doc. A/34/46 (1979). As of January 1992, 131 states have ratified this Convention; see Appendix A, p. 585.

6. For the text of Egypt's reservations, see Richard Lillich, ed., *International Human Rights Instruments* (Buffalo, NY: W.S. Hein, 1985), 11. Other Islamic countries have also entered similar reservations. See Donna J. Sullivan, "Gender Equality and Religious Freedom: Toward a Framework for Conflict Resolution," *N.Y.U. J. Int'l L. & Pol.* 24 (1992): 835–45.

On the question of reservations to this Convention in general, see Rebecca Cook, "Reservations to the Convention on the Elimination of All Forms of Discrimination Against Women," *Va. J. Int'l L.* 30 (1990): 643–716.

7. On the issues that might arise in this connection see generally Daniel P. O'Connell, *International Law*, 2d ed. (London: Stevens & Sons, 1970), 1:246–80; or Harris, *Cases and Materials*, note 4 at 729–816.

8. For such an argument see Anna Jenefsky, "Permissibility of Egypt's Reservations to the Convention on the Elimination of All Forms of Discrimination Against Women," *Md. J. Int'l L. & Trade* 15 (1991): 208–13, 226–31.

9. See generally Hurst Hannum, ed., *Guide to International Human Rights Practice*, 2d ed. (Philadelphia: University of Pennsylvania Press, 1992).

10. For a recent collection of studies on relevant issues from a variety of perspectives, see Martin Koskenniemi, ed., *International Law* (Aldershot, England: Dartmouth Publishing Co., 1992), 3–60.

11. The fact that changing religious and customary laws is made the subject of "state responsibility" raises issues of sovereignty and indicates the limitations on direct enforcement in international law. On the nature and scope of state responsibility in international law see Brownlie, *Principles of Public International Law*, note 3 at 431–35. For a more comprehensive treatment of relevant issues see Harris, *Cases and Materials*, note 4 at 460–93.

12. Although I will refer to these two examples to illustrate my argument in some parts of this paper, it is not possible to discuss these practices in detail here. On land tenure issues in Africa see generally Richard G. Lowe, *Agricultural Revolution in Africa? Impediments to Change and Implications for Farming, for Education, and for Society* (London: Macmillan, 1986); Jean Davison, ed., *Agriculture, Women, and Land: The African Experience* (Boulder, CO: Westview Press, 1988); R. E. Downs and Stephen P. Reyna, eds., *Land and Society in Contemporary Africa* (Hanover, NH: University Press of New England, 1988); James C. Riddell and Carol W. Dickerman, *Country Profiles of Land Tenure: Africa 1986* (Madison: University of Wisconsin-Madison Land Tenure Center, 1986); and Carol W. Dickerman, *Security of Tenure and Land Registration in Africa: Literature Review and Synthesis* (Madison: University of Wisconsin-Madison Land Tenure Center, 1989).

On female genital mutilation see generally, Fran P. Hosken, *The Hosken Report*, 3rd rev. ed. (Lexington, MA: Women's International Network News, 1982); and Fran P. Hosken, *Female Sexual Mutilation: The Facts and Proposals for Action* (Lexington, MA: Women's International Network News, 1980). These two sources contain useful bibliographies.

13. See, generally, Abdullahi An-Na'im and Francis M. Deng, eds., *Human Rights in Africa: Cross-Cultural Perspectives* (Washington, DC: Brookings Institution, 1990); and Abdullahi An-Na'im, ed., *Human Rights in Cross-Cultural Perspectives: A Quest for Consensus* (Philadelphia: University of Pennsylvania Press, 1992).

The question of the legitimacy of internationally recognized standards of human rights should be seen in the context of the broader issue of the legitimacy of international law itself. On this broader issue see Thomas M. Franck, "Legitimacy in the International System"; Martin Koskenniemi, "The Normative Force of Habit: International Custom and Social Theory"; and Surakiart Sathirathai, "An Understanding of the Relationship Between International Legal Discourse and Third World Countries," all in *International Law,* ed. Koskenniemi, note 10 at 157, 213, and 445 respectively.

14. See, for example, Virginia A. Leary, "The Effect of Western Perspectives on International Human Rights," in *Human Rights in Africa,* ed. An-Naʿim and Deng, note 13 at 15–30.

15. For an elaboration on these remarks see Abdullahi A. An-Naʿim, "Problems of Universal Cultural Legitimacy for Human Rights," in *Human Rights in Africa,* ed. An-Naʿim and Deng, note 13 at 346–53.

16. For an elaboration of these remarks see Abdullahi A. An-Naʿim, "Toward a Cross-Cultural Approach to Defining International Standards of Human Rights," in *Cross-Cultural Perspectives,* ed. An-Naʿim, note 13 at 27–28.

17. The concept of global overlapping consensus is similar to that proposed by John Rawls for social justice at the domestic level. See Tore Lindholm, "Prospects for Research on the Cultural Legitimacy of Human Rights," in *Cross-Cultural Perspectives,* ed. An-Naʿim, note 13 at 400; and John Rawls, "The Idea of an Overlapping Consensus," *Oxford J. Legal Stud.* 7 (1987): 1–25.

18. Richard Falk, "Cultural Foundations for the International Protection of Human Rights," in *Cross-Cultural Perspectives,* ed. An-Naʿim, note 13 at 45–46.

19. For further explanation of the proposed approach, see Falk, "Cultural Foundations," note 18; and An-Naʿim, "Universal Cultural Legitimacy," note 15 at 339–45 and 361–66.

20. See, for example, Sullivan, "Gender Equality," note 6, especially 848–54.

21. For a general explanation of what are known as African traditional religions, and a critique of terms and classifications applied to them in earlier western scholarship, see, Berta I. Sharevskaya, *The Religious Traditions of Tropical African in Contemporary Focus* (Budapest: Center for Afro-Asian Research of the Hungarian Academy of Sciences, 1973), 13–66.

See generally Terence O. Ranger and Isaria N. Kmambo, eds., *The Historical Study of African Religions* (Berkeley and Los Angeles: University of California Press, 1972); Charles E. Fuller, "Native and Missionary Religions," in *The Transformation of East Africa,* ed. Stanley Diamond and Fred G. Burke (New York: Basic Books, 1966), 511–35; Matthew Schoffeleers and Wim Van Binsbergen, eds., *Theoretical and Methodological Explorations in African Religions* (London: Kegan Paul International, 1985); and Thomas D. Blakely et al., eds., *Religion in Africa: Experience and Expression* (London: James Currey, 1991).

22. On the case of the Sudan, see Hosken, *Hosken Report,* note 12 at 95–119.

23. In this case, a native (Indian or Aboriginal) woman challenged before the UN Human Rights Committee a Canadian statute that discriminated against female members of native bands in Canada. See "*Lovelace v. Canada,* 1983," *Can. Hum. Rts. Y.B.* 1 (1983): 305–14; and William Pentney, "*Lovelace v. Canada:* A Case Comment," *Can. Legal Aid Bull.* 5 (1982): 259.

24. For brief comments on *Shah Bano Begum,* see my chapter, "Islam, Islamic Law and the Dilemma of Cultural Legitimacy for Universal Human Rights," in *Asian Perspectives on Human Rights,* ed. Claude E. Welch, Jr. and Virginia A. Leary (Boulder, CO: Westview Press, 1990), 43–46; and Sullivan, "Gender Equality," note 6 at 849–52.

25. See, for example, Allan McChesney, "Aboriginal Communities, Aboriginal Rights and the Human Rights System in Canada," in *Cross-Cultural Perspectives,* ed. An Naʿim, note 13 at 221–52.

26. I have explained and discussed these and related matters in detail in *Toward an Islamic Reformation: Civil Liberties, Human Rights and International Law* (Syracuse, NY: Syracuse University Press, 1990).

27. For a general discussion of Shari'a and the human rights of women, see Abdullahi A. An-Na'im, "The Rights of Women and International Law in the Muslim Context," *Whittier L. Rev.* 9 (1987): 491–516. A more empirical discussion of the process of changing Shari'a law from a human rights point of view can be found in my "Human Rights in the Muslim World: Socio-political Conditions and Scriptural Imperatives," *Harv. Hum. Rts. J.* 3 (1990): 13–52.

28. An-Na'im, "Dilemma of Cultural Legitimacy," note 24.

29. There are some theoretical exceptions. For instance, according to some jurists of Shari'a, a woman can stipulate in the contract of marriage that the man may not take another wife while married to her, and can "persuade" her husband to divorce her on the payment of monetary compensation known as *khul'*. However, in practice few women know about these exceptions or can afford to exercise them. Moreover, the terms of the exceptions themselves are premised on male guardianship of women and the inferior status of women in the relationship, rather than as a challenge or repudiation of those principles of Shari'a.

30. On this point and the following methodology of Islamic law reform, see An-Na'im, *Toward an Islamic Reformation*, note 26, especially chapters 2 and 3.

31. See generally my translation of his major work, Mahmoud M. Taha, *The Second Message of Islam* (Syracuse, NY: Syracuse University Press, 1987). It is important to note that Taha's methodology does not affect the devotional and ritual aspects of Shari'a, known as *'ibadat*.

32. See my chapter, "Toward a Cross-Cultural Approach to Defining International Standards of Human Rights: The Meaning of Cruel, Inhuman or Degrading Treatment or Punishment," in *Cross-Cultural Perspectives*, ed. An-Na'im, note 13 at 29–39.

33. It is not possible to discuss here the question of when and how international human rights law might be subjected to critical examination and reformulation. In any case, it is too early for me to express definite views on this aspect of the intermediatory or cross-cultural approach to human rights. For a brief review of my tentative thinking, and proposals for research, on this and other relevant issues, see An-Na'im, "Cross-Cultural Approach," note 32 at 427–35.

Chapter 8
Toward More Effective Enforcement of Women's Human Rights Through the Use of International Human Rights Law and Procedures

Andrew Byrnes

Introduction

The proliferation of human rights standards at the international level in the last forty-five years has been a striking feature of the development of international law in that period. While there had previously been international concern with issues that we would now characterize as human rights issues, the volume and scope of international and regional instruments in the field of human rights is now extensive.

This period has also seen some important developments in the recognition by the international community that sex/gender is an important category of analysis when it comes to examining the enjoyment of human rights, a recognition reflected in particular in the elaboration of a number of important instruments dealing with discrimination against women.[1]

As a result, the extent of formal protection of the rights of women under general human rights law and gender specific regimes is quite extensive (although largely worked out through a non-discrimination framework). This is not to say that there are not important areas in which the further elaboration or formulation of substantive norms is desirable.[2] Furthermore, like other areas of international human rights, the gap between the formal guarantees and the extent to which the rights are actually enjoyed in practice is frequently a wide one.

In addition to the development of substantive norms, many bodies and procedures have been established to promote the implementation of those norms. While within the European Convention system there was an enforcement procedure much earlier (and within the International Labour Organisation even before that), the elaboration of procedures within the United Nations human rights machinery to promote the implementation of human rights standards was a notable feature of the 1970s and 1980s. Inter-governmental organizations, non-governmental organizations (NGOs) and some states devoted a great deal of energy and resources to making these enforcement and implementation mechanisms as effective as such international mechanisms can be, and significant progress has been made in some respects. In this chapter I am adopting a fairly broad understanding of the term "enforcement" and do not confine it to those (quasi-) judicial complaint procedures that result in binding or quasi-binding adjudications in individual contentious cases.[3]

Nonetheless, there are many who consider that the attention given by many international human rights bodies to issues that predominantly or overwhelmingly affect women or to the extent to which women may be the victims of rights violations identical or similar to those suffered by men (though mediated through gender as well) has been inadequate. Many of those critics have called for a strengthening of the procedures and bodies that have primary responsibility within "women's issues," as well as arguing for greater attention to violations of the human rights of women within the so-called "mainstream" bodies. Others have queried whether the international system can adequately respond to the legitimate claims of women because of its conceptual and institutional limitations.[4]

This chapter discusses whether and how a greater use and more effective deployment of international human rights procedures and substantive law might help to promote the enjoyment of human rights by women. My major focus is the use of international procedures to advance human rights claims of particular importance to women. My primary emphasis is the organs of the United Nations, mainly because I have some familiarity with them. In many respects resort to regional mechanisms of enforcement may well provide a much more effective route for action than the UN mechanisms.[5] I also briefly consider the use of international standards in the national arena as a means of advancing those claims.[6]

The chapter touches on the following matters:

- the variety of procedures which are available at the international and regional level for the reception of allegations of human rights violations;
- some of the limitations and drawbacks of these procedures;

- procedures that might be profitably used for pressing claims of violations of women's rights (and which are presently underutilized);
- Using international material domestically.

The International Perspective

General

Traditionally, the role of international systems for the protection of human rights has been viewed as supplementary to that of the national authorities, with whom the primary responsibility for the implementation of binding international standards rests. It is up to the national authorities in the first instance to prevent violations of human rights or to provide remedies for those violations. It is when these fail to ensure the observance of applicable standards that the international system may have a role to play.

This traditional view needs to be qualified in important respects in the light of the many developments in the international system for the protection of human rights, although it still provides the conceptual underpinning for most of the procedures that permit complaints of violations of human rights to be brought to the international level. There are now many ways in which the international system scrutinizes and pronounces upon the human rights situation in individual countries, ranging from overtly political fora, to consideration by expert bodies or country mechanisms, to the consideration of complaints lodged by individuals or groups. Some of these may involve consideration of alleged violations of human rights in a given country long before any domestic remedies for the alleged violations have been exhausted.

One of the promises of recent developments in the international system(s) for the protection of human rights is not just the elaboration of norms intended to bind or guide national authorities in the manner in which they treat persons under their jurisdiction, but also the prospect that, if the national system fails to ensure the observance of human rights, some redress may be available through the international system.

The Appeal to International Law and Rights Discourse—International Human Rights Law and Procedures as a Strategic Resource

Although this chapter focuses on a number of procedural and substantive aspects of international human rights practice, it does not do so out of any belief that international human rights law and procedures have any talismanic quality. The limitations of international law generally when it comes to enforcement of binding standards are well known, and international human rights law is no exception in that regard. Even the strongest supporters of the international human rights "system" and its myriad procedures recognize the limitations of the system and, although there are many concrete cases in which it can be seen to have made a difference, it is frequently difficult to evaluate the importance of the role played by the deployment of international procedures. The assumption that the effort put in at the international level is a cost-effective use of time and resources is to some extent an article of faith.

While in some cases the utilization of an international procedure can produce a direct effect at the national level, perhaps the most realistic and pertinent way to approach the question of using international human rights mechanisms is to view them as one of a number of ways to pressure governments or others in order to achieve one's specific goals in the promotion of the enjoyment of human rights by women.

Thus my starting point is that recourse to international procedures is likely to have a very limited direct impact in redressing violations of human rights in many of the cases that might be brought before international bodies under one procedure or another. Some of the reasons for that position are mentioned below. It follows—and it is perhaps only those with a tendency to fetishize law, such as international human rights advocates, once described as "notoriously wishful thinkers," who need to be reminded of this—that any use of international procedures must form part of a broader political strategy. Recourse to international bodies and procedures may provide some additional leverage to a campaign at the national level, but will only infrequently do more than that. Indeed, in some circumstances the appeal to an international forum and international standards may be counter-productive. This chapter nevertheless proceeds on the basis that using an international forum can sometimes help to bring about change.

Using international human rights procedures involves the invocation not just of an international law discourse but of a rights discourse as well. The various critiques of rights are well known, as are many of the responses to those critiques.[7] Many of the concerns about appeals to rights that have been expressed in national contexts, are applicable to the international level as well. In the international context, one may pursue a much broader range of rights claims than is often possible under domestic legal systems, at least if one is trying to utilize a judicial or quasi-judicial procedure. The whole gamut of economic, social and cultural rights as well as the traditional catalogue of civil and political rights may, depending on the forum, be invoked. That said, it is still the case that the strongest enforcement procedures from a "judicialized" perspective are those that relate to the privileged civil and political rights catalogues.

There has been much recent writing from feminist perspectives about whether the so-called mainstream human rights framework has sufficiently addressed violations of women's human rights and whether this neglect is something that can be remedied by methodological or institutional changes, or that reflects an androcentric model of human rights which simply cannot be adapted but must be radically transformed. While not attempting to argue that all the claims women might wish to advance can be accommodated within the "human rights framework" or even within that of the specialized instruments and bodies dealing with "women's rights," the operating premise of this chapter is that the rights framework and the internationalization of a claim as a human rights claim may provide some assistance in pursuing one's goals.[8]

This chapter advocates an essentially instrumentalist approach to the deployment of international human rights law and procedures. That this may give rise to difficulties is clear from the experiences of those who have sought to pursue rights-based litigation strategies at the national level.[9] In some cases, existing doctrine can be useful in achieving goals, in other cases there appear to be good prospects of molding the doctrine in a useful direction. However, it is probably the case that both the mainstream human rights framework and the women's rights framework will simply not serve beyond a certain point; at that stage it is necessary to continue to rely on other sources of moral, political, or other normative changes.

Similarly, while accepting that international institutions (no matter how good their substantive jurisprudence or practice) are subject to fundamental limitations in the influence they can exert on developments at the national level, in essence I am arguing that there are nonetheless improvements that can be made to existing structures and practices that may go some way to optimizing the impact such institutions may have. This is not to say that such changes will fundamentally change the impact at the national level; nor is it to suggest that recourse to these institutions should be viewed as other than one plank in a broader strategic approach.

"Women's human rights" or "women's rights"

This chapter focuses on what might be termed violations of "women's rights"; this focus (and the conceptual categorization it is based on) itself gives rise to some difficulties. The dangers of constructing the category of "women" without having sufficient regard to the many different perspectives of women and the way in which not just sex/gender but race, class, and other social characteristics constitute the subordination that women face in different societies have been cogently pointed out time and time again.[10]

Women suffer from violations of their human dignity and human rights in many different ways. While it may be that these violations are always mediated through gender, in many cases race, nationality, class, or some other group characteristic may be the primary determinant; accordingly, the violations that women suffer may appear basically indistinguishable from those suffered by men of the same social group. Even in these cases, however, the form that a violation takes is frequently influenced by gender. Political opponents of either sex may be imprisoned, but the sexual violence inflicted on female detainees is a marked feature of women's experience in detention. A denial of the right to adequate housing or food may affect all the poor of a society, but if, for example, the division of labor within that society assigns primary responsibility to women for such tasks as collecting firewood, water, and food, then women's experience of the denial of those rights will be different in important respects from that of men.

There are, of course, many violations of rights that appear to affect women overwhelmingly, even though women of different races, classes or nations may experience them differently. Violence against women in the home as well as outside it, denial of control over one's own body, and trafficking in women are just a few of these gender-specific violations.

Whether one describes some or all of these violations of rights as violations of the "human rights of women" or violations of "women's rights" is a question that has given rise to a certain amount of perplexed discussion. It may be that the "right(s)" way to classify particular types of violations depends on the classification's context. In any event, it would be a mistake to assume that these are dichotomous categories and that violations can be assigned clearly or always into a particular category.

In this chapter I am not concerned to categorize particular types of violations. The general discussion of international procedures has relevance for most sorts of violations that may be suffered by women, whether they be gender-neutral (where women "just happen" to be the victims)—if there is such a thing—or gender-specific violations. That said, more emphasis is given in the discussion to violations that can loosely be described as gender-specific and how both mainstream and gender-specific mechanisms can be used in response.

International Human Rights Mechanisms

At the international and regional levels a wide range of bodies and procedures provide avenues for raising human rights grievances. The mandates, the composition of the bodies, the types of complaints that may be brought, the procedures followed, and the possible outcomes vary widely. These mechanisms have been described and discussed in many works and only a broad outline is attempted here.[11]

I will refer not only to those procedures which have been established in order to deal with complaints of human rights violations, but also to a number of other human rights implementation or monitoring procedures that can be utilized as part of a strategy of bringing the international system to bear on the national system. However, my primary emphasis will be the complaint procedures and those procedures which may have similar functions.

In examining the range of international procedures for monitoring human rights, one can conveniently distinguish between *complaint* and *non-complaint* procedures. *Complaint procedures* expressly permit or contemplate the submission of complaints by individuals or groups of individuals to a body for consideration by that body. Under most of the UN human rights treaties, and within the regional frameworks as well, there is provision made for one state party to lodge a complaint against another, alleging its failure to comply with its obligations under the relevant treaty. While in theory a possible avenue for recourse, in practice inter-state complaints are extremely rare.[12]

The nature of the consideration of complaints varies according to the nature of the procedure, in particular whether the procedure is a *complaint recourse* or a *complaint information* procedure.[13] Examples of complaint recourse procedures are the individual complaint procedures established under the First Optional Protocol to the International Covenant on Civil and Political Rights (ICCPR), the European Convention, and the American Convention, while examples of complaint information procedures include the Resolution 1503 procedure established by the Economic and Social Council (ECOSOC) and the communications procedure of the UN Commission on the Status of Women.

Maxime Tardu has formulated the distinction between a complaint recourse procedure and a complaint information procedure:[14]

Under *complaint-recourse* procedures, the competent international organ is legally bound to take a decision on each and every case brought before it, be it only on admissibility. The goal of the procedure is the redress of specific grievances. The plaintiff is entitled—to various extents—to participate in the proceedings. Such procedures are meant to approximate—however loosely—the judicial model of domestic law. . . .

Complaint-information schemes seek not the redress of individual grievances, but the identification of human rights problems affecting whole populations—e.g., Apartheid or Forced Disappearances—in order to define remedial strategies. Under such procedures, petitions are received only as elements of information. Even well-founded, the complaint may be discarded if it does not bring fresh data. Accepted petitions lose their individuality, merged into a mass of data. The author has none of the entitlements pertaining to "a party," often not even the right to be informed of the fate of his communication.

The variety of international procedures available defies quite such tidy categorization and there are a number of complaint procedures that have both a recourse and information component. These *hybrid procedures* include the Special Rapporteurs appointed by the UN Commission on Human Rights, who have responsibility not only for investigating the extent and nature of particular problems (ranging from summary or arbitrary executions to trafficking in children), but who may also raise individual cases with governments as part of their work. This flexibility can be particularly valuable, since it is one of the few procedures under which an individual case may be raised with a government on an urgent action basis, which can be of considerable importance in averting a threatened violation or stopping an existing one.

Non-complaint procedures are procedures before bodies which do not have an explicit mandate to consider complaints about violations of human rights, but which may nonetheless receive such complaints as a matter of practice on a formal or informal basis. While not competent to investigate allegations in a (quasi-) judicial mode, these bodies may nonetheless act on the information with which they have been provided. These procedures include not only the reporting procedures under the major UN human rights treaties, but also the work of the more politicized (though independent) bodies (such as the Sub-Commission on the Prevention of Discrimination and Protection of Minorities) and even the overtly political bodies (such as the Commission on Human Rights), which may consider the human rights situation in individual countries.

The primary focus of this section is on the complaint procedures and the "non-political" bodies; while some reference is made to the "political" fora, these are not dealt with in any detail.

Complaint Procedures

(a) Individual complaint procedures

This section consists of a brief description of the types of individual complaint procedures available internationally, followed by mention of some of the problems involved in using them and assessment of their contribution so far to advancing women's rights and their potential use for that purpose.

Under a number of the UN human rights treaties and within the framework of the European Convention on Human Rights and the

American Convention on Human Rights, provision is made for the receipt of individual complaints by the monitoring body concerned. The United Nations Educational, Scientific and Cultural Organization (UNESCO) has also established an individual complaint procedure for dealing with allegations of violations of human rights within its areas of competence.[15] Furthermore, the International Labour Organisation has a number of procedures under which complaints of violations of workers' rights or ILO conventions can be considered, although these complaints cannot be directly lodged by individuals, but must be lodged through a workers' (or employers') organization.[16]

At the United Nations level, the range of treaties under which individual complaints can be lodged is limited.[17] One omission of particular importance for present purposes is the lack of any procedure under the Convention on the Elimination of All Forms of Discrimination Against Women for receiving individual complaints. Nor is there a complaints procedure under the International Covenant on Economic, Social and Cultural Rights or the Convention on the Rights of the Child.

As a formal matter, this may not appear to be of any great moment, since a complaint of discrimination on the ground of sex in the enjoyment of almost any human right may be brought under Article 26 of the ICCPR, provided that the state concerned is a party to the First Optional Protocol to the Covenant. However, in practical terms it might well have a major impact on the outcome of a given case. Not only might one receive a more receptive hearing from CEDAW for a complaint alleging violations of women's human rights, but the substantive law to be applied might be somewhat more favorable under the Women's Convention. For example, the Women's Convention makes clear that a state party is under an obligation to eliminate all forms of discrimination including private acts of discrimination (Article 2); this obligation may be interpreted as more far-reaching than the obligations under the ICCPR to prevent or punish violations by private actors, which have been little explored in the case law of the Human Rights Committee.[18]

Admissibility criteria. In order for a complaint to be considered on the merits under one of the international communications procedures, *admissibility criteria* must be satisfied. These criteria normally prescribe the time limits for lodging complaints, the persons who may submit a complaint, requirements that domestic remedies be exhausted, and in some cases restrictions on considering complaints already considered under some other international procedure or currently being considered. Of course, the substantive coverage of the individual instruments is of considerable importance; any complaint lodged under one of these procedures may only be considered on the merits if it alleges a violation of one of the rights guaranteed by the governing instrument.

Procedures for processing a complaint vary. Before the UN treaty bodies, the hearing is on the papers, with both the complainant and the state concerned given the opportunity to respond to each other's submissions. Under the European Convention and the American Convention, there may be opportunities for oral hearings at different stages of the procedure. Under nearly all the procedures the decision adopted by the body examining the complaint is made public (the UNESCO procedure is an exception in this regard).

The decisions reached by the various bodies vary in their legal effect. While the decisions of the European Court and the Inter-American Court are binding on the states parties to a case, the views adopted by the UN treaty bodies or the reports adopted by the European Commission are not formally binding as a matter of international law.

(b) Problems with using individual communications procedures: general

The opportunity of bringing an individual complaint before a body that will consider it within the framework of a quasi-judicial model can be valuable in some cases and has a particular appeal from a legal perspective because of the possibility of a clear result.

However, the procedures that permit such complaints to be brought, while they bring the benefits of a procedure whose outcomes are legally binding either formally or in practice, have a number of drawbacks. For example, of the Human Rights Committee procedures, Bernard Graefrath has written: "But to protect the affected individual, let alone guarantee its subjective rights, the procedure can do little. It starts too late, takes too much time, does not lead to binding results and lacks any effective enforcement."[19] The utilization of these procedures to advance women's human rights may encounter not just the obstacles that meet nearly any attempt to use international mechanisms, but further obstacles as well.

(i) *Finding a procedure to which the state concerned is subject.* One of the difficulties frequently experienced in seeking to use individual complaint procedures (particularly at the universal level) arises from the voluntary nature of many of these procedures: the procedures or body that appears to provide the most effective avenue of redress does not have jurisdiction over the state against which a complaint is to be made. In the case of the UN human rights treaties, all individual complaint procedures are optional and require the state party to the treaty to accept the jurisdiction of the monitoring body to entertain complaints from individuals or groups alleging violations of rights protected by the treaties. Thus a state may be a party to a treaty and have accepted substantive obligations under it, but not necessarily have accepted the procedure in the treaty that allows individual complaints to be brought against it. As a result, it can often be the case that one's procedure of choice is not available and that one may have to make do with another procedure that may not be as good a fit for the substantive claim being advanced or that may provide a less hospitable forum for such a complaint or less effective remedies.[20]

The problem is less pronounced in the context of the European and American Conventions. Under the European Convention nearly all of the states parties to the Convention have accepted the competence of the European Commission and European Court to consider individual complaints, and within the Inter-American system all members of the Organization of American States are subject to the jurisdiction of the Inter-American Commission of Human Rights to entertain complaints alleging violations of the American Declaration of the Rights of Man. Furthermore, all 23 states parties to the American Convention are subject to a similar jurisdiction in relation to the Convention, and of these 14 have also accepted the jurisdiction of the Inter-American Court. The complaint procedure under the African Charter on Human and Peoples' Rights has not been used to protect women's rights, and there is no regional human rights treaty in the Asian region.

Under the UNESCO communications procedure, a complaint may be lodged against any member of the organization. As far as the ILO is concerned, freedom of association complaints can be lodged against any member of the ILO, while complaints alleging violations of specific ILO conventions can only be lodged against states parties to those conventions.

(ii) The slowness of the procedure. One major drawback in using individual complaint procedures is that it can take considerable time for any decision on the merits to be reached. Each of the individual complaints procedures (with the exception of the ILO procedures) is based on the traditional model of international redress, namely, that it is for the national system in the first instance to remedy violations of rights, and only if the national system has failed to do so, or is incapable of doing so, should an international body be presented with the complaint.

Accordingly, each procedure requires that domestic remedies be exhausted prior to the lodging of the complaint with the international body concerned. If legal or other remedies are arguably available within the national system, then the time taken to pursue them may be considerable, in most cases probably a matter of some years.

Even when domestic remedies have been exhausted and the matter can be taken up by an international body, the consideration of a case by such a body can itself take a considerable time, in some cases running into years. As happens so often in litigation at the national level, the person who wins a case may not derive particular benefit from the victory; in a sense, the successful complainant may have won the case for other people.

Whether the delay is worth putting up with will depend on the nature of the problem being addressed and the time frame within which those seeking to change law and practice are working. There may be other procedures or bodies available to which a complaint can be taken immediately (even though the same quasi-judicial procedure is not available) and it may be possible to pursue different avenues simultaneously.

(iii) *Composition of the bodies.* One of the factors that may impede efforts to utilize the various individual complaint procedures to advance women's rights is the composition of the adjudicatory bodies. Although the membership of these bodies is generally balanced to reflect diversity of regions, legal or cultural systems, and stages of development, they are overwhelmingly male. While men may indeed be sensitive to gender issues, it seems clear that the presence of (feminist) women on bodies of this sort generally can make an important difference.[21] Where novel claims or arguments that draw heavily on women's experiences are being presented, the male domination of these bodies may significantly reduce the chances that such an argument will be successful.

(iv) *The nature of the international decision-making process—institutional constraints and compromises.* One of the problems with taking an ultimately unsuccessful case to an international body is that it is very easy for the international standard (which should function as a floor below which national standards should not slip) to function at the national level as a ceiling for human rights protection.[22] If the national legislature, administration, and courts resist change in a given area and attempts to move them by appealing to national constitutional values (or even international standards when these form part of national law) have been unsuccessful, then taking the case to the international level may appear an attractive proposition. However, for various reasons an international tribunal may have considerably less freedom of movement than a national court in adopting a higher standard of rights protection. Losing a case at the international level may impede prospects for political and legal change at the national level, since a government may claim that the changes advocated are not required by international law.

Losing even a good case at the international level may be the result of the institutional demands on the system and the nature of the constituency of states that a particular treaty regime serves. Within the European Convention system, for example, the high volume of applications has meant that a large number of applications are screened out at the admissibility stage, in many cases summarily or with scanty and uninformative reasoning. It is often difficult to see why some cases with an apparently good factual and legal basis are excluded without any real consideration of the merits, but excluded they are and without the possibility of an appeal. A case that is advancing a novel reading of a guarantee—and this might include cases seeking to develop established jurisprudence for the promotion of women's rights—may be particularly vulnerable to this sort of summary procedure.

In such cases it is very easy for a national government to maintain, when a case has been dismissed on admissibility grounds, that its position has been vindicated by an international body (which, in a sense, it has) and that no further steps need to be taken since its position is in conformity with international law.

Similar results may follow even when there is full-fledged consideration of the merits. In most cases international bodies of this sort seek to reach decisions by consensus (although provision is made for individual opinions to be expressed). When a body consists of members from a wide range of national backgrounds who may have varying views, the result can easily be a compromise at the least common denominator level or a decision with little or no supporting reasoning.

(v) Margin of appreciation. Another feature of the approach developed by some international bodies when deciding whether a state has impermissibly restricted the enjoyment of a right is the concept of the *margin of appreciation*. When deciding whether a state has committed a violation of a guaranteed right, international bodies will frequently defer to the judgment of national authorities in areas where they consider that the state has an area of discretion and is particularly well placed to make an assessment of the appropriate course of action. The notion of a margin of appreciation at the international level, while somewhat analogous to national doctrines of the deference of the courts to the conclusions of the legislature, appears to give the national authorities a much greater freedom of movement than many of those doctrines.

This notion, largely developed in the jurisprudence of the European Court of Human Rights, is a malleable one, and the extent to which a national government may be afforded the benefit of the notion varies considerably from right to right and case to case.[23] This notion of the margin of appreciation has also been adopted by other international bodies (the Human Rights Committee, for example).[24]

The European Court has granted states a considerable margin of appreciation in the areas of national security, the protection of morals, and economic policy involved in expropriation and regulation of the use of property. In the area of "protection of morals," the various Strasbourg organs have allowed the national authorities considerable discretion where the activities that the state seeks to restrict or punish are "public," such as the distribution of publications like the *Little Red Schoolbook*[25] or "obscene" paintings.[26] Yet the doctrine has been not so generously applied in the context of sexuality (or, at least, in relation to homosexual acts in private between consenting adults).

One might expect that when considering controversial and sensitive issues, characterized by governments as issues of "morality" or "national or ethnic cultural identity," international supervisory organs would be more likely to defer to the judgment of the national authorities. While the European experience in this regard has been varied, it does appear that over time the Strasbourg organs have been less ready to defer in this way where they consider (some) fundamental questions of identity, sexuality, and family life to be concerned.[27] However, developments under the European Convention in relation to questions of discrimination and women's human rights have a mixed record; in any event it is probably unwise to generalize about possible outcomes under other treaties on the basis of the relatively small and homogeneous group of states that are parties to the European Convention.

In fact, one would surmise that the invocation of a doctrine like the margin of appreciation is more likely the broader the constituency of the supervisory body. Under a regional treaty such as the European Convention, where the Convention authorities are dealing with a reasonably homogeneous group of nations (at least until recently), it may be easier to identify a "European standard" of a "high" level. Under a universal human rights treaty, on the other hand, to which more than 100 states parties with a wide variety of cultures, legal systems, and stages of development are party, an international body might not so easily identify an actual or evolving international standard or, if it can do so, that standard may be heavily influenced by the least common denominator "drag"—the feeling that any decision must command a broad level of acceptance within the relevant constituency. Thus, a complaint brought to a regional organ might succeed, while the same complaint brought before an international body might fail, even though identical or similarly worded guarantees were invoked. For example, the first complaint against Australia under the Optional Protocol to the ICCPR alleges that laws criminalizing homosexual acts between consenting adults in private violate a number of articles of the Covenant, including those relating to discrimination and the right to privacy. Similar legislation has been held to be a violation of the guarantee of the right to respect for private life under the European

Convention (to which Australia is not and cannot become a party), but this does not automatically mean that the Human Rights Committee will hold that the legislation violates the Covenant.[28] The possibility of such an outcome has obvious implications for choice of venue—assuming there is a choice.

(vi) Legal effect of decisions of the adjudicative body. The nature of the decision that emerges at the end of an individual complaint procedure varies. In the case of the judgments of the European Court and the Inter-American Court, the decisions are binding on the state that is a respondent in the case. The views expressed by the European Commission of Human Rights in its reports, however, are not formally binding, though the decision on the case made by the Committee of Ministers (if the case has not been referred to the European Court) is binding as a matter of international law.

Under the UN procedures, the "views" adopted by the treaty committees are not formally binding as a matter of international law, although of the Human Rights Committee it has been said that "Normally, it may be expected that States ratifying the Protocol will show themselves inclined to follow the opinion of the Committee, even when it goes against them."[29]

In general, it is true to say that where decisions are rendered against a state under one of these procedures, the state will take steps to bring its domestic law and practice into conformity with the international law position as determined or opined by the relevant supervisory body. However, this is not to say that there are not exceptions or that the steps taken by a state party to rectify inconsistencies will adopt a generous approach to remedying the defects identified by the international body.

(vii) Conceptual framework of human rights adjudication. The limitations of the conceptual framework of the mainstream human rights framework(s) have often been raised. It is certainly the case that advancing particular types of claims within the mainstream is more difficult than pressing other claims that more closely fit the dominant conceptual framework. For example, mainstream bodies can deal reasonably well with straightforward claims of differential treatment on the basis of sex in law or the practice of public authorities. However, they have considerably more difficulty in responding to claims that challenge the distinction between public and private and that seek to attribute responsibility to a state for violations committed by private individuals acting as such. Since so many of the violations of human dignity are suffered at the hands of private individuals, the question of the responsibility of the state for private violations is of fundamental importance for women's rights.

(viii) "One Statism"? The individual complaints procedures are generally "one statist" in nature, focusing on the acts of a state within its physical territory or within its jurisdiction in the extended sense of that term. This means that there may be problems in using such procedures to address violations in which two or more states may be implicated, for example, trafficking in women and children across national boundaries or sex tourism. Although there would appear to be nothing to prevent complaints being brought against two states if both had submitted to the relevant procedure, such cases are relatively unusual.[30] It may be that it is easier to bring such cases under procedures other than the individual complaint procedures. In such a case, resort to one of the political fora or to one of the policy-making bodies that is prepared to receive communications as part of its general work may be the only alternative available.

This statist orientation of the individual complaints procedures also makes it difficult to bring a complaint where the gist of the violation alleged arises from international power imbalances and exploitation, for example, the role that multinational companies may play in the free economic zones in various countries in Asia.

(ix) The possibilities and the dangers. There are obvious dangers in bringing a case before an international body and losing. However, there are also dangers in bringing a case and winning. *Abdulaziz v. United Kingdom*[31] illustrates how a success internationally may have unanticipated effects at the national level if the government found to have violated rights guarantees seeks the least generous interpretation of those guarantees consistent with the decision of the international body concerned.

In *Abdulaziz*, a challenge to provisions of the United Kingdom's immigration law that permitted men who were citizens of the United Kingdom or residents there to bring their wives into the country but which did not provide the same entitlement to women in the same position succeeded on the basis that this amounted to discrimination against the women concerned in the enjoyment of their right to respect for family life. The reaction of the United Kingdom's government to the judgment of the European Court was not to extend to women the entitlement to bring in their spouses, but to restrict considerably the entitlement of the categories of men who were so entitled and to apply those entitlements across the board.[32]

(c) Petition information mechanisms or procedures

In addition to the complaint recourse mechanisms, there are a number of other procedures for the reception and consideration of complaints, not as part of a process leading to a resolution or adjudication of the individual complaints themselves but as a source of information on the human rights situation in individual countries or for policy development along thematic lines.

Within the UN system, the best known of these is the Resolution 1503 procedure, the first major procedure for the consideration of individual complaints which took effect within the UN human rights framework; also of interest is the communications procedure of the Commission on the Status of Women.

The procedure for the receipt of communications laid down in ECOSOC Resolution 1503 (XLVIII) is intended to identify situations in which there appears to be a consistent pattern of gross and reliably attested violations of human rights so that appropriate action may be taken by the Commission on Human Rights. The procedure has three stages. First, an initial examination of communications by a working group of the Sub-Commission on Prevention of Discrimination and Protection of Minorities is made to select those communications that appear to reveal a consistent pattern of gross violations. These are then referred to the full Sub-Commission, which may then refer situations to the Commission on Human Rights for its consideration. Communications must satisfy admissibility criteria, and the whole procedure is confidential unless and until the Commission on Human Rights decides to make recommendations to ECOSOC. Those who submit communications play no formal role in the process after their communications have been submitted.

While the 1503 procedure was an important step forward when it was adopted over twenty years ago, there has been much criticism of its operations and of its limitations for providing timely and effective responses to gross violations of human rights. The development of the wide variety of alternative mechanisms for dealing with complaints since the adoption of the 1503 procedure now means that there may be more effective and more transparent alternative procedures available.

So far as addressing issues of sex discrimination or violations of human rights that have a significant gender dimension, it seems that the Resolution 1503 procedure has made little contribution.[33]

(i) The communications procedure of the Commission on the Status of Women. The UN Commission on the Status of Women (CSW) also has the power to receive communications relating to the status of women. The procedure is a relatively little known and little used one.[34] The communications (UN jargon for "complaints") are received as a source of information for the Commission on which it can draw in its own policy making and its recommendation to the ECOSOC. The communications are considered by a working group of the Commission, which

reports to the Commission on the trends and patterns of discrimination against women revealed by the communications. The proceedings are confidential and the persons who submit the communications have no role in their consideration (and until recently, were not even informed of any recommendations the Commission might have made in response to the communications received). It has not made a major contribution to the policy-making work of the Commission and does not appear to have provided as a by-product an avenue for redress of specific grievances.

The procedure was recently the subject of a comprehensive review[35] and the Commission considered what improvements (if any) should be made at its 1991 and 1992 sessions. However, the Commission was reluctant to make more than minor changes to the procedure and the procedure still remains essentially unchanged.[36] This is not to say, however, that more creative and effective use of this procedure is not possible.

(ii) Working Group on Disappearances and Working Group on Detention. In addition to the mechanism of the Special Rapporteur there are two thematic working groups of the Commission on Human Rights which, although perhaps not formally designated as such, have a complaint recourse function. The Working Group on Disappearances was established in 1979 and in fact pre-dated any of the thematic Special Rapporteurs.[37] The Working Group on Arbitrary Detention was established only in 1991. The group was entrusted with the task of investigating cases of detention imposed arbitrarily or inconsistently with international law standards. In performing its task, it is to seek and receive information from governments and from individuals, their families, and their representatives.[38] While neither procedure at first sight appears to offer an avenue for pursuing gender-specific human rights violations, the new Working Group on Detentions may well offer some opportunities.

(iii) Thematic rapporteurs. An important development in the Commission on Human Rights in the last ten years has been the adoption of the mechanism of the thematic special rapporteur. The Commission has appointed four special rapporteurs with mandates covering summary and arbitrary executions, torture, religious intolerance, the sale of children, racism and xenophobia, freedom of opinion and expression, mercenaries, and internally displaced persons.

The functions of the Special Rapporteurs were recently described in the following terms:

133. The functions of the individual Rapporteurs vary according to the different mandates granted to them by the Commission. They include the collec-

tion of information about the observance or violation of specific rights, the receipt and forwarding to Governments of communications received from individuals or organizations alleging violation of the rights which fall within the relevant mandate (in some cases as a matter of urgent action), reporting on the extent and practice of the violations of the relevant rights, formulating policy recommendations and, in some cases, visiting individual countries at the invitation of those countries.

134. The report of each rapporteur to the Commission on Human Rights is a public document that contains summaries of communications and of replies from Governments, as well as more general material. The Rapporteurs do not adjudicate on the accuracy of the allegations contained in material which they receive from individuals and organizations or from Governments in reply.[39]

A number of the Rapporteurs could provide a useful avenue for filing claims of violations of women's human rights. Relatively little use of these procedures has been made to date.

Other Procedures

(a) Reporting procedures under the treaties[40]

Under all major UN human rights treaties, a system of reporting by states parties is provided for. States parties are required to report on a regular basis to the responsible supervisory body on the steps that they have taken to implement their obligations, and the difficulties they have experienced in doing so. These reports are then examined by the relevant treaty body in the presence of representatives of the state concerned. All the committees receive information informally from non-governmental organizations which they may use in their questioning of states.

The examination of a state's report under a treaty can provide an occasion for exerting international pressure on the state. If members of a supervisory body are strongly critical of a state, or express the view that the state has not carried out its obligations under the treaty, this can serve to put some pressure on a government, particularly if the proceedings receive publicity internationally or nationally.

It can be difficult to use this procedure effectively. First, even the knowledge that a country is party to an instrument that requires it to report is not likely to be widespread, and even those in the know may have trouble in tracking the submission of government reports and the timetable for their consideration by the committee concerned. Second, national groups who might be able to exploit such an opportunity may know little about the procedure, the appropriate format for the submission of material and how most effectively to lobby members of the committee or to generate publicity. Furthermore, the consideration of a state's report by the monitoring body is generally contingent on the submission of a report by that state. Many states have fallen well behind in fulfilling their reporting obligations (and some have even failed to submit any reports under individual treaties). It is also a matter of chance whether a state is scheduled to appear before a treaty body that will be considering the substantive issues one may wish to raise before it. Add to this the fact that the meetings of these bodies are held in Geneva, New York, or Vienna and the cost of bringing people to brief members may quickly become prohibitive. While there are many international NGOs with a presence in these places, there appear to be only a few which make a conscious effort to keep national NGOs informed of when a country's next report is due and to liaise with them.

Despite these difficulties, with a certain amount of preparedness, the proceedings before the treaty bodies can be used quite effectively. For example, after the 1989 crackdown on the pro-democracy movement in China, NGOs in Hong Kong and international NGOs took the issue to a number of UN fora, including not just the Sub-Commission and the Commission on Human Rights but also the Committee Against Torture and the Committee on the Elimination of Racial Discrimination, before which China happened to have reports considered in the period following the 1989 crackdown. To date, with the exception of CEDAW, there has been relatively little material relating to gender issues placed before the various treaty bodies. A recent exception before the Human Rights Committee was the case of Hong Kong at the hearing on the United Kingdom's report held in April 1991. The Hong Kong Council of Women submitted a detailed report on the nature of discrimination against women in Hong Kong. Unfortunately, due to the time constraints of the Committee, relatively little in that report was followed up in questioning by the Committee.

(b) "Political" and "policy" bodies

In addition to the procedures that are formally designated as complaint procedures, or under which allegations of human rights violations may be taken to treaty bodies as part of their review of country reports, a number of other procedures are available. They might be described as the "thematic" and expert bodies, on the one hand and the political bodies on the other.

Within the UN system there are various bodies which examine particular themes and which, although they may not have a specific mandate to consider complaints of human rights violations, may nonetheless receive these as part of the information-gathering. For example, the Working Group on Contemporary Forms of Slavery, a working group of the Sub-commission on Prevention of Discrimination and Protection of Minorities, is a body that considers among other issues the question of trafficking in women and children. (Since there is no monitoring or enforcement mechanism provided for under a number of the major conventions dealing with prostitution and trafficking in women,[41] this body has assumed something of that task.) In so doing it receives information and complaints from NGOs. Considerable use has been made of this forum in recent years by NGOs working in the field. Although taking a matter to this body essentially only provides a forum for publicity, states referred to in NGO submissions frequently attend and respond to allegations of rights violations.[42] The Working Group on Traditional Practices of the Sub-Commission played a similar role in investigating the existence and extent of various traditional practices affecting the health of women and children (including female circumcision, son preference, and similar practices).[43]

The Sub-Commission on Prevention of Discrimination and Protection of Minorities also provides a forum in which country-specific allegations of rights violations may be raised in public debate.[44]

The "political" organs of the UN also provide a forum for airing human rights grievances in public session. These may provide an opportunity to place the spotlight on abuses in an individual country, and publicity is the major benefit to be gained from using such fora. In fairly egregious cases of rights violations it may be that such a body would be prepared to place additional pressure on a state by adopting a resolution ranging from expressions of concern to expressions of condemnation and even the establishment of a special mechanism to investigate the condition in a country.

The main forum of this sort within the United Nations is the Commission on Human Rights, which meets annually early in the year. On its agenda is a wide range of issues and it considers allegations of human rights violations in individual countries as well as thematic issues.[45]

The Commission on the Status of Women is also an available forum. Technically of the same status as the Commission on Human Rights, the CSW meets once a year for a relatively brief period of two weeks. Interestingly, the CSW has not followed the path of the Commission on Human Rights in debating alleged violations of human rights in particular countries (although as mentioned above, it does consider these by way of its rather ineffectual confidential communications procedure). As Laura Reanda comments,

there has been no concerted attempt to expand the role of the Commission [on the Status of Women] into a monitoring mechanism with powers of investigation, such as is the case with the Commission on Human Rights.

Clearly, the problem of implementation of women's rights was posed differently from that of human rights. Policies were directed not at attempting to detect violations and ensure respect for basic rights, but rather at assisting governments in identifying needs and encouraging them to adopt enlightened social policies which would promote the "advancement" of women.[46]

The difficulties with using such procedures can be surmised. The politicized nature of such bodies can make the merits of a complaint seem almost irrelevant, and whether action of any sort is taken depends largely on success in building coalitions between various countries and regional groups. This requires presence at such meetings and familiarity with the procedures. Nonetheless, the use of a political forum may be one way of bringing a matter quickly to the international level.

What Fruit Has the Use of International Procedures Borne So Far?

The international procedures for the consideration of individual complaints appear to have borne relatively little fruit in terms of women's rights. Overall, it seems that relatively few complaints of gender-specific violations have been brought under the procedures. There have, it is true, been a number of important cases in which the right to nondiscrimination has been firmly upheld[47] or in which a decision based on violation of a substantive right has advanced women's interests.[48] But there have also been cases one would have thought relatively straightforward in terms of sex discrimination that have come out unfavorably. Furthermore, in the area of reproductive rights the record has been somewhat mixed, with decisions that promote the rights of women,[49] but also those which both in their reasoning and their result are less satisfactory.[50]

There have been relatively few attempts to bring a broad range of issues before these bodies, in particular issues relating to economic, social, and cultural rights or to the responsibility of states for rights violations by private individuals.[51]

The same pattern has been replicated in the other procedures; there has been relatively little use of the ILO or Resolution 1503 procedures to raise women's rights violations. There have been some efforts made under the aegis of the Special Rapporteurs and within the framework of the various thematic working groups. As part of a recent review of the communications procedure of the UN Commission on the Status of Women by that Commission, the extent to which violations of women's human rights or human rights violations of special concern to women have been taken up and addressed within the communication procedures of the United Nations human rights bodies, ILO and UNESCO was reviewed. The conclusion was that there had been relatively little attention devoted to violations of women's rights within the framework of the mainstream procedures.[52]

The reasons are no doubt many. Primary among them must be the lack of knowledge about the available procedures and how to go about using them. For those who are familiar with them, a reluctance to use procedures under which redress may be long in coming (if it comes at all) or ineffectual, or which (for whatever reason) offers limited prospects of success may also be evident. Within the European context the law of the European Community may offer a more satisfactory and expeditious route. An assessment that energies would be better spent in activism at the national level and the possibility of an unfavorable or unhelpful result may also deter groups from bringing cases before international bodies.

The Possibilities

This rather somber recounting of the limitations of international procedures and the problems that can arise in attempting to use them is not intended to suggest that the use of international procedures is hardly worth considering. In fact my view is that considerably more effective use of some of these procedures is possible with an appropriate coordination of groups at the national and international levels.

Some Suggestions for Action

The following section contains a number of suggestions for action that may promote the enforcement and implementation of human rights standards so far as women are concerned. They concern action that could be taken by those working at the international and national level and jointly.

(a) Making international law for use internationally and domestically

The rights guaranteed by international instruments and the practices that surround their interpretation and implementation are not set in concrete, nor are those who have until now dominated the exegesis of those rights fated or entitled to remain the sole decoders of the meaning of human rights guarantees. Portrayals of rights discourse as a "site of struggle" or a "site of dialogue"[53] are useful in this context, since they make clear the negotiability and the political process that is the interpretation of rights, even (or particularly) in formalized (quasi-)judicial contexts. The critiques of the limitations of international rights discourse for women have included arguments that those "dialoguing" are simply not talking about issues of fundamental concern to women. Part of any overall strategy to use international human rights discourse more extensively must be a concerted effort to expand the range of participants in that dialogue. Karen Engle argues that the history of the development of human rights law has been the history of challenges from the margins by those who have been excluded from participation in the discourse.[54] Accordingly, there is a need to appropriate some of the power of defining the content of human rights in order to challenge narrow androcentric models and to address issues of central concern to women. Standard renderings of the dynamic nature of the interpretation of human rights norms and procedures highlight the need to respond to changing social conditions and concerns; expanding the range of participants and perspectives in that dialogue is certainly a start.

(b) Strengthening existing enforcement mechanisms and developing new ones to address human rights violations of particular concern to women

It is important that the existing enforcement mechanisms under which violations of women's human rights be strengthened and that new enforcement procedures be adopted for that purpose. There are at least three areas in which action could be taken to this end. The first is to press for further, substantial improvements to the communications procedure of the CSW. While at present there may seem to be little prospect for a total revamping of the procedure, this and other alternatives (such as a Special Rapporteur on specific issues such as violence) are still worth pursuing. This is largely a political strategy, but support from non-governmental organizations may play a role in advancing those developments that have already taken place.

Second, there is much to be said for supporting the establishment of individual complaint procedures under treaties that do not yet have them. Of particular importance in this regard are both the Convention on the Elimination of All Forms of Discrimination Against Women and the International Covenant on Economic, Social and Cultural Rights. While CEDAW (and the CSW) have discussed in a rather cursory fashion the possibility of an individual complaints procedure under the Women's Convention, that discussion has not progressed very far, although the idea did receive support at the June 1993 World Conference on Human Rights. The Committee on Economic, Social, and Cultural Rights has taken the discussion a little further, though the matter does not seem to have progressed beyond discussions in the Committee of a number of the substantive and procedural issues to which such a procedure might give rise. The prospect of an Optional Protocol to both these treaties gives rise to similar types of issues, in particular objections suggesting that the rights guaranteed are to be implemented progressively and are not suitable for (quasi-)judicial enforcement procedures.

In this area both NGOs, states, and institutions (including donors) may have a role to play. One way to develop serious momentum for an Optional Protocol to, say the Women's Convention, would be a thematic conference at which human rights experts, women's groups, and others (including representatives of sympathetic states) could discuss the issue. For example, much of the impetus within the UN for the elaboration of the Draft Declaration on Violence Against Women can be attributed to the Government of Canada, which funded an expert group meeting in October 1991 to discuss the development of an instrument concerning violence against women.

(c) Increasing the feminist presence on human rights bodies

One obvious goal that needs to be more vigorously pursued is that of increasing the representation of women on the various human rights bodies. Such a course of action involves close liaison between national and international NGOs, and the support of sympathetic governments.

(d) Using existing procedures to greater effect

There are many opportunities within the current range of procedures for increasing the visibility of violations of women's human rights, developing law and practice to take greater cognizance of them, and deploying international procedures to enhance the enjoyment of human rights for women.

In terms of strictly judicial proceedings, one strategy that might be explored further than it has been already is the possibility of intervention before such a body by an organization with a demonstrated interest in the subject matter of the litigation. Intervention by *amici curiae* may often have a critical impact on a case, as the result of putting before the court relevant material it might not otherwise have received. While this sort of intervention is well developed in a number of national legal systems, it is less so at the international level (although there have been a number of cases in which NGOs have intervened in cases before the European Court and the Inter-American Court).[55]

Among the procedures that appear to be underutilized are the complaint procedures of the ILO. It is possible under Article 24 of the ILO for a complaint to be lodged against a member state of the ILO that the state has failed to secure the observance of a convention to which it is a party. The ILO has adopted a number of conventions dealing with issues of importance for women. The most prominent are the two antidiscrimination conventions dealing with equal pay and discrimination in employment and occupation (ILO Nos. 100 and 111), but there are many other conventions dealing with labor and social issues which could be used as vehicles for pressing human rights claims for women. While individuals cannot lodge complaints, it may be possible to find a national or international workers' organization prepared to do so.

The procedures of the Committee Against Torture may also provide some scope for bringing issues relating to violence against women to the international level. Although the Committee has so far shown a considerable degree of myopia in relation to torture of women (even in the context of traditional violations where the torture is inflicted by a state agent),[56] it may be that in the course of time the Committee will be persuaded to take an expansive view of the definition of torture in the Convention and apply the Convention to private violence against women in which the state acquiesces.

Article 22 of the Convention Against Torture creates an individual complaint procedure that must be accepted by a state if a complaint is to be brought against it).[57] Article 20 of the Convention establishes a procedure whereby the Committee may initiate an inquiry into the situation in a state if the Committee has received "reliable information which appears to it to contain well-founded indications that torture is being systematically practised in the territory of a state party."[58] A state is bound by this procedure unless it opts out of it at the time of ratification. Of the 71 states parties to the Convention as of 31 December 1992, 65 were bound by the article 20 procedure.

As a matter of practice it is likely to be information supplied by NGOs that triggers the invocation of the Article 20 procedure.

The *communications procedure of the CSW* remains considerably under-utilized in terms of its potential. While the procedure is flawed in important respects, it may be possible to use it to greater effect. At present many of the communications submitted to the Commission are fairly brief and lack full documentation, thus permitting them to be dismissed easily by governments. The confidential nature of the procedure also permits governments to escape accountability.

However, there appears to be nothing to prevent an NGO that submits a communication from sending a copy of the full communication not just to the government concerned, but to all members of the CSW (who typically receive only summaries). Furthermore, there appears to be no reason why the contents of the communication cannot be made public by the body that submits it with a request to the government concerned to make public its response to the CSW (some governments have already expressed their willingness to provide their replies to the complainant and some have indeed done so). If an approach of this sort were combined with close liaison with members of the CSW, the procedure could provide a greater measure of leverage on governments than it has to date.

A greater use could also be made of the *thematic procedures* of the Commission on Human Rights, in particular the thematic Special Rapporteurs. As already mentioned, these procedures can provide a means of urgent action in appropriate cases as well as a public revelation of complaints and government replies. The appropriate mechanism to use depends, of course, on the nature of the violation. However, the Special Rapporteur on Torture may provide an important forum in which to raise issues of violence against women, both state-inflicted and state-condoned.

The Special Rapporteur has, for example, accepted that rape may constitute "torture" as that term is defined in his mandate. For example, his first report listed rape under the general heading of "sexual aggression" as a form of torture.[59] In discussing the "grey" area of his mandate (conduct that falls between "torture" and other forms of ill treatment, which are not explicitly included in his mandate), he refers also to other forms of sexual abuse, although his main concern seems to be sexual abuse of male prisoners by other males.[60] He also refers on a number of occasions to traditional practices affecting the health of women and children and notes that the state may incur responsibility for such actions as a result of its attitude to such acts committed by private persons and, more generally, in relation to the practices per se.[61] Consistent with this approach he has forwarded to governments allegations of rape inflicted on female detainees or female relatives of detainees.[62]

This procedure, which is quite accessible and cheap to use, may therefore provide an opportunity to bring cases relating to violence against women to the international forum where the state concerned will be under a certain amount of pressure.

(e) A more effective use of reporting procedures under the various UN human rights treaties

The opportunities presented by the consideration of country reports by the various treaty bodies may be useful for exerting additional pressure on a national government. At present, with the exception of CEDAW, relatively little use is made of such occasions by national groups (or, indeed, international groups) to present information about rights violations of particular concern to women. Even in the case of CEDAW, while the flow of information and the attendance of national groups at its sessions has been increasing, the publicity given to these sessions at the international and national levels and the follow-up at the national level still have a long way to go before the full potential of the reporting procedure can be utilized.

All the treaty bodies offer opportunities for a gender perspective to be advanced. While the general human rights treaties (the ICCPR and the ICESCR) together with the Women's Convention offer the broadest range of substantive rights, issues of discrimination against women belonging to a racial or ethnic minority can be raised under the Racial Discrimination Convention.[63] Mention has already been made of some of the issues that could be raised under the Torture Convention, and the Convention on the Rights of the Child also covers a number of areas in which there are important gender-related violations that could be addressed.

It is also important to bring these matters before the Human Rights Committee under the ICCPR, since that body has considerable status in defining discourse within the UN structure. Equally important is the exploitation of the opportunities offered by the Committee on Economic, Social, and Cultural Rights, a body still in the early stages of its work with the Economic Covenant and thirsty for information from NGOs and for thematic input on which it can draw to develop its jurisprudence. For example, the Committee has already formulated a number of general comments, including one dealing with nondiscrimination in the enjoyment of the rights guaranteed by the Covenant and, most recently, on the right to adequate housing. Since many violations of women's rights occur in the area of economic, social, and cultural rights and this is one of the few international fora concentrating on these rights, it is an important committee to work with for those who wish to advance women's rights in the area of economic, social and cultural rights. Whether one treaty body or another can be utilized will depend not just on the substantive issue one wishes to raise (there is after all considerable overlap between some of the treaties), but also on whether the country in question has submitted a report which is to be reviewed at a suitable time.

For more effective use of reporting procedures, much needs to be done to disseminate knowledge about the process and its potentialities, as well as to ensure that national groups are made aware of the submission by governments of reports and the time when they are to be examined by the relevant treaty body. There may be a need for further training programs in which national NGOs can be involved, to build connections between them and organizations active at the international level and be able to follow the day to day activities of the treaty bodies. In some cases greater efforts may need to be made by the secretariat to make documents available to NGOs in particular countries who are not on the regular distribution lists and therefore unlikely to be aware of recent events. Responsibility also devolves on the members of the committees assigned to act as country rapporteur for a report. Sometimes little or no effort may be made to contact groups in the countries concerned (and these are unlikely to be women's groups). Reliance on these NGOs that regularly support the mainstream committees may also fail to ensure that a gender perspective is brought to the committee, since many of those groups have no special interest in this and may not have good contacts at the national level.

(f) The substantive issues

The suggestions above relate to the more effective use of procedures and do not deal with questions of substance (except to the extent that only complaints that fall within the scope of the relevant treaty will be maintainable under the respective procedures). However, it may be that a broad-ranging thematic strategy adopted across a range of bodies and procedures would be effective. Amnesty International, for example, was extremely effective in its campaign against torture, bringing the matter to the center of the international human rights stage by a concerted campaign. Other issues pursued in this way included the question of disappearances. It may be that one major issue or a selected range of issues could be actively brought before a number of human rights bodies, ranging from the political bodies to the treaty committees in both their monitoring and adjudicative roles. To put violence against women on the agenda of every major human rights body at the international and regional level, for example, has become a goal that has recently been pursued with some success.

The substantive rights that will be of particular interest to those interested in utilizing the international system will be the product of the experiences of those whose rights are violated. Nonetheless, there appear to be two general areas in which the substantive law of human rights as it may particularly affect women needs theoretical and practical development. Those areas are the responsibility of the state arising out of human rights violations perpetrated by private individuals (and perhaps also the international responsibility of private individuals themselves) and the area of women's enjoyment of economic, social, and cultural rights. Both are themes which so far as women's human rights are concerned (and perhaps generally) are deserving of considerable development in the substantive law and practice of the international human rights regime.

(g) Creating one's own jurisprudence

As suggested above, the substantive content of human rights guarantees is malleable in many respects and the struggle over meaning is a political struggle carried out through legal discourse. Thus there are opportunities to influence decisively the direction in which international jurisprudence relating to the human rights of women develops and to take that international jurisprudence back to the national level.

While one can influence the development of case law by bringing appropriate cases and perhaps intervening in others, this process can be somewhat sporadic, though valuable. However, one other area in which significant contributions could be made in the development of international standards is in developing the *jurisprudence* in a broad sense of the various treaty bodies. The UN treaty bodies have power to make general comments, or general recommendations, a power that the Human Rights Committee has seized on to elaborate its understanding of individual articles of the Convention. It has been followed in that endeavor by the Committee on Economic, Social and Cultural Rights and also by the Committee on the Elimination of Discrimination Against Women.

These detailed general comments can be particularly useful for invoking a detailed elaboration of the broadly worded guarantees of the various treaties and may be particularly useful for that purpose in the domestic political and even judicial context. For example, the general comments of the Human Rights Committee under the ICCPR have been regularly cited to and by courts in relation to the interpretation of the Hong Kong Bill of Rights, which incorporates the ICCPR as part of domestic law.[64] With the exception of CEDAW's general recommendations, gender plays a relatively minor role in the general comments of the other committees.

In the case of the ESCRC and CEDAW, the formulation of general comments and general recommendations of a detailed sort is still in its early stages. The committees are grateful for and in need of expert input from NGOs and this provides an excellent opportunity for women's groups to help shape the jurisprudence that emerges through this process. The most recent general comment of the ESCRC dealing with the right to adequate housing was heavily influenced by the contribution of Habitat International, and the recent CEDAW general recommendation on violence (1992) had considerable input from NGOs. The International League for Human Rights organized, in collaboration with the International Women's Rights Action Watch, a pre-session seminar dealing with violence against women in the context of international human rights law and the Convention, which a number of CEDAW members attended.[65] The work of all the treaty bodies in this regard provides an important opportunity to help shape human rights jurisprudence in a way that will benefit women.

(h) Using international procedures—some necessary steps

Any consideration of whether to take a case internationally involves the consideration of a large number of issues.[66] It will normally involve the following steps (the order is not necessarily linear):

- Identifying the violations (and their causes) and conceptualizing them in terms of international human rights instruments at an early stage (even when initiating domestic proceedings). Knowledge of the admissibility requirements of an international communications procedure that may eventually be used may be crucial for planning a case at the national level that will satisfy these criteria. The requirement that local remedies be exhausted, for example, may require that applicable international standards have been invoked formally or in substance in the national proceedings. Failure to do so (even if the invocation would very likely not have any impact on the outcome of the national proceedings) may mean that domestic remedies have not been exhausted and the complaint cannot proceed at the international level.
- Identifying an appropriate body or procedure.
- Identifying the goals to be achieved by taking the issue or case to an international body.
- Assessing whether the time and energy required in a particular case is a useful and efficient utilization of precious resource.
- Liaison with a local or international NGO with experience in dealing with the body concerned or using the procedure.
- Preparation and submission of the complaint or other documentation.
- Follow up/lobbying/presentation of the material.
- Bringing the international back home (publicity).

Bringing the International Back Home: Using International Law in the National Forum

I have suggested above that there is something to be said for steps to promote the greater use of international standards and comparative material at the national level in the legal and political contexts. To do so effectively requires the collection and dissemination of information about developments at the international level and in other countries and the provision of resource centers which are available to provide assistance as and when it is needed. Some of this is already happening, both in relation to human rights issues generally and in relation to women's rights in particular.[67] One may have to exercise some care in the selection of appropriate case law, since much national case law interpreting international human rights guarantees of concern to women seems to run counter to the underlying principles embodied in those guarantees.[68]

However, the Commonwealth Secretariat has been especially supportive of a number of judicial colloquia to introduce judges in Commonwealth countries to international human rights standards and jurisprudence—a strategy that appears to be having some impact. A similar strategy focusing on women's rights might well bring similar benefits. However, although such a colloquium has been proposed to the Commonwealth Secretariat, the Secretariat has not apparently viewed this as a priority, even though it has already organized five judicial colloquia on the application of international human rights norms domestically, none of which dealt in any detail with women's rights.

Obviously, the legal efficacy of invoking international standards will vary from country to country, as will the strategic and tactical benefits or drawbacks of appealing to an international forum or invoking international standards. For example, the Australian federal Sex Discrimination Commissioner has intervened in a number of cases before industrial courts in order to present arguments based on the Women's Convention and its implementing legislation.[69]

International standards can be invoked not just in the curial context but also in the legislative and administrative contexts. The invocation of international standards in the curial context will be influenced by the nature of the legal system involved and the extent to which international treaty or customary law forms part of national law and the extent to which specific treaty obligations have been translated into domestic law.

In common law systems, apart from the situation where a treaty has been directly incorporated or there is a statute that is clearly intended to implement specific treaty obligations, the system (its judges and legal practitioners) has a certain resistance to the invocation of international legal standards. Quite apart from systemic and conceptual barriers, working with international materials in a context where positive law "counts" can be difficult.[70] International law sources are often unfamiliar in origin and presentation and often frustratingly elusive in their vagueness or statement of principle, and applying them to the facts of a particular case can easily perplex a judge trained in common law tradition. Nonetheless, much can be done, both to acculturate lawyers at the national level to international standards (the process is likely to take some time) and also to make law at the national level that may inform the further elaboration of international standards in a manner that can be put to use in the context of other national systems.

The Need for Knowledge and Access

A common thread running through many of the suggestions made above is the need to spread knowledge about the existence and potential of the various international procedures available and to build better linkages between organizations working at the national level and those working at the international level. One suggestion I have made elsewhere is that of a manual that would present, from a gender-specific perspective, the ways in which international procedures might be exploited as part of the struggle to advance women's position, as well as to identify ways international and comparative law might be brought back home and incorporated to the domestic legal system.

Conclusion

The range of human rights guarantees and bodies with responsibility for developing, monitoring compliance with, or enforcing these standards means that there are significant opportunities for bringing violations of women's human rights to international fora as part of a campaign to respond to these violations. The gains that can be achieved by resorting to such procedures will vary considerably, but in many cases additional international pressure on a government may be a path worth pursuing. While ultimately an assessment has to be made whether the time and resources required to take matters to the international level are an efficient way to proceed, there are many possibilities for advancing the human rights of women in the short and long term.

There are many situations in which national law and practice appeared incapable—in the short term at least—of responding adequately to violations of women's human rights. At the end of the day, the question is whether any of the myriad procedures referred to in the course of this chapter offer any further possibilities for responding to such violations.

With thanks to Julian, whose teething troubles helped shape the form and content of this paper.

Notes

1. See Laura Reanda, "The Commission on the Status of Women," in *The United Nations and Human Rights: A Critical Appraisal,* ed. Philip Alston (Oxford: Clarendon Press, 1992), 265, 281–89.

2. The development of a new international instrument on violence against women, currently before the Commission on the Status of Women, is an example of this. See U.N. Doc. E/CN.6/1992/WG.2/L.3 (1992) for the draft as of the end of 1992.

3. Compare Bernard Graefrath, "Reporting and Complaint Systems in Universal Human Rights Treaties," in *Human Rights in a Changing East/West Perspective,* ed. Allan Rosas and Jan Helgesen (London and New York: Pinter, 1990), 290–91.

4. See generally Karen Engle, "International Human Rights and Feminism: When Discourses Meet," *Mich. J. Int'l L.* 13 (1992): 517.

5. See generally Chaloka Beyani, "Toward a More Effective Guarantee of Women's Rights in the African Human Rights System," Chapter 11 in this book; and Cecilia Medina, "Toward a More Effective Guarantee of the Enjoyment of Human Rights by Women in the Inter-American System," Chapter 10 in this book.

6. See generally Anne Bayefsky, "General Approaches to Domestic Application of Women's International Human Rights Law," Chapter 15 in this book.

7. See, for example, Radhika Coomaraswamy, "To Bellow like a Cow: Women, Ethnicity, and the Discourse of Rights," Chapter 2 in this book; Celina Romany, "State Responsibility Goes Private: A Feminist Critique of the Public/Private Distinction in International Human Rights Law," Chapter 4 in this book; and Adetoun O. Ilumoka, "African Women's International Economic, Social, and Cultural Rights—Toward a Relevant Theory and Practice," Chapter 12 in this book.

8. See generally Ratna Kapur, "Feminism, Fundamentalism, and Rights Rhetoric in India," in *Women Living Under Muslin Law, Special Bulletin on Fundamentalism and Secularism in South Asia* (Lahore: Shirkat Gah, 1992), 35–36.

9. See generally Elizabeth A. Sheehy, "Feminist Argumentation Before the Supreme Court of Canada in *R v. Seaboyer*"; *R v. Gayme:* "The Sound of One Hand Clapping," *Melb. Univ. L. Rev.* 18 (1991): 450.

10. See generally Chandra Mohanty, "Under Western Eyes: Feminist Scholarship and Colonial Discourses," in *Third World Women and the Politics of Feminism,* ed. Chandra Mohanty, Ann Russo, and Lourdes Torres (Bloomington and Indianapolis: Indiana University Press, 1991), 51; Elizabeth V. Spelman, *Inessential Woman: Problems of Exclusion in Feminist Thought* (Boston: Beacon Press, 1988).

11. For a recent overview, see Andrew Byrnes, "International Human Rights Procedures," Appendix IV in Commonwealth Human Rights Initiative, *Put Our World to Rights* (London: Commonwealth Secretariat, 1991). For more detailed discussions, see Hurst Hannum, ed., *Guide to International Human Rights Practice,* 2d ed. (Philadelphia: University of Pennsylvania Press, 1992); Leo F. Zwaak, *International Human Rights Procedures: Petitioning the ECHR, CCPR, and CERD* (Nijmegen: Ars Aequi Libri, 1991); Maxine Tardu, "Human Rights Complaint Procedures of the United Nations: Assessment and Prospects," in *Des Menschen recht zwischen Freiheit und Verantwortung: Festschrift für Karl Josef Partsch zum 75. Geburtstag,* ed. J. Jekewitz, K. Klein, J. Kuehne,

H. Petermann, and R. Wolfrum (Berlin: Duncker & Humblot, 1989), 287. See also the articles in *Netherlands Q. Hum. Rts.* 6(2) (1988): 5–102.

12. See generally Scott Leckie, "The Inter-State Complaint Procedure in International Human Rights Law: Hopeful Prospects or Wishful Thinking?" *Hum. Rts. Q.* 10 (1988): 249.

13. The terminology is that used by Tardu, "Complaint Procedures," note 11.

14. Tardu, "Complaint Procedures," note 11 at 291–92.

15. Philip Alston, "UNESCO's Procedures for Dealing with Human Rights Violations," *Santa Clara L. Rev.* 20 (1980): 665; Stephen Marks, "UNESCO and Human Rights: The Implementation of Rights Relating to Education, Science, Culture, and Communication Violations," *Texas Int'l L. J.* 13 (1977): 35; S. Bastid, "La mise en oeuvre d'un recours concernant les droits de l'homme dans le domaine relevant de la compétence de l'UNESCO," in *Völkerrecht als Rechts-ordnung—internationale Gerichtsbarkeit—Menschenrechte: Festschrift für Hermann Mosler,* ed. R. Bernhardt, W. Geck, G. Jaenicke, and H. Steinberger (Berlin: Springer, 1983), 47.

16. Virginia Leary, "Lessons for the Experience of the International Labour Organisation," in *A Critical Appraisal,* ed. Alston, note 1, 580 at 595–612; E.A. Landy, "The Implementation Procedures of the International Labor Organization," *Santa Clara L. Rev.* 20 (1980): 633.

17. Convention on the Elimination of All Forms of Racial Discrimination 1965, art. 14; (First) Optional Protocol to the International Covenant on Civil and Political Rights 1966; Convention Against Torture and Other Forms of Cruel, Inhuman or Degrading Treatment or Punishment 1984, art. 22. See Graefrath, "Complaint Systems," note 3 at 317–27; Torkel Opsahl, "The Human Rights Committee," *A Critical Appraisal,* ed. Alston, note 1, 369 at 420–32; Andrew Byrnes, "The Committee Against Torture" in *A Critical Appraisal,* ed. Alston, 509 at 534–39.

18. See generally Andrew Byrnes, *Austl. Y.B. Int'l L.* 12 (1992): 205. There has been considerably more attention to this in the context of the American Convention on Human Rights. See, e.g., *Velásquez Rodríguez v. Honduras,* Inter-Am. C.H.R. ser. C, No. 4 (1988), 28 I.L.M. 291 (1989). See generally Naomi Roht-Arriaza, "State Responsibility to Investigate and Prosecute Grave Human Rights Violations in International Law," *Cal. L. Rev.* 78 (1990): 449.

19. Graefrath, "Complaint Systems," note 3 at 327.

20. As of 31 December 1992 the following numbers of states parties to the major UN treaties with individual complaints mechanisms had accepted the competence of the relevant treaty body to consider individual complaints: First Optional Protocol to the ICCPR, 66 (of 115 state parties); art. 22 of the Convention Against Torture, 30 (of 71 states parties); art. 14 of the Racial Discrimination Convention, 17 (of 133 states parties).

21. See, e.g., in the context of the Supreme Court of Canada, Mary Eberts, "Feminist Perspectives on the Canadian Charter of Rights and Freedoms," in *International Human Rights Law: A Comparative Perspective,* ed. Philip Alston (Oxford: Clarendon Press, forthcoming 1994).

22. A point recently made by Andrew Clapham, "The European Convention on Human Rights in the British Courts: Problems Associated with the Incorporation of International Human Rights," forthcoming in *International Human Rights Law,* ed. Alston, note 21 and Craig Scott, "International Review and European Human Rights and Interpretive Authority," paper presented at the conference, Human Rights and Australia: Where to Now? August 1992.

23. See generally Peter van Dijk and Godefridus J.H. van Hoof, *Theory and Practice of the European Convention on Human Rights,* 2d ed. (Deventer: Kluwer, 1990), 583–606; John G. Merrills, *The Development of International Law by the European Court of Human Rights* (Manchester: Manchester University Press, 1988), 136–59; Walter J. Ganshof van der Meersch, "Le caractère 'autonome' des termes et la 'marge d'appréciation des gouvernements dans l'interpretation de la Convention européenne de Droits de l'Homme," in *Protecting Human Rights: The European Dimension,* ed. Franz Matscher and Herbert Petzold, 2d ed. (Cologne: Carl Heymann, 1990), 201 at 206–20.

24. *Hertzberg v. Finland,* Communication No. 61/1979, Vol. 1, Selected Decisions Under the Optional Protocol (second to sixteenth sessions) (New York: United Nations, 1985), 1: 124.

25. *Handyside v. United Kingdom,* Judgment of 7 December 1976, ser. A, No 24, 58 I.L.R. 150, *Eur. H.R.R.* 1 (1976): 737.

26. *Müller v. Switzerland,* Judgment of 24 May 1988, ser. A, No. 133, *Eur. H.R. R.* 13 (1988): 212.

27. See, e.g., the progression of the Court on issues related to the recognition for the purposes of civil status of the change of sex of transsexuals, culminating in the recent decision of the Court in *B v. France,* Judgment of 25 March 1992, ser. A., No. 232-C, *Hum. Rts. L. J.* 13 (1992): 358. For earlier cases which went the other way, see *Cossey v. United Kingdom,* Judgment of 27 September 1990, ser. A, No. 184, *Eur. H.R. R.* 13 (1990):622; and *Rees v. United Kingdom,* Judgment of 17 October 1986, ser. A, No. 106, *Eur. H.R. R.* 9 (1986): 56.

28. See Hilary Charlesworth, "Equality and Non-Discrimination Under the Optional Protocol," in *Internationalising Human Rights: Australia's Accession to the First Optional Protocol* (Melbourne: Centre for Comparative Constitutional Studies, 1992), 51 at 57–59.

29. Torkel Opsahl, "The Human Rights Committee," in *A Critical Appraisal,* ed. Alston, note 1 at 431.

30. For a recent example of a case brought against two states (France and Spain) in relation to events in Andorra, see *Drozd and Janousek v. France and Spain,* 240 Eur Ct. H.R. (ser. A) (1992) *Hum. Rts. L.J.* 13 (1992): 445.

31. *Abdulaziz, Balkandali and Cabales v. United Kingdom,* 94 Eur. Ct. H.R. (ser. A) (1985), 81 I.L.R. 139.

32. See Andrew Byrnes, "Recent Cases: *Abdulaziz et al. v. U.K.,*" *Austl. L. J.* 60 (1986): 182 at 185–86.

33. See U.N. Doc E/CN.6/1991/10, para. 131.

34. For discussions of the communications procedure of the Commission, see Reanda, "Status of Women," note 1 at 295–97; Sandra Coliver, "United Nations Machineries on Women's Rights: How Might They Better Help Women Whose Rights Are Being Violated?" in *New Directions in Human Rights,* ed. Ellen L. Lutz, Hurst Hannum, and Kathryn J. Burke (Philadelphia: University of Pennsylvania Press, 1989), 25; Herta Kaschitz, "The Commission on the Status of Women," *Netherlands Q. Hum. Rts.* 6(4) (1988): 22; Margaret E. Galey, "International Enforcement of Women's Rights," *Hum. Rts. Q.* 6 (1984): 463; Laura Reanda, "Human Rights and Women's Rights: The United Nations Approach," *Hum. Rts. Q.* 3 (1981): 11; Margaret E. Galey, "Promoting Non-Discrimination Against Women: The U.N. Commission on the Status of Women," *Int'l Stud. Q. 23* (1979): 273.

35. See generally "Examining Existing Mechanisms for Communications on the Status of Women," *Report of the Secretary-General,* U.N. Doc E/CN.6/1991/

10. (The present author was responsible for preparing the draft of this report for the UN Division for the Advancement of Women.)

36. See ESC Res. 1992/19; and Report of the Commission of the Status of Women on its thirty-sixth session, U.N. Doc. E/1992/24 at 16 (Draft Resolution VI) and 56–60.

37. See generally J. Daniel Livermore and Bertie G. Ramcharan, "Enforced or Involuntary Disappearances: An Evaluation of a Decade of United Nations Action," *Can. Hum. Rts. Y. B.* 6 (1989–1990): 217. For a recent update, see Penny Parker and David Weissbrodt, "Major Developments at the U.N. Commission on Human Rights in 1991," *Hum. Rts. Q.* 13 (1991): 574 at 594–95.

38. C.H.R. Res. 1991/42, U.N. Doc. E/1991/22 at 105; Parker and Weissbrodt, "Major Developments," note 37 at 599–602.

39. U.N. Doc. E/CN.6/1991/10, paras.133–34.

40. The reporting procedures under ILO conventions and under the European Social Charter also provide some opportunities, but they do not seem to allow for the level of direct involvement of NGOs that the UN procedures do.

41. See U.N. Doc. E/CN.4/Sub.2/1989/37.

42. See, e.g., *Report of the Working Group on Contemporary Forms of Slavery*, 16th Session, U.N. Doc. E/CN.4/Sub.2/1991/41, paras. 18–96 (1991).

43. For the final report on the work of the group, see U.N. Doc. E/CN.4/Sub.2/1991/6.

44. Asbjørn Eide, "The Sub-Commission on Prevention of Discrimination and Protection of Minorities," in *A Critical Appraisal*, ed. Alston, note 1 at 248–52; Karen Reierson and David Weissbrodt, "The Forty-Third Session of the UN Sub-Commission on Prevention of Discrimination and Protection of Minorities: The Sub-Commission Under Scrutiny," *Hum. Rts. Q.* 14 (1992): 232.

45. On the powers and actions of the Commission on Human Rights, see Philip Alston, "The Commission on Human Rights," in *A Critical Appraisal*, ed. Alston, note 1, 126 at 155–164.

46. Reanda, "Status of Women," note 1, 265 at 301–302.

47. *Abdulaziz, Balkandali and Cabales v. U.K.*, note 31 at 471 (claims to the same entitlements in relation to immigration or nationality law for foreign husbands as husbands enjoyed in respect of their foreign wives); *Aumeeruddy-Cziffra v. Mauritius*, Communication No. 35/1978, Vol. 1, *Selected Decisions Under the Optional Protocol* (second to sixteenth sessions) (New York: United Nations, 1985), 67 I.L.R. 285, *Hum. Rts. L. J.* 2 (1985): 139; *Proposed Amendments to the Naturalization Provisions of the Political Constitution of Costa Rica*, Inter-Am. C.H.R., Advisory Opinion OC-4/84 of 19 January 1984, OEA/Ser. A No. 4, 79 I.L.R. 282, *Hum. Rts. L.J.* 5 (1984): 161. *Broeks v. Netherlands*, Communication No 172/1984, Vol. 2, *Selected Decisions of the Human Rights Committee Under the Optional Protocol* (1990), 196 (same entitlements to social security benefits as similarly situated men); *Zwaan de Vries, Selected Decisions*, vol. 2 at 209; *Ato del Alvellanal v. Perú*, Communication No. 202/1986, *Report of the Human Rights Committee in 1989*, U.N. Doc. A/44/40, Annex X.C, 196 (same formal legal rights to legal personality). *Schuler-Zgraggen v. Switzerland*, 263 Eur. Ct. H.R. (ser. A) (1993) (denial of social security benefit on basis of assumption that women gave up work after they gave birth to a child, discrimination on the basis of sex).

48. E.g., *Lovelace v. Canada*, Vol. 1, *Selected Decisions*, 83 at paras. 17–18; 68 I.L.R. 17, *Hum. Rts. L.J.* 2 (1981): 158.

49. For brief summaries of international cases raising sex discrimination and

other relevant issues, see Rebecca Cook, "International Human Rights Cases Relating to Women: Case Notes and Comments," *Vand J. Transnat'l L.* 23 (1990): 779. See generally Maud Buquicchio-de Boer, *Sexual Equality in the European Convention of Human Rights: A Survey of Case Law* (Strasbourg: Council of Europe, 1989); Maud Buquicchio-de Boer, "Sexual Discrimination and the European Convention on Human Rights," *Hum. Rts. L.J.* 6 (1985): 1; Torkel Opsahl, "Equality in Human Rights Law with Particular Reference to Article 26 of the International Covenant on Civil and Political Rights," in *Fortschritt im Bewusstsein der Menschenrechte: Festschrift für Felix Ermacora,* ed. Manfred Nowak, D. Steurer, and H. Tretter (Arlington: N.P. Engel, 1988), 51–67; Anne Bayefsky, "The Principle of Equality of Non-Discrimination in International Law," *Hum. Rts. L.J.* 11 (1990): 1; Andrew Byrnes, "Equality and Non-Discrimination," in *Human Rights in Hong Kong,* ed. Raymond Wacks (Hong Kong: Oxford University Press, 1992), 226 at 234–42.

50. See, e.g., the permissibility of abortions in the light of the right to life, *Baby Boy* case, Inter-American Commission of Human Rights, case 2141 (United States of America), Resolution No. 23/81, 6 March 1981, *Hum. Rts. L.J.* 2 (1981): 110; alleged rights of father of child to prevent woman from obtaining an abortion: *Paton v. United Kingdom,* European Commission of Human Rights, App. No. 8416/78, *Eur. Comm'n H.R. Dec. 8 Rep.* 19 (1980): 224, *Eur. H.R. Rep.* 3 (1980): 408. See also *Brüggeman and Scheuten v. Federal Republic of Germany,* App. No. 6959/75, *Eur. Comm'n H.R. Dec. 8 Rep.* 10 (1977): 100, *Eur. H.R. R.* 3 (1977): 244 (permissibility of restricting access to abortions).

51. One exception is *X and Y v. Netherlands,* 91 Eur. Ct. H.R. (ser. A) (1985), 81 I.L.R. 91. In the case involving a challenge to Irish law prohibiting the dissemination in Ireland of information about abortion services in England: *Open Door Counselling Ltd. and Dublin Well Woman Centre Ltd. v. Ireland, Hum. Rts. L.J.* 13 (1992): 378, *Eur. H.R. R.* 15 (1992): 244, the European Court of Human Rights held that the prohibition was a violation of freedom of expression found in art. 10, since it was a disproportionate measure, despite the legitimate goals it pursued.

52. U.N. Doc. E/CN.6/1991/10, paras. 95–135.

53. See Scott, "International Review," note 22 and sources cited there.

54. Engle, "When Discourses Meet," note 4 at 519–20.

55. Anthony Lester, "Amici curiae: Third-Party Interventions Before the European Court of Human Rights," in *Protecting Human Rights,* ed. Matscher and Petzold, note 23 at 341.

56. Byrnes, "Committee Against Torture," note 17 at 516–20.

57. Byrnes, "Committee Against Torture," note 17 at 534–539.

58. Byrnes, "Committee Against Torture," note 17 at 530–533.

59. U.N. Doc. E/CN.4/1986/15, para. 119.

60. U.N. Doc. E/CN.4/1988/17, paras. 40–48; UN Doc. E/CN.4/1986/15, para. 104.

61. U.N. Doc. E/CN.4/1986/15, paras. 38 and 49.

62. U.N. Doc. E/CN.4/1990/17, paras. 55 and 56.

63. See, e.g., *Yilmaz-Dogan v. Netherlands,* Communication No. 1/1984, *Report of the Committee on the Elimination of Racial Discrimination* in 1988. U.N. Doc. A/43/18, Annex IV.

64. See Andrew Byrnes and Johannes Chan, eds., *Bill of Rights Bulletin* (Hong Kong: Faculty of Law, University of Hong Kong, 1991).

65. For the results of the Seminar, see Donna Sullivan, ed., *Combating Violence Against Women* (New York: International League of Human Rights, 1993).

66. For an extremely helpful checklist, see Hannum, *International Human Rights Practice*, note 11, App. B.

67. See, e.g., *Dow v. Attorney General for Botswana* [1991] L.R.C. (Const.) 623; Ct. of Appeal of Bots., on appeal from [1991] L.R.C. (Const.) 574 and reproduced in *Hum. Rts. Q. 13* (1991): 614. The result in this case (a finding that law relating to nationality which discriminated against women was in violation of the equality guarantees of the Botswana Constitution) has recently been upheld on appeal.

68. See, e.g., the Japanese experience: Yuji Iwasawa, "The Impact of International Human Rights Law on Japanese Law—The Third Reformation for Japanese Women," *Japanese Ann. Int'l L.* 21 (1991): 56–61.

69. Quentin Bryce, "The Convention at Work: Submission to the Industrial Relations Commission in Support of the ACTU Test Case on Parental Leave," in *Ten Years of the Convention on the Elimination of All Forms of Discrimination Against Women*, Occasional Paper from the Sex Discrimination Commissioner No. 4 (Sydney: Human Rights and Equal Opportunity Commission, 1990).

70. See, e.g., the survey of the practice of the Canadian courts in Anne Bayefsky, *International Human Rights Law: Use in Canadian Charter of Rights and Freedoms Litigation* (Toronto: Butterworths, 1992). See also Peter P. Bayne, "Human Rights and Administrative Law," *Commonwealth L. Bull.* (1991): 320; and Andrew Byrnes, Review of *Developing Human Rights Jurisprudence* (London: Commonwealth Secretariat, 1988) in *Hong Kong L.J.* 20 (1990): 409, 412–14.

Chapter 9
State Accountability Under the Convention on the Elimination of All Forms of Discrimination Against Women

Rebecca J. Cook

Introduction

The time has come to recognize that denials of individuals' rights on the ground only that they are women are human rights violations, and to require state practices that expose women to degradation, indignity, and oppression on account of their sex to be independently identified, condemned, compensated, and, preferably, prevented. The purpose of changing ubiquitous state practice may appear ambitious, but it is not too ambitious for the needs of our times. Egregious and pervasive violations of women's rights often go unrecognized. Moreover, when they are recognized, they go unpunished and unremedied, and are all too often defended as a necessary part of a culture or religion or as a quality of human nature. While violations of women's rights vary in different cultures, victims all share a common risk factor: that of being female.[1]

States are likely to contest not only their legal responsibility for such wrongs but also their accountability. Legal responsibility denotes liability for breach of the law, but accountability is a wider concept that requires a state to explain an apparent violation and to offer an exculpatory explanation if it can.[2] States may deny that there are binding international obligations, that they have violated binding duties, that particular tribunals have jurisdiction over them, or that particular claimants have standing to launch legal claims. States are seldom held responsible for ignoring their international obligations to respect women's human rights, but may more often be called to account for the status of women in their territory. A survey of international human rights jurisprudence shows that international and regional human rights conventions have been applied only sparingly to address violations of women's rights.[3]

State responsibility is a fundamental principle of international law. It provides that a state is legally accountable for breaches of international obligations under customary international or treaty law that are attributable or imputable to the state. The international law of state responsibility for human rights violations has evolved significantly in recent times.[4] It has developed to require governments to take preventive steps to protect the exercise and enjoyment of human rights, to investigate violations that are alleged, to punish violations that are proven, and to provide effective remedies, including the provision of compensation to victims. Modern developments in international human rights law have widened the network of international obligations through state adherence to multilateral human rights conventions, and have thereby enhanced prospects of enforcing state responsibility.[5]

The purpose of this chapter is to explore how developments in the international law of state accountability and responsibility can be applied to ensure more effective protection of women's human rights. It will address the potential for enforcement of state accountability and responsibility primarily under the Convention on the Elimination of All Forms of Discrimination Against Women (the Women's Convention).[6]

The discussion will identify acts of states parties' executive, legislative, and judicial branches of government that can create state legal responsibility for breaches of obligations under the Women's Convention. Convention provisions will be addressed that require states parties to ensure elimination of discrimination against women, and instances will be considered of enactment or maintenance of apparently discriminatory legislation, governmental conduct, and judicial decisions. It will also examine the emergence of an international standard of treatment owed to women under the Women's Convention that may be different from the national standards of the states parties.

Legal analysis will address which acts of violation of women's rights are imputable to a state party. For instance, acts of private persons that are violent to women or discriminatory against women do not necessarily implicate the responsibility of the state. If a state facilitates, conditions, accommodates, tolerates, justifies, or excuses private denials of women's rights, however, the state will bear responsibility. The state will be responsible not directly for the private acts, but for its own lack of diligence to prevent, control, correct, or discipline such private acts through its own executive, legislative, or judicial organs.

In determining whether states can be held accountable for violations of women's human rights under the Women's Convention, one has to examine the nature of the right in question by reference to the actual text of the Convention, its overall object, and purpose, its *travaux préparatoires* in the event of uncertainty of interpretation, how the right has been interpreted by the Convention's monitoring body and human rights tribunals, and state practice with respect to that right. Where the obligation with respect to a right is not clear from interpretation of the Convention or its subsequent application, then one must turn to the general principles of international law governing state responsibility.

The Nature of the Obligations of States Parties

Determination of which state acts or omissions are breaches of the Women's Convention depends on the nature of the undertakings to which states pledged themselves when they became states parties. Article 2 of the Women's Convention requires that:

> States parties condemn discrimination against women in all its forms, agree to pursue, by all appropriate means and without delay, a policy of eliminating discrimination against women and, to this end, undertake:
> (a) To embody the principle of the equality of men and women in their national Constitutions or other appropriate legislation if not yet incorporated therein, and to ensure, through law and other appropriate means, the practical realization of this principle;
> (b) To adopt appropriate legislative and other measures, including sanctions where appropriate, prohibiting all discrimination against women;
> (c) To establish legal protection of the rights of women on an equal basis with men and to ensure through competent national tribunals and other public institutions the effective protection of women against any act of discrimination;
> (d) To refrain from engaging in any act or practice of discrimination against women and to ensure that public authorities and institutions shall act in conformity with this obligation;
> (e) To take all appropriate measures to eliminate discrimination against women by any person, organization or enterprise;
> (f) To take all appropriate measures, including legislation, to modify or abolish existing laws, regulations, customs and practices which constitute discrimination against women;
> (g) To repeal all national penal provisions which constitute discrimination against women.

Article 2 is the general undertaking article that applies with respect to rights recognized in Articles 5–16 of the Women's Convention. It generally requires states parties "to ensure" compliance by their governments' organs with the Convention and "to take all appropriate measures" to effect "the elimination of discrimination in all its forms" by "any person, organization or enterprise" and "to modify or abolish existing laws, regulations, customs and practices." Analogies may be drawn to Article 2 of the International Covenant on Civil and Political Rights and Article 1(1) of the American Convention on Human Rights, both of which require that states parties shall respect and ensure the rights recognized in those respective conventions.

Article 2 has not been subject to a General Recommendation by the Committee on the Elimination of Discrimination Against Women (CEDAW), established to monitor compliance by states parties with the Women's Convention. Such a General Recommendation would help to specify the nature of the obligation of the states parties. The Human Rights Committee, established to monitor compliance with the International Covenant on Civil and Political Rights and the Committee on Economic, Social, and Cultural Rights, established to monitor compliance with the International Covenant on Economic, Social, and Cultural Rights, have each issued General Comments on the respective articles that establish the general undertakings of states with regard to that Covenant. These articles are referred to here as the "general undertaking" articles.

The Human Rights Committee's General Comment 3 stresses that "the obligation under the Covenant is not confined to the respect of human rights, but that States parties have also undertaken *to ensure* the enjoyment of these rights to all individuals under their jurisdiction. This aspect calls for specific activities by the States parties to enable individuals to enjoy their rights"[7] (emphasis added). The Committee on Economic, Social, and Cultural Rights explains that

the phrase "by all appropriate means" must be given its full and natural meaning. While each state party must decide for itself which means are the most appropriate under the circumstances with respect to each of the rights, the "appropriateness" of the means chosen will not always be self-evident. It is therefore desirable that States parties' reports should indicate not only the measures that have been taken but also the basis on which they are considered to be the most "appropriate" under the circumstances.[8]

These interpretations of the phrases "to ensure" in the Political Covenant and "by all appropriate means" in the Economic Covenant could also be applied in a General Recommendation by CEDAW to the same phrases used in Article 2 and subsequent articles of the Women's Convention.

Obligations of Results and of Means

A distinction has traditionally been drawn in international law between obligations of means and obligations of ends, that is, between obligations to act by specified means toward the achievement of aspirational goals[9] and obligations to achieve certain results by whatever means are determined to be appropriate.[10] Under the Women's Convention, states parties have assumed obligations both of results and of means.

The general undertaking clause that "states parties . . . agree to pursue, by all appropriate means and without delay, a policy of eliminating discrimination against women" imposes an obligation of result to eliminate "discrimination against women in all its forms." The International Law Commission has interpreted Article 2(1) of the International Convention on the Elimination of All Forms of Racial Discrimination, which has almost identical language[11] to the general undertaking clause of the Women's Convention, as imposing an obligation of result.[12] States parties to the Women's Convention have also assumed obligations of means outlined in the seven subsections of Article 2 and subsequent articles. For example, obligations under Article 2(c) "to pursue by all appropriate measures and without delay"

To establish the legal protection of the rights of women on an equal basis with men to ensure through competent national tribunals and other public institutions the effective protection of women against any act of discrimination

leave states parties a choice of means, and create legal duties to exercise choice diligently. States parties are therefore obligated to take the measures prescribed in the subsections as state policy and to achieve reasonable results in eliminating all forms of discrimination.

The Women's Convention does not create absolute liability offenses regarding deficient results, but only requires states parties to exercise due diligence in execution of the specified means. States can never guarantee that discrimination against women will not occur, and therefore cannot be held absolutely liable for all or any acts of discrimination. Parties are liable only for their failures to implement the means prescribed in the Convention, which were considered by the drafters to be reasonably likely to achieve the result of eliminating all forms of discrimination against women.

International Standards of Conduct

States that enter international treaty regimes undertake to do more than maintain their domestic law and customary practice. Concerning the law itself, the Vienna Convention on the Law of Treaties provides that "A party may not invoke the provisions of its internal law as justification for its failure to perform a treaty."[13] The same is true regarding standards of conduct. Historically, when nationals of country B were lawfully present in country A, particularly detained in its prisons, country A would accept that they were not to be granted lesser rights than nationals of country A. Country A was bound by the principle of nondiscrimination against nationals of country B on grounds of their nationality, but international law was satisfied by applying the national standard of country A. If the national standard of country A fell below "the standard of civilization," meaning an international minimum standard, country B could protest regarding its nationals, and demand their treatment according to the higher international minimum standard. For instance, in the Neer Claim, the U.S.-Mexican General Claims Commission applied the criterion of whether a state's response to private conduct amounted to

an outrage, to bad faith, to wilful neglect of duty, or to an insufficiency of governmental action so far short of international standards that every reasonable and impartial man would readily recognize its insufficiency.[14]

Country B would have no voice, and country A would have no international obligations, regarding nationals of country A. International human rights law now requires, however, that all persons be treated, including in their own countries, in accordance with international minimum standards of respect for human rights.

States parties to the Women's Convention accept obligations of both results and of means. They accept a duty to act "by all appropriate means"[15] and "to take all appropriate measures"[16] to achieve stated objectives. Determination of what is "appropriate" must be sensitive to national legal, political, and social environments, but it is not within the exclusive control of each state party. They accept accountability to act appropriately in accordance with international standards of performance. Even though many states parties to the Women's Convention have reserved the jurisdiction of the International Court of Justice under Article 29(1), that in any "dispute between two or more states parties concerning the interpretation or application of the present Convention,"[17] the potential for international adjudication of disputes remains, and the performance of states parties would be measured according to international standards. International human rights tribunals may apply a generous "margin of appreciation" in favor of each country's chosen method of observance of human rights obligations, but nevertheless hold countries to international account according to international standards.

Autonomous Interpretation of Treaty Terms and Their Application

International and regional human rights tribunals have uniformly held that international standards, and not those of states parties, will be used to determine whether there has been a violation of international human rights laws. This is consistent with the general rule of interpretation as specified in Article 31(1) of the Vienna Convention on the Law of Treaties: "A treaty shall be interpreted in good faith in accordance with the ordinary meaning to be given to the terms of the treaty in their context and in the light of its object and purpose." Article 31(2) explains that the "context for the purpose of the interpretation of the treaty shall comprise . . . its preamble and annexes." Subsection (3) adds that account may be taken of "any subsequent agreement between the parties regarding the interpretation of the treaty or the application of its provisions" and "any subsequent practice in the application of the treaty which establishes the agreement of the parties regarding its interpretation." Article 31(4) provides that "a special meaning shall be given to a term if it is established that the parties so intended." Terms given a special meaning are known as autonomous terms.

The Human Rights Committee, for example, explained that

its interpretation and application of the International Covenant on Civil and Political Rights has to be based on the principle that the terms and concepts of the Covenant are independent of any particular national system of law and of all dictionary definitions. Although the terms of the Covenant are derived from long traditions within many nations, the Committee must now regard them as having an autonomous meaning.[18]

In the Lawless Case,[19] the European Court of Human Rights decided that it would determine the standards by which it would measure whether the facts that led to the declaration of a state of emergency were justified by the European Convention on Human Rights.[20]

CEDAW will give autonomous meaning to the terms of the Women's Convention according to the terms themselves, the Convention's object and purpose, and the subsequent practice of states.

The Obligation to Eliminate All Forms of Discrimination Against Women

"In All Its Forms"

By becoming states parties to the Women's Convention, states agree to "condemn discrimination in all its forms." The Preamble to the Women's Convention notes that the UN Charter, the Universal Declaration of Human Rights, the Declaration on the Elimination of Discrimination Against Women (the Women's Declaration), the two international human rights covenants, and UN and specialized agency resolutions, declarations, and recommendations promote equality of rights of men and women. However, the drafters expressed concern in the Preamble "that despite these various instruments extensive discrimination against women continues to exist."[21] The Preamble concludes with an expression of determination "to adopt the measures required for the elimination of such discrimination in all its forms and manifestations."[22]

In agreeing "to pursue, by all appropriate means and without delay, a policy of eliminating discrimination against women,"[23] states parties are obligated to address the particular nature of each discrimination. The Women's Convention clearly reinforces sexual nondiscrimination, but its purpose is not simply to achieve gender neutrality. In contrast to previous human rights treaties, the Women's Convention frames the legal norm as the elimination of all forms of discrimination against women, as distinct from opposing sex discrimination per se. That is, it develops the legal norm from a sex neutrality norm that requires equal treatment of men and women, usually measured by how men are treated, to recognize that the distinctive characteristics of women and their vulnerabilities to discrimination merit a specific legal response.

For the purposes of the Women's Convention, a legal definition of "discrimination against women" was required. Discussions leading to the evolution of the Women's Declaration into the Women's Convention showed an intention to define discrimination against women for purposes of legal application and enforcement of the Convention.[24] According to Article 1,

the term "discrimination against women" shall mean any distinction, exclusion or restriction made on the basis of sex which has the effect or purpose of impairing or nullifying the recognition, enjoyment or exercise by women, irrespective of their marital status, on a basis of equality of men and women, of human rights and fundamental freedoms in the political, economic, social, cultural, civil or any other field.

Where a law does make a distinction that has the effect or purpose of impairing women's rights in any way, then it constitutes discrimination under this definition, violates the Convention, and must accordingly be remedied by the state party.

Not all laws or practices that place women at a disadvantage constitute "discrimination against women" within the meaning of Article 1. A law that makes no express distinction on the basis of sex in its language cannot be impugned under this definition despite its having a discriminatory effect. For example, employment and apprenticeship programs that are neutral on their face often have discriminatory effects because girls cannot meet educational eligibility standards. Family conditions may require that school-age girls remain in the home, for instance to care for siblings while their mothers work outside the home. Admission criteria for apprenticeship programs may not offend Article 1 of the Women's Convention, because they do not discriminate in their terms, but they may violate Article 3, which echoes the Preamble in requiring states parties

to ensure the full development and advancement of women, for the purpose of guaranteeing them the exercise and enjoyment of human rights and fundamental freedoms on a basis of equality with men.

In addition to impugning laws and practices that are detrimental in their effect but neutral on their face, Article 3 prohibits practices that are detrimental to women as such, including for instance non-provision of obstetric services. This article, therefore, catches those discriminatory practices that do not come within the scope of the Article 1 definition.

The goal of Article 3 is reinforced by Article 4, which specifies that "temporary special measures aimed at accelerating de facto equality between men and women shall not be considered discrimination as defined by the Convention." This allows for determinate, concrete practices to secure "equality of opportunity and treatment."

The elimination of discrimination on grounds of marital status is a goal in addition to and separate from that of securing equal developmental opportunities for women and men. This objective is shown in the provision in the Article 1 definition that offensive conduct is that which distinguishes on the basis of sex, and which has the effect or purpose of denying women their human rights and fundamental freedoms "irrespective of their marital status" in the "civil or any other field." For example, a practice of health clinics to require wives, in contrast to unmarried women, to show the authorization of their husbands in order to receive health care constitutes marital status discrimination that violates the Convention and would accordingly have to be changed.[25]

"By Any Person, Organization or Enterprise"

The Women's Convention in Article 2(e) requires states parties:

To take all appropriate measures to eliminate discrimination against women by any person, organization or enterprise.

Under this provision, a state may well be obliged to prevent and deter private acts of discrimination, to investigate and negate their harmful consequences, and to provide for compensation or sanctions for the performance of such acts, for instance by penalties of a civil or criminal nature. Private discriminators, such as religious organizations, may also be required to forfeit public advantages such as licensure, tax-exempt status, and direct or indirect government grants or subsidies.

States are not responsible in principle for the actions of private persons, either natural persons or artificial legal persons such as private corporations, that are incompatible with standards of conduct that states themselves are obliged to observe under customary international law or treaties that states have voluntarily assumed, including international human rights conventions.[26] Although individuals have achieved status under modern international human rights law, this is as beneficiaries of rights and as litigants against state defendants rather than as perpetrators of wrongs.

International criminal law has considered pirates and more recently international war criminals to be *hostis humani generis* (enemies of humankind) and individually accountable under international law, but these exceptions prove the general rule that private individuals, corporations, and unincorporated associations are not directly bound by the provisions of international law. Accordingly, individuals whose acts or omissions are incompatible with the terms of the Women's Convention, for instance in creating or maintaining discrimination in women's tenure or inheritance of land or other property, bear no legal liability on that ground under the Women's Convention.

States are responsible, however, not only for the effects deliberately achieved by different state organs, but also for their failures to act appropriately to meet the international obligations by which the states are bound by customary or treaty law, even when the substantive breach originates in the conduct of private natural or legal persons. Although a state is not internationally responsible for a private act of sexual discrimination, it is bound to undertake means to eliminate or reduce and mitigate the incidence of private discrimination, and to achieve the result that such private discrimination should not recur.

State responsibility arises when a state fails to act appropriately under its municipal law to punish and/or allow compensation for violations of international human rights law. A state bears similar liability when it has failed to act to prevent anticipated violation of human rights.[27] A state will not be directly accountable for the behavior of private individuals or agencies, but their behavior indirectly implicates the state through its lack of due diligence in awareness of the risk of violation of human rights, or the failure of its punitive and/or compensatory responses to such violations. Indeed, a state may be considered to have facilitated an international wrong or to be complicit in its commission when the wrong is of a pervasive or persistent character.

The law on state responsibility has been developed beyond its classical origins by international human rights tribunals to apply to international human rights conventions. The Inter-American Court of Human Rights established this in its important *Velásquez Rodríguez* decision in 1988[28] when it imposed liability on Honduras for lack of due diligence in preventing unexplained "disappearances." Liability of the state arose through its failure to keep the obligation "to ensure" respect for human rights, whose violation in the form of "disappearances" could not be attributed either to state officers or private persons.

Where state responsibility does not arise directly, therefore, a state may nevertheless be internationally responsible for its failure, usually through its executive branch of government but potentially through its judicial or legislative branches, to act appropriately in anticipation of or in consequence of private acts. The responsibility of the state is to respond appropriately to potential or actual private conduct and

to organize the governmental apparatus and, in general, all the structures through which public power is exercised, so that they are capable of juridically ensuring the free and full enjoyment of human rights.[29]

The state must accordingly, inter alia, investigate, correct, compensate, and appropriately punish private violations of human rights, including those expressed in the Women's Convention.

It is possible to build on this jurisprudence to amplify state responsibility for violations of the rights that states have undertaken "to ensure" through their ratification of the Women's Convention. The identity of language contained in the American Convention, which was at issue in the *Velásquez Rodríguez* case and that found in the Women's Convention opens considerable potential for the enforcement of states' obligations under the Women's Convention.

Responsibility of a state is particularly significant when human rights are implicated, because the principal beneficiaries of international human rights are private individuals, who are as vulnerable to the depredations and discrimination of their peers as to those of officers of the state. The responsibility of states is not simply not to engage in human rights violations themselves, but to meet international obligations to deter and condemn such violations initiated by private persons. State responsibility includes taking appropriate action to prevent objectionable private action, to monitor private acts that constitute violations, for instance through human rights monitors and police monitors, and to sanction and remedy acts of violation that are identified.

States are required under Article 16 to "take all appropriate measures to eliminate discrimination against women in all matters relating to marriage and family relations." CEDAW's General Recommendation 19 on Violence Against Women makes clear that "Gender-based violence is a form of discrimination that seriously inhibits women's ability to enjoy rights and freedoms on a basis of equality with men."[30] It explains that

Family violence is one of the most insidious forms of violence against women. It is prevalent in all societies. Within family relationships women of all ages are subjected to violence of all kinds, including battering, rape, other forms of sexual assault, mental and other forms of violence, which are perpetuated by traditional attitudes.[31]

The General Recommendation requires states parties to take "appropriate and effective measures to overcome all forms of gender based violence, whether by private or public act." With respect to family violence, the Recommendation obligates states parties to provide criminal penalties and civil remedies, to remove the defense of protection of family honor by legislation, and, among other programs, to provide support services for victims of violence including incest. States are internationally responsible not simply to legislate against such wrongs, but to make their legislation effective through their judicial, police, and other organs of state power.[32]

"Customs and Practices"

The Forward Looking Strategies for the Advancement of Women adopted at the 1985 UN Conference on Women in Nairobi (the Nairobi Strategies)[33] explain how more subtle forms of exploitation are correlated with cultural, religious, and family conditions that have constrained the advancement of women and intensified their marginalization and oppression.[34] The Women's Convention in Article 2(f) requires states parties

To take all appropriate measures, including legislation, to modify or abolish existing laws, regulations, customs and practices which constitute discrimination against women.

Article 5(a) elaborates on this duty by explaining that states parties agree

To modify the social and cultural patterns of conduct of men and women, with a view to achieving the elimination of prejudices and customary and all other practices which are based on the idea of the inferiority or the superiority of either of the sexes or on stereotyped roles for men and women.

By Article 2(f) taken together with Article 5(a), states parties agree to reform personal status laws[35] and to confront practices, for instance of religious institutions, that, while perhaps claiming to regard the sexes as different but equal, in effect preclude women from senior levels of authority and influence. These articles strongly reinforce the commitment to eliminate all forms of discrimination, since many pervasive forms of discrimination against women rest not on law as such but on legally tolerated customs and practices of national institutions. These may hold a revered and privileged status in national life, such as organizations that recognize the sacrifice of military veterans, and the sanctity of religious faith.

Obligations that states parties have assumed directly and indirectly under the Women's Convention also arise when women suffer from operation of customary laws with respect to property, when family members execute discriminatory wills, or banks obstruct women's equal opportunities for commercial initiatives by denial of equitable mortgages and loans.[36] States are obligated under Article 13(b) to take all appropriate measures to eliminate discrimination against women in areas of economic and social life and in particular the "right to bank loans, mortgages and other forms of financial credit."

The special significance of land rights to rural women is recognized in Article 14, which requires states parties to "take into account the particular problems faced by rural women and the significant roles which rural women play in the economic survival of their families." Article 14(2)(g) requires appropriate measures to ensure the equal right of women with men

To have access to agricultural credit and loans, marketing facilities, appropriate technology and equal treatment in land and agrarian reform as well as in land resettlement schemes.

States parties accordingly are responsible for taking "appropriate measures" to eliminate discrimination in relevant "customs and practices."

A willingness to discount religious traditions that subordinate women is evident in Article 4 of the 1993 Declaration on the Elimination of Violence Against Women proposed by the UN Commission on the Status of Women and adopted by the General Assembly.

States should condemn violence against women, and should not

invoke any custom, tradition or religion or other consideration to avoid their obligation with respect to its elimination.[37]

Similar repudiation of customs and practices of particular religions that disadvantage women can be achieved through withholding or withdrawing privileges that states give to such religious institutions. Respect for freedom of religion necessarily precludes states from directing religious authorities on matters of doctrine, ritual, and practice. Freedom of religion is a negative right, however, not dependent on privileges. Where religious institutions discriminate against women in practice, they are not necessarily to be censured by governments, but may forfeit their entitlement to legal privileges such as tax exempt status as charitable institutions.

State denial of tax privileges on income and land to institutions whose customs and practices disadvantage women does not inhibit the freedom of religious institutions any more than it does that of secular, non-charitable institutions. States parties' duties of due diligence to take all appropriate measures to prohibit all forms of discrimination against women, and state liability for omissions to enforce human rights nondiscrimination provisions may require that they treat religious institutions whose practices do not conform to international human rights standards as secular, non-charitable organizations.

Identifying Other Forms of Discrimination

States are obligated to identify and eliminate "all forms" of discrimination against women. This requires understanding perceptions of women in all walks of life and how they perceive laws, policies and practices as discriminatory. A common theme in feminist discourse is that women's experiences and capacities for distinctive understandings and proposed solutions of their disadvantage, based on sex and gender, be given voice. Development of feminist scholarship has added dimensions to the significance of experience, revealing contrasts between, for instance, the social situations of women in diverse racial and other communities.[38] Feminist analysis of law has generated approaches and schools of doctrine of rich diversity.

In international law, this development serves to demonstrate that the understanding and application of uniform principles of respect for human rights must be informed by the experiences of women within their own countries and cultures.[39] For instance, what appears to be oppression from outside a culture may be found tolerable and even advantageous by women within it, and what they find discriminatory and subordinating may not be apparent from outside. Feminist doctrine stresses approaches that afford women voice, visibility, and power within their communities. At the international level, feminism and international legal scholarship can each inform the other of its strengths and limitations, creating a self-critical exchange that will reduce limitations and apply strengths to enhance the achievements of both in their common quest for advancement of women's international human rights.

In feminist legal analysis, a method to determine women's needs has come to be called "asking the woman question."[40] The question arises from analysis that is conscious that much standard setting in law is derived from ostensibly objective criteria that, as a matter of history and legal culture, were fashioned through the male gender. Reasonable person standards, frequently described as the standards of "the reasonable man," center on men with whom senior lawyers, judges, and legislators have been able to identify. Such officers have in the past been members of socioeconomic elites, aware of the lives of women, racial minorities, and people of low income and influence only through stereotypes. Their attitudes patronized women and sought to protect them from vulnerability in the world of men's affairs through exclusion. They did not truly answer, because they never truly asked, what impact the laws and social institutions they had created had on women. Answers are compelled by "asking the woman question."

The challenge to which the "woman question" responds is to apply feminist methods of legal, ethical, and related analysis to the circumstances of women's lives in order to lift their invisibility and better understand and remedy injustice. A legal analyst explains:

In law, asking the woman question means examining how the law fails to take into account the experiences and values that seem more typical of women than of men, for whatever reason, or how existing legal standards and concepts might disadvantage women. The question assumes that some features of the law may be not only non-neutral in a general sense, but also "male" in a specific sense. The purpose of the woman question is to expose those features and how they operate, and to suggest how they might be corrected.[41]

In asking this question, in the context of international women's human rights law as in other legal contexts, one is contesting assumptions of the law's gender neutrality:

Without the woman question, differences associated with women are taken for granted and, unexamined, may serve as a justification for laws that disadvantage women. . . . In exposing the hidden effect of laws that do not explicitly discriminate on the basis of sex, the woman question helps to demonstrate how social structures embody norms that implicitly render women different and thereby subordinate.[42]

A consequence of answering the "woman question" in domestic legal systems is development of new theories that require women's equal access to public sector institutions and the law's remedial involvement in spousal and family relations that exploit the vulnerability and powerlessness of women.[43]

Similarly, doctrines of international human rights law can be opened to development through analysis of their historic failure to recognize women's oppression and through realization of their potential for application to women's experiences.[44] Applications of international legal doctrine to women's human rights through, for example, CEDAW General Recommendations affect state responsibility for state organs' omissions to meet international commitments. For instance, states that possess laws against young and non-consensual marriages, marital violence and rape, and mistreatment of widows and of elderly people, the majority of whom tend to be women, frequently fail to enforce such laws or acquire adequate statistics of instances of their breach when the victims are women. Whether or not failures are conditioned by sexual or gender bias against women victims of illegal conduct, the effect of states' neglect of events and records of such victimization is to deny the application of preventive and remedial resources and to compound and perpetuate women's vulnerability. Legal theories that relate state organs' omissions to develop strategies and apply resources in order to reduce women's victimization would expose states to accountability under international human rights law.

Internationally Wrongful Acts

In international law, states bear responsibility for their own wrongs, meaning the wrongs they actively perform and the wrongs legally attributable to them through culpable omissions. The International Law Commission Draft Articles on State Responsibility open by providing:

Article 1. Responsibility of a State for its internationally wrongful acts
Every internationally wrongful act of a State entails the international responsibility of that State.

Article 2. Possibility that every State may be held to have committed an internationally wrongful act
Every State is subject to the possibility of being held to have committed an internationally wrongful act entailing its international responsibility.

Article 3. Elements of an internationally wrongful act of a State
There is an internationally wrongful act of a State when:
(a) Conduct consisting of an action or omission is attributable to the State under international law; and
(b) That conduct constitutes a breach of an international obligation of the State.

States are liable for the acts of, authorized by, and attributable to their different organs. Organs of state are usually dominated and characterized by the executive branch of government, meaning not only the political officers and departments of government but also the head of state and police, military, and diplomatic agents of the state, whether they act politically or apolitically. The legislative branch of government is also an organ of state, however, as is the judiciary, including both courts and quasi-judicial tribunals, for instance those dealing with immigration and refugee claims. A state will bear legal responsibility for international wrongs that are done directly or indirectly by any such organs of state authority.

States normally take policy direction from the executive branch of government, frequently referred to simply as "the government," whose policies may be implemented by police, military, diplomatic, consular, and other officers. The relationship of the executive to the legislative branch of government is a matter of national constitutional law, and is immaterial for purposes of state responsibility. For instance, when a state fails in its obligation to enact legislation, the state itself is in breach of its duty, whether the failure stems from an executive failure to propose legislation to the legislature, the legislature's failure to enact the measure, or an executive veto of a measure that the legislature has approved.

Similarly, the acts and omissions of a constitutionally independent judiciary can render the state liable for failure to respect an international commitment. Before a domestic grievance can be heard at an international level, local remedies must usually be exhausted. When local remedies have been exhausted through a state's highest court, an international tribunal may find that an international wrong has remained unremedied. It is of no international legal consequence that the judiciary claims that it is simply giving effect to the intention enacted by the national legislature.

Reliance on the constitutional concept of the Separation of Powers that distinguishes executive, legislative, and judicial authority is convenient for purposes of analysis. Ian Brownlie has observed, however, that the emphasis should be on

whether in the given case the system of administration has produced a result which is compatible with the pertinent principle or standard of international law. In many instances, the source of the breach will be a particular official or a particular organ such as the judiciary. However, in a number of important cases the breach of international law is the product of a combination of factors. . . . In such cases it is the system or general policy, and the implementation thereof, which is in issue, rather than responsibility for the acts of particular officials or particular types of organ.[45]

Executive Acts

Since governments provide the principal motivation for the exercise of state power, executive action and failure to act most frequently raise questions of state responsibility. It is a matter of national constitutional law whether such action can be corrected, nullified, or compensated through the national judiciary. The requirement in international adversarial adjudication that local remedies must be exhausted before an issue rises to the level of an international wrong may afford a state means to forestall an international legal challenge. Nevertheless, a state cannot invoke a defense that the action of an executive organ or officer is not attributable to the state simply because the action is illegal or *ultra vires* under domestic law.[46]

Under Article 2(d) of the Women's Convention, states parties undertake

To refrain from engaging in any act or practice of discrimination against women and to ensure the public authorities and institutions shall act in conformity with this obligation.

Such restraint is not dependent on legislation, although the absence of required restraint may be remedied and compensated through the national judiciary. The provision makes it clear, however, that the executive branch of government must observe the practice of non-discrimination.

Executive responsibility of a state for violations of international human rights law arises when its military personnel engage in acts of inhumanity, whether against aliens outside its territory or against its own citizens within its territory. Torture and causing "disappearances" implicate state liability.[47] The rape of women is also an international human rights outrage,[48] but it has tended to go unobserved because it has been considered an inescapable element of subjugation of a population. The plight of violated women is aggravated when they lose status in the eyes of their families, husbands, and communities by this victimization. A similarly unacknowledged form of torture consists in violating men's wives or daughters before their eyes, or threatening rape, to force men's confessions or to induce them to supply information.

Varieties of state responsibility through executive misconduct are numerous,[49] and now go beyond crude outrages to address passive failures to meet positive obligations. In the case of *Airey v. Ireland*,[50] for instance, the European Court of Human Rights found Ireland at fault through its failure to provide adequate legal aid or simplified procedures to achieve remedies through its courts. Mrs. Airey, an Irish national, alleged that the state failed to protect her because the prohibitively high cost of lawyers prevented her from obtaining a judicial separation from her alcoholic husband who had abused her. The Court held that Mrs. Airey's right under Article 6(1) "to a fair and public hearing within a reasonable time by an independent and impartial tribunal established by law" had been violated.

The Court found that the fulfillment of a duty under the European Convention "necessitates some positive action on the part of the State; in such circumstances, the State cannot simply remain passive."[51] The Court stated that providing a lawyer to such individuals is

indispensable for an effective access to court either because legal representation is rendered compulsory, as is done by the domestic law of certain contracting States for various types of litigation, or by reason of the complexity of the procedure or of the case.[52]

The Court also held that the state had violated Mrs. Airey's right under Article 8 to respect for private and family life. Noting that Article 8 does not simply compel the state to abstain from interference but that positive obligations must be discharged to protect the respect due to private and family life, the Court stated that the entitlement to a decree of judicial separation recognizes that protection of private or family life may, under Irish law, involve a husband and wife being relieved of the duty to live together.[53] The Court concluded:

Effective respect for private or family life obliges Ireland to make this means of protection effectively accessible, when appropriate, to anyone who may wish to have recourse thereto.[54]

Legislative Acts

When states assume membership in international human rights conventions, they agree to give effect to treaty obligations owed to individuals, principally although not exclusively their own nationals, in their municipal legal systems. These treaty responsibilities exist for all states parties, no matter whether their law is codified, as for instance in the civil law tradition, or whether they are so-called common law states whose law is customary through judicial declaration but liable to be superseded by legislation. States that do not adhere to either of these European traditions may not distinguish secular from religious laws but derive significant portions of their law from interpretations of sacred texts.

Legislative incompatibility with the Women's Convention exists when a state fails in its obligation "To repeal all national penal provisions which constitute discrimination against women."[55] In contrast to this negative duty of repeal is the positive obligation of states

To adopt appropriate legislative and other measures, including sanctions where appropriate, prohibiting all discrimination against women.[56]

The Women's Convention makes explicit the legal expectation of conformity with its obligations through national measures, of which laws are frequently the most obvious and direct. Article 24 provides that

States parties undertake to adopt all necessary measures at the national level aimed at achieving the full realization of the rights recognized in the present Convention.

The Women's Convention intends to be comprehensive, but recognizes that some national laws and other international agreements may in fact be more conducive to the elimination of all forms of discrimination against women. Article 23 provides that

Nothing in this Convention shall affect any provisions that are more conducive to the achievement of equality between men and women which may be contained:
(a) In the legislation of a state party; or
(b) In any other international convention, treaty or agreement in force for that State.

More significant for sexual equality de jure and de facto, however, is the obligation in Article 24 to introduce necessary national measures.

Article 24 may afford states discretion to adopt methods that suit the political traditions, constitutional conventions and idiosyncrasies of their legal and political orders for the purpose of moving towards achievement of the equality goals of the Women's Convention. For instance, instead of introducing a piecemeal review of its national legislation, a state may introduce a Bill of Rights or Charter of Rights and Freedoms, perhaps a constitutional instrument, in light of which all legislation is subsequently to be applied. More modestly, a state may introduce an Interpretation Act providing that all legislation is to be understood as equating the rights of women with those of men insofar as a particular context will permit, or that all laws are to be interpreted as applicable equally to both sexes as far as is practicable.[57]

A failure of a state's legislation to give effective protection to private and family life under Article 8 of the European Convention on Human Rights was found in the case of X and Y v. The Netherlands.[58] The defendant state was found in breach of its obligation "to respect" private life by having no criminal law mechanism by which an alleged rapist of a mentally handicapped girl could be prosecuted. The Court noted that, although Article 8 is primarily concerned with protecting individuals from aggressive interference of public authorities by requiring them to refrain from actions, there may be positive obligations inherent in an effective respect for private or family life. These obligations may involve the adoption of measures designed to secure respect for private life even in the sphere of the relations of individuals between themselves.[59]

The court acknowledged that the choice of means designed to achieve compliance with Article 8 is a matter that falls within the contracting state's margin of appreciation. While there are different means of ensuring "respect for private and family life," so that recourse to criminal law is not necessarily mandated, prevailing civil law remedies were insufficient in this case.[60] Effective deterrence was crucial, because the offense alleged in the X and Y case involved fundamental values and essential aspects of private life. The state was found able to achieve such deterrence only through criminal law provisions.[61] This claim is underscored in that other states normally undertake this protection of personal privacy under criminal statutes. Thus the Court held unanimously that, since the Netherlands Criminal Code failed to provide Miss Y with practical or effective protection from this sort of assault, the state had violated Article 8 of the European Convention. The Court awarded Miss Y compensation of 3,000 Dutch guilders.[62]

It is a failure of a state's executive organ when its legislature is ineffective to repeal offensive legislation or to enact mandatory legislation because an executive officer vetoes what the legislature has approved, or, where a parliamentary executive exists, because an influential minister fails to initiate legislation. The failure is particularly glaring when a state party to a convention maintains a law similar to that of another state party that has been held to be violative of the convention. A state party should not wait until its own legislation has been challenged, but should move readily to change it. Whether legislation is subject to an executive veto or requires executive initiation, a state remains responsible for the condition of its legislation, and cannot invoke the terms of its own constitution as a defense against its international liability.

Legislative failures arise, for instance, when legislation discriminates against women by permitting male nationals who marry alien wives to afford them and children of the union the husbands' nationality, but does permit national women who marry alien husbands to afford them and resulting children their national status.[63] Moreover, legislation affording all males priority over females in intestate succession to land or other advantage would discriminate on its face, in violation of the Women's Convention.

When provisions discriminatory against women, for instance on inheritance to or ownership or use of land, are expressed in laws or customs, states parties to the Women's Convention have accepted an obligation of result to reform or repeal such laws or customs.[64]

The state obligation to reform discriminatory customary law extends to an obligation to introduce legislation or constitutional provisions to reform non-codified customary law. Under Article 2(a) of the Women's Convention states parties have agreed

To embody the principle of the equality of men and women in their national constitutions or other appropriate legislation if not yet incorporated therein, and to ensure, through law and other appropriate means, the practical realization of this principle.

A particular difficulty is presented, however, when a state has a constitution such as Kenya's, which explicitly provides that the prohibition of discrimination does not apply to matters governed by personal law, matters including property, and matters governed by customary law.[65] It is a general principle of international law that states cannot invoke the provisions of their own constitutions to justify or excuse derogation from their internationally binding legal obligations.[66] Accordingly, Kenya faces the dilemma of being obliged either to amend its Constitution compatibly with the obligations it has assumed, as a state party to the Women's Convention, or to be in perpetual violation of its obligations while its customary law is discriminatory.

Judicial Acts

States parties agree to take "all appropriate measures" in Article 2(c) of the Women's Convention

To establish the legal protection of the rights of women on an equal basis with men to ensure through competent national tribunals and other public institutions the effective protection of women against any act of discrimination.

The article leaves states parties a choice of means and creates legal obligations to exercise choice diligently.

Domestic law furnishes relatively few instances of legal responsibilities arising from the official conduct of judges, because of doctrines of judicial immunity. At the international level, a state's responsibility for the conduct of its judiciary is frequently masked because judicial acts of an administrative nature appear as executive action and acts of adjudication may interpret legislation or determine the legal character of executive action, so that attention is deflected from the judiciary itself onto the legislature or the executive.

The judiciary has the responsibility to determine the application of principles of international human rights law, including relevant conventions, at the national level. If final courts of accessible appeal consider themselves bound by national legislation or legal doctrines in ways that obstruct enforcement of human rights, national judicial remedies will be exhausted and the claim will assume an international character:

> if . . . the courts commit errors in that task [of treaty interpretation] or decline to give effect to the treaty or are unable to do so because the necessary change in, or addition to, the national law has not been made, their judgments involve the State in a breach of treaty.[67]

For instance, the European Court of Human Rights found the United Kingdom in breach of the European Convention on Human Rights because of a judgment of its highest court that denied the Convention's guarantee of freedom of expression.[68]

Important powers and responsibilities lie in the hands of the judiciary to give effect to women's rights. In many non-codified legal systems, development of the law of inheritance, tenure, and transfer of land is customary in origin, and is amenable to development through the courts. Judges have the power to respect the claims of women, such as to just inheritance, possession, and use of land, and can invoke international human rights conventions to condition the evolution of the law. Judges' failure or refusal to apply human rights principles to this effect will implicate the responsibility of the state, although the state organ that appears at fault may be the legislature that failed to reform the law or the executive that failed to urge revision.

The judiciary of both secular and religious courts[69] may serve as a primary instrument through which states parties to the Women's Convention discharge their responsibility "To modify the social and cultural patterns of conduct . . . which are based on the idea of the inferiority or the superiority of either of the sexes or on stereotyped roles for men and women."[70] Because senior judges tend to be the elders of their communities, trained in traditions and values of earlier times, and to favor the predictability of stable rules over the unpredictable results of innovation, judges are often slow to modify social and cultural patterns of conduct. Their perceptions are often shaped by stereotypical thinking about the social roles of men and women, and they accept as self-evident truths, for instance, that women cannot compete in the rough and tumble worlds of industry or the market place, and that men living alone cannot rear young children.

An instance of the judiciary playing a leading role in the elimination of stereotypical thinking about women comes from Tanzania. In *Ephrahim v. Pastory,* [71] the High Court of Tanzania faced an inherent conflict between Haya customary law and the Tanzanian Bill of Rights.

The High Court invoked the sexual nondiscrimination provisions in the Tanzanian Bill of Rights and human rights conventions, including the Women's Convention, the African Charter on Human and Peoples' Rights, and the International Covenant on Civil and Political Rights, all of which Tanzania has ratified, to conclude that customary law has been modified to afford men and women equal rights to inherit, own, and sell land.[72] The case involved a challenge against a woman's right to dispose of land rather than to inherit land, but the Court ruled that in all incidents of land ownership the Bill of Rights operated to equate the rights of women with those of men.

It would therefore be neither accurate nor fair to presume that judges are the source of the inequality that women frequently face in the courts.[73] Instances exist in which national judges have brought legal systems into conformity with the standards laid down by international human rights conventions. It cannot necessarily be presumed either, however, that national judiciaries can be relied upon to take the initiatives at their disposal, nor that advocates appearing before them will be uniformly inspired by the values of international human rights. The price of women's human rights to enjoy freedoms remains the eternal vigilance of national judiciaries.

The Way Forward: Improving State Practice

Developing international human rights law through treaties such as the Women's Convention, and recognizing international customary law on human rights, are necessary but in themselves not insufficient steps to the achievement of women's human rights through international law. The legal foundation of rights serves only as a basis on which to build structures that will protect the security and integrity of women and provide them an equitable opportunity for individual and collective development. Treaties offer an architecture of rights, but the realization of treaty goals requires further construction. Treaties must be followed by an effective method to monitor and police states' observance of the obligations to which they have committed themselves; and national and international mechanisms to maintain treaties in effect and to enforce state responsibility for violations of treaty rights.

The enormity of the task that the Women's Convention tackles should not be minimized. The Race Convention similarly concerns the way in which some races treat others, but reflects the popular conception that "human rights" concern treatment of minorities. The origin of modern human rights law concerns vulnerable individuals at the margins of their societies, such as ethnic and religious minorities, political activists, and, for instance, prisoners. The Women's Convention is designed to change how half of humanity treats the other half, and to compel the dominant half to elevate the subordinate half to the functional status of equals.

Effective power in every state is in the hands of men whose self-interest as such may appear to lie in maintenance of the status quo. Their definition of normality, nature, or divine will centers on male ascendancy and female servitude. They do not find it oppressive of women or unjust that man should be the hunter, provider, and protector or that women should care for the home and the children. The values of their cultures, religions, and homes often appear to idealize relations between men and women that perpetuate a conservative imagery in which men are active and visible, women passive and invisible. The Women's Convention requires not that this pattern be inverted but that it be equalized. Nevertheless, the change the Convention requires compels the male leadership of states to reconsider and change the states' most fundamental political, social, economic, and religious structures, and to revise the culture through which its peoples define and comprehend themselves.

International law is the product of states' collective vision and practice. It may progress more rapidly through the cumulative effect of small changes rather than depend on the revolutionary impact of a new doctrine. The Women's Convention is explicable as a stage in the evolution of human rights, traceable to treaties adopted early in this century and reinforced in its middle period. The deficiency remains that its thrust, effective at the level of rhetoric, has not yet been effective through the inspiration or compulsion of state practice. Neither domestic nor international orders have been effective in delivering the promise of the Convention to advance the frontiers of women's de facto equality with men. Many states parties to the Convention have structured their resistance through reservations in law, and many more demonstrate resistance through reservation in practice. Few states have objected to others' legal reservations, and fewer to others' tardiness in practice, in fear, perhaps of exposing their own records of practice.

Legal strategies are needed not simply to monitor but to effect state practice to implement specific provisions of the Women's Convention.[74] The duty to report to CEDAW keeps states parties conscious of their legal accountability for violations of the Women's Convention, and of their legal obligation to eliminate private discriminatory behavior. CEDAW might facilitate the duty of states parties to report by developing a comprehensive General Recommendation on Article 2 similar to its General Recommendation on Violence Against Women and to the General Comment developed by the Committee on Economic, Social, and Cultural Rights on Article 2 of the Economic Covenant.

A General Recommendation on Article 2 of the Women's Convention could make clear that CEDAW will apply international standards of conduct to state practice with respect to women. Moreover, the General Recommendation could explain that CEDAW will give autonomous interpretations to terms, such as "in all its forms," of the Women's Convention and their application.

CEDAW's effectiveness in monitoring state compliance is greatly enhanced by non-governmental organizations that provide them with information and alternative reports about violations of women's rights in reporting countries.[75] These reports expose violations that often go unrecognized and show how they might have been prevented or at least remedied by the state. Moreover, the alternative reports are far less sympathetic than the state reports to justifications and excuses of human rights violations offered by states on the grounds that the denial of such human rights is compatible with preservation of indigenous social, cultural, and religious traditions.

The dissonance between women's organizations' criticisms of states' inadequate protection of women's rights and states' explanations that such rights are subject to wider cultural and traditional imperatives poses the questions whether states can be relied upon to compel respect for women's human rights and whether they are parties to or complicit in their violation. The doctrine of state responsibility raises this question to an international concern amenable to scrutiny and perhaps resolution before international tribunals. The doctrine has the merit of affording states the right to contest international jurisdiction on the ground that their domestic remedies are available and adequate, and of affording the international community the means to hold states to account whose remedies are unavailable or ineffective and whose practices deny women the protection of international human rights law.

Notes

1. Charlotte Bunch, "Women's Rights as Human Rights: Toward a Re-Vision of Human Rights," *Hum. Rts. Q.* 12 (1990): 486.

2. Menno T. Kamminga, *Inter-State Accountability for Violations of Human Rights* (Philadelphia: University of Pennsylvania Press, 1992), 4–5.

3. Rebecca Cook, "International Human Rights Law Concerning Women: Case Notes and Comments," *Vand. J. Transnat'l L.* 23 (1990): 779.

4. Kamminga, *Inter-State Accountability,* note 2; Oscar Schachter, *International Law in Theory and Practice* (New York: Kluwer Academic Publishers, 1991).

5. See generally Philip Alston and Gerard Quinn, "The Nature and Scope of States Parties' Obligations Under the International Covenant on Economic, Social, and Cultural Rights," *Hum. Rts. Q.* 9 (1987): 156; Ahcene Boulesbaa,

"The Nature of the Obligations Incurred by States Under Article 2 of the U.N. Convention Against Torture," *Hum. Rts. Q.* 12 (1990): 53; Thomas Buergenthal, "To Respect and To Ensure: State Obligations and Permissible Derogations," in *The International Bill of Rights: The Covenant on Civil and Political Rights,* ed. Louis Henkin (New York: Columbia University Press, 1981), 72; Dominic McGoldrick, *The Human Rights Committee: Its Role in the Development of the International Covenant on Civil and Political Rights* (Oxford: Clarendon Press, 1991), Chap. 6; Manfred Nowak, *U.N. Covenant on Civil and Political Rights: CCPR Commentary* (Strasbourg: N.P. Engel, 1993), part 2.

6. 18 Dec. 1979, U.N. GAOR Supp. 34th Sess., No. 21 (A/34/46) at 193, U.N. Doc. A/RES/34/180 (entry into force 3 Sept. 1981); as of January 1994, 131 countries are states parties; see Appendix A, p. 285.

7. Human Rights Committee General Comment 3(13) CCPR/C/21/Rev.1 (1989).

8. U.N. GAOR, 5th Sess., Supp. No. 3, U.N. Doc. E/1991/23 at para. 4.

9. International Law Commission Draft Articles on State Responsibility, art. 20.

10. ILC Draft, note 9, art. 21.

11. It provides that "States Parties condemn racial discrimination and undertake to pursue by all appropriate means and without delay a policy of eliminating racial discrimination in all its forms."

12. 1L Y.B. Int'l Comm'n Pt. II at 27 (1977).

13. 23 May 1969, 1155 U.N.T.S. 331, art. 27.

14. *U.S. v. Mexico,* 4 R.I.A.A. iv, 60, para. 4 (1926).

15. See, for example, Women's Convention, art. 2.

16. See, for example, Women's Convention, art. 2(e), (f).

17. Rebecca Cook, "Reservations to the Convention on the Elimination of All Forms of Discrimination Against Women," *Va. J. Int'l L.* 30 (1990): 643, 713.

18. In the Matter of *Van Duzen v. Canada,* Communication No. R. 12/50, Views of the Human Rights Committee, 7 Apr. 1982, U.N. Doc. CCPR/C/DR (xv)/R.12/50 para. 10.2.

19. *Y.B. Eur. Conv. H.R.* 4 (1961): 438.

20. *Y.B. Eur. Conv. H.R.* 4, note 19 at 474.

21. Women's Convention, Preamble, para. 6.

22. Women's Convention, Preamble, para. 15.

23. Art. 2.

24. U.N. ESCOR Supp. No. 5 at 54, at paras. 9 and 23; U.N. Doc. E/CN.6/573 (1973).

25. Rebecca Cook, "International Protection of Women's Reproductive Rights," *N.Y.U. J. Int'l L. & Pol.* 24 (1992): 645, 682–83, 697–98.

26. M. Forde, "Non-Governmental Interferences with Human Rights," *Brit. Y.B. Int'l L.* 56 (1985): 253.

27. Case of *Plattform Artze für das Leben,* 139 Eur. Ct. H.R. (ser. A) (1988).

28. Annual Report, Inter-Am. C.H.R. 35, OAS/Ser. L./V./III.19, doc. 13 (1988).

29. Inter-Am. C.H.R., *Velásquez Rodríguez,* note 28 at 70, para. 166.

30. *Report of the Committee on the Elimination of Discrimination Against Women,* U.N. Doc. A/47/38 (1992) at 5.

31. U.N. Committee Report, note 30 at 8.

32. See generally Kenneth Roth, "Domestic Violence as an International Human Rights Issue," Chapter 13 in this book.

33. *Nairobi Strategies,* U.N. Doc. A/Conf.116/28/Rev.1 1985.

34. *Nairobi Strategies,* note 33 at para. 4.

35. See Asma Mohamed Abdel Halim, "Challenges to the Application of International Women's Human Rights in the Sudan," Chapter 17 in this book; Sara Hossain, "Equality in the Home: Women's Rights and Personal Laws in South Asia," Chapter 20 in this book; and Kirti Singh, "Obstacles to Women's Rights in India," Chapter 16 in this book.

36. See Florence Butegwa, "Using the African Charter on Human and Peoples' Rights to Secure Women's Access to Land in Africa," Chapter 21 in this book.

37. G. A. Res. 104, U.N. GAOR 48th sess. (1993).

38. Marianne Hirsch and Evelyn Fox Keller, eds., *Conflicts in Feminism* (New York: Routledge, 1990).

39. Marnia Lazreg, "Feminism and Difference: The Perils of Writing as a Woman on Women in Algeria," in *Conflicts in Feminism,* ed. Hirsch and Keller, note 38 at 326.

40. K. T. Bartlett, "Feminist Legal Methods," *Harv. L. Rev.* 103 (1990): 829–88.

41. Bartlett, "Feminist Legal Methods," note 40 at 837.

42. Bartlett, "Feminist Legal Methods," note 40 at 843.

43. Carrie Menkel-Meadow, "Mainstreaming Feminist Theory," *Pac. L. J.* 23 (1992): 1493.

44. Hilary Charlesworth, "What Are 'Women's International Human Rights'?" Chapter 3 in this book; Radhika Coomaraswamy, "To Bellow like a Cow: Women, Ethnicity, and the Discourse of Rights," Chapter 2 in this book, Celina Romany, "State Responsibility Goes Private: A Feminist Critique of the Public/Private Distinction in International Human Rights Law," Chapter 4 in this book.

45. Ian Brownlie, *System of the Law of Nations, State Responsibility,* Part I (Oxford: Clarendon Press, 1983), 150.

46. Brownlie, *Law of Nations,* note 45 at 145.

47. Inter-Am. Ct., *Velásquez Rodríguez,* note 28.

48. See generally Rhonda Copelon, "Intimate Terror: Understanding Domestic Violence as Torture," Chapter 5 in this book; and Joan Fitzpatrick, "The Use of International Human Rights Norms to Combat Violence Against Women," Chapter 23 in this book.

49. Brownlie, *Law of Nations,* note 45 at 132–42.

50. *Airey v. Ireland,* 32 Eur. Ct. H.R. (ser. A) (1979).

51. *Airey v. Ireland,* note 50, para. 25.

52. *Airey v. Ireland,* note 50, para 26.

53. *Airey v. Ireland,* note 50, para. 33.

54. *Airey v. Ireland,* note 50.

55. Women's Convention, art. 2(g).

56. Women's Convention, art. 2(b).

57. See, e.g., The United Kingdom Interpretation Act 1978, sec. 6 stating that "In any Act, unless the contrary intention appears,—(a) words importing the masculine gender include the feminine; and (b) words importing the feminine gender include the masculine; . . ."

58. *X and Y v. The Netherlands,* 91 Eur. Ct. H.R. (ser. A) (1985).

59. *X and Y v. The Netherlands,* note 58, para. 23.

60. *X and Y v. The Netherlands,* note 58, paras. 24–25.

61. *X and Y v. The Netherlands*, note 58, para. 27.

62. *X and Y v. The Netherlands*, note 58, para. 40.

63. At least nine states parties to the Women's Convention have reserved the nationality provision of Article 9. Cook, "Reservations," note 17 at 693–96, 714–15.

64. Women's Convention, art. 2(f); see section above on "Customs and Practices."

65. Constitution of Kenya, Sec. 82(4)(b), (c); see generally Perpetua W. Karanja, "Women's Land Ownership Rights in Kenya," *Third World Legal Stud.* (1991): 109.

66. Vienna Convention, art. 27, note 13.

67. Arnold D. McNair, *Law of Treaties* (Oxford: Clarendon Press, 1961), 346.

68. *The Sunday Times case,* 30 Eur. Ct. H.R. (ser. A) (1979).

69. See generally Donna Sullivan, "Gender Equality and Religious Freedom: Toward a Framework for Conflict Resolution," *N.Y.U. J. Int'l L. & Pol.* 24 (1992): 795, 848–54.

70. Women's Convention, art. 5(a).

71. (PC) Civil Appeal No. 70 of 1989 (unreported).

72. Civil Appeal, note 71 at 4.

73. See generally Kathleen E. Mahoney, "Canadian Approaches to Equality Rights and Gender Equity in the Courts," Chapter 19 in this book.

74. See Abdullahi Ahmed An-Na'im, "State Responsibility Under International Human Rights Law to Change Religious and Customary Laws," Chapter 7 in this book; Andrew Byrnes, "Toward More Effective Enforcement of Women's Human Rights Through the Use of International Human Rights Law and Procedures," Chapter 8 in this book; Chaloka Beyani, "Toward a More Effective Guarantee of Women's Rights in the African Human Rights System," Chapter 11 in this book; Cecilia Medina, "Toward a More Effective Guarantee of the Enjoyment of Human Rights by Women in the Inter-American System," Chapter 10 in this book; and Anne F. Bayefsky, "General Approaches to Domestic Application of Women's International Human Rights," Chapter 15 in this book, for discussion of such strategies.

75. See, e.g., Association of Development Agencies in Bangladesh, *Alternative Report on Implementation of United Nations Convention on the Elimination of All Forms of Discrimination Against Women in Bangladesh* (Dhaka, Bangladesh: the Association, 1992); Sharon Ladin, "IWRAW to CEDAW: Country Reports," *International Women's Rights Action Watch* (Minneapolis: Humphrey Institute, University of Minnesota, 1992).

Chapter 10
Toward a More Effective Guarantee of the Enjoyment of Human Rights by Women in the Inter-American System

Cecilia Medina

Introduction

Before addressing the substance of my chapter, I think it useful to state my position on some points. First, I have consciously changed the title of my chapter and refrained from using the expression "women's rights." My starting point is that human rights are those rights that each and every human being has on the sole merit of being human; thus it does not seem possible to use an expression that suggests the idea that some human beings, women, have different rights from those of other human beings, men. A first consequence of this position is that I find in the existence of human rights the moral justification to fight for women. I can think of no other reason that I should be entitled to plead for the improvement of women's lot in life. Consequently, my approach is that the struggle for women forms part of the general struggle to develop respect for the dignity of all human beings, and it is from the latter that it obtains the necessary force and legitimacy that will ultimately ensure its success.

A second consequence of this approach is that, in order to justify enjoyment by women of their rights, I do not find it necessary to point out that some characteristics inherent to women are better than those of men for an adequate functioning of society, or to argue that women have a higher morality or a higher intellect than men and that their serving in leading positions in society will result in an improved form of community life. In my view, women do not need to "earn" human rights; they should be encouraged, not hindered, to achieve leading positions in society, and have their fair share of power, education, financial resources, and so forth, only because they are human beings, and discrimination on any basis is not tolerated by international law. This notwithstanding, in the struggle to improve the situation of any sector of society that has been postponed in terms of human rights, it is legitimate and useful to create new formulations for existing human rights and/or establish actions one wishes to combat as specific violations of human rights, even though they might be subsumed within the general norms. In this way, women could acquire useful instruments to achieve the final aim they pursue, namely, nondiscrimination in the enjoyment of human rights. Thus, at this point in history, there is a need for stronger international human rights law especially for women and there is a need for women to make this happen.

This statement may appear self-evident, but it is not without controversy. So far, women have not really enjoyed human rights and, perhaps influenced by this fact, some sectors of the women's movement question the validity or the usefulness of resorting to human rights to carry out their struggle.[1] In this respect, and as a second point, I think it useful to state briefly my perception of international human rights law to explain why I think it is wrong to discard that body of law as a main arena in which to fight for the improvement of women's lot in society and, above all, for fairness in treatment. Societies usually try to embody in legal provisions the values they cherish, and I conceive international human rights law as a response of the community to the violation of, or ever-present threat to, the dignity of human beings throughout the world. As a consequence, I consider catalogues of human rights as historically determined, thus containing what at a certain moment of history appears to be threatening this core, which is human dignity. The historical character of the catalogue makes international human rights law essentially evolutionary: on the one hand, new categories of individuals may accede to the status of human beings in the eyes of the community (something that blacks and women are finally achieving); on the other hand, the community may perceive new threats or lower its threshold of tolerance toward intrusions or omissions of the state concerning their human dignity. A perfect example is the development of the concept of privacy through the progressive interpretation of Article 8 of the European Convention of Human Rights by the European Court of Human Rights.[2]

Thus the negative situation of women vis-à-vis international human rights law—largely due to the absence of women's participation in its creation and interpretation—can be reversed if women begin consistently to use international human rights law for their own benefit. This is all the more likely when one considers that international human rights law is created and developed in various arenas, not only inter-governmental fora, and by various actors, ranging from non-governmental organizations (NGOs), through national courts and parliaments, to individuals. These actors reciprocally influence each other, the contents and application of international human rights law being the result of a synthesis of all their activities. By involving themselves in the creation and functioning of international human rights law, women may stride toward their goal.

A last point to be made is that I start from the premise that the purpose of human rights law is to allow individuals to exercise their human rights fully, and not to have to resort constantly to remedies. Because of the nature of human rights, this is better accomplished at a national level. Therefore it is my understanding that the ultimate aim of international human rights law is to strengthen national law as much as possible, international law itself remaining a subsidiary instrument to recognize and protect human rights and a main instrument to support and give legitimacy to the changes needed at a national level.

In this chapter I will work from an international human rights law perspective, distinguishing four areas in which international law operates. The first is standard setting, that is to say, the creation of legal norms establishing the catalogue of human rights that states should promote and protect. The second is promotion, this being the effort of developing awareness in the international community of the existence of the standards and campaigning for their acceptance. The third is the implementation of rights at a national level, an area in which international law plays the role of forcing, or persuading states to take the necessary steps so that human rights can be fully enjoyed by all. The fourth is protection, where international law grants international organs the competence to investigate, and eventually condemn and order the redress of human rights violations.

I intend, first, merely to point out the problems women face in the area of human rights, either de jure or de facto, and the importance of the political, social, and economic context for the solution of these problems.[3] I do not pretend to give an exhaustive list of the problems, to address the many differences existing among the various countries on the continent, or to substantiate my perception with many references to statistical data. Second, I will describe the main characteristics of the inter-American system for the promotion and protection of human rights, selecting those I consider suitable to help the particular situation of women. Third, in light of the above I will offer a few examples of what women can do within the system, as it is now. Fourth, I will indicate some tasks that in my opinion should be undertaken to achieve the aims pursued by women.

I am aware, and I think it is important that the reader also be aware, that the struggle for the real enjoyment of human rights by women is multidimensional and heterogeneous, so that my contribution addresses merely one of the many forms that the struggle must take in order to achieve its purpose.[4]

The Problems Women Face in Latin America

The position of women in Latin America does not constitute an exception. Statistics show, in general, the same weaknesses as in other parts of the world. The position of women in society is well reflected in the legal order of their countries, where it is possible to find discriminatory provisions, although most states have ratified international treaties that create for them the legal obligation of doing away with, among other things, legal discrimination. Affairs are improving at a very slow pace,[5] and it is still possible to find discriminatory provisions in civil law, especially with regard to married women and their capacity to administer marital or even their own property, or in criminal law, where differences between men and women, or between "honest" or "pure" women and dishonest women, amount to blatant discrimination.[6] For example, a single act of sexual intercourse of a married woman with a man other than her husband constitutes a criminal offense, called adultery, while it is not so for married men, who can only be punished for concubinage, that is to say, keeping a woman for a certain period of time. The penalty for rape does not depend on the gravity of the offense but on the qualities of the victim, as the law distinguishes between married and unmarried women (the penalty is higher if the victim is married), "honest" and "not honest" woman (naturally the penalty is higher if the victim is "honest"). It should also be remembered that in almost all Latin American countries abortion is a criminal offense, even in cases of rape.

Even where legal discrimination has decreased, women continue to be treated—at home, at work, at school, in social life—as subordinate beings, and often continue to behave as subordinate beings, adding a de facto discrimination to the legal one.[7] If we take political participation, although women began to acquire political rights by the end of this century's third decade[8] and by now enjoy these rights throughout the Americas, the percentage of women in public office is minimal. In Chile, for instance, there are more women registered to vote than men (51.5 percent against 48.5 percent), and almost all registered women vote;[9] nonetheless, we barely find 1 Cabinet Minister (Women's Affairs), 3 under-secretaries, no governors, and 63 mayors out of 325; in Congress, there are 7 women representatives out of 120 and 3 senators out of 47; in the judiciary, there are no women on the Supreme Court, and only 25 out of 120 in Courts of Appeals, despite the fact that women constitute 43.6 percent of the judiciary.[10] In Central America and Panama, women fare no better.[11]

As to the economic situation, the enormous gap between rich and poor particularly affects women. Although there has been some improvement, women, who constitute half or more of the population in each state of the American continent, still constitute only around one-third of the economically active population, and are significantly poorer than men; they occupy less skilled jobs, have difficulty in achieving higher positions, earn less than men, and are at greater risk of losing their jobs.[12] The low level of education constitutes a significant disadvantage in reversing the situation. There are countries in Latin America, such as Nicaragua, Guatemala, and Honduras, where illiteracy rates for women are between 25 percent and 40 percent.[13]

Women's personal integrity is often exposed to violence at home. The problem of domestic violence has just begun to be acknowledged; not only are the figures staggering, but so is the way the law and society react to it.[14] Women's personal freedom is severely curtailed. For example, a study made for Central America and Panama states that between 50 percent (Costa Rica) and 85 percent (El Salvador) of women living with a man, either married or unmarried, do not wish to have more than two or three children, and yet access to contraceptives is, as a matter of policy, extremely difficult. As a result, fertility rates in those countries between 1985 and 1990 were the following: Honduras, Guatemala, and Nicaragua, around six children; El Salvador, around five children.[15]

The problem of the subordination of women is a problem of power, deeply embedded in the culture of Latin America. To end subordination, the culture must change. This is no easy task and requires a thorough knowledge of the political, social, economic, and racial context of Latin America. Otherwise, strategies to improve the situation will not be effective. Two factors to consider are the still prevalent "Marianism" in Latin America's culture, which is the complement to "machismo," and the way in which Latin America's population came to exist. In an interesting study three authors analyze the influence of "mestizaje" in the identity of Latin American men and women. They suggest that the mixing of European males with indigenous women, realized by violence and in the context of war, and the blending of the indigenous religious beliefs, where woman represented the giver of life, the earth, with European Catholicism and its adoration of the Virgin Mary put women in a double bind. On the one hand, women find their worth in motherhood; on the other, they identify themselves with the Virgin Mary, thereby striving to be as pure and unselfish as "She" was.[16]

Concerning the political sphere, in many Latin American countries democracy is not often experienced, and men and women live in a context of authoritarianism, which is not conducive to realizing equality. Repression or subordination are facts of life with which many have to live. Political polarization is also a handicap: the right-wing ideology considers woman as mother and housewife; the left pays lip service to equality, but ascribes the subordination of women to capitalism and refuses to fight for women's liberation on the pretext that it will weaken the struggle to change society as a whole.[17] Progressive women have not succeeded in finding, or have not attempted to find, sound arguments to belie the latter. As a result, significant sectors of progressive Latin American women do not have a very positive reaction to "feminism."[18] They do not describe themselves as "feminists," even though they may behave as such. It seems that many women are scared of the word, since it has very radical connotations for the culture they have shared for so long; in this sense, declaring themselves "feminist" may be tantamount to declaring open war on their families and social relations.

Furthermore, the feminist movement is very often negatively perceived in Latin America as "petit bourgeois"; poor to lower-middle-class women's movements, although they may pursue the same cultural changes as those pursued by feminists, do not belong to feminism but to what is called "popular movements."[19] A possible explanation is that feminism has been promoted mainly by intellectual or upper-middle-to upper-class women, those with access to "first world" developments, and it addresses the issue of the advancement of women from a very individualistic position that requires attitudes on the part of women that those of poorer strata are in no psychological, mental, or physical condition to adopt, since the struggle for survival occupies all their strength. The importance of the context in which women live was made clear by Haydee Birgin, who wonders about the possibilities of carrying out the postulates of feminism in the middle of a very severe economic crisis in Argentina.[20] Her reflections are based on Ludolfo Paramio's "La libertad, la igualdad y el derecho a la infelicidad,"[21] where he states that women who are unqualified workers, and who therefore have no advantage to compete in the labor market, may be confronted with a dilemma if they are urged to work outside the home. They are told that, if they remain home, they will be their husbands' slaves, but if they work outside the home, they will lead a harder life and not necessarily achieve better living conditions. Given a choice between the devil and the deep blue sea, Paramio thinks it probable that a woman may prefer to confront the devil and deny the evidence of her unhappiness or of her oppression.[22] Reflections such as these, taken from the reality of most Latin American women, beg careful consideration of the context surrounding women, before deciding on any action. In societies such as those of Latin America, which are characterized by a significant gap between classes, this is an important point to take into consideration when deciding how, where, and when to act.

The Inter-American System for the Promotion and Protection of Human Rights

The Substantive Rules

The inter-American system[23] for the promotion and protection of human rights operates for all member states of the Organization of American States (OAS).[24] Twenty-five of them[25] are evaluated against the catalogue of human rights set forth in the American Convention on Human Rights,[26] being monitored by the Inter-American Commission on Human Rights (hereafter the Commission) acting as an organ of the Convention, and, if certain conditions are met, also by the Inter-American Court of Human Rights[27] (hereafter the Court), another organ of the Convention. The remaining OAS member states are evaluated against the standards set in the American Declaration on the Rights and Duties of Man,[28] and monitored by the Inter-American Commission on Human Rights, this time acting as an organ of the OAS Charter.

Both the American Declaration (despite its title and preamble) and the American Convention sustain as a fundamental principle that of nondiscrimination, among other things, on the basis of sex. Article II of the Declaration sets forth that:

All persons are equal before the law and have the rights and duties established in this Declaration, without distinction as to race, sex, language, creed or any other factor.

All the other rights in the catalogue are recognized for "every human being" or for "every person," except Article VII, which recognizes the right to special protection, care and aid for all children and for women during pregnancy and the nursing period. The American Convention, in its turn, states in Article 1:

1. The States Parties to this Convention undertake to respect the rights and freedoms recognized herein and to ensure to all persons subject to their

jurisdiction the free and full exercise of those rights and freedoms, without any discrimination for reasons of race, color, sex, language, religion, political or other opinion, national or social origin, economic status, birth, or any other social condition.
2. For the purposes of this Convention, "person" means every human being.

The catalogue in the Declaration comprises not only civil and political rights, but also social, economic, and cultural rights.[29] The catalogue in the American Convention establishes civil and political rights only. With regard to economic, social, and cultural rights, Article 26 sets forth that the states parties

undertake to adopt measures with a view to achieving progressively the full realization of the rights implicit in the economic, social, educational, scientific and cultural standards set forth in the Charter of the Organization of American States as amended by the Protocol of Buenos Aires.

On 17 November 1988, at San Salvador, an Additional Protocol to the American Convention on Economic, Social and Cultural Rights (Protocol of San Salvador) was adopted within the framework of the OAS and is open for signature and ratification.[30]

Besides these treaties of a general nature, there exist also a Protocol to the American Convention on the Abolition of the Death Penalty, adopted in Paraguay on 8 June 1990,[31] and the Inter-American Convention to Prevent and Punish Torture, adopted at Cartagena de Indías, Colombia, on 9 December 1985.[32] Specifically for women, there exist the Inter-American Conventions on the Granting of Political Rights and of Civil Rights to Women adopted at the Ninth International Conference of American States, held in Bogotá, Colombia, 30 March to 2 May, 1948.[33]

A rule that should also be mentioned is Article 29 of the American Convention, which provides a framework for states to interpret the Convention:

No provision of this Convention shall be interpreted as:
a. permitting any State Party, group, or person to suppress the enjoyment or exercise of the rights and freedoms recognized in this Convention or to restrict them to a greater extent than is provided for herein;
b. restricting the enjoyment or exercise of any right or freedom recognized by virtue of the laws of any State Party or by virtue of another convention to which one of the said states is a party;
c. precluding other rights or guarantees that are inherent in the human personality or derived from representative democracy as a form of government; or
d. excluding or limiting the effect that the American Declaration of the Rights and Duties of Man and other international acts of the same nature may have.

The Supervisory Organs and Their Functions

The Inter-American system possesses two organs to watch over the compliance of states with international human rights law: the Inter-American Commission on Human Rights (the Commission), and the Inter-American Court of Human Rights (the Court).

(a) The Inter-American Commission on Human Rights

The Commission,[34] an organ composed of seven independent experts, performs its activities with regard to OAS member states not parties to the Convention, under the authority of the OAS Charter and the Commission's statute, and its activities vis-à-vis states parties to the American Convention, under the authority of that Convention. The latter states are also subject to the supervision of the Commission on the authority of the Charter, in those aspects not covered by the Convention.[35]

The Commission has varied functions. Article 41 of the Convention sets forth, among other functions and powers, those of:

- developing an awareness of human rights among the peoples of America;
- providing the member states of the OAS with advisory services in the field of human rights;
- making recommendations to those states for the adoption of progressive measures in favor of human rights; and
- investigating and giving an opinion about complaints of human rights violations.

Furthermore, the Commission has, through its practice, given broader scope to its powers, having played an important role in the area of good offices and even mediation.[36] Thus the Commission has promotional and protective tasks.

Pursuant to its promotional function, the Commission prepares studies and reports, advises states, performs a modest educational role, organizing seminars and conferences, and executes quasi-legislative activities by drafting human rights conventions.[37] As stated above, this function is exercised vis-à-vis all OAS member states.

In exercise of its protective function, the Commission has devised two procedures, one of which is the procedure to examine communications regarding specific instances of human rights violations. This procedure can be set in motion by any person, group of persons, or non-governmental entity legally recognized by one or more OAS member states (Article 44 of the Convention) or by a state if conditions set forth in Article 45 thereof are met. The Commission's Regulations establish somewhat different rules to deal with communications against states parties to the Convention and those that are not parties thereto.[38] Finally, according to Article 26(2) of those Regulations, the Commission may initiate a case on its own motion. The second procedure is meant to examine the general situation of human rights in a country. Although it is not always so, the Commission usually carries out the latter type of procedure when the state is engaging in gross, systematic violations of human rights. Furthermore, sometimes the Commission also scrutinizes economic, social, and cultural rights in this procedure, under the authority of the American Declaration.[39]

Broadening its powers in comparison with other human rights organs, and as a matter of course, the Inter-American Commission monitors the conduct of the states not only with regard to the international obligations established either in the American Convention or the American Declaration, but also to all other obligations in the field of human rights.[40] The Commission is then competent to supervise the compliance of states with the United Nations Convention on the Elimination of All Forms of Discrimination Against Women or any other international treaty that may give support to women's human rights.

The procedure to deal with communications of specific instances of human rights violations ends with an opinion of the Commission, the case being able to go to the Court if certain conditions are met. Before the Court can hear a case it is necessary, first, that the procedure before the Commission be completed; second, that the Commission or a state party submit the case to the Court; and third, that the states parties to the case recognize or have recognized the contentious jurisdiction of the Court.[41] The procedure to examine the general situation of human rights in a country usually ends with a "country report," which is almost always published, and is discussed at the public forum of the OAS General Assembly.

To perform its protective function, the Commission has several legal mechanisms with which it investigates the conduct of states with regard to human rights. It can request the state for information, use communications as a source of information, conduct hearings, and carry out observations in loco. Once the situation is investigated, or sometimes while the situation is being investigated, the Commission may take action, such as make recommendations, offer its good offices or mediation, and use publicity.

Finally, it seems worthwhile to mention the fact that, since the Commission has operated for almost twenty years on the basis of its own regulations, its procedural rules are very flexible and fit the situation of human rights in a continent where very often the rule of law does not prevail.

(b) The Inter-American Court of Human Rights

A seven-member organ composed of "jurists of the highest moral authority and of recognized competence in the field of human rights," the Court has two types of jurisdiction, a contentious jurisdiction and an advisory one. The Court may exercise the former only with regard to states parties to the Convention, while it may exercise the latter at the request of any OAS member state or, within their sphere of competence, of any of the OAS organs listed in Chapter 10 of the OAS Charter.[42]

The advisory jurisdiction allows the court to interpret Article 64(1) of the American Convention or "other treaties concerning the protection of human rights in the American states." The Inter-American Court interpreted the expression "other treaties" in Article 64(1) stating that

> the advisory jurisdiction of the Court can be exercised, in general, with regard to any provision dealing with the protection of human rights set forth in any international treaty applicable in the American States, regardless of whether it be bilateral or multilateral, whatever be the principal purpose of such a treaty, and whether or not non-Member States of the inter-American system are or have a right to become parties thereto.[43]

It also allows the Court, at the request of a member state of the Organization, to give opinions regarding the compatibility of any of its domestic laws with the international obligations of the state in the field of human rights. The Court has interpreted the expression "domestic laws" as comprising "all national legislation and legal norms of whatsoever nature, including provisions of the national constitution," and with a caveat, also legislative proposals not yet adopted as law.[44]

The Court has rendered twelve advisory opinions, of which one is directly related to discrimination on the basis of sex.[45] Advisory Opinion No. 4 was requested by Costa Rica in conformity with Article 64(2) of the American Convention in order to have the Court's opinion on the compatibility of a constitutional amendment on naturalization being discussed in Congress. The Court was of the opinion that the proposed amendment in Article 14.4 of the bill, which established preferential conditions for naturalization of spouses of men as compared to those of women, constituted discrimination incompatible with Articles 17.4 and 24 of the American Convention.

The contentious jurisdiction empowers the Court to settle controversies about the interpretation and application of the provisions of the American Convention. Cases may be submitted to the Court by the Inter-American Commission on Human Rights or by the states. A case may finish by a decision in which the Court may "rule that the injured party be ensured the enjoyment of his right or freedom that was violated" and that "the consequences of the measure or situation that constituted the breach of such right or freedom be remedied and that fair compensation be paid to the injured party" (Article 63). Article 68 sets forth that "the States Parties to the Convention undertake to comply with the judgment of the Court in any case to which they are parties"; it establishes further that when the judgment stipulates compensatory damages, it can be executed in the country concerned.

Eight cases have reached the Court so far, of which three finished with a judgment of the Court, one is about to be settled because the state accepted responsibility, and four others are pending. The first three cases concerned disappearances and were submitted against Honduras. In two of them[46] the Court found a violation by Honduras of the right to life (Article 4), the right to humane treatment (Article 5), and the right to personal liberty (Article 7) of the American Convention. In the third, *Fairén Garbi* case,[47] the Court could not reach a conviction that the victim had disappeared within the territory of Honduras, so it did not find that the responsibility of that state had been proven.

There are two cases against Suriname that affect the rights of Articles 4 and 7. In one of them, the Court noted the admission of responsibility made by Suriname and left pending the decision on reparation.[48] The last three pending cases are against Peru and deal with violations of the rights in Articles 4, 5, and 7, plus the right to a fair trial (Article 8), right to property (Article 21) and the right to judicial protection (Article 25) concerning various Peruvian citizens who resided in Ayacucho.

A Brief Evaluation of the System

(a) Standard setting

As far as standard setting is concerned, international human rights law provides us, basically, with the means to fight private or public violation of human rights of women. The base is certainly the principle of nondiscrimination, set forth in Articles 1, 17, 24, and 27 of the American Convention and in Article 2 of the American Declaration. In my view, nondiscrimination on the basis of sex—as well as on the basis of race or of religion—is not just another human right, it is a principle, a fundamental one underlying human rights law in general and inter-American human rights law in particular, so much so that to deny it would amount to denying the existence of this law altogether. This quality is reflected in the American Convention on Human Rights, which does not allow states parties thereto even to suspend it in times of emergency.[49] This leads me to conclude that reservations to the American Convention might affect specific rights, but not the general principle of nondiscrimination on the basis of sex; otherwise, they would be incompatible with the object and purpose of the Convention, thereby not complying with the provisions of the Vienna Convention on the Law of Treaties, which govern the institution of reservations to the American Convention.[50]

States that are measured against the American Declaration are also bound to respect the principle, enshrined in its Article 2 and in the formulation of the rights, which are recognized for "every human being" or for "every person." A different interpretation would amount to excluding women, or other individuals, from the category "human being," and it would be rare to find somebody who would now sustain such an argument.

It could be argued that there is a significant difference in the treatment by international law of racial discrimination as compared to sexual discrimination, to the disadvantage of the latter. It is true that currently there seems to be agreement that the principle of non-discrimination on the basis of race has become *jus cogens,* while the same cannot be said about nondiscrimination on the basis of sex. However, if one analyzes the elements of *jus cogens,* one does not find any logical reason to differentiate between racial and sexual discrimination. The conclusion, apparently, has been reached from the prejudices that permeate legal thinking and not from an unbiased reading of the law. Although he is critical of the existence of *jus cogens,* this seems to be Brownlie's position, who lists the principle of racial discrimination among the least controversial examples of the class, adding in a footnote

The principle of religious non-discrimination must have the same status as also the rather neglected principle of non-discrimination as to sex.[51]

To return to what I said in the introduction, the system could be improved, as far as standard setting is concerned, by a careful revision of international norms with a view to (i) finding out the best formulation possible in order to prevent their misinterpretation to the detriment of women; and (ii) to spelling out in detail the international obligations of the states for allowing women full enjoyment of human rights, for example, by putting in international legal form violations of rights perpetrated against women as a matter of course.

(b) Promotion, implementation, and protection

Promotion of women's human rights has simply not happened at the level of the general human rights organ, that is to say, the Inter-American Commission on Human Rights. The Commission has not carried out properly its promotional function in general, but promotion is particularly absent with regard to enjoyment of human rights by women. The same can be said about the task of persuading states to implement the principle of nondiscrimination on the basis of sex in their national legal orders, which has not been attempted by the Commission. It is true that there is a specialized organ to perform this task, the Inter-American Commission on Women, but this should have been no obstacle for the Commission to do its share, specially since it has the advantage of a thorough knowledge of the general situation of human rights in the territories of the member states of the Organization of American States.

The task of protecting human rights of women, which is—unlike the other two mentioned above—strictly the Commission's and the Court's business, has not been carried out either. The Commission has neither investigated obvious discriminatory situations affecting women nor has it declared that by allowing the existence of these situations states are violating inter-American human rights law. The Court cannot use its powers unless it is requested to do so, and therefore it is no wonder that it has not dealt so far with any contentious case about discrimination against women. Thus the Commission has failed to exercise its powers with respect to protection of women's human rights, and the Court has not been given the chance to pronounce on women's issues.

Toward a More Effective Guarantee of the Enjoyment of Human Rights by Women in the Inter-American System

It is my contention that the failure of inter-American supervisory organs to address the violation of women's human rights is often not the result of a lack of legal provisions, but of their reluctance to apply them and of the fact that women do not resort to them. To reverse the situation, women should make a consistent effort.

It seems essential that women start to make international organs their own; for this, women have to be aware that international human rights law exists, that there are international obligations for the states in this field, and that there are organs with the power to monitor the behavior of states in human rights issues. Subsequently, they have to start using the system by putting their problems before the supervisory organs and making them face their bias, in order to convince those who apply the law to shed their prejudices and apply it to all situations that fit the norm, without regard to past practices. Furthermore, they should take a greater interest in controlling the membership of these organs, applying pressure so that women with a "gender awareness" are appointed thereto. Attention should also be devoted to monitoring the performance of the members of international organs, with a view to calling them to account and attempting to prevent their re-election.

International organs themselves have a significant responsibility in this regard. It seems incredible that even though they are ours, most individuals do not even know they exist. It is their duty to develop mechanisms to reach those who are the main subjects of their protective powers, and to publicize their work so that a positive dynamic starts to operate between the organs and the individuals they are supposed to serve.

How to Use the International Norms: A Few Examples

(a) Before the Inter-American Commission on Human Rights

Individual communications. The general principle of nondiscrimination and the specific provisions concerning sexual discrimination are enough to challenge any domestic legal provision that discriminates against women, such as legal incapacity, exclusion from administering marital property, exclusion from representing their children, or others. This could be done by means of a communication lodged with the Inter-American Commission that could eventually go to the Court.

It has been argued that the principle of nondiscrimination in international human rights law does not protect women against de facto discrimination. In my opinion this is not so. Article 1 of the American Convention establishes for states parties the obligation to "respect" and to "ensure to all persons subject to their jurisdiction the free and full exercise of" the rights and freedoms recognized in the Convention. Article 2 sets forth that the states parties undertake to adopt such legislative or *other measures* "as may be necessary to give effect to those rights or freedoms." State obligations arising from the American Convention, consequently, comprise not only an abstention by the state from violating a human right, but positive action to ensure the "free and full exercise" of these rights.

The Inter-American Court elaborated upon these legal provisions in its first judgment.[52] The matter under controversy was the disappearance of Mr. Velásquez Rodríguez in the territory of Honduras and the eventual responsibility of the state for this crime. The case was built by, first, proving that during a certain period of time many individuals, who shared certain characteristics such as political ideas, had disappeared in Honduras under similar circumstances, and second, proving that Velásquez Rodríguez had disappeared during that same period of time and under similar circumstances. Even though the case dealt with a disappearance, the importance of the Court's judgment for non-state violations merits relating some of the statements made by the Court. On analyzing Article 1.1, paragraph 166 of the judgment sets forth that:

The second obligation of the States Parties is to "ensure" the free and full exercise of the rights. . . . This obligation implies the duty of the States Parties to organize the governmental apparatus and, in general, all the structure through which public power is exercised, so that they are capable of juridically ensuring the free and full enjoyment of human rights. As a consequence . . . the States must prevent, investigate and punish any violation of the rights recognized by the Convention.

Paragraph 167 continues:

The obligation to ensure . . . is not fulfilled by the existence of a legal system designed to make it possible to comply with this obligation—it also requires the government to conduct itself so as to effectively ensure the free and full exercise of human rights.

Finally, on the state's responsibility, paragraph 172 states:

Thus, in principle, any violation of rights . . . carried out by an act of public authority or by persons who use their position of authority is imputable to the State. However, this does not define all the circumstances in which a State is obligated to prevent, investigate and punish human rights violations, nor all the cases in which the State might be found responsible for an infringement of those rights. An illegal act which violates human rights and which is initially not directly imputable to a State (for example, because it is the act of a private person or because the person responsible has not been identified) can lead to international responsibility of the State, not because of the act itself, but because of the lack of due diligence to prevent the violation or to respond to it as required by the Convention.

There does not seem to be a valid argument that would prevent an application of the Court's considerations in *Velásquez* to situations such as, for example, domestic violence against women or systematic de facto discrimination in labor law, if it could be proven that a practice exists that leaves domestic violence unpunished, or that the state is not undertaking any efforts to attempt prevention of the phenomenon. It would be important to test the capacity of the Court for being consistent and start an individual case at the Inter-American Commission with the special request that it be sent to the Court once the procedure before the Commission is ended.

Country reports and annual reports. With a view to monitoring the general compliance by states with the principle of nondiscrimination, the Inter-American Commission has the power to examine the situation of women's human rights in a specific state. This is a protective function and, in this sense, one that is the exclusive responsibility of the Commission. Up to now, country reports have never contained any mention of even legal discrimination against women, and it may not be realistic to expect that the Commission will do so on its own (though there have been women members of the Commission in the past). National women's associations could contact the Commission and provide it with pertinent information about the situation of human rights of women in any state about which the Commission is carrying out an investigation. They could also request the Commission to start a general investigation to be followed by a country report on the problem of domestic violence, for example, particularly since the *Velásquez* precedent could be used to identify this type of situation as one of "gross, systematic violations of human rights." In current international human rights law, the expression "gross, systematic violations of human rights," which triggers international action, is identified as such when the right to life, or the right to be free from torture, or the right not to be subjected to prolonged, arbitrary arrest are massively and systematically violated.[53]

We should not forget that the Commission has the power to make recommendations to the states for the adoption of progressive measures in favor of human rights, and it should be noted that it has not been shy in the exercise of this power. In its Annual Report 1979–1980, for example, the Commission recommended the government of El Salvador adopt the following measures:

(a) effective, real steps to disarm individuals and prevent the entry of weapons from abroad;
(b) a massive campaign against violence in the schools and the mass media;
(c) the reopening of the dialogue among all sectors of Salvadorian society without exception, including, therefore, the dissident forces of the left and of the right, with a view to establishing the conditions that would make it possible in the short term to hold elections which would reveal the true will of the people and

legitimize the government that wins such an election. For this purpose, a new election law and a reorganized Central Election Council are needed.[54]

If no country reports are forthcoming, it could be possible for the Commission to exercise its supervisory functions by means of its annual report, since it reports once a year, among other things, on the "Areas in which steps need to be taken towards full observance of the human rights set forth in the American Declaration of Rights and Duties of Man and the American Convention on Human Rights." The Commission addresses in that section of its Annual Reports varied topics of general concern, such as the situation of indigenous peoples (although there is an Inter-American Indian Institute), the status of economic, social and cultural rights, the rights of minors and the independence of the judiciary.[55]

Using these same procedures, the Inter-American Commission could start monitoring the de facto situation of women in the field of economic, social, and cultural rights. The Commission has done some pioneering work in this connection,[56] and nothing prevents it from adding gender as a category to its analysis. Moreover, by applying the precedent in *Broeks v. The Netherlands* (where the Human Rights Committee, an organ of the International Covenant on Civil and Political Rights, declared that the Netherlands had violated Article 26 of the Covenant when granting unequal unemployment benefits to married women as compared to those of married men, setting forth that, although the right to social security was not covered by the Covenant, once a state establishes social security, it must provide the benefits in an equal manner),[57] and by invoking Article 24 of the American Convention—similar to Article 26 of the International Covenant on Civil and Political Rights—any legal differences made on the basis of sex in the enjoyment of social, economic, or cultural rights could be challenged in the procedure meant to complain against civil and political rights violations, established in Article 44 and subsequent articles of the Convention.

Cooperation between the Commission and the Inter-American Commission on Women. The Inter-American Commission on Women, whose mandate is to identify women's human rights problems and promote the advancement of international human rights law in this area, could also do its share of protecting human rights by working in cooperation with the Inter-American Commission on Human Rights. The latter may start cases on its own motion, and it could be prompted to do so by the Women's Commission informing it whenever it detects massive violations in a country. The importance for the promotion of women's human rights of a serious involvement of the Inter-American Commission on Human Rights in scrutinizing the situation of women in this field seems self-evident.

(b) Before the Inter-American Court of Human Rights

Advisory jurisdiction of the Court. Another possibility for use of the system would be to lobby at the governmental level, or in the legislature, to persuade the state to make a formal request for an advisory opinion of the Court on the compatibility of legal provisions with the state's international obligations in the field of human rights. We should remember that the Court may examine domestic legal provisions in the light of other international human rights obligations, such as those in the Convention on the Elimination of All Forms of Discrimination Against Women.

The Inter-American Commission on Women has the power to consult the Court as well, concerning the interpretation of provisions set forth in any treaty containing human rights norms legally binding on the member states of the Organization of American States. It is true that this Commission is formed of government representatives, so it is not to be expected that it will break much ground if this means exposing OAS member states to what should be properly called "the mobilization of shame." Nevertheless, using the precedent of the request for an advisory opinion on the restrictions to the death penalty,[58] where the Court agreed to advise on a matter that was under discussion before the Inter-American Commission on Human Rights, the Inter-American Commission on Women might take legal provisions of several states to use as an example to have the Court clarify, for example, the meaning of Article 11(2) on privacy, Article 17(4) on equality in marriage, or Article 24 on equal protection of the law. A favorable opinion of the Court on the position of women with respect to these articles would be a welcome support to women's efforts to change national law.

Some Tasks for the Future

(a) A first task: research

Latin America suffers from a lack of financial resources to do research, particularly if its usefulness is not apparent in the short term. Thus cooperation between international organs and local researchers should be promoted. I believe that national women's organizations should work in close contact with the Inter-American Commission on

Women to develop a comprehensive plan of research on issues identified as relevant by the women themselves. Such research, carried out similarly in different countries, would facilitate further fruitful action. The struggle for the improvement of the position of women in society has reached a point where neither dilettantism nor prejudiced investigation will do. Some areas for possible research are suggested below.

Earlier in this chapter, I stated that the lack of enjoyment of human rights by women is a problem of culture. It is important to realize that culture is shared by men and women and that there are a significant number of women who oppose change. Many researchers point to the fact that women have misgivings about "feminism" and that they have very little "gender awareness." Others state that women have a conservative attitude and regard themselves as custodians of the status quo.[59] I agree in this with Susana Bianchi's statement that the "masculine/dominant culture" is not imposed on an "inert mass constituting half of humanity, but on subjects which accept the hegemony and find in it something useful for their own needs."[60] If this is so, I think we have to forget declaratory statements and voluntaristic options, and set ourselves to the task of investigating what it is that women feel prevents them from attempting to change a culture that places them in a subordinate position, in order to find a way to dissipate their fears or reluctance. In this process, we should proceed with an open mind and no preconceptions, carefully reviewing the postulates of feminism to find out whether adaptations should be made to achieve the ultimate purpose of improving women's lot in life.

In this same line of thought, I believe we should investigate and debate with the concerned women themselves about ways of facing the transitional period inherent in any major change of society. Before the time comes when men and women take up together the care of children, and society is organized in such a way as to acknowledge that caring for the family is the responsibility of all members of the community (I am thinking here of the organization of work in terms of part-time jobs for parents, nurseries in factories and offices, and so forth), there will be a long period in which women will bear the brunt alone. If we are not able to devise solutions for the transitional period, there is a risk that women will remain very reluctant to change. Latin American women will live their own emancipation with difficulty if it is perceived as being achieved to the detriment of their children.

Another area that still needs to be researched is the extent of the subordination of women to men in Latin American societies and the various forms this subordination takes. This is a task that has not been thoroughly done in the continent. In this regard, an important subject of research is the reaction of the public apparatus toward discrimination against women, including legal norms, the attitude of the judiciary, and the attitude of the administration.

Also needed is research to find support—aside from the ethical justification and the existence of an international law that prohibits discrimination—to demonstrate that real equality has its advantages. A very important field is that of development. In this almost frenetic race toward· modernization, the incorporation of educated, imaginative, free-thinking women is a must. One cannot conceive that a country can go far if one half of the population attempts to keep the other half in a situation where they cannot function, either because they are not intellectually prepared or because they cannot make decisions without consulting or requesting consent from others. Suppose it could be demonstrated with statistical data, and a case subsequently made that in order to incorporate women it is necessary, first, to educate them, and, second, to offer them their due—which is not uninteresting, poorly paid work plus two full-time jobs (work outside and inside the home). I am sure that then politicians, business people and others will start to see the light and yield more rapidly to women's demands.

For similar reasons, it would be useful to be able to demonstrate that the way society has been handled until now could improve if new approaches to conflict-solving are tried, approaches that individuals in a subordinate position have learned as a necessary instrument for their own progress.

(b) Publicity and lobby

Research should lead to further action. A primary target in the struggle for women is a change in the culture shared by society in general. Thus exposure of the real situation of women is essential, and this can be achieved by giving ample publicity to research. Research should also become a sound basis to lobby for legal changes. In this sense it should be used in combination with everything that international human rights law offers: international standards, precedents of international human rights organs that interpret and apply international human rights law, and international remedies. The legitimacy of human rights today is such that governments and legislatures will have a hard time rejecting changes that appear needed to bring national law in conformity with international human rights law. Amendments of national legislation might be slightly easier to enact, and the law might then serve to promote cultural change.

(c) Education in human rights

Research would help to carry out the second type of tasks needed to improve the position of women in society: education in human rights. The Inter-American Commission on Human Rights could play an important role in this task. Its mandate includes developing an awareness of human rights among the peoples of America, and women should profit therefrom, calling the Commission to account for its lack of activity in that regard.

Women and men have to be educated in human rights.[61] It is fairly safe to assume that a number of people would be willing to change, if they could realize the implications of their actions and statements. Human beings are prone to repeat discriminatory words and attitudes automatically, so making them aware of the negative connotations that this repetition has for human rights would promote change. It is also fairly safe to assume that if a number of people change, those who do not change will have a more difficult time keeping on as before. It is clear that if a substantial majority of women change, we will be more than half way toward success.

Education in human rights requires very accurate knowledge of the characteristics of those who will be taught. The subject-matter of human rights touches intimate aspects of our individuality, and thus one has to deal with a natural reluctance on the part of the student to open up to new ways of looking at life, a reluctance that can be more easily counterbalanced by using appropriate language and examples to carry the message. I would strongly advise training local trainers who subsequently will carry out the same task in their own countries. It is they who will have the necessary sensibility to prevent situations of embarrassment that may lead students to withdraw their willingness really to listen and try to understand and feel. This is a task that needs time, patience, and good judgment, lest the results achieved be precisely the opposite of those sought.

Target groups for this type of education should be selected with a view to increasing the multiplier effect. Certainly, the legal community has to be educated in human rights; lawyers and judges have to learn about international human rights law and about its development on other continents. Teachers in the primary and secondary schools are a must, as are journalists. Informal education at a community level should also be started; a combination of courses, some only for women, some only for men, and some mixed courses, in sequence, may be an idea to consider.

To reach all these target groups, but particularly those at the community level, careful consideration should be given to the appropriate methodology for teaching human rights; methodology is central in the attempts to change cultural traits, often making the difference between failure and success. The place and occasion where human rights are taught is also especially important in reaching ordinary individuals. With regard to women, the possibility should be explored of introducing human rights teaching not in a classroom but as part of the activities women have to carry out daily. In several parts of Latin America, it seems a fact that great numbers of women rally around "popular movements," that have as a primary purpose not the advancement of women in orthodox feminist terms, but the solution of problems of survival and/or minimum welfare, such as obtaining food, shelter, and medical care, or training to acquire skills needed to find a job. Concrete examples taken from the activities in these movements could be used to explain human rights, develop "gender awareness" among women, make them realize that the skills they use in the limited frame of their group are the same skills that can be used outside the group, and that ultimately there is no gap between the private and the public world, so that conquering one empowers you to conquer the other.

A Final Caveat

At the beginning of this chapter I stated my conviction that the ultimate aim in human rights law is to strengthen national law as much as possible, leaving international law as a subsidiary instrument to recognize and protect human rights. I then analyzed the possibilities offered by the inter-American system, as it is, to achieve this aim. One should be aware that these are only possibilities. To turn them into certainties several obstacles have to be overcome, among which a major one is cultural, since with respect to women the international community is not considerably better than national communities. This should not deter us from attempting changes in interpretation. Experience in the field of human rights shows that the road is paved with stumbling blocks, but with patience and ingenuity they can be eroded and, perhaps, even eliminated.

Notes

1. See Hilary Charlesworth's description of the feminist critiques of rights, "What are 'Women's International Human Rights'?" Chapter 3 in this book.
2. See Peter van Dijk and Godefridus J. H. van Hoof, *Theory and Practice of the European Convention on Human Rights,* 2d ed. (Dordrecht: Kluwer, 1990), 368–97, 530–31.
3. Although the inter-American system operates for the whole of the Ameri-

can continent, including the United States, Canada, and the Caribbean Islands, in this paper I address the problems of women in Latin America.

4. See in this regard V. Vargas Valente, "Movimiento de mujeres en América Latina: un reto para el análisis y para la acción" (Women's Movement in Latin America: A Challenge for Analysis and Action), *Revista Paraguaya de Sociologia* 77 (1990): 53–69. This article was published in English in *Revista Europea de Estudios Latinoamericanos y el Caribe* (1990).

5. In Chile, for example, a bill is about to be proposed in order to decrease subordination of married women to husbands. Costa Rica, Honduras, and Nicaragua have changed the most discriminatory aspects of their civil law. See Ana Isabel García, "Situación general de las mujeres en Centro América y Panamá" (General Situation of Women in Central America and Panama) in *Las juezas en Centro América y Panamá: Un enfoque ampliado con los casos de Chile y Estados Unidos,* ed. T. Rivera Bustamante (San José, Costa Rica: Center for the Administration of Justice, Florida International University, 1991), 15–40.

6. See Cecilia Medina, "Women's Rights as Human Rights: Latin American Countries and the Organization of American States," in *Women, Feminist Identity and Society in the 1980s,* ed. Myriam Díaz-Diocaretz and Iris M. Zavala (Amsterdam/Philadelphia: John Benjamins, 1985), 63–79.

7. See James Russell, "Reproductive Health: The United Nations Convention on the Elimination of All Forms of Discrimination Against Women as a Catalyst for Change in Colombia," *U. Toronto Fac. L. Rev.* 49(2) (1991): 106–46. See also Medina, "Women's Rights," note 6.

8. In Chile, for example, women were granted the right to vote in municipal elections in 1931, and the right to vote in congressional and presidential elections in 1949. See FLACSO, *Mujeres Latinoamericanas en cifras: Avances de investigación: Chile, Documento VI. Situación jurídica de la mujer* (Latin American Women in Numbers: Advances in Research: Chile, Document VI. Legal Status of Women) (Santiago: FLACSO, 1991), 3. In Central American countries, the right to vote was granted in the 1950s. See García, "Situación general," note 5 at 34.

9. In the referendum held in 1988 to decide whether General Pinochet would remain in office, 97.7 percent of registered women voted. A similar percentage voted in the presidential elections that followed in 1989. See UNICEF-SERNAM, *Perfil de la mujer, argumentos para un cambio* (Santiago: UNICEF, 1991). See also García, "Situación general," note 5 at 22–27.

10. Nancy de la Fuente, "Situación y desempeño de la jueza en Chile" (Status and Fulfillment of the Judge in Chile), in *Las juezas,* ed. Bustamante, note 5, 125–40 at 130.

11. The proportion of women in the legislature throughout Latin America and the Caribbean Islands is 10 percent; that in the executive branch at a ministerial level is 4 percent. See Ana Cecilia Escalante, "Las mujeres y los procesos de toma de decisiones en Centroamérica y Panamá" (Women and the Decision-Making Processes in Central America and Panama), *Las juezas,* ed. Bustamante, note 5 at 49.

12. García, "Situacíon general," note 5 at 22–27; and UNICEF/SERNAM, *Perfil de la mujer,* note 9.

13. García, "Situación general," note 5 at 27.

14. For Chile see Gloria Guerra, *Muestreo sobre violencia doméstica en postas y comisarías de la comuna de Santiago* (Statistics on Domestic Violence in Emer-

gency Units and in Police Stations in the District of Santiago) (SERNAM, Documentos de Trabajo, Santiago, December 1990). For Brazil, see Human Rights Watch/Americas Watch, *Criminal Injustice: Violence Against Women in Brazil* (New York: Human Rights Watch, 1991). For Colombia, see Profamilia, *La violencia y los derechos humanos de la mujer* (Violence and Women's Human Rights) (Bogotá: Printex Impresores Ltda., 1992).

15. See García, "Situación general," note 5 at 21 and 33.

16. See Sonia Montecino, Mariluz Dussuel, and Angélica Wilson, "Identidad femenina y modelo mariano en Chile" (Feminist Identity and the Marianist Model in Chile), in *Mundo de mujer: continuidad y cambio* (Woman's World: Continuity and Change), Centro de Estudios de la Mujer (Santiago: Ediciones CEM, 1988), 501–22.

17. Medina, "Women's Rights as Human Rights," note 6 at 63–65.

18. See Nancy de la Fuente, "Situación y desempeño de la jueza en Chile," in *Las juezas*, ed. Bustamante, note 5 at 137. See also Valente, "Movimiento," note 4 at 53–69.

19. See Valente, "Movimiento," note 4 at 58. See also *Proceedings of the V Encuentro Feminista Latinoamericano y del Caribe*, San Bernardo, Argentina, November 1990, at 35–36, where the feminist movement acknowledges the difference between it and women's movements and admits the need to recognize that the former is just a part of the many movements that struggle to improve the condition of women, stating that it is more important to carry out actions in specific areas within the women's movement using a feminist approach, than to assert their actions as "feminist."

20. Haydee Birgin, "Repensando nuestras categorías de análisis" (Rethinking our Categories for Analysis), in *Argentina: Varones y mujeres en crisis* (Argentina: Men and Women in Crisis), ed. Virgina Haurie, Blanca Ibarlucía, and Norma Sanchís (Buenos Aires: Edición Lola Moras, Ediciones Imago Mundi, 1990), 28–36.

21. Cited in Birgin, "Repensando," note 20 at 31.

22. Cited in Birgin, "Repensando," note 20 at 31.

23. In this paper, I will deal only with the organs the functions of which are to promote and protect human rights in general. By making this choice I do not wish to convey the impression that the specific inter-American organ for the problems of women, the Inter-American Commission on Women, is useless, but I think that the possibilities that general organs provide for women are not well known among them.

24. The member states are Argentina, Barbados, Bolivia, Chile, Colombia, Costa Rica, Dominican Republic, Ecuador, El Salvador, Grenada, Guatemala, Haiti, Honduras, Jamaica, Mexico, Nicaragua, Panama, Paraguay, Peru, Suriname, Trinidad and Tobago, Uruguay, and Venezuela (all are also parties to the American Convention on Human Rights); and Antigua and Barbuda, Bahamas, Belize, Brazil, Canada, Dominica, Guyana, St. Kitts and Nevis, Saint Lucia, Saint Vincent and the Grenadines, and the United States (not parties to the American Convention). Although the OAS considers Cuba a member state, I exclude it, since the government of Cuba has been expelled from the organization, and thus Cuba cannot operate within the system, which renders efforts by the system to monitor the human rights situation in that country quite useless.

25. See Appendix A, p. 385.

26. The American Convention on Human Rights was adopted at the Specialized Conference held in San José, Costa Rica, in 1969. It entered into force on 17 July 1978. Text reproduced in OAS, IACHR, Inter-Am. C.H.R., *Basic Documents Pertaining to Human Rights in the Inter-American System,* OEA, 1988, at 25–55.

27. American Convention, art. 62.

28. The American Declaration of the Rights and Duties of Man was adopted in Bogotá, Colombia, in 1948, as a non-binding set of human rights standards. Currently, however, it is almost impossible to maintain that the Declaration is not a source of legal obligations for the member states of the OAS. See in this regard P. Nikken, *La protección internacional de los derechos humanos: su desarrollo progresivo* (International Protection of Human Rights: Its Progressive Development) (Madrid: Instituto Interamericano de Derechos Humanos, Editorial Civitas S.A., 1987), 284–308. Text of the Declaration in *Basic Documents,* note 26 at 17–24.

29. See arts. VII (right to protection for mothers and children), XI (right to the preservation of health and to well-being), XII (right to education), XIII (right to the benefits of culture), XIV (right to work and to fair remuneration), XV (right to leisure time and the use thereof), and XVI (right to social security).

30. Until now, 15 states have signed the Protocol, but only Suriname has ratified it.

31. This Protocol has been signed by six states and ratified by one, Panama.

32. The Convention has been signed by 20 states and ratified by 11 states, having entered into force on 28 February 1987.

33. Pursuant to Res. AG/RES.1128 (XXI-0/91), the Inter-American Commission on Women drafted a project for an Inter-American Convention Against Domestic Violence, which is still in the process of being examined by all OAS member states. See OEA/Ser.P, AG/Doc.2914/92 rev. 1, 23 May 1992.

34. A thorough analysis of the Inter-American Commission on Human Rights can be found in Cecilia Medina, *The Battle of Human Rights: Gross, Systematic Violations and the Inter-American System* (Dordrecht: Martinus Nijhoff, 1988), chap. 4 at 67–92, chap. 6 at 113–59.

35. See Cecilia Medina, "Procedures in the Inter-American System for the Promotion and Protection of Human Rights: An Overview," *SIM Newsletter* 6(2) at 83–102.

36. See in this regard, Medina, *Battle,* note 34 at 139–43.

37. See Medina, *Battle,* note 34 at 122–26.

38. See for the former, art. 31 through 50, and for the latter, art. 51 through 53 of the Regulations.

39. See Medina, *Battle,* note 34 at 125.

40. Medina, *Battle,* note 34 at 126–27, 154.

41. See Articles 61 and 62 of the Convention. This means that only cases against states parties to the Convention can ever reach the Court. As of December 1991, 14 states have recognized the jurisdiction of the Court: Argentina, Chile, Colombia, Costa Rica, Ecuador, Guatemala, Honduras, Nicaragua, Panamá, Perú, Suriname, Trinidad and Tobago, Uruguay, and Venezuela.

42. These organs are the General Assembly, the Meeting of Consultation of Ministers of Foreign Affairs, the three Councils, the Inter-American Juridical Committee, the Inter-American Commission on Human Rights, the General Secretariat, the Specialized Conferences, and the Specialized Organizations. The latter are, among others, the Pan American Health Organization, the

Inter-American Children's Institute and the Inter-American Commission of Women.

43. Inter-Am. C.H.R. "Other treaties" subject to the advisory jurisdiction of the Court: art. 64, American Convention on Human Rights, Advisory Opinion OC-1/82 of 24 September 1982, Ser. A No. 1, first conclusion, at 43.

44. American Convention, art. 64. See Inter-Am. C.H.R., Proposed Amendments to the Naturalization Provisions of the Constitution of Costa Rica, Advisory Opinion OC-4/84 of 19 January 1984, Ser. A No. 4, para. 14 at 87 and para. 28 at 92.

45. Proposed Amendments, note 44.

46. *Velásquez Rodríguez* (Inter-Am. C.H.R., Judgment of 29 July 1988, Ser. C No. 4), and *Godínez Cruz* (Inter-Am. C.H.R., Judgment of 20 January 1989, Ser. C No. 5).

47. Inter-Am. C.H.R., Judgment of 15 March 1989, Ser. C No. 6.

48. *Aloeboetoe et al. v. Suriname,* Judgment of 4 December 1991, *Informe Anual de la Corte Interamericana de Derechos Humanos 1991,* OEA/Ser.L/V/III.25, doc. 7, 15 de enero de 1992, Original: Español at 58–64.

49. See American Convention, arts. 1, 27.

50. American Convention, art. 75.

51. See Ian Brownlie, *Principles of Public International Law,* 3d ed. (Oxford: Clarendon Press, 1979), 513. See also Warwick McKean, *Equality and Discrimination under International Law* (Oxford: Clarendon Press, 1985), 264–84. Finally, see the American Restatement of Foreign Relations Law: "Freedom from gender discrimination as state policy, in many matters, may already be a principle of customary international law" (quoted in Anne F. Bayefsky, "The Principle of Equality or Non-Discrimination in International Law," *Hum. Rts. L.J.* 11 [1990]: 1–34 [22]).

52. Inter-Am. C.H.R., *Velásquez Rodríguez* case, Judgment of 29 July 1988, Ser. C, No. 4, paras. 169–73.

53. See Medina, *Battle,* note 34 at 7–19. For the use of the concept with regard to women, see Celina Romany, "State Responsibility Goes Private: A Feminist Critique of the Public/Private Distinction in International Human Rights Law," Chapter 4 in this book.

54. OAS/IACHR, *Annual Report of the Inter-American Commission on Human Rights 1979–1980,* OEA/Ser.L/V/II.50 Doc. 13 rev. 1, 2 October 1980, original: Spanish, at 147. For a more thorough examination of the Commission's powers, and particularly of recommendations, see Medina, *Battle,* note 34 at 135–38.

55. See as an example the Annual Report of the Inter-American Commission on Human Rights 1991 (OEA/Ser.L/V/II.81 rev. 1, Doc. 6, 14 February 1992), Chap. 6 at 282–321.

56. See note 39.

57. Communication 172/1984, 42 U.N. GAOR Supp. No. 40, U.N. Doc. A/42/40 (1987).

58. See Inter-Am. C.H.R., Restrictions to the Death Penalty (arts. 4(2), 4(4), American Convention on Human Rights), Advisory Opinion OC-3/83 of 8 September 1983, Ser. A, No. 3.

59. See de la Fuente, "Situación y desempeño," in *Las juezas,* ed. Bustamante, note 5 at 137–38. See M. del Rocío Carro et al., "Las administradoras de justicia en Costa Rica" (The Administration of Justice in Costa Rica), in *Las juezas,* ed. Bustamante, 143–66 at 164–66.

60. Susana Bianchi, "Femenino/masculino o acerca de la cultura como campo de tensión" (Feminine/Masculine or the Culture as a Field of Tension), in *Argentina,* ed. Haurie, Ibarlucía, and Sanchís, note 20, 13–23 at 19.

61. Miguel Murmis, "El feminismo: tarea conjunta de varones y mujeres" (Feminism: Joint Homework of Males and Females), in *Argentina,* ed. Haurie, Ibarlucía, and Sanchís, note 20, 37–40.

Chapter 11
Toward a More Effective Guarantee of Women's Rights in the African Human Rights System

Chaloka Beyani

Introduction

This chapter is intended to contribute modestly toward the effective protection of the rights of women under the African Charter of Human and Peoples' Rights 1981 (the African Charter).[1] This Charter was adopted under the auspices of the Organization of African Unity in 1981, and came into force in 1986. It establishes human rights standards of regional application and a machinery for the protection of human rights in Africa.

A notable significance of the adoption of the Charter by African states is that human rights is not a foreign concept in Africa. Moreover, as a human rights instrument, the Charter contains regional standards of conduct by African states in the matter of human rights. By establishing human rights standards relating to the performance of African domestic legal systems, the essence of the Charter is that the relationship between African states and populations within their territories is not an exclusive function of domestic jurisdiction. The latter is a relative concept fettered by international standards of human rights, both of regional and international scope.

Some aspects of the Charter provide evidence of acceptance of general human rights standards in Africa. This is true where the Charter embodies standards[2] which are also contained in other human rights instruments, especially those of general international scope. The fact that such standards are carried in several instruments denotes that they are generally accepted and may have a particular status within general international law. In the context of the rights of women, such standards include nondiscrimination, fundamental freedoms, and liberties. However, in examining the protection of rights of women generally, it should be acknowledged that the claims of women to adequate protection of their interests, and to equality of treatment, are centered on human rights and pose a challenge regarding application of human rights standards to women as a specific category.

The approach adopted by this chapter is to seek to unravel the content of the standards of the African Charter which directly bear on the status of women, in particular, certain aspects of the Charter that reflect conceptions of human rights standards which are purportedly unique to Africa. Such standards supposedly underpin what is seen as cultural diversity in the conception of human rights. So far as such standards are relevant to the status of women in Africa, the Charter raises the delicate issue of relative diversity versus universality in the protection of human rights of women. Thus provisions in the Charter concerning traditional values bear adverse consequences for the status and protection of rights of women if they are applied on a prima facie basis. The argument for cultural relativity or cultural diversity cannot be used to undermine or evade human rights obligations. Rules governing state responsibility in international law require that the propriety of government acts in the performance of international obligations must satisfy international standards, including those of human rights, notwithstanding a state's internal deficiencies. As far as international law is concerned, it matters less that the deficiency results from the municipal legal system or culture, or both. Consequently, certain standards of the African Charter pertaining to culture or traditional values must thus be applied constructively and in accordance with the fundamental obligation to respect and observe human rights for all.

This is the framework within which this chapter sets out to discuss the effective protection of the rights of women in the African human rights system. The chapter will first place the relevant standards of the African Charter in the context of those of general application to women. The Convention on the Elimination of All Forms of Discrimination Against Women (the Women's Convention) is taken to provide evidence of human rights standards that are specifically applicable to women on a general basis. Particular attention will be paid to the effect of human rights on traditional values and custom in Africa, with a view to enhancing the protection of rights of women under the African Charter. The chapter will then examine the conformity of domestic law to international standards of human rights relating to women in Africa. Finally, it will explore the role the African Commission can exert in protecting rights of women under the African Charter of Human and Peoples' Rights.

The African Charter and the Rights of Women in International Law

In general terms, the African Charter as a regional human rights instrument has to be seen in the light of the international human rights system as a whole. The concept of universal protection of human rights is an essential underlying feature of the system of international protection of human rights in contemporary international law. A major issue is whether claims concerning protection of the rights of women have been adequately addressed as a human rights issue under the concept of universal protection of human rights.

When the Charter of the United Nations[3] established the obligation to promote and encourage respect for human rights and for fundamental freedoms for all without distinction as to race, sex, language, or religion, it presumed that human rights of all human beings would be enjoyed and protected on a universal basis. Article 56 of the Charter pledged all member states to take joint and separate action in cooperation with the United Nations for the achievement, amongst other things, of "universal respect for, and observance of, human rights and fundamental freedoms for all without distinction as to race, sex, language, or religion."[4]

Subsequent elaboration of the United Nations Charter's obligations by instruments of general application in the field of human rights confirms the integrity of the supposition underlying the standard of universal protection of human rights. The objective was to ensure that human rights were enjoyed by all, and protected for all, without any unjustified discrimination based on race, color, sex, language, religion, political or other opinion, national or social origin, property, birth, or other status.[5] Hence the European Court of Human Rights has correctly decided that the provision entitling the enjoyment of human rights without discrimination on specified grounds, including sex, applies to each provision of the European Convention on Human Rights.[6] This reasoning applies mutatis mutandis to human rights instruments that contain nondiscriminatory provisions underlying the entitlement of the rights enshrined in them.

But in addition to the general formulation envisaged in the standard of universal protection, the Covenant on Civil and Political Rights goes further and establishes an express principle of equality between men and women in Article 3:

The present States Parties to the present Covenant undertake to ensure the equal right of men and women to the enjoyment of all civil and political rights set forth in the present Covenant.

Article 3 of the Covenant on Civil and Political Rights provides support for the existence of the principle of equality between men and women in general international law.[7] But notwithstanding general existence of the principle of equality of men and women, and the inclusion of sex as a category in which discrimination in the exercise and enjoyment of human rights is prohibited, principles of human rights have not been employed adequately to improve the position and general well-being of women in Africa and elsewhere. This makes the question of the position and treatment of women central to human rights in modern international law.

However, it is an issue that has not received deserved attention from the perspective of human rights. The reason for this is obvious. Claims of women to equality of treatment and exercise of human rights on an equal basis with men challenge long-standing male dominance over women. Male attitudes toward the treatment of women have dominated the conception of human rights, and permeated their application to women in a lopsided manner. The subordination of women to men in all communities is a fact that has led women to conclude that it is as if "these abstract ideals" of human rights had never been intended to apply to them.[8]

The lopsided application of human rights has led women to urge for the development of international standards of general application designed for the protection of rights of women, as signaled by the conclusion of the Convention on the Elimination of All Forms of Discrimination Against Women in 1979. Contemporary developments in international law and international relations as marked by this Convention show that the issue of the treatment of women on the basis of human rights is a measure of the international standard of civilization with which the international system must be concerned.

However, the international system of human rights protection is neither holistic nor homogeneous. It extends to standards of regional application set by regional instruments which establish regional machinery for the protection of human rights. The point is that regional systems of human rights protection are an essential part of the international system, and should not be viewed as self-contained regimes. In any case, certain standards of human rights, such as nondiscrimination in specific contexts, are of general application on the basis of customary international law. Therefore, regional systems of protecting human rights cannot depart from generally accepted principles of human rights.

For this reason, and as a caution against developing regional standards that undermine general principles of human rights, the standards of the African Charter have to be examined in light of the international framework for the protection of human rights. This is an effective legal strategy in strengthening the protection of the rights of women and human rights generally in Africa.

The standing of the African Charter in the international system of human rights protection rests on institutional and normative links. Institutionally and legally, the machinery of the African Charter exists under the Organization of African Unity (OAU). With regard to human rights, the Charter of the OAU, 1963 denotes freedom, equality, justice, and dignity as essential objectives in achieving the legitimate aspirations of the African people. Within this framework, the African Charter on Human Rights must be seen as a means to realizing those aspirations. Women constitute the majority of people in Africa and their demand for freedom, equality, justice, and dignity has unequivocal support in the objectives of the OAU itself.

As a regional body, the Organization of African Unity is connected to the United Nations. Existence of the OAU as a regional entity under the Charter of the United Nations is shown by its preamble which affirms adherence to the Charter of the United Nations and the Universal Declaration of Human Rights as a solid foundation for peaceful and positive cooperation among states. Such preambular *consideranda* are a constitutive part of the text of the Charter of the OAU for purposes of its interpretation.[9]

Under the Charter of the United Nations, regional organizations including the OAU and their machinery for protecting human rights are permitted to exist, provided they are consistent with the purposes and principles of the United Nations.[10] Moreover, in the event of a conflict between the obligations of the members of the United Nations under the Charter, and their obligations under any other international agreement, obligations under the Charter shall prevail.[11] These provisions put the matter of regional arrangements for the protection of human rights in perspective. Their effect is that regional bodies and human rights systems established under their framework are not exclusive regimes isolated from the objectives and purposes of the United Nations, including the protection of human rights. Many African states are parties to several human rights instruments as well as to the African Charter. However, they cannot be excused from fulfilling their international human rights obligations arising from such instruments on grounds of being states parties to the African Charter.

Important normative consequences flow from the connection of regional human rights systems to obligations concerning human rights under the UN Charter. Modern international standards of human rights, and the international machinery erected for their protection are rooted in the obligations established by the UN Charter to promote universal respect for, and observance of, human rights and fundamental freedoms for all without distinction as to race, sex, language, or religion.

In reaffirming faith in fundamental human rights, in the dignity and worth of the human person, the Charter proclaims the equal rights of men and women, and of nations large and small. Preambular statements of the African Charter on Human and Peoples' Rights pledge inter alia promotion of international cooperation, with due regard for the UN Charter and the Universal Declaration of Human Rights,1948.

Standard-setting instruments as well as regional instruments in the field of human rights have their genesis in the UN Charter's human rights obligations. The Convention on the Elimination of All Forms of Discrimination Against Women clearly elaborates upon the content of nondiscrimination in the specific context of protecting the rights of women. It may be viewed as a direct amplification of the UN Charter's obligation to promote universal protection of human rights for all without discrimination as to sex and in relation to women.

With reference to protection of the rights of women in Africa, the African Charter encapsulates the principles contained in the Convention on the Elimination of All Forms of Discrimination Against Women. Article 18(3) of the Charter provides that

The State shall ensure the elimination of every discrimination against women and also ensure the protection of the rights of the woman and child as stipulated in international declarations and Conventions.

Four observations may be made with respect to the content of this provision. First, it lays a gender-specific obligation upon states in Africa to eliminate discrimination against women, and not merely on grounds of sex as such. Second, the language employed admits of no exception in requiring states to eliminate *every* discrimination against women. Third, it distinctly acknowledges the existence of the rights of women and children, and recognizes the necessity for the protection of those rights by the state. Fourth, it incorporates the application, within the African Charter, of international standards protecting the rights of women and children as stipulated in international conventions and declarations.

Article 18(3) of the Charter is remarkably important to protecting the rights of women because not only does it make pertinent international conventions applicable, but it also renders certain relevant declarations that do not normally carry the force of law directly applicable. Since the African Charter establishes binding obligations for states parties, the consequence of Article 18(3) is to transform the non-binding declaratory character of such declarations into legally binding instruments. In its text, the African Charter incorporates as law the normally moral persuasive value of international declarations that are concerned with the rights of women.

Such declarations include the Universal Declaration of Human Rights, the declaration that certain customs, ancient laws, and practices relating to marriage and the family are inconsistent with the principles of the UN Charter and the Universal Declaration of Human Rights,[12] the Declaration on the Elimination of Discrimination Against Women 1967,[13] and possibly the Teheran Proclamation of 1968 and the Vienna Declaration of 1993. There could be others. Similarly, a host of conventions concerning the rights of women come into play.[14] The most relevant of these is the Convention on the Elimination of All Forms of Discrimination Against Women.

As well as obliging African states parties to ensure the elimination of every discrimination against women, and mandating these states to protect the rights of women in accordance with accepted international standards, the Charter introduces notions of perceived African values. There is reference in Article 18(2) of the Charter to the family as the custodian of morals and traditional values recognized by the community. In addition, the African Charter establishes a duty to preserve the harmonious development of the family and to work for the cohesion and respect of the family.[15]

These provisions reflect the importance attached to the family in Africa and must be read in light of the provisions in the Covenants that categorize the family as a natural and fundamental group unit of society.[16] In effect, the family is both depicted and established as a unit in which individual and collective rights of the members of the family coexist intractably. Collective rights are inherent in the concept of human rights in general, and rights pertaining to the family have been recognized as collective.[17] Within this context, the relation between individual and collective rights is that individual rights within the family regulate internal family relations and provide the basis for the constitution of the family as a collective unit.

In order to preserve the family as a unit, and to the extent that it continues to exist as such, individual rights of the members of the family[18] are generally exercised within the parameters of the collective interests of the family. Where interests of individual members of the family (e.g., parties to a marriage) do not, or cease to, coincide with those of the family as a collectivity, individual rights can be exercised to opt out of a family in cases where a marriage or partnership or family form has failed. Tension between collectivity and individuality may thus be inevitable in family relations.

Collective rights pertaining to the family circumscribe its profile and regulate its external relations in the community. Their purpose is to protect interests that preserve the subject of the rights to the exclusion of other interests. For example, Article 17 of the Covenant on Civil and Political Rights prohibits arbitrary or unlawful interference with the family and thereby reinforces collective rights of the family, such as rights to family life and family union.

However, the concept of family is changing rapidly and varies from place to place.[19] Family relations in Africa are extensive, and the concept of the family is correspondingly wide. As noted elsewhere,[20] the family is ordinarily conceived as the embodiment of culture and traditional values. Yet it is generally within the family that stereotypic attitudes and power relations have weighed heavily against women for centuries.

By setting standards based on the equality of men and women as well as equality of treatment of women in exercising human rights, the Convention on the Elimination of All Forms of Discrimination Against Women evidences international acceptance of the principle to alter the present imbalance of power relations between men and women, and to eliminate male stereotypic attitudes that prejudice women.[21] Article 16 of the Convention confers equal rights on women with men within the family and in matters connected with the family. The combined effect of the standards in the African Charter and those of the Convention is such that the meaning to be given to "morals and cultural values" in the Charter must be consistent with human rights standards.

This means that whatever their nature, the morals or cultural values in question must neither discriminate against women, nor impair their enjoyment of human rights on an equal basis with men, and they ought to be consistent with human rights standards. A similar conclusion was reached regarding the effect of standards of human rights on traditional custom by the High Court of Tanzania in the case of *Ephrahim v. Pastory and Kaizingele*.[22] The Appellant was a nephew of the first Respondent. He challenged her right to sell clan land that she had inherited from her father under a valid will. She sold the land to the second Respondent, whereupon the Appellant sought a declaration that the sale was void because under the first Respondent's Haya customary law, the power to sell clan land was vested in men and not in women.

In the first instance, the Primary Court had held that the sale was void, and it ordered the first Respondent to return the monies received for the purchase of the land in question. On appeal to the District Court, the decision of the Primary Court was set aside on the basis that the Tanzanian Bill of Rights forbade discrimination on grounds of sex with the consequence that male and female clan members had the same powers of disposition over clan land.

The Appellant sought to overturn this decision in the High Court where the appeal was dismissed, and the decision of the District Court was affirmed. In determining that the sale of land was valid, the High Court expressed the view that the Tanzanian Constitution incorporated a Bill of Rights and the Universal Declaration of Human Rights both of which prohibited discrimination on grounds of sex. The High Court also took into account the effect of several international conventions pertaining to human rights and the elimination of discrimination against women, which Tanzania had ratified.

It stated that it was clear that Haya customary law was in conflict with the Constitution of Tanzania and its international obligations towards human rights. In particular, it found that the prohibition on women selling clan land was discriminatory and contrary to human rights and decided that women were now vested with the same rights as men with regard to the inheritance of clan land and the power to sell such land.

The reasoning behind the decision of the Court was that any existing customary law that is inconsistent with the Bill of Rights should be regarded as modified or qualified by the Bill of Rights. The modification of Haya customary law made by the Court meant that any member of the clan, male or female, could dispose of the clan land to strangers without the consent of the clansmen and could redeem that clan land on payment of the purchase price to the purchaser.

Although the Court may be criticized for its circular approach, it may be commended for not preserving the essential character of the customary law in issue. It qualified the nature of the custom by applying the standard of nondiscrimination between men and women with respect to the disposition of clan land on the basis of human rights standards.[23] By doing so, the decision of the Court reflected the concern addressed by the important obligation in Article 5(1) of the Women's Convention. This requires the adoption of measures to modify the social and cultural patterns of conduct of men and women, with a view to achieving the elimination of prejudices and customary and all other practices based on the idea of the inferiority or superiority of either of the sexes or on stereotyped roles for men and women. In the case at hand, Judge Mwalusanya declared:

From now on, females all over Tanzania can at least hold their heads high and claim to be equal to men as far as inheritance of clan land and self-acquired land of their fathers is concerned. It is part of the long road to women's liberation. But there is no cause for euphoria as there is much more to do in other spheres.[24]

No doubt a necessary caution, but the decision has a certain value in international law because it dealt with the application of nondiscrimination as an international standard in the specific context of the rights of women. It also shows the position taken by Tanzania on the question of the effect of human rights standards on the right of women to own, inherit, and dispose of clan land.

An important factor in the protection of the rights of women in Africa against oppressive social and traditional practices involves a grasp of the interaction of the standards of the Charter and the Convention. By providing within its text that states shall ensure the elimination of every discrimination against women and protection of the rights of women as stipulated in international declarations and conventions, the Charter presupposes that its own standards are to be applied in compliance with the standards of those conventions and declarations.

However, in addition to rights, the African Charter establishes certain duties on individuals. Provisions[25] of the African Charter concerning duties of the individual are said to reflect aspects of African values according to which individuals within the community have certain duties in addition to rights. But these values are not independent of human rights. This is the significance of the inclusion of the notion of cultural values in the Charter as a human rights instrument.

Consequently, a broad view of what constitutes "values" under the African Charter ought to be taken as inclusive of values embellished in principles of human rights. In the matter between the *Attorney General v. Unity Dow*,[26] the Appeal Court of Botswana used the values enshrined in the Bill of Rights of the Constitution of Botswana to override traditional custom relating to the treatment of women in Botswana.

The *Unity Dow* case arose out of certain provisions of the Citizenship Act 1984 which caused an awkward differentiation of citizenship status between the children of the Respondent. The Respondent was a female citizen of Botswana born of indigenous parents in Botswana. In 1979, a child was born to her and Peter Nathan Dow, an American citizen who lived in Botswana for nearly 14 years. In terms of the law then in force, this child was a citizen of Botswana.

On 7 March 1984, Unity married Peter Nathan Dow, and two children were born of the marriage in 1985 and 1987. Earlier in 1984, Botswana had enacted the Citizenship Act as a result of which, under its terms, the children born of the Respondent after 1984 were not eligible to attain the citizenship of Botswana because their father was a foreign citizen.[27] This meant that Unity's first child was a citizen of Botswana, while her two children born after 1984 when the Citizenship Act came into force were not citizens of Botswana. Before the High Court of Botswana, the Respondent successfully established that the provisions in question infringed some of her fundamental rights and freedoms under the Constitution of Botswana. Her application was allowed and the Attorney General appealed against that decision.

The thrust of the Appellant's case rested on the premise that while S. 3 of the Constitution of Botswana conferred rights and freedoms irrespective of sex, the word "sex" was not mentioned as a category in relation to which discrimination was prohibited in S. 15, the provision of the Constitution of Botswana that defined the term "discrimination." On this basis it was argued that omission of the category of sex from the definition of discrimination was intentional in order to allow sex based discrimination in Botswana because Botswana society was patrilineal and, therefore, male oriented. The Appellant sought to justify the constitutional validity of the Citizenship Act on account of the necessity to preserve the male orientation of the society of Botswana, and that as a piece of legislation based on descent, the real objective of the Act was to promote the male orientation of society and to avoid dual citizenship.

In addressing these arguments, the Court made an important and instructive response on the issue of the effect of the Bill of Rights under the Constitution:

Our attention has been drawn to the patrilineal customs and traditions of the Botswana people to show, I believe, that it is proper for Parliament to legislate to preserve or advance such customs and traditions. Custom and tradition have never been static. Even then, they have always yielded to express legislation. Custom and tradition must *a fortiori,* and from what I have already said about the pre-eminence of the Constitution, yield to the Constitution of Botswana. A constitutional guarantee cannot be overridden by custom. Of course, the custom will be read so as to conform with the constitution. But where this is impossible, it is custom not the constitution which must go.[28]

The Court rejected grounds of traditional custom and the avoidance of dual citizenship as justification for permitting legislation that discriminated between the "sexes" of the parents in matters of citizenship of the children. Its opinion was that where the legislature is confronted with passing a law on citizenship, its only course is to adopt a prescription that complies with the imperatives of the Constitution, especially those that confer fundamental rights on individuals within the state.

When dealing with the issue of the omission of the category of sex in the provisions concerning discrimination, the Court took a textual approach, but regarded the Constitution as a "constitutive whole." It considered the relation of S. 15(3) of the Constitution, which omitted the term "sex" in its definition of discrimination, to S. 3 of the Constitution which provided for the right of the individual to equal protection of the law regardless of sex. The court declined to accept that equal protection of the law as a fundamental right conferred by the Constitution could be circumscribed by the provision defining discrimination.

By a vote of 3 to 2, it held that the provisions of the Citizenship Act in question were discriminatory against the Respondent. The Judge President, Mr. Justice Amissah, had this to say:

If the makers of the Constitution had intended that equal treatment of males and females be excepted from the application of subsections 15(1) or (2), I feel confident after the examination of these provisions, that they would have adopted one of the express forms of words that they had used in this very same section and in the sister section referred to. I would expect that, just as section 3 boldly states that every person is entitled to the protection of the law irrespective of sex, in other words giving a guarantee of equal protection, section 15 in some part would also say, again equally expressly, that for the purpose of maintaining the patrilineal structure of the society, or for whatever reason the framers of the Constitution thought necessary, discriminatory laws or treatment may be passed for or meted to men and women. Nowhere in the Constitution is this done. Nowhere is it mentioned that its objective is the preservation of the patrilineal structure of the society.[29]

Reference was made by the Court to the effect of the African Charter on the protection of human rights under the Constitution of Botswana. Although Botswana is a state party to the African Charter, like many African states, it has not enacted legislation adopting or incorporating the provisions of the Charter. In this respect, the majority decision adopted a progressive stand and considered that the Charter was an aid to the construction or interpretation of the Constitution, and concurred with the High Court's determination that domestic legislation should as far as possible be interpreted not to conflict with Botswana's obligations under the Charter or other international obligations. According to the Court, such obligations reinforced its view that the intention of the framers of the Constitution could not have been to permit discrimination purely on the grounds of sex.

The Court placed particular reliance on provisions in international human rights instruments concerning entitlement of rights and freedoms for all irrespective of, among other things, sex,[30] equal protection of the law,[31] and the elimination of discrimination against women.[32] Judge Aguda expressed the view that Article 18(3) of the Charter constituted an emphatic obligation on the part of Botswana and all other African states to ensure the elimination of every discrimination against their women folk.

But the Court failed to examine other provisions of the Charter which are relevant to the protection of the rights of women. There is a personal duty in the Charter to respect and consider fellow human beings without discrimination, as well as to maintain relations that promote, safeguard, and reinforce mutual respect and tolerance. With special reference to protecting the rights of women, this duty is binding upon male individuals not to discriminate against women, as human beings, and for men to conduct themselves with a sense of mutual respect toward women.

When portrayed positively, this duty may be seen as providing a basis for not subordinating women to men, as well as outlawing violence against women. Values of mutual respect and tolerance are in consequence, unfettered by the human rights principle of nondiscrimination against women, and non-impairment of women's enjoyment of human rights.

In Article 29, the Charter establishes, among others, a duty to preserve and strengthen positive African cultural values in relations with other members of society in the spirit of tolerance, dialogue, and consultation and, in general, to contribute to the promotion of the moral well-being of society. Close attention must be paid to the inclusion of the term "positive" African cultural values in the African Charter.

Allusion to "positive values" indicates an awareness of the necessity, if not the willingness, to discard aspects of culture or tradition that are deemed negative and retrogressive in Africa. There is implicit recognition in the Charter of the fact that cultural values in Africa cannot remain static. As Judge Aguda observed,

it appears to me that, now more than ever before, the whole world has realised that discrimination on grounds of sex, like that institution which was in times gone-by permissible both by most religions and the conscience of men of those times, namely, slavery, can no longer be permitted or even tolerated, more so by the law.[33]

Principles of human rights, as shown in the cases of *Ephrahim v. Pastory and Kaizingele* and *Attorney General v. Unity Dow,* provide a basis for negating retrogressive traditions and customs which are adverse to the position of women in society and in their enjoyment of human rights. Another technique of potential significance is the repugnancy clause which, in Anglophone countries, has for long been used to check the application of custom against the written law. This view recently found support among judges in the jurisdictions of the Commonwealth at a Judicial Colloquium held at Balliol College, Oxford, 21–23 September 1992.

The character of the repugnancy clause essentially remains the same in African countries of the Commonwealth, but its scope varies from country to country. In Zambia, it is applicable to local courts which ordinarily adjudicate matters involving customary law. Thus S. 12(1) of the Local Courts Act, Cap. 54, empowers local courts to administer

African customary law relating to any matter before it insofar as such law is not repugnant to natural justice or morality or incompatible with the provisions of any written law. In Kenya the repugnancy clause may apply to matters before the High Court, the Court of Appeal, and all subordinate courts, and its scope is wider. Section 3(2) of the Judicature Act provides that these courts shall be guided by African customary law in civil cases in which one or more of the parties is subject to it or affected by it, so far as it is applicable and is not repugnant to justice or morality or inconsistent with any written law.

Advances that have now been made in the field of human rights, such as standards of conduct, the increasing participation of women in public life, as well as their engagement in economic life, leave no doubt that customs and traditional practices that subordinate women to men are repugnant to justice and morality. The repugnancy clause may be used on the basis of standards of human rights to effect a process of change in order to ensure the adequate protection of the rights of women in Africa. One specific example of special legislation whose effect is broader than the repugnancy clause, and which is aimed at establishing conformity between custom and human rights is the Constitutional (Consequential, Transitional and Temporary Provisions) Act of 1984 of Tanzania. Section 5(1) of that act empowered the courts, with effect from March 1988, to construe the existing law including customary law with such modifications, adoptions, qualifications, and exceptions as may be necessary to bring it in conformity with the provisions of the Bill of Rights. This legislation shows that customary law can be changed; the presence of human rights standards provides the guide toward which the change may be directed.

Change or modification of custom is desirable because customary law is the "infertile" ground on which women suffer perverse discrimination in the enjoyment of their rights as well as in their individual and collective livelihood. It is not surprising that some countries, including Kenya, Tanzania, and Zambia, have used legislation to intervene in matters of customary law in order to alleviate the plight of women in areas such as succession and inheritance.

It is obvious that more human rights based measures are required to modify traditional custom; once such measures are in place, the courts have shown a willingness to apply them to improve the status of women. Thus, in *Ephrahim v. Pastory*, Judge Mwalusanya expressed this view regarding the Tanzanian legislation:

There can be no doubt that Parliament wanted to do away with all oppressive and unjust laws of the past. It wanted all existing laws (as they existed in 1984) which were inconsistent with the Bill of Rights to be inapplicable in the new era or be treated as modified so that they are in line with the Bill of Rights. It wanted the Courts to modify by construction those existing laws which were inconsistent with the Bill of Rights such that they were in line with the new era. We had a new *grundnorm* since 1984, and so Parliament wanted the country to start with a clean slate. That is clear from the express words of Section 5(1) of the Act 16/1984. The mischief it is intended to remedy is all the unjust existing laws, such as the discriminatory customary law now under discussion. I think the message the Parliament wanted to impart to the courts is loud and clear and needs no interpolations.[34]

Without recourse to standards of human rights as a guide for modifying custom, the danger is inherent that the general process of modifying custom will largely depend on power relations that disadvantage women in African societies. This is due to the fact that custom has traditionally reflected male interests, dominance and power over women. Ensuring the full benefit of human rights to women means empowering women to overcome male dominance, and to redress abuses leveled at them on account of their gender. Therefore, any measures by states in Africa to modify custom in line with human rights have to be clear and unambiguous.

Conformity of Constitutional and Regional Standards

Conformity between constitutional and regional standards of human rights relating to the rights of women is important in order to govern and regulate civilized conduct toward women, and to ensure protection by the state of rights of women in accordance with generally accepted standards of human rights everywhere in the world. Where effective regional or international mechanisms of human rights protection exist, the conformity of domestic standards as such is not an essential requirement, because the regional or international mechanisms check the performance of the domestic legal systems concerned. It is a trite principle of international law that a state is responsible for failing to carry out its international obligations on account of the deficiency of its legal system. Municipal courts therefore should seek to interpret domestic legislation consistently with regional and international human rights obligations. Happily, this was the course pursued by the Appeal Court of Botswana in the case examined above.

In Africa the machinery of protection of human rights is relatively new, and perhaps somewhat timid. Therefore domestic compliance with international standards concerning the rights of women is vital. The African Charter obliges member states of the OAU and states parties to recognize the standards enshrined in it, and to adopt legislative or other measures to give effect to the standards of the Charter.

Few, if any, African countries have fulfilled this obligation. Though

African states are enthusiastic in ratifying international human rights instruments, they do not usually enact enabling legislation incorporating human rights obligations in domestic legal systems. Be that as it may, African countries cannot avoid their obligations towards human rights by failing to incorporate them in their domestic legal systems. Indeed many domestic courts, as evidenced by the Appeal Court of Botswana, have assumed a clear stand in such situations. Clearly, international obligations may be used as an aid to the interpretation of provisions relating to Constitutional Bills of Rights. The position taken by international tribunals in corresponding circumstances is that the international obligations are a factor to take into account in the application of domestic law.[35] Even where human rights contained in international instruments are to be applied in accordance with the law of a state party, it should be noted that there is an applicable international standard regarding the quality of the law in question.[36]

As African states lurch towards constitutional democracy, the time is opportune to formulate constitutional systems that meet the obligation to implement the standards of the Charter and other international instruments so as to advance the protection of human rights, including those of women. Most constitutions in Africa formally discriminate against women and thus confer an inferior status on women by deliberately omitting sex as a ground upon which discrimination is prohibited.[37]

The aim of this, as the Attorney General of Botswana argued in the *Unity Dow* case, is formally to deny women equal rights with men as well as equality of treatment in the exercise of human rights. And the minority dissenting opinions in *Unity Dow*[38] show that the omission of sex in the definition of discrimination may provide a conservative basis for denying women legal protection of claims that may enhance their dignity and status.[39] For this reason, *Unity Dow* is an important persuasive decision in municipal jurisdictions whose Constitutional format omits sex as a category on which discrimination is prohibited. It is also significant in international law because it deals with questions of international law in relation to human rights.

Moreover, the sheer numerical strength of women in Africa, manifested in their voting power, means that women are in a position to influence democratic constitutional change in such a way as to protect their rights in the transition to constitutional democracy. An example is how women fought to include the prohibition of discrimination on grounds of sex and marital status in the new constitution of Zambia.[40] But even here, adequate representation of women in government and public institutions must be secured as a matter of participation and enabling better protection of their rights. Attention must now turn to the role of the African Commission in the protection of the rights of women in Africa.

The African Commission and the Rights of Women

The African Commission was created in 1987 under the African Charter of Human and Peoples' Rights. Its mandate extends to undertaking studies on problems of human rights in Africa, and to formulating principles and rules aimed at solving legal problems relating to human rights and fundamental freedoms.[41] Exercise of human rights by women on an equal basis with men is a priority for the African Commission to undertake to investigate. Special attention ought to be paid by the Commission to particular categories of women, including rural women, women caught in internal conflict, refugee women, and to the problem of women's enforced prostitution.

Rights of women in Africa may be enhanced by informed techniques of interpretation of the provisions of the Charter. The African Commission may have limited experience in this respect, given its short history. Nevertheless, there is a wealth of legal experience emanating from other regional systems upon which it can draw in safeguarding human rights in Africa.

The experience gained by the inter-American system of human rights is particularly useful to the African Commission because of the similarity of the human rights problems with which the Inter-American system is faced. Reliance can also be placed by the Commission on information from investigations carried out by nongovernmental organizations (NGOs) in their reports on violations of human rights in Africa. It is one of the stated functions of the Commission under the African Charter to cooperate with other African and international institutions concerned with the promotion and protection of human and peoples' rights.[42]

Furthermore, the African Charter enjoins the Commission to draw inspiration from the international law of human rights and other international human rights instruments. When invoked collectively, these provisions considerably expand upon the legal jurisdiction of the Commission, and would enable it to establish a working and collaborative relationship with the Committee on the Elimination of All Forms of Discrimination Against Women (CEDAW) in safeguarding women's rights.

A functional collaboration between the African Commission and CEDAW in the protection of the rights of women is indispensable because:

(a) the standards of the Convention are either incorporated or rendered applicable within the Charter by its Article 18(3);

(b) some of the states parties to the African Charter are also states parties to the Convention; and

(c) some states parties to the African Charter are not States Parties to the Convention.

Nevertheless, Article 18(3) of the African Charter obliges this latter category of African states to eliminate every discrimination against women and ensure protection of their rights as stipulated in the Convention. On the basis of the combined effect of Articles 18(3), 45, and 62, the African Commission can ensure the obligation of states parties to the African Charter to report on their own measures to eliminate discrimination against women and protect their rights as stipulated by the Convention.

On a practical basis, the Commission may receive communications from states[43] and individuals[44] which allege abuse of human rights. As a matter of procedure, complaints are subject to the rule of prior exhaustion of domestic remedies, and other conditions stipulated under Article 56 of the African Charter. The complaints procedure can be used effectively by the Commission to protect rights of women against abuse in cases where such women have moved beyond the jurisdiction of the Commission. If the Commission demonstrated objectivity in examining complaints arising from violations of the rights of women, it would inspire confidence in women to assail such violations. Hence the members of the Commission may need to have their consciousness raised in order to avoid the "male lopsided" application of human rights standards to women. In fact it is important to the adequate protection of rights of women to secure a balanced membership of men and women on the Commission. At the very least, a number of qualified women who are conscious of issues affecting the welfare of women merit appointment.

The African Commission possesses powers to investigate violations of human rights on its own motion.[45] It may also investigate special cases that reveal the existence of a series of serious or massive violations upon the request of the Assembly of Heads of the OAU.[46] In addition to the complaints and investigative procedures, the African Commission may make use of certain powers to call states to account with regard to their performance of human rights obligations under the Charter.

Article 62 of the Charter obliges every state party to submit a report on the legislative and other measures it takes in order to give effect to the rights guaranteed in the Charter every two years from date of entry of the Charter. A point to note is that the effectiveness of the African Commission in protecting the rights guaranteed under the Charter is likely to be eroded by vertical and rather bureaucratic connections with the Assembly of Heads of States of the OAU.

An assessment of the functioning of the African Charter is made difficult by its relatively short period of existence and the fact that very little of its activities is either known or effectively publicized. Generally, the effectiveness of an international tribunal is a question of its structure, jurisdiction, and method of operation. The structure of the Commission, particularly its Secretariat, composition, and relationship with the Assembly of Heads of State of the Organization of African Unity all pose significant operational problems in exercise of its jurisdiction.

Rules of Procedure adopted by the African Commission allow individuals to lodge complaints with the Commission regarding alleged violations of human rights. Some flexibility on the part of the Commission has been demonstrated here, since it has not insisted that individual complaints should be based on a series of serious or massive violations of human rights.

So far, it is estimated that the Commission has received around 35 individual complaints but the individual complaints procedure is confidential and it is not clear how these cases have been dealt with by the Commission. It may be prudent for the Commission, in the face a restrictive Charter, to use its Rules of Procedure to interpret the Charter liberally and to establish a practice based on such rules. Most of all, it is the technique of exposing human rights violations that embarrasses states and that has proved effective in the experience of the inter-American human rights system.

NGOs have been granted observer status and may put forward items for the Commission's agenda as well as participate in its public sessions. The presence of NGOs means that they may exert some pressure on the Commission and also monitor its progress. However, caution ought to be taken in dealing with NGOs as such because they usually have their "private agendas" to pursue.

The absence of female Commissioners is a poor reflection of the Commission's capacity to inspire confidence about its ability to protect the rights of women and to promote the equal treatment of women. The issue is not simply about the representation of women on the Commission as window-dressing. In truth, there are women within Africa who deserve appointment to the Commission on merit, qualification, and understanding of the issues affecting rights of women.

Conclusion

The question of the protection of the rights of women has gained prominence in the past decade, and will become an even more pressing issue in this decade. Given the current advancement of human rights standards, it is simply unacceptable to subject women to subordinate treatment that enslaves them to men. Human rights is about regulated civilized behavior and conduct toward all human beings. It is not a benefit to be monopolized by men. In Africa, the subordination of women to men is buttressed by certain traditional practices that cannot remain unaffected by human rights standards. Accordingly, the impact of the standards of the African Charter and the Women's Convention require careful appraisal. The net effect of these standards is that, at a minimum, women must not be subordinated by men, and they must be able to exercise their rights without being discriminated against, or impaired in the enjoyment of human rights just because they are women. The obligations to fulfill these standards under the African Charter rest primarily with the African states.

It is inescapably the primary responsibility of domestic legal systems in Africa to ensure that African states discharge their human rights obligations, including those relating to women. Some municipal decisions have taken a lead here; it is not more than a passing coincidence that this lead has arisen from cases that have been initiated by women, and that the cases have involved application of international human rights obligations contained in the Charter and other instruments. Municipal legal standards in Africa are generally heavily weighted against women.

In such systems, international standards of human rights are helpful in constructing a legal basis for interpreting municipal standards to enable their equality of treatment. If its standards are applied purposefully and interpreted progressively, the African Charter will become an important regional system for measuring the performance of domestic legal systems in matters of human rights in Africa. Domestic courts have begun to take the initiative in recognizing the importance of protecting rights of women. The African Commission must give a pride of place to the protection of women's rights under the African Charter.

Notes

1. See 21 I.L.M. 1982 for text, and generally Emmanuel G. Bello, "The African Charter on Human and Peoples' Rights: A Legal Analysis," *Hague Recueil* 5 (1985): 70.

2. See. e.g., arts. 2–16 of the African Charter.

3. U.N. Charter, art. 1(3).

4. U.N. Charter, art. 55(c).

5. See particularly art. 2 of the Universal Declaration of Human Rights 1948; art. 2 of the International Covenant on Civil and Political Rights, and art. 2(2) of the International Covenant on Economic, Social and Cultural Rights.

6. *Belgian Linguistics* case (Merits), Eur. Ct. H.R. Judgment of 23 July 1968; *Abdulaziz* case, 94 Eur. Ct. H.R. (ser. A) (1985).

7. See, e.g., International Covenant on Civil and Political Rights, art. 3; Convention on the Elimination of All Forms of Discrimination Against Women (Women's Convention); Convention on the Political Rights of Women.

8. Susan G. Bell and Karen M. Offen, eds., *Women, the Family, and Freedom: The Debate in Documents,* vol. 1, *1750–1880* (Stanford, CA: Stanford University Press, 1983), 1, 3.

9. Vienna Convention on the Law of Treaties, 1969, art. 31(2).

10. Vienna Convention, art. 52.

11. Vienna Convention, art. 103. With regard to the significance of this provision, see Theodor Meron, "On a Hierarchy of International Human Rights," *Am. J. Int'l L.* 80 (1986): 3.

12. G.A. Res. 843(IX) of 17 December 1954.

13. G.A. Res. 2263.

14. See Natalie K. Hevener, *International Law and the Status of Women* (Boulder, CO: Westview Press, 1983).

15. This duty extends to respecting one's parents at all times and to maintaining them in case of need.

16. International Covenant on Civil and Political Rights, art. 23; International Covenant on Economic, Social, and Cultural Rights, art. 10.

17. Ian Brownlie, "The Rights of Peoples in Modern International Law," in *The Rights of Peoples,* ed. James Crawford (Oxford: Oxford University Press, 1988), 1–5

18. See, e.g., Women's Convention, art. 16.

19. See Thandabantu Nhlapo, "The African Family and Women's Rights: Friends or Foes," *Acta Juridica* (1991): 135.

20. Alice Armstrong et al., "Uncovering Reality: Excavating Women's Rights in African Family Law," *Int'l J. Fam.* 7 (1993): 314.

21. See the Preamble, and art. 5, of the Women's Convention.

22. Judgment of the High Court of Tanzania of 22 February 1990, 87 I.L.R. 106.

23. Tanzania, note 22 at 118–19.

24. Tanzania, note 22 at 119.

25. See arts. 27–29.

26. *Attorney-General v. Unity Dow,* C.A. Civil Appeal No. 4/91 Botswana (unreported).

27. Sections 4 and 5 of the Citizenship Act of Botswana (1984).

28. Per Judge Amissah, *Attorney General v. Unity Dow,* note 26 at 24.

29. Per Judge Amissah, *Attorney General v. Unity Dow,* note 26.

30. Universal Declaration of Human Rights, art. 2; African Charter, art. 2.

31. African Charter, art. 3.

32. United Nations Declaration on the Elimination of Discrimination Against Women; African Charter art. 18(3).

33. Amissah, *Unity Dow,* note 28 at 79.

34. *Ephrahim,* note 22 at 115.

35. For example, *Abdulaziz,* note 6 at 471.

36. "The Word 'Laws' in Article 30 of the American Convention on Human Rights," Advisory Opinion OC-6/86 of May 9, 1986; *Sunday Times v. United Kingdom,* 2 H.R.R. 245.

37. See, e.g., Alice Armstrong and Welsham Ncube, eds., *Women and Law in Southern Africa* (Harare: Zimbabwe Publishing House, 1987); Alice Armstrong and Julie Stewart, eds., *The Legal Situation of Women in Southern Africa* (Harare: University of Zimbabwe Publications, 1990).

38. See the opinions of J. A. Schreiner, and J. A. Puckrin, *Attorney-General v. Unity Dow,* note 26 at 108, 132 respectively.

39. Chaloka Beyani, "Constitutional Reform, Human Rights and Democracy in Zambia," paper presented to the Constitutional Reform Commission in Zambia (Lusaka, 1990), 17.

40. Constitution of Zambia Act (1991), s. 23(3).

41. African Charter, art. 45.

42. African Charter, art. 45.

43. African Charter, art. 47.

44. African Charter, art. 55.

45. African Charter, art. 46.

46. African Charter, art. 58.

Chapter 12
African Women's Economic, Social, and Cultural Rights—Toward a Relevant Theory and Practice

Adetoun O. Ilumoka

Introduction

The assertion of rights presumes their existing or probable violation, and a desire to remedy or prevent violation. It has been argued that many of the standards embodied in human rights instruments today have been recognized by most societies at some point in history.[1] They are articulated as rights largely vested in individuals and asserted against the state or other individuals, and their expression in specific international or national legal and policy instruments is specific to certain historical periods and social formations. Is the widespread acceptance of vague general principles, such as the right to life, health, and work, sufficient reason for asserting that the concept of human rights is universal?

The ascendancy of an international human rights discourse dominated by western liberal thought, with its emphasis on individual, civil, and political rights, has given rise to some controversy over the relevance of existing concepts of human rights in Africa.[2] However, the contribution of non-western societies to the broadening of the content of international human rights since the 1940s has been significant, resulting in the articulation of so-called second and third generation rights such as those to be found in the International Covenant on Economic, Social, and Cultural Rights (ICESCR) and the African Charter on Human and Peoples' Rights (the Banjul Charter). Considerable emphasis has been placed by non-western countries, including those in the socialist bloc, on economic, social, and cultural rights. Differences in emphases constitute a significant challenge to the universality of the human rights discourse. Women's groups have also posed challenges to the universality of human rights. In so doing, they have made significant contributions to the broadening of the content of international human rights, their efforts culminating in the far-reaching provisions of the Convention on the Elimination of All Forms of Discrimination Against Women. Do human rights mean different things to different people? Is the concept dogged by its history and origins, or can its content continue to expand without exploding the form?

Clearly the enforcement of the rights enunciated in the Convention on the Elimination of All Forms of Discrimination Against Women, as of economic, social, and cultural rights generally, has far-reaching implications for social organization and the balance of power nationally and internationally. The attempt since the 1940s to draw up legal instruments or bills of rights at the national and international levels is indicative of an attempt to make the rights justiciable, and to prevent violation. Despite decades of articulation of human rights in various international and national legal instruments, however, systematic violation appears to be more the rule than the exception in most parts of the world. This raises questions as to the nature of the international consensus on human rights.

This chapter focuses on the significance of human rights discourse to African women and the problems of promoting and enforcing existing internationally recognized economic, social, and cultural rights for women in Africa. It will briefly examine the nature of these rights and state practice in relation to them, taking Nigeria as an example. In the light of this analysis, the relevance of international human rights and the tasks before the "international human rights movement" will also be addressed. Arguably, the situation of African women as a disadvantaged group within the present world system has great potential for providing a stronger conceptual foundation for improved practice, and more balanced approaches towards the realization of truly universal respect for human dignity and well-being.

The Concept of International Human Rights

The assertion of rights embodies both "is" and "ought" statements. It proclaims what "ought" to be by reference to what "is." The claim in relation to international human rights is that they inhere in all human beings and therefore ought to be respected. It is not surprising that the growth of the human rights movement has been described as part of the "revival of natural law."[3] This notion has its antecedents in earlier European natural law theories and in the civil and political liberties articulated in the constitutions of some European nations and the

United States of America in the seventeenth to nineteenth centuries, notably the English Bill of Rights 1689, the U.S. Bill of Rights amending the U.S. Constitution of 1789 in 1791, and the French Declaration of the Rights and Duties of Man and of the Citizen, 1789.

The Universal Declaration of Human Rights (UDHR) of 1948 refers in its Preamble to the "inherent dignity and of the equal and inalienable rights of all members of the human family" as being "the foundation of freedom, justice and peace in the world," and to the need to protect human rights by the rule of law, in order to avoid tyranny and oppression that lead to rebellion. It proclaims a common standard of achievement for all peoples and all nations in its 30 articles. The International Covenant on Civil and Political Rights (ICCPR) and the International Covenant on Economic, Social, and Cultural Rights (ICESCR) expanded the provisions of the UDHR to provide further details of human rights standards and to make them legally binding on states.

The process of arriving at these standards was protracted, largely because of ideological differences between states. Reference to the "rule of law" in the preamble to the UDHR, and the importance attached to private property and civil and political liberties over economic, social, and cultural rights,[4] even in that first and most general of international human rights documents, reflect the dominant western liberal tradition in international human rights discourse. Other examples of the way in which the articulation of international human rights standards reflects a particular way of life and mode of social organization are to be found in all three instruments.[5]

The debate on the universality of human rights standards has thus been raging since the 1950s when the Covenants were being drafted. An aspect of the debate has focused on the relationship between and the status of the rights contained in the ICCPR and the ICESCR. The emphasis has been placed in western traditions on civil and political rights, while socialist and third world countries have insisted on the importance of economic, social, and cultural rights as the foundation on which civil and political rights rest.

The definition of economic, social, and cultural rights as rights rather than as policy goals has been questioned. These rights are contrasted with civil and political rights, which, it is argued, are immediately realizable or enforceable.[6] Economic, social, and cultural rights are among the most disregarded all over the world. States' obligations to enforce them "progressively" rather than immediately, and the consequent implications for their status and observance, continue to generate controversy.

In response to the assertion that the concept of human rights is western in origin and therefore not universally applicable, several scholars have sought to demonstrate the universality of human rights through studies of value systems and social organization in non-western societies.[7] Not surprisingly, the goal has colored the enterprise, and much of the scholarship that falls into this category proceeds from a definition of respect for human dignity as the essence of human rights, begging the essential question of what constitutes human dignity. The absence of universal standards for measuring adherence would make the assertion of human rights a mere tautology. The articulation of international human rights today is an attempt to set universal standards and procedures for enforcing them. It is the processes by which these standards are set and enforced, and the priorities evident from them, that have been challenged.

The Problem with Rights

The language of rights has been the language of groups seeking to establish a new legitimacy. In medieval Europe, the language was used to justify the exercise of power by an aristocracy that claimed a divine or God-given right to rule. Between the seventeenth and nineteenth centuries in Europe and the United States, it was used by a nascent capitalist class to establish its hegemony. It was in this period that the idea of rights attaching to all individual human beings, equality before the law, and the "rule of law" were popularized as part of the ideology of an emergent bourgeoisie confronting an authoritarian state.

This conception of rights, with its emphasis on individual civil and political liberties, property rights, and the rule of law, which has been internationalized today, is premised on a notion of society as a collection of isolated, autonomous individuals, free and equal, interacting in a marketplace. It advocates formal equality before the law, laying down general, universally applicable rules while often ignoring rather than abolishing real inequalities existing between people (and in effect sometimes intensifying them). The implications and limitations of this quest for formal equality have been manifested in women's struggles, expressed in terms of equality rights, as a tension between "equality" and "difference."[8] The discourse of rights also seeks to establish the parameters for change by establishing a due process of law whereby aggrieved parties may seek redress. Other processees for seeking redress are then often delegitimated. The preamble to the UDHR, which refers to the need to avoid rebellion against tyranny and oppression,[9] exemplifies this goal. In seeking to define acceptable change and the process for effecting it, the concept of human rights can be a powerful tool for legitimation of existing institutions and the concentration of power in the hands of powerful groups.

The rights discourse is the discourse of a conflict-ridden society. It often presumes the existence of intractable conflict, which it seeks to manage, positing oppositional interests in a struggle for supremacy conducted in courts of law or similar tribunals.

The assertion of rights also presumes aspirations for and a consciousness of the capacity to prevent violation. Rights thus cannot in any meaningful way be given to a people; rather, a people must assert them. The attempt by asserting rights to impose a new legitimacy and to challenge monopoly of the definition of morality can be revolutionary. However, it often merely challenges existing definitions of morality and monopoly by a particular group that is seeking to supplant them with its own alternative version. The attempt rarely challenges the very fact of monopoly, and is thus open to further challenges for greater democratization.[10] Rights discourse is therefore in the final analysis open to use by any group of people. The discourse does not resolve the basic policy issues and the need to prioritize from which it sprang.

Women's International Human Rights: The Feminist Challenge

Women's preoccupations, reflected in international human rights instruments, have changed from an emphasis on the negative principle of nondiscrimination to more substantive eradication of discrimination by giving women positive rights, and now to an insistence on increased priority being given to prevention of violations and enforcement of all women's rights. These concerns are reflected most comprehensively in the Convention on the Elimination of All Forms of Discrimination Against Women. The Convention elaborates on the right to nondiscrimination as it affects women. It details the economic and social conditions necessary for the elimination of discrimination against women, setting out standards in the form of positive rights and thus recognizing the importance of economic, social, and cultural rights in women's struggles.

Since 1990, women's challenge to the international human rights movement has moved from calls for equality or nondiscrimination and positive rights of guarantee, to a call for the international system to go beyond mere recognition of women's rights to addressing violations of those rights through preventive action and enforcement of the law. Women's human rights have been described both as rights that women have by virtue of being human and as rights specific to women. It has therefore been pointed out that, in some situations, women suffer human rights abuses in a specific form related to their being female.[11] It has also been argued that sexual abuse, violence against women, and other attempts to control women's bodies, which constitute violations of women's human rights, are not recognized as human rights violations and do not generate the same public outcry as other human rights violations.[12]

As a result of this oversight or bias in the international human rights system, a focus on women's human rights is advocated. Once again, an attempt is being made to universalize this agenda. However, to talk of universal women's rights presumes a self-conscious, coherent group of persons that cuts across class and cultural lines and has an identity of interests. Furthermore, there is an underlying presumption of the existence of abiding conflict between monolithic male and female interests. These presumptions have been questioned times without number.[13] Has the context of women's struggles to be full and equal human beings in societies all over the world been such as to constitute women into a self-conscious, coherent group? What have been the struggles of women in Africa in the economic, social, and cultural realm?

African Women's Economic, Social, and Cultural Rights

International and Regional Treaties

Economic, social, and cultural rights of women in Africa are enunciated in three main international legal treaties—the International Covenant on Economic, Social and Cultural Rights; the Convention on the Elimination of All Forms of Discrimination Against Women; and the African Charter on Human and Peoples' Rights.

General rights recognized in the Covenant on Economic, Social and Cultural Rights include the rights to work; to fair wages and conditions of service; to an adequate standard of living and freedom from hunger; to mental and physical health; to education and freedom from discrimination; to establish and join trade unions; to strike; and to have social security and insurance.

Feminists early in their struggles recognized the importance of economic and social conditions and practices in establishing and maintaining female subordination. Positive rights for women contained in CEDAW include equal rights to property; to financial credit and assistance; to training; to choice of marriage partner; to family benefits; to equal rights on dissolution of marriage; to reproductive health care; and to maternity leave and benefits, among many others.

At the regional level in Africa, guarantees of human rights are contained in the African Charter on Human and Peoples' Rights. This Charter, adopted in 1981, endorses the United Nations Declaration on Human Rights and the Human Rights Covenants.[14] It provides for equality before the law and freedom from discrimination, and recognizes economic, social, and cultural rights[15] similar to those guaranteed under the ICESCR. Duties of states include the duty to promote and protect morals and traditional values recognized by the community and to ensure "the elimination of every discrimination against women . . . and . . . the protection of the rights of the woman . . . as stipulated in international declarations and conventions."[16] Chapter 1 spells out "peoples'" rights, including their right to economic, social, and cultural development.[17] The duties of individuals toward their families, the community, the state, and the international community are also stipulated,[18] which is one of the novel aspects of the Charter.

The framing of the Charter's provisions represents a significant shift away from the western preoccupation with individual rights, and in a sense highlights the tension between individual rights and social duties. Several commentators have expressed the fear that the Charter does not offer sufficient protection to women.[19] Very few of its provisions relate specifically to women, and it has been argued that a state's duty to promote and protect the morals and traditional values recognized by the community, and the individual's duty to preserve and strengthen positive African cultural values in relations with other members of the society, stated in Article 29(7), represent areas of potential conflict with women's rights. In this writer's view, such conflict will depend entirely on how the provisions of the Charter are interpreted.

Under these three international human rights instruments, it would therefore appear that women in Africa (like women elsewhere in the world) can lay claim to the right to equality before the law, to freedom from discrimination, and to certain economic, social, and cultural benefits and freedoms. Furthermore, as a result of the broad terms in which the provisions of these three instruments are phrased, various practices in different parts of the world may be measured against these standards, and rights of women may be inferred from them. In that sense, the ambit of women's economic, social, and cultural rights would appear to have an infinite capacity to expand, but like all standards and aspirations, the significance of these rights ultimately depends on the ability to enforce them.

The weakness of enforcement mechanisms at the international level has been noted countless times. This applies even more regarding human rights instruments, because they are often concerned with the claims of individuals and groups against states, in a system that continues to be state-centric. As noted earlier,[20] significant differences exist in the phrasing of obligations arising from the various conventions, as well as in the enforcement mechanisms they provide. It may be argued that there is a continuing emphasis in the international system on the enforcement of civil and political rights, while economic, social, and cultural rights are deemed unenforceable in the short term. This is evident from the debates in the UN system on the right to development and the debates within the Human Rights Commission on the realization of economic, social, and cultural rights. It is especially so in relation to the question of the external debt and structural adjustment programs in countries in Africa, Asia, and Latin America.[21] The mechanisms for the enforcement of rights guaranteed under the African Charter have generated even more pessimism.[22]

From the provisions of these international instruments we can infer that they anticipate that one of the most significant ways states will give effect to the rights articulated in the Covenants and Charter is by adopting legislative measures.[23] Do policy, law, and practice within different countries in Africa today reflect these internationally recognized standards?

National Constitutions, Legislation, and Customary/Religious Laws

The constitutions of most African countries today affirm the right to nondiscrimination on the basis of sex. Other rules of law and legislation may, however, discriminate against women in certain instances. Even where provisions of law are not overtly discriminatory, their application to women may yield discriminatory results due to women's economic and social positions in society. In Nigeria, for example, guarantees of economic, social, and cultural rights for women are considered briefly.

Chapter 4 of the Constitution of the Federal Republic of Nigeria 1989 (provisions of which are almost identical to the 1979 Constitution) sets out the fundamental human rights to which all persons are entitled. These are a catalogue of the usual civil and political rights contained in most modern constitutions today. Chapter 2 of the Constitution, described as "Fundamental Objectives and Directive Principles of State Policy," contains principles of economic, social, and cultural rights relating to equal access to resources; provision of basic needs and an adequate means of livelihood; and provision of adequate health facilities for all and free education. The state has a duty to conform to, observe, and apply these principles and provisions, but they are not justiciable.

While a recognition of some internationally accepted economic, social, and cultural rights outlined earlier may be inferred from these principles, the distinction made between them and fundamental human rights in the Nigerian Constitution clearly indicates that there was no intention to enforce them. This distinction is reminiscent of the differences in the provisions of the international human rights covenants and the predominant attitude toward the enforcement of economic, social, and cultural rights.[24] According to one commentator,

The Nigerian Constitution has entrenched fundamental rights and made them justiciable but economic and social rights have been relegated to mere declaration of pious hopes because it is believed that they can only be achieved progressively according to available resources of the Nation and the policies pursued by Government.[25]

Section 18(2a) of the Fundamental Objectives and Directive Principles of State Policy states that "every citizen shall have equality of rights, obligations and opportunities before the law." These principles are restated as a fundamental human right in Section 41 and provide a legally enforceable guarantee against discrimination, on the basis of sex and other characteristics, in these terms:

A citizen of Nigeria of a particular . . . sex . . . shall not, by reason only that he is such a person—
(a) be subjected either expressly by, or in the practical application of, any law in force in Nigeria or any executive or administrative action of the government to disabilities or restrictions to which citizens of Nigeria of other . . . sex . . . are not made subject; or
(b) be accorded either expressly by, or in the practical application of, any law in force in Nigeria or any such executive or administrative action, any privilege or advantage that is not accorded to citizens of Nigeria of other . . . sex . . .

Although Nigeria has ratified the Convention on the Elimination of All Forms of Discrimination Against Women, some legal scholars are of the view that Section 41 is far-reaching, rendering unconstitutional any form of "affirmative action" or special privileges (such as those relating to working conditions for nursing mothers) for women.[26] This of course depends on whether specific considerations or measures recognizing the peculiar situation of women or their disadvantaged position can be defined as the award of a privilege or advantage. If Section 41 of the Constitution is interpreted in the light of Nigeria's obligations under Article 18 of the African Charter, which it has ratified, then affirmative action by the state toward "the elimination of every discrimination against women . . . and . . . the protection of the rights of the woman" is not only desirable but required.

Section 41 renders all laws including customary and religious laws, subsidiary legislation, regulations, and official government practices that permit discrimination against women unconstitutional, null and void, with the exception stipulated in subsection 3 relating to appointments in the public service, armed forces, and police force. The section covers not just promulgated laws and regulations but their "practical application." Also significant is the exclusion of Section 41 from the omnibus clause in Section 43, which restricts and limits the ambit of fundamental human rights in the interests of defense, public interest, public order, public morality, or public health.

In effect, women in Nigeria therefore have all the human rights stipulated in the Constitution including the right to nondiscrimination on the basis of sex, but no positive rights specifically addressed to their particular needs or vulnerabilities nor a recognition of the need for such rights.

Specific rights for women are expressed in some legislation, notably employment laws that offer special protection to women during pregnancy, guarantees of maternity leave with pay, and job security during and after childbirth.[27] Specific legal provisions such as those relating to abortion in Nigeria,[28] it could be argued, in effect deny women legal access to the best attainable state of health. The application of certain laws also results in discrimination against women. For example, Nigerian women have challenged the existing application of tax laws in the country as discriminatory. Married women who wish to claim tax relief for expenses related to rearing children are required to show documentary evidence of those expenses and evidence that the father of the children is not responsible for their upkeep. Men are not required to produce such documents.

Several areas of actual and potential conflict between constitutional provisions and Islamic law in terms of equality of men and women have been pointed out by various commentators.[29] Notable among these are rules relating to maintenance of women during marriage and dissolution of marriages; rules of inheritance that provide for smaller shares for females than males in family estates; and rights of men to beat their wives.

Often cited examples of customary laws that violate provisions for equality before the law and nondiscrimination in Nigeria are those relating to inheritance and ownership of land, and to custody of children. In some parts of the country, females do not have the same rights of inheritance as males, or rights to own and dispose of family or communal land, nor do they have the same rights to be considered heads of families.

Colonial/modern and customary/religious systems of law co-exist within the legal systems of most African countries. The rules of law examined above that involve some discrimination against women have not been contested in the courts as unconstitutional and a violation of human rights, so it is difficult to make categoric statements on the probable outcome of such challenges. Challenges have not been posed for several reasons, including the irrelevance of modern legal discourse to the vast majority of people in these countries, as well as the problem of access to modern legal processes and institutions.

The Context of African Women's Human Rights Struggles

Today, the majority of people in Africa live under extremely difficult conditions with their ability to subsist threatened by international and national policies and practices. Women suffer in particular as a result of patterns of division of labor and the spread of modern capitalist relations of production in the colonial and post-colonial period, which has resulted in the devaluation of their work. Colonial education and employment policies, the development of a distinction between the public and private spheres, the relegation of household work to the latter sphere, and its redefinition as women's work, have all had serious implications for the status of women vis-à-vis men.

Under many pre-colonial systems of social organization, sexual division of labor did not necessarily imply patriarchal oppression. The work of both sexes and all groups was valued as necessary to the functioning of the society, and women's reproductive roles were sometimes given great premium. In modern capitalist societies, where enterprises are increasingly mechanized and seek, above all, to maximize profit, value is measured in terms of profit, and childbearing becomes a disability for women workers. Property has become alienable by individuals and groups, and status in the family is often linked to effective control of property to the exclusion of others. Women in some parts of Africa have now lost their rights to the use of land, and there is no corresponding responsibility placed on men to provide them with a means of livelihood. The social practices that ensured that a widow remained part of a family and was cared for on the death of her husband were altered, and no limitations were placed, in the new dispensation, on her husband's family's claims to all his belongings, leaving her and her children destitute.

Various practices relating to reproduction continue to place women at risk of disease and death in spite of advances in medical knowledge and technology. New forms of social and political organization have eroded communal support systems, placing an immense burden on women for supporting the extended family in many areas.

The impact of economic and social changes in the colonial and post-colonial period, combined with vestiges of "tradition"—decontextualized, proclaimed as customary law,[30] and applied to the lives of the majority of African women by new tribunals dubbed "customary"—has been profound.

Since the 1980s, the debt crisis and the imposition of structural adjustment programs (SAPs) inspired by the World Bank and the International Monetary Fund (IMF) have further impoverished the majority of African peoples. The pillars of structural adjustment programs have been devaluation of local currencies; rationalization of industry, including privatization of public enterprises; and reduction of government expenditure on social services. The results have been spiraling inflation, massive retrenchment of workers, and severely restricted access to education and to health facilities.

Women, already laboring under severe disadvantage, have been severely affected by SAPs. Employment opportunities have been restricted, access to education rendered more difficult, and to the double burden of work they bear as household managers has been added an increasing role as providers of social security including health care for the sick and elderly. In the severely strained economic circumstances, violence against women and sexual exploitation have risen to alarming levels.

Women's capacity to change their lives has been restricted in this process by their limited exposure to alternatives, and by their economic position. The effect of their political and economic position is a structural dependence on men for access to resources that subjects even relatively privileged women to a certain insecurity. Questions of social justice and social capacity to bring about change for women are inextricably linked to economic power, and to control of the processes that confer economic power in a society.

It is within this context that women's rights to an adequate standard of living, to freedom from hunger, to work with fair wages and fair conditions of service, to mental and physical health including reproductive health care, and to education and training, among many other rights outlined in the ICESCR and CEDAW, are violated *systematically and on a daily basis.*

In the face of all these obstacles and disenabling conditions, African women have organized at various levels to try to change practices, policies, and laws that they consider to be discriminatory, unjust, or harmful, whether perceived as customary or modern practices, policies, or laws.[31] They have organized both as interested human beings and as women suffering specific oppression to promote their interests. Their goals and patterns of organization vary considerably depending on whether they function in rural or urban areas and on the class and cultural backgrounds of the women involved. Some of their most important struggles in recent times have centered on taxation and levies, education, improved conditions of employment, traditional practices, property rights, and inheritance.

It is noteworthy that in many of their struggles, even where they have organized against discriminatory practices perpetrated by males, African women have not necessarily acted in opposition to men as a group. These struggles have not generally taken the form of assertions of rights made by groups of women most affected, or by others acting on their behalf. Calls for justice and improved conditions of health have often been the bases for demanding change. Change has come with the organization and mobilization of women, in many cases as a result of joint action by men and women.

Toward a Relevant Theory and Practice

Today in Africa, the rights discourse has been made relevant by changes in political organization based on new socioeconomic arrangements. Old forms of organization with which many women were familiar have changed and continue to change. New forms are sometimes used to oppress women, and require new forms of resistance in reaction.

There are various forms of struggle that develop in response to a situation of oppression. The discourse of rights has had little resonance for the majority of African women, and the national and international rules and procedures for enforcement of rights have rarely been their arenas of struggle. The language of freedom, justice, and fair play[32] has had greater resonance among the "masses" in Africa[33] than has the language of "rights," especially in relation to struggles against social and cultural practices. This may be partly because women have generally not seen themselves as organizing *in opposition* to men, but *for* social justice. In this sense, although many women see their rights as unquestionably human, they do not define themselves solely in relation to men.

The discourse of rights has been more popular in struggles by sections of the political elite for political and civil liberties against repressive governments in Africa. This is not surprising, since the assertion of rights has traditionally been a cry for political space within which to maneuver.[34] Economic, social, and cultural rights are concerned with complex social relations and are sometimes denied by layers of institutional and systemic hostility to conditions necessary to human dignity and well being.

Existing declarations of universal human rights have become so broad and all-encompassing that they are difficult to criticize even at the national level. As was shown earlier, much depends on interpretation and enforcement of the principles and rules, which in turn depend on challenges posed within the system.[35] The often-noted failure of enforcement mechanisms for international human rights may more accurately be described as a problem of selective enforcement. Selection reflects the priorities of powerful groups in the international system, and the weakness of relevant protesting parties.

The human rights movement today has gone beyond a quest for formal equality to articulate as rights some of the conditions necessary to establish real equality. In retaining the language of universal rights, but failing to link these rights to the total social context in which the problem of violation of human dignity arises, the modern human rights movement lays itself open to accusations of promoting sectional interests. African, socialist, and other "third world" states have been forcing a confrontation of the issue of selective definition and enforcement of human rights in the international system by insisting on greater attention to economic, social, and cultural rights. Paradoxically, on the national front many of these states are doing exactly what they complain of at the international level, namely, relegating economic and social rights to the background,[36] even when paying only lip service to civil and political rights.

The international women's rights movement, like the international human rights movement, largely projects the concerns of privileged women who are able to make their voices heard. The voices of middle-class European and American women, because of their cultural affinity with and access to centers of power from whence the dominant discourse emanates, are often loudest. The attack by western feminists on male, white privilege within the international human rights system can become the quest for male *and female* white privilege in the system, or simply male and female privilege in the system.

As remarked earlier, the discourse of rights can privilege certain relatively empowered groups within a specific context, whilst operating to neutralize or delegitimize other forms of struggle for human dignity and well-being. It could, on the other hand, be a mode of naming a legal claim and acquiring political space to advance certain goals, and so be empowering in the struggle for social justice. The goals of the struggle within a specific society must, however, be defined, and form the reference point for the definition and assessment of rights.

Rights have never been absolute and universally applicable. At best, they have been declarations of aspirations or ideals. Promulgation of Bills of Rights or Constitutions in various societies can be seen as an attempt to institute a new order. The new order is built on the old order; there is never a vacuum. The inadequacy of the old order or dissatisfaction with it, expressed in different terms including armed struggle, is what leads to calls for a new order. However, ignoring the old order, or making pious declarations that have no basis in reality, can defeat efforts to effect social change. Examples of this kind of situation abound in Africa. When it is asserted that "constitutionalism" has failed in most parts of Africa because written constitutions have not operated according to their texts, it may be countered that what has happened is that the *real* constitution—social relations and an existing distribution of power—has endured unchanged and rendered the new written text, which ignored it, irrelevant and unworkable. A similar view is expressed by Albie Sachs, writing on the tasks ahead in drawing up a bill of rights for a New South Africa. He puts forward his idea of a progressive concept of a bill of rights as "a true consolidator of the gains of a people in struggle," going on to state that "A Bill of Rights can be either an enduring product of history shaped by lawyers, or a transitory product of lawyers imposed upon history."[37] The point is that rights cannot be seen outside the context of a movement or struggle to achieve specific goals.

African women's struggles for human dignity and well-being are located in the context of political, economic, and cultural domination within an unjust international system of allocation of resources. For the large majority of women in Africa and other parts of the world whose struggle for basic needs and subsistence alongside men prevents them from changing their lives for the better, addressing the problem of poverty is a priority human rights issue. In their situation, international economic policies like those expressed in structural adjustment programs are a main source of violation of their human rights. Yet such programs are expounded and supported by UN agencies and countries of the North, which have, nonetheless, constituted themselves watch-dogs against the violation of international civil and political liberties. It is at this level that violation of African women's economic, social, and cultural rights is most direct, and that the language of rights is most appropriate to prevent such violation. Yet it is also at this level that African women are least empowered to take action. Their strategic alliances with groups challenging this violation therefore become imperative.

At the regional level, the emphasis on safeguarding tradition could indeed be used against women.[38] The challenge is for women seeking to use the African Charter and contest the constitutionality of provisions of customary and religious law to advance interpretations that promote justice, based on the context in which the laws are applied.

At the national level, African women confront social practices with peculiar implications for women that now operate within contexts different from those in which they originated. African women need to be empowered to develop appropriate modes of resistance to unjust and oppressive outcomes of such practices.

Conclusion

The impact on the lives of peoples throughout the world of capitalist economic expansion and the development of a new international division of labor in the nineteenth and twentieth centuries has been profound. The new economic environment has brought with it a certain uniformity of modes and sources of oppression, which has inspired different groups to try to build international solidarity movements in reaction. Indeed, the growth and significance of transnational policymaking in today's world make transnational organization by interest groups imperative if they are to really influence policies.

This chapter has sought to examine existing claims of the existence of universally applicable human rights and women's rights and the relevance and significance of such claims for African women. It has been argued that the rights discourse, although relevant to specific struggles, is only one of many forms of resistance to oppression. The international system has been an arena of struggles for the realization of the end of oppression. It has also been argued that the tendencies towards "enforcing a consensus" or universalizing specific interests or priorities, evident both in the international human rights movement and the women's rights movement, defeat the laudable general goals of achieving respect for human dignity and well-being.

The challenge before women in Africa, especially those who are relatively empowered to bring about change, is how to use the language of rights to advance our claims for social justice at the international and local levels. However, we need to be careful how we use the loaded language of rights, even as we develop innovative approaches and perhaps a different, less alienating, language appropriate to the search for enduring solutions to our problems. In this enterprise, the facilitation of broader participation in the definition of standards reflecting our aspirations for a better society is vital. The proclamation of rights is one strategy in the process of delegitimating existing violations but the forum for such proclamation must be carefully considered and chosen.

The challenge before the international women's rights movement is to recognize and build on different experiences within it rather than suppress them, and to link hands to oppose domination in any form and advance democratization; as human beings, to pose an alternative by drawing on the movement's perspective on each specific form of domination and its linkages with other forms of domination. To advance common goals, women need to organize to empower each other. Women must collaborate in localized struggles through the sharing of experiences, information, and other resources; in opposition to violations of their interests; and to confront selective recognition and enforcement of claims to human dignity and well being, at all levels. Can the international women's rights movement rise to the challenge? If so, will it?

Notes

1. Paul Sieghart, *An Introduction to the International Covenants on Human Rights* (London: Commonwealth Secretariat, 1988), 1.

2. See generally Abdullahi A. An-Na'im and Francis M. Deng, eds., *Human Rights in Africa: Cross-Cultural Perspectives* (Washington DC: Brookings Institution, 1990).

3. Carl J. Friedrich, *The Philosophy of Law in Historical Perspective* (Chicago: University of Chicago Press, 1963), 178.

4. See art. 17 of the Universal Declaration, which states that everyone may own property *alone,* in spite of the fact that such ownership was not recognized in certain communities. Art. 22 states the right to social security and realisation of economic, social, and cultural rights indispensable for dignity and free development of personality, are limited in accordance with the organization and resources of each State; yet no such limitation is acknowledged with regard to private property.

5. For example, the right to form trade unions and to strike. This is not an attempt to argue that the form of social organization presumed is European or American but merely to highlight the origins and historical specificity of the reflected traditions.

6. See, e.g., comments by Oji Umozurike, "The African Charter on Human and Peoples' Rights," paper presented at the Judicial Colloquium on Developing Human Rights Jurisprudence: The Domestic Application of Human Rights Norms, Banjul, November 1990 at 24–25. See also Sieghart, *International Covenants,* note 1 at 4–7 for comments on the alleged differences between the two covenants.

7. See, e.g., Kwasi Wiredu, "An Akan Perspective on Human Rights," and Francis Deng, "A Cultural Approach to Human Rights Among the Dinka," in An-Na'im and Deng, *Human Rights in Africa,* note 2 at Part IV. See also Lakshman Marasinghe, "Traditional Conceptions of Human Rights in Africa" in *Human Rights and Development in Africa,* ed. Claude Welch and Ronald Meltzer (Albany: State University of New York Press, 1984).

8. See Introduction to Anne Phillips, ed., *Feminism and Equality* (Oxford: Basil Blackwell, 1987) for a summary of some of the issues raised in this debate.

9. Phillips, *Feminism and Equality,* note 8 at 3.

10. Significant expansion of the dominant concept of rights has taken place with the articulation of group and peoples' rights (including the right to development), with definitions of groups still expanding and subject to much controversy.

11. See Charlotte Bunch, "Women's Rights as Human Rights: Towards a Re-Vision of Human Rights," *Hum. Rts. Q.* 12 (1990): 486–98 at 486–89.

12. Bunch, "Re-Vision," note 11 at 489.

13. Marie Angélique Savane, "Another Development with Women," *Dev. Dialogue* 1 (2) at 8–16; Anne Marie Goetz, "Feminism and the Claim to Know: Contradictions in Feminist Approaches to Women in Development," in *Gender and International Relations*, ed. Rebecca Grant and Kathleen Newland (Bloomington: Indiana University Press, 1991); Hilary Charlesworth, Christine Chinkin, and Shelley Wright, "Feminist Approaches to International Law," *Am. J. Int'l L.* 85 (1991): 613–45.

14. African Charter on Human and Peoples' Rights, 1981, art. 18 (3).

15. African Charter, arts. 14-17.

16. African Charter, arts. 17 and 18.

17. African Charter, art. 22.

18. African Charter, Chapter II of Part 1.

19. Deborah Wean, "Real Protection for African Women? The African Charter on Human and Peoples' Rights," *J. of Int'l Disp. Resolution* 2 (Spring 1988): 425–28.

20. Wean, "Real Protection," note 19.

21. "Realisation of Economic, Social and Cultural Rights," *Report of the Special Rapporteur to the United Nations Commission on Human Rights, U.N. Doc.*, E/CN.4/Sub.2/1991.

22. See, e.g., Osita Eze, "The Organisation of African Unity and Human Rights: Twenty-Five Years After," *Nigerian J. Int'l Aff.* 14 (1) (1988): 154–88.

23. Art. 4 of ICESCR also stipulates that states may only subject the rights to limitations that are determined by law, for the purpose of promoting general welfare in a democratic society, and that are compatible with the nature of the rights.

24. See Umozurike, "The African Charter," note 6 at 24–25.

25. Jadesola O. Akande, "A Decade of Human Rights in Nigeria," in *New Dimensions in Nigerian Law*, ed. M.A. Ajomo (Lagos: Nigerian Institute of Advanced Legal Studies, Law Series No. 3 1989), 123.

26. B.O. Nwabueze, "Equality Before the Law," in *Fundamentals of Nigerian Law*, ed. Ayo Ajomo (Lagos: Nigerian Institute of Advanced Legal Studies Law Series No. 2, 1989), 54.

27. See secs. 53–55 of Labour Decree No. 21, 1974.

28. Secs. 228, 229, and 297 of the Criminal Code and secs. 232 and 235 of the Penal Code. These provisions of the law make abortion illegal unless it is performed to save or preserve the life of the mother. Similar provisions are to be found in the laws of various other African countries including the Sudan, Senegal, Botswana, and Malawi.

29. See essay by Bassam Tibi in *Human Rights in Africa*, ed. An-Na'im and Deng note 2 at 104.

30. There is a wealth of literature on the "creation" of customary law in Africa. See, for example, Ajayi, "The Judicial Development of Customary Law in Nigeria," in *Integration of Customary and Modern Legal Systems in Africa* (Ile-Ife: University of Ife, 1981); Francis Snyder, "Colonialism and Legal Form: The Creation of Customary Law in the Senegal," *J. Leg. Pluralism* 19 (1981): 49.

31. Women's struggle against widowhood rites and customs relating to inheritance in Nigeria is a case in point.

32. This is reflected even in the difficulty of translating the term "rights" in some languages.

33. See Adetoun O. Ilumoka, "The Marginalisation of the Legal Profession

in Nigeria 1984–1985: A Sign of Things to Come?" paper presented at the European Critical Legal Studies Conference, Kent University, 1986. I have argued there that, in relation to reactions of the Nigerian populace to the military coup that brought General Buhari to power, and the opposition of lawyers to that regime, that "justice" rather than the "rule of law" was what generated initial support of people for a military regime that seized power from a civilian one. This is true also to a large extent of the Rawlings regime in Ghana.

34. Ilumoka, "Marginalisation," note 33 at 7.

35. Ilumoka, "Marginalisation," note 33 at 13, 17 and 19.

36. See Akande's comments on the situation under the Nigerian Constitution, "Decade," note 25 at 13.

37. Albie Sachs, *Protecting Human Rights in a New South Africa* (Cape Town: Oxford University Press, 1990), 13–14.

38. For discussion on the African Charter, see text, pp. 312–14.

Chapter 13
Domestic Violence as an International Human Rights Issue

Kenneth Roth

Introduction

In this chapter I will discuss some of the methodological problems that the Human Rights Watch Women's Rights Project has encountered in addressing domestic violence against women. I have chosen to focus on domestic violence both because of the severity of the problem and because of the complexities of the legal and conceptual issues that arise in treating it as a human rights violation. By highlighting these complexities, I hope to illustrate how international human rights law can most effectively be used to combat domestic violence. The discussion will also have obvious relevance to other efforts to address de facto discrimination in the application of facially neutral criminal laws to private actors.

I will begin by tracing the evolution of the traditional human rights movement for the purpose of showing both why that movement has neglected the problem of domestic violence and why such neglect can no longer be justified in light of comparable issues that the movement now addresses. I will then outline the type of evidence that in my view is needed to treat the problem of domestic violence as a human rights issue, while noting the ways in which this proof often differs significantly from the evidence required for more traditional human rights inquiries.

Finally, I will discuss the experience of the Human Rights Watch Women's Rights Project in collecting this evidence. In doing so, I will note a troubling void that we have observed in the work of local human rights and women's rights organizations. By highlighting this void, I hope to help spawn the factual research needed to address the problem of domestic violence more effectively as a human rights issue.

A Narrow Reading of International Human Rights Law

Until very recently, international human rights organizations, including Human Rights Watch, have neglected the problem of domestic violence against women. In discussing international human rights organizations I will limit myself to two: Human Rights Watch, because it is the organization with which I am most familiar, and Amnesty International, because of its defining role in the field. One cause of this neglect was their narrow reading of the broad language of the International Covenant on Civil and Political Rights (the Covenant). I will limit my legal discussion to the International Covenant on Civil and Political Rights, because this treaty is the most influential within the traditional human rights movement, and because it addresses problems of violence more directly than the Convention on the Elimination of All Forms of Discrimination Against Women. The Covenant contains powerful, expansive phrases, with obvious potential relevance to the fight against domestic violence—particularly violence that amounts to murder, and arguably also lesser assaults. For example, Article 6(1) provides: "Every human being has the inherent right to life. This right shall be protected by law. No one shall be arbitrarily deprived of his life." Article 7 provides that "No one shall be subjected to torture or to cruel, inhuman or degrading treatment." Article 9(1) provides that "Everyone has the right to . . . security of person." All these guarantees are arguably implicated by domestic violence.

Political Motivation

Despite the broad potential reach of the Covenant's guarantees, international human rights organizations, particularly in their early days, treated these provisions as if they applied only to the victims of politically motivated abuse (and even then only if the abuse was at the hands of a government agent). It was as if the sweeping language of these provisions—"Every human being," "Everyone"—were replaced by the far narrower phrase, "every dissident."

Part of the reason for this narrow reading of the Covenant is historical accident: the large human rights organizations were born out of a concern with politically motivated abuse. Amnesty International was founded to protect people who had been imprisoned for their peaceful political beliefs. The classic prisoner of conscience was a man or woman who had been detained because of his or her nonviolent political opposition to a government. Human Rights Watch, in the form of Helsinki Watch, originated in an effort to protect human rights monitors who had begun to emerge in the former Soviet Union and

Eastern Europe following the signing of the Helsinki Accords in 1975. These "Helsinki monitors" arose in response to Principle VII of the Final Act of the Conference on Security and Cooperation in Europe, which proclaimed "the right of the individual to know and act upon his rights." In each case, dissidents were the main focus of concern.

There may have been good reasons for this focus, given the limited resources available at the time for human rights work and the need to create a public consciousness about (and sympathy for) human rights. But justification for this narrow interpretation of the human rights cause cannot be found in the Covenant's text.

Although both Amnesty International and Human Rights Watch have gradually expanded their mandates beyond the classic prisoner of conscience, the paradigm of a government seeking to still dissent remains powerful. For example, while the fight against torture and extra-judicial execution encompasses those detained because of common as well as political crimes, the political prisoner remains a principal concern. Campaigns waged against violations of physical integrity still tend to feature dissidents rather than common criminal suspects.

In recent years, however, international human rights organizations have begun to move beyond an exclusive focus on prisoners of conscience. For example, Human Rights Watch has documented summary executions by the police of common criminal suspects, with substantial reports devoted to this topic in Argentina, Brazil, and Jamaica. Amnesty International has engaged in similar work. Torture in countries like Turkey and India, where it affects vast numbers of common criminal suspects, has also received heightened attention. In addition, Human Rights Watch launched a Prisoners' Rights Project, which monitors prison conditions faced by those held for common crimes as well as political offenses, and has reported on prison conditions in some dozen countries around the world.

Of course, there is often a political dimension to abuses against alleged common criminals, in that the victims are usually poor and the abuses tend to serve as a method of social control. But the victims generally are targeted not because of their political views—indeed, these often are not known—but because of their social status and presumed aspirations. Yet the broad language of the Covenant clearly encompasses these governmental abuses, and it has become increasingly accepted that they should be part of the international human rights mandate.

By the same token, the lack of a traditional political motivation behind domestic violence against women should no longer preclude its consideration by international human rights organizations. Like violence against presumed common criminals, violence against women can be said to have a political dimension in that it arguably serves as a form of social control by reinforcing the subjugation of women. But even that political dimension should not be necessary to address the issue. If international human rights organizations no longer ask the political views of a victim of execution, torture, or inhuman prison conditions, why should they care that domestic violence has little if anything to do with the political views of its victims? A woman killed by her husband for a supposed offense to his "honor" is deprived of her life in as "arbitrary" a fashion (to use the language of Covenant article 6(1)) as a common criminal suspect who is summarily executed by the police.

State Action Versus Inaction

A second conceptual obstacle to the treatment of domestic violence against women has been the focus of the human rights movement, and human rights law, on violations by the state. Anyone can commit a common crime, but only a state and its agents can commit a human rights violation under international law. Since the perpetrators of domestic violence are by definition private, they cannot be treated as appropriate subjects of international human rights law unless the state can in some sense be held responsible.

The necessary theory of accountability can be found in the traditional human rights movement's gradual acceptance of the argument that the state can be held responsible under international human rights law for its inaction as well as its action. The trend toward broader acceptance of this analytic approach was sparked to a significant extent by the effort to grapple with the phenomenon of death squads. Although in places like El Salvador and Guatemala there was strong evidence linking death squads with governmental forces, the international human rights movement did not rely exclusively on a theory of government agency. It also used an argument of complicity, by contending that the government should be held responsible simply because of its systematic failure to attempt to halt the death squads.

Human Rights Watch used a similar theory of government complicity to address private violence against landless peasants in the course of rural land disputes in such countries as Brazil and Paraguay. Although at times the violence is committed by state agents, often it occurs at the hands of private militias in the employ of large landowners who have no direct relationship with the state. To hold the state responsible for this otherwise private violence, we have highlighted the state's systematic failure to enforce criminal laws against this category of violence. The state's abdication of its duty to protect its citizens from crimes of violence amounts to a tacit endorsement of that violence. That complicity provides the requisite governmental dimension to consider the violence a human rights issue.

The same theory of state responsibility by omission rather than commission can be seen in Human Rights Watch's treatment of a range of other abuses, including sectarian violence, violence against labor activists, violence against political opponents, slavery, and forced labor. When the Egyptian government turns a blind eye toward private violence against Copts, or the Romanian government does the same toward private violence against Gypsies, Human Rights Watch has not hesitated to hold the government responsible under international human rights law. Similarly, we have condemned as human rights violations:

- the systematic failure of the government in Miami to prosecute those responsible for violent attacks on moderate voices in the Cuban-American community on issues relating to the Cuban government;
- the systematic failure of the governments of Guatemala, El Salvador and South Korea to prosecute those who, at the behest of large private employers, have attacked union organizers and labor activists;
- the systematic failure of the Mauritanian government to act against private citizens who continue to enslave blacks;
- the systematic failure of the Brazilian government to move against large private landowners who employ forced labor.

Implicit in this approach is that a state has some duty to protect those within its territory from private acts of violence and illicit force. When the state makes little or no effort to stop a certain form of private violence, it tacitly condones that violence. This complicity transforms what would otherwise be wholly private conduct into a constructive act of the state.

While the Covenant does not explicitly establish a state's duty to combat private violence, its broad language is fully compatible with this duty. For example, the right not to be "arbitrarily deprived of [one's] life" could be read as imposing a duty on the state to address both official and private violence. Since the international human rights movement has been willing to hold the state responsible under the Covenant for its complicity in various other forms of private violence, there is no reason why it should refrain from using the same analytic approach to address domestic violence. Just as the state's systematic failure to act against private violence directed at landless peasants, labor activists, or disfavored religious or ethnic minorities can give rise to a human rights violation, so this theory of liability by omission can be used to treat the state's systematic failure to confront domestic violence against women as a human rights issue.

For example, in studying domestic violence in Brazil, the Human Rights Watch Women's Rights Project devoted considerable attention to the courts' and prosecutors' persistent acceptance of the "honor" defense—the illegal but widely used claim that instances of domestic violence can be justified or excused because the actions of a man's wife or lover allegedly offended his honor. The continued existence of this defense made the state complicit in the phenomenon of "honor" killings because it signaled a tacit official acceptance of the practice.

The Limits of State Liability by Omission

Even if one accepts that a state can be held responsible under international human rights law for its failure to address certain categories of violence, the limits to such liability must be defined. When does a state's failure to stop private violence constitute a human rights violation, as opposed to a mere policy failure?

Theoretically, one could treat each act of private violence as a human rights violation, in that the state has failed to prevent it. But such an absolutist approach to the intractable problem of private violence would trivialize the special stigma behind the label "human rights violator."

Rather, in my view, the limits to state responsibility for private violence must be found in the same notion of complicity that made such violence a human rights matter in the first place. The more vigorous a state's efforts to prosecute violent criminals, the less it can be said to condone, or be complicit in, their crimes. Once this link of governmental complicity is broken, private violence ceases to present a human rights issue.

In this sense, the theory of complicity used to transform private violence into a matter of state responsibility is a relative one. Unlike the absolute duty imposed on the state to prevent acts of unlawful violence by its own agents, a state's duty under international human rights law to prevent private violence extends only so far as a private actor can be said effectively to have become a state agent. It is a human rights violation for a state to commit even a single act of torture, for example. But a single act of domestic violence is not a human rights violation unless the state can be said through its systematic inaction to have condoned the violence.

Unsatisfied with this limited notion of state responsibility, some women's rights activists have suggested an alternative theory. They argue that, unlike other common crimes, domestic violence is inherently an issue under international human rights law because it systematically subordinates women. Victims of ordinary assaults range across all segments of society, the argument goes, but domestic violence is directed primarily at women, with the aim of maintaining male supremacy and depriving them of a range of political, social, and economic benefits. Because of this systematic subordination, these advocates contend, domestic violence constitutes a violation of international human rights law in and of itself. That is, the state has a duty to eradicate domestic violence not simply as it has a duty to counter common crime but akin to its absolute duty to eradicate torture or summary execution by government agents. Or, put another way, they argue that the state must go beyond simply not condoning domestic violence (the standard with respect to most private violence) to ending it (the standard for violence by state agents).

There are two main problems with this approach. First, it fails to distinguish domestic violence from a range of other forms of violence that also systematically subordinate a class of people. Violence in the context of land disputes systematically subordinates landless peasants. Violence against labor activists systematically subordinates workers. Forced labor and slavery systematically subordinate still other categories of people. The list could go on. As the number of classes of victims who can claim systematic subordination at the hands of violent private actors grows, so do the forms of violence that must be considered in and of themselves to be violations of international human rights law and thus to trigger the state's duty of eradication (as opposed to the lesser duty simply not to condone). In the process, the defense of human rights under international law is gradually transformed into an exercise of crime control.

This transformation would have disastrous consequences for the cause of international human rights law because it would devalue the special stigma attached to a violation of that law. If a state's violation of international human rights law had no more stigmatizing effect than the police's failure to prevent a common crime, human rights would be reduced from a series of fundamental legal guarantees limiting the scope of government to mere policy prescriptions.

Second, the effort to distinguish a class of people who merit special protection by the state—whether because of their systematic subordination or any other characteristic—should give pause because it breaches the universality that underlies international human rights law. An important strength of most, if not all, international human rights law is that its guarantees apply universally. Rights generally exist equally for all. Any theory that creates special rights for a class of people undermines this universality and risks setting a precedent for exempting classes of people from the full protection of international human rights instruments that can easily be abused. Given the long and continuing history of women's suffering under non-universal systems of rights, women's rights advocates should be particularly reluctant to breach this principle of universality.

I do not deny that the rhetoric of human rights can be a useful political tool for those seeking special protections for women. Speaking in terms of human rights can be highly effective in rallying political support for one's cause. But that rhetorical use of human rights discourse to impose special obligations on the state with respect to women is quite different from the universal meaning that human rights concepts should retain under international law. It is one thing for an organization devoted exclusively to the protection of women to use such rhetoric for political ends. It is quite another thing for an international human rights organization, which must be devoted to protecting the rights of all people, to forsake the principle of universality—particularly when, as I will show, an alternative approach exists for defining the limits of a theory of state complicity in private violence.

Nondiscrimination

If the Covenant's provisions are not absolute with respect to domestic violence, what do they demand? The substantive provisions of the Covenant provide no clear answer. What steps must a government take against domestic violence to avoid becoming complicit and thus transforming the problem from one of common crime to a human rights issue? Is it enough simply to outlaw the practice? Is it enough to make an occasional arrest, launch a periodic prosecution, or secure a sporadic conviction? Human rights advocates would argue that such desultory efforts are not enough for a state to avoid being held complicit in domestic violence, but the provisions of the Covenant that protect the physical integrity of the person provide no textual guidance on this matter.

The antidiscrimination provisions of the Covenant are more helpful in this regard. They impose an independent duty on the state not to discriminate on a number of specified grounds, including gender, in the protection of various rights. Failure to fulfill this duty constitutes a human rights violation independent of the substantive rights at stake.

The advantage of adding this argument to the theory of state responsibility by utter indifference is that it permits evaluation of a state's efforts to eradicate domestic violence well beyond the stage when it is doing nothing. While a discrimination-based theory of state responsibility does not dictate the precise level of effort to be devoted to combating domestic violence, it does provide important supplemental standards in comparative terms. That is, in the case of the state that is doing the bare minimum in combating domestic violence to avoid charges of complicity, a discrimination theory allows one to insist on greater diligence as a matter of international human rights law. It provides justification for the demand that the state's efforts to combat domestic violence are at least on a par with its efforts to fight comparable forms of violent crime.

Of course, if a state's inaction in the face of violence is nearly complete, there is no need to make an argument in terms of discrimination. The state's complicity in itself allows domestic violence to be treated as a human rights issue. But once a state moves beyond the stage of obvious complicity, a discrimination-based theory of state responsibility permits an additional argument: a state can be said to condone a particular form of violence because it pays inadequate attention to prevent it in relation to comparable forms of violence.

The textual basis for a discrimination-based theory of liability can be found in several provisions of the Covenant:

- Article 2(1): "Each State Party to the present Covenant undertakes to respect and to ensure to all individuals within its territory and subject to its jurisdiction the rights recognized in the present Covenant, without distinction of any kind, such as race, color, sex, language, religion, political or other opinion, national or social origin, property, birth or other status."
- Article 3: "The States Parties to the present Covenant undertake to ensure the equal right of men and women to the enjoyment of all civil and political rights set forth in the present Covenant."
- Article 26: "All persons are equal before the law and are entitled without any discrimination to the equal protection of the law. In this respect, the law shall prohibit any discrimination and guarantee to all persons equal and effective protection against discrimination on any ground such as race, color, sex, language, religion, political or other opinion, national or social origin, property, birth or other status."

These provisions require, in essence, that whatever efforts a state makes to combat private violence, it must proceed in a nondiscriminatory way. Or, in terms more directly applicable to the problem of domestic violence, whatever level of resources a state decides to devote to enforcing criminal laws against private acts of violence, it must ensure that crimes against women receive at least as thorough an investigation and as vigorous a prosecution as crimes against men. Lesser attention constitutes not only a violation of the antidiscrimination provisions of the Covenant but also evidence of the complicity needed to make out a substantive violation.

There is an additional advantage to relying on Covenant Article 26 in particular as an alternative theory of state liability, in that it allows one to sidestep the potentially thorny issue of whether the Covenant applies to domestic violence short of murder. Some of the Covenant's guarantees with potential relevance to domestic violence are contained in provisions that have no other relevance to private conduct. For example, the "security of person" guarantee found in Covenant Article 9 is crafted onto a section that otherwise addresses only arrest and detention.

A discrimination approach avoids potential difficulties in arguing that these provisions also apply to private actors. Even if they do not encompass private assaults, the nondiscriminatory provision of Article 26 (unlike similar provisions in Articles 2(1) and 3) is not tied to particular rights secured by the Covenant, but mandates the "equal protection of the law" in all respects. Thus Article 26 can be used to address not only discriminatory enforcement of other human rights guarantees but also discriminatory enforcement of any criminal law. Discriminatory enforcement of laws applicable to domestic violence thus would constitute a human rights violation—because of the unequal protection of the law—even if domestic violence is deemed not to violate the physical-integrity guarantees of the Covenant.

Documenting Discrimination

Unfortunately, the type of comparative fact-finding needed to make out a case of discrimination can be considerably more complex than the inquiries traditionally undertaken by international human rights organizations (though arguably much less complex than proving empirically that a particular form of violence is responsible for the subordination of a class of people). For most fact-finding conducted by international human rights organizations, the case speaks for itself. As noted, it is enough to document an instance of torture by a state agent to establish that a human rights violation has occurred. In the case of overt complicity in private violence—such as a state's authorization of an honor defense like Brazil's—this remains true. But to make out a case of discriminatory non-enforcement of the criminal laws beyond such overt complicity, it is necessary not only to establish that there has been an unprosecuted crime, but also that the lack of prosecution is due to a prohibited form of discrimination. This comparative element introduces a new dimension requiring a broader analysis of the criminal justice system than is needed for traditional human rights fact-finding.

Nonetheless, many of the tools used in traditional human rights documentation can also be employed to prove discrimination. The most readily available—and the one principally relied on so far by the Human Rights Watch Women's Rights Project—is anecdotal testimony, taken from either victims or their lawyers. We describe particularly compelling cases of domestic violence that the criminal justice system has not adequately addressed. Implicit in this approach is the argument that, if even the egregious cases of domestic violence are not prosecuted, one can hardly expect better results in run-of-the-mill cases. It still is necessary to show that these cases of non-prosecution are not aberrational—that they reflect a pattern that is fairly attributable to the state rather than to the exceptional behavior of isolated functionaries. But by assembling a variety of such cases, the pattern needed to establish state responsibility for the prosecutorial neglect of domestic violence can be demonstrated.

We have also relied on "expert" testimony taken from actors in the criminal justice system to establish a pattern of discrimination. Judges, lawyers, prosecutors, and police officers can describe their experiences across a range of cases to assess how the criminal justice system generally treats domestic violence. Sometimes they can provide compelling anecdotes of their own. By introducing a broader view of the criminal justice system, these accounts can provide an important supplement to the case-oriented testimonies of victims and their advocates to show whether domestic violence is treated with less seriousness.

A particularly useful form of evidence is statistical. If it can be shown through statistics that domestic violence is systematically prosecuted less often (or less rigorously) than comparable acts of violence, a strong case of discrimination can be made. But gathering such statistics has been difficult, since few governments maintain systematic data on their criminal justice system. And even countries that do maintain such statistics may neglect to collect data on the gender of the victim, the relationship to the offender, or the locale of the crime. That such data should be collected and maintained should be a standard recommendation of those who examine the state's response to domestic violence.

The Role of Human Rights and Women's Rights Organizations

In most human rights inquiries, local human rights monitors play a critical role. With their superior knowledge of a country's legal and political system, they can provide invaluable guidance to the research of an outside organization. Judgments made without such consultation are inevitably inferior. Given the complexity of investigations into systematic discrimination, the need for informed local consultation is all the more important. Yet our experience in enlisting local human rights monitors in our inquiries into women's rights issues has been mixed at best.

Aware of the importance of local expertise on the issues under investigation, we have made the existence of a well-developed women's rights movement an important factor in our initial selection of countries for investigation. For example, our decision to examine domestic violence in Brazil[1] and violence against women in custody in Pakistan[2] was deeply influenced by this consideration. In each case, local women's rights advocates played a critical role in initiating the investigation, providing us with an overview and analysis of the problem we were studying and directing us to victims and "experts." Indeed, these advocates themselves were highly valuable "experts" whose experiences and views were repeatedly reflected in our final reports.

Unfortunately, these two experiences appear to be atypical. In most countries that we have examined, we have encountered a gaping lack of reliable, systematically collected evidence about the scope and nature of domestic violence and other women's rights issues. This void is attributable, in different respects, to both the traditional human rights movement and the women's rights movement.

I have already discussed how international human rights organizations have only gradually moved from their narrow focus on the state's treatment of dissidents to a broader sense of state responsibility based on a duty to redress violence by private actors. A similar evolution can be found at the local level. In countries where politically motivated, state-sponsored violations of human rights continue to be the primary human rights issue, these organizations may continue to work within the classic paradigm. In other countries where politically motivated abuses have diminished, many local organizations have begun to expand their mandates to address non-politically motivated abuses or even state-tolerated, as opposed to state-sponsored, abuse. An evolution of this sort is particularly apparent in recent years in certain countries of Latin America. However, even in countries in which local human rights organizations have completed this progression, we have found a marked failure to address domestic violence, as if violence against women is somehow outside the human rights domain.

This neglect is particularly unfortunate because local human rights organizations have developed fact-finding skills that would be extremely useful in demonstrating systematic discrimination against women in the workings of the criminal justice system. The ability to conduct detailed and accurate case studies is hardly innate; it requires experience in locating and interviewing witnesses, and in producing reports that can stand up to public scrutiny. Since such case studies are routinely produced by the traditional human rights movement, local human rights organizations would be well equipped to conduct similar investigations for women's rights issues. Moreover, although neither local nor international human rights organizations have as much experience examining the systematic workings of a criminal justice system as they do in documenting particular cases, these organizations' familiarity with pertinent laws and their contacts with lawyers and judges can be quite useful for such studies.

By contrast, most of the women's rights organizations that we have encountered have not had the opportunity to develop skills in human rights fact-finding. Given the frequent lack of domestic (let alone international) consensus behind norms of nondiscrimination on the basis of gender, it is natural that the women's rights movement in most countries has devoted itself to such tasks as political organizing and public education. But as important as these efforts are, they are quite distinct from the detailed factual documentation that is necessary to establish a human rights violation (case studies also can be used quite profitably for political organizing and public education). As a result, we have found that local women's rights groups generally have not been able to fill the fact-finding void left by the failure of local human rights organizations to address women's rights issues.

This is obviously an undesirable state of affairs. We have attempted to fill this void ourselves by conducting our own fact-finding. But as I noted, this can never be a fully adequate substitute for the active involvement of local monitors. Aware of the importance of local monitoring efforts, we have sought to use our own investigations and reports as a catalyst to the work of others, with the hope that we might stimulate an understanding of the sort of inquiries needed to treat women's rights issues under international human rights law. We encourage others to do the same, since an important goal of both the traditional human rights movement and the women's rights movement must be an introduction of human rights fact-finding to the problem of women's rights.

Ideally this will come from two directions: human rights organizations will begin to see women's rights issues as an integral part of their mandate, while women's rights organizations will begin to supplement their advocacy with attention to fact-finding and the collection of well documented data. At a minimum, one of the two types of organizations must move to fill the void. Until that happens, the problem of domestic violence and other women's rights issues will never move beyond the political domain to the realm of human rights where they also belong.

Notes

1. Human Rights Watch, *Criminal Injustice: Violence Against Women in Brazil* (Washington, DC: Human Rights Watch, 1991).

2. Human Rights Watch, *Double Jeopardy: Police Abuse of Women in Pakistan* (Washington, DC: Human Rights Watch, 1992).

Chapter 14
The Developing Approaches of the International Commission of Jurists to Women's Human Rights

Mona Rishmawi

Introduction

In recent years the international women's rights movement has been successful in addressing universal gender discrimination. It is due to this success that human rights groups have begun to address questions of the human rights of women. For instance, the International Commission of Jurists (ICJ), Amnesty International, Human Rights Watch, and the International Human Rights Law Group have all created programs that specifically deal with gender-specific issues. While it is too early to evaluate the effectiveness of these programs, it is certain that this interest is long overdue.

This chapter attempts to explore:

1. Some conceptual and methodological obstacles inherent in the traditional international human rights movement that may hamper its effectiveness in addressing the human rights of women; and
2. The attempt of the ICJ to deal with those problems in order to enhance its relevance and effectiveness.

In composing this chapter I do not intend to enter into a philosophical debate on what constitutes women's human rights. I am simply adopting as a framework for this discussion the principles codified in the 1967 Declaration on the Elimination of Discrimination Against Women (DEDAW),[1] as well as the 1979 Convention on the Elimination of All Forms of Discrimination Against Women (CEDAW).[2]

Human Rights and Women's Rights: Conceptual and Methodological Concerns

When attempting to work on the human rights of women, traditional human rights groups encounter two conceptual problems. These obstacles have direct implications on their methods of operations. The first relates to the definition of human rights, the second to the nature of state obligations. Each will be further explored below.

The Definition of Human Rights: The Private/Public Distinction

Human rights are traditionally defined as individual claims against the state. Violations of these rights are perpetrated by state officials or in the state's domain. Hence state responsibility is direct and clear. For instance, torture is committed by state agents in prisons that are part of the public domain and censorship of free speech is conducted by a state official. Clear and direct state responsibility is what distinguishes human rights abuses from ordinary crimes, human rights scholars argue.

In contrast, violations of women's rights take place in public as well as in private spheres.[3] Many of these violations are perpetrated by private individuals. Genital mutilation, dowry-killing, and wife beating commonly occur within the family. Since these acts are not committed by the state, human rights advocates argue that they constitute ordinary crimes that fall outside their mandates. State responsibility in such cases is confined to ensuring the proper administration of justice, that is, that domestic law prohibits such acts, and the perpetrator is found and tried according to the provisions of international and domestic laws.

Meanwhile, the human rights of women underline another dimension in the human rights debate. Women's rights go beyond the relationship between the individual and the state. Indeed, the human rights of women often clash with other powers within the society that are no less powerful than state institutions. These powers include culture, tradition, custom, religion, and patriarchy which institutionalize the debasement of the status of women in the society.[4]

This analysis makes it particularly difficult for human rights groups whose mandates are focused around traditional human rights issues to deal adequately with women's human rights matters. As a result, Amnesty International reports on rape only as a method of torture in prisons.[5] Human Rights Watch monitors reports on domestic violence concentrating on police performance.[6] This approach, however, is insufficient to address institutionalized gender discrimination.

The Nature of State Responsibility: Negative or Positive Duties

Another conceptual problem facing the adequate redress of violations of women's human rights is the debate on whether human rights impose negative or positive obligations on states. Some scholars argue that state obligations to respect human rights are negative as they require the state not to interfere with individual rights and freedoms. For example, states are obliged not to interfere in free expression and movement of persons.

Such a restrictive approach to the nature of state obligations excludes from the category of human rights, claims such as shelter, health care, food, and other economic, social and cultural rights that impose positive duties. These rights, however, are essential to the human rights of women.

CEDAW imposes significant positive economic, cultural and social duties on state parties. Article 5 alone requires states

to take all appropriate measures to modify the social and cultural patterns of conduct of men and women, with the view of achieving the elimination of prejudices and other customary practices and all other practices that are based on the idea of the inferiority or the superiority of either of the sexes or on stereotyped roles for men and women.

This positive social and cultural duty imposed on states is essential to eliminate historical discrimination against women. Indeed, institutionalized cultural protection of gender-based discrimination, clearly demonstrated in such matters as genital mutilation[7] and denial of property rights,[8] must be challenged. The state's role is crucial in modifying such cultural practices through promoting concepts favorable to women, and passing adequate laws that prohibit discriminatory practices.

Restricting the human rights discourse to the negative obligations of states, therefore, has significant practical implications. Human rights groups focus their programs on issues arising from these negative duties. Consequently, in designing human rights activities, civil and political rights are given precedence over economic, cultural, and social rights. Thus a significant segment of women's concerns is automatically excluded from the scope of human rights activities.[9]

The Developing Approach of the International Commission of Jurists

The International Commission of Jurists (ICJ) is conscious of the difficulties inherent in the traditional human rights movement when dealing with the totality of the human rights of women. Currently, the

ICJ is developing its approach in order to be more relevant and effective in responding to women's rights concerns.

Organizational Profile

The ICJ was founded in 1952. Its mandate has been broadly defined as promoting the rule of law and the legal protection of human rights. Headquartered in Geneva, the ICJ has 75 sections and affiliated organizations throughout the world.

Since its establishment, the ICJ has been working on the elaboration of legal principles that bring about societal justice. During the 1950s and 1960s it examined principles in criminal, civil, administrative, and international law to achieve the legal protection of human rights. Concepts such as the independence of the judiciary and the legal profession, states of emergency, and the role of lawyers in a changing world have been among its key concerns.

The ICJ operates on three levels: international, regional, and domestic. Among its main achievements are the elaboration of instruments such as the European Torture Convention, the African Charter on Human and Peoples' Rights, the Basic Principles of the Independence of the Judiciary, and the Basic Principles on the Role of Lawyers.

In carrying out its task, the ICJ conducts studies and fact-finding missions on alleged violations of human rights[10] to assess the administration of justice in various parts of the world.[11] It also sends observers to trials, organizes meetings and seminars, and assists as well the establishment of local groups to carry out similar tasks.

Taking Up Third World Concerns

The flexibility of the ICJ mandate has allowed the organization to develop its focus over the years. For more than two decades after its creation, the ICJ, similar to other western-based groups, had focused its activities on the concerns of western legal systems. Only in the late 1970s did it begin to approach the concerns of the countries of the South. A number of jurists from the south joined the ICJ at both the Commission (the highest ICJ policy-making body) and the Secretariat levels.

Struck by problems of extreme poverty, illiteracy, and the existence of dictatorial regimes in these countries, the ICJ explored concepts to respond to the needs of the underprivileged poor. It organized seminars and meetings around the question of the right to development, sharply distinguishing that issue from the economic growth being promoted by the World Bank and other international financial institutions.

One basic idea became obvious from the above-mentioned activities: legal services in rural areas had to be improved to make law accessible to the general public. The ICJ therefore trained paralegals to become a bridge between the people and the lawyers. Programs around this theme were developed in Asia, Africa, and Latin America.

It soon became obvious from these programs that women constitute the most underprivileged sector of societies. Hence the ICJ initiated legal services programs targeting women's groups. The driving force behind these activities was the concern over the right to development rather than women's rights. The ICJ believed that, if women do not enjoy the right to organize themselves and formulate their demands, the right to development would degenerate into a meaningless cliché.

As more of these programs were conducted, the approach of the ICJ developed into a women's rights approach. The organization added to its perspective the conviction that women who are educated about their basic rights are more able to assert themselves and to seek prompt assistance if their rights are violated, as will be further elaborated below.

Developing a Women's Rights Approach

The above activities made the ICJ confront the daily reality of women throughout the world: the universal debasement of women's status, the laws that treat women differently from men, and women's ignorance of their few legally protected rights. To confront the problems it diagnosed, the ICJ has undertaken the following activities:

(a) Women in decision making

The ICJ has realized that, if women's concerns are to be brought to the attention of the mainstream human rights movement, women have to be part of the decision-making process in human rights structures. Starting to reform its own institution, the ICJ recognized that, despite the growing organizational awareness about women's needs and realities, the ICJ itself remains dominated by men. To remedy the situation, a special effort has been made to add women to the ICJ Commission as well as to the professional staff. At present two of the four ICJ vice-presidents and two of the four legal officers are women.

The ICJ believes that such egalitarian rule should be reflected in all regional and international human rights bodies. The ICJ therefore has taken the lead in pressing for the appointment of women to the African Commission on Human and Peoples' Rights. It has also brought the same concern before the UN Human Rights Commission, lobbying not only for the appointment of a special rapporteur on discrimination against women, but also for women as thematic and country rapporteurs.

(b) Promoting the legal rights of women

Building on its experience in promoting economic and social rights, the ICJ adopted the theme of empowerment in addressing women's concerns. The ICJ program in this area is mainly devoted to designing training programs on the legal rights of women. This methodology attempts to demystify law and to empower women to confront violations of their rights.

In various parts of the world, paralegal training seminars for women have been conducted with ICJ support.[12] Those who have been trained are expected, in turn, to train others. The objectives of these seminars have been identified as follows:

1. to explore the legal status of women in various societies and to train persons working in women's organizations on how to address these issues;
2. to create awareness about the various UN bodies dealing with women's issues and to discuss how to make use of these fora;
3. to introduce and/or review the paralegal training methods used by women's organizations.

Further, the ICJ promotes national follow-up to these activities. One national seminar on paralegal training for Indian women's organizations, for instance, discussed the launching of a campaign for India's ratification of CEDAW and the development of a manual on paralegal training for women.[13]

The ICJ also encourages institution-building such as the establishment of legal aid units and paralegal training programs. Several programs have been established in a number of countries. These include organizations such as the Legal Resource and Research Development Centre in Nigeria, which focuses on the training of women paralegals. In Cotonou, Benin, a paralegal organization, Association pour le Développement des Initiatifs Villageoises (ASSODIV), supported by the ICJ, scored a significant point by legally challenging juvenile forced marriages. Additional ICJ activities aimed at enhancing the process of demystifying laws include ICJ assistance in translating to local languages laws that advance the status of women.

Moreover, in conducting all other training seminars irrespective of their subject, the ICJ seeks gender balance among the participants. It also brings up for discussion relevant women's rights issues. This was the case, for instance, in the Third ICJ Workshop on NGO participation in the work of the African Commission on Human and Peoples' Rights, which took place in October 1992 in Banjul, the Gambia. One day of the three-day workshop was devoted to women's rights under the African Charter. The ICJ also makes special effort to include women as resource persons and speakers at these meetings.

Perspectives for the Future

From the above, it is clear that four elements give the ICJ the potential to develop a human rights approach that would respond more adequately to the concerns of women. These are

1. the flexibility of its mandate (the promotion of the rule of law and the legal protection of human rights) as well as its willingness to adapt this mandate to the needs of its constituency;
2. its focus not only on political and civil rights, but also on economic, social, and cultural rights;
3. its method of operation, not confined to research, monitoring, and reporting but including training and institution-building; and
4. the wealth of experience it accumulated over the years in dealing with underprivileged sectors of societies.

Until today, the ICJ has built its approach toward the human rights of women around the theme of empowerment. Some achievements have been scored in this field, mainly in Africa and Asia. Similar efforts ought to be invested in Latin America, Europe, and the Middle East, taking into account the specific needs of women in these societies.

While training should remain a key method to raise awareness about the human rights of women, the ICJ has the capacity to engage in a number of other activities. For instance, the ICJ should be more vigorous in elaborating legal concepts relevant to women's human rights. One suggestion is that it embark on a series of workshops and seminars examining the relationship among human rights, culture, and state responsibility, with special emphasis on women's concerns. Another worthwhile effort is to engage in programs that spell out in practical and specific terms the state's positive duties in relation to women's rights, and to launch campaigns to implement these obligations.

Through its seminars on the independence of the judiciary and the legal profession, the ICJ and its Centre for the Independence of Judges and Lawyers need systematically to include questions related to

gender equality as essential in promoting fairness in the judicial process. The ICJ should also systematically include CEDAW in its training
programs on domestic implementation of human rights norms.

Moreover, similar to other traditional human rights organizations,
the ICJ has yet to integrate women's rights concerns into its fact-
finding and reporting efforts. The ICJ continues to restrict its human
rights monitoring to violations committed by the state. Abuses that are
sanctioned by culture are not examined. The ICJ needs to explore
conceptual and methodological frameworks of monitoring the cultural
abuses of rights. The question of remedies must also be addressed.

In addition, the ICJ must also become vigorous in reviewing local
laws legalizing the status of women and examine them against state
obligations and practice. More effort should be invested in addressing
the legality of the reservations to CEDAW and other relevant human
rights instruments.

Conclusion

In conclusion, I would like to stress that indeed there are conceptual
and methodological questions facing the integration of women's rights
into the human rights discourse. However, organizations with broad
human rights perspectives, like the ICJ, can play an important role in
addressing these questions. Such organizations can serve as a bridge
between the human rights movement and the women's rights movement. This effort is crucial, not only for eliminating the historic injustice perpetrated against women, but also for creating healthy and
fair societies based on the respect and integrity of all human beings,
irrespective of their gender.

Notes

1. Proclaimed by G.A. Res. 2263 (XXII) of 7 November 1967 as cited in
A Compilation of International Instruments (New York: United Nations, 1988),
108.

2. Adopted and opened for signature, ratification and accession by G.A. Res.
34/180 of 18 December 1979. It entered into force on 3 September 1981.
Compilation, note 1 at 112.

3. See Celina Romany, "State Responsibility Goes Private: A Feminist Critique of the Public/Private Distinction in International Human Rights Law,"
Chapter 4 in this book; and Hilary Charlesworth, "What are 'Women's International Human Rights'?" Chapter 3 in this book.

4. See Radhika Coomaraswamy, "To Bellow like a Cow: Women, Ethnicity
and the Discourse of Rights," Chapter 2 in this book; and Abdullahi An-Na'im,
"State Responsibility Under International Human Rights Law to Change Religious and Customary Laws," Chapter 7 in this book.

5. See, e.g., Amnesty International, *Rape and Sexual Abuse: Torture and Ill Treatment in Detention* (London: Amnesty International, 1991).

6. See, e.g., Human Rights Watch, *Criminal Injustice: Violence Against Women in Brazil* (Washington, DC: Human Rights Watch, 1991).

7. See Joan Fitzpatrick, "The Use of International Human Rights Norms to Combat Violence Against Women," Chapter 23 in this book.

8. See Florence Butegwa, "Using the African Charter on Human and Peoples' Rights to Secure Women's Access to Land in Africa," Chapter 21 in this book.

9. See Adetoun O. Ilumoka, "African Women's International Economic, Social, and Cultural Rights—Toward a Relevant Theory and Practice," Chapter 12 in this book; and Akua Kuenyehia, "The Impact of Structural Adjustment Programs on Women's International Human Rights: The Example of Ghana," Chapter 18 in this book.

10. See, e.g., Ustinia Dogopol and Snehal Paranjape, *Comfort Women: The Unfinished Ordeal* (Geneva: International Commission of Jurists, 1993).

11. See, e.g., *Attacks on Justice: The Harassment and Persecution of Judges and Lawyers, 1989, 1990, 1992* (Geneva: International Commission of Jurists).

12. Seminar on Legal Services for Rural and Urban Poor and the Legal Status of Rural Women—Anglophone West Africa, organized by the International Commission of Jurists in collaboration with FIDA and WILDAF (Ghana), 19–23 July 1993, Accra, Ghana; Séminaire sur les Services Juridiques en Milieux Ruraux et Urbains, et le Statut de la Femme dans le Monde Rural—Afrique de l'Ouest Francophone, organized by the ICJ in collaboration with MBDHP and REFAD, 27–31 July 1993, Ouagadougou, Burkina Faso.

13. The seminar was organized by the ICJ and the Shrima Nathibi Damodar Thackersey (S.N/D.I.) Women's University Legal Aid Cell in Bombay, 24–26 September 1991.

Part IV
National Approaches

Chapter 15
General Approaches to the Domestic Application of Women's International Human Rights Law

Anne F. Bayefsky

The Rationale

International standards in the field of human rights are numerous and their quantity continues to grow rapidly. But the eagerness of the international community to set standards masks a deep-seated reluctance to design adequate corresponding implementation schemes.

The consequence of this hypocrisy has been the establishment of international supervisory bodies with different enforcement tools. The Human Rights Committee set up by the International Covenant on Civil and Political Rights, with additional powers granted by an Optional Protocol, considers individual communications concerning violations of the Covenant. The power of individual petition is not available, however, with respect to violations of the Convention on the Elimination of All Forms of Discrimination Against Women (the CEDAW Convention), signed some 15 years later. In general enforcement machinery for the human rights treaties has tended to weaken in the 25 years since the Optional Protocol was signed.

Perhaps nowhere is the gulf between standards and enforcement more evident than in the context of women's rights. There are over 20 treaties devoted specifically to women and issues related to sexual discrimination.[1] All human rights treaties that contain provisions for equality or nondiscrimination and that list prohibited grounds of discrimination include "sex." The general derogation clause of the Covenant on Civil and Political Rights disallows derogations from the requirement of nondiscrimination on the basis of sex.[2] And in particular, women's rights are the subject of a comprehensive treaty, the CEDAW

Convention. Furthermore, states continue to concern themselves with drafting new standards in the context of women's rights, including the recently adopted declaration on violence against women.

On the other hand, even the CEDAW Convention itself reflects the marginalization of women's rights with respect to the implementation of international human rights law. This is evident from a number of factors. First, although over 120 states have ratified the Convention, many have done so conditionally. Approximately 40 states have made a total of roughly 105 reservations and declarations to the Convention. Many of the substantive reservations are wide-ranging and profoundly affect the integrity of the Convention. For example, Article 2 of the Convention contains a general statement of the obligations of states parties, requiring them to pursue without delay a policy of nondiscrimination using all appropriate means, including the amendment of national laws. It also requires the repeal of discriminatory penal provisions. But Bangladesh has made the following reservation: "The Government of . . . Bangladesh does not consider as binding upon itself the provisions of Article 2 [and other articles] as they conflict with Shari'a law based on Holy Qur'an and Sunna."[3] Other states such as Egypt, Iraq, and Libya have also made similar broad reservations.[4] Such general reservations strike at the essence of the Convention. Other more specific reservations are directed, for instance, at the preservation of domestic laws that deny women equal rights with respect to the nationality of their children, equal rights to divorce, to choose a profession or occupation, and to acquire, dispose of, and manage property. Second, the Convention assigns the CEDAW Committee an annual meeting period of two weeks. Every other human rights treaty body meets for a greater length of time than the CEDAW Committee, specifically from three to nine weeks per year. The Torture Committee, for example, meets for four weeks a year, although the Torture Convention has about half the number of ratifications. Obviously this smaller allotment of resources to the supervisory organ of the CEDAW Convention dramatically reduces its ability to monitor implementation. Third, many states fail to adhere to their reporting obligations. As of the end of its 1992 meeting, the Committee had examined 92 reports since its beginning in 1983; 112 reports were overdue. The Committee has taken the view that it can examine no more than 10 reports in its two-week sessions if it is to perform its task effectively. Fourth, the General Assembly has treated the Committee with disrespect. For example, in 1987 the CEDAW Committee requested that the UN system as a whole "promote or undertake studies on the status of women under Islamic laws and customs." This request was met with hostility in ECOSOC and the General Assembly. CEDAW was even asked to review its decision. (Such pressures unfortunately seem to have succeeded in intimidating the Committee. The Committee has, for example, dealt with the subject of "female circumcision" or genital mutilation conservatively, apparently to avoid alienating certain states parties and the General Assembly. The Committee made a general recommendation in 1990 on the subject which addressed the problem merely as a practice harmful to the health of women, rather than torture, cruel, and inhuman treatment.) And last, there is no individual petition mechanism associated with the CEDAW Convention. This is in marked contrast to the Covenant on Civil and Political Rights, the Racial Discrimination Convention, and the Convention Against Torture.

Even where international human rights law has created more adequate enforcement machinery, it is often inaccessible to individual grievors. Correspondence with an international agency is beyond the reach of many potential clients. This can result from a lack of resources, ignorance of local counsel of international remedies, or a failure by national authorities to disseminate information about the international human rights obligations of the state.

For all these reasons, it is imperative to identify other means by which international standards, such as those affecting women, can be enforced. The concern of most states in refusing to participate in the creation of significant international machinery is the preservation of national sovereignty. Recourse to national enforcement agencies would therefore seem to offer a logical alternative.

International agencies readily concede their status as fora of last resort. The European Court of Human Rights, for example, reminds states that international machinery for protecting fundamental rights is subsidiary to national systems of safeguarding rights. The Court has stated that the national authorities are in a better position than the international judge to determine the appropriateness of limitations upon rights.[5] International treaties that do permit a right of individual petition contain a standard clause requiring grievors to first exhaust domestic remedies before coming forward. In other words, there is an initial reliance on national agencies to protect human rights. It would be a natural extension of such reliance to encourage national judicial bodies to enforce international human rights standards.

Domestic courts can serve as a missing link between promulgation and realization of international human rights norms to the benefit of both international and domestic law. International bodies, whose work tends to be far more interstitial than that of national judicial organs, can benefit from more frequent interpretations of international standards by a variety of national courts. More enlightened interpretations of domestic human rights laws may also be fostered through reference to international law.

Standards of Judicial Review

The use of domestic courts to realize international human rights standards raises the important issue of the scope of judicial review, both from the perspective of international enforcement bodies and from the perspective of domestic judicial agencies.

From an international perspective, a balance must be struck between the protection of rights by national agencies on the one hand and international agencies on the other. In the first instance, recourse to the international body requires the exhaustion of domestic remedies. In the words of one member of the Human Rights Committee, this requirement gives the state "an opportunity to redress, by its own means within the framework of its domestic legal system, the wrongs alleged to have been suffered by the individual."[6] The international machinery is clearly intended to be subsidiary; the initial onus for protecting human rights and defining the methods or means of protecting rights rests on local authorities. The local authorities are in a better position than the international judge to assess indigenous conditions and needs. Second, the exhaustion of domestic remedies brings the international remedy into play. The treaty requires the international body to supervise the legislative, administrative, and judicial acts of national authorities.

The international agency is confronted with balancing those factors in particular situations, a task that cumulatively will set an international standard of review. More specifically, the issue will take the form of the following quandary. What account should be taken of local definitions of rights and their limitations in determining the content of international standards? How much scope should be given to national authorities to set limits on rights? How much deference should be paid to national decision makers? How much allowance should be made for national variations in the definition of rights? Where should uniformity among contracting state parties be encouraged and regional diversity be tolerated?

Two international human rights monitoring bodies that face these issues are the European Court of Human Rights and the Human Rights Committee. Since the *Belgian Linguistics* case of 1968, the European Court of Human Rights has struggled to define the scope of international judicial review, or, in its terms, set the parameters of a margin of appreciation allocated to national authorities. The phrase is unfortunate, since it suggests a margin of error within which there is no international review at all for satisfaction of Convention standards. And there are indeed cases where a wide margin of appreciation has been synonymous with a failure by the Court to apply Convention obligations. But, in general, the width of the margin of appreciation connotes a conclusion about the appropriate attitude of the international court toward the national authorities in a particular case.

According to European case law, the margin is given to the domestic legislator and to the bodies, including the judiciary, that interpret and apply the laws. The margin applies to the identification of a legislative aim—a local problem or the necessity for restricting rights—and to the selection of the means for achieving that aim or implementing measures of control. There are very few cases in which the European Court actually speaks of limiting review, and only one dissenting opinion in which a member of the Court explicitly identifies the invocation of the margin of appreciation as a form of judicial restraint. But in effect when the European Court determines there is a wide margin of appreciation, it adopts a limited scope of judicial review or an attitude of judicial restraint. However, identification of the relevant factors in determining the standard of international judicial review by the European Court of Human Rights is at a rudimentary stage. Overall, there is an insufficient attempt to rationalize the circumstances that justify different levels of review.

The Human Rights Committee has also been operating under some general convictions about the appropriate scope of international review. But the constituent elements of those assumptions have barely been defined. In characterizing its relationship with national authorities, the Committee in one case spoke of a "margin of discretion." It has also stated that it is not a court of fourth instance and is not empowered to consider whether domestic law has been properly applied. Overall, the Human Rights Committee has given little consideration to the problem of articulating the scope of international review. Many of the cases that come before the Committee are obvious, egregious violations of the Covenant, calling for only minimal reasoning in the course of applying the law. Where, on the other hand, cases have involved more subtle human rights issues, the Committee has tended to reach conclusions in a perfunctory fashion and has not identified the considerations that lead it to exercise restraint or otherwise.[7]

From a national perspective, the effort to strike a balance between international supervision and national responsibility requires definition of the scope of domestic judicial review. To varying degrees, national courts may be permitted to measure governmental activities against international human rights principles. Where domestic agencies perceive themselves to be in such a symbiotic relationship with international law, international supervisory organs may adjust their approach accordingly. At the very least, such national judicial use of international law will provide an opportunity to apply international standards with greater sensitivity to local circumstances and needs.

The national standard of review involves balancing two elements. On the one hand, the judiciary will be concerned not to bring the state into violation of its international obligations. On the other hand, they will also seek to protect domestic sovereignty and employ local attitudes and insights. In some states, international law may not be introduced directly into national litigation. The major human rights treaties do not require that grievors be able to invoke treaty provisions directly before national courts, or that domestic law be subject to challenge in domestic courts as contrary to the treaty.[8] But even where treaties have not been incorporated into domestic law, in many states the balance is struck by compelling the judiciary, where possible, to construe domestic law in conformity with international obligations, customary or conventional.[9]

Where national courts apply a presumption in favor of conformity with international law, direct conflicts between national judicial bodies and international organs may be avoided. For example, in *Norris v. Ireland*[10] the European Court of Human Rights was forced to find Ireland in violation of a Convention immediately after the Irish Supreme Court refused to be guided by a previous decision of the European Court having essentially the same facts. Furthermore, application of this presumption can improve human rights protection by domestic courts.

The successful implementation of international human rights law requires a greater understanding of the interrelationships between international and national agencies. International supervisory bodies need to articulate the rationale for different levels of review, or for tolerating national variations in the nature of human rights protection. National judicial bodies need to appreciate and explore the contexts in which international law can serve the human rights needs of their communities. A mutually reinforcing association is both possible and desirable.

One important example of the potential usefulness of international law in addressing a recurrent problem of national law in the realm of gender equality is the definition of discrimination itself. Finding discrimination requires a court to draw lines between justified and unjustified distinctions. The outcome of the line-drawing exercise will depend on the degree of deference to legislative authority that the adjudicator, national or international, adopts. Both national and international adjudicatory bodies have held that the deference paid, or the stringency with which legislative distinctions are examined, will vary with the ground of distinction at issue. International bodies have found that in the context of sex discrimination deference to the legislative body should be minimized. In other words, the requirements necessary to justify distinctions based on sex ought to be very stringent; international law indicates that distinctions based on sex are deserving of the highest degree of judicial scrutiny.[11] This is an approach to the identical problem of defining and applying norms of discrimination in domestic law which could be adopted by national courts. International law can therefore be used here, not directly to determine the outcome of a particular case, but to set the standard for the national courts' evaluation of whether a given law is discriminatory on the basis of sex.

The Anti-Democratic Objection[12]

Embedded in the query over the scope of domestic judicial review, and whether and how domestic courts should refer to international law, is the more general concern over the legitimacy of judicial "activism." The judiciary is frequently depicted as a counter-majoritarian body with suspect legitimacy.[13] When the claimed fundamental rights have their source in international law, the impulse to defer to law-making authorities and withhold a judicial remedy is likely to be even greater. Many American judges, for example, tend to place a strong emphasis on the imponderables of foreign affairs and the need for a single voice by the American government.[14]

It is therefore important to counter the concern that the reference to international human rights law by domestic courts raises the identical problem of judicial "activism" in all cases.

With respect to the direct enforcement of uncodified customary international law, the counter-majoritarian objection might seem to counsel against enforceability. This would be inconsistent, however, with the common law presumption that imputes an intention to the law-making authorities of acting in conformity with binding international law.

Constitutional norms concerning most significant issues of individual rights are inevitably indeterminate. Theorists of constitutional interpretation seek to prove that their interpretive framework for judicial review is bounded and determinate enough not to leave judges free to impose their personal values. As a source of meaning for unclear domestic texts, the norms of customary human rights law have several attractive characteristics. Customary international law is made by an extremely decentralized and "democratic" process. All states may participate. Furthermore, though the relevant practice is that of states and the predominant players therefore governments, this is not exclusively true. In the human rights field, non-governmental organizations have been influential in exposing abuses and articulating norms.[15] Compared to reliance on abstract political or moral philosophy, reference to customary human rights law has the advantage of being grounded in the articulated values of a real historical community.

In the case of ratified treaties, the existence of implementing legislation adopted within the constitutional framework refutes any objection to the treaty's non-democratic origin. But at the same time it is the implementing legislation, rather than the treaty, that supplies the rule of decision.

Interpretive use of ratified treaties rests on the common law presumption where it is available. Where the presumption is false, the law-making authority need only correct the court's error by a clear statement of repudiation of the treaty's obligations. Thus there is no real counter-majoritarian problem, only an issue as to where the risks of inertia should be placed.

With respect to interpretive uses of international human rights norms that are not legally binding, one can argue that international standards have legitimacy within the republican tradition as expressive of community values, broadly conceived. Reference to certain international documents that are the careful product of serious and open discussion among informed experts from diverse cultures appears preferable to the ad hoc articulation of values by an individual judge. Denial of all relief to human rights victims until the preoccupied legislature lays down a specific rule likewise lacks appeal.

There are those who reject the majoritarian criticism of judicial review for the protection of individual rights on the basis that judicial review does and ought to provide moral guidance, which legislators sometimes cannot give. The issue from this perspective for the legitimation of reference to customary international human rights norms will not be one of majoritarianism, but of justice. Is the international community, which evolves these norms through practice and opinion, and in which the government in question is simply one of many participants, a community with shared and just values?

While the justness of customary human rights law cannot be guaranteed, the likelihood of its embodying right answers, or at the very least, its harmlessness, can more readily be assured. First, customary international human rights law is very restricted in scope. It requires a significant degree of generality among nations to generate such a norm, and it is extremely improbable that such a norm will be created where there is dissent by any of the world's major legal systems. Second, in any case, there may be additional domestic rules concerning the relationship between international and municipal law which protect municipal law from too much encroachment. For example, customary international human rights law may not bind a domestic court in the face of inconsistent constitutional or subsequent statutory law. Within these limits, a particular society is a potential beneficiary, in the context of constitutional or statutory indeterminacy, of a general collective wisdom.

Domestic Rules of the Relationship Between Municipal Law and International Law

Utilizing domestic courts to enforce women's international human rights law or enhancing domestic law by way of international human rights standards will be a function of domestic legal rules. The relevant domestic rules concern:

1. the relationship between customary international law and domestic law; in a federal state there will be the further issue of the relationship between customary international law and each of state/provincial law and federal/national law; and
2. the relationship between conventional international law and domestic law; in a federal state there will be the further issue of the relationship between conventional international law and each of state/provincial law and federal/national law.

These rules must be stated on a country-by-country basis. They do not differ, however, on the basis of the substance of international law. In other words, the domestic legal rules governing the relationship between international and municipal law will not be unique to international human rights law concerning women.

The relative importance of customary versus conventional international law for a particular state will depend on the extent to which the state has ratified human rights treaties. In those states that have ratified such treaties, greater emphasis will likely be placed on these international rules. It will be easier for a domestic court to take account of a rule that the state has clearly adopted as constituting a binding obligation. In those states that have not ratified treaties, individuals will be forced to place greater reliance on customary international law.

The rules governing the relationship of international law to municipal law are attempts to reconcile a variety of policies: protection of national sovereignty, protection of the supremacy of domestic law-making institutions from the powers of the executive, satisfaction of the state's international obligations, and realization by individuals of the benefits of international norms. Different considerations for harmonizing these policies arise for conventional and customary international law. The result is that in some states the relationship between international law and municipal law is different in respect of customary international law as compared with conventional international law.

The different ways of reconciling these policies are formulated in two general theories about the relationship between municipal law and international law: the adoption[16] and the transformation theory. The adoption theory states that international law is part of domestic law automatically, that is, without an act of incorporation, except where it conflicts with statutory law or well-established rules of the common law. Transformation theory states that international law is only part of domestic law when it has been incorporated into domestic law.

Again, whether a particular state and its legal system embraces the adoption theory or transformation theory must be stated on a country-by-country basis. A corollary of an adoption theory would be acknowledgment by domestic courts of the capacity for municipal law to change as international law changes.

Customary International Law and Municipal Law

(a) Proving customary international law

The most difficult problem with introducing customary international human rights law into domestic courts is proving that it exists. International jurisprudence sets two conditions for the existence of a customary rule of international law: (a) evidence of a sufficient degree of state practice and (b) a determination that states conceive themselves as acting under a legal obligation.[17] This obligation has been stated as the requirement for a "constant and uniform usage, accepted as law."[18] Usage (meaning the usage found in the practice of states) must involve[19] substantial uniformity or consistency and substantial generality.[20] Second, the requirement that states "feel that they are conforming to what amounts to a legal obligation,"[21] that is, exhibit *opinio juris*, is to be contrasted with motives of courtesy, fairness, and morality. In this regard, there is some suggestion that establishment of a general practice will give rise to a presumption of the existence of *opinio juris*.[22]

The International Court of Justice has commented upon the difficulty of defining precise rules of customary international law. Albeit not in a human rights context, but rather in a case involving the delineation of a maritime boundary between Canada and the United States in the Gulf of Maine, the Court stated that a body of detailed rules is not to be looked for in customary international law which in fact comprises a limited set of norms for ensuring the co-existence and vital co-operation of the members of the international community, together with a set of customary rules whose presence in the opinio juris of States can be tested by induction based on the analysis of a sufficiently extensive and convincing practice, and not by deduction from preconceived ideas.[23]

A degree of judicial crystallization of a rule embodied in state practice and intentions will often be necessary. But the project is clearly analogous to the task of the domestic judge in defining common law.

Proving that norms particularly affecting women constitute customary international law would require consideration of at least the following elements: the numerous international conventions dealing with women's rights,[24] the large number of ratifications of such treaties by a variety of states representing the world's major legal systems and cultural contexts, the recurrent United Nations General Assembly resolutions concerning women's rights, and statements by government officials of the country concerned recognizing women's rights as rights.[25]

(b) Identifying customary international human rights norms

A limited list of customary international human rights has so far been identified by national and international bodies, such as the American Law Institute and U.S. courts. Considering case law primarily from the United States, the list includes:

(a) the right not to be murdered;[26]
(b) freedom from torture;[27]
(c) standards for the treatment of prisoners embodied in the United Nations Standard Minimum Rules for the Treatment of Prisoners;[28]
(d) freedom from arbitrary detention;[29]
(e) the right not to be subjected to cruel, inhuman, or degrading treatment or punishment;[30]
(f) the right not to be a slave;[31]
(g) freedom from disappearance, defined as (1) abduction by state officials or their agents, followed by (2) official refusals to acknowledge the abduction or to disclose the detainee's fate;[32]
(h) freedom from loss of consortium;[33]
(i) freedom from racial discrimination;[34]
(j) freedom from genocide; and
(k) freedom from a consistent pattern of gross violations of internationally recognized human rights.[35]

On the subject of gender discrimination and customary international law, the Restatement of the Foreign Relations Law of the United States has the following comment: freedom from "gender discrimination as state policy . . . may already be a principle of customary international law."[36] The Restatement is careful to note that customary international human rights law continues to develop and the list of customary human rights laws "is not closed."[37]

There are also suggestions, albeit not generally supported, that the entire Universal Declaration of Human Rights has entered the status of customary international law.[38] Although General Assembly resolutions do not, alone, constitute international legal obligations, they are evidence of *opinio juris* and state practice. The determination of whether such resolutions express customary international law will depend on additional factors, such as the degree of unanimity with which they were adopted, whether they were intended by supporting governments to state legal principles, and the existence of contrary state practice.[39] It is more probable that the usefulness of the Universal Declaration as identifying binding human rights standards comes indirectly by way of Articles 55 and 56 of the UN Charter, a treaty whose general obligations to protect human rights are specified by at least some of the rights in the Declaration. The 1986 Restatement of the Foreign Relations Law of the United States concludes:

The language [of the Charter] imports legal obligation, but there has been no agreement or authoritative determination as to the character and extent of the obligation. . . . Few states would agree that any action by a state contrary to any provision of the [Universal] Declaration is, for that reason alone, a violation of the Charter or of customary international law. On the other hand, almost all states would agree that some infringements of human rights enumerated in the Declaration are violations of the Charter or of customary international law.[40]

(c) Using customary international human rights law to found a right of action

In the context of an adoption theory relationship between customary international law and domestic law, customary international human rights law will be part of the law of the land—at least in the absence of conflicting statutes, well-established rules of the common law, or provisions of a Constitution. In theory, as part of the law of the land, customary international human rights law could be directly invoked to itself provide the basis for a remedy. However, in the domestic law of Canada, the United States, and the United Kingdom, for example, there are very few instances of this actually occurring.[41]

(d) Using customary international human rights law to assist in the interpretation of domestic law

A second distinct use that can be made of customary law in domestic courts is as assistance in interpreting and applying domestic law. In this context, customary law can influence the interpretation of a state's common law, statutory law, or constitutional rights.

In common law countries there is a presumption that the law-making authority(ies) do not intend to act in breach of international law, both customary and conventional, which is binding upon the state.[42] Concomitantly, there is a principle of construction that the domestic law should be interpreted as far as possible consistently with binding international law. This would include any domestic law (including a constitution) that articulated human rights norms.[43]

Conventional International Law and Municipal Law

(a) General

In contrast to the limited scope of customary international human rights law, there are an abundance of international treaties devoted to women and issues related to sexual discrimination.[44] In states where such treaties have been ratified, they may serve as a useful tool in domestic litigation.

In states where treaty-making is an executive act, and the consent of domestic law-making institutions is not required, domestic courts will try to protect the authority of the law-making bodies from any attempt by the executive to change the law merely by way of ratification. (This is less a concern with respect to customary international law, where obligations arise over time from the consent and practice of nations, not merely from acts of executive authority.) That protection is achieved by way of the transformation theory for the relationship between conventional international law and municipal law. In these states an important initial question for domestic courts will be whether the relevant treaty has been incorporated. This will likely require evidence that the law-making body intended to make the treaty part of the law of the land, either by passing a law that states simply that the treaty has the authority of domestic law, or by passing law(s) drawn from the treaty.

In common law countries the presumption that the law-making body(ies) do not intend to act in breach of the state's international obligations also applies to conventional international law. In the context of implementing legislation, this means that domestic courts should interpret domestic implementing legislation in conformity with a convention insofar as the domestic legislation permits. In other words, they should do so where there is no obvious inconsistency between the domestic law and the international law.[45]

At the same time, if the domestic legislation cannot be given a possible meaning in conformity with the treaty, or if there is a conflict between the domestic legislation and international law, it is the domestic legislation which will prevail.

Even in the absence of implementing legislation, the presumption that the law-making institutions do not intend to legislate in violation of the state's treaty obligations still operates; wherever possible, statutes ought not to be interpreted as violating international conventional law.[46] In this context, however, the transformation theory's rule that without implementing legislation the treaty is not part of domestic law suggests that a strong need for having recourse to international conventional law should first be established. This need could, for example, take the form of a requirement that an ambiguity in the domestic law must be established by considering the domestic law on its own, before recourse to the treaty as an interpretive aid becomes acceptable.

(b) A Canadian example

Many of these general rules are illustrated in the few Canadian court cases that mention the CEDAW Convention, which Canada has ratified. Canadian law takes a transformation theory approach to the relationship between domestic law and treaties.[47]

Of the approximately 225 cases that both interpret Canadian human rights legislation and mention international human rights law, seven refer specifically to the CEDAW Convention. Of these, one stated that the Convention could not be used to interpret Canadian law where there had been a definitive interpretation by the Supreme Court of Canada that was inconsistent with the Convention.[48] Two mentioned the Convention only in passing or in a manner irrelevant to the outcome of the case.[49] One mentioned the Convention in the context of a very confused statement of the relevance of international law in Canadian courts; the court refused to use the CEDAW Convention as an aid to interpretation in the absence of a thorough examination of international human rights instruments having a "broader perspective"—and then failed to undertake such an examination.[50] In two cases the reference to the CEDAW Convention, although not directly determinative, supported the outcome of the case. In the first instance, the Convention supported the court's finding that "marital status" was a ground of discrimination under the constitutional Charter of Rights equality provision.[51] In the second instance, the Convention was used to "reinforce the view that Canadian society is committed to equalizing the role of parents in the care of children as much as possible, . . . in particular for the achievement of greater equality in the work place for women."[52] There is a third case in which a lower court used the Women's Convention, as well as the Racial Discrimination Convention and I.L.O. Convention No. 111 on Discrimination in Education, to support its definition of the equality rights provision of the constitutional Charter of Rights.[53] However, when the issue came before the Supreme Court of Canada it arrived at a different definition of discrimination in the context of interpreting the same provision without considering international law.[54]

Overall, the Canadian experience with the use of the CEDAW Convention (and other international human rights instruments) to construe domestic law indicates that courts tend to be result-oriented. Where courts are inclined to come to a conclusion consistent with the CEDAW Convention, but on the basis of quite independent reasons, they may point to the Convention for support. Where courts are inclined to come to conclusions incompatible with the Convention, they will simply ignore it. Legal commentators are left to object that this result-oriented approach is inconsistent with the common law presumption that domestic law ought to be construed in conformity with Canadian international obligations in the absence of clearly inconsistent domestic provisions.

(c) Use of international material collateral to treaties

Encouraging domestic courts to use treaty obligations in interpreting and applying domestic law should go beyond consideration of the language of the treaty. In a number of contexts, international human rights law affecting women has been interpreted by international bodies. As the extent of this collateral material grows, it will be increasingly important to examine it along with the treaties themselves.

For example, domestic courts have difficulty distinguishing between positive laws designed to provide women with assistance that is not available to men, and discrimination. International human rights law is not so confused. The CEDAW Convention explicitly deems certain special measures not to be discrimination. The Convention makes obvious the link that is understood between providing special measures and preventing discrimination or implementing equality. Article 4(1) states:

Adoption by States Parties of temporary special measures *aimed at accelerating de facto equality* between men and women shall not be considered discrimination as defined in the present Convention, but shall in no way entail as a consequence the maintenance of unequal or separate standards; these measures shall be discontinued when the objectives of equality of opportunity and treatment have been achieved.[55]

Special measures can thus be aimed at achieving equality, and while that objective remains unfulfilled, they are not discrimination.[56]

The Human Rights Committee under the Civil and Political Covenant has made a General Comment on nondiscrimination which helps to expand the point; it states that, "as long as such action is needed to correct discrimination in fact, it is a case of legitimate differentiation under the Covenant."[57] CEDAW has affirmed the importance of this obligation in its General Recommendations contained in its annual report. General Recommendation No. 5[58] states:

Taking note that . . . there is still a need for action to be taken to implement fully the Convention by introducing measures to promote de facto equality between men and women, . . . Recommends that States parties make more use of temporary special measures such as positive action, preferential treatment or quota systems to advance women's integration into education, the economy, politics and employment.

The Human Rights Committee has similarly interpreted the Civil and Political Covenant to require affirmative action programs in certain circumstances. In its General Comment on nondiscrimination the Committee states that

the principle of equality sometimes requires States parties to take affirmative action in order to diminish or eliminate conditions which cause or help to perpetuate discrimination prohibited by the Covenant. For example, in a State where the general conditions of a certain part of the population prevent or impair their enjoyment of human rights, the State should take specific action to correct those conditions. Such action may involve granting for a time to the part of the population concerned certain preferential treatment in specific matters as compared with the rest of the population.[59]

Thus discussion before domestic courts of the nature of certain treaty obligations concerning equality is usefully elaborated through the comments of the relevant treaty bodies.

Another example, is the closely related issue of remedies. A domestic court concerned with the question of fashioning an appropriate remedy for a discriminatory law or practice may usefully consider CEDAW's comments on the nature of the CEDAW Convention's duties. CEDAW's comments make it clear that adequate implementation of the equality rights in the Convention requires positive state action or imposes positive duties for achieving equality. In 1988 CEDAW remarked in General Recommendation No. 8:[60]

The Committee . . . Recommends that States parties take further direct measures in accordance with Article 4 of the Convention to ensure the full implementation of Article 8 of the Convention and to ensure to women on equal terms with men and without any discrimination the opportunities to represent their Government at the international level and to participate in the work of international organizations.[61]

Thus the recommendations of CEDAW give detailed guidance as to the content of particular articles and the types of steps that should be taken to give effect to those obligations. As the considered collective pronouncements of the body entrusted with monitoring the implementation of the Convention, general recommendations should have considerable authority, even if formally they do not constitute a binding interpretation of the Convention. They should therefore be an integral part of the domestic application of international law.

International Law That Does Not Bind the State

In some instances, domestic courts may still make use of international law as an aid to interpreting domestic law even where such international law does not bind the state concerned.[62] In this context, regardless whether the domestic rules embrace the adoption or transformation theory, the international law in question is not part of the law of the land. Its relevance may result from other considerations. For instance,

(a) Courts often make some reference to non-binding sources of law from other jurisdictions, for the purpose of formulating informed responses to domestic legal questions.

(b) Sometimes domestic law suggests that the courts consider the requirements of a free and democratic society. In so doing, it invites comparison with the legal responses of other free and democratic societies.

(c) The drafting history and actual provisions of an international law that is not binding on the state may be closely related to an international law that is binding on the state (for example, the European Convention is closely related to the Covenant on Civil and Political Rights).

(d) Non-binding international conventional law may be associated with a sophisticated quasi-judicial and judicial system—like the European Convention on Human Rights—which makes its jurisprudence useful.

There is a danger, however, that the reasons domestic courts make use of such international law will not be articulated. And in the absence of explicit justification, reference to such sources will often be haphazard. In other words, such international law may simply be invoked where it supports a conclusion already determined. If it suggests any contrary result, it will often be ignored.

Expressions by Government Officials of the Relevance of International Human Rights Law in Applying Domestic Law

General

Government officials will be asked by members of international bodies about the relevance of international law in domestic courts. Those questions may be put in the context of consideration of government reports to the various human rights treaty bodies. The responses of government officials will be found in the summary records of those committees and (more briefly) in their annual reports.

These comments could be valuable in the context of domestic litigation—particularly in opposition to government counsel. An individual within a state wishing to convince a domestic court to use international law to interpret domestic law could usefully refer to an affirmation by government officials of the relevance of international law for this purpose. Furthermore, remarks by government officials—often heard in international fora—that domestic law provides rights protection at least as great as that provided by international law can also be helpful in encouraging domestic courts to take account of international law.

A Canadian Example

Canada's First Report to CEDAW on the Convention, of May 1983, stated:

The provincial and federal human rights acts/codes are important statutes implementing the Convention.[63]

In 1988, the Second Report of Canada on the CEDAW Convention gave a detailed account of

measures adopted by each government to implement the provisions of the Convention in areas within its jurisdiction.[64]

Among other things, the Report stated:

Another primary means of implementing the Convention in Canada is through human rights legislation which prohibits discrimination on various grounds, including sex and marital status.[65]

The Report went on to refer specifically to

measures adopted by each government to implement the provisions of the Convention in areas within its jurisdiction. . . . Article 2: . . . In July 1983, the Act [Canadian Human Rights Act] was amended to specifically prohibit discrimination on the ground of pregnancy or childbirth.[66] . . . Changes were made to the Unemployment Insurance Act conditions for maternity benefits described under Article 2(f). . . . Article 4.1: . . . An Act Respecting Employment Equity, adopted by Parliament in June 1986.[67]

During the consideration of Canada's Second Report to CEDAW in February 1990, the Committee was told by the Canadian delegation that "the Charter [the constitutional Charter of Rights] was an important means of implementing the Convention in Canada."[68]

Thus, in different international contexts, Canadian government officials have represented Canadian law as implementing international human rights obligations of Canada. Domestic courts could be encouraged to take such representations into account when interpreting domestic law.

This is at least one important reason why the comments of state officials before human rights treaty bodies should be closely monitored.

Mistakes

Judicial comprehension of public international law is frequently minimal. The rules of the relationship between international law and municipal law, which must be identified on a state-by-state basis, are often poorly understood. References to international law include many examples of errors concerning basic principles governing the relationship between domestic and international law, as well as the substance of international law.

Improvement of the familiarity of both bench and bar with international human rights law will require at least the following changes in domestic legal systems: increased judicial education, expansion of the number of law students reached by related law school courses, and significantly enriched library collections. Ultimately, these items turn on improving access to information and securing adequate financial resources, developments that in most states depend on a political will to recognize and enforce international human rights standards.

Notes

1. International Convention Respecting the Prohibition of Night Work for Women in Industrial Employment, (1906), 2 Martens *Nouveau Recueil* (ser.

3) 861, 4 *Am. J. Int'l L. Supp.* 328; Convention Concerning Employment of Women During the Night (ILO 4) (1919), 38 U.N.T.S. 67; Maternity Protection Convention (ILO 3) (1919), 38 U.N.T.S. 53; International Convention for the Suppression of Traffic in Women and Children (1921) and Protocol (1947), 9 L.N.T.S. 416, 18 *Am. J. Int'l L. Supp.* 130; International Convention for the Suppression of the Traffic in Women of Full Age (1933), 150 L.N.T.S. 431, and Protocol (1947), 52 U.N.T.S. 49; Inter-American Convention on the Nationality of Women (1933), P.A.U.T.S. 37, 28 *Am. J. Int'l L. Supp.* 61; Convention Concerning Employment of Women during the Night (ILO 41) (Rev. 1934), 40 U.N.T.S. 33; Convention Concerning the Employment of Women in Mines of All Kinds (ILO 45) (1935), 40 U.N.T.S. 63; Inter-American Convention on the Granting of Political Rights to Women (1948), P.A.U.T.S. 3; Inter-American Convention on the Granting of Civil Rights to Women (1948), P.A.U.T.S. 23; Convention (No. 89) Concerning Night Work for Women Employed in Industry (Rev. 1948) (ILO 89) (Revised 1948), 81 U.N.T.S. 147; Convention for the Suppression of the Traffic in Persons and of the Exploitation of the Prostitution of Others (1950), 96 U.N.T.S. 271, and Final Protocol (1950), 96 U.N.T.S. 316; Convention Concerning Equal Remuneration for Men and Women Workers for Work of Equal Value (ILO 100) (1951), 165 U.N.T.S. 303; Maternity Protection Convention (Revised) (ILO 103) (1952), 214 U.N.T.S. 321; Convention on the Political Rights of Women (1953), 193 U.N.T.S. 135; Convention on the Nationality of Married Women (1957), 309 U.N.T.S. 65; Convention on Consent to Marriage, Minimum Age for Marriage, and Registration of Marriages (1962), 521 U.N.T.S. 231; Convention on the Elimination of All Forms of Discrimination Against Women, G.A. Res. 34/180, U.N. GAOR 34th Sess. Supp. 46, at 193, 19 I.L.M. 33; Workers with Family Responsibilities Convention (ILO 156) (1981), Cmnd. 8773.

2. This is in addition to a few other grounds.

3. U.N. Doc. CEDAW/SP/1992/2, 1 Nov. 1991 at 9.

4. U.N. Doc., note 3 at 11, 15 and 16.

5. *Handyside v. United Kingdom,* 24 Eur. Ct. H.R. (ser. A) (1976) at para. 48.

6. *Ominayak v. Canada,* Communication No. 167/1984, 28 March 1990, CCPR/C/38/D/167/1984, Appendix II, Individual opinion of Mr. B. Wennergren.

7. For a more detailed discussion of this subject see Anne Bayefsky, "The Scope of Judicial Review in the International Human Rights Context," *Proceedings of the 85th Annual Meeting of the American Society of International Law,* Washington, DC, April 17–20, 1991 (Washington, DC: American Society of International Law, 1991), 337–41.

8. See, for example, *Leander v. Sweden,* 116 Eur. Ct. H.R. (ser. A) (1987) at para. 77.

9. The Canadian Supreme Court has said, for example, that the constitutional Charter of Rights and Freedoms "should generally be presumed to provide protection at least as great as that afforded by similar provisions in international human rights documents which Canada has ratified." *Davidson v. Slaight Communications,* 59 D.L.R. (4th) 416 (1989) at 427–28; [1989] 1 S.C.R. 1038 at 1056–57.

10. 142 Eur. Ct. H.R. (ser. A) (1988).

11. See list of treaties devoted to women and issues related to sexual discrimination in note 1; *Abdulaziz, Cabales, and Balkandali v. U.K.,* Eur. Comm'n H.R. Dec. 8 Rep. 12 (1983) (art. 31 Report) at 102–3; 94 Eur. Ct. H.R. (ser. A),

(1985), at para. 91, 8. See also the non-derogation clause of the Civil and Political Covenant, art. 4(1) and gender discrimination provision of the American Law Institute, Restatement of the Law: *The Foreign Relations Law of the United States,* §702 Comment (1986). For a greater discussion of these issues, see Anne Bayefsky, "The Principle of Equality or Non-Discrimination in International Law," *Hum. Rts. L.J.* 11(1–2) (1990): 1–34.

12. Anne Bayefsky and Joan Fitzpatrick, "International Human Rights Law in United States Courts: A Comparative Perspective," *Mich. J. Int'l L.* 14 (1992): 1.

13. See, for example, Robert Bork, "Neutral Principles and Some First Amendment Problems," *Ind. L.J.* 47 (1971): 1.

14. This is especially true of cases raising the act of state or political questions doctrines. For an analysis of this "one-voice" concern, see Steinhardt, "Human Rights Litigation and the 'One-Voice' Orthodoxy in Foreign Affairs," in *World Justice: U.S. Courts and International Human Rights,* ed. Mark Gibney (Boulder, CO: Westview Press, 1991).

15. See customary international law prohibition on torture.

16. This is sometimes also confusingly called incorporation theory, although it refers to automatic "incorporation."

17. Statute of the International Court of Justice, art. 38(1)(b).

18. *Asylum Case (Colombia v. Perú),* 1950 I.C.J. 266.

19. These are characteristics for establishing a general, rather than a local, custom.

20. Generality refers to widespread and representative practice of at least those states whose interests are specially affected. *North Sea Continental Shelf Cases (Federal Republic of Germany v. Denmark; Federal Republic of Germany v. The Netherlands),* 1969 I.C.J. 3. Substantial uniformity and generality is to be contrasted with absolute or universal conformity. In the words of the International Court of Justice in the case of *Nicaragua v. United States,* 1986 I.C.J. 14 at 98: "The Court does not consider that, for a rule to be established as customary, the corresponding practice must be in absolutely rigorous conformity with the rule. In order to deduce the existence of customary rules, the Court deems it sufficient that the conduct of States should, in general, be consistent with such rules, and that instances of State conduct inconsistent with a given rule, should generally have been treated as breaches of that rule, not as indications of the recognition of a new rule."

21. *North Sea Continental Shelf Cases (Federal Republic of Germany v. Denmark; Federal Republic of Germany v. The Netherlands),* I.C.J. Rep., note 20 at 3.

22. Judge Sorensen, dissenting in *North Sea Continental Shelf Cases,* note 20 at 246–47; Hersch Lauterpacht, "Sovereignty over Submarine Areas," *Br. Y.B. Int'l L.* 27 (1950): 376 at p. 395.

23. *Gulf of Maine* case, 1984 I.C.J. 246 at p. 299, para. 111.

24. See note 1.

25. See, for example, representations made to CEDAW by government officials in the course of examining state reports.

26. *De Sanchez v. Banco Central de Nicaragua,* 770 F.2d (5th Cir. 1985) at p. 1397; *Forti v. Suárez-Mason,* 672 F.Supp. 1531 (N.D. Cal. 1987) at pp. 1541–42, modified on other grounds 694 F.Supp. 707 (N.D. Cal. 1988).

27. *Filártiga v. Peña-Irala,* (1980) 630 F.2d 876; *De Sanchez v. Banco Central De Nicaragua,* note 26; *Forti v. Suárez-Mason,* note 26.

28. *Lareau v. Manson,* 507 F. Supp. 1177 (D. Conn., 1980), Aff'd in part,

modified and remanded in part. 651 F. 2d 96 (2nd Cir. 1981). Only the District Court decision spoke of the Standard Minimum Rules as relevant by way of customary international law.

29. *Rodríguez-Fernández v. Wilkinson*, 654 F.2d 1382 (10th Cir. 1981); *De Sanchez v. Banco Central de Nicaragua*, note 26; *Forti v. Suárez Mason*, note 26.

30. *De Sanchez v. Banco Central de Nicaragua*, note 26; but see *Forti v. Suárez-Mason*, modified, note 26, which held that "cruel, inhuman, or degrading treatment" was not a violation of customary international law.

31. *Barcelona Traction Case*, 1970 I.C.J. 3, at p. 32, paras. 33 and 34. *De Sanchez v. Banco Central de Nicaragua*, note 26.

32. *Forti v. Suárez-Mason*, note 30 at p. 711.

33. *Siderman v. Republic of Argentina*, No. 82-1772-RMT (C.D. Cal. March 12, 1984) vacated, No. 82-1772-RMT (C.D. Cal. March 7, 1985). After first entering a default judgment for the plaintiffs, Judge Takasugi eventually dismissed on the ground that the lack of an explicit exception in the Foreign Sovereign Immunities Act for human rights claims based on torts committed abroad deprived the court of jurisdiction.

34. *Barcelona Traction Case*, note 31 at paras. 33 and 34. The Restatement of U.S. Foreign Relations Law limits this right to systematic racial discrimination. It states that the customary law of right of freedom from systematic racial discrimination is only racial discrimination practiced systematically as a matter of state policy, such as apartheid (Foreign Relations Law, note 11 at sec. 702, Comment i at p. 165).

35. *Foreign Relations Law*, note 11 at sec. 702 at p. 161. In total the Restatement lists the following other rights and prohibitions as having the status of customary international human rights law: slavery or slave trade, the murder or causing the disappearance of individuals, torture or other cruel, inhuman, or degrading treatment or punishment, and prolonged arbitrary detention, sec. 702 at p. 161.

36. *Foreign Relations Law*, note 11 at sec. 702, Comment 1 at p. 166. On the subject of religious discrimination and customary international law, the Restatement of the Foreign Relations Law of the United States has the following comment: "there is a strong case that systematic discrimination on grounds of religion as a matter of state policy is also a violation of customary law" (*Foreign Relations Law*, note 11 at sec. 702, Comment j at p. 165).

37. *Foreign Relations Law*, note 11 at sec. 702, Comment at 161–62.

38. John P. Humphrey, "The Implementation of International Human Rights Law," *N.Y.L.S. L. Rev. J.* 24 (1978–79): 31, 32.

39. See generally Oscar Schachter, "International Law in Theory and Practice," *Rec. des Cours* 178 (1982): 114–21.

40. *Foreign Relations Law*, note 11 at Introductory Note, Part VII at 146–47.

41. See the following U.S. court decisions: *Fernández v. Wilkinson*, 505 F. Supp. 787 (D. Kan. 1980; aff'd 654 F.2d 1382 10th Cir. 1981) for different reasons); *Soroa-Gonzales v. Civiletti* (515 F. Supp. 1049 (N.D. Georgia, 1981) at p. 1061, n. 18); *Ishtyaq v. Nelson* (627 F. Supp. 13 (E.D. New York, 1983)). But see *Tel-Oren et al. v. Libyan Arab Republic, the Palestine Liberation Organization et al.*, 726 F.2d 774 (D.C. Cir. 1984) at 810–11.

42. See *Bloxam v. Favre*, 8 P.D. 101 (1883) (U.K.) at p. 197: "Every statute is to be so interpreted and applied, as far as its language is mixed, as not to be inconsistent with the comity of nations or with the established rules of international law." *The Ship "North" v. The King*, 37 S.C.R. 385 (1906) (Canada) at 398:

"No prudent sovereign power would willingly, in these modern times, invite conflict with a neighbour by enacting a statute directing that to be done which international law had clearly forbidden or that which had been denied as an inherent right. This statute now in question must be read in light of the well-known, recognized, customary or international law that has preceded it, and is yet in force, and receive interpretation thereby." *Salomon v. Commissioners of Customs and Excise,* 2 Q.B. 116 (1967) (U.K.) at 143 in the context of conventional international law, but expressed in general language, Diplock L.J. said: "there is a prima facie presumption that Parliament does not intend to act in breach of international law, including therein specific treaty obligations" and at 141 "we ought always to interpret our statutes so as to be in conformity with international law."

43. See the Canadian cases of *Reference Re Public Service Employee Relations Act,* 38 D.L.R. 4th 161 (1987) (Can.) at 184; 1 S.C.R. 313 (1987) (Can.) at 348. Chief Justice Dickson was writing in dissent but his remarks in this respect were later adopted in majority decisions. See *Davidson v. Slaight Communications,* note 9.

44. See note 1.

45. See the Canadian case *Daniels v. The Queen,* 2 D.L.R. 3d 1 (1968) (Can.) at 23; 1 S.C.R. 517 (1968) (Can.) at 541.

46. See, e.g., the Canadian Supreme Court case of *Davidson v. Slaight Communications,* note 9, per Chief Justice Dickson (at 427–28 D.L.R. and at 1056–57 S.C.R.).

47. Anne Bayefsky, *International Human Rights Law: Use in Canadian Charter of Rights and Freedoms Litigation* (Toronto: Butterworths, 1992).

48. *Canada (A.G.) v. Stuart,* 137 D.L.R. 3d 740 (F.C.A.), (1982). Leave to appeal to S.C.C. refused, 45 N.R. 531 (S.C.C.) (1982).

49. *Andrews v. Law Society (B.C.) et al.,* 4 W.W.R. 242 (1986) (B.C.C.A.) (Can.) (aff'd 1 S.C.R. 143 (1989)); *Can. Trust Co. v. Ontario (Human Rights Commn.),* 74 O.R. 2d 481 (1990), 37 O.A.C. 191 (Can.).

50. *Gould v. Yukon Order of Pioneers,* Y.J. No. 637 (Yukon Territory Sup. Ct.) (1992), 22–24.

51. *Leroux v. Co-operators General Insurance Co.; Superintendent of Insurance, Intervenor,* 71 O.R. 2d 641 (Ont. H.C.) (1990), 652.

52. *Schachter v. Canada,* 52 D.L.R. 4th 525, at 542 (F.C.T.D.) (1988); upheld on appeal S.C.C., July 9, 1992, No. 21889, but no mention was made by the higher court of international law.

53. *Reference re Use of French in Sask. Criminal Proceedings,* 44 D.L.R. 4th 16 (Sask. C.A.) (1987). Leave to appeal to S.C.C. sought; notice of discontinuance filed, 43 C.R.R. 189 (1988) (note).

54. *Andrews v. Law Society (B.C.) et al.,* note 49.

55. Convention on the Elimination of All Forms of Discrimination Against Women, emphasis added.

56. Bertie G. Ramcharan, "Equality and Nondiscrimination," in *The International Bill of Rights: The Covenant on Civil and Political Rights,* ed. Louis Henkin (New York: Columbia University Press, 1981), 246, 259–61.

57. Adopted by the Human Rights Committee under art. 40(4) of the International Covenant on Civil and Political Rights at its meeting 21 November 1989. *Report of the Human Rights Committee,* U.N. Doc. A/45/40, 1990, Vol. 1, Annex VI, pp. 173–75, para. 10. The Committee is authorized to formulate General Comments by Covenant Article 40(4) and has been doing so since 1981.

58. 7th session, 1988, U.N. Doc. A/43/38 (1988), 109.

59. CCPR/C/21/Rev. i/Add.1 at para. 10.

60. 7th session, 1988, A/43/38 (1988), 111.

61. For an expansion of this point see Bayefsky, "Principle of Equality," note 11 at 28–33.

62. The Supreme Court of Canada, for example, has used non-binding international human rights law as support for a dozen cases that concerned the interpretation of the constitutional Charter of Rights and Freedoms. See, for example, *R. v. Oakes* 1 S.C.R. 103 (1986) at 120 and 140–41; 26 D.L.R. 4th 200 (S.C.C.) (1986) at 213 and 228–29; *Schmidt v. The Queen*, 39 D.L.R. 4th 18 (S.C.C.) (1987) at 39; 1 S.C.R. 500 (1987) at 522; *Rahey v. The Queen*, 39 D.L.R. 4th 481(1987) at 513; 1 S.C.R. 588 (1987) at 633; *Tremblay v. Daigle*, 62 D.L.R. 4th 634 (1989) at 661–62; 2 S.C.R. 530 (1989) at 567–68; *R. v. Keegstra*, 1 C.R. 4th 129 (S.C.C.) (1990) at 177–78; *Canada (Can. H.R. Commn.) v. Taylor*, 75 D.L.R. 4th 577 (S.C.C.) (1990) at p. 594.

With respect to the use of non-binding international norms directly affecting women's rights in Canadian courts, see the reference to the Inter-African Committee on Traditional Practices Affecting the Health of Women and Children in Africa and the UN Seminar on Traditional Practices Affecting the Health of Women and Children, F.C.J. No. 1068 (F.C.T.D.) (1991) at 3.

See the U.S. Supreme Court's use of non-binding international human rights law as support for its judgments: *Trop v. Dulles* 356 U.S. 86 (1957) at 101–2; *Estelle v. Gamble* 429 U.S. 97 (1976) at 103–4, n.8; *Coker v. Georgia* 433 U.S. 584 (1977) at 596, n.10; *Enmund v. Florida* 458 U.S. 782 (1982) at 796, n.22; *United States v. Stanley* 483 U.S. 669 (1987) at 709, 710; *Thompson v. Oklahoma* 487 U.S. 815 (1988) at 830–31, and n. 34, 851–52; but see *Stanford v. Kentucky* 492 U.S. 361 (1989) at 369 and n.1 and *Wilkins v. Missouri* (same cite as *Stanford v. Kentucky*). Note the dissenting judges in contrast at 389–90.

63. *Report of Canada,* Convention on the Elimination of All Forms of Discrimination Against Women, May 1983, Department of the Secretary of State, at 3.

64. *Second Report of Canada,* Convention on the Elimination of All Forms of Discrimination Against Women, Human Rights Directorate, Department of the Secretary of State, January 1988, at 21.

65. *Second Report,* note 64 at 2.

66. *Second Report,* note 64 at 21.

67. *Second Report,* note 64 at 21–23. The report also contained statements by each of the provinces. For example, in the section on Quebec it said: "The Government of Quebec undertook to abide by the Convention on the Elimination of All Forms of Discrimination Against Women. . . . The present report covers the legal and other measures that have been taken to implement the Convention" (81).

68. Summary Record of the 167th Meeting, Committee on the Elimination of All Forms of Discrimination Against Women, February 1990, U.N. Doc. CEDAW/C/SR.167 at 6, per Ms. Stanley.

Chapter 16
Obstacles to Women's Rights in India
Kirti Singh

Introduction

While the Constitution of India adopted in November 1949 contains articles mandating equality and nondiscrimination on the grounds of sex, several laws that clearly violate these principles continue to exist, especially in the area of personal laws or family laws. Most of these laws, which contain provisions that are highly discriminatory against women, have either remained static or have changed in retrogressive ways.[1]

The Indian state has, however, made no effort to change these laws or introduce new legislation in conformity with Constitutional principles. In fact, the Indian government seems to have chosen to ignore these principles completely and acts as if they did not exist.

The only personal laws in India that have been reformed to some extent have been the Hindu personal laws. Personal laws have been retained for reasons of political expediency and electoral gain and to deny equality to women.[2] The only justification put forth by the state, however, has been that it does not want to interfere in the personal matters of a minority community. In fact, while signing the Convention on the Elimination of All Forms of Discrimination Against Women (the Women's Convention) on 30 July 1980, the Indian government made a unilateral declaration that "with regard to Articles 5(a) and 16(1) . . . the Government of India declares that it shall abide by . . . these provisions in conformity with its policy of non-interference in the personal affairs of any community without its initiative and consent."[3] But the government ratified the Women's Convention on 9 July 1993 without reservations and is therefore obligated to implement the entire Convention.

While some reforms have been introduced in the criminal laws, ostensibly to deal with the issue of violence against women, these reforms have been half-hearted and inadequate. There is also an almost complete absence of laws dealing with the majority of women workers, who work in the rural unorganized sector.[4] It is significant to note that even the changes brought about in the criminal laws during the last decade were largely due to massive and sustained campaigns by women's groups and others. These campaigns forced a reluctant state to give more rights to women.[5] On several occasions, however, the Indian government has paid lip service to the cause of women while acting in a totally contradictory manner. The Rajiv Gandhi government, for instance, after passing the Muslim Women's (Protection of Rights on Divorce) Act of 1986, which deprived divorced Muslim women of their right to maintenance, actually came out with a "National Perspective Plan" for Women[6] that recommended, among other things, a complete overhauling of the discriminatory laws and the passing of a common civil code by the end of the century, that is, by the year 2000. As anticipated, no action to change any laws as recommended in this plan has yet taken place. The government thus seems to have formulated this plan only to put up a false front that it was interested in advancing women's rights.

The most significant barrier to women's rights in India, therefore, is a hostile state that is not actually interested in giving them any rights. Other factors that have adversely affected women's rights in India include the lack of implementation of laws by the state law and order machinery and the gender bias pervasive in the judiciary at all levels. In spite of the amendments to the rape and dowry laws during the 1980s, these laws have not been enforced or implemented by the state and its administrative machinery. Further, though certain challenges to personal laws as being discriminatory and violative of the right to equality are pending before the Supreme Court of India,[7] the Supreme Court and other courts have in the past mostly interpreted laws relating to women in an extremely narrow, conservative, and anti-women manner without taking into account the women's perspective and their situation in India. Illiteracy and poverty also have a major role to play. Most Indian women have no access to the courts or knowledge of the laws and, because of the dismal conditions in which they live, they cannot afford to fight for their rights in a hostile social and economic environment. These are the reasons at the domestic level that are primarily responsible for inhibiting the growth of women's rights in India.

After outlining the Constitutional position, this paper briefly discusses various personal laws and analyzes whether they are violative of the Indian Constitution or can be justified on the basis of freedom of religion. It discusses the reforms brought about in the Hindu personal laws, which were based on the concepts of equality and nondiscrimination against women, and the objections to these reforms raised by Hindu fundamentalists, which were very similar to the objections raised by Muslim fundamentalists at the time of the *Shah Bano* decision by the Supreme Court of India in 1985. Following this is a brief discussion of how Indian courts have interpreted personal and related laws in the context of the Constitution. Thereafter the paper deals with the other factors responsible for denial of women's rights in India, primarily the inadequacy of criminal laws and their lack of implementation because of the anti-woman and grossly negligent attitude of the law and order machinery, including the reaction of the police and the courts to cases of violence against women. The paper concludes by showing how the stand of the Indian government is violative of both the provisions of the Constitution at the national level and the obligation of India to uphold the provisions of international conventions and treaties which it has signed or ratified.

The Constitutional Position

The Indian Constitution has a "Fundamental Rights" chapter that guarantees various rights. The rights of special importance to women are the Right to Equality in Article 14 and the Express Prohibition Against Discrimination in Article 15. Article 14 mandates that "the state shall not deny to any person equality before the law or the equal protection of the laws within the territory of India." Article 15(1) prohibits discrimination against any citizen by the state "on grounds only of religion, race, caste, sex, place of birth or any of them." Article 15(3) also allows for special provision for women and children by clarifying that "Nothing in this Article shall prevent the state from making any special provision for women and children." This article has been used by courts to justify reservation in favor of women[8] and to justify a provision, Section 497(1) of the unamended Indian Criminal Procedure Code of 1898, which gave special treatment to women and children and prescribed leniency in granting them bail.[9]

In addition, Article 16(1) mandates equality of opportunity for all citizens in matters relating to employment or appointment to any office under the state. Article 16(2) clarifies that "no citizen shall, on grounds only of religion, race, caste, sex, descent, place of birth, residence or any of them, be ineligible for, or discriminated against in respect of, any employment or office under the State." Article 19[10] guarantees the basic freedoms of speech and expression, movement, and peaceable assembly, and the right to form associations or unions. Another important right is the protection of life and personal liberty provided in Article 21,[11] since this right has been very widely interpreted by the courts and has been held to include the right of privacy[12] and the right of an individual to live with dignity. These Fundamental Rights in Chapter III of the Constitution are obviously enforceable in a court of law.

Chapter IV of the Constitution of India contains principles of law known as the "Directive Principles of State Policy," which, though not enforceable, are supposed to be fundamental in the governance of the country. It is also supposed to be the duty of the state to apply these principles in making laws. These principles direct the state, in Article 39(a), to ensure that all citizens, men and women equally, have the right to an adequate means of livelihood. In Article 39(d), the state is directed to ensure that there is equal pay for equal work for both men and women. The Equal Remuneration Act passed by the Indian Parliament in 1975 does provide that men and women will be paid equally for doing the same work or work of a similar nature. This act also states that there will be no discrimination against women at the time of recruitment or later at the time of promotion. In Article 39(e) of the Constitution, the state is directed to secure that the health and strength of workers, men and women, and the tender age of children are not abused and citizens are not forced by economic necessity to enter occupations unsuited to their age or strength. Article 42 of the Directive Principles directs the state to make provisions for securing just and humane conditions of work and for maternity relief. The Maternity Benefit Act of 1961 was ostensibly passed to achieve this purpose.

Another very important article[13] of the Directive Principles of State Policy aims at ending the regime of personal laws and states that "the State shall endeavour to secure for the citizens a uniform civil code throughout the territory of India."

Personal Laws

Personal laws in India deal with marriage and divorce, maintenance, guardianship, adoption, wills, intestacy and succession, joint family, and partition, and can broadly be characterized as "family laws." These laws are basically divided along religious lines, whether or not they are based on religion.[14] Thus Hindus in India are governed by the Hindu Marriage Act of 1955, the Hindu Succession Act of 1956, the Hindu Guardianship and Minorities Act of 1956, and the Hindu Adoption and Maintenance Act of 1956. Indian Muslims are governed by the Shari'a Act of 1937, the Muslim Women's Dissolution of Marriage Act of 1939, the Muslim Women's (Protection of Rights on Divorce) Act of 1986, and uncodified Muslim personal laws. Christians are governed by their own Christian Marriage Act, the Indian Divorce Act, and the Indian Succession Act, while Parsis, too, have codified laws of marriage and divorce and of succession.

The main characteristic of all the personal laws is that they are anti-women, anti-liberal, and anti-human. It is ironic that while all Indian women suffer from the same or similar discrimination at home or within their families, the family or personal laws applicable to them are different and subject them to varying degrees of discrimination. We are thus confronted with a strange situation that while a Hindu, Christian, or Parsi woman can sue her husband for bigamy under the criminal law code for punishment of up to seven years imprisonment, Indian Muslim personal law allows a Muslim man to marry up to four times.

One of the main arguments advanced against reform of personal law has been that such reform violates the right of all Indian citizens to freedom of religion. If one examines Article 25 of the Constitution which gives all persons freedom of conscience and the right to profess, practice and propagate religion, it will be seen that this article is specifically subject to the following provisions:

(a) Public order, morality and health;
(b) The provisions of Part III of the Constitution including the right to equality and Article 15.

This article also makes it clear that

(a) The state can regulate any economic, financial, political or other secular activity that may be associated with religious practice;
(b) The state can make any law providing for social welfare and reform.

Article 25 therefore clearly states the parameters within which the right freely to practice, propagate, and profess religion is limited. It in fact defines the content of secularism by stating that the right to freely propagate and practice religion is not an unlimited right but is subject to the constitutional rights of equality and freedom from discrimination.[15] It also enables the state to regulate any economic, financial, political, or other secular activity associated with religious practice. The state has also been empowered to make any laws for social welfare and reform which may interfere with the right to freedom of religion. A bare reading of this article shows clearly that the Constitution restricts the scope of the right to freedom of religion.

The question, however, of enacting a common civil code has never been on the agenda of the government, in spite of the fact that from time to time various committees, women's organizations, and others interested in women's rights have asked for a uniform secular family law based on equality. In fact, until the judgment of the Supreme Court in Shah Bano's case, several women's groups and others were actively working toward a uniform civil code based on equality[16] that would apply to all Indian women regardless of their community. After witnessing the opposition to a uniform civil code from sections of the Muslim population, however, women's groups and others have been demanding reforms in the personal laws of the different communities.

A look at the various reforms in Hindu personal laws shows that they have come about due to the separation of family laws from religion. In fact, the progressive changes that have been brought about in Hindu personal law have nothing to do with religion, but were instead based on the concept of equality and had nothing to do with *smritis* (old Hindu texts) and the laws of Manu[17] (an ancient law-giver who prohibited divorce).

Prior to Independence, the British rulers also followed a policy of retaining and not reforming the family laws applicable to Hindus, Muslims, and Parsis.[18] In fact, during this entire period the personal laws of various communities remained static, and the British system of courts relied heavily on religious pundits and the *ulama* for interpreting the personal laws applicable to Hindus and Muslims. In several instances, this resulted in further communalizing the law.[19]

Family laws were therefore extremely backward at the time of Indian Independence and needed to be extensively amended. Changes, however, took place only in Hindu law. This law was codified and separate acts dealing with marriage and divorce, adoption and maintenance, succession and minority, and guardianship were passed. The concept of monogamy was introduced for the first time in the Hindu Marriage Act of 1955. Concomitantly, certain limited grounds of divorce were introduced into Hindu law for the first time. Prior to the change, while a man was free to marry an unlimited number of times without getting divorced, the woman could not do so and once married had to remain married until she died.

The passing of the Hindu Marriage Act with its provision for divorce was opposed by conservative members of Parliament who were members of Hindu communal organizations like the Jan Sangh and the Hindu Maha Sabha. These members claimed that the bill had been passed to "wound the religious feelings of the Hindus"[20] and was "against the fundamental principles of Hinduism."[21] It is interesting that one Hindu fundamentalist member of Parliament at that time,

V.M. Trivedi, actually proposed an amendment to the effect that if the wife agreed that she did not object to her husband's having a second wife, this condition should not apply. Strangely enough, the fundamentalists demanded that a uniform civil code be introduced and stated that Hindus were being discriminated against since the bill did not apply to Muslims. It was only because the government of the day was in favor of reforming and codifying Hindu law that the Act was passed despite fierce opposition. In fact the Minister of Law in Parliament at the time, while introducing the bill, said it was a measure of great social importance to do good to women because men had been enjoying disproportionate rights and privileges as compared with women and the government could not, in the name of preserving the sanctity of any ancient culture, try to treat women differently in the present time and conditions. The Minister also pointed out that ancient Hindu law had already been altered from time to time.[22]

Similarly, the Hindu Succession Act was passed in 1956, giving more property rights to women, including the complete right of disposal of their property. Previously women could not sell or alienate their property and had only what was known as a "limited estate" in their property. This bill did not grant equal rights of inheritance to women. In fact, at that time the All India Women's Conference, a women's organization allied to the Congress Party, objected to the Hindu Succession Act on the grounds that "The Bill, although a step in the right direction, falls far short of what is required due to the fact that it excludes from its application the Mitakshara joint family property. As the Mitakshara Law with its various sections prevails over more than two-thirds of India, a substantial number of women will be debarred from inheriting property on the same terms as their male relatives, thus leading to discrimination on grounds of sex which is contrary to the provisions of the Indian Constitution."[23] The Hindu Succession Act, however, contained several retrogressive features in addition to not conferring equal property rights on women. In section 4(2), "laws providing for the prevention of fragmentation of agricultural holding" were left out or exempted from the application of the act. This meant that in the name of "prevention of fragmentation of agricultural land," Hindu women could be deprived of their right to property. Further, section 23 stipulated that if a woman inherited a house in which members of the family were living, she had no right to ask for a "partition" of the house and could only reside in it if she was not married or had been separated. The act also provided that if a female Hindu died intestate and left behind no children or husband, her property would devolve on her husband's heirs. The only exception to this rule was that property inherited by a woman from her parents would revert, in the absence of a son or daughter (or their son or daughter), to the heirs of her father. These provisions have not been altered or amended to date.[24] The passage of this act was also vehemently opposed by orthodox Hindu members.

The Hindu Guardianship and Minority Act was also passed at this time, though it made no radical departure from old Hindu law. The father is the natural guardian of the child under this act and only in the absence of the father can the mother be the natural guardian. A proviso, however, gives the custody of the minor child who has not completed the age of five years to the mother. A suggestion during the Parliamentary debates at the time the act was being discussed, that custody of the minor child remain with the mother till the age of fourteen years, was not accepted. Only in respect to illegitimate children has the mother been given the privilege of being the natural guardian. The Hindu Adoption and Maintenance Act provided a Law of Adoption only for Hindus. No other community in India has the right to adoption. This was the first act that allowed Hindu daughters as well as sons to be adopted. Hindus earlier believed that only a son should be adopted as only the son inherited the property of the father. It is interesting that even at the time of its passage conservative Hindu members of Parliament protested various features of this act; one conservative member actually said,

I am again entering my protest against this kind of communal legislation. You are going against your Constitution and the Directive Principles. Though they are not justiciable as per the Fundamental Rights, still you solemnly enacted them for the purposes of giving guidance to the Parliament and the state Legislatures. It is not proper on the part of the Government which has been responsible for ushering in that Constitution to enact this law in defiance of the Directive Principles. They say that there shall be a uniform Civil Code for all the citizens of India. Have it for everybody. As Mahamahopadhyaya Kane himself said, why run after the Hindus only.[25]

The preceding discussion shows that the subject of reform was hotly debated in the 1950s. All sorts of arguments, including cries that religion was in danger and that reforms were against secularism and against the Constitution of India were put forward to stop any reform from taking place. After the 1950s these laws have remained largely static; only some changes like divorce by mutual consent and on the grounds of cruelty and desertion were introduced in 1976. No reforms were brought about in the laws of other communities. As far as the Christian law of marriage and divorce is concerned, it is extremely backward, since both the Christian Marriage Act and the Indian Divorce Act were framed by the British rulers on the then prevailing English law of marriage and divorce, and no changes or reforms have been brought about in these laws. The Indian Divorce Act recognizes only adultery as a ground for divorce for men. The wife is subject to even harsher grounds of divorce and can ask for divorce only if the husband has changed his religion and married another woman or has been guilty of adultery along with bigamy or rape, sodomy, bestiality, cruelty, or desertion. This act, besides being archaic, obviously discriminates against women on the grounds of sex alone. No reforms have been brought about in this law in spite of demands from various liberal Christian and women's organizations. This is because the orthodox Christian clergy have been opposed to these reforms and the government policy of "no interference in the religious affairs of the minorities" has been a convenient tool to avoid reform.

As far as Muslim personal law is concerned, not only has the law remained static, but as noted above, there has been a steady retrogression, which culminated in the introduction of the Muslim Women's (Protection of Rights on Divorce) Act of 1986. This act restricts the right of Muslim women to maintenance only to the *iddat* period, approximately three months after divorce, and stipulates that thereafter her own family and the Waqf board would be responsible for her maintenance. As stated earlier, the act debars Muslim women from claiming maintenance under the general criminal law under Section 125, Code of Criminal Procedure. It further states that, where the woman herself maintains the children, maintenance is to be paid by her former husband for a period of two years from the dates of birth of such children. This act clearly violates the right to equality and discriminates against Muslim women on the ground only of religion. The history of how this act came to be passed is interesting. For over a century, since 1898, a provision in the Criminal Procedure Code of India provided for maintenance for neglected and deserted wives and children unable to maintain themselves. This provision has been applicable to all Indian women, irrespective of their religion. In 1974, the Criminal Procedure was amended to include within the definition of "wife" a divorced wife. This had become necessary since divorced wives were often in urgent need of maintenance and the Code of Criminal Procedure provided a relatively speedy remedy, even though the amount of maintenance was more in the nature of a dole and was and is restricted to a maximum sum of Rs. 500 per person per month. Fundamentalist and orthodox Muslim opinion, however, opposed the inclusion of a "divorced wife" in the definition of a "wife," as they argued that under Muslim personal law, a divorced wife could only receive maintenance for the *iddat* period. The government succumbed to this opinion and added a section to this law that stated that, if the woman had received "the whole of the sum which, under any customary or

Personal Law, applicable to the parties, was payable on such divorce," she was not entitled to any maintenance. Even after this amendment, however, the Supreme Court in a series of judgments held that a divorced Muslim woman was entitled to adequate maintenance and that the provision in the Criminal Penal Code was meant for destitute women and to prevent vagrancy.[26]

In 1985 the famous *Shah Bano* judgment[27] on the right of a divorced Muslim woman to get maintenance was pronounced by the Supreme Court. The case was filed by Shah Bano, who had been thrown out of her house by her husband after thirty years of marriage. When she asked for maintenance in the Court of the Judicial Magistrate, she was divorced by her lawyer husband who maintained that he had already given her her *mehar* (dowry) and maintenance and was not liable to pay any further amounts. The Magistrate awarded a princely sum of Rs. 25 per month to Shah Bano and this sum was enhanced to Rs. 179.20 per month by the High Court. Not willing to pay even that amount, the husband appealed to the Supreme Court, saying that he was not liable to pay any maintenance beyond the *iddat* period according to his personal law. The Court held that the provisions regarding maintenance were applicable to all communities, that Section 125 of the Criminal Procedure Code had been enacted in order to provide a quick and summary remedy to a class of persons unable to maintain themselves, and, further, that the religion professed by the party cannot have any repercussion on the applicability of such laws. The Court also quoted certain provisions of the Qur'an and stated that it imposes an obligation on a Muslim husband to make provision for or to provide maintenance to the divorced wife. It further held that *mehar*/dowry was not a sum payable on divorce by the husband but was a sum payable in consideration of the marriage. The Court also stated that it was a matter of deep regret that Article 44 of the Constitution had remained a dead letter. It stated that, though the article provides that the state shall endeavor to secure for its citizens a uniform civil code for the country, "there is no evidence of any official activity for framing a common civil code for the country" and that a beginning has to be made if the Constitution is to have any meaning.

This judgment was vehemently criticized by fundamentalist Muslims, who described the judgment as an unacceptable interference in Muslim personal law. The Muslim Personal Law Board, which was an intervenor in the Court, and other Muslim religious leaders and organizations launched a huge campaign alleging that Islam was in "danger," and that the government should introduce a bill exempting Muslim women from Section 125 of the Criminal Procedure Code.[28] While various reasons have been advanced for the support the fundamentalists could master[29] on this occasion it is in some respects easy to understand how economically poor and socially oppressed illiterate minority populations can react to the highly emotional cry of "religion in danger."

Some Indian Muslims were also forced to take this stand as Hindu fundamentalists, represented by the Vishwa Hindu Parishad, the Rashtriya Sewak Sangh, and the Bharatiya Janata Party, decided to use the issue as a convenient whip against Muslims and demand a uniform civil code that in their understanding probably meant a Hindu civil code.

But it would be wrong to state that the entire Muslim population supported the fundamentalists. Women's groups also carried out massive campaigns in support of the *Shah Bano* judgment as it was a vital issue for them that the Supreme Court had upheld a deserted and destitute divorced woman's right to maintenance, whatever her religion.[30]

The women's groups and other liberal organizations carried out a campaign throughout the country,[31] convening meetings and holding demonstrations and mass signature campaigns. Women blocked traffic outside Parliament in Delhi for hours when the bill was introduced in Parliament to deny divorced Muslim women their right to maintenance. Fifteen women's organizations held a demonstration in Delhi on 6 March 1986 to protest the government action. In Bombay, thirty-five women's organizations led by the Women's Liberation Movement held a rally demanding a secular civil code; 1,500 Muslim women demonstrated in Delhi in April 1986;[32] one organization alone collected the signatures of 100,000 women, 20,000 of whom were Muslim.[33]

The government, however, paid no attention to the women's voices and, though it had initially supported the *Shah Bano* judgment through the speech of its Minister of State for Home Affairs in the Lower House of Parliament[34] (Lok Sabha), completely changed its stand and introduced the Muslim Women's Act containing all the provisions which the fundamentalists desired.[35]

It is mostly believed that the government changed its stand because it felt it could not afford to alienate the Muslim fundamentalist leaders who were valuable vote banks.[36] This opportunist stand of the Indian government sealed the fate of millions of Muslim women in India.

As far as the other personal laws were concerned, attempts had earlier been made to introduce a uniform Indian Adoption Act as well. This, too, was opposed by orthodox Muslims, including the Muslim Personal Law Board, who claimed that adoption was against the Qur'an and that any change in Muslim personal law would impinge on the secular character of the Constitution. It is important to note that even an optional law governing adoption was vehemently opposed by fundamentalists, who claimed that members of their community should not have the option to adopt even if they wanted to. Fundamentalist leadership and other politicians have always used religion to promote their own vested interests and to preserve the status quo regarding women's rights, preventing reform in the family laws relating to women.

Courts on Personal Law

As far as the courts are concerned, other than a few judgments like *Shah Bano*, they have been mainly concerned with preserving the status quo. It was only in the 1950s that the courts showed a determination to uphold the reforms passed in the Hindu Law. In the 1950s there were some challenges to certain laws prohibiting bigamy that had been passed in some states prior to the Hindu reforms referred to above. In *State of Bombay v. Narasu Appa Mali*,[37] the Bombay High Court held that the "Bombay Prevention of Hindu Bigamous Marriage Act was a measure of social reform and the state was empowered to legislate with regard to Article 25(2)(b), notwithstanding the fact that it may interfere with the right of a citizen to freely profess, practice, and propagate religion." Similarly, in *Srinivasa v. Saraswati Ammal*,[38] it was held that the freedom to practice religion was not an absolute right as Article 25 itself states, but that it is subject to the other provisions of Part III of the Constitution. It was further held that Article 25(2) empowered the legislature to enact a law providing for social welfare and reform and that religious practice, therefore, may be controlled by legislation if the states think that it is necessary to do so in the interest of social welfare and reform. Both cases also made a sharp distinction between religious belief and practice. In the former case it was held that what the state protects is religious faith and belief and quoted with approval an American case, *Davis v. Beason*,[39] in which it had been held that "laws are made for the Governments of action and while they cannot interfere with mere religious beliefs and opinions, they may with practices." The court held that it was difficult to accept the proposition that polygamy is an integral part of the Hindu religion. In the latter case also the court quoted another American case, *Reynolds v. U.S.*,[40] in which religious belief and practice were distinguished, to show that the freedom to practice religion is not an absolute right, though it went on to justify the Madras Hindu (Bigamy and Divorce) Act of 1949, on the basis of Article 25(2). The two courts also held that there was no discrimination between Hindus and Muslims in spite of the fact that Muslims could marry more than once, because the classification between Muslim and Hindu was based on a reasonable and rational consideration and thus did not offend Article 15 of the Constitution.

Thus in these cases the courts were mainly concerned with justifying the reforms in the laws.

Later challenges to various personal laws have not been upheld, even though the laws challenged blatantly discriminate against women. In a challenge to Section 10 of the Indian Divorce Act, the Madras High Court[41] refused to hold that the said section was in violation of Articles 13, 14, and 15 of the Constitution of India. Section 10 of the Indian Divorce Act applies to Christians in India; as stated earlier, under this section adultery is the only ground of divorce for the husband whereas the wife has to prove that the husband was guilty of adultery plus another ground. The wife challenged that this section violates Articles 13 to 15 of the Constitution of India as it discriminates against women on the grounds of sex. The court held that adultery by a wife is different from adultery by a husband. Since a wife can bear a child as a result and the husband will have to maintain the said child, this difference in the result of their acts was said to show that the classification is not based on sex alone.

In another judgment the Supreme Court of India refused to strike down a provision[42] of the Indian Penal Code which allows a husband to prosecute the man with whom his wife has committed adultery and provides for punishment up to five years fine or both.[43] The court held that this section was not in violation of Articles 14 or 15 as it makes a rational classification between men and women by a rather strange reasoning.

The court also held that since under the section the wife is not liable to be prosecuted for the offense of adultery, "no grievance can then be made that the section does not allow the wife to prosecute the husband for adultery." The court further stated that "the offence of adultery, as defined in Section 497, is considered by the legislature as an offence against the sanctity of the matrimonial home, an act which is committed by a man, as it generally is. Therefore those who defile the sanctity are brought within the net of law." This judgment shows the conservative and outdated attitude of the judges since they refused to acknowledge that this archaic provision of law is blatantly anti-woman and treats her as the property of her husband.

Only in a couple of cases has the judiciary seen the woman as an independent human being who is capable of making her own decisions. In a landmark judgment,[44] a judge of the Andhra Pradesh High Court held that the remedy of restitution of conjugal rights "violates the right to privacy and human dignity guaranteed by and contained in Article 21 of our Constitution." The restitution of conjugal rights is an old English remedy retained by the Indian legislature in both the Hindu Marriage Act and the Special Marriage Act of 1954, which is the only optional civil law of marriage and divorce. It was pointed out by the judge that the purpose of the remedy was through the judicial process to coerce the unwilling party to have "sex" against the person's consent and free will, since conjugal rights necessarily connote "the right which husband and wife have to each other's society" and "marital intercourse." The judgment further stated that a decree for restitution of conjugal right constitutes the grossest form of violation of an individual's right to privacy. It "deprives a woman of control over her choice as to when and by whom the various parts of her body should be allowed to be sensed" and "when and how her body is to become the vehicle for the procreation of another human being." This judgment is significant because it makes a clear break from the earlier judgments and upholds the right of an Indian woman to live with dignity, and lays stress on an individual's happiness and the woman's right to decide when and with whom she wants to live.

The Supreme Court, however, in a later judgment[45] held that there were sufficient safeguards in Section 9 of the Hindu Marriage Act, which allows a spouse to sue for restitution of conjugal rights, to prevent it from being a tyranny, as only financial sanctions could be applied under the law to the earning spouse who willfully refused to obey the decree for restitution of conjugal rights. The Supreme Court also held that the decree "serves a social purpose as an aid to the prevention of break-up of marriage." In upholding the remedy, the Supreme Court totally ignored the effect that such a decree could have on an Indian woman, who, under the threat of judicial and social pressure and financial sanctions may well be forced to go back to the matrimonial home and, because of her vulnerable position in it, be forced to have sex and live a life of misery in an atmosphere she obviously abhors. This judgment is thus a denial of the fundamental right of every human being to privacy and a right to decide at least with whom they want or wish to live. It is also relevant to mention that several of the earlier judgments of various High Courts had taken the extremely backward view that a Hindu woman's duty is to live with her husband in the matrimonial home.[46] The said judgments completely overlook the fact that marriage is supposed to be a voluntary union and the state cannot force two people to remain married.

As far as bigamy is concerned, the Indian Supreme Court has held that in order to prove bigamy it is essential for the prosecution to prove that the second marriage has been solemnized with proper ceremonies[47] and in due form. In *Bhurao v. State of Maharashtra*, the court held that "if a marriage is not a valid marriage, it is not a marriage in the eyes of law. The bare fact of a man and woman living as husband and wife does not, at any rate normally, give them the status of husband and wife even though they may hold themselves out before society as husband and wife and the society treats them as husband and wife." In this case, the court held that, since the prosecution had failed to establish that the second marriage had been performed in accordance with the customary rites as provided by the act or in accordance with the essential requirements for a valid marriage under Hindu law, bigamy was not proved. In subsequent cases[48] the Supreme Court has held that both the marriages must be valid and strictly proved according to the law governing the parties in order for the offence to be proven. It is obvious that if a person wants to commit bigamy he is not likely to do so openly, as he knows that he is about to commit an offense. The Supreme Court has thus sided with the bigamist by taking too technical a view, and a complainant has to prove factually that the second marriage was performed strictly in accordance with all the requirements of a valid marriage under the law.

In fact in many cases[49] husbands have married again without bothering to take a divorce and give maintenance. Most such marriages are performed secretly and it is impossible to find evidence about where and how they were performed since marriages need not be registered according to Hindu law.

Crimes Against Women

On 9 April 1992, a Minister of State of Home Affairs in the Government of India admitted in the Lok Sabha that there was a sharp rise in atrocities against women, by almost 104 percent during the last decade. In fact, government statistics over the past few years have shown a phenomenal rise in crimes against women. It is also a well-acknowledged fact that these statistics represent only the tip of the iceberg, since most violence against women is not reported to the police.

Violence against women in India has assumed terrifying proportions, both within the family and outside. In the family the woman is often subjected to all forms of domestic violence, harassment for dowry, and sometimes rape. Outside the family she is subjected to rape, molestation, and sexual harassment at work, among other forms of violence. Further, new forms of violence like female feticide and a regeneration of older forms like sati have taken place. This increase in crime reflects the worsening status of Indian women, which also shows itself in the falling sex ratio, rising unemployment, and wide-scale discrimination and harassment at work.

One of the main problems is that, though many changes have taken place in the criminal laws, through the ceaseless efforts of women's groups and others, the government has made little effort to implement the laws. These laws have either remained unused or been flouted with impunity, often by the law and order machinery itself. In fact when a woman victim of violence goes to a police station she comes face to face with a police force that is corrupt and inefficient, and that basically has an anti-woman attitude. If the woman is poor, the police are very likely to throw her out on the street or mistreat her themselves.[50]

The catalyst for change in the laws relating to rape involved a policeman who raped a girl in the police station. A young girl, Mathura, was raped inside a police station by one policeman and molested by another. Mathura had gone to the police station at night for interrogation along with her boyfriend on a complaint filed against both by her brother. The boyfriend and brother were told to go outside after interrogation while Mathura was taken to a bathroom at the rear of the police station and raped. Mathura sustained no bodily injuries and no semen was found on her pubic hair or in vaginal smears when she was medically examined twenty hours later. The policeman's clothes however, were stained. It is said that the case was investigated at all only because Mathura immediately told her brother and friend about the rape and a huge crowd had gathered outside the police station demanding justice. The Sessions Court held that Mathura had voluntarily had sexual intercourse with the policeman. The High Court, however, reversed the findings and held that "mere passive surrender" did not mean that the sexual act was voluntary. The Supreme Court of India,[51] however, held that, since Mathura had not raised any alarm, her allegations were untrue. This decision of the Supreme Court generated massive protest marches organized by various women's organizations and groups. Three eminent professors of law from Delhi addressed an open letter to the Chief Justice of India. Women members of Parliament and various women's groups demanded changes in the laws relating to rape. One of the demands was that, if sexual intercourse is proved and the woman, who is alleged to have been raped says that she has not consented to the act, the onus of proof should be shifted to the accused to prove that the woman consented. Some women's groups felt that given the social backwardness of Indian women they would never make an allegation of rape. This demand was partly conceded. Widespread amendments to the law on rape were enacted. By these amendments, a special category of rape known as "custodial rape" was introduced. Under this amendment, rape by a man in a position of authority over a woman is considered more serious than ordinary rape. In this category were included rape by a policeman in a police station or of a woman in his custody or on the premises of a police station; rape by a public servant of a woman in his custody; rape by a person on the staff or management of a jail or remand home or any other place of custody of any woman inmate; rape by a person in the management of a hospital; rape of a pregnant woman; rape of a girl under twelve years of age; and gang rape.

The punishment prescribed for this category of rape was made more severe—rigorous imprisonment for ten years or a life sentence. Punishment by way of imprisonment for an ordinary case of rape was also increased to a minimum of seven years. In a major concession to women's groups, the onus of proof was shifted in cases of custodial rape after the fact of sexual intercourse had been proved.

Increasing punishment to a minimum of seven or ten years has not made much difference in the actual sentences that rapists have to serve. On many occasions reduced sentences have been given by the courts, ostensibly for special reasons. In one case,[52] because the doctor who had conducted the medical examination testified that the girl was used to sexual intercourse, the court reduced the sentence for three policemen who had raped her to five years. When a women's group and others filed a review petition,[53] the court justified the reduction in sentence by saying that when they spoke of "conduct" of the victim they meant her conduct in not logging the first information report till five days after the event. It often happens in India that the victim does not report the crime for a few days, because rape victims are often viewed with suspicion and their families are reluctant to report the matter to the police. Courts have also recognized this tendency in the past.[54] Later rape judgments have also been retrogressive with the judges in one case saying that if there was no injury on the rapist's penis in a minor rape case, rape was not proved.[55] Judges have also differed about the kind of corroboration required in a rape case. In certain cases the court has held that the victim's testimony should ordinarily be accepted,[56] and in other cases the court has insisted on direct evidence or circumstantial evidence in corroboration.[57] It is important to note that in the Indian situation doctors are often not available, particularly in rural areas, and a rape victim is therefore sometimes not medically examined at all.

Among other problems that rape victims face is that the police do not investigate the case properly. They also do not collect basic evidence as they are required to do. Often the sheet on which the rape took place, the clothes of the victim, and other evidence like fingerprints are not collected by the police. The medical examination is often carried out after a long waiting period. This results in loss of valuable evidence. The medical examination of the victims is also often cursory, and the doctors are sometimes obviously biased.[58]

Other victims of domestic violence face similar problems when they complain to the police. Even in big cities like Delhi, the police do not ensure that a victim who has obviously been beaten is medically examined. Instead, they try to dismiss the whole incident as a domestic brawl and often try to send the woman back to the matrimonial home. Even cases of dowry deaths are deliberately not properly investigated. This has been noticed in cases even by the Supreme Court of India.[59]

In the early 1980s, another struggle was launched by women's organizations to change the laws relating to dowry. As a result, the Dowry Prohibition Act of 1961 was amended in 1984 and again in 1986. In the 1986 amendment a provision was made for the appointment of dowry prohibition officers. These officers were meant to prevent dowry from being given or taken and to see that all the provisions of the act were complied with. Only a couple of states, however, have appointed dowry officers. There has been a complete lack of will on the part of the union and state governments to check the rampant custom of dowry. Other amendments were also brought about in the Indian Penal Code. A section that defined a special kind of murder, dowry death,[60] was introduced. This amendment provided that when a woman dies by burning or other bodily injury or under unnatural circumstances within seven years of marriage, and it can be shown that she was subjected to cruelty or harassment by her husband or any of his relatives in connection with dowry, such deaths will be known as "dowry death." The person, the amendment stated, "who commits a dowry death shall be punishable for a prison term not less than seven years but which may extend to life." Another amendment to the Evidence Act provided that, once it was shown that a person harassed a woman for dowry prior to her death, the court should presume that such a person had caused the death. Another amendment to the Penal Code made cruelty to a woman a criminal offense[61] and it has been found that many victims of domestic violence lodge their complaints under this section, at least in the cities.

These changes in the dowry laws, however, did not make any attempt to change the basic structure of inheritance and other property laws. Thus, though the giving and taking of dowry, which was largely perceived as the woman's share in the property, was made illegal, women were not given equal inheritance rights. Thus the phenomenon continued to occur, except that dowry was usually used and retained by the husband and his family. The Indian woman, too, has no right to date in the matrimonial property at the time of breakdown of the marriage unless she can prove that she has contributed toward buying it. All this makes her financially dependent on her husband and makes it extremely difficult for her to opt out of a violent home. On the other hand, her own family does not encourage her to come back, since after she has been given her share, a married woman is supposed to belong to her husband's family.

The inaction on the part of the Indian state in not reforming personal law is against the Fundamental Principles of the Constitution, which clearly elevates the Fundamental Rights to equality and freedom from discrimination above the right to freedom of religion. India is also a party to the Universal Declaration of Human Rights 1948. It has ratified the International Convention on Civil and Political Rights and has signed the Convention on the Elimination of All Forms of Discrimination Against Women. The International Covenant on Civil and Political Rights in Article 18(3) also subjects the freedom to manifest religion or belief to limitations prescribed by law which are necessary to protect public safety, order, health, or morals or the fundamental rights and freedoms of others. Thus even this Covenant states that, where religious practices impinge on the fundamental rights and freedoms of others, they can be restricted. India is bound by the terms of this Covenant. Its action in taking divorced Muslim women out of the purview of the prescribed law, that is, Section 125 of the Code of Criminal Procedure,[62] can easily be argued to be violative of its obligation under the Covenant. Also, at the time of signing the Women's Convention, although India undertook "to refrain from acts which would defeat the object and purpose of the treaty," India in total disregard of this obligation passed the Muslim Women's (Protection of Rights on Divorce) Act of 1986, which actually deprived Muslim women of a pre-existing right.[63] Further, the Indian government's decision of noninterference in the personal affairs of any community is incompatible with the purpose and object of the Women's Convention to improve the status of women.[64] This is also violative of provisions of the Indian Constitution, and the state cannot justify inaction regarding women's rights on this basis. The state is bound by the provisions of the Constitution to which it owes its existence, but by consistently listening to the most orthodox and obscurantist sections of the Indian population, namely, the religious leaders and their allies who are interested in preserving patriarchy, the state is perpetrating a fraud on the women of India.

Notes

1. Kirti Singh, "Women's Rights and the Reform of Personal Law," in *The Hindus and Others: The Question of Identity in India Today*, ed. Gyanendra Pandey (Delhi: Penguin, 1993), 177–97.
2. Singh, "Reform of Personal Law," note 1.
3. Quoted by Anika Rahman, "Religious Rights Versus Women's Rights in

India, A Test Case for International Human Rights Law," *Col. J. Transnat'l L.* 28 (1990): 473 at 486.

4. See Shramshakti, *Report of the National Commission on Self-Employed Women and Women in the Informal Sector in India,* 1988.

5. Indu Agnihotri and Rajni Palriwala, "Tradition, the Family, and the State: Politics of Contemporary Women's Movement," in *Terms of Political Discourse in India,* vol. 3, ed. T. V. Sathyamurthy (London: Oxford University Press, 1993).

6. *National Perspective Plan for Women,* Department of Woman and Child Development, Ministry of Human Resource Development, Government of India, 1988.

7. For instance, Criminal Writ Petition No. 1055 of 1986 in the Supreme Court of India titled *Susheela Gopalan v. Union of India,* challenging the constitutionality of the Muslim Women's (Protection of Right on Divorce) Act of 1986.

8. *Dattatreya v. State of Bombay,* A.I.R. (1953) Bombay 311.

9. *Mt. Choki v. State,* A.I.R. (1957) Rajasthan 10.

10. Indian Constitution, art. 19:

(1) All Citizens shall have the right:
  (a) to freedom of speech and expression;
  (b) to assemble peaceably and without arms;
  (c) to form associations or unions;
  (d) to move freely throughout the territory of India;
  (e) to reside and settle in any part of the territory of India; . . .
  (g) to practice any profession, or to carry on any occupation, trade or business.

11. Indian Constitution, art. 21: Protection of life and personal liberty—"No person shall be deprived of his life or personal liberty except according to procedure established by law."

12. AIR 1983 A.P. 356.

13. Art. 44 of the Directive Principles of State Policy.

14. Singh, "Reform of Personal Law," note 1.

15. Singh, "Reform of Personal Law, note 1.

16. Agnihotri and Palriwala, "Tradition," note 5.

17. Singh, "Reform of Personal Law," note 1.

18. See Tahir Mahmood, *Civil Marriage Law: Perspectives and Prospects* (Bombay: N.M. Tripathi Pvt. Ltd., 1973).

19. Singh, "Reform of Personal Law," note 1.

20. *Lok Sabha Debates,* Part II, Vol. IV (1955): 6889 on the Hindu Marriage Bill.

21. *Lok Sabha Debates,* note 20 at 6892.

22. *Lok Sabha Debates,* note 20 at 6465.

23. *Lok Sabha Debates,* Part II, 3 May (1956): 7110.

24. Singh, "Reform of Personal Law," note 1.

25. Singh, "Reform of Personal Law," note 1.

26. Singh, "Reform of Personal Law," note 1.

27. *Mohammad Ahmed Khan v. Shah Bano,* A.I.R. (1985) S.C. 945.

28. Asghar Ali Engineer, ed., *The Shah Bano Controversy* (Hyderabad: Orient Longman Ltd., 1987), 9, 12–13.

29. Engineer, ed., *Shah Bano,* note 28 at 12–13.

30. Agnihotri and Palriwala, "Tradition," note 5.
31. Agnihotri and Palriwala, "Tradition," note 5.
32. Agnihotri and Palriwala, "Tradition," note 5.
33. Agnihotri and Palriwala, "Tradition," note 5.
34. Engineer, ed., *Shah Bano*, note 28 at 112.
35. Engineer, ed., *Shah Bano*, note 28 at 14.
36. Engineer, ed., *Shah Bano*, note 28 at 114.
37. *State of Bombay v. Narasu Appa*, A.I.R. (1952) Bombay 1984.
38. *Srinivasa v. Saraswati Ammal*, A.I.R. (1952) Madras 193.
39. *Davis v. Beason* 133 U.S. 333 (1890).
40. *Reynolds v. United States* 98 U.S. 145 (1879).
41. *Dr. Swarka Bhai v. Nainan Mathews*, A.I.R. (1953) Madras 792.
42. Section 497 of the Indian Penal Code states:

Adultery—whoever has sexual intercourse with a person who is and whom he knows or has reason to believe to be the wife of another man, without the consent or connivance of that man, such sexual intercourse not amounting to the offence or rape, is guilty of the offence of adultery, and shall be punished with imprisonment of either description for a term which may extend to five years or with fine or with both. In such case the wife shall not be punishable as an abettor.

43. *Sumithri v. U.O.I.*, A.I.R. (1985) S.C. 1618.
44. *T. Sareetha v. T. Venkata Subhaiah*, A.I.R. (1983) A.P. 356.
45. AIR 1984 S.C. 1562.
46. A departure was made from this viewpoint in a Delhi High Court Judgment in *Garg v. Garg*, A.I.R. (1978) Delhi 269.
47. *Bhurao v. State of Maharashtra*, A.I.R. (1965) S.C. 1564.
48. 2 S.C.R. 1019 (1979) and 2 S.C.R. 1171 (1979).
49. We come across many such cases in the legal cell for women run by the Janvadi Mahila Samiti, New Delhi.
50. We have also experienced this while working with the Janvadi Mahila Samiti.
51. *Tukaram v. State of Maharashtra*, A.I.R. (1979) S.C. 185.
52. *Premchand and Another v. State of Haryana*, A.I.R. (1989) S.C. 937.
53. *State of Haryana v. Premchand and others*, A.I.R. (1990) S.C. 538.
54. See *Harpal Singh v. State of H.P.*, A.I.R. (1981) S.C. 753; and *Bhoginibhai Hirjabhai v. State of Gujarat*, A.I.R. (1983) S.C.
55. *Mohamad Habib v. State*, Delhi, *Criminal Law Journal* (1989): 137.
56. *Rafiq v. State of U.P.* 1 S.C.R. 402 (1981).
57. *Sheikh Zakir v. State of Bihar*, A.I.R. (1983) S.C. 911.
58. In a case that AIDWA, a women's organization, investigated concerning the rape of two nuns in August 1990 in Gauraula, a small town in U.P., they found that the police had not bothered to collect evidence like the clothes sheet on which the rape was committed. The police took the nuns (young girls) for medical examination after 12 hours. The doctor's report was also cursory and showed her bias; in one report the doctor had concluded by saying that the nun, just because her hymen was broken, was used to sexual intercourse and no rape had taken place. The doctor disregarded all marks of physical injury observable on the victim.

59. E.g., *Lichhamadevi v. State of Rajasthan*, A.I.R. (1988) S.C. 1785.
60. Section 304B, Indian Penal Code.
61. Section 498A, Indian Penal Code:

498 A Husband or relative of husband of woman subjecting her to cruelty. Whoever being the husband or the relative of the husband of a woman subjects such woman to cruelty shall be punished with imprisonment for a term which may extend to three years and shall also be liable to fine.
Explanation—for the purpose of the section:
"Cruelty" means—
(a) Any wilful conduct which is of such a nature as is likely to drive the woman to commit suicide or to cause grave injury or danger to life, limb or health (whether mental or physical of the woman);
         or
(b) harassment of the woman where such harassment is with a view to coercing her or any person related to her to meet any unlawful demand for any property or valuable security or is on account of failure by her or any person related to her to meet such demand.

62. Rahman, "Test Case," note 3 at 490, where the author argues that the *Shah Bano* decision cannot be considered a limitation prescribed by law. Rather, the *Shah Bano* judgment was only an interpretation of Section 125 of the Criminal Procedure Code.
63. Rahman, "Test Case," note 3 at 487.
64. Rahman, "Test Case," note 3.

Chapter 17
Challenges to the Application of International Women's Human Rights in the Sudan

Asma Mohamed Abdel Halim

Introduction

The struggle for women's rights in the Sudan started nearly fifty years ago. At that time, few women were educated and those who were lived mainly in the major cities. The Sudanese Women's Union fought fiercely for women's rights and promoted women's education. The Women's Union and other groups had a great impact on changing the personal law rules at that time so that they were less harsh.

The struggle for women's rights continues today. Only recently have women begun to address women's rights as human rights. Women, particularly those active on a grass-roots level, have never addressed their problems in terms of international law, but women have challenged discriminatory laws by relying strictly on those mechanisms available within the domestic law. This chapter will address the challenges to the application of international law of human rights in the Sudan.

As a religious state the Sudan has adopted, since 1983, laws based on Islamic law. The fundamental sources of Islamic law are the Qur'an, which is believed to be the literal word of God, and the Sunna, the traditions of the Prophet Mohammed. Both the Qur'an and the Sunna have been subjects of extensive interpretation and counter-interpretation since the death of the Prophet in 632.[1] This process has resulted in the Shari'a, the comprehensive codes governing subjects ranging from religious dogma and practice to ethical norms and rules of private law. Individual rights are governed by the Shari'a. Customary law governs the parts of the country that are predominantly Christian.

The interpretation of Qur'anic verses is an important part, perhaps the most important part, of law-making in Muslim nations. Sudanese law-makers have, unfortunately for women, adhered to an interpretation of the Qur'an that has resulted in laws that discriminate on the basis of gender.

The Sudan has, at times in the recent past, had various constitutions that guaranteed equality of the sexes. These constitutional guarantees have not protected women from inequalities written into domestic law. For example, Article 17(1) and (12) of the 1973 Permanent Constitution guaranteed equality of all people before the law and equality of all citizens in duties, rights, and employment opportunities without discrimination on the basis of place of birth, race, color, sex, religious, or political stand. This article was disregarded when Shari'a law was applied in 1983. Additionally, the Evidence Act of 1983, which is part of the Islamic Codes, provides that the testimony of one woman is not considered credible, whereas the testimony of two women or one man is. A group of women and men, the Republican Brothers, challenged the law in the courts but were hindered by a procedural rule requiring litigants to be personally aggrieved by the particular law challenged. Moreover, the Transitional Constitution of 1985, which likewise granted equality, was not invoked to strike down discriminatory provisions in important legislation, such as the Civil Procedure Act and the Evidence Act, enacted in 1983. These same rules, with the addition of the expressly discriminatory Personal Law for Muslims Act of 1991, continue to exist today without any real legal challenge by women.

Based on the nation's history of disregarding its own constitutional provisions, it is not surprising that international law protecting the rights of women was not respected during the law-making process. International norms against discrimination on the basis of religion have also been disregarded by the Sudan. For example, the Supreme Court has allowed evidence given by non-Muslims to be treated as of a lesser value when given against a Muslim.[2] Sudanese authorities are inclined to justify their disregard of international law on the grounds of religion. In the Sudan, law is equated with religion, and therefore, as the governmental authorities argue, it should remain free from interference by the international community.

In this chapter, I will describe a brief history of the law in the Sudan and the current legal status of women. Women seeking greater rights in the Sudan face great challenges posed by the current method of interpretation of the Shari'a, by religious conventions, and by resistance to the use of international law. An understanding of these challenges is a precursor to exploring means of obtaining greater rights for women. This chapter does not purport to offer concrete solutions to existing problems but rather tries to focus on the challenges facing women in the Sudan.

Historical Background

Throughout its history the Sudan has endured governance under differing constitutional and legal systems. The Funj Sultanate period applied Islamic or Christian rules to its subjects. The Turkish Colonization period (1821–84) applied Islamic rules to personal law and a secular system to other affairs. The Mahadist State (1884–99) applied the Islamic code to all aspects of its subjects' lives. The fall of the Mahadist State in 1899 was followed by an Anglo-Egyptian government. In this period, three systems were applied in the Sudan:

(1) Common Law applied to civil transactions.
(2) Shari'a or Islamic Codes governed personal law.
(3) Customary law or other religious rules governed those who belong to traditional religions and different religious groups, especially in the Southern Provinces.

Over the years from 1899 to 1983, the Sudan evolved into a common law country. In the absence of applicable Sudanese law, courts employed a provision of the Civil Procedure Act regarding "Equity and Good Conscience" as the basis for the use of common law.[3] The statutes adopted during this period (except for a short period of application of the civil law adopted from the Egyptian Codes), were drafted and interpreted according to common law rules. The first and second Constitutions were also adopted during this period, in 1964 and 1973 respectively.

Islamization of all laws took place suddenly in September 1983. The Islamic Codes implemented at the time are still known as the September Laws. Islamization of all laws resolved any conflict of law questions that arose during the pre-1983 era when the common law and Shari'a law were in simultaneous use. As one scholar commented, "The conflict between Shari'a and other rules has been resolved in favor of the former. One can safely state now that under these laws, Shari'a rules are supreme."[4]

Islamization was clearly a political move, following a three-month-long judges' strike that created a constitutional vacuum. The military regime in power at the time felt that it was losing ground and sought to strengthen its position among the people by enacting the Islamic Codes. Yet, due to the regime's extremely harsh interpretation and application of the codes, the move was one of the reasons leading to the regime's downfall in April 1985.

A coup in 1985 ushered in a democratic government. This government enacted a transitional constitution in 1985, which, like its 1973 precursor, prohibited sex discrimination and conferred equality between the sexes. Despite these constitutional guarantees, the major legislation enacted while these constitutions were in effect subordinated women. The Revolutionary Council of the 1985 Coup did, however, ratify the International Covenant on Civil and Political Rights (ICCPR) in 1986[5] and now the Sudan is also party to the Optional Protocol to the Covenant allowing individuals to file communications alleging violations of the Covenant.[6]

Despite all the defects that appeared in the Islamic Codes (even by the standards of traditional schools), and the defects that accompanied their application, the democratic government did not effect any major change or repeal the codes. Every political party at that time benefited from the Islamic commitment of the people of Northern and Central Sudan. Thus political parties thought of easing the rigor of the Codes but did not repeal them. In any event, a general relief could be felt when the Constituent Assembly, the legislative body, voted to halt execution of judgments of amputation.

The democratic era was short-lived. It ended in 1989 when another military coup, referred to as the "National Salvation Revolution," succeeded. In June 1989 the Constitution was suspended. The regime advocated its version of "Islamization," in which Islamic rules were to be applied to all aspects of life. In order to attain such Islamization, the regime advocated the reconstruction of all aspects of social life through a program of education. It included measures requiring the veiling of women. The most important law enacted since the coup has been the dominant Personal Law for Muslims Act of 1991 (another translation of the title of this law adopted by some lawyers is "The Personal Matters for Muslims Act of 1991"), which explicitly subordinates women.

Since the 1989 coup's suspension of the transitional constitution, there has not been any single document that can be referred to as a constitution. Laws have been passed according to Constitutional Decrees (*Marsoum Dustoury*), which the Revolutionary Council of National Salvation has issued from time to time. Six Constitutional Decrees have been issued so far, and none mentions individual rights. In the first decree, the government ordered that all existing laws be enforced until amended in accordance with that decree. This means that all the acts ratifying international conventions remain in force, which in turn, means that the government has not repudiated its obligations under the international and regional conventions and treaties.

Despite the Sudan's two previous constitutions, which both prohibited gender discrimination and its ratification of international and regional human rights instruments, subordination of women has always been and continues to be part of the law.

The Status of Women Under Islamic and Customary Law

In many countries, written law expressly guarantees equal rights and opportunities for women. Despite this, women may still face difficulties overcoming a patriarchal administration of the law. The case of the Sudan is different. The letter of the law is discriminatory: women are considered expressly unequal and subordinate. Much attention is given to women in the law. Unfortunately, to the detriment of women, all this attention is given to women solely to ensure that no one mistakenly believes women to be equal to men. The law does, however, hold all women to be equally unequal to men.

The Shari'a, which has governed Muslims, accords partial and very limited rights to women. Under the Shari'a, women have the rights to a full and independent legal personality, to make contracts (excluding marriage contracts), to own property, and to share in inheritance. There is, however, no semblance of equality between men and women. Men have dominant rights regarding marriage and serve as the guardians of women.

The Shari'a still governs the rights of women. In addition, a recent statute, the Personal Law for Muslims Act (hereinafter Personal Law Act) was enacted in 1991. In regard to women's rights, the Personal Law Act does not deviate much from the Shari'a. Under this law, private matters between a husband and wife have become the concern of the public. As discussed in detail below, the act's stringent and close regulation of the private sphere between women and men, coupled with a judicial circular that women should dress in loose long dresses and cover their heads, will have tremendous impact on the education and employment of women outside the home.

According to the Personal Law Act, a woman cannot contract her own marriage. She has to have a male guardian (*wali*). Even in the absence of a male in the family, a woman may not contract her own marriage nor can she be guardian to another woman, such as her daughter.

A male guardian is responsible for concluding a marriage for a woman, but the woman's consent to the marriage is required. If the woman does not consent to the proposed marriage, she has the right to challenge the guardian in court. However, if the woman does not challenge the marriage in a court, or if the court upholds the marriage contract, the woman will be bound by the marriage.

If a woman marries against the guardian's will or in his absence, the wali may annul the marriage. The guardian of an adult woman may seek to annul her marriage if it is contracted against his will, and if he deems the husband to be unsuitable. The law affords the woman a chance to challenge her guardian in court, but there is no guarantee that she will be able to have the judge contract her marriage, for the court may well agree with the guardian that he has the right to annul or stop the marriage.

The Personal Law for Muslims Act specifies that a guardian has the right to determine the suitability (*Kafaa*) of a husband for a woman. Section 19 of the act, addressed to men only, lists the women whom a man cannot marry. There is no corresponding section delineating the men a woman could or could not marry. According to the law-makers such a section is unnecessary because a woman does not have a say on the suitability of her husband to be. Her guardian has the exclusive right to judge the suitability of a husband.

The Personal Law for Muslims Act further provides that during marriage the wife is required to obey the husband and care for him by protecting herself and his property. In return, she has the right to maintenance and permission to visit parents and relatives. Permission by the husband should be granted "within reason," although he does have discretion which he may reasonably use to regulate visitation rights. Under the Shari'a, a woman's right to leave her home to visit others was customarily subject to her husband's approval. Although a woman's ability to go where she wished was customarily conditioned on her husband's approval, the restrictions were rather relaxed. Under the Personal Law Act, these restrictions are written into law.

There are parts of the country where women are not confined to their homes, such as western Sudan where women are the providers of food for their family from the small plots they farm. Nevertheless, even in these areas, the law may be used against a woman who shows the slightest resistance to the husband's authority, in that he may be able to confine her to the home by saying that he will take the responsibility for providing food for the home. The law will serve then as a tool of subordination—a woman in such a situation may offer no resistance when her husband claims her money or causes her to spend that money to fulfill his duties (e.g., buying clothes for the children). Knowing that the husband has the authority to regulate her life, a wife may submit to a treatment harsher than that provided for by the law.

Moreover, the Personal Law Act allows the marriage contract to contain conditions stipulated in favor of the wife. However, even if the husband agrees to a condition at the time the contract is concluded, he will not be obligated to adhere to it if it is deemed to violate the essence of the marriage contract. For example, a condition that the wife will not go to live in a home other than the one prepared by the husband at the time of the marriage will be deemed not to violate the essence of the marriage contract, and the husband will be obligated by it. However, a husband may breach a condition that the wife will keep her job after marriage and forbid her to go to work, unless he is being "unreasonable." To my knowledge, the only time that a husband may be held "unreasonable" on this issue is when he cannot provide the necessities of life. In that case, the wife is entitled to a divorce anyway. Similarly, a condition that the husband will not be allowed to take a second wife will be held to violate the essence of the contract and, therefore, will not be binding on the husband.

Another instance of inequality under the Personal Law Act is the status of women in the dissolution of marriage. The man has an unfettered right to divorce. He, of course, may be urged to honor the marriage and warned that divorce, although permitted, is a hated act. Nevertheless, if a man says the words "You are divorced," a divorce takes place. On the other hand, a woman must go to court and establish an acceptable basis for divorce, such as impotence, violence, or the inability to provide necessities of life.

After the divorce, a three-month period of "constructive" marriage begins. During this three-month period, the husband has the option of having his wife "returned" regardless of her consent. If she does not obey the husband, she is considered *nashiz* (disobedient). The *ragaa* or right to reclaim a divorced wife within a period of three months is exclusively a husband's, and the wife should comply.

Even a woman's job as a homemaker is threatened by male dominance in all spheres of domestic life. Wives perform duties according to the husband's directions. A divorced mother who has custody of her children is responsible for their physical well-being, but a father (or a guardian on their father's side) is responsible for their moral and intellectual upbringing.

In addition to matters of marriage and divorce, women's rights are restricted in other regards. A woman's testimony is only given limited effect: the testimony of two women is given the same credibility as the testimony of one man. A woman is precluded from testifying in certain crimes, for instance *zina* (fornication). Witnesses to documents may be either two men or one man and two women.[7] Thus a woman may conclude a contract of a million pounds for her own business, but she is not recognized as a witness in a similar contract. A woman who cannot be her own guardian and who cannot be trusted to give a credible account of any event under oath is obviously precluded from public office and decision-making positions.

A woman's freedom of movement is also subject to discrimination. A woman cannot travel on her own: she must have a man travel with her or, alternatively, she must have written permission from her guardian. A woman can only be accompanied by her husband or by a *mahram*—someone she cannot be married to, such as a brother or an uncle. Travel for religious pilgrimages is not possible except with a mahram, or, for a woman over 50 years old, a trustworthy companion. A woman traveling with a mahram other than a husband or a father should get the written consent of her husband, if married, or of her father. If the father is dead, she needs the consent of the guardian who replaced the deceased father.

In addition to the prohibition against women traveling alone, a woman is subject to differing treatment regarding the issuance of a visa. Both men and women have to obtain an exit visa to be able to travel abroad, but a woman has to appear before a "Women's Committee" that interviews the woman on the reasons why she wants to travel. If the written permission of the guardian is not produced before that committee, which may consist of just one person conducting the interview, no exit visa will be issued. Women traveling for educational purposes (to attend universities, brief conferences, or workshops) will be issued an exit visa when they submit documents showing the invitation with the clear address of the invitor.

Most other statutes, such as the Public Employment Act which provides for near equality in public employment situations, remain almost free of any discrimination or subordination. But, because all women are subordinate to their husbands, these statutes pertain only to the few women who are allowed by their husbands and other male guardians to work outside their homes. Thus, the Personal Law for Muslims Act has rendered equality in any other statutes valueless.

The Islamic Codes of 1983 were not enacted in a vacuum. At the time of their enactment, the Sudan was a Muslim society in which women were already serving as judges, managers, lawyers, and other professionals. The conflicts in this situation are apparent. Female judges are necessarily guardians who attest to documents that they lack the ability to witness. In a personal law court, a female judge may issue a judgment that divorces a woman from her husband, or a judgment that a woman can marry a certain man against her guardian's will, but at the same time she (the judge) cannot contract her own marriage. This double standard in the status of women is tolerated for political reasons: the ruling regimes want to avoid the international reaction that would ensue if professional women were suddenly reduced to second class citizens. It also serves as a buffer for the attacks already being launched by and on behalf of women. The state may give token recognition to equality of men and women by placing some women in governmental offices and appointing some to the appointed legislative body. Lip service may be paid to the important role of women in the development of the country, but women are only permitted to perform the role designed for them by the ruling patriarch.

The Islamic Shari'a rules that are applied in the Sudan are not the only rules that deny women's rights. Customary law in some parts of the Sudan treats a woman as property bought by her husband from her father. On the husband's death she is inherited by the oldest son, who is not her own son, or the nearest of kin of the deceased. The law allows non-Muslim groups to keep their customs. No attempt is made to educate these groups for change because the only change anticipated is Islamization of those groups.[8] Women are the victims of both situations. In customary law they are property and in the patriarchal version of Islamic law they are minors, who are mainly dependent on husbands or the nearest of kin.

In sum, under both Islamic law and customary law in the Sudan, it is the prerogative of the husband to subordinate his wife. Any argument that this subordination is restricted only to the home is defeated by the fact that outside the home, women's existence is barely noticed. Subordination in the home leads to discrimination in public as well.

Subordination of women leads to discrimination in the distribution of whatever resources the state has. A dependent woman may not be given an equal share in development schemes such as mechanized farms, and even worse, development schemes may deprive women of whatever traditional farming or milk production occupations they may have. This has in fact already taken place. Mechanized agriculture proved to be designed for, and to employ, men. As a result women fell back into poverty as they were deprived of their traditional occupations of producing food for family consumption and milk for sale.[9]

Obstacles to Women Seeking Equality in the Sudan: The Difficulties and Prospects of Progress

Women in the Sudan face many obstacles in the equal rights espoused in international human rights law. One very serious barrier to gender equality is the manner in which Islamic law has been interpreted.[10] New laws enacted since the Islamization of 1983, including the Personal Law for Muslims Act, have been based on an interpretation of the Qur'anic verses intended to keep the culture and customs that subordinate women intact. The culture and customs that subordinate women are not inseparable from Islam. As discussed in more detail below, interpretation of Shari'a in a discriminatory manner is, in the least, unnecessary. The same broad guarantees found in international human rights documents such as the Universal Declaration of Human Rights can be found in an "enlightened construction" of the Qur'an and Sunna.[11]

Thus the development of new scholarship regarding the interpretation of Islamic rules is a necessary step in the move forward for women. The reinterpretation of Islamic law in a manner consistent with equality for women is very significant. It will not only help women seeking equal rights strictly within the Islamic tradition, but will also decrease the resistance to the use of international human rights norms. International human rights standards have a greater chance of being accepted if they reflect cultural norms.

A second formidable obstacle facing human rights advocates is resistance by Sudanese legislators or judges to the application of the notions of equality found in international and regional human rights instruments. These are seen as secular intrusions into the Muslim religion.

Finally, it is important to understand the difficulties faced by women living in the Sudan, in a culture where the notion of liberation of women has been manipulated by the dominant patriarchy in an attempt to persuade women that what they want is liberation from secular international/western ideas rather than from the Islamic patriarchy that protects and cares for them. I will begin with this last issue first.

Manipulation of the Concept of Women's Liberation

In general, the notion of women's liberation is conceived of as women's struggle against male dominance and patriarchy, in the quest for equal rights and an end to gender discrimination. In the Sudan, the notion of the liberation of women is being twisted. Muslim women are being told, by Muslim men, that patriarchy is not what is hindering them, that international law (seen as inseparable from western ideas and ideals) is the real obstacle to women. As Abdul Karim Shiraz asserts, women should be liberated from western ideas that are subjecting them to the double burden of domestic and public work responsibilities.[12] Evidently the men advocating these concepts of liberation believe that there is no need for women to take up the task of this liberation, as the men will gladly do it for them, ensuring that it will then be a smooth "Islamic" process as long as it is kept outside the ambit of secular international law.

The patriarchs working to promote such "liberation" of women have felt no obligation to look into the responsibilities assigned to women in traditional Shari'a interpretation. The role of a woman under a traditional interpretation of the Shari'a is that of a wife and child-bearer. There is no obligation on the woman to provide housekeeping services for the matrimonial home. According to traditional Shari'a, any housework done by the woman entitles her to payment. Even that traditional role tried to strike a balance of justice in the status of women. Since they were totally subject to the authority of men and to a strict rule of seclusion, they were entitled to protection from abuse. Omer ibn Ilkhatab presents a clear example in his well-known answer to the question why he bore his wife's ill-temper. His answer was that she cooked for him, cleaned the house, washed his clothes, combed his hair, and that none of that was her responsibility.[13]

However, even though it contradicts traditional Shari'a interpretation, the role of housekeeper has been customarily and historically assigned to women. Housekeeping duties were passed to women without any consideration in return. Scholars have found no need to address the issue from an "Islamic" point of view, nor has it been seen as necessary to find a proper explanation of these rules for the time we live in. The issue is simply avoided, even though it reduces women to less than their historical role.

Even aside from any considerations of secular international law, Muslim men should take up the task of giving women credit for housekeeping "labor" or "liberate" them from that burden of unpaid labor. That step by men is hardly foreseen, because "we are a backward society that has inherited a heavy load of traditions and ideas that are not only repugnant to our time and life but are, at the same degree, repugnant to the correct Islamic Shari'a."[14]

The Patriarchal Interpretation of Islamic Law

The interpretation and application of the Shari'a are products of human efforts in the particular historical context of the eighth and ninth centuries.[15] Given this historical context, it is understandable that the Shari'a would be greatly affected by the historically patriarchal attitude toward women.

For example, in an Islamic community that existed during Mohammed's time, both women and men occupied public space while participating in the social and economic life of the community. This historical model has been overshadowed by the customs of secluding and veiling women, which are the result of the patriarchy that dominated interpretation of Islamic rules for centuries.

A closer look at the veiling of women, known as *Ziyy al-Islami,* which intensifies gender discrimination, helps to show how interpretation of the Shari'a is affected by patriarchy. Some women who say they are religiously conscious accept veiling as a way of bringing women to the outside world of males. In her article, Margot Badran adopts the argument that

If the new dress is a strategy for helping women enter the "male" public sphere, as El Gunidi asserts, the *mitadayyinat* [the pious] are acknowledging a fundamental inequality in the definition of that space. They do not perceive that the notion of male public sphere may be simply a patriarchal construct nor do they invoke, as they might, the historical model of the *Umma* or the Islamic Community of Mohammed's time, when both women and men occupied public space while participating in the social and economic life of the community.[16]

It is clear how the patriarchal notion of the male public sphere has affected interpretation of Islamic law regarding women entering the public sphere. Moreover, a patriarchal version of history is responsible for subordinating women and infecting them with the belief that they are to be guided and guarded. It suggests that women, once unveiled, cannot think properly and become a source of evil—the very weak point of a nation through which an enemy may enter and destroy the society. Historically, the fall of great nations was attributed to the unveiling of women.[17]

"Unveiling" the falsity of the above idea is possible through interpretations that are not compelled by patriarchy and that are sensitive to women's perspectives. Indeed, an understanding that many of the discriminatory aspects of the Shari'a can be understood in light of the patriarchal historical context does not serve as any basis for concluding that those interpretations are still justified. Rather, advocates of women's rights should examine methods of reforming Islamic law to eliminate its gender discriminatory aspects without losing its religious legitimacy for Muslims.

The process of reformulating Islamic law to adapt to changed circumstances is not new: it has been an ongoing process. Throughout fourteen centuries of Islamic knowledge, Islamic rules were reinterpreted, modified, or simply treated as inapplicable to changed circumstances. There are many examples of this. Qur'anic verses dealing with slavery serve as good examples. No Muslim scholar, as far as my humble knowledge goes, will argue that the institution of slavery is presently sustainable in Islam, even though the practice of taking slaves through warfare was permissible under the Qur'an in earlier Islamic history. Moreover, the practice of distributing certain tax monies (*zakat*) to certain persons as described in Qur'anic verses was abandoned when circumstances dictated. Specifically, Omer Iln Elkhatab, the second

Khalifa after the Prophet's death, stopped giving zakat to those who had recently joined Islam or expected to join and financial help was one way to assure they stayed in or joined the faith. The cessation of this practice was not seen as a violation of Islamic law, even though it was contrary to a provision of the Qur'an.

In addition, the commercial activities of banking and insurance were not part of traditional Islamic knowledge. Yet that knowledge is elastic and flexible enough to accommodate such commercial activity. The broad basics of Islamic rules have been employed to create a new version of banking and insurance that are labeled Islamic.

Progress in the reinterpretation of Islamic law to adapt to modern circumstances with regard to women has been very limited. It is interesting to note that women have made at least one small step in this regard. Islamic rules regarding marriage have evolved from total dominance of the patriarch to a stage where the marriage can be annulled for lack of consent of the woman. Initially, the rules gave the male guardian absolute authority to marry off the woman under his control. Due to an increased rate of suicide among young girls unwilling to consummate these forced marriages and active attacks by women's groups, these harsh rules were changed.[18] The new rules repealed the guardian's power to compel a marriage. An adult woman's consent became essential before marriage, and a minor girl could only be married with the permission of the court. The law kept the concept of guardianship intact, but equipped women with a tool of protection. Women in urban areas were not reluctant to take their guardians to court to annul forced marriages. The few who took this step discouraged many fathers and other guardians from concluding marriages without consent.[19]

It is clear that the fundamental sources of Islamic law can be interpreted in a manner supportive of equality for women, and that the patriarchal system established in the name of Islam can likewise be changed in the name of religion. Despite this, women have been prisoners of old interpretations of the Qur'an and Sunna. Although Islamic rules were reinterpreted, modified, or simply treated as inapplicable to deal with changing circumstances in regard to slavery, modern commercial practice, and other matters, no such flexibility has been shown with regard to women's rights. For women the trend of interpretation has worked almost exclusively in the opposite direction, as the new status attained by women has been forced into the stringent old mold, where it does not fit. Instead of modifying the mold, the patriarchy tries to shrink the women.

Thus it is apparent that flexibility in religious interpretation has generally only been used to accommodate the needs of men, not women.

Women's status as reserve workers illustrates this. Rules denying women's rights to work were stretched or changed when men deemed it necessary to keep an industry alive. For example, in the textile factories women were given good employment terms, flexible hours, and transportation.[20]

Reference to interpretations of the Shari'a in other Muslim countries may be useful in the attempt to achieve an enlightened interpretation of the Shari'a. As an example, Egypt has adopted the Hanafi interpretation, which is by no means modern but which allows a woman to contract her own marriage without any guardianship. Unfortunately, in many Islamic communities the trend has been to adapt Islamic rules to a patriarchal society and not vice versa.

One serious obstacle facing women who seek a reinterpretation of the Islamic sources is the fact that in the Sudan, the interpretation of Qur'an has been, and remains, the domain of males. Women's attempts at interpretation of Qur'anic verses and Sunna, a recent development, have met harsh resistance in all Islamic countries.

Women today in the Sudan are faced with the dangerous dilemma that certain religious ideas and interpretations are viewed as the only correct ones. Perhaps the only answer to this dilemma lies in realizing that when solutions are sought within the boundaries of religion, there may be no ultimate solution. Rather, the solution will be in providing a clear basic idea of justice and equality for all the members of humanity. It is in this regard that resort to international human rights documents may be necessary for women in the Sudan.

Resistance to the Use of International Human Rights Law to Improve the Status of Women in the Sudan

(a) Resistance to international human rights conventions

The Sudan as a state party to the International Covenant on Civil and Political Rights and its Optional Protocol is obligated to bring its laws, policies, and programs into compliance with the terms of the Covenant. Thus, the government is required to change those provisions of the Islamic codes that discriminate against women or otherwise deny them their civil and political rights. For example, the Personal Law for Muslims Act breaches articles 23(3) and (4) of the International Covenant for Civil and Political Rights. These articles hold states responsible for ensuring that no marriage shall be entered into without the free and full consent of both spouses, and the equality of rights and responsibilities of spouses during marriage and at its dissolution.

One approach for women's rights advocates lies in challenging gender discriminatory laws under mechanisms available in domestic law. During the time that the 1985 Constitution was in effect (prior to its suspension in 1989), a constitutional provision specifically afforded individuals the right to challenge violations of their rights under all domestic law, including any international conventions that were ratified by the Sudan. Thus a legal challenge might have resulted in a finding that these regulations were unconstitutional or in violation of the state's international obligations. Presently, in the absence of the Constitution and its provision affording individuals the right to challenge violations of their rights, there is a likelihood that a court may conclude it lacks the authority to determine such a claim.

In fact, since the Islamization of 1983, no cases challenging sex discrimination have been filed. The absence of litigation on this issue may be attributed to women choosing to raise their issues directly with governmental officials instead of litigating, or it may be due to fear of some sort of retaliation, since going to court is seen as an act against government. Alternatively, the lack of legal challenges may be due to the absence of the clear legal provision, such as that in the 1985 Constitution, which directly gave individuals the right to challenge a violation of their rights in court.

Even if a court in the Sudan were to hear a challenge to discriminatory domestic law, women would still face many obstacles in persuading the governmental authorities in the Sudan to respect the norms of international law. First of all, there is serious resistance to the Civil and Political Covenant and all international human rights conventions as western constructs. The belief that change and equality are western notions hinders the application of international human rights norms. Everything western, including music, literature, education, and art, is condemned, and men and women are told that western ideas contradict a good religious life. "Western ideals" are condemned, not for their content, but for being western. This allows equality to be confused with promiscuity.

It is thus left to human rights advocates to try to challenge the belief that international law should be disregarded because of its western influences. One effective approach may be to point out the tolerance of western ideas everyday in our lives. Western-style clothes are worn by men despite the different climate. Western education is our passage to development. If blind rejection of western influences could be overcome, people could freely choose the ideas, practices, and developments (including international standards of conduct) they find most appropriate for themselves.

Moreover, authorities will try to evade the applicability of the international conventions by an attack on "universality" and by emphasis on the differences between nations because of religion or customs, especially in the case of women's issues. Based on this, most Islamic and African countries seem to prefer to adopt regional or religious instruments instead of international ones. For example, many Islamic states have refused to ratify the Convention on the Elimination of All Forms of Discrimination Against Women (CEDAW) or have ratified it with reservations such as those entered by Bangladesh and Egypt. Like the Sudan, they may prefer to adhere to a regional religious instrument such as the Cairo Declaration of Human Rights in Islam.[21]

Perhaps most significant, religion is used as an excuse to breach and overlook international conventions.[22] Islam is both a religion and a legal system. Islamic law is believed to be divinely inspired, and thus seen as supreme to all other law, even international law. The tensions between Islamic law and international human rights law may cause some Islamic nations to justify on religious grounds their refusal to sign or ratify a treaty such as CEDAW or their reservations to such treaty. In the words of one scholar:

Here the latent tensions between Islamic and international law become, at least ostensibly, the cause of conflict—but there may be other reasons for rejecting international law. An official policy of repudiating international human rights standards in order to follow *shari'a* law may not necessarily be dictated by the religious piety of the persons who wield power, but may be a convenient pretext for denying freedoms that the government wishes to curtail for reasons of self-interest.[23]

As discussed above in the Sudan, the prevailing interpretations of the Shari'a are intended to keep the culture and customs that subordinate women intact. Women's rights advocates must demonstrate that such interpretations are not essential to the Islamic religion, and therefore cannot be sheltered from the obligations of international human rights law under the guise of religious freedom. In summary, women face serious difficulties in persuading Sudanese officials of their obligation under the International Covenant on Civil and Political Rights to eliminate any law or practice that subordinates women.

In addition to attempts to work domestically for the advancement of women's rights, human rights advocates in the Sudan may pursue the remedies available under international law for the violation of international law. This includes using the procedure under the Optional Protocol to the Covenant on Civil and Political Rights to file individual communications with the Human Rights Committee, established by the Covenant, concerning violations of women's civil and political rights in the Sudan. Although these options warrant further study,[24] the pursuit of international remedies in itself poses great difficulty and danger for women in Sudan.

Women in the Sudan would benefit greatly from any assistance by the United Nations, the Human Rights Committee, or other international bodies in persuading the nation to respect its international obligations. Unfortunately, little has been done in this regard. For example, the Human Rights Committee should scrutinize reports of states parties to ensure that they comply with their obligations under the Covenant even if those obligations are inconsistent with obligations the state has assumed under other international, regional, or religious instruments. Women's groups need to provide information to the Human Rights Committee that show where these inconsistencies exist and how they are detrimental to women's civil and political rights.

(b) Resistance to recognition of the equality guarantees in regional human rights law—the African Charter

In 1986 the Sudan ratified the African Charter on Human and Peoples' Rights, which is also referred to as the O.A.U. Convention on Non-Discrimination.[25] The Charter is enforceable in the Courts of Law of the Sudan after its ratification. Article 2 of the Charter stipulates that

Every individual shall be entitled to the enjoyment of the rights and freedoms recognized and guaranteed in the present Charter without distinction of any kind such as race, ethnic group, color, sex, language, religion, political or any other opinion, national and social origin fortune, birth or other status.

How does the Charter guarantee these rights? Article 18(3) stipulates that "The State shall ensure the elimination of every discrimination against women and also ensure the protection of the rights of the woman and child as stipulated in international declarations and conventions."

As a state party, the Sudan is bound to respect the Charter's obligations. However, authorities in the Sudan will likely deny that the Sudan's clearly discriminatory laws violate the state's obligation under the African Charter to eliminate sex discrimination. They may argue that the African Charter's obligation to eliminate discrimination is subject to domestic law, and that there is no obligation on the state to limit the rigor of its laws. For example, Article 12(1) of the Charter gives every individual the right to freedom of movement and residence within the borders of a state provided that he *abides by the law.* There is no explicit provision in this article as to the obligation of the state to make this law in accordance with any international law or convention. In addition, Article 12(2) provides that the right to leave or return to any country, including one's own country, may only be subject to restrictions "provided for by law for the protection of national security, law and order, public health or morality."

To buttress their argument, such authorities may compare this with Article 12 of the International Covenant on Civil and Political Rights, which provides that the right of the individual to liberty of movement may only be subject to restrictions that are provided by law and necessary for protection of national security, public order, public health, or morals, or the rights of others *and* which are consistent with other rights recognized in the Covenant.

In addition to article 12, other rights recognized by the African Charter are in most cases subject to domestic law. Articles 8, 9, 10, 11, and 14 expressly subject the rights embodied in them to the domestic law. For example, Article 14 guarantees the right to property but allows encroachment on that right "in the interest of public need or in the general interest of the Community and in accordance with provisions of appropriate laws." Authorities in the Sudan may well try to justify discriminatory practices on these grounds.

To illustrate this, consider the case of women in certain areas, particularly in the south, who may be deprived of the right to own land in the interest of tribal community and in accordance with appropriate laws. In all regions, a woman may be denied the right to allocation of plots distributed for housing because her husband is allocated one, or may be forced to take the plot provided that half of it is registered in her husband's name. Authorities can argue that such measures are permissible under Article 14 of the Charter.

In essence, the government may argue that discriminatory limitations upon rights are permissible under the Charter if domestic law so provides. A human rights advocate seeking to establish that any restriction on rights guaranteed by the Charter must be gender neutral must be prepared to meet these arguments. Although the African Charter is not as explicit as the ICCPR in declaring that all limitations upon rights must be consistent with other rights guaranteed in the Charter, it can be interpreted as implicitly limiting any domestic law restricting rights to those consistent with the other rights recognized in the Charter. In other words, gender discriminatory domestic laws are not to be tolerated under the Charter. In a recent case, the highest court in Botswana found this interpretation to be correct, holding that the Article 12 freedoms cannot be limited by discriminatory domestic laws.

In that case, a woman, Unity Dow, challenged the nation's nationality law, which indisputably discriminated against women, as a violation of the Botswana Constitution.[26] The Constitution prohibited discrimination based on race and origin, but did not specifically mention sex. The government argued that the omission of the word "sex" from the list of impermissible types of discrimination was intentional. The government argued that sex discrimination was essential to maintain and promote the patriarchal nature of the society.

The decision ruled unconstitutional the provision of the 1984 Citizenship Act that denied a female citizen of Botswana married to a foreign man the right to pass citizenship to her children born during the marriage in Botswana. The Court of Appeal held that this provision infringed on Dow's fundamental rights and freedoms, her liberty of movement, and her right to nondiscrimination. This Court, noting the obligations of Botswana as a party to the African Charter, stated that, even if the Charter was not given the power of law in the nation, Botswana was obligated to interpret its domestic law in a manner consistent with international obligations unless it would be impossible.[27] The Court of Appeal specifically cited Article 12 of the African Charter. The Court clearly interpreted the African Charter as imposing an obligation on parties to "ensure the elimination of every discrimination against their women folk."[28] This case clearly indicates that Botswana's highest court did not interpret the "as provided by law" language in Article 12 of the African Charter as an "escape clause" allowing the state to restrict the rights of women pursuant to discriminatory domestic law.

If women's rights advocates are unable to persuade Sudanese officials of the applicability of the Charter, or that discriminatory laws or practices violate Sudan's obligations under the Charter, recourse to the regional body set up to enforce the Charter is available. The African Charter provides for a Commission that may accept communications from individuals, states parties, or organizations. However, its power is severely limited. It may only make confidential recommendations to the government involved, ruling out any possible deterrent effect from public exposure. There is no entity that can function as a court with the power to make judgments upon human rights violations.[29] Women in the Sudan would benefit from greater assistance from regional bodies in an effort to enforce the equality provisions of the African Charter.

(c) The obstacle of regional Islamic human rights declarations

The member states of the Organization of the Islamic Conference adopted the Cairo Declaration of Human Rights in Islam in August 1990.[30] The Declaration appears to be a formulation of human rights as found in the Shari'a. Article 1 of the Declaration states that:

(a) All human beings form one family whose members are United by Submission to God and descent from Adam. All men are equal in terms of basic human dignity and basic obligations and responsibilities, without any discrimination on the grounds of race, color, language, sex, religious belief, political affiliation, social status or other considerations. True faith is the guarantee for enhancing such dignity along the path to human perfection.

(b) All human beings are God's Subjects, and the most loved by Him are those who are most useful to the rest of His Subjects, and no one has superiority over another except on the basis of piety and good deeds.

The article recognizes equality in "basic human dignity" without regard to sex. It makes express reference to superiority according to piety and good deeds without any reference to gender. Equality in basic human dignity does not mean equality of rights.

The only article that deals expressly with women, article 6, sheds light on the meaning implied by the term "basic human dignity." It provides:

(a) Woman is equal to man in human dignity, and has rights to enjoy as well as duties to perform, she has her own civil entity and financial independence, and the right to retain her name and lineage.

(b) The husband is responsible for the support and welfare of the family.

Article 6 indicates that human dignity is viewed as a concept inseparable from the differing roles assigned to men and women. Section (b) of the article draws the line and divides the responsibilities on basis of sex. Only husbands are to be the breadwinners. The term "human dignity" thus incorporates the view that differences between the tasks assumed by men and women are inevitable. It is consistent with a view in which tasks are assigned by the ruling patriarch, and usually based on gender. Women are responsible for household work and men for jobs outside the home.

Notwithstanding the granting of two important rights in section 6(a), the Cairo Declaration reconfirms the impaired and subordinate status of women in traditional Shari'a. The Cairo declaration plays a role supportive of male domination by putting the power to protect "morals" in the hands of men. The move towards making women's affairs "personal," and the concern of male guardians violates the international human rights of women. The Cairo Declaration, as such, is of no help to women's rights in the Sudan as it merely reiterates the status quo for women in the Sudan.

Women can nevertheless use the Declaration as a basis to push for further rights. The strength and empowerment Muslim women seek should stem from the two important rights set out in the Declaration. A woman with full capacity to manage her own financial affairs should have the capacity to contract her own marriage, and should be seen as responsible for her own acts and not be subject to a constant and absolute guardianship that overshadows her whole life.

The Cairo Declaration does not provide room for interpretation of its articles according to existing international conventions. Article 25, the last article of the Declaration, emphatically states that "The Islamic *Shari'a* is the only source of reference for the explanation or clarification of any of the articles of this Declaration."

Article 24 restricts all rights and freedoms by stating that "All rights and freedoms stipulated in this Declaration are subject to the Islamic Shari'ah." Article 23(b) has a condition for the "right to assume public office," that is, that it should be in accordance with the provisions of Shari'a. Thus the Shari'a eliminates the possibility that women may enjoy any of the freedoms provided for "all human beings" in any international convention or domestic law. This status is upheld by the declaration that all rights and freedoms are subject to Islamic Shari'a.

It is of interest to note that the Cairo Declaration in its rights granting provisions uses the terms "all human beings" (Articles 1, 2) and "everyone" (Articles 22 and 23). Article 19 refers to "all individuals." Article 12 is the only article that, in its English translation, addresses "man." It provides that "Every man shall have the right, within the framework of *Shari'ah,* to free movement and to select his place of residence whether inside or outside his country." In the Arabic text, Article 12 uses the term "person" instead of "man."

A human rights advocate may argue that the words "human beings," "all individuals," "everyone," and "every man," are being used interchangeably. Tempting as this argument may be, it is seriously weakened by the fact that Article 12, the only article that starts with the words "Every man," where the phrase is immediately followed by the words, "within the framework of *Shari'ah.*" Within the framework of the male-dominated Shari'a, a woman's movement has been directed and wholly governed by male restriction.

Thus the use of "every man" in the English translation of Article 12, or even the use of "every person" in the Arabic text, is limited by the phrase restricting the rights within the framework of the Shari'a. Since the right to free movement is only given to men under the Shari'a, Article 12 does not extend rights to women.

The Impact of International Organizations in the Struggle for Women's Rights in the Sudan

The pressures of the Civil War, economic change, and natural disasters have forced most of the ethnic groups ruled by customary law out of their traditional domains. In the east, west, and south, women have been forced out of their traditional status by pressing financial need. By moving toward the big northern and central cities they have been subjected to poverty and homelessness. In response to these pressures, the United Nations and other international bodies have maintained a daily presence in certain areas as providers of food and medicine. In addition to providing food and medicine, the United Nations has provided education in cooperation with the government.

Human rights advocates in the Sudan would be aided by greater contributions by the United Nations and other international agencies. I am not speaking of any direct intervention affecting the sovereignty of the state, such as taking up the task of setting up the curricula in schools. Rather, direct pressure on the state to live up to its commitment to the conventions it has ratified would be most helpful. In particular, the United Nations or other international agencies could encourage the government to recognize and cooperate with non-governmental organizations (NGOs).

The international community has come to know the blessing of non-governmental organizations who may have international or regional membership. NGOs proved to be active and effective in providing different types of help in times of need. Seen as a "western" activity, they may not be able to provide direct assistance on human rights, but they are an excellent source of support for their international members and contacts. They provide training for paralegal workers, networks for sharing information, and support systems for activists in hostile zones. As a result, the chances for organized groups to provide services locally are far greater than before.

Public denunciation of human rights abuses by those groups that function outside particular countries are effective in reducing the abuse of human rights. Again they may be dubbed "secular western voices," but the international acclaim accorded those bodies makes them difficult to ignore. As a matter of fact, the reports of those same NGOs on the progress of human rights in a certain area will be broadcast and printed in the press as strong proof, given by the state, of its good human rights record.

Education, popular and formal, of human rights is an issue that has not yet been seriously addressed in the Sudan. Again, collaboration and coordination between scholars and advocacy groups is essential for local government and non-governmental groups. The Sudan needs its women in its development process, and it has used them when pressed. Women proved to be a major force in the development process. Without getting equal rights in the development schemes and without being empowered to participate as partners, the subordinate status of women will result in their poverty and isolation.

Conclusion

As a state party to the International Covenant on Civil and Political Rights, its Optional Protocol, and the African Charter on Human and Peoples' Rights, the Sudan is obligated to launch a campaign to rid the nation of discrimination on the basis of gender. However, as described above, the state prefers to maintain the status quo. The state has avoided challenging customs alone for fear of provoking the patriarchs involved. In light of the Sudan's failure to assume responsibility for protecting women's rights, the duty must shift to advocates and scholars alike. Scholars and advocates must inspire and mobilize women to force the state to change its stand and to assume its responsibility for protecting women's rights.

In their struggle for equality, women in the Sudan must take on difficult obstacles, including the patriarchal interpretation of Islamic law and the corresponding resistance to the use of international human rights law. An active move by scholars to uncover methods of reformulating Islamic law that eliminate gender discrimination without losing its religious legitimacy will provide an important tool in achieving a paradigm shift in favor of women. Scholarship that leads to a reinterpretation of the Shari'a in a manner consistent with the international women's rights norms will provide a strong foundation for advocates and educators of human rights. Despite obstacles to the use of international and regional law, its use warrants further study and effort.

Coordination between human rights education groups, advocacy groups, and scholars is essential in the struggle for women's rights in the Sudan. As advocates of women's rights, scholars and activists must take new approaches. We must not be content with merely reporting on the status of women or merely using facts about the status of women for purposes of scholarship. Rather, we must communicate this information in a very simple, easily understood form to women and our society at large.

The obstacles are formidable and the tasks we need to undertake to achieve equal rights for women will not be easy. The patriarchs will be provoked by any move to liberate women from the bane of customs and tradition that are without value.

Notes

1. See generally Abdullahi Ahmed An-Naʿim, "State Responsibility Under International Human Rights Law to Change Religious and Customary Laws," Chapter 7 in this book; and Abdullahi Ahmed An-Naʿim, "Problems of Univer-

sal Cultural Legitimacy for Human Rights," in *Human Rights in Africa: Cross-Cultural Perspectives*, ed. Abdullahi An-Naʿim and Francis Deng (Washington, DC, Brookings Institution: 1990), 359.

2. *The Sudan Government v. Abdien Khieri & Others*, SC/83/1991, unreported.

3. See generally Z. Mustafa, *Common Law of the Sudan* (Oxford: Clarendon Press, 1971).

4. Dina S. Osman, "The Legal Status of Women in the Sudan," *Journal of East African Research and Development* 15 (1985): 134.

5. Legislative Supplement to the *Gazette* (Sudan) 1388 (15 March 1986).

6. United Nations, *Human Rights International Instruments Chart of Ratifications* as of 31 January 1993 U.N. Doc. St/HR/4/Rev. 7 (1993) at 8.

7. Civil Procedure Act 1983, First Schedule—Attestation of Documents.

8. For more details on customary law in the southern region, see Stubbs, "Customary Law of the Aweil District Dinkas," *Sudan Law Journal and Report* (1962): 450; Francis M. Deng, "The Family and Law of Torts in African Customary Law," *Sudan L.J. & Rep.* (1965): 535.

9. Balghis Bedri, "Women, Land Ownership, and Development," in *Empowerment and the Law: Strategies of Third World Women*, ed. Margaret Schuler (OEF International: McNaughton & Gunn Inc., 1986), 76.

10. See generally Abdullahi Ahmed An-Naʿim, *Toward an Islamic Reformation: Civil Liberties, Human Rights, and International Law* (Syracuse, NY: Syracuse University Press, 1990).

11. For further discussion of approaches to reconcile the fundamental sources of Islamic law with international human rights norms (including an argument for the abrogation of discriminatory verses of the Qur'an and the enactment of other verses of the Qur'an and sunna that support equality for women), see Abdullahi Ahmed An-Naʿim, "Islam, Islamic Law and Human Rights," in *Asian Perspectives on Human Rights*, ed. Claude Welch, Jr. and Virginia Leary (Boulder, CO: Westview Press, 1990), 47–48.

12. Abdul Karim Biazar Shiraz, *The Oppression of Women Throughout History* (Iran: BaʾThat Publishers, Islamic Lunar Year 1405 H), 88.

13. Ali al-Tantaway and Nagi al-Tantaway, *Akhbar Omer wa Akhbar Abdullah Ibn Omer*, 2d ed. (Beirut: Al-Maktab Al-Islami, 1983), 298.

14. Ahmen Ali ElWadiey, *Status of Women in Yemani Law*, vol. II (Cairo: Arab Lawyers Union, 1989).

15. An-Naʿim, "Universal Cultural Legitimacy," note 1 at 359.

16. Margot Badran, "Islam Patriarchy and Feminism in the Middle East," Dossier 4, *Women Living Under Muslim Laws* (Montpellier, France: Women Living Under Muslim Laws, 1984).

17. Shirazi, *Oppression of Women*, note 12.

18. Judicial Circular No. 54 of 1960.

19. Osman, "Legal Status," note 4.

20. Asha Abdulla, *Women and Social Security* (Khartoum: Welfare Department of the Sudan, 1991).

21. Columbia University Center for the Study of Human Rights, *Twenty-Four Human Rights Documents* (New York: Center for the Study of Human Rights, 1992), 180–83.

22. See Virginia Leary, "When Does the Implementation of International Human Rights Constitute Interference into the Essentially Domestic Affairs of a State? The Interaction of Articles 2(7), 55, and 56 of the UN Charter," in

International Human Rights Law and Practice, ed. James C. Tuttle (Philadelphia: International Printing, 1978), 15–21.

23. Ann Elizabeth Mayer, "Current Muslim Thinking on Human Rights," in *Human Rights in Africa,* ed. An-Naʿim and Deng, note 1 at 36.

24. See generally Rebecca J. Cook, "Women's International Human Rights Law: The Way Forward," Chapter 1 in this book.

25. Adopted June 27, 1981, O.A.U. Doc. CAB/LEG/67/3 Rev. 5, entered into force October 21, 1986; see generally Claude E. Welch, Jr. "Human Rights and African Women: A Comparison of Protection Under Two Major Treaties," *Hum. Rts. Q.* 15 (1993): 549–74.

26. *Attorney General v. Unity Dow,* Ct. of App. of Bots., Civil Appeal No. 4/91 (unreported 1992). See generally Lisa C. Stratton, "The Right to Have Rights: Gender Discrimination in Nationality Laws," *Minn. L. Rev.* 77 (1992): 195–239.

27. *Unity Dow,* note 26 at 53. Domestic law should be interpreted in accord with international human rights standards unless such interpretation would do violence to the language of the domestic provision.

28. *Unity Dow,* note 26 at 83 (concurring opinion of Justice Aguda).

29. Issa G. Shivji, *The Concept of Human Rights in Africa* (London: CO-DESIRA, 1989), 104–05.

30. Cairo Declaration, in *Twenty-Four Human Rights Documents,* note 21 at 180–83.

Chapter 18

The Impact of Structural Adjustment Programs on Women's International Human Rights: The Example of Ghana

Akua Kuenyehia

Introduction

This paper is not an economic analysis of Economic Recovery Programs, neither does it seek to put forward any economic ideas. It is simply an attempt to put in the context of human rights the privations suffered by a section of one society as a result of programs fashioned by international financial institutions for the solution of the economic problems that have beset our nation for many years. The paper looks at the nature of these programs in the special context of Ghana and advocates that, important as it is that the economy be put on a sound basis, it is also necessary that the social cost of these programs be considered carefully and that every attempt be made to alleviate them so that the people most affected adversely would have a chance to enjoy their human rights.

The discourse on rights, and specifically human rights, has assumed immense significance and has become increasingly sophisticated in recent years. The question, however, is how women's rights and their international human rights feature in all these discussions. Even though women have enjoyed civil and political rights for some time, it has been contended that international human rights law has as yet not been applied to redress the disadvantages that are suffered by women for various and complex reasons. For women in Africa, there is the added complication of the effect on them of structural adjustment programs that have been going on for a decade or more. The severity of the socioeconomic conditions in African countries undergoing structural adjustment is such that it is questionable whether the whole discourse on rights and international human rights is at all relevant to African women.

The paper seeks in the following paragraphs to relate the scenarios of the circumstances of women and children in one African country undergoing structural adjustment to demonstrate the fact that, for women in this country and in many African and third world developing countries, the concerns really center around basic needs. Thus it is put forward the view that, in drawing up the agenda of issues of concern in women's international human rights, it is necessary to develop strategies that will address these basic needs and thus free the women to look at issues of other rights. The paper is divided into three parts: the nature and form of structural adjustment and how it impacts on the lives of women; what has been done to address some of the negative effects of the adjustment programs; and, finally, where that puts the African woman in the context of international human rights law.

The population of Ghana is currently estimated at 14.6 million.[1] In 1988 the national population was 48.1 percent male and 51.3 percent female. The proportions in rural areas were 48.8 percent and 51.2 percent; in urban areas excepting Accra, 47.1 percent and 52.1 percent; in Accra, 50.3 percent and 49.7 percent.[2] Of the total population, 30 percent are presently located in the urban areas and 70 percent in the rural areas.[3]

The Economic Recovery Program in Ghana (ERP)

In 1983 Ghana initiated an adjustment process the main objective of which was to arrest the decline in the economic and human conditions that characterized the 1970s and early 1980s. The country has since implemented a number of stabilization/adjustment programs: ERP (I) 1983–86 and ERP (II) comprising the Structural Adjustment Program (SAP I) in 1987–88 and SAP (II) in 1989–90.

The Economic Recovery Program I, 1983–86, was a traditional stabilization program whose major objectives were to shift relative prices and incentives in favor of production within the framework of fiscal and monetary discipline and to increase domestic saving and investment. In line with the stated objectives, the exchange rate was realigned to more realistic levels, government borrowing was reduced, interest rates were raised, and producer prices of cocoa, the main export, were increased. ERP (I) was succeeded by Structural Adjustment (SAP) I, which had two major objectives. First, it aimed to establish an incentive framework for stimulating growth, encouraging savings and investment, and strengthening the balance of payments.

Second, it aimed to improve use of resources, especially in the public sector, and ensure fiscal and monetary stability. The third phase of the stabilization/adjustment program was marked by SAP (II), which was directed at the continuing macroeconomic reforms initiated earlier. It was designed to provide the necessary infrastructural and institutional support to encourage private investment and production. SAP (II) also put some emphasis on alleviating poverty through the achievement of growth and employment objectives. From the above, it is clear that the objectives of the various stages of the Economic Recovery Program could not be achieved without some hard sacrifices on the part of the population. One of the first consequences of the program was the increased cost of imported goods as a result of the massive devaluation of the currency which is still ongoing. Devaluation meant that the cost of every imported item and service went up, immediately making it impossible for the most vulnerable people within the society, notably women and children, to obtain such goods and services. Coupled with the high prices of imported goods due to the realignment of the exchange rate, the prices of some other goods and services also rose because of higher taxes and cost-recovery in the provision of government services, for example, petroleum prices and utility tariffs.

The consequence of devaluation and an end to the administration of commodity prices is an increase in food prices and this represents a threat to the nutritional well-being of poor urban consumers and rural households who are net purchasers of food. The majority of the affected group happen to be women and children.

In line with the stated objectives of the Economic Recovery Program, there was a need to reduce the levels of employment within the government sector as well as the organized private sector. The Civil Service and Education Service had to reduce its staff by 45,000 during 1987–89 and the State Enterprises had to reduce staff by 20,000 during the same period. Even though the ERP is expected to generate increased employment in the medium to long term, there will be a significant time lag before the economy begins to absorb more labor. The hardships suffered by retrenched workers and their families is a real problem that needs to be addressed. Most displaced workers are clerical or unskilled workers and relatively young, thus creating a major problem of unemployment for a time.

Another consequence of the ERP is the cutback in government spending, stressing self-sustaining government agencies and institutions. Cutbacks in government spending affecting the health sector, education, and social services usually has adverse effects on the vulnerable groups in the short term, even though it is expected that in the medium to long term, under the ERP, there will be increases in public expenditure so that more resources can be devoted to social development.

Because women are in the majority of the groups that are vulnerable, they have suffered severe short-term hardships as a result of these adjustment programs. In Ghana, women play a variety of roles in the home and within the society and these roles place significant stress on them and their families. They are responsible for the welfare of their households and as a consequence are engaged in various activities. In addition to their reproductive function, they perform tasks such as undertaking income generating activities, providing food, fetching water and fuel, and taking care of children, the sick, and the aged. All these are at a great cost to their physical and mental health.

The ERP influences the export of agricultural produce, which has had an adverse effect on rural women who are mostly engaged in subsistence farming. As more land has been devoted to the production of export crops, some women have been rendered landless, while the whole process of commercialization has increased their workload without necessarily making them better off economically. This is because, even though women are actively engaged in the back-breaking work of clearing the land, planting, and harvesting, the actual marketing of the produce is done by men. Within their own subsistence farming, they have very little help from extension services, so that they are unable to take advantage of new ideas in farming that would help reduce the drudgery of their work, neither do they have access to new simple technologies.

It is obvious therefore that, in a situation where the ongoing economic adjustment programs produce increased costs, women are the first to be hit, and they and their children suffer most. The majority of these women are either among the urban poor or in the rural areas engaged in subsistence agriculture. Most often, these women are engaged in activities that are geared toward their very survival, and it is therefore questionable whether any talk of international human rights is relevant to them. The ERP is said to have achieved satisfactory growth rates of GDP and increased real government expenditure in the social sectors. However, at the household level, the living conditions of many Ghanaians continue to be generally poor, and the benefits of the economic recovery have yet to be widely distributed among the population.

Women still trek for hours looking for water and wood for fuel to cater for their families. They till the land using age-old farm implements to produce food. Their lot is not an easy one. Additionally, the short-term effect of the adjustment programs has been to further impoverish these women. There has been an increase in the number of children who have dropped out of school and have taken to the streets as a result of the substantial cuts in subsidies in the education sector. Some of these children are engaged in a variety of economic activities to support themselves and sometimes to help support their families. As subsidies have been removed from other sectors such as health, many women have been unable to use the health services where they do exist.

Measures to Address the Cost of Adjustment

The government of Ghana, in 1987, introduced a Programme of Actions to Mitigate the Social Costs of Adjustment (PAMSCAD). In the document introducing the program in 1987, the government said, "Even in today's improving conditions the plight of the poor and vulnerable remains desperate with limited access to health, education or good drinking water and severe constraints on their ability to produce and/or earn enough to meet their basic needs."[4] The dimensions of the problems generated by the Economic Recovery Programme were such that there had to be measures aimed at alleviating some of the hardships suffered by the most vulnerable groups. In the PAMSCAD document the government stated: "Conscious that the very sustainability of the economic reform effort could be endangered by inadequate attention to the social dimensions of economic recovery, the government has deemed it timely and indeed necessary to establish consistent action orientation aimed at redressing the plight of the poor and disadvantaged groups."[5] The government therefore introduced a program addressing the plight of specific groups that had been adversely affected by the Economic Recovery Programme; among these groups are women and their children. Among the stated rationales of the programs are that:

(a) The present and likely short-term conditions of poverty and deprivation of the poor groups, stemming either from pre-existing poverty or from measures in the design of the adjustment program (e.g., redeployment and price increases from further depreciation) warrant that a targeted, additional action program be implemented to alleviate the hardships of these groups.[6]

(b) PAMSCAD seeks to enhance the sustainability of the ERP. General improvements in the economy must be related to the condition of specific groups within the economy, bearing in mind that the experiences of some groups may create resistance to the implementation of the whole program. It is important to develop an action program that cushions the high costs of the ERP on the groups that have been particularly hit and those who are not experiencing the benefits of economic recovery.[7]

The program was introduced and implemented with donor support. The vulnerable groups identified for the purposes of the program were:

(1) Rural households especially in the northern and upper regions of the country that have low productivity and poor access to social services. These households also suffer from unemployment and hunger during the lean season.
(2) Low-income, unemployed, or under-employed urban households that lack productive economic opportunities and have suffered from the increase in prices of essential commodities.
(3) Retrenched workers from the civil service, state enterprises, and private enterprises, who lack productive employment opportunities. From the point of view of government, "the source of vulnerability of each of these groups points to areas where targeted interventions would prove to be most beneficial."

For example, for the small rural households in the north and other regions, income and nutrition supplements are required in the lean seasons; in the long term, their productivity needs to be increased. The programs have a strong poverty focus aimed at benefiting vulnerable groups. The projects for the interventions should have a high economic and social rate of return but with a recognition that for some of the projects, for example, supplementary feeding, it is not possible to quantify economic rates of return. Again in "sensitive areas (such as redeployment and education) which had been particularly adversely affected by the ERP, interventions should have high visibility, and should assure the target groups of the sincere efforts being made to cushion adjustment costs. This would serve to ensure the sustainability of the ERP, while alleviating the burden on the vulnerable groups."[8]

Within the stated rationale and objectives, a number of projects were chosen that included community initiative projects designed to enable communities themselves to identify and implement projects that would rehabilitate and construct the social and economic infrastructure, generate employment, and address the needs of vulnerable groups; a set of targeted employment generation projects that would provide productive jobs to the rural and urban unemployed and under-employed through public works projects and credit schemes for small-scale enterprises; a package of compensation, placement, and limited training for the redeployed; a number of projects designed to meet the basic needs of vulnerable groups through interventions in the areas of water and sanitation, health, nutrition, and shelter; and projects to improve access to the education infrastructure by vulnerable groups.

Thus came into being a program (PAMSCAD) designed to relieve and alleviate some of the harsh consequences of the ERP and its adjustment programs. Because women form a large proportion of the vulnerable groups and had suffered and are still suffering from the removal of subsidies from sectors such as health, education, and social services, as well as the realignment of the currency that has resulted in the escalation of prices of essential commodities, it was decided to set aside a part of the money to specially address their needs. Of the total amount of US$83.9 million, of which US$37.6 million is the foreign exchange component, US$2 million was given for the women's component of the program. The government further contributed 150 million local cedis as counterpart support in kind for staff salaries, fuel, and so forth. The women's component of PAMSCAD started in 1990 and is to last for an initial period of three years. The program has three clear objectives:

(1) To provide credit to enable women who are already engaged in income-generating activities to improve upon their performance and expand their operations where necessary.

(2) To provide training in basic bookkeeping and management techniques for those women as well as training for skills diversification.

(3) To assist them in acquiring simple appropriate technological implements in order to lighten their work load and relieve the drudgery of their lives.

The women's program is initially being carried out in three regions of the country and is expected to benefit a total of 7,200 women in these three regions. The credits under the PAMSCAD scheme are directed away from agricultural activities and are focused on other income-generating activities. The target beneficiaries are rural women and poor urban women. But in order to qualify for assistance, the woman must have been engaged in the particular income generating activity for at least twelve consecutive months. Thus the program effectively excludes, not only women engaged in agricultural activities, but also those who because of poverty are not able to engage in income generating activities. It must be noted that the majority of the vulnerable women in Ghana are rural women engaged in subsistence agriculture.

From 1990 to date, a total of 120 million local cedis has been disbursed to 3,120 women in the three pilot regions. The program assists women by giving them loans to help improve their business. The rate of interest is 20 percent and the loan cycle is six months. Repayments are on a weekly basis since their production and activities are normally organized around weekly market days. There are various savings incentives attached to the program designed to help the women mobilize savings, and one of the expected results of the program is to link the women to commercial banks for credit facilities to help their businesses in the future. Within the normal framework of things most rural women and urban poor women do not have access to credit from commercial banks because they are unable to meet the requirements of the banks.

From the size of the program it is obvious that, for the time being, a large majority of the women adversely affected by the ERP remain beyond any attempt at alleviating their hardships. What then are the implications of the consequences of structural adjustment for the human rights of women both within the domestic sphere and within the international community? How do states deal with the issue of human rights of women when their own policies implemented by them lead to violations of these rights? It is not possible for anyone to enjoy any human rights when basic needs are not met. What then can be done? Even though a state may have ratified the various international instruments on human rights, it still remains a fact that women in most African countries, especially those countries undergoing structural adjustment programs, are far from the realization of many of the rights identified in these international instruments. Many of these women continue to live in absolute poverty. Most have no access to safe drinking water or basic primary health care. Many cannot read or write and lack safe sanitation. There is therefore a need to devise strategies to address the relationship between structural adjustment programs of the World Bank, the IMF, and other international financial institutions and the enjoyment or fulfillment of economic, social, and cultural rights. As has been noted by the Special Rapporteur, "The conditions generally set by the IMF, which must be fulfilled by a recipient country prior to receiving financing from the World Bank or before being considered as internationally credit worthy, concern areas of state involvement which can have a decidedly negative influence, both directly and indirectly, on the attainment of economic, social and cultural rights."[9] The very notion of human rights obligations of the states undergoing structural adjustment is challenged by these conditions because they demand reductions in the expenditure that is aimed at creating the conditions for the enjoyment of the rights. Invariably these conditions demand the reduction of expenditure in the social sector and the removal of subsidies so that previously public services have to be paid for by users. This naturally excludes the vulnerable groups unable to pay from access to these essential services, notably health services and education. It has been asserted that "The negative consequences of structural adjustment on the human condition resulted in retrogression, rather than development, in the areas of nutrition, education, employment and social welfare. Human rights to food, education, work and social assistance have been rendered meaningless."[10] Women in Ghana and other African countries undergoing structural adjustment are thus doubly jeopardized because they already suffer sociocultural discrimination and the consequences of adjustment programs also fall heavily on them. With the reduction in public social expenditure, the pressures on women have increased in the recessional conditions created by these programs.

International Human Rights Law and Women

In the context of international human rights, it has been advocated that there must be a recharacterization of human rights in order to better make the concept more responsive to women's needs. To this end it would be necessary to make international human rights law more gender conscious and to recharacterize some if not most of the concepts. For example in relation to nondiscrimination, it has been advocated that there must be a move away from the "similarity and difference" model for determining what amounts to discrimination and to adopt the more appropriate "disadvantage" test in determining what constitutes discrimination against women. In relation to civil and political rights, it has been argued that the right to life ought to be expended from the traditional obligation of states to observe due process of law before the imposition of capital punishment, to include the situation where thousands of women die annually in third world countries from avoidable pregnancy-related causes. It is in this regard that the issue of structural adjustment ought to be taken account of as it has impacts on economic, social, and cultural rights of women.

So far, in spite of what the economists assert as to the value of structural adjustment programs, the indications are that these programs are not achieving their objectives. In spite of the growth of the GDP and exports, and in spite of improvements in such areas as external payments, there are still massive problems of malnutrition, abject poverty, and even starvation in African countries undergoing the programs. It has been observed that

it is essential to evaluate these programs with respect to their implications for the achievement of Africa's development and transformation objectives rather than merely on the basis of orthodox performance criteria such as GDP and export growth, balance of payments and budget balance which among others, are only at best marginally related to the achievement of Africa's central development objectives such as food self-sufficiency, poverty alleviation, sustainable growth and self-reliance.[11]

There is no doubt that the international community is actively engaged in rethinking the present form of these adjustment programs. In fact, it is this process that led UNICEF to advocate adjustment with a human face.

For women in Ghana and other African countries facing structural adjustment, the problems seem endless. They continue to have the responsibility for child care, producing food, gathering fuelwood and water, and taking care of sick members of the family. Those functions are economically invisible and yield little or no cash. Additionally, they have to engage in economic ventures to earn income in a climate that has been rendered increasingly hostile by a process of adjustment that has completely marginalized their productive activities. The implications for their human rights are enormous. Even at the best of times, most African governments pay only lip service to human rights. The fact that they are signatories to various international human rights treaties does not make the situation any better. Most of these governments fail to take the legislative steps necessary to make the provisions of these international human rights instruments directly applicable to their citizens. For example, the Convention on the Elimination of All Forms of Discrimination Against Women is a framework for the full and free participation of women in society. It guarantees to women their legal capacity to act as full citizens and spells out in great detail what discrimination needs to be ended to achieve that end. However, it will remain just rhetoric unless states parties take positive steps in the form of legislation to make the contents part of the national laws. The question that needs to be confronted, however, is whether the state can make these rights a reality for its women given the strict conditionalities that often accompany the funds that they so desperately need in order to put their economies in order. There is a real dilemma here to which a solution must be found if the women that are affected are to extricate themselves from the vicious cycle in which they are locked.

Because international human rights law has not been gender conscious in the past, the concerns of women generally and of African women in particular have not always received the attention that they need. This point has been made forcefully by many feminist writers as well as others.[12] As one writer put it,

substantively considered, the situation of women is not really like anything else. Doing something legal about something that is not like anything else is hard enough in a legal system that prides itself methodologically on reasoning by analogy. Add to this the specific exclusion or absence of women and women's concerns from the definition and design of this legal system since its founding, combined with its determined adherence to precedent, and you have a problem of systemic dimension.[13]

It is important that gender be taken account of in international human rights because many of the violations that women suffer are bound up with the various disadvantages that they suffer in the economic and social field. Any lack of attention to these economic, social, and cultural rights, therefore, leads to neglect of areas that are important for the advancement of women.[14]

What Can Be Done to Help?

The impact of structural adjustment on vulnerable groups, notably women and children, has received attention within the context of international human rights law and there is an ongoing discussion to find solutions to the problems raised. Various critical questions have been raised as to the appropriateness of the adjustment programs operated by the World Bank and the IMF. For example, the Special Rapporteur in his final report, *The Realization of Economic, Social, and Cultural Rights,* noted that "despite their obviously different economic structures, the structural adjustments negotiated with Sri Lanka, Ghana, Kenya, Zimbabwe, Costa Rica, Nicaragua, Nigeria and the Philippines were essentially the same." The report went on to say that "At an absolute minimum, the overriding tendency of adjustment measures to take on virtually the same components, notwithstanding the specific conditions prevailing within the adjusting country requires reconsideration."[15] So far, the theoretical framework being used has been the starting point for any requests for reconsideration. The problem is that it is obvious the conventional structural adjustment programs are not adequate in addressing the real causes of economic, financial, and social problems facing African countries. They have not succeeded in bringing about economic recovery and socioeconomic transformation. This is probably because the model—emphasizing the use of competitive domestic and external market forces—is not adapted to the African situation, which is said to be characterized by weak production structures and imperfect markets. The UN Economic Commission for Africa in advocating an African alternative framework to structural adjustment programs for socioeconomic recovery and transformation says:

Therefore, a more holistic approach is called for. This approach is in contrast to that of conventional stabilization and adjustment programs which isolate and address only a few aspects of the overall macro-economic set-up. While such partial approach of the conventional program could achieve its limited objectives, it could at the same time bring about adverse consequences for other aspects of sustainable development, such as growth, social welfare, equity, employment, and socio-economic transformation. More often than not, even the positive results that might be achieved through the conventional programs could be outweighed by such negative consequences.[16]

It goes on to say,

This holistic approach should identify the principal positive and negative factors impinging on development, the human and material resources whose constructive interactions provide the dynamism for development, and the network of institutions that should be fashioned to provide a suitable environment for the forces of change and development. It should also properly assess the possible interactions among different elements during the process of adjustment with transformation, so that appropriate strategies and policies can be formulated and implemented.[17]

The need for a reappraisal of structural adjustment from the point of view of international human rights has been recognized, and various approaches have been advocated. This is because there is no doubt that the adjustment policies presently being pursued by the international financial institutions in many cases have worsened rather than improved the situation of the poor. Real wages have fallen while there has been a reduction in access to health, sanitation, and education, especially among the vulnerable groups, notably women and their children. There is a need, therefore, for a concerted effort by human rights groups to try and influence the policies of international financial institutions so that they develop appropriate responses to the problems so far identified. If, as has been asserted, adjustment programs are unavoidable to resuscitate African and other third world economies, then it is suggested that the programs be reappraised in view of the experiences of the social impact that they have had so far and modified accordingly.

In order to address the human rights dimension of these programs, especially as they affect women, it is necessary to give a gender dimension to international human rights norms so that the experiences of these women will be brought into the redefinition of the various economic, social, and cultural rights. As has already been mentioned, even without the burden of adjustment programs most African governments at best pay lip service to human rights and are most reluctant to take legislative and other steps to incorporate rights contained in international human rights instruments into national laws. With the added burden of adjustment programs, they give up all pretense of adhering to their obligations, using these programs as their excuse. Even where, as in Ghana, attempts have been made to put in place a program to mitigate the social cost of adjustment, the component of that program allocated to women is so small as to make little if any impact on the plight of these women. Obviously women are yet to move from the background into the mainstream. There is a danger in such a situation because it is possible for these inadequate programs designed to mitigate the social impact of adjustment to be used as part of the rhetoric on the observance of human rights. One of the ways in which the vulnerable who are adversely affected by the adjustment process can be helped is by encouraging their participation in the development process at the national level. So far, the call for increasing participation in the development process has not really been heeded. As noted by the Special Rapporteur, "Decades of pleas for increasing levels of participation in the development process, principles about which are included, for instance, in the 1986 Declaration on the Rights to Development, have clearly yet to bear fruit."[18] If the people most affected by these programs are consulted on the measures designed to alleviate their hardships, the resulting program is more likely to be of benefit and achieve a measure of success. The UNDP in its Human Development Report noted, "And participation is a means to ensure the efficient provision and more equitable distribution of goods and services. If people are involved in decision-making, policies and projects tend to be more realistic, more pragmatic and more sustainable."[19]

Conclusion

This has been an attempt to relate some of the experiences of women in one country undergoing structural adjustment and to raise questions as to the impact of these adjustment programs on their economic, social, and cultural rights. The paper is by no means exhaustive even of the experiences. It simply seeks to raise questions which are important for women in this country as well as other countries undergoing the process of adjustment. So far the experiences of the women are such that it is necessary to incorporate their concerns into any rethinking and recharacterization of international human rights norms if these norms are to become relevant to them.

Despite claims to the contrary by economists and others it is true that as a result of structural adjustment programs, the total burden of women's work has increased and pressures on them have also increased. This is because they already bear the burden of child care, provision of food for the family, and care of the aged as well as the sick in the family. Therefore the cutbacks on social expenditure resulting in diminished access to social services such as health, sanitation, and education only add to their problems. Since the majority of those women live in rural areas, engaged in subsistence agriculture, the concentration of resources on export crops under structural adjustment has worked to their disadvantage. As more land has been devoted to the production of export crops, some of them have become landless, and even where they are involved in the production of these export crops, they have no hand in marketing these crops. They thus do not enjoy the benefits, though they do the work. Those who are engaged in small-scale subsistence farming do not enjoy the benefits of extension services or new technological advances. Employment creation under these programs has been weak, especially for women. In the project document for the Programme of Action to Mitigate the Social Cost of Adjustment (PAMSCAD) of the government of Ghana in 1987, it was noted that "while the ERP is expected to generate increased employment in the medium to long term, it is important to recognise that there will be a significant time lag before the economy begins to absorb more labor."[20] The adjustment programs have so far done very little by way of addressing gender inequalities in the formal and informal sectors of the economy. Because of their marginalization and the scale of their economic activities, many women still have no access to credit and therefore are unable to expand their activities and improve their performance.

It is therefore imperative that there be a radical rethinking of human rights, a process that should accommodate the experiences of the burdens of these adjustment programs on the women concerned. Such rethinking and redefinition, it is hoped, will enable the international financial institutions, in collaboration with the affected states, to develop appropriate action programs responsive to the needs of women and other vulnerable groups, in the process of structural adjustment.

In order to address the human rights dimensions adequately within the framework of adjustment, the Special Rapporteur proposed the drafting of a possible set of basic policy guidelines on structural adjustment, which was approved by the Sub-Commission in resolution 1991/27. The process of drafting such basic policy guidelines, set within a human rights framework, could serve to display coherently the main concerns of the human rights bodies vis-à-vis adjustment, offer a significant contribution to the adjustment debate as well as provide an opportunity for the exchange of views with the international financial institutions, member states and non-governmental organisations about the still under-emphasized human rights angle of the adjustment process.[21]

This quote captures the spirit of the current debate and points in the direction of the future.

Notes

1. Ghana Statistical Survey, 1989.

2. Ghana Living Standards Survey, 1989.

3. MFEP/UNICEF 1990.

4. Republic of Ghana, *Programme of Actions to Mitigate the Social Costs of Adjustment* (Accra: Government Publication, Nov. 1987), 1, para. 5.

5. *Mitigate Social Costs,* note 4 at 1, para. 5.

6. *Mitigate Social Costs,* note 4 at 8 at 23.

7. *Mitigate Social Costs,* note 4 at 8 at 25.

8. *Mitigate Social Costs,* note 4 at 10 at 30(f).

9. Danilo Turk, Special Rapporteur, *The Realisation of Economic, Social and Cultural Rights,* U.N. ESCOR, U.N. Doc. E/CN.4/Sub.2/1992/16., 3 July 1992, 14 at 50.

10. Katarina Tomaševski, "The World Bank and Human Rights," in *Yearbook of Human Rights in Developing Countries,* ed. Manfred Nowak (Oslo: Norwegian Institute of Human Rights, 1987), 95.

11. UN Economic Commission for Africa, *African Alternative Framework to Structural Adjustment Programmes for Socio-Economic Recovery and Transformation,* U.N. Doc. E/ECA/CM 15/6/Rev. 3 (1989), 25 at 71.

12. See, e.g., Hilary Charlesworth, Christine Chinkin, and Shelley Wright, "Feminist Approaches to International Law," *Am. J. Int'l L.* 85(4) (1991): 613.

13. Catharine A. MacKinnon, "Pornography, Civil Rights, And Speech," *Harv. C.R.-C.L. L. Rev.* 20(1) (1985): 8.

14. For a fuller discussion of some of the reasons for the exclusion of gender in the definition of international human rights norms, see Andrew Byrnes, "Women, Feminism and International Human Rights Law—Methodological Myopia, Fundamental Flaws or Meaningful Marginalisation? Some Current Issues," *Austl. Y.B. Int'l L.* 12 (1992): 205.

15. Turk, *Economic, Social and Cultural Rights,* note 9, 14 at 49.

16. UN Economic Commission for Africa, *African Alternative Framework to Structural Adjustment Programmes for Socio-Economic Recovery and Transformation (AAF-SAP),* E/ECA/CM 15/6/Rev. 3 (1989): 26 at 74.

17. UN Economic Commission, *Framework,* note 16 at 75.

18. Turk, *Economic, Social and Cultural Rights,* note 9, 46 at 177.

19. UNDP, *Human Development Report* (1991): 71.

20. Republic of Ghana, *Programme of Actions to Mitigate The Social Cost of Adjustment* (Nov. 1987): 7 at 20.

21. Turk, *Economic, Social and Cultural Rights,* note 9, 18 at 63.

Chapter 19
Canadian Approaches to Equality Rights and Gender Equity in the Courts

Kathleen E. Mahoney

Introduction

[T]he history of tne struggle for human rights from the eighteenth century on has been the history of men struggling to assert their dignity and common humanity against an over-bearing state apparatus. The more recent struggle for women's rights has been a struggle to eliminate discrimination, to achieve a place for women in man's world, to develop a set of legislative reforms in order to place women in the same place as men. . . . It has not been a struggle to define the rights of women in relation to their special place in the societal structure and in relation to the biological distinction between the two sexes. Thus, women's needs and aspirations are only now being translated into protected rights.[1]

Equality has always been a very difficult concept for judges, lawyers, law professors, and other students of the law to define or describe. The reason is, as Justice Rosalie Abella of the Ontario Court of Appeal puts it, that

Equality is evolutionary, in process as well as in substance, it is cumulative, it is contextual, and it is persistent. Equality is, at the very least freedom from adverse discrimination. But what constitutes adverse discrimination changes with time, with information, with experience and with insight. What we tolerated as a society 100, 50 or even 10 years ago is no longer necessarily tolerable. Equality is thus a process, a process of constant and flexible examination, of vigilant introspection, and of aggressive open-mindedness. If in this on-going process we are not always sure what "equality" means, most of us have a good understanding of what is "fair."[2]

And the way women's rights are treated in all areas of the world, in many ways is not fair. It is now widely documented and accepted that international norms and institutions were designed by men primarily to serve men's interests.[3] Women have barely been visible in systems that create, interpret, and apply laws.[4] If women are served by them, it is in a derivative way—when they suffer violations in the same way as men. This privileges the male world-view and supports male dominance in the international order. Issues of concern to men are seen as general human concerns, while those of women are relegated to a specialized limited category of women's rights that under analysis, do not amount to "human rights" as we know them.

The purpose of this paper is to first show how barriers to the achievement of gender equality for women are created by theories of equality that do not work and by gender bias in judicial decisions. Unless both these problems are dealt with, women will not achieve legal or social equality. The second purpose of the paper is to suggest some theoretical and practical strategies that may improve the status, recognition, and implementation of women's rights such that they are given the same weight and respect as men's rights.

The Problem

One of the primary emphases of the United Nations Charter as well as the Universal Declaration is equality.[5] The International Covenants on Civil and Political Rights and on Economic, Social, and Cultural Rights both give legal force to the equality guarantees but do not define them. To fill the gaps, the United Nations Commission on the Status of Women labored for many years—more than thirty—to amplify the general discrimination prohibitions. It brought to light almost all the areas of life in which women are denied equality with men. As a result of these efforts, several declarations and conventions were drafted and subsequently ratified by many countries[6]—the central, most important, and comprehensive document being the Convention on the Elimination of All Forms of Discrimination Against Women (the Women's Convention).[7] It deals with civil rights and the legal status of women, reproduction, and the impact of cultural norms on gender relations. It emphasizes rights of political participation, nationality rights, non-discrimination rights in education, employment, and economic and social activities. It asserts equal rights and obligations of women and men with regard to choice of spouse, parenthood, personal rights, and command over property. It requires that rules intentional or unintentional treating women differently from men cannot be tolerated, particularly when they are based on prejudice and inaccurate generalizations about women. Although there are a number of provisions requiring women to be treated the same as hypothetical men in similar situations, read as a whole, the concept of equality in the Women's Convention clearly extends beyond formal de jure equality to address unintentional, systemic forms of discrimination and equality of result.

In the area of reproduction, for example, it recognizes that equality requires legal norms to go beyond gender neutrality or treating women in the same way as men. It makes the connection between discrimination against women and women's unique reproductive role. By recognizing that women's equality requires states parties to guarantee women's rights to decide on the number and spacing of pregnancies and to have access to information and means to exercise these rights, the Women's Convention comes to grips with the realities of gender difference and the social and economic consequences of pregnancy. It acknowledges that gender discrimination is often caused by stereotyped sex roles when it demands fully shared responsibility for child-rearing by both sexes. Maternity protection and child care are proclaimed as essential positive rights saying that states have an obligation to provide services to enable individuals to combine family responsibilities with work and participation in public life.

Finally, the Women's Convention identifies the generic, structural sources of inequality. It identifies culture and the use of stereotypes, customs, and norms as potential barriers to women's enjoyment of equality. States are exhorted to modify such customs and practices when they encourage the domination of women by men. In other words, it obliges them to change not only negative laws but negative culture. In summary, it recognizes that, in order to achieve gender equality, a multifaceted approach is required. In some instances, equality requires that women cannot be denied opportunities and benefits enjoyed by men. In others, women must be empowered to determine their own destinies, defined by their own priorities and needs. Unlike the non-interference role required for the protection of civil liberties, states have a crucial, proactive role to play if gender equality is to be achieved. Unfortunately, very few states have either accepted or performed this role.

The Women's Convention was adopted by the UN General Assembly in 1979 and ratified or acceded to by 126 countries as of August, 1993, but the global status of women shows no significant improvement since the Convention was drafted. Many reasons have been suggested for the abysmal lack of progress[8] not the least of which are the large number of reservations to the Convention;[9] its much weaker implementation procedures compared to other antidiscrimination conventions; and a male-centered conceptualization of rights that determines the interpretation and application of modern human rights law.

Male-centered conceptualizations of rights have tended to ignore or diminish women's experiences in the application and interpretation of human rights in the courts and other decision-making bodies.[10] Although judicial and quasi-judicial bodies are not entirely to blame for the low status of women, numerous studies show that one of the most formidable barriers to women's equality is gender bias in the courts.[11] The results of judicial decisions are often discriminatory and harmful to women. For example, the freedom of religion guarantee more often than not has been interpreted by the judiciary to operate to the detriment of women. When certain religious practices undermine women's bodily security, social position, and status[12] and women's rights are not considered, religion-related issues such as marriage, divorce, custody, property rights, and participation in public life allow men to exercise their freedoms at the expense of women.[13] Internationally recognized rights applicable to the family raise the same problems, couched in different terms.[14] If the perspective of women is not considered when family rights are challenged or interpreted, the unequal power division and stereotyped sex roles within families, which usually favor men, are institutionalized. This results in legalized male dominance and female subordination on such "family" matters as birth control, access to abortion, spousal violence, citizenship, and economic independence.

Women's gender equality rights and traditional values may also clash in the context of the right to development. When it is interpreted in a gender-blind way, traditional theories, strategies, and solutions to deal with development, growth, and under-development tend to ignore the role of women. In Africa, for example, where women produce 75 percent of the agricultural food products,[15] development policies and strategies that fail to take women's concerns and realities into account not only violate women's human rights to development but doom themselves to failure.[16] Furthermore, when the "neutral" language of development and economics fails to challenge the sexist assumption that women's work is of a different or lesser order than that of men, the work women do is often rendered invisible. Universally, reproduction, child care, domestic work, and subsistence production have been excluded from the measurement of economic productivity and growth. This has been particularly detrimental to women in developing countries.[17]

Many other examples can be offered from areas such as refugee law, humanitarian law, children's rights, and environmental law. All demonstrate the same point. Where general "human" norms are equated with male norms, the interests, rights, and concerns of women tend to disappear. Feminist analyses of international law suggest that the problem is global. Men of all nations have used the statist system to establish economic and nationalist priorities to serve males while the basic human, social, and economic needs of women are not met. In both developed and developing countries, the power structures and decision-making processes exclude women, who, in every society, are the poorest and least privileged.

It is clear that if women's rights are to be recognized and protected and if women are to achieve equality, existing models and values must be questioned and traditional theories, foundations, and boundaries challenged. More women must participate in male-dominated human rights institutions, in the courts and in other centers of legal decision making. Most important, the international human rights emphasis must shift from the discussion and setting of norms to implementation of rights. One of the challenges is to discover ways to use the Women's Convention effectively to deliver substantive gender equality in countries bound by its terms. One approach lies in an interpretation of the Women's Convention that invalidates narrow, male-centered conceptualizations of equality and other rights that disadvantage women. Strategies must be developed to ensure that women's voices are heard, that gender-biased myths that buttress the law are removed, that principles applied to the law involve and support women in the legal system, and that judges and other actors in the administration of justice respond to women's needs.

In the next section, a theory of equality is described which if applied in the Courts could achieve equality under the law for women and lead to social equality in real life. I explain that an understanding of equality in terms of socially created advantage and disadvantage instead of sameness and difference, applied to international human rights law including the Women's Convention, could profoundly influence domestic law. In the second section I describe a judicial education strategy designed to implement the theory at the grass-roots level of domestic law as well as at the international level. The suggestions are based on experiences in Canada where such strategies have achieved some notable results and have provided a focus for action and consciousness-raising.[18] It is my view that the Canadian model could be adapted to achieve a similar result at the international level.

Theories of Equality

In order for women to engage the law's transformative potential, there must be a legal framework with enough flexibility to permit the development of a theory of equality that will advance women's interests, identify and recognize violations of their rights, and lead to effective remedies. It is clear from the extraordinary number of reservations to the terms of the Women's Convention[19] that countries have widely different views on what constitutes discrimination against women. Drawing the line between "justified" and "unjustified" distinctions, determining whether or not intention is a requirement for discrimination, deciding on the relevance of purpose and effect—all these choices have led to different interpretations and different results in equality cases.[20] The reason is that the theories behind the choices lack a principled base, a clear, unequivocal purpose to eliminate disadvantage and reliance on unjustified stereotypes which relegate women to second class status from the outset.

In most countries of the world, if equality for women is legally acknowledged at all, it is understood in the Aristotelian sense.[21] Equality norms require that likes be treated alike and permit unalikes to be treated differently. Put another way, equality law is a law of sameness and difference. This is a problem for women because their social reality consists of systemic deprivation of power, resources, and respect. Men do not experience long-term, widespread social conditioning in systemic subordination as women do. Most often, the second class citizenship women endure ensures their difference from men, so it makes no sense to require them to be the "same" as socially advantaged men in order to be entitled to be treated equally. Moreover, the sameness/difference model does not allow for any questioning about the ways in which law has maintained and constructed the disadvantage of women, nor does it allow for an examination of the extent to which the law is male-defined and built on male conceptions of problems and of harms. Simply put, it does not permit effective implementation of equality rights when their infringement arises from female-specific circumstances.[22] For example, legal treatment of sexual harassment, prostitution, sexual assault, reproductive choice, and pornography cannot be characterized or questioned as sex equality issues because the male comparators have no comparable disadvantage or need. Women will always be "different." Even governmental action or inaction that furthers women's disadvantage in these sex-specific areas is not considered to be a violation of domestic sex equality guarantees or a violation of the Women's Convention.[23] The sameness/difference model is one of the reasons that rape of women in conditions of war has never been prosecuted as a war crime, yet torture, genocide, and other "gender-neutral" crimes have.

In addition to the male comparator problem, when equality is defined according to the sameness/difference model, the assumption is made that equality is the norm and that, from time to time, autonomous individuals are discriminated against. Systemic, persistent disadvantage is not contemplated. The Aristotelian model is incapable of proposing or restructuring or even identifying systematic discrimination in educational institutions, the workplace, the professions, the family, or the welfare system. It assumes these societal institutions should continue to exist as they are. To be equal, women just need the same chance as men to be able to participate in them.[24] This universalistic, gender-neutral approach does not recognize that institutional structures may impinge differently on men and women. Such an interpretation of discrimination cannot provide women with the systemic remedies they need such as employment equity, equal pay for equal work, adequate child care facilities, access to abortion and contraception, and literacy rights. Without systemic remedies, female occupational job ghettos will persist, women's lives will continue to be biologically determined and their low status will not improve.

Despite its superficial attractiveness and historical longevity, in practice the Aristotelian doctrine is more likely to perpetuate rather than eradicate inequality. When its use by legislators or the courts obstructs the achievement of equality for women, states should be challenged for violating the substance, intent, and spirit of the Committee for the Elimination of Discrimination Against Women as well as other international instruments that mandate gender equality.[25] This cannot be done however, until courts, human rights commissions, human rights committees, and other decision-making bodies reject the Aristotelian model and replace it with a more effective and principled approach.

The history of gender discrimination cases decided by the Canadian Supreme Court over the past ten years provides excellent illustration of the change in thinking that is required. Two earlier cases demonstrate how the Aristotelian theory was used to perpetuate gender inequality and why such use should be recognized as a violation of international law. More recent cases apply a different theory that is far more likely to achieve de facto equality.

The first case, *Bliss v. Attorney General of Canada*,[26] was decided in 1979. In the *Bliss* case, the Supreme Court of Canada was asked to consider whether an employment benefit provision was discriminatory when it required pregnant workers to meet more stringent requirements to access unemployment benefits than it required of men or non-pregnant workers. In deciding that there was no sex discrimination, the Court came to the bizarre conclusion that discrimination on the basis of pregnancy did not amount to discrimination on the basis of sex. The Court said if the government treats unemployed pregnant women differently from other unemployed persons, be they male or female, it is because they are pregnant and not because they are women.

It is easy to see that interpretation of sex discrimination in this case was so narrow as to be perverse. Failure to acknowledge pregnancy as a component of femaleness when interpreting discrimination not only exacerbates the social and economic disadvantage of women by forcing them to absorb all the costs of pregnancy, it distorts women's reality and perpetuates gender bias in the law. What is not so evident at first glance is the role played by the underlying theory of equality in driving the result.

The outcome of the *Bliss* case was effectively predetermined through the use of the male comparator or the sameness/difference approach. Compared to men, pregnant women will always be different and they will always be vulnerable to discriminatory treatment. One can readily see how women's opportunity to be treated equally is diminished. They can only demand equal treatment to the extent that they are the same as men. Compounding the difficulties was the further reasoning that even if the discrimination test was satisfied, it was not discriminatory to confer benefits in an unequal way, as the equality guarantees were interpreted as being applicable only to imposed burdens. This, of course, ignored the reality that for those who need them, discriminatory allocation of benefits can be just as damaging as or even more damaging than discriminatory burdens.

A second example of a perverse application of the theory was the case of *Attorney General of Canada v. Lavell; Issac v. Bedard.*[27] In this case, the sameness/difference definition of discrimination was used to perpetuate and condone flagrant discrimination against aboriginal women. The case arose when two native women challenged a section of the Federal Indian Act[28] that disqualified them from claiming their Indian status if they married outside their race. The challenge was made under the sex equality provision that guaranteed equality before the law and equal protection of the law,[29] because Indian males who married non-Indian women did not suffer the same disqualification. Upon marrying non-Indian women, males not only retained their Indian status, they automatically conferred Indian rights and status on their non-Indian wives and children. The effect of losing statutory Indian status meant that, on marriage to a non-Indian, women were required to leave their reserve. They could not own property on that reserve and were required to dispose of any property they might have held up to the time of marriage. They could be prevented from inheriting property and could take no further part in band business. Because their children were not recognized as Indian, they too were denied access to cultural and social amenities of the community. The women could also be prevented from returning to live with their families on the reserve notwithstanding dire need, illness, widowhood, divorce, or separation. The discrimination even reached beyond life—they could not be buried on the reserves with their ancestors.[30]

When this institutionalized gender inequality was put before the Supreme Court of Canada, it found that the legislation did not violate sex equality rights. Without providing any principled rationale, the Court merely said that Indian women were not the same as Indian men and could not be compared to them. As long as all Indian women were treated the same, no violation of "equality before the law" or "equal protection of the law" occurred. The Court interpreted the section to guarantee only procedural, not substantive equality. It refused to consider the inherent unfairness or adverse effect of the law on women.

It is difficult to see how either of the above decisions could amount to anything but violations of the Women's Convention and other gender equality provisions of international and regional human rights conventions. At the international level, a state is responsible for the conduct of its judiciary when the use of its legal doctrine violates human rights norms. This is especially true when, as in both *Bliss* and *Lavell,* the decisions came from the court of last resort.[31] Nevertheless, this situation in Canada persisted until 1989, when the Supreme Court, in the first case requiring an interpretation of the equality guarantee in Canada's newly entrenched Charter of Rights and Freedoms, threw out the Aristotelian similarly situated test in no uncertain terms saying it could justify even Hitler's Nuremberg Laws.[32] It was replaced with a new test that focuses on the impact of laws and on the context of the plaintiff. This test, I believe, corrects the gender bias problem, is fairer, has a much greater chance of achieving real equality, and is consistent with the norms set out in the Women's Convention.

The new Canadian test determines discrimination in terms of disadvantage. No comparator, male or otherwise, is required. If a person is a member of a persistently disadvantaged group and can show that a distinction based on personal characteristics of the individual or group not imposed on others continues or worsens that disadvantage, the distinction is discriminatory whether intentional or not. Disadvantage is determined contextually by examining the plaintiff's social, political, and legal reality. Unlike the test of "similarity and difference," the test of "disadvantage" requires judges to look at women or other claimants in their place in the real world and to confront the reality that the systemic abuse and deprivation of power women experience is because of their place in the sexual hierarchy. When a constitutional case is taken, women have the opportunity to challenge male-defined structures and institutions and demonstrate how it is only through norms based on their own needs and characteristics that equality will be achieved. This is not to rule out that in some cases appropriate remedies will require identical treatment with men. In others, however, the male comparator will be irrelevant. Only this type of result-oriented, contextual view of equality, permitting both facially neutral and gender-specific laws or policies to be questioned for a disparate impact on individual women or women as a group, will deliver de facto equality.

In the remedial context, the effects-based approach opens the door for development and growth of positive rights. For example, a purposive response to under-inclusive benefits legislation would be to "read-in" the excluded group rather than to strike down the legislation[33] in order to alleviate the disadvantage it causes or exacerbates. While striking down under-inclusive legislation may meet technical constitutional requirements, in reality it increases disadvantage. It is a kind of "dog-in-the-manger" remedy that helps no one. An example would be striking down under-inclusive welfare legislation allowing only single mothers to apply for benefits. Reading in single fathers rather than striking down legislation solves the constitutional problem and keeps food on the table whether needy parents be female or male.

It is interesting to look at the difference the new equality theory made when it was applied to a pregnancy discrimination case decided ten years after *Bliss* in the same Supreme Court of Canada. In *Brooks v. Canada Safeway Ltd.*,[34] pregnant women workers had received disfavored treatment in comparison with males and non-pregnant women in terms of benefit provisions. This time, the Court not only found it unnecessary to find a male equivalent to the condition of pregnancy, it specifically held that the disadvantage the pregnant women suffer comes about because of their condition—because of their difference. In order to determine whether discrimination on the basis of sex occurred, the Chief Justice situated the pregnant women in reality, in their own context. Once this step was taken, it was impossible not to find that differential treatment on the basis of pregnancy was anything but discrimination on the basis of sex. The Court stated:

Combining work with motherhood and accommodating the childbearing needs of working women are ever-increasing imperatives. That those who bear children and benefit society as a whole thereby should not be economically or socially disadvantaged, seems to bespeak the obvious. It is only women who bear children; no man can become pregnant. As I argued earlier, it is unfair to impose all the costs of pregnancy upon one half of the population. It is difficult to conceive that distinctions or discriminations based upon pregnancy could ever be regarded as other than discrimination based upon sex, or that restrictive statutory conditions applicable only to pregnant women did not discriminate against them as women.[35]

In the same vein, a case dealing with sexual harassment and the issue of sex discrimination was resolved by situating sexually harassed women in the context of their own workplace reality of economic disadvantage and lack of access to power. The Supreme Court unanimously overturned a lower court's decision that had left the plaintiffs without a remedy by concluding that sexual harassment did not constitute sex discrimination.[36] In rejecting the lower court's decision, the Supreme Court explained the relationship between sexual harassment and gender, how sexual harassment has a differential, negative impact on women in terms of the gender hierarchy in the labor force and the inherent "abuse of both economic and sexual power."[37]

The Court understood that, in the context of a deeply sexist society that objectifies women's bodies and perpetuates a male-defined image of sexual attractiveness, the practice of sexual harassment cannot be separated from the unequal relations of sexual interaction that disadvantage women.[38] The Court noted with approval the view that a hostile or offensive working environment created by sexual harassment is every bit the arbitrary barrier to sexual equality at the workplace that racial harassment is to racial equality.[39] This contextual approach to women's sexuality if applied to other gender-specific laws would be of great assistance to women. Reproductive self determination and sexual assault are good examples. If laws limiting women's access to reproductive control were to be examined in terms of whether or not they increase the persistent disadvantaged status of women, I think they would be found to be discriminatory. Similarly, laws that require sexual assault survivors to be subjected to degrading forms of questioning; or to meet evidentiary requirements not demanded of other victims of violent crime (such as recent complaint or corroboration); or sentencing patterns that show batterers of women treated more leniently than other assaulters; or police practices showing slack enforcement of sexual assault or wife abuse laws—all of these matters could be framed as discrimination cases if discrimination were defined in terms of disadvantage to already disadvantaged claimants.[40]

The disadvantage test is also effective when used as a shield rather than as a sword. The Canadian Supreme Court's decision in *R. v. Keegstra*[41] illustrates the point in the context of race, ethnicity, and religion. This was a case involving a constitutional challenge to hate propaganda laws in the Criminal Code[42] as a violation of freedom of expression. The Court upheld the anti-hate law, advancing an equality harm-based rationale to support limitations on speech. It said that not only can the constitutional guarantee of equality be used to strike down laws that discriminate, it can also be used to constitutionally *support* laws that further equality. It held that the objective of promoting social equality that lies behind constitutional guarantees is relevant to the inquiry about justifiable limits on freedom of expression. Just as in the cases where the equality guarantee was directly engaged, the Court in *Keegstra* examined the larger social, political, and legal context of the target groups protected by the hate propaganda provisions and balanced them against the free speech interests between equality and freedom of expression of hate mongers. In other words, the Court contemplated the social meaning of hate propaganda and uncovered its harmful effects. Once revealed, the balancing of interests favored equality. The decision demonstrates that equality is a positive right, that equality provisions have a large remedial component, and that legislatures should take positive measures to improve the status of disadvantaged groups. Most important, the *Keegstra* decision identifies the transformative potential of equality rights when they are properly interpreted.

The Court further clarified and strengthened this position in the first case to challenge obscenity laws as a violation of the freedom of expression guarantee under the Charter.[43] Once the Court examined the threat pornography posed to women's equality rights, it unanimously found that pornography presents an even stronger case for regulation than hate propaganda does. The Court adopted a contextualized approach which revealed that pornography is much more commonplace, socially accepted, and widely distributed across class, race, and geographical boundaries than hate propaganda, and that it exists in a context of social inequality. It said that the most serious risk of harm arises when the material in question presents sexual representations that degrade and dehumanize the participants, subjects them to violence, and reduces them to mere objects of sexual access. Women's disadvantage viewed in the larger context—including rape, battery, prostitution, incest, and sexual harassment, when placed beside the encouragement and promotion of women's subordination in pornography, demonstrated its undermining effects on women's legal and social equality as well as their bodily security rights.

The Court logically concluded that the deeper, wider, and more damaging harm to social life caused by pornography, as compared to hate propaganda, outweighs any free speech interest of pornographers or their consumers. In a society where gender inequality and sexual violence exist as entrenched and widespread social problems, it makes sense that criminal legislation with the objective of prohibiting material that attempts to make degradation, humiliation, victimization, and violence against women appear normal and acceptable is constitutionally valid.

The foregoing cases demonstrate a re-thinking of equality. They exemplify an analytical approach that favors context rather than detached objectivity—an approach that expands the perimeters of the discussion, exposing underlying facts and issues. The cases demonstrate that in order to redress past wrongs, equality must be taken beyond formalistic, abstract principles. Where barriers impede fairness for some individuals, they must be removed. This mandates a theory that permits flexibility, understanding, and empathy in judicial response.

Judicial Gender Bias

The foregoing analysis underscores the crucial role that judges and other actors in the administration of justice play in the achievement of rights for women. In many ways, the judiciary in particular is the institution on which women's rights ultimately depend. Judges are responsible for deciding how and when international human rights law generally and the Women's Convention specifically will be applied at the local level and the degree to which legal systems can be made to conform to international standards.[44] An effective theory of equality is essential, but just as important is the use judges make of it. Experience has shown that even the most progressive legal reforms can be thwarted by a stroke of the judicial pen.[45] Extensive research over the past twenty years demonstrates that judicial decisions in many other areas of the law are influenced by biased attitudes, sex stereotypes, myths, and misconceptions about the relative worth of men and women, and the nature and roles of the sexes.[46] Consequently, women are often denied equal justice, equal treatment and equal opportunity by the courts as well as by governments. In addition to areas of law already discussed above, distortions of substantive law through gender bias occur in areas such as damage awards, treatment of wife abuse, criminal law, matrimonial law, and sentencing practices, to name a few. Brief descriptions of the effect of judicial gender bias in each of these areas follow.

Damages

In tort law one sees judicial gender bias at the theoretical level as well as in process and application of the common law including in the assessment of damages. Gender bias becomes embedded in the substantive law from actions such as the *actio per quod*, which recognizes a husband's claims when his wife is injured. The action treats the marital relation as one of master-servant. When a wife is injured, the husband is compensated for the loss of his wife's services including homemaking and sexual relations. At the same time, the action is not available to wives whose husbands are injured. This gender bias influences much of the present day tort law as it applies to homemakers. The concept of equal interdependency in marriage is not accepted by judges in their personal injury damage assessments. It is only very recently that judges in Canada have recognized that impairment of homemaking capacity can be a compensable loss to the homemaker rather than her spouse. But even where assessments have been granted, they have been pathetically meager, especially when compared to damages awarded for impairment of working capacity outside the home. On the other hand, where actions for compensation are based on wrongful death of wives the damages assessments are much higher.[47] This is because the husband's claim is on a basis similar to the old *actio per quod* and the cost of a market replacement for the wife must be calculated. Judges who are more used to being homemakees rather than homemakers,[48] recognize that husbands whose wives have been killed will have to hire child care workers, cooks, chauffeurs, and housekeepers and award damages accordingly.

Family Law

In family law, gender bias exists in underlying assumptions and stereotypes that affect division of property, alimony, child support, and custody awards. In the western world, researchers have traced the "feminization of poverty" directly to judicial misinformation and misunderstanding about the economic and social realities of women and men. They have concluded that inequitable apportionment of the economic burdens of divorce has created an entire underclass of women and children.[49] Some of the misinformation judges rely on include inaccurate economic assumptions about the costs of raising children and unrealistic expectations about women's ability, especially that of middle aged and older women, to earn future income. When the earning power of women who have been out of the job market for many years is overestimated, alimony awards are seriously deficient. The research data show that men experience a 42 percent improvement in their post-divorce standard of living, while women experience a 73 percent loss.[50] In addition, division of property decisions show that judges undervalue the contribution of the wife-homemaker to the marriage. Seldom do judges take a homemaker's foregone income-generation potential and retirement funds into account in any significant way in considering contributions the wife makes to the marriage and career of her husband.[51]

With respect to child support, researchers have discovered that judges, for the most part, have unrealistic ideas of the costs of running a family and raising children[52] and award inadequate amounts of support payments. Some posit that the awards are based on what the father can afford without suffering a decline in his standard of living rather than on the children's needs. When payments fall into arrears, they are frequently forgiven by judges without justification.[53]

On the custody issue, the case law indicates that judges are influenced by traditional stereotypes that disadvantage non-traditional women who work outside the home and men who are primary caregivers. They assume children raised in homes with full-time homemakers are better off. The limits this places on the aspirations and goals of women affects their independence, economic security, and equality in a way that does not affect most men. It also fails to recognize that more often than not, the mother is the primary parent notwithstanding the fact that she may have responsibilities outside the home,[54] and that removing children from her custody does them more long-term harm than the lack of an idealized, stereotypical home life. Women often find themselves in a double bind when they are awarded custody but insufficient support to remain homemakers. Once they leave their homemaking jobs for the marketplace, they then lose custody when the fathers remarry and tell the judge their new wives will stay at home and be "proper" mothers for the children. Similarly, women who are battered often lose custody to fathers because of the lifestyle they are forced to adopt to protect themselves. Frequent changes of address are viewed as evidence of instability and the new wife of the batterer, especially if she is a "traditional" mother, will be viewed as the better caretaker for the children.[55]

Criminal Law

In criminal law, gender bias is found in many areas, but probably most notoriously in the judicial treatment of sexual assault and wife abuse. In many jurisdictions, there is a sweeping uncritical acceptance of the view that rape complainants are inherently suspect and may well make false accusations against men.[56] This puts the woman victim on trial in an unsympathetic, insensitive courtroom environment. The nature of the crime of rape, long-term psychological injury to the victim and the prevalence of the crime, especially acquaintance-rape, are subjects that researchers have discovered judges know little about.[57] This is often reflected in judge-made rules that require corroboration (or at least a warning of the dangers of convicting on the uncorroborated evidence of a rape complainant), or evidence of a recent complaint to support the credibility of the victim, or which permit questions on the past sexual history of the victim to attack her credibility. This not only relies on the sexist assumption that women who are sexually active with more than one man are liars, it turns the trial into a pornographic spectacle. As a result, victims of rape are often reluctant to report the crime and suffer unequal protection of the law.[58] In sentencing practices, gender-biased mitigation principles partially or sometimes totally excuse male sexual violence through a "blame the victim" ideology, which limits women's freedom to dress as they like, walk when and where they choose, and drink as much as they want—limitations that are not placed on males. Some more extreme examples of this problem include cases where judges have blamed female children as young as three years of age for their abuse because of "sexual provocation."[59]

Victims of wife abuse face serious gender bias due to widespread judicial misunderstanding of the dynamics and seriousness of a battering relationship. This often leads to unjust conclusions being drawn about victims who are reluctant to leave a battering relationship or who do not cooperate in testifying.[60] When a woman is burdened by multiple disadvantages because of her race, disability, or other immutable characteristic, the harmful effects are magnified. Victims who stay in battering relationships are often blamed in a gender-biased way by judges who assess their behavior from a dominant, male perspective which demonstrates a lack of understanding of the context of inequality within which women live. First-hand accounts by many battered women demonstrate that they are often trapped in their relationships. A decision to stay with an abusive husband is perfectly reasonable if, from the wife's point of view, there is no other place to go. Financial and emotional dependence on their husbands; concern for the welfare and their custody of the children; lack of emergency housing and day care; lack of support from law enforcement agencies; the fear of public exposure; inadequate social support networks; the fear of greater injury; and the tendency of society to blame women rather than their assailants are some of the reasons battered women cite for staying in violent relationships.[61] All are related to the unequal social position of women.

These are but a few examples of gender bias. Many more could be offered to illustrate its existence. What must be understood is that gender bias in the application and interpretation of laws is important not only for individual women before the courts. To the extent that the justice system suffers from gender bias, the system fails in its primary societal responsibility to deliver justice impartially. As a consequence, the administration of justice as a whole suffers. The legitimacy of the entire system is brought into question.

What is the most troublesome and insidious aspect of the problem of gender bias in the courts is the failure of the legal establishment to recognize its existence. It often exists without the cognizance of either the individuals or institutions where it is practiced, be they courtrooms, law schools or law firms. Ironically, the judiciary—the very institution that determines the effectiveness of efforts to achieve equality and which can undermine even the most progressive legal reforms through the exercise of judicial discretion and through courtroom behavior—is not scrutinized by social reformers and analysts for discriminatory biases. Why? Probably the main reason lies in the unquestioned and commonly held belief that judges are completely objective, disinterested, and impartial in all their work. The pervasive hold of the appealing and powerful idea of judicial neutrality has affected even those whose job it is to criticize and evaluate the judiciary. Lawyers and law professors have historically limited their inquiry and critiques of judgments to the logic and sensibility of the legal analysis they contain and their relationship to precedent. Occasionally the social, economic, or policy implications of judgments are discussed or evaluated, but rarely, if ever, are questions asked about judicial use of societally induced assumptions and untested beliefs—about the use of stereotypes that judge individuals on their group membership rather than on their individual characteristics, abilities, and needs. Law review articles are rarely written about judges who view issues solely from the dominant perspective, who neglect to consider alternative views, who over-simplify or trivialize the problems of women, or who fail to treat children seriously. The importance of variability of cultural, racial, and gender perspectives; of context, contingency, and change are neither discussed in classrooms nor in courtrooms.[62]

Another reason is the courts themselves. Until recently, the judicial arm of government has been loath to accept any culpability with regard to the disadvantaged status of women or other minority groups. The idea that courts could be acting in a manner prejudicial to a specific group in society is generally rejected outright.[63] The failure to entertain this possibility precludes any attempt to begin to rectify or redress the situation. To further complicate matters, the issue of bias is often personalized and reduced to assertions of individual judges denying prejudice on their part or on the part of their associates. This reaction is inappropriate because it confuses the concepts of overt discrimination with systemic discrimination. While there may still be some incidents of overt prejudice, they are relatively easy to identify and rectify. Systemic discrimination, on the other hand, is far more insidious and much more difficult to eradicate; to do so requires knowledge of its existence, its pervasiveness, and its consequences and an unremitting commitment to ending it. In Canada this reality is now accepted and recognized at the highest levels of the judiciary, the government, the bar, and in the legal academy.[64] To remedy this the following reform efforts are underway.

Judicial Education Programs to Eliminate Gender Bias in the Courts

In order to remove gender bias from the judicial processes, judges must be able to understand the impact of sex-role stereotypes, myths, and biases on their thinking and decision making. Deeply held cultural attitudes and beliefs about the "proper" roles for women and men must be examined and challenged where they interfere with the fair and equitable administration of justice. This requires education programs that stimulate a sense of personal discovery and enable judges to identify and eliminate their own biases. Presentation of new facts and sensibilities assists this process as does the involvement and commitment of non-judges. The key element to sustainable and successful reform, however, is the realization that change must come from within the judiciary and that judges must lead the program. Not only does this give the program legitimacy and credibility in the eyes of the judges, it addresses the requirement of judicial independence.

Two of the most active participants in judicial reform in Canada are the Western Judicial Education Centre (WJEC), a cooperative project of the Canadian Association of Provincial Court Judges and the International Project to Promote Fairness in the Administration of Justice, which operates in and outside of Canada.[65] The WJEC organizes continuing education programs for Provincial and Territorial Court Judges from western and northwestern Canada and the International Group, often working with WJEC, promotes judicial education in other countries through the presentation of seminars, teaching demonstrations, consultations, and dissemination of materials. Since 1988, the members of this cooperative group, assisted and supported by legal academics, the bar, community groups, and representatives of minorities have focused on developing programs dealing with delivery of justice to Aboriginal people, gender equality in judicial decision making, and racial, ethnic, and cultural equity. A central objective of the WJEC is to show judges how their own beliefs and attitudes affect impartiality and fairness. In addition, a "participatory" model of program delivery has been adopted which is capable of implementation in any part of the country at any level of court. A close association has been developed with law schools and continuing legal education societies in western Canada as well as with non-legal professionals and private citizens. Advice and direct resource commitment of these organizations and individuals is obtained, often at no charge. As a result, a strong community support base as well as a high-quality product has been created.

One of the key elements of WJEC programs is peer leadership. Judges are trained by credible "outsiders" to instruct and lead other judges in training-the-trainer sessions. While initially there was some concern expressed about "imposed agendas of special interest groups," it soon became apparent to the judges that, on the contrary, such sessions provided new facts and more precise knowledge which only helped them maintain their genuine commitment to fairness and impartiality. This method of delivery also challenges judges to participate and to take responsibility for their own continuing education, while at the same time allowing members of the broader community concerned with improving the quality of justice delivery to participate in the workshops and other sessions. Women, Aboriginal people, racial, cultural, and ethnic minority group members—people very unlike most judges—supply knowledge judges require but seldom receive. They describe and discuss the problems they experience in their daily lives as well as in the courts. They lead discussions, present papers, participate in social events, and sometimes provide entertainment to educate judges about their cultural and social reality. Over time these programs have grown significantly in scope and quality.

In May 1993, the fourth annual WJEC workshop attracted 330 judges and more than 60 faculty and advisors to Victoria, British Columbia for what was probably the best example to date of "hands-on" judicial education using the best adult education techniques and high quality interdisciplinary resources. Notwithstanding the WJEC's considerable progress, much remains to be done. If gender, race, and other forms of bias are to be eradicated from judicial decision making, the education of judges on these issues must be comprehensive, consistent, systematic, and of high quality. At the present time, there is no comprehensive long-term pan-Canadian plan for judicial education, no clearinghouse for materials, no consistent evaluative process providing reliable, comparative results. In order to support and validate the programs in the future as well as to document specific problems and trends, empirical data must be collected as an ongoing part of judicial education.

There is a danger that as the programs grow and develop, organizers may lose sight of the original goals. As new people with different agendas enter the programs, there are tendencies to alter directions and perspectives. One increasingly discernible trend in Canada is the tendency to focus on courtroom interaction rather than on substantive law. The pressures to emphasize this aspect of bias are considerable and must be avoided if the integrity of the fundamental premises of judicial education is to remain intact. Gender, race, and ethnic biases in courtroom interaction are important for judges to address but they are only symptomatic of deeper, doctrinal problems. Learning about more sensitive courtroom behavior does not require judges to re-think the fundamental premises of their decision making and the patterns they form. Substantive inequities must be explained, understood, and changed if real, lasting reform is to occur in the administration of justice as a whole.

Conclusion

Canada has progressed on two fronts in ensuring that women's rights will be recognized and protected and that women will achieve de facto equality. The first is at the theoretical level in the adoption of a theory of equality that allows Canadian women to address, in equality terms, the deepest roots of discrimination that occurs to them as women, not just as women compared to men. If courts in other jurisdictions were to similarly interpret equality requirements in domestic and international law, a major barrier to the achievement of gender equality would be removed. The second is at the practical level in identifying and attempting to correct gender and race bias in the courts through judicial education programs. This is based on the understanding that equality will never be achieved unless the administration of justice is free from gender bias.

The acknowledgment in Canada that unequal and unfair treatment of women and racial minorities occurs within the judicial system was the important and crucial first step toward equality. The second step was the recognition that in order to remove these biases judges need better to understand the impact of variables such as gender, poverty, race, illiteracy, disabilities, discrimination, alcohol and drug abuse, sexual and physical abuse on social behavior and on their own decisions. This led to the further recognition that legal principles must be linked to the social context in order to achieve complete justice and fairness within the legal system.

By virtue of the fact that judges have taken a leadership role in opening the channels of communication, they have not only removed artificial barriers to the acquisition of important knowledge required to address issues previously unaddressed, but have set an important example for other actors in the legal system about self-examination and improvement. What is innovative and exciting about the new judicial education initiatives in Canada is the idea that the community, as well as judges, has a direct connection to and investment in the work that judges do.

One can only hope that this development will continue and flourish within the Canadian judiciary and expand into other jurisdictions.[66] It may be that a solution to the implementation of women's human rights will be found in the direction and leadership the judiciary in all countries of the world can provide. While it is fundamental that individual judges cannot substitute personal values and moral choices for those of elected legislatures—statutes, constitutions, and international human rights conventions do not interpret themselves. They are abstract concepts that require courts to breathe life into them. The judiciary has the power to permit equality to grow and flourish to meet the legitimate demands and aspirations of the female majority of the world's population. They also have the power to deny it. The ideas proposed here are only a means to an end. Their realization depends on judicial fidelity to their own ideals of objectivity, fairness, and impartiality.

Notes

1. Noreen Burrows, cited in *R. v. Morgentaler,* 1 S.C.R. 30 (1988) at 171–72 per Wilson, J.
2. Rosalie Abella, "The Evolutionary Nature of Equality," in *Equality and Judicial Neutrality,* ed. Kathleen E. Mahoney and Sheilah L. Martin (Toronto: Carswell, 1987), 4.
3. Laura Reanda, "Human Rights and Women's Rights: The United Nations Approach," *Hum. Rts. Q.* 3 (Spring 1981): 11; see also Margaret Schuler, ed., *Empowerment and the Law: Strategies of Third World Women* (Washington, DC: OEF International, 1986); and the North-South Institute, *Ours by Right,* ed. Joanna Kerr (London and New Jersey: Zed Books, 1993).
4. United Nations Department of International Economic and Social Affairs, *Compendium of Statistics and Indicators on the Situation of Women 1986* (New York: United Nations Statistical Office, Social Statistics and Indicators Series K, No. 5, 1989) 558–77; *Equal Time* (July 1985): 5; Brian Urquhart and Erskine Childers, "A World in Need of Leadership: Tomorrow's United Nations," *Development Dialogue* 1–2 (1990): 29; Andrew Brynes, "The 'Other' Human Rights Treaty Body: The Work of the Committee on the Elimination of All Forms of Discrimination Against Women," *Yale J. Int'l L.* 14 (1989): 1; Hilary Charlesworth, Christine Chinkin, and Shelley Wright, "Feminist Approaches to International Law," *Am. J. Int'l L.* 85 (4) (1991): 613.
5. See Rebecca Cook, "International Law and Women," in *The United Nations Legal Order,* ed. Oscar Schachter and Christopher C. Joyner (Cambridge: Grotius Press, 1994).
6. For example, the Convention for the Suppression of the Traffic in Persons and of the Exploitation of the Prostitution of Others, 96 U.N.T.S. 272 (1950); the Convention on the Political Rights of Women, 193 U.N.T.S. 135 (1953); the Convention on the Nationality of Married Women, 309 U.N.T.S. 65 (1957); and the Convention on Consent to Marriage, Minimum Age for Marriage, and Registration of Marriages, 521 U.N.T.S. 231 (1962).
7. Convention on the Elimination of All Forms of Discrimination Against Women, 18 December 1979, 34 U.N. GAOR Supp. (No. 21) (A/34/46) at 193, U.N. Doc. A/Res/34/180 (entered into force 3 September 1981).
8. See, e.g., Charlotte Bunch, "Women's Rights as Human Rights: Toward a Re-Vision of Human Rights," *Hum. Rts. Q.* 12 (1990): 486; Charlesworth, Chinkin, and Wright, "Feminist Approaches," note 4.

9. At least 21 of the 126 states parties have filed a total of over eighty reservations to the Women's Convention, thereby limiting their obligations to ensure women's equality rights. By contrast, of the 123 states parties to the Convention on the Elimination of All Forms of Racial Discrimination, only two countries have filed reservations. Rebecca Cook, "Reservations to the Convention on the Elimination of all Forms of Discrimination Against Women," *Va. J. Int'l L.* 30 (1990): 643, 644.

10. Rebecca Cook, "International Human Rights Law Concerning Women: Case Notes and Comments," *Vand. J. Transnat'l L.* 23 (1990): 779–818.

11. Schuler, ed., *Empowerment*, note 3. Kathleen Mahoney and Sheilah Martin, eds., *Equality and Judicial Neutrality* (Toronto: Carswell, 1987); Elizabeth A. Sheehy and Susan B. Boyd, *Canadian Feminist Perspectives on Law* (Toronto: Resources for Feminist Research, 1989); Dorothy E. Chunn and Joan Brockman, "Researcher Index and Research Subject Index on Gender Bias in the Law," Feminist Institute for Studies in Law and Society, Simon Fraser University, Burnaby, British Columbia, Publication #2 (May 1992); Department of Justice of Canada, *Gender Equality in the Canadian Justice System* (Ottawa: Department of Justice, 1993). The World Conference on Human Rights also identified gender bias in the administration of justice as one of the barriers to the equal status and human rights of women. See *Report of the Drafting Committee: Final Outcome of the World Conference on Human Rights,* A/CONF.157/DC/1/Add. 1, June 25 (1993): 23 at 3.

12. Arvind Sharman, ed. *Women in World Religions* (Albany: State University of New York Press, 1987); Donna J. Sullivan, "Advancing the Freedom of Religion or Belief Through the UN Declaration on the Elimination of Religious Intolerance and Discrimination," *Am. J. Int'l L.* 82 (1988): 515–17; Donna Artz, "The Application of Human Rights Law in Islamic States," *Hum. Rts. Q.* 12 (1990): 202.

13. For example, see Frances Raday, "Constitutional Evolution in Israel and Equality Between Men and Women," *Conference Proceedings,* Chartering Human Rights, Canada-Israel Law Conference, Faculty of Law, Mount Scopus Campus, Hebrew University of Jerusalem, 1992.

14. For example, Article 16(3) of the Universal Declaration proclaims that the family is the "natural and fundamental group unit of society and is entitled to protection by society and by the State."

15. Sény Diagne, "Defending Women's Rights—Facts and Challenges in Francophone Africa," in *Ours by Right,* ed. Kerr, note 3.

16. Florence Butegwa, "The Challenge of Promoting Women's Rights in African Countries" in *Ours By Right,* ed. Kerr, note 3 at 40–43.

17. Marilyn Waring, *If Women Counted: A New Feminist Economics* (San Francisco: Harper and Row, 1988), 134; Waring, "The Exclusion of Women from 'Work' and Opportunity," in *Human Rights in the Twenty-First Century: A Global Challenge,* ed. Kathleen E. Mahoney and Paul Mahoney (Dordrecht: Martinus Nijhoff, 1993), 109; Schuler, ed., *Empowerment,* note 3.

18. Norma Juliet Wikler, *Educating Judges About Aboriginal Justice and Gender Equality,* Western Workshop Series, 1989, 1990, 1991, An Evaluation Study Report, Department of Justice of Canada (Dec. 1991).

19. See note 9.

20. For example, the Human Rights Committee in its General Comment on nondiscrimination adopts a definition of discrimination that looks to discriminatory effects or purposes, yet their decisions indicate a lack of commitment to

the concept and a consequent lack of leadership. See Communication No. 212/1986, (1988), A/43/40, p. 244; *Vos v. The Netherlands,* Communication No. 218/1986, (1989), A/44/40, p. 232 (CCPR/C/21/Rev. 1/Add. 1).

21. The largely unquestioned theory developed by Aristotle is found in his *Nicomachean Ethics.* See, e.g., trans. by David Ross, World's Classic Series (Oxford: Oxford University Press, 1980).

22. For a discussion, see Margaret Thornton, "Feminist Jurisprudence: Illusion or Reality?" *Austl. J. L. & Soc.* 3 (1986): 5, 8.

23. Catharine MacKinnon has observed that, in practice, this approach means that if men don't need it, women don't get it. "Reflections on Sex Equality Under Law," *Yale L.J.* 5 (1991): 1281.

24. Clare Dalton, "Where We Stand: Observations on the Situation of Feminist Legal Thought," *Berkeley Women's L. J.* 3 (1987–88): 1, 5.

25. For a discussion on judicial responsibility see Rebecca Cook, "State Accountability Under the Convention on the Elimination of All Forms of Discrimination Against Women," Chapter 9 in this book.

26. [1979] 1 S.C.R. 183 (1978). I have discussed this theme more extensively in "The Constitutional Law of Equality in Canada," *N.Y.U. J. Int'l L. & Pol.* 24(2) (1992): 759 at 765–68.

27. [1974] S.C.R. 1349.

28. Indian Act, R.S.C. Ch. 1–5, sec. 12(1)(b) (1985).

29. See Canadian Bill of Rights, R.S.C., app. III, sec. 1(b) (1970).

30. For a discussion of discrimination of Aboriginal people generally, see Thomas R. Berger, *Fragile Freedoms: Human Rights and Dissent in Canada* (Toronto: Clarke, Irwin, 1981).

31. Cook, "State Accountability," note 25; Ian Brownlie, *System of the Law of Nations, State Responsibility, Part 1* (Oxford: Clarendon Press, 1983), 150.

32. See *Andrews v. Law Society of British Columbia,* 1 S.C.R. 143 (1989). See also two subsequent decisions that added further clarification to the principles articulated in *Andrews,* namely, *Reference Re Workers' Compensation Act* 1983 (Nfld.), 1 S.C.R. 992 (1989); *R. v. Turpin* 1 S.C.R. 1296 (1989).

33. The Supreme Court of Canada recognizes this possibility in *The Queen v. Schachter* 139 N.R. 1 (S.C.C.) (1992).

34. 1 S.C.R. 1219 (1992).

35. 1 S.C.R., note 34 at 1243–44.

36. *Janzen and Govereau v. Platy Enterprises* [1989] 1 S.C.R. 1252 (1989), 59 D.L.R. 4th 352 (1989), 10 C.H.R.R.D/6205.

37. *Janzen and Govereau,* note 36, 1 S.C.R. at 1284.

38. See N. Colleen Sheppard, "Recognition of the Disadvantaging of Women," *McGill L.J.* (1989): 207 at 215; see also Catharine MacKinnon, *The Sexual Harassment of Working Women: A Case of Sex Discrimination* (New Haven: Yale University Press, 1979), chapter 5.

39. *Janzen and Govereau,* note 36.

40. See also decisions of the Supreme Court of Canada, including *R. v. Lavallee,* 1 S.C.R. 852 (1990) in which the traditional concept of self-defense was found to be based on a male-centered "bar-room brawl" model and thus adapted the legal concept of reasonableness in self-defense to recognize the reality women face in battering situations; *R. v. Morgentaler,* 1 S.C.R. 30 (1988) in which criminal legislation relating to abortion was struck down for violating the constitutional guarantee of life, liberty, and security of the person, when the law forced a woman to carry a fetus to term unless certain criteria unrelated

to her own priority and aspirations were met; *Moge v. Moge*, 1 W.W.R. 496 (1993) in which it was held that women are economically disadvantaged in most marriages and that judges must not treat most divorcing women as if they have achieved equality; *Norberg v. Wynrib*, 2 S.C.R. 226 (1992), in which it was held that a doctor had demanded and received sexual favors from a drug addicted patient in return for drugs, and there could be no genuine consent to sexual activity given the power imbalance; and *McCraw v. The Queen*, 3 S.C.R. 72 (1991), in which it was held that rape is always harmful to women, and that to ignore the serious psychological harm it causes would be a retrograde step, contrary to any concept of sensitivity in the law.

41. 3 S.C.R. 697 (1990).

42. Criminal Code, R.S.C., Ch. C-46, sec. 319(2) (1985).

43. *R. v. Butler*, 1 S.C.R. 452 (1992).

44. Cook, "State Accountability," note 25.

45. Norma J. Wikler, "Water on Stone: A Perspective on the Movement to Eliminate Gender Bias in the Courts," paper presented at the National Conference on Gender Bias in the Courts, Williamsburg, Virginia, 18 May 1989.

46. See references in note 11.

47. Ken Cooper-Stephenson, "Past Inequities and Future Promise: Judicial Neutrality in Charter Constitutional Tort Claims," in *Equality and Judicial Neutrality*, ed. Kathleen Mahoney and Sheilah Martin (Toronto: Carswell, 1987), 226.

48. Cooper-Stephenson, "Past Inequities," note 47.

49. In the American context see Lenore J. Weitzman, *The Divorce Revolution: The Unexpected Social and Economic Consequences for Women and Children in America* (New York: Free Press, 1985). For the Canadian context see E. Diane Pask and Marnie L. McCall, *How Much and Why? Economic Implications of Marriage Breakdown: Spousal and Child Support* (Toronto: Canadian Research Institute for Law and the Family, 1989).

50. Pask and McCall, *How Much and Why?* note 49.

51. See, e.g., *Report of the New York Task Force on Women in the Courts*, Exhibit A (New York: Office of Court Administration, March, 1986); *New Jersey Supreme Court Task Force on Women in the Courts*, June 1984 (first report) (Trenton, NJ: Administrative Office of the Courts, 1986).

52. Lynn Hecht Shafran, "Documenting Gender Bias in the Courts: The Task Force Approach," *Judicature* 70(5) (1987): 280, 285.

53. Shafran, "Documenting Gender Bias," note 52.

54. See Phyllis Chesler, *Mothers on Trial: The Battle for Children and Custody* (New York: McGraw-Hill, 1986).

55. Shafran, "Documenting Gender Bias," note 52.

56. John Henry Wigmore, *Evidence in Trials at Common Law*, rev. ed., vol. 3A (Boston: Little, Brown, 1970), 924a at 736. Leigh B. Bienen attacked Wigmore's views as being unscientific, based on manipulated authorities, and selectively and untruthfully used, "A Question of Credibility: John Henry Wigmore's Use of Scientific Authority in Section 924a of the Treatise on Evidence," *Cal. W. L.R.* 19 (1983):235.

57. See Mona Brown, ed., *Gender Equality in the Courts: Criminal Law*, A Study by the Manitoba Association of Women and the Law (Winnipeg: Manitoba Association of Women and the Law, 1991); Department of Justice Canada, *Conference Proceedings*, National Symposium on Women, Law and the Administration of Justice (Ottawa: Ministry of Supply and Services Canada, 1991);

Gender Equality in the Justice System, A Report of the Law Society of British Columbia Gender Bias Committee (The Law Society of British Columbia, 1992); National Center for State Courts, Williamsburg, Virginia, *Conference Proceedings,* National Conference on Gender Bias in the Courts (Williamsburg: National Center for State Courts, 1989), which summarizes the findings of state task forces in the United States; *Report of the Committee on Violence Against Women,* Department of Supply and Services Canada (Ottawa: Queen's Printer, 1993).

58. Lorenne M.G. Clark and Debra J. Lewis, *Rape: The Price of Coercive Sexuality* (Toronto: Women's Press, 1977); Christine Boyle, *Sexual Assault* (Toronto: Carswell, 1984); B. Roberts, "No Safe Place: The War Against Women," *Our Generation* 15(4) (1983): 7.

59. Brad Daisley, "B.C.C.A. Affirming Penalty in Sexually Aggressive Tot Case," *Lawyer's Weekly* (9 Feb. 1990); *Sunday Times,* "Judges in the Dock," Judge Ian Starforth Hill, 13 June 1993, p.1, Section 2.

60. Mona G. Brown, Monique Bicknell-Danaker, Caryl Nelson-Fitzpatrick, and Jeraldine Bjornson, in *Gender Equality in the Courts,* ed. Brown, note 57 at 3–51. See also Kathleen E. Mahoney, "Legal Treatment of Wife Abuse: A Case of Sex Discrimination," *U.N.B.L.J.* 41 (1992): 23.

61. Women in Transition, a Canada Works Project, Thunder Bay, Ontario (1978) cited in Linda MacLeod, *Wife Battering in Canada: The Vicious Circle* (Ottawa: Canadian Advisory Council on the Status of Women, 1980), 29. See also R. Emerson Dobash and Russell Dobash, *Violence Against Wives: A Case Against Patriarchy* (New York: Free Press, 1979); L. Chalmers and P. Smith, "Wife Battering: Psychological, Social and Physical Isolation and Counteracting Strategies," in *Gender and Society: Creating a Canadian Women's Sociology,* ed. Arlene T. McLaren (Toronto: Copp Clark Pitman Ltd., 1988), 221; Lisa Freedman, "Wife Assault," in *No Safe Place: Violence Against Women and Children,* ed. Connie Guberman and Margie Wolf (Toronto: Women's Press, 1985), 41; Lee Ann Hoff, *Battered Women as Survivors* (London: Routledge, 1990).

62. See generally Mahoney and Martin, *Judicial Neutrality,* note 2.

63. Norma Juliet Wikler, "Water on Stone: A Perspective on the Movement to Eliminate Gender Bias in the Courts," *Court Review* 26(3) (1989): 6.

64. See Mahoney and Martin, *Judicial Neutrality,* note 2; Brown, ed., *Gender Equality,* note 57.

65. This is a project of the University of Calgary, Group for Research, Education, and Human Rights, chaired by the author.

66. For example, see Kathleen Mahoney, *Report on the Geneva Workshop on Judicial Treatment of Domestic Violence,* February 5, 1992, Palais des Nations, Geneva (Calgary: University of Calgary International Project to Promote Fairness in Judicial Processes, 1992).

Part V
Guaranteeing Human Rights of Particular Significance to Women

Chapter 20
Equality in the Home: Women's Rights and Personal Laws in South Asia

Sara Hossain

Introduction

Every state in South Asia is bound by the norm of equality and non-discrimination between men and women as defined by international human rights instruments. The norm of equality is also reflected in domestic law, in entrenched and justiciable provisions of national constitutions. In its domestic application, however, the norm is severely impaired by unjustifiable deviations in the sphere of women's rights within the family.

The application of the norm in South Asia is asymmetric. It subjects relations in the public sphere, the world of political participation, employment, and education, to minimum standards of equality. In contrast, it relegates the private sphere of the home and the family, to an arena "beyond justice," regulated by variable sets of norms.[1] Rights within the family are determined by personal laws, based on religious traditions, customs, and practices. These personal laws sanction discrimination between men and women and between members of different religious communities regarding their rights to marriage, divorce, maintenance, guardianship, custody, adoption, and inheritance. They violate fundamental rights to equality and are inconsistent with the secular basis of most national constitutions in South Asia. Campaigners for women's rights have vociferously demanded the replacement of personal laws with uniform civil laws based on principles of equality. Piecemeal judicial and legislative reforms have partially mitigated the grossly discriminatory impact of personal laws. In contrast, the state's accommodation of orthodoxies whose agenda involves the control of women's autonomy, and in particular women's subjugation within the family, has resulted in its continued resistance to challenging personal laws. Thus blatant and pervasive inequalities have been entrenched in the arena in which most women's lives are spent.

This chapter argues that personal laws in South Asia constitute a violation of women's rights to equality and nondiscrimination under international and domestic law. It examines the relationship between equality rights as defined by international instruments and national constitutions and the provisions of personal laws. Although personal laws apply in every South Asian state and to every religious community, the discussion here focuses primarily on the personal laws of Muslims in Bangladesh.

Part I briefly discusses the scope of the equality norm, as established by international human rights instruments, and lists specific extensions to the family and its comprehensive elaboration in the Convention on the Elimination of All Forms of Discrimination Against Women (the Women's Convention).[2] Part II outlines the international obligation to guarantee equality. It considers the pervasive practice of states entering reservations to the Women's Convention to limit their obligations to ensure equality within the family. In this context, it evaluates the extent to which South Asian states are bound by equality guarantees and examines in particular Bangladesh's reservation to the Women's Convention. Part III explores the constitutional protection of women's rights and the effect of countervailing religious and community rights that constrain the scope of equality rights and prevent their extension into the family. It describes examples of direct and indirect discrimination sanctioned and effected by the continued existence of personal laws. It then traces legislative and judicial interventions into personal laws, and the balance between measures incorporating a progression toward uniformity and equality and those involving retrogression to further divisions and discrimination. Part IV discusses possible strategies for challenging the application of personal laws and for enforcing equal rights in the family in South Asia. Given the limitations of international enforcement procedures, and the absence of a regional human rights system, domestic courts continue to provide the most effective fora for establishing equal rights. Constitutional guarantees, when interpreted in consonance with international human rights standards, clearly apply in all spheres, including the family. Such guarantees, together with judicial and legislative reforms moving toward uniformity indicate a means for the restructuring of personal laws toward equality.

I. The International Norm of Equality

Scope and Definition of the Norm

Equality and nondiscrimination between women and men and equal protection before the law are among the cardinal principles regulating the enforcement and enjoyment of human rights.[3] The equal rights provisions in international instruments are broad and expansive and distinctly admit interpretations extending their application to all spheres of life.

The United Nations Charter affirms "faith in fundamental human rights, in the dignity and worth of the human person and the equal rights of men and women"[4] and imposes upon member states the obligation to promote "universal respect for and observance of human rights and fundamental freedoms for all without distinction as to . . . sex."[5]

The Universal Declaration of Human Rights provides for the enjoyment of human rights "without distinction of any kind, such as . . . sex"[6] and also states that "all are equal before the law and are entitled without any discrimination to equal protection of the law."[7] These principles are reaffirmed in many other international and regional instruments, including the International Covenant on Civil and Political Rights[8] (the Political Covenant) and the International Covenant on Economic and Social Rights.[9]

It is well established that any legal discrimination against women must be closely examined and may be justified only against a very high standard.[10] A test for discrimination formulated by the European Court of Human Rights requires that any distinction in treatment must have an "objective and reasonable justification" or "pursue a legitimate aim" and that there is a "reasonable relationship of proportionality between the means employed and the aim sought to be realized."[11]

Establishing Equal Rights in the Family

International human rights instruments specifically prescribe the content of equal rights in the private sphere, imposing an obligation upon states to make substantive interventions into the world of the home and the family.

The bare notion of equal rights for men and women in the UN Charter has been supplemented and reinforced through its articulation in other instruments in the context of the family.[12]

The Universal Declaration prohibits "arbitrary interference with privacy and the family,"[13] and provides for "the right of all men and women, without any limitation due to race, nationality or religion the right to marry and found a family" and for "equal rights as to marriage, during marriage and at its dissolution"[14] and states that marriages shall only be contracted "with the free and full consent of the intending spouses."[15] Similar guarantees may be found in the Political and Economic Covenants.[16] International tribunals have interpreted these provisions as clearly traversing the public/private divide to enforce women's rights within the family,[17] to administer property,[18] and, for example, to social security benefits.[19]

Comprehensively Defining Equality—The Women's Convention

As the equality principle has moved from the peripheries to the center of human rights discourse, it has become more comprehensive in its reach. Today, women's rights in all spheres of society are elaborated in the Women's Convention. Article 1 of the Women's Convention constitutes a statement of "international consensus"[20] on the definition of discrimination against women and proscribes:

any distinction, exclusion or restriction made on the basis of sex which has the effect or purpose of impairing or nullifying the recognition, enjoyment or exercise by women, irrespective of their marital status, on a basis of equality of men and women, of human rights and fundamental freedoms in the political, economic, social or cultural, civil or any other field.[21]

Articles 6 through 14 of the Women's Convention set out in detail the content of equality rights in every field. Article 15 establishes the right to full equality in all civil legal matters, both in substance and practice, and specifies that this is inclusive of the right to make contracts, and administer property.[22] Article 16 explicitly details the content of women's equal rights within the family, regarding entry into marriage, choice of spouse, rights during marriage and at the dissolution of marriage, rights to guardianship and adoption, and rights relating to property. This article also prohibits child marriages and requires the compulsory registration of marriages.[23]

II. South Asia and the International Obligation to Implement Equality

Extent of the Obligation

The elimination of formal discrimination is only a necessary first step to implementing equality in the family. Substantive changes in women's situations also need to be attempted and achieved. In doing so, the state may be required to abandon its traditional noninterventionist stance, and to adopt positive measures to ensure equality between individuals in the family:[24]

there may be positive obligations inherent in any effective respect for private or family life. These obligations may involve the adoption of measures designed to secure respect for private life even in the sphere of the relations of individuals between themselves.[25]

To deal with the complex nature of women's subordination and its embeddedness in culture and society, a comprehensive strategy is needed. This is well reflected in the Women's Convention, which articulates multidimensional means to eliminate discrimination against women, imposing obligations not only to eradicate formal inequality but also to ensure substantive equality.

Article 2 of the Women's Convention imposes a clear obligation on all states parties to undertake a policy of eliminating discrimination "by all appropriate means and without delay." It specifies the means to include providing for constitutional equality in substance and practice, legislation, equal and effective judicial and administrative protection, modification and repeal of existing laws, customs and practices, and penal provisions where necessary. Article 3 further binds all states parties to "take all appropriate measures, including legislation" to eliminate discrimination in the "political, economic, social or cultural, civil or any other field." Article 4 further clarifies that "temporary special measures aimed at accelerating de facto equality" will not constitute discrimination but are to be welcomed as necessary interim steps towards eliminating discrimination. Recognizing the existence of inequality in women's daily lived realities, Article 5 requires states to modify "social and cultural patterns of conduct . . . with a view to achieving the elimination of prejudices and customary and all other practices which are based on the idea of the inferiority or the superiority of either of the sexes or on stereotyped roles for men and women." Article 24 further imposes an obligation to take "all necessary domestic measures at the national level aimed at achieving the full realization of the rights recognized."

Thus a state will violate its obligations under Articles 2, 3, and 24 if it passes or fails to repeal legislation that incorporates standards of inequality, or if its judicial organs enunciate decisions that perpetuate inequality.[26] A state may be held responsible for private acts that discriminate against women as a result of existing legislation or customary practices by virtue of Article 2(e) and Article 5.[27]

Acceptance of the Obligation to Implement Equality in South Asia

In South Asia, every state is obliged to ensure the equality of men and women both under customary principles of international law and under the terms of the UN Charter as elaborated by the Universal Declaration. Several states—India, Pakistan, Sri Lanka—are parties to the Political and Economic Covenants. Most important, Bangladesh, India, Nepal, and Sri Lanka are parties to the Women's Convention.[28]

Bangladesh has purported to restrict its obligations under the Women's Convention by entering reservations regarding the provisions relating to the means of implementing the Convention (Article 2), the equal rights of men and women to family benefits (Article 13(a)) and the equal rights of men and women to marriage, dissolution of marriage, guardianship and custody (Article 16.1(c) and (f)):

> The Government of the People's Republic of Bangladesh does not consider as binding upon itself the provisions of articles 2, 13(a) and 16.1(c) and (f) as they conflict with *Shari'a* law based on the Holy Qur'an and *Sunna.*[29]

Restricting the Obligation to Implement Equality Through Reservations to the Women's Convention

The impact of international obligations to implement women's rights has been much less far-reaching than envisaged. This is largely due to the pervasive practice of states entering reservations to limit their obligations under the Women's Convention. Approximately 38 of the 127 states parties have entered 105 substantive reservations to the Women's Convention,[30] many framed in very wide and general terms and relating to women's rights to legal capacity or equality within the family. The permissibility of reservations under the Women's Convention is in stark contrast to those under other human rights treaties.[31]

Such reservations are governed by the general rules of treaty law, as contained in the Vienna Convention on the Law of Treaties 1969. They are permitted unless prohibited under the terms of the treaty, not specifically provided for by the treaty, or "incompatible with the object and purpose of the treaty."[32] The Women's Convention expressly allows reservations that relate to the dispute resolution procedure or are compatible with its objects and purposes.[33] In the absence of any authoritative definition, the question whether reservations are compatible risks is left to the subjective satisfaction of the reserving State. Objections to reservations on grounds of incompatibility also appear to have negligible effect.

Commentators on the Women's Convention have forcefully argued that reservations should be very strictly construed.[34] This is in part because, as was explained in the *Belilos* case, the objects and purposes of human rights treaties are "not to create but to recognize rights which must be respected even in the absence of any instrument of positive law."[35] Moreover, reservations may fall foul of the specificity criterion, which requires that reservations be sufficiently precise to make it possible to determine their scope.[36] The vagueness and generality of the reservation "may be construed not to permit the reserving state to claim a legal justification for its refusal or failure to respect the fundamental goal of the Convention to which the State claims to be a party."[37] The need to provide adequate legal justification for reservations is enhanced in the case of human rights treaties. Finally, reservations must be consistent with the general principle of international law that all treaties are binding upon states parties and must be performed "in good faith."[38]

The Effect of Bangladesh's Reservations to the Women's Convention

It is argued here that Bangladesh's reservations to the Women's Convention are invalid on the grounds that they are (i) incompatible with the object and purpose of the Convention; (ii) inconsistent with existing international obligations; and (iii) vague and unspecific.

(a) Incompatibility

Bangladesh's reservations are incompatible with the object and purpose of the Women's Convention. They have been denounced by several states including Germany, Mexico, Netherlands, and Sweden on this ground.[39] Mexico, in its objection, explained that "if implemented, [the reservations] would inevitably result in discrimination against women by reason of their sex, contrary to the entire intent of the Convention."[40]

The object and purpose of the Women's Convention is to eliminate discrimination against women in substance and practice. Any reservation to Article 2, which sets out the means to implement the Women's Convention, appears designed to avoid any need to modify domestic law. Such a reservation cannot be in conformity with "the overriding duty to establish means, i.e. proper instrumentalities, institutions, laws and administrative actions" aimed at achieving equality.[41] It renders ratification little more than a symbolic exercise, by seriously reducing the content of the obligation to take appropriate measures to eliminate discrimination.[42]

The elimination of discrimination in both the public and private spheres is clearly envisaged by the Women's Convention. Thus women's rights, in particular women's rights in the family, are placed at the heart of human rights discourse, and of the agenda of the Women's Convention. Reservations to Article 16 derogate from the aim of ensuring equality in every sphere, and hence are incompatible with the objects and purposes of the Women's Convention and invalid.

(b) Inconsistency with existing obligations

It is a principle of international law that a state is bound by its international obligations. Bangladesh is bound to respect women's rights to equality and nondiscrimination as enshrined in the UN Charter and other international instruments. Mexico's objection to Bangladesh's reservation explains that: "The principles of equality between men and women and of nondiscrimination on the basis of sex are enshrined in the second preambular paragraph and in Article 1, paragraph 3, of the Charter of the United Nations, and Bangladesh has accepted the obligations contained therein, as well as in other internationally recognized instruments."[43]

(c) Vague and unspecific

The general and imprecise nature of Bangladesh's reservation makes it difficult to determine its scope. The language of the reservation fails to particularize the grounds on which the Shari'a is an insuperable obstacle to implementing the provisions of Articles 13(a) and 16.1. Indeed, it is difficult to ascertain the reason for the reservation to Article 13(a), which relates to family benefits; it has been conjectured that it might have been considered to relate to shares of inheritance.[44] It has also not been indicated how and why the means of implementing equality as set out in Article 2 are contrary to Shari'a.

The reservation is ambiguous with regard to the scope of its application. It could be argued either that the reservation is absolute, *because* the reserved provisions are in conflict with Shari'a, or that it applies *only* to the extent that the provisions are in conflict with Shari'a. Bangladesh has a sizeable non-Muslim population.[45] The former interpretation would result in an untenable conclusion in terms of the reservation's being applicable throughout Bangladesh, to Muslim and non-Muslim alike, although the latter are not governed by Shari'a law. The latter interpretation would lead to an equally inconsistent result, with the reservation restricting the rights of Muslims, and the full protection of the Convention being available only to non-Muslims.

(d) Obligation to perform treaty in good faith

The breadth of the reservations to the treaty, in particular to Article 2, would appear to be designed to avoid any obligation to bring domestic laws into conformity with the obligation to eliminate discrimination against women and is inconsistent with the obligation to perform treaties in good faith.

It is important to determine the effect of Bangladesh's reservations. A noted commentator on the Women's Convention has argued that any state that has entered reservations impermissible on the grounds of incompatibility should be held to have ratified the Women's Convention unreservedly.[46] Thus Bangladesh could be considered bound by all the provisions of the Women's Convention. Any other interpretation would render ratification a purely formal exercise, severely constraining and limiting the obligations to change the structures and sources of inequality.[47]

III. South Asia, the Asymmetric Application of the Equality Norm, and Personal Laws

Personal Laws and the Violation of Women's Rights

Domestically, the equality principle is eroded by the continued existence of personal laws that discriminate against women. In violation of constitutional guarantees and the principles of secularism and pluralism, and in stark contrast to the prevalence of civil law in every other sphere, discriminatory personal laws continue to govern relations in South Asian families. Based on religious laws as modified by legislation, case law, and custom, personal laws determine rights in matters relating to marriage, divorce, maintenance, guardianship, and custody. They perpetuate women's subordination within the family and also constitute discrimination between different religious and ethnic groups. Clearly discriminatory on their face, personal laws obstruct women's participation in political and public life, and significantly contribute to the causes of continuing violence against women.

In South Asia, discrimination effected by personal laws is perpetuated by the state's accommodation of powerful orthodoxies. Such discrimination is exacerbated by the state's characterization of women's rights in the family as issues not of individual equality or dignity but of community or religious rights. Consequently, constitutional guarantees are reduced in this context to mere aspirations, and are rarely applied to their full extent to enforce the equality standard in domestic relations. Judicial and legislative interventions have shown a gradual trend towards extending equality and uniformity, whether based on constitutional interpretations or on extrapolations of principles internal to religious systems of law. However, recent shifts in the political climate have witnessed an abandonment of the secular pluralist consensus; fundamentalist and communal forces have strengthened and consolidated, and have received, directly or indirectly, support and patronage from the state. This has prompted retrogressive state interventions against reform, which have reinforced divisions among religious communities and justified the perpetuation of egregious violations of women's rights, thus emphasizing the fragile nature of constitutional protection of women's rights.

Constitutional Guarantees of Equality and Their Asymmetric Application

In conformity with every other constitution in South Asia, the Constitution of Bangladesh 1972 recognizes, in Articles 27 and 31, the fundamental right to equality before the law and equal protection of the law.[48] Article 28 stipulates that the state shall not discriminate against any citizen on the grounds only of sex and guarantees women's equal rights with men in all spheres of the State and of public life.[49] It specifies that there shall be no discrimination in the context of access to educational institutions or places of public entertainment, and provides that special provision may be made for women.[50] Article 29 establishes that the principle of nondiscrimination applies to government service.[51] The state may, however, make special provision in favor of women.[52]

Despite the expansive scope of these provisions, equality rights have traditionally been considered inapplicable to personal laws. This limitation has been implied from the inherently ambiguous nature of the equality guarantee itself—as in Bangladesh, where it appears to be qualified by the phrase "state and public life"—or from conflicting provisions that allow for a saving for pre-existing legislation.[53] It has also been suggested that if personal laws are characterized as an aspect not of the equality right but of religious rights, they may be constitutionally protected as part of the right to profess, practice, and propagate religion, as guaranteed by Article 41 of the Constitution.

There appears to be no inherent bar to the application of equality rights in every sphere. Adopting a "creative and purposive" approach to interpreting the relevant constitutional provisions would allow for the establishment of women's rights. In particular, the argument in favor of the protection of personal laws by the right to religious freedom is difficult to sustain given the strictly circumscribed limits on the latter which make it subject to law, public order, and morality.

First, the right to religious freedom extends only to matters considered to be of the essence of religion. Courts may determine which practices are essential to religion;[54] so, for example, it has been held that the right does not protect the practice of polygamy under Muslim and Hindu personal law.[55]

Second, the right may be limited on the grounds of morality. Courts appear to have accepted by implication the need to take into account changing notions of morality, which include changing notions of relations between man and woman in society and the gradual progress towards the recognition of equity in the family.

Third, the right must be read in the context of the Constitution as a whole. It should not therefore restrict the exercise of other fundamental rights provisions, in particular those relating to equality. Though the preamble and fundamental principles are nonjusticiable, they have been used to define the content of fundamental rights and may also be taken into consideration. They reaffirm the pledge to establish a democratic society guaranteeing "fundamental human rights and freedom, equality and justice, political, economic and social."[56] In a democratic society, rights cannot be selectively applied; they must permeate all spheres of life, including the domestic, and must recognize the dignity and worth of every man and woman, irrespective of community or religious identity.

There being no restrictions on the scope of the equality guarantee, personal laws sanctioning discrimination against women within the family should be treated as violations of constitutional rights and therefore void and of no legal effect.[57]

Legislative Encroachments on Inequality

In South Asia, the colonial state intervened to ensure the uniform application of civil law in relation to criminal law, civil procedure and evidence, revenue, land tenure, and, partially, the transfer of property.[58] Reinforcing the division of the personal and the political, it refused to make a similar modification in the particular arena of family law. Subject to a few statutory ameliorations, the colonial state left women's position within the family to be governed by the customary laws and practices of different communities.[59] At the same time, it discarded the interpretive guidelines internal to indigenous systems, which allowed for a degree of flexibility and change. Instead it applied common law rules with varying degrees of latitude: these were significantly narrower in the case of family relations.[60] This further contributed to the petrification of personal law and of women's rights, and in certain cases, such as the Muslim law of inheritance, in fact effected further retrogressions.

Following independence, personal laws have undergone piecemeal reforms through judicial and legislative intervention. Such reforms have, however, been largely limited to the laws of the majority community in every country. Hindu law in India has been modified by a series of statutes; Muslim law has been reformed by the Muslim Family Laws Ordinance of 1961 in Pakistan, and supplemented by the Muslim Marriages and Divorces (Registration) Act of 1974 and the Family Courts Act of 1985 in Bangladesh. In contrast, laws applicable to minorities in each country remain as crystallized during the colonial period.[61]

A few examples are discussed below of statutory reforms in favor of establishing women's rights in the family. The implementation of such reforms is constrained, and their impact is limited given the differential and discriminatory basis of the underlying substratum of personal laws.[62]

The Special Marriage Act of 1872, which provides for civil marriage, is rarely used, since it requires the parties to the marriage to renounce their personal laws and also limits rights to divorce, succession, and adoption.[63] The vast majority of marriages are therefore contracted under personal laws, which restrict the right freely to choose a spouse.[64] For example, under Muslim law, while a man may contract a marriage with a non-Muslim, a woman's marriage to a Christian or Jew would be considered irregular and she would not inherit her husband's property; her marriage to a Hindu would be considered invalid and her children would be illegitimate. The Child Marriage Restraint Act of 1929[65] establishes a minimum age for marriage at 18 for women and 21 for men. The Act does not, however, invalidate child marriages, which, in the absence of effective enforcement, remain a common practice.

The Muslim Family Laws Ordinance of 1961 (the MFLO) imposes some limitations on polygamy. In order to contract a second marriage, a Muslim man must obtain a prior consent of the Arbitration Council (consisting of representatives of both parties and of the local authority).[66] If he fails to do so, he is liable to a fine or imprisonment, and to the repayment of dowry to his previous wife.[67] In addition, any of his wives may claim maintenance or demand a divorce on the grounds of inequitable treatment.[68] However, a polygamous marriage contracted without the necessary permission remains valid; this, coupled with the man's right to unilateral divorce and the fact that maintenance is not available to divorced women, forces many women to continue to suffer the humiliation and indignity of such a relationship, given that the only alternative is destitution.

The MFLO has curtailed a husband's right to unilateral divorce and enhanced that of a wife. Previously, a declaration of divorce by a Muslim man repeated three times would suffice to dissolve a marriage. The MFLO requires that the chairman of the local authority must be apprised of any such declaration, and he is then bound to constitute an Arbitration Council and to attempt reconciliation within 30 days. The divorce takes effect after 90 days (or, if the wife is pregnant, on delivery), whether or not such meetings have been held or attended.[69] This procedure is also available to Muslim women, provided a right of divorce has been delegated by the husband in the marriage contract.[70] In addition, the MFLO has restricted the practice of requiring a woman to undergo an intervening marriage (*hila*) in order to remarry her divorced husband.[71] It should be emphasized that these reforms only apply to Muslim men and women; the right to divorce is not recognized at all under Hindu law, and is very restrictively available to women under Christian law.

Registration of marriages contracted under Muslim[72] or Christian[73] law is compulsory. Where registration is not required, as in Hindu marriages, the courts' technical approach, in particular the failure to recognize customary forms of marriage, may cause considerable difficulty to women who seek to validate their rights.[74]

Colonial legislation, in the form of the Guardian and Wards Act of 1890,[75] determines rights to guardianship and custody over children on the basis of the "welfare of the child" in consistency with the personal law of the minor. The courts have interpreted the welfare criterion expansively to minimize the effect of Muslim personal law, which makes the father the natural guardian of the child and limits women's right to custody over sons to the age of seven years and over daughters to puberty (see below).

The Bangladesh Abandoned Children (Special Provisions) Order of 1972[76] is an interesting example of a statute enacted in response to an urgent social need which swept away personal law limitations on adoption. In response to the need to provide for the large numbers of unwanted babies born as a result of the mass rapes committed during the Liberation War, the personal law basis of adoption law was replaced by a uniform civil law. However, reports of the ill treatment of children adopted and taken abroad, followed by a campaign that whipped up sentiment over the alleged conversion of Muslim children, led to repeal of the law.[77] Today adoption is again governed by personal law—it is prohibited under Muslim law, and is allowed in very limited circumstances under Hindu law (only sons may be adopted, and a woman may not adopt unless so authorized by her husband).

Women's rights to inherit property are directly affected by personal laws. Although general statute governs property relations in every other arena, Shari'a governs the question of inheritance,[78] and grants a woman only one-half of the male share. Hindu law similarly, restricts the right of Hindu women.

Two Steps Forward—Judicial Interventions Toward Equality

It has been pointed out that the state is liable for violations of women's rights in the family by its involvement in the enforcement of personal laws. However, there have been few direct challenges to personal laws as constituting violations of the constitutional guarantee of equality. In the rare cases where the equality right has been invoked, judicial comments are usually limited to a reflection of stereotyped notions of women's roles and functions.[79]

In a series of landmark cases, the courts have shifted the limits of personal law in favor of greater protection of women's rights.[80] Such decisions have interpreted existing laws in the light of constitutionally and internationally accepted equal rights provisions, and have emphasized the need to ensure progress and modification of the law toward achieving the goal of equality. The cases discussed below represent examples of gender-positive judicial interpretation in the context of women's rights in the family under Muslim law in Bangladesh. They also indicate possible strategies for future reform of personal laws, drawing not only on constitutional equality rights but also on principles of progressive interpretation internal to personal law systems to establish women's rights within the family.

(a) Extending equality in every sphere

In *Nelly Zaman v. Ghiyasuddin*,[81] following a violent and abusive marriage, a woman sought to exercise her right to a delegated divorce. The husband challenged the legality of the divorce and also claimed restitution of conjugal rights. The lower court held that the woman had "no right to divorce at her own sweet will and without any reasonable excuse," although in fact her right to divorce was clearly established by the marriage contract. Ultimately, her rights were vindicated by the High Court, which not only upheld the divorce but commented, *obiter,* on the remedy of restitution of conjugal rights constituting a violation of equality rights:

The very concept of the husband's unilateral plea for forcible restitution of conjugal rights had become outmoded and . . . does not fit with the State and Public Principle and Policy of equality of all men and women being citizens equal before the law and entitled to be treated only in accordance with the law as guaranteed in Articles 27 and 31 of the Constitution.

The Court appeared to read the equality clause disjunctively as applicable beyond the public to all spheres of life, including the family:

A reference to Article 28(2) of the Constitution of Bangladesh guaranteeing equal rights of women and men in all spheres of the State and public life would clearly indicate that any unilateral plea of the husband for forcible restitution of conjugal rights as against a wife unwilling to live with her husband is violative of the accepted State and Public Principle and Policy.[82]

(b) Deviating from personal laws

Abu Bakar Siddiq v. AB Siddiq[83] concerned a dispute over the custody of an eight-year-old boy. It thus squarely raised the question of the scope of women's custody rights in Muslim law,[84] which grants a mother custody of a male child until he completes his seventh year. The Appellate Division of the Supreme Court upheld the mother's right to custody of her eight-year-old son on the basis that although "the principle of Islamic law has to be regarded, but deviation therefrom would seem permissible as the paramount consideration should be the child's welfare." On the facts, the mother was best qualified to look after the child, who was afflicted with a rare disease: she was a doctor, she had sacrificed a highly remunerative job in order to care for her son, and she had arranged and financed his medical treatment.

The Court stated that such departure from the rules of Muslim law was justifiable on the basis of the lack of uniformity among the jurists of different schools of Islamic law and on the facts and circumstances of the case. It was stressed that such rules would be followed if found in the Qur'an or Sunna or in principles based on Qur'anic text and represented by a dominant opinion of a particular school of Muslim law. In this case, the law on custody was neither founded directly on the Qur'an or Sunna, nor uniformly interpreted by the different schools. In these circumstances, the Court upheld the mother's rights, reasoning that there was room for difference of opinion on the issue and that the father's prima facie right to custody of a seven-year-old son could not "have any claim to immutability." The Court thus indicated that personal laws should not be seen as fixed and defined in perpetuity but could be progressively re-interpreted in certain circumstances.

(c) Changing interpretations in a changing society

In *Hasina Ahmed v. Syed Abul Fazal*,[85] the Court reaffirmed[86] that a woman's right to *'khula* (divorce by consent or agreement with her husband in consideration of the surrender of all her claims), may, in the absence of such consent or agreement, be obtained from the court.

In this context, the need for flexibility in defining the content of rights in the family was emphasized; the application of the principle of *ijtehad* or progressive interpretation, internal to Muslim law, was suggested as a possible means for "bringing about change in the concept of the Muslim personal law with regard to their application in a changing society." The Court responded positively to the exhortation:

while adjudicating on and administering Personal law [to] take into account not only the factual and the legal position and questions involved in a particular case but also consider the social dynamics when [the] concept of law is changing in a changing society . . . with the changing society women are coming of their own and their independen[ce] of mind and will must be respected while considering the legal and contractual obligation in marriage between man and woman as such.[87]

These decisions significantly extend the contours of women's rights in the family. They recognize that the personal law system exists in tension with rapidly transforming notions of personal relations, and that traditional, religious laws and precepts relating to marriage need to be brought into line with the reality of women's needs in the family.

The ramifications of these decisions are much wider than the confines of the particular judgment. They are examples of creative and gender-positive judicial interventions, which reject rigid religious interpretations in favor of establishing equal rights. Nelly Zaman's case sets out a framework based on Articles 27, 28 and 31 of the Constitution which would enable the equality of principle to be molded to fit more closely the needs of women in all spheres: state and civil, public and private. This framework, informed by the principle of interpreting existing laws in consonance with changing social mores, allows for the possibility of a major overhaul of all discriminatory personal laws, on the basis of their violation of the generally accepted principle of equality.[88]

One Step Back—Communalizing the Law

The progressive development of legal reforms has been affected by the growing forces of fundamentalism across the subcontinent, reinforced by cultural and religious resistance to equality. Discriminatory values embedded in personal laws have split into many other areas to affect women. Existing rights, previously uniformly available, have been whittled down or reformulated to include communal and discriminatory criteria in their application.

(a) Retreating from secularism

Throughout the South Asian subcontinent, the shift away from the principle of secularism has created a climate for the legitimization of discrimination against women. The most extreme situation prevails in Pakistan, now an Islamic state. The replacement of civil law with Islamic law, in particular in criminal law and the rules of evidence, has resulted in egregious violations of women's right to life and liberty and to equality under the law. For example, the state has been empowered to police private morality through the criminalization of purely private acts between consenting adults, such as *zina* (adultery and fornication).[89] It has been argued that Islamization has affected personal laws, which have by constitutional amendment been made dependent on the interpretation of the sect to which they are to be applied, and have thus been removed from the possibility of progressive interpretation. It has also indirectly restricted the availability of rights under personal laws: for example, it has been pointed out that the law on zina has deterred divorce under Christian law, since any person seeking such a divorce would need to show proof of adultery by the other spouse, leaving the offending spouse vulnerable to criminal prosecution.[90]

In Bangladesh the Constitution has been amended[91] to include the words "Bismillah ar Rahman ar Rahim"; secularism, one of the "four pillars" of the Constitution, has been replaced with "trust and faith in almighty Allah,"[92] and the fundamental principles guiding that state's international relations now include "fraternal relations among Muslim countries based on Islamic solidarity."[93] These amendments culminated in the adoption of Islam as the state religion.[94]

Women's organizations denounced the use of religion for political gain, and protested the amendment as an imminent threat to women's rights. Constitutional experts argued that the principle of secularism could not be amended as it was part of the basic structure of the Constitution,[95] and others pointed to the risk of an "end to demands for equal rights, certain amounts of judicial discrimination and religious injunctions in various spheres of personal life."[96] Political opposition was followed by legal challenges to the amendment as violating equal rights and nondiscrimination on the grounds of both sex and religion, in contravention of the Constitution, the UN Charter and the Universal Declaration.[97]

(b) Turning back the tide—limiting the application of secular laws

The spillover effect of the retreat from secularism may be discerned in a number of recent cases and statutes that reinforce divisions between communities.

Perhaps the most graphic illustrations may be found in the recent restrictions of the right to maintenance. Throughout South Asia, women have been entitled to a choice of remedies for maintenance, under the provisions of the Criminal Procedure Code, which is available uniformly,[98] or under personal laws. The criminal remedy is often preferable for both substantive and procedural reasons. It allows a claim by illegitimate children, involves less delay and expense, and is more easily enforced. Recent interventions, through statutes and through judgments of the superior courts have severely limited access to the criminal law remedy of maintenance, with Muslim women's rights being constrained by wholly inadequate provisions of their personal law.

In India, the Supreme Court's decision in the *Shah Bano* case, recognizing the extension of the statutory right to a divorced Muslim woman, was reversed by legislation in the face of a country-wide campaign by fundamentalists.[99]

In Sri Lanka, maintenance cases brought by Muslim women are heard in separate *qazi* courts; although these courts used to apply a uniform Maintenance Ordinance, a commentator sees a foreshadowing of the application of Muslim personal law in this arena in recent Supreme Court decisions.[100]

In Bangladesh, the High Court has recently held that women are no longer entitled to a choice of remedy for maintenance.[101] Selina Begum filed a claim for maintenance under the Criminal Procedure Code, having been deserted by her husband following his second marriage, and her refusal to accept the return of the dowry. Her husband argued that she could not resort to the remedy under the Criminal Procedure Code following the establishment of the Family Courts Act, which had been invested with exclusive jurisdiction to hear, inter alia, maintenance matters. The Court held in his favor. In a peculiar twist, it was held that these courts could only hear claims relating to family disputes under Muslim law. As a result, the more effective statutory remedy continues to be available to non-Muslims, while the civil remedy in the Family Court is the only remedy open to a Muslim woman. Ironically, the Family Courts were established precisely to provide a forum for speedy and effective resolution of disputes regarding family matters; conservative judicial interpretation, based on a distinction according to religious identity, has ensured that legislation intended to be ameliorative has instead narrowed and truncated the choice of remedies available to women.

Piecemeal reforms to personal laws to ameliorate the most outrageous forms of discrimination against women have only touched the majority community in every state; the laws of the minority communities have been left largely untouched, for fear of a political backlash. While the existence of personal laws violate the rights of all women, a "triple oppression" is suffered by women of minority communities.[102]

They are subject to discrimination and communal violence as members of a minority community, to gender discrimination and violence as women; they are further condemned to bear the brunt of the resistance to change by conforming to discriminatory traditions and customs practiced by their community.

The state justifies its retention of personal laws as an aspect of the policy of pluralism and the protection of minority and ethnic communities. In doing so, it detracts from basic democratic norms, in that it accepts the arrogation by so-called community leaders of the right to represent the community and ignores women's voices that point to an underlying unity of common oppression and subordination within the family.

Women who have challenged such discriminatory laws and practices within their communities have been roundly denounced by the male "leaders" of their communities. In the *Shah Bano* case tensions supported demands for reform of Muslim law; this provoked a hardening of attitudes in the threatened minority community and the backlash in turn led to reinforcing both the state's commitment to remain within the personal law framework and the "community's" resistance to change. The "cultural and religious" resistance to amending or abolishing personal laws as articulated by strong and organized religious and fundamentalist lobbies has ensured that any attempts at more comprehensive reform have been stifled. Despite repeated demands by concerned groups and in particular women's organizations, there has as yet been no overhaul of the legal system ensuring gender equality.[103]

Given the backlash that has followed interventions into the personal laws of minority communities, a useful strategy may be to emphasize reform of all religious laws together, rather than focusing on any one community, which will only increase women's sense of insecurity. It is important also to note that discrimination against women is marked by its "invisibility in fundamental rights litigation, reflecting their lack of access to justice through the court system."[104] Test cases to challenge personal laws as violative of equality rights, utilizing articulations of the equality norm in international human rights law, may provide a catalyst for change.

IV. Enforcement of the Equality Principle

International Enforcement

The inadequacy of international enforcement mechanisms is magnified and compounded when applied to the protection of women's rights. International complaints procedure remain distant and inaccessible. Recourse to the Human Rights Committee is not possible given that most South Asian states (except Sri Lanka) have not accepted its jurisdiction. The International Court of Justice (ICJ) is also an improbable forum for redress of women's rights since individuals may not approach it directly.[105] There is as yet no regional human rights regime in South Asia, and the prospect of one's coming into being is remote.

The primary enforcement mechanisms regarding women's rights in the family continue to be those of reporting and monitoring. A first step in the application of the equality norm to the violations of women's rights in the personal sphere is to lobby all relevant international bodies, in particular the Committee on the Elimination of Discrimination Against Women. A crucial aspect of the lobbying is to urge ratification of the Women's Convention and to call for the withdrawal of reservations to the Convention.

International bodies have expressed their concern at the breadth and number of reservations to the Women's Convention. They have adopted a number of strategies to counteract what is perceived as the diluting effect of reservations on the equality principle. Resolutions of the meeting of states parties regarding the incompatibility of some of the reservations to the Women's Convention have formed the basis of reports by the Secretary-General, but have so far produced no results.[106] The Committee on the Elimination of All Forms of Discrimination Against Women has recommended that states parties consider withdrawing such reservations, questioning their validity and legal effect, or introducing procedures comparable to those in other treaties to govern them.[107] The Committee has stressed when evaluating the reports of states parties that constitutional equality rights should be adhered to even where traditional and religious practices prevail.[108]

Most recently, the Sub-Commission on the Prevention of Discrimination and the Protection of Minorities has commented that certain reservations, including those to Article 2 and Article 16, might diminish the international legal norm and legitimize its violation, and that failure to meet the objects of the Convention is contributing to the exploitation of women. In this context, the Sub-Commission has explored the idea of seeking an advisory opinion from the International Court of Justice on the validity and legal effect of reservations to the Women's Convention and, whether the Vienna Convention on the Law of Treaties requires reservations to be specific.[109] The states parties to the Women's Convention can also request an advisory opinion through the Economic and Social Council.

Domestic Enforcement

Whatever the difficulties of international enforcement, the equality norm constitutes "invaluable ammunition"[110] for expanding, establishing, and enforcing standards in domestic law. Applying the international equality norm to inform the content of constitutional and legislative provisions in domestic courts remains the most effective mechanism for protecting women's rights in the family as elsewhere.

In common law countries, international law obligations must be specifically incorporated in domestic law. Customary norms will be automatically incorporated, while convention obligations often require enabling legislation.[111] A number of commentators suggest that non-discrimination on the grounds of sex has achieved the status of a customary norm.[112] However, it is difficult to argue in the face of overwhelmingly contrary state practice that this norm applies equally in both the public and private sphere.

Even where international law is not found to be incorporated in domestic law, it may affect its content as a result of the presumption that states will, as far as possible, construe their domestic law in consistency with their international obligations.[113] Principles of international law, customary or conventional, may be referred to in explicating ambiguities in domestic law.[114] Also, international conventions may reflect government policy which the courts may respect.[115] Thus it has been stated that:

The domestic application of human rights norms is now regarded as a basis for implementing constitutional values beyond the minimum requirement of the Constitution. The international human rights norms are in fact part of the constitutional expression of liberties guaranteed at the national level. The domestic courts can assume the task of expanding these liberties.[116]

The decisions of international tribunals applying the equality principle to the private sphere may be persuasive in the domestic courts of South Asia. They suggest that international obligations should be considered as evolving in accordance with the dynamic principle of treaty interpretation.

Interpreting constitutional guarantees in conformity with international equality norms, in particular the standards established by the Women's Convention, would ensure their application to the private, thus creating space for a challenge to personal laws as violative of such constitutional guarantees.

Conclusion

In considering the impact of personal laws on women's rights, this chapter has considered the scope of the international norm of equality.

The equality guarantee has to be applied universally and in the area where inequality hurts most; to do this it must breach the citadel of the private sphere—the family.

The equality norm under international law governs relations in the family. Personal laws are clearly violative of equality guarantees contained in the UN Charter and other international human rights instruments, and in particular Articles 1, 2, 3, 5, and 24 of the Women's Convention. Enforcing women's equal rights in the family requires a combination of strategies at the international and domestic level. Internationally the ratification of all human rights instruments and the withdrawal of reservations to the Women's Convention should be emphasized. Reservations assume rights will be frozen within a particular social and cultural context but this context can be reshaped in accordance with evolving notions and human rights standards.

The critical sphere for enforcement remains the domestic legal system and, in particular, the substance and procedure of family law. Domestically, constitutional equality clauses may be construed purposively to extend into the family. In South Asia, human rights norms have traditionally been seen as irrelevant to the private world of the family. These restrictive interpretations have been compounded in their effect by the conflict set up between human rights principles, in particular between religious rights, family rights, community or cultural rights, and equality rights.

The state's prioritizing of the protection of a religious or ethnic community over the protection of women—the individuals who make up half of every such community—has allowed it to ignore or excuse blatant violations of the principle of equality. Statutory reforms have mitigated the discriminatory impact of personal laws; some progress toward uniformity can also be discerned in judicial decisions on questions of family and inheritance laws.

Invoking international norms of equality, together with principles of progressive interpretation or of justice, equity, and good conscience to the end of establishing women's rights, suggests a framework for reforming personal laws. Such reforms indicate that the state's reluctance to infuse personal laws with the minimum standard of equality is not based on any overriding and inflexible principle but is purely a product of political expediency and is therefore amenable to change if supported by a sufficiently wide political consensus. At the same time these reforms indicate further strategies for change, and point to means for the restructuring of personal law toward equality.

In this context it is imperative to insist on the incorporation of universally accepted norms to prioritize the rights of women over those of the traditionally defined community. State sanction of such norms would assist in the process of their legitimization, critical in a situation where traditional and customary notions of women's roles hold sway. Popular legitimization of these principles would provide leverage not only for substantive internal reform of each community's laws but perhaps also for the eventual overhaul of the personal law system to guarantee women's rights in the home and the world.

Notes

1. See generally for critiques of the public/private divide, Katherine O'Donovan, *Sexual Divisions in the Law* (London: Weidenfeld and Nicolson, 1985); Hilary Charlesworth, Christine Chinkin, and Shelley Wright, "Feminist Approaches to International Law," *Am. J. Int'l L.* 85(4) (1991): 625–26.

2. 18 December 1979, 34 U.N. GAOR Supp. (No. 21) A/34/46 at 193 U.N. Doc. A/Res/34/180 (1979).

3. See generally Anne Bayefsky, "The Principle of Equality or Non-Discrimination in International Law," *Hum. Rts. L.J.* 11 (1990): 1.

4. U.N. Charter, Preamble.

5. U.N. Charter, arts. 1(3), 55(c).

6. Universal Declaration of Human Rights, art. 2, U.N. GAOR, G.A. Res. 217A (III), U.N. Doc. A/810 (1948) (the Universal Declaration).

7. Universal Declaration, note 6, art. 7.

8. International Covenant on Civil and Political Rights 1966, G.A. Res. 2200 (XXI), 21 U.N. GAOR Supp. No. 16 at 52, U.N. Doc. A/6316 (1966) (the Political Covenant) specifies the obligation to respect and ensure all rights set out in the Covenant "without distinction of any kind, including . . . sex" (art. 2); the obligation to ensure equal rights with regard to all civil and political rights set out in the Covenant (art. 3); the prohibition on any derogations that are discriminatory from the obligations set out therein (art. 4); the obligation to ensure equality before courts and tribunals (art. 14) and the obligation to ensure equality before the law and equal protection before the law (art. 26).

9. International Covenant on Economic and Social Rights 1966, G.A. Res. 2200 (XXI), 21 U.N. GAOR, Supp. No. 16 at 49, U.N. Doc. A/6316 (1966) (the Economic Covenant) imposes an obligation to guarantee rights contained in the Covenant "without discrimination of any kind as to . . . sex" (art. 2(2)) and to ensure the equal rights of men and women to all the economic social and cultural rights in the Covenant (art. 3).

10. *Abdulaziz, Cabales, and Balkandali v. U.K.*, 94 Eur. Ct. H.R. (ser. A) (1985).

11. *Belgian Linguistics Case*, 23 Eur. Ct. H.R. (ser. A) (1968).

12. See generally Anne Bayefsky, "Principle of Equality," note 3; Rebecca Cook, "International Human Rights Law Concerning Women: Case Notes and Comments," *Vand. J. Transnat'l L.* 23 (1990): 779; Rebecca Cook, "International Protection of Women's Reproductive Rights," *N.Y.U. J. Int'l L. & Pol.* 24 (1992): 645 at 684–88; Rebecca Cook, "Sectors of International Cooperation Through Law and the Legal Process: Women" in *The United Nations Legal Order*, ed. Oscar Schachter and Chris Joyner (Cambridge: Grotius Press, 1993) and particularly Donna J. Sullivan, "Gender Equality and Religious Freedom: Toward a Framework for Conflict Resolution," *N.Y.U. J. Int'l L. & Pol.* 24 (1992): 795–856.

13. Universal Declaration, art. 12.

14. Universal Declaration, art. 16(1).

15. Universal Declaration, art. 16(2).

16. The Political Covenant, note 8, prohibits "arbitrary or unlawful interference with privacy, family or the home" (art. 17) and provides equal rights to marry and found a family, equal rights and responsibilities as to marriage, during marriage, and at its dissolution (art. 23). The Political and Economic Covenants both provide that marriage is subject to the full and free consent of the intending spouses" (art. 23, Political Covenant; art. 10, Economic Covenant).

17. *Aumeeruddy-Czifra v. Mauritius,* Communication No. 35/1978, U.N. Doc. A/36/40 (1981); *Amendments to the Naturalization Provisions of the Constitution of Costa Rica,* Inter-American Court of Human Rights, Advisory Opinion of 19 Jan. 1984.

18. *Avellanal v. Perú,* Communication No. 202/1986, U.N. Doc. A/44/40 (1989).

19. *Broeks v. The Netherlands,* Communication No. 172/1984, U.N. Doc. A/42/40 (1987); *Zwaan de Vriez v. The Netherlands,* Communication No. 182/1984, U.N. Doc. A/42/40 (1987).

22. See Women's Convention, art. 15:

1. States Parties shall accord to women equality before the law.
2. States Parties shall accord to women in all civil matters, a legal capacity identical to that of men and the same opportunities to exercise that capacity. In particular, they shall give them equal rights to conclude contracts and to administer property and shall treat them equally in all stages of procedure in courts and tribunals.
3. States Parties agree that all contracts and instruments of any kind with a legal effect which is directed at restricting the legal capacity of women shall be deemed null and void.

23. See Women's Convention, art. 16:

1. States Parties shall take all appropriate measures to eliminate discrimination against women in all matters relating to marriage and family relations and in particular shall ensure on a basis of equality of men and women:
(a) The same right to enter into marriage;
(b) The same right freely to choose a spouse and to enter into marriage only with their free and full consent;
(c) The same rights and responsibilities during marriage and at its dissolution;
(d) The same rights and responsibilities as parents, irrespective of their marital status, in matters relating to their children; in all cases the interest of the children shall be paramount; . . .
(f) The same rights and responsibilities with respect to guardianship, wardship, trusteeship and adoption of children, or similar institutions whether these concepts exist in national legislation; in all cases the interests of the child shall be paramount;
(h) The same rights for both spouses in respect of the ownership, acquisition, management, administration, enjoyment and disposition of property, whether free of charge or for a valuable consideration.

2. The betrothal and marriage of a child shall have no legal effect and all necessary action, including legislation, shall be taken to specify a minimum age for marriage and to make the registration of marriages in an official registry compulsory.

24. See generally Bayefsky, "Principle of Equality," note 3; Cook, "Reproductive Rights," note 12 at 709–10.

25. *X & Y v. The Netherlands,* 91 Eur. Ct. H.R. (ser. A) (1985) at 11; see also *Marckx v. Belgium,* 3 Eur. Ct. H.R. (ser. A) (1979) at 31; *Airey v. Ireland,* 32 Eur. Ct. H.R. (ser. A) (1979) at 25: "fulfillment of a duty under the Convention on occasion necessitates some positive action on the part of the State."

26. See Rebecca Cook, "State Accountability Under the Convention on the Elimination of All Forms of Discrimination Against Women," Chapter 9 in this book.

27. The Committee on the Elimination of Discrimination Against Women (CEDAW) has drawn on Article 2 of the Women's Convention in its General Recommendation #19, to require states to take action to eliminate discrimination against women by private persons. *IWRAW Bulletin* (1992).

28. Bangladesh deposited its instrument of accession on 6 November 1984, India signed on 30 July 1980, and deposited its instrument of ratification on 9 July 1993, and Sri Lanka deposited its instrument of ratification on 5 October 1981.

29. U.N. Doc. CEDAW/SP/1992/2 at 9.

30. U.N. Doc. CEDAW, note 29.

31. Article 9 of the Supplementary Convention on the Abolition of Slavery, Slave Trade and Customs and Practices Similar to Slavery prohibits reservations, and art. 20(2) of the United Nations Convention on the Elimination of All Forms of Racial Discrimination provides for rejection of reservations if a two-thirds majority of contracting states object to the reservation.

32. Vienna Convention on the Law of Treaties (1969), art. 19 reflects the compatibility rule enunciated in the I.C.J Advisory Opinion on Reservations to the Convention on the Prevention and Punishment of the Crime of Genocide, 1951 I.C.J. (May 28) (Advisory Opinion).

33. Women's Convention, art. 29.

34. See generally on reservations to the Women's Convention, Belinda Clark, "Vienna Convention Reservations Regime and the Convention on the Elimination of All Forms of Discrimination Against Women," *Am. J. Int'l L.,* 85 (1990): 281; Rebecca Cook, "Reservations to the Convention on the Elimination of All Forms of Discrimination Against Women," *Va. J. Int'l L.* 30(3) (1991): 643; Anna Jenefsky, "Egypt and the Convention on the Elimination of Discrimination Against Women," *Md. J. Int'l L. and Trade* 15 (1991): 199.

35. See *Belilos,* 132 Eur. Ct. H.R. (ser. A) 132 (1988) at 28, concurring opinion of Judge de Meyer.

36. See *Belilos,* note 35 at paras. 54 and 55.

37. See Cook, "Reservations," note 34 at 691–92.

38. Vienna Convention, arts. 26 and 31, note 32.

39. U.N. Doc., note 29 at 29, 30, 32 and 33 respectively.

40. U.N. Doc., note 39 at 31.

41. Clare Palley, *Report of Working Group on Contemporary Forms of Slavery,* Sixteenth Session, U.N. Doc. E/CN.4/Sub.2/1991/41 at 16.

42. Cook, "Reservations," note 34 at 689.

43. U.N. Doc., note 29 at 31.

44. *Bangladesh Strategies for Enhancing the Role of Women in Economic Development* (Washington, DC: World Bank, 1990).

45. Eighty percent of the population of Bangladesh are Muslims, 10 percent Hindus, and the remaining 10 percent Buddhists, Christians, and Animists.

46. Cook, "Reservations," note 34.

47. Charlesworth et al., "Feminist Approaches," note 1.

48. The Constitution of Bangladesh 1972 provides for equality before the law and equal protection of the law (art. 27) and for treatment in accordance with the law (art. 31). See *Hamidul Huq Chowdhury v. Bangladesh* 34 D.L.R. 190 (1982) at paras. 11 and 12: "Equal protection under the constitution means the right to equal treatment in similar circumstances . . . harmony is to be established between a statute seeking the welfare of the community and fundamental right and to that end the executive is authorized to make a reasonable classification as to the subject matter of the statute. The reasonableness is justiciable by the Supreme Court and must be judged by standards of an ordinary prudent and reasonable man. It should be determined by intelligent differentia which would be available firstly in the statute or by external evidence."

49. Constitution of Bangladesh, 1972, art. 28.

50. Constitution of Bangladesh, art. 28(4).

51. Constitution of Bangladesh, arts. 28(3), 29(3)(c). It is important to note that any class of employment or office may be reserved on the grounds that "it is considered by its nature unsuited to members of the opposite sex."

52. Constitution of Bangladesh, art. 28(4).

53. See Constitution of Sri Lanka.

54. Durga Das Basu, *Shorter Constitution of India* (Calcutta: S.C. Sarkar 1988), 205. Commentary on the Indian Constitution (1965).

55. See *Badruddin v. Aisha,* A.L.J. 300 (1957) and *Ramprasad v. State of UP,* A.L.J. 411 (1957) respectively.

56. Constitution of Bangladesh, Preamble and art. 11.

57. Constitution of Bangladesh, art. 26.

58. See, for example, the Penal Code of 1860, the Code of Criminal Procedure, 1898, the Code of Civil Procedure 1872, and the Evidence Act 1872.

59. For example, Muslim Personal Law (Shari'a) is applicable in questions relating, *inter alia,* to "intestate succession, special property of females, including personal property inherited or obtained under . . . any other provision of personal law, marriage, dissolution of marriage . . . , maintenance, dower guardianship" (sec. 2, Shari'a Act 1937, Pakistan Code, vol. 9, 404) subject to statutory modification (sec. 37, East Bengal Civil Courts Act 1887 Pakistan Code, vol. 3, 257).

60. Sir Abdur Rahim, *Principles of Muhammadan Jurisprudence* (Lahore: Indus Publishers, 1982), 34, cited in Khawar Mumtaz and Farida Shaheed, *Women of Pakistan* (London: Zed Books, 1987), 37.

61. Hindus continue to be governed by *shastric* laws as modified by colonial legislation, such as the Hindu Widows Remarriage Act 1856, Hindu Women's Right to Property Act of 1937, and the Hindu Women's Right to Separate Residence and Maintenance Act of 1946; see generally Werner Menski and Tahmina Rahman, "Hindus and the Law in Bangladesh," *South Asia Research* 8 (1988): 111. For developments in Hindu law in India, see Kirti Singh, "Obstacles to Women's Rights in India," Chapter 16 in this book.

62. See generally on personal laws and women's rights in Bangladesh, Salma

Sobhan, *Legal Status of Women in Bangladesh* (Dacca: Bangladesh Institute of Law and International Affairs, 1974); Menski and Rahman, "Hindus and the Law," note 61; *Report of the Task Force on Women in Development* (Dhaka: 1991).

63. Pakistan Code, vol. II, 62; significantly modified in India by the Special Marriage Act 1954; see M.A. Jinnah's speech on a proposed amendment to the 1872 Act seeking to make civil marriage available irrespective of faith (cited in Tahir Mahmood, *Civil Marriage Law, Prospectives and Prospects* [Bombay: Indian Law Institute, 1978], 6): "There is a good number of progressive, educated, and enlightened Indians, whether Hindu, Muslim or Parsi, who want to adopt such laws which conform to modern trends, why should they be deprived of justice: more so since it is not prejudicial to the interests of either the Hindus or the Muslims?"

64. See also *Sukhendra Chandra Das v. Home Secretary* 1990 D.L.R. 79; *Monindra Kumar Malakar v. State* 1990 D.L.R. 349; and *Krishna Pada Datta* 1990 D.L.R. 297, in the context of the resistance to interreligious marriages and the use of criminal law to prevent women from freely choosing a spouse. The facts of the cases are similar. A Hindu woman marries a Muslim man, her family brings criminal charges of kidnapping and abduction against the man, and the woman is kept in safe custody by the police; in court the woman claims she is a major and has married and converted to Islam of her own volition. (In *Sukhendra* and *Krishna,* the woman was returned to her parents' custody.)

65. Pakistan Code, vol. VIII, 430.

66. Muslim Family Laws Ordinance 1961 (henceforth, MFLO), s. 6.

67. MFLO, sec. 6(5).

68. MFLO, secs. 9, 13 respectively.

69. MFLO, sec. 7. See, for the limited function of the Arbitration Council in restricting the husband's power of unilateral divorce, *Abdus Sobhan Sarkar v. Md. Abdul Ghani,* 25 D.L.R. 227 (1973); *Abdul Aziz v. Rezia Khatoon,* 21 D.L.R. 733 (1969).

70. MFLO, sec. 8.

71. MFLO, sec. 7(6).

72. Muslim Marriages and Divorces Registration Act, 27 D.L.R. 4 (1974).

73. Births, Deaths, and Marriages Act, P.C. vol. III 189 (1886).

74. See *Amulya Chondro Modak v. State,* 35 D.L.R. 160 (1983), where a woman had brought criminal charges under section 493 of the Penal Code 1860 against the accused of having deceitfully induced her to have sex with him in the belief that she was lawfully married to him. The Court laid great stress on the definition of belief in a *lawful* marriage, to the detriment of the appellant; see for discussion Menski and Rahman, "Hindu Law," note 61.

75. Bangladesh Code, vol. 3, 292.

76. 24 D.L.R. 240 (1972).

77. The Bangladesh Abandoned Children (Special Provisions) Repeal Ordinance, 34 D.L.R. (1982).

78. See sec. 37, East Bengal Civil Courts Act 1887, and section 2, Shari'a Act, note 56.

79. See, e.g., *Dr. Swarka Bai v. Prof. Narain,* A.I.R. Mad 792 (1953), where it was held that sec. 10 of the Divorce Act which restricts Christian women's rights to divorce is not discriminatory since: "it appears to be based on a sensible classification and after taking into consideration the abilities of man and woman, and the results of their acts, and not merely based on sex . . . also an adultery of a wife is different from an adultery by a husband . . . if the wife

commits an adultery she may bear a child and the husband will have to treat it as legitimate and be liable to maintain it."

80. See Shahdeen Mallick, "Once Again Shah Bano, Maintenance and the Scope for Marriage Contracts," *D.L.R. J.* 42 (1990): 34, and *Case Studies on Family Law in Bangladesh: Gender and Access to Justice* (APWLD Report, 1993).

81. 34 D.L.R. 221 (1982).

82. The formulation of the quality guarantee is ambiguous and appears to suggest that its application is restricted only to the State and public sphere, and does not extend into the private: see *Task Force Report on Women in Development,* note 62.

83. 38 D.L.R. (AD) 108 (1986).

84. The Muslim law of *hizanat* or custody perpetuates stereotyped notions of women's functions—see Hedayta Chapter XIV (cited in *Abu Bakar Siddiq,* para. 12): "the right of a male child appertains to the mother until he becomes independent of himself . . . capable of shifting, eating, drinking . . . but the right with respect to a girl appertains until . . . she attains the age of puberty, because a girl has occasion to learn such manners and accomplishments as are proper to women . . . and after that period it belongs to her father who is most appropriate to superintend her conduct."

85. 32 D.L.R. 294 (1980).

86. See P.L.D. (1967) S.C. 97.

87. 32 D.L.R. 294 (1980), note 85 at 297, emphasis added.

88. See, e.g., a trend toward uniformity discerned in Muslim law on succession: *Mobinnessa v. Khalidur Rahman* 37 D.L.R. (AD) 216 (1985); *Ummida Khan v. Salahuddin Khan,* 37 D.L.R. 117; *Musa v. Tazul Islam,* 38 D.L.R. 134 (1986), and *Sahimon Bewa v. Spiruddin Mohammed,* 38 D.L.R. 265 (1986); *Bangladesh v. Abani Kanti Chakraborty,* 38 D.L.R. (AD) 93 (1986).

89. Pakistan has recently enacted the Shari'a Act, which has provoked fears that it takes the country "closer towards theocracy and strengthens a handful of anti-democratic obscurantist forces, who have always taken positions against women." *Special Bulletin on the Erosion of the Judiciary and Human Rights Through Legislation (Pakistan), Women Living Under Muslim Laws* (January 1992); for more detail on violation of women's rights through "Islamization" of laws in Pakistan, see Mumtaz and Shaheed, *Women in Pakistan,* note 60 at 99–123.

90. Paper presented by Hina Jilani at the Regional Workshop on Human Rights in South Asia in the 1990s. Law and Society Trust, Colombo, November 1990.

91. Proclamations (Amendment) Order, 1977 (Proclamations Order No. 1 of 1977), 29 D.L.R. 128 (1977).

92. Constitution of Bangladesh, arts. 8(1), (1A).

93. Art. 25(2), note 92.

94. Constitution (Eighth Amendment) Act, 40 D.L.R. 95 (1988): "The state religion of the Republic is Islam, but other religions may be practised in peace and harmony in the Republic."

95. See *Keshavananda v. Kerala,* A.I.R. (1973) S.C. 1461 at 1534: "It seems also to have been a common understanding that the fundamental features of the Constitution, namely secularism, democracy and freedom of the individual would always subsist in the welfare state"; *Indira Gandhi v. Raj Narayan,* A.I.R. (1975) S.C. 2299: "It is beyond the pale of reasonable controversy that if there be any unamendable features of our Constitution on the score that they form part of our basic structure of the Constitution they are: . . . equality of status

and opportunity shall be secured to all its citizens. . . . The state shall have no religion of its own and all persons shall have equally entitled to freedom of conscience and right freely to profess practice and propagate religion."

96. Justice K.M. Subhan, Courier, 22 April 1988, cited in Naila Kabir, "The Quest for National Identity: Women, Islam and the State in Bangladesh in *Women, Islam and the State,* ed. Deniz Kandyotti (Houndmills, UK: Macmillan, 1991), 139.

97. See Kabir, "The Quest," note 96.

98. See sec. 488, Code of Criminal Procedure, 1898, Bangladesh Code, vol. 4, 90; sec. 125, Criminal Procedure Code, India.

99. For further discussion, see Kirti Singh, "Obstacles to Women's Rights in India," Chapter 16 in this book; and Radhika Coomaraswamy, "To Bellow like a Cow: Women, Ethnicity, and the Discourse of Rights," Chapter 2 in this book.

100. See *Marzoona v. Samad,* 79 N.L.R. 209 (1977); *Burhan v. Ismail,* 1978–1979 2 Sri L.R. 218, cited in S. Goonasekara, "Women, Equality Rights and the Constitution," *Thatched Patio* 3 (1990): 41, see also comments at 42 regarding the application of a uniform adoption act so as to restrict a Muslim adopted child's inheritance rights.

101. *Abdul Khaleque v. Selina Begum,* D.L.R. 450 (1990).

102. See Rohini Hensman, "Oppression Within Oppression: The Dilemma of Muslim Women in India," *Thatched Patio* 3 (1990): 22.

103. A number of petitions have been filed in the Indian High Court challenging personal laws as violative of equality guarantees, regarding Muslim law of marriage and inheritance, Christian law of succession, tribal law on succession: see Indira Jaising, "Women and Law," in *A Decade of Women's Movement in India,* ed. Neera Desai (Bombay: Himalaya Pub. House, 1988).

104. See Goonesekara, "Women, Equality Rights," note 100.

105. Any disagreement between parties on the interpretation or application of the Women's Convention may be submitted to arbitration or to the International Court of Justice. Art. 29, the Women's Convention.

106. See Cook, "Reservations," note 34 at 708.

107. Committee on the Elimination of Discrimination Against Women, General Recommendation #20, in IWRAW Report (1992) at 33.

108. See, for example, comments on Sri Lanka report in IWRAW Bulletin (1992) at 13.

109. U.N. Doc. E/CN.4/Sub.2/1991/41 at paras. 51–59 and L. 49.

110. Noreen Burrows, "International Law and Human Rights: The Case of Women's Rights," in *Human Rights: From Rhetoric to Reality,* ed. T. Campbell et al. (London: Blackwell, 1986), 92.

111. See, e.g., Constitution of India, art. 253: "Notwithstanding anything in the foregoing provisions of this chapter, Parliament has the power to make any law for the whole or any part of the territory of India for implementing any treaty, agreement or convention with any other country of countries or any decision made at any international conference, association or other body."

112. See Ian Brownlie, *Principles of International Law* (Oxford: Clarendon Press, 1990); Bayefsky, "Principle of Equality," note 3; and Bayefsky, "General Approaches to the Domestic Application of Women's International Human Rights Law," Chapter 15 in this book; "American Restatement of International Law," in *Cases and Materials in International Law,* ed. D.J. Harris (London: Sweet and Maxwell, 1991), 695.

113. Justice Md. Haleem in *Developing Human Rights Jurisprudence, the Domes-*

tic Application of International Human Rights Norms (London: Commonwealth Secretariat, 1988), 101: "A State has an obligation to make its municipal law conform to its undertakings under treaties to which it is party."

114. *Keshavananda v. Kerala,* A.I.R. (1973) S.C. 1461 at 1510; *Bombay Education Society v. Bombay,* I.L.R. (1954) Bombay 1333; *Maneka Gandhi v. India,* A.I.R. (1978) S.C. 597 (India); *M. K. Silva v. Piyasena Senaratne* (S.C. App. No. 7 of 1988) (Sri Lanka); see also the International Law Association's interim report on *Status of Universal Declaration in National and International Law* (London: International Law Association, 1992).

115. *Jolly George Verghese v. Bank of Cochin,* A.I.R. (1980) S.C. 470 at 473.

116. Haleem, *Developing Human Rights Jurisprudence,* note 113.

Chapter 21
Using the African Charter on Human and Peoples' Rights to Secure Women's Access to Land in Africa

Florence Butegwa

Introduction

Insofar as there exists a de jure or de facto significant difference in opportunities for access to land in any country, and that difference is based purely on whether one is a man or a woman, there is discrimination. Such discrimination violates international human rights law if it is unable to pass the international standards of "objective and reasonable justification"[1] or of reasonable relationship of proportionality between the means and the aim sought.[2] In many African countries, there is both de jure and de facto discrimination against women in opportunities to acquire, hold, and deal in land. This chapter explores possibilities and difficulties of using the African Charter on Human and Peoples' Rights to secure women's access to land.

The chapter is divided into four sections: an overview of the situation regarding women's access to land in Africa; the international principle of nondiscrimination and its relevance to women's access to land; the African Charter, possibilities and constraints; and some strategies for the future.

Women and Access to Land in Africa

Access to land in many African countries is governed by a dual system of law. Customary law and statutory law apply alongside each other often raising situations of internal conflict of laws and general confusion in case law and in popular understanding of the law. The diversity of customary and legislative frameworks for land ownership in Africa do not render themselves to easy combined analysis. Therefore, for purposes of this chapter, the situation of women regarding access to land is presented here with special reference to Tanzania and Uganda.

In both countries, land is owned by the state and individuals can only acquire rights of occupancy and usufructuary.[3] The technical difference between usufructuary rights and ownership as understood in western legal theory is not material in this chapter. Both confer rights of control and power to deal in the land and the interest of the holder may be transferred by will, under laws of intestacy or through commercial transactions. Tanzania has attempted to codify its customary law rules and provides some insights into land ownership among matrilineal societies in Africa. In both countries, access to land is mainly through "family transfers," direct allocation from a state agency or through a commercial transaction. The situation of women under each method is dealt with separately.

Family Transfers and Women's Access to Land

The term "family transfers" is used here to refer to three methods of acquiring land. The first is the case where a man transfers land to his son when he is ready to marry and is quite common in the rural areas, where land is not registered. The transfer is accomplished by simply showing the son that part of the land on which he can establish his new home. Daughters are never beneficiaries of this type of land acquisition.

The second covers the rare instances where a woman is given a share of her husband's landed property on divorce. In Uganda, legislation and courts do not regard a married woman's domestic duties as contributions toward the accumulation of property by her husband. A woman will only share in the distribution of matrimonial property if she can prove actual monetary contribution toward the purchase.[4] In Tanzania, however, the Law of Marriage Act provides that property acquired during the subsistence of the marriage shall be presumed as belonging to both parties.[5] Courts are given wide powers when called upon to divide matrimonial property between the parties on divorce. They may take into account, inter alia, "the contributions by either party in money, property or work towards the acquisition of the assets."[6] Courts have differed in their interpretation of this provision. In *Hamid Amir v. Maryam Arris*, a woman's claim to a share in the matrimonial property was rejected, and the judge stated:

With due respect I'm unable to agree because the wife runs a household, washes, cleans, cooks and saves money each month, this should be termed as her contribution and joint effort towards acquisition of property during subsistence of marriage.[7]

In *Bi Hawa Mohamed Ally Sefu,* however, the Tanzania Court of Appeal held a different view:

It is apparent that the Act seeks to liberate married women from such exploitation and oppression by reducing the traditional inequality between them and their husbands in so far as their respective rights and duties are concerned. Although certain features of traditional inequality [remain] under the Act . . . , these do not detract from the overall purpose of the Act as an instrument of liberation and equality between the sexes.[8]

It is hoped that the Court of Appeal has set a precedent that is soundly based on considerations of women's human rights and will pave the way for further inroads into customary law-based sex discrimination.

The third method of family transfers is through the inheritance of a deceased relative's parcel of land. As virgin land available for state allocation decreases, succession to a relative's land may be the only viable avenue left for many people in Africa. This is especially so for those without the economic means to purchase land on the market or to qualify for land allocation by State agencies. Allocation is normally dependent on financial ability to develop the land within a specified period.[9]

Customary law governs succession to land held under customary tenure. In Uganda the Succession Act[10] and the Succession (Amendment) Decree 1972[11] allow a surviving widow to inherit any property, including land, bequeathed to her under her deceased husband's will. In practice very few people make wills in Uganda. It is considered a bad omen for one to make a will.[12]

In case of intestacy, the widow has no claim to her late husband's land. The land goes to the customary law heir, normally the deceased's eldest son. The widow was traditionally allowed to remain on the matrimonial land until her death or remarriage. The past decade, however, has seen a marked erosion of this custom. Heirs tend to sell off the land and use the proceeds for their own benefit. The Uganda Succession Act[13] allows a widow a 15 percent share in the estate of a deceased husband, but this percentage is very rarely calculated to include any land.

In Tanzania's matrilineal societies, where property is inherited through a wife's lineage, women do not have effective control or ownership of the family land. Contrary to popular belief, land and other valuable property is controlled by the male members of the woman's family, normally her father, brothers, or uncles. They are responsible for showing her and her husband a piece of land to use as family land.[14] In patrilineal societies, a wife is not regarded as a member of the family for land ownership and inheritance purposes. The widow's contribution toward the acquisition of the property is not taken into consideration either.[15] Under the Local Customary Law (Declaration) Order, the eldest son in the deceased's first marriage[16] has the primary right to the family land.[17] Failure of a male issue in this marriage passes the right to sons in subsequent marriages. As a Tanzania High Court ruling puts it aptly,

a widow does not acquire any proprietary rights in her husband's landed property simply because she contributed labour in developing them [sic] and therefore she gains no inheritance rights therein.[18]

Daughters of the deceased cannot inherit land. They are allowed to live on and cultivate the family land as long as they are not married. Progressive judges have attempted to interpret Rule 19 more liberally. In *Ndewawosia d/o Ndeamtzo v. Imanuel s/o Malasi*, for instance, the judge said:

this custom, which bars daughters from inheriting clan land and sometimes their own fathers' estate, has left a loophole for undeserving clansmen to flourish within the tribe. . . . These men are not entitled to take property towards the acquisition of which they have contributed absolutely nothing. . . . In Tanzania . . . and elsewhere the idea of equality between men and women has gained much strength. . . . The time has come when the rights of daughters in inheritance should be recognized.[19]

Unfortunately this decision does not appear to have been followed consistently by other high court judges.[20] The inconsistencies in case law are indicative of the fact that the issue remains undecided. The judge in *Ephrahim v. Pastory* and like-minded judges are pioneers in safeguarding women's human rights while reminding the government that it is a signatory to international human rights instruments guaranteeing equality and freedom from discrimination on the basis of sex.[21] The situation might be clearer when the issue has been considered and determined by the Court of Appeal.

Access to Land Through Direct Purchase

The acquisition of land through direct purchase is generally governed by the law of contract. Contractual capacity is based on age. Once one has attained the age of majority in Uganda and Tanzania, he/she is eligible to contract. Theoretically, therefore, women have access to land on an equal footing with men. In practice, however, women remain at a significant disadvantage. Financial credit to purchase land requires security in the form of a developed piece of land. The majority of women do not have it since they do not inherit land. An outright purchase is even rarer as the majority of women do not earn enough from petty trading, formal employment, or the informal sector to raise the purchase price.

Women's Access to Land and International Human Rights Law

The whole question of women's access to land and other economic resources is one that is rarely discussed in the context of international human rights law. Freedom from discrimination is a central theme in international human rights law. The United Nations has as one of its purposes the promotion and encouragement of a "respect for human rights and for fundamental freedoms for all without distinction as to . . . sex."[22] The International Covenant on Civil and Political Rights states:

All persons are equal before the law and are entitled without any discrimination to the equal protection of the law. In this respect, the law shall prohibit any discrimination and guarantee to all persons equal and effective protection against discrimination on any ground such as . . . sex.[23]

The African Charter on Human and Peoples' Rights simply states that "Every individual shall be equal before the law."[24] The Charter further provides in Article 18(3) that states shall ensure the elimination of every discrimination against women and also ensure the protection of the rights of the woman as stipulated in international declarations and conventions.

Freedom from discrimination is a substantive and independent human right in the context of these instruments.[25] The Human Rights Committee has confirmed in relation to Article 26 of the International Covenant on Civil and Political Rights that the right to freedom from discrimination is an autonomous right. It prohibits discrimination in law or in practice in any field regulated and protected by public authorities.[26] The concept of discrimination is understood to mean

any distinction, exclusion, restriction or preference which is based on any ground such as race, colour, sex, language, religion, political or other opinion, national or social origin, property, birth or other status, and which has the purpose or effect of nullifying or impairing the recognition, enjoyment or exercise by all persons, on an equal footing, of all rights and freedoms.[27]

Such discrimination is against women if it is made solely on the basis of sex and it impairs or nullifies the recognition and enjoyment by women on an equal footing with men of human rights and fundamental freedoms.[28] As indicated by Bayefsky, the definition of discrimination has two key requisites: a distinction that is not based on objective and reasonable justification and the absence of a reasonable relationship of proportionality between the aim and the means employed to attain it.[29]

The state of the law in Tanzania and Uganda determines access to land on the basis of sex. This discrimination against women is not based on any objective and reasonable justification. Much as the customs of the people of Uganda and Tanzania may have barred women from inheriting clan land, the tenets underlying the custom are no longer valid. It was feared that clan land would fall into the hands of non-clan members through marriage. It could even be said that this fear and consequent prohibition applied equally to men. No man had a right to sell clan land to a non-clan member. Clan membership was customarily the effective criterion on which usufructuary rights and control over the land was based.

This is no longer the case. Men, increasingly appreciative of commercial credit, have applied for and obtained direct grants (long-term leaseholds) and title deeds from government. The title documents are issued in the name of the individual rather than the clan. The deeds are then used as security for loans from commercial banks. Men are also increasingly selling land to non-clan members. Urbanization and ease of geographical mobility have allowed more and more people to settle in areas far from their original clan territory. The individualization of land through individual titles, coupled with the fact that families can settle anywhere in the country, is indicative of the erosion of clanism as a basis for access to land. These developments mean that the retention of the custom that discriminates against women is not justifiable. The discrimination in cases of land that is not held under customary tenure is even less justifiable. Consequently, it is clear that both law and practice in Tanzania and Uganda relating to access to land unlawfully discriminates against women contrary to international human rights law.

The African Charter and Women's Access to Land

The question is the extent to which the African Charter can be used to secure and promote women's access to land in Africa. Both Tanzania and Uganda have ratified the Charter. As states parties they are bound to "recognize [the right to freedom from discrimination] . . . and shall undertake to *adopt legislation* or other measures to give effect to [it]."[30] State parties undertake to recognize the rights and freedoms guaranteed by the Charter and to adopt legislation or other measures to give effect to them.[31] Tanzania and Uganda have failed in their obligations under the Charter. They have not adopted legislation that would guarantee access to land for women on an equal footing with men. In fact by allowing discriminatory customary rules of inheritance to apply, the laws of Tanzania and Uganda are in direct conflict with the obligation of these states under the African Charter.

Neither have they taken other appropriate measures to remove discrimination against women. What "other measures" states parties are required to take under Article 1 are not specified. The only guiding principle is that such other measures should be designed to give effect to the protected right. The wording of this article in the African Charter is modeled on other international human rights instruments. States parties to the International Covenant on Civil and Political Rights undertake "to take the necessary steps . . . to adopt such legislative or other measures as may be necessary to give effect to the rights."[32] In *Airey v. Ireland,* the European Court of Human Rights confirmed that fulfillment of a state's obligation under the European Convention "necessitates some positive action on the part of the state; in such circumstances, the state cannot simply remain passive."[33] The United Nations Committee on Economic, Social, and Cultural Rights has also emphasized that while the adoption of legislation may be a desirable step toward the protection of guaranteed human rights, it did not exhaust state obligation under the treaty. States must take all appropriate means.[34]

These interpretations give a good indication of the extent of the obligation of states parties to the African Charter in eliminating discrimination against women in the area of access to land. Article 25 of the Charter is crucial and perhaps goes further than other instruments. It reads:

States parties . . . shall have the duty to protect and ensure through teaching, education and publication, the respect of the rights and freedoms contained in the present Charter and to see to it that these freedoms and rights as well as corresponding obligations and duties are understood.

The significance of this provision is that not only is state responsibility invoked if the state fails to pass laws which guarantee freedom from discrimination, but also if private individuals continue to run their affairs in accordance with discriminatory customs because they are unaware of the statutory laws or internationally guaranteed rights. The framers of the African Charter were obviously aware that many

African customs and practices were based and modeled on the principle of unequal relations and status between the sexes. A conscious decision was, therefore, taken to require each state to teach and educate its population on the changed values and laws. Each state party to the Charter is obliged to publicize the rights guaranteed by the Charter and the obligations of private individuals and state organs to respect those rights. It is an explicit state obligation to ensure that nondiscriminatory laws are clearly understood by the populace and its own agents.

What is the extent of this duty? Is it fulfilled if a state merely passes nondiscriminatory statutes that nobody (save the few lawyers) is aware of? Internal rules in most African states provide that a law becomes enforceable once it is published in the *Official Gazette,* a government publication that is not sold anywhere except at government printers in the capital city of the country. In many countries, the *Gazette* is published in English. The statute is in the legal language whose technical nature and incomprehensibility only serves to keep lawyers employed. Does such publication satisfy the requirements of the African Charter in Article 25? It is submitted here that merely passing laws or publishing them in a publication whose circulation is severely limited and whose language is not understood by the majority of the people in a country falls far short of the Charter's requirements. States have a duty to ensure the respect of rights and freedoms and to see to it that these freedoms and rights as well as corresponding obligations and duties are understood.

Article 28 of the African Charter enunciates the obligation of every individual in the following terms:

> Every individual shall have the duty to respect and consider his fellow beings without discrimination, and to maintain relations aimed at promoting, safeguarding and reinforcing mutual respect and tolerance.

It is not just the state that is obliged to stop discrimination but all individuals within it. The state itself is obliged to ensure that this obligation of each individual within its purview not to discriminate against a fellow human being is clearly understood. It is clear from the first part of this chapter that Tanzania and Uganda, prototypes of many other countries in Africa, have failed in their obligations under the African Charter. Women continue to be discriminated against in matters concerning access to land.

Possibilities of Using the Charter

Can the Charter effectively be used to promote and protect women's right to freedom from discrimination in access to land? In attempting to answer this question, one important matter must be emphasized. The fact that the provisions of the Charter explicitly prohibit discrimination on the basis of sex and impose stringent obligations on states parties opens up real possibilities for using the African Charter to secure access to land for women in Africa. This section looks at six inter-related aspects which may affect positively or negatively the realization of this possibility: (1) the apparent contradictions in the provisions of the Charter; (2) the institutional framework for enforcement established under the Charter, including its powers and independence; (3) the institutional support available to the African Commission on Human and Peoples' Rights; (4) the national, regional, and international political environment within which the African Commission is posited to function; (5) the knowledge and ability of women and women's and/or human rights organizations to use the African Charter; and (6) opportunities for internal application of Charter provisions and/or ideals.

(a) Apparent contradictions in the Charter

Does the African Charter combine concepts and values which are inherently contradictory, thereby nullifying one of them? Does the Charter nullify the individual fundamental rights and freedoms guaranteed in Articles 1–17 by the so-called group rights? Specifically and of particular relevance to this chapter, are the provisions prohibiting discrimination on the grounds of sex necessarily nullified by Article 18 (1) and (2)? Ronald T. Nhlapo raises the same issue when he asks:

Can a state guarantee equality before the law for its citizens whilst taking into consideration "the virtues" of . . . [its] historical tradition . . . ?[35]

At issue here are the terms of the preamble to the Charter in which African states agree to take into consideration the virtues of their historical tradition and the values of African civilization as an inspiration in reflecting on concepts of human rights. Also at issue is Article 18, which reads:

1. The family shall be the natural unit and basis of society. It shall be protected by the state which shall take care of its physical health and moral.
2. The State shall have the duty to assist the family which is the custodian of morals and traditional values recognized by the community.

It has been argued that unequal relations and status between men and women were part and parcel of traditional African values and the concept of family.[36] It is not necessary here to engage in a discussion as to whether or not discrimination against women has always been part of African traditional culture. The Charter itself makes it clear that whatever the traditions were, any discrimination against women is not permissible. This is why this assertion is made right within the Article dealing with family. Thus Article 18(3) provides:

The State shall ensure the elimination of every discrimination against women and also ensure the protection of the rights of the woman and the child as stipulated in international declarations and conventions.

The Charter obliges states to ensure that whatever cultural values and practices are permitted by domestic law must comply with the human right principle of freedom from discrimination on the basis of sex. It is, consequently, submitted that there is no real contradiction between the right of women not to be discriminated against and the protected position of the family.

(b) The institutional framework

The African Charter establishes the African Commission on Human and Peoples' Rights (the Commission) "to promote human and peoples' rights and ensure their protection in Africa."[37] The Commission consists of eleven members chosen from amongst African personalities of the highest reputation, known for their high morality, integrity, impartiality, and competence in matters of human and peoples' rights.[38] The method of appointment of the Commissioners presents the first weakness in the potential effectiveness of the Commission. The Commissioners are to be elected by the Assembly of Heads of State and Government (Assembly) from amongst persons nominated by states parties.[39] The practice of state parties has shown that individual states give special attention to loyalty to the government in power when nominating candidates for election. As a result many of the current Commissioners are also ministers in their countries. This raises questions of their potential ability to act impartially, especially in cases in which the human rights record of their respective states is called into question. Professor Nguema, a member of the Commission, has admitted that issues of credibility do arise out of the fact that candidates are presented by the state.[40] The Commission is seen as an extension of national governments. The selection of government officials also means that Commissioners are often too busy to attend to Commission affairs. There have been occasions when the Commission has not been able to transact its business at its biannual sessions due to lack of quorum.[41]

The Commission has power to receive communications from both states parties and individuals. According to its Rules, a complaint may also be submitted by a non-governmental organization (NGO) if the person(s) directly affected by the alleged human rights violation is unable to submit the complaint. This rule offers a real possibility for using the Commission to protect human rights. The likelihood of reprisals against an individual often means that victims of abuse are unwilling to file the complaints directly. Individuals also lack the resources necessary to represent their complaints in the manner required by the Commission. Affected individuals may also be in detention and therefore unable to contact the Commission or to research into matters relating to their own case. Allowing non-governmental organizations to play a role is very progressive of the Commission.

The Commission has no right to grant a remedy or to bind a state party to any particular decision. Its power is limited to submitting a report of its findings to the Assembly which determines the course of action, if any, to take.[42] A further limitation to the potential effectiveness of any intervention by the Commission is the obligation to keep any action it takes confidential until the Assembly decides otherwise.[43] This means that the Commission cannot publish the names of the parties to a dispute, the issues raised or the action taken. One of the most important "enforcement mechanisms" in international human rights law is publicity. The Commission is denied this tool.[44] The potential preventive, educational, and promotional role of publicizing of the identity of the offending state and the action taken to redress the situation is entirely lost. It was claimed that Article 59 was justified by the fact that African traditions favored conciliation rather than judicial settlement. The same argument was used to explain the inappropriateness of establishing an African court of human rights.[45] Such an argument is only partly true. While conciliation was and still is the preferred method of conflict resolution, African societies always had a judicial option in case reconciliation failed. A look at the congestion and backlog of cases in the national courts of African states clearly indicates the need for judicial settlement, if only as a last resort. It is not clear why African leaders maintain this facade within the context of the African Charter. One possibility is, of course, the fear that an African court of human rights would question their own human rights record.

Women's access to land could also be promoted by calling upon the Commission to interpret the Charter to show that it is covered by the equality provision in Article 3. States would then be obligated to include in their periodic reports information on the steps they have taken to remove discrimination against women. Unfortunately, the Charter provides that only state parties or an African organization recognized by the Organization of African Unity (OAU) may request the Commission to interpret the Charter.[46] It is not clear whether a non-governmental organization granted observer status at the Commission is thereby "recognized by the OAU." No provisions of the Charter have been interpreted by the Commission because no state party has requested such interpretation.[47]

Another primary function of the Commission is to collect documents and to undertake studies and research on African problems in the field of human and peoples' rights.[48] This mandate is crucial for any efforts in promoting women's access to land on the continent. There is general lack of empirical data on many aspects of the problem. Most important is the extent to which African social structures have broken down and the selectivity in which those customs that keep women in subordinate positions are kept while others are abandoned.

(c) Institutional support

The Commission, though hampered by the institutional problems outlined above, remains with some potential to promote women's access to land. In order to exploit this potential, however, the Commission requires institutional support including finances, an efficient and functional secretariat, and sufficient time for the Commissioners to transact Commission affairs. Toward this end, the African Charter provides that the Secretary-General of the OAU shall provide the staff and services necessary for the effective discharge of the duties of the Commission. The OAU shall bear the costs involved.[49]

Despite this assurance, it is common knowledge that the OAU has failed to provide institutional support adequate to enable the Commission to carry out its functions. Limited finances have severely affected the capacity of the Commission to carry out its functions. The Commission can only have two biannual meetings of eight days each. These meetings are clearly insufficient if the Commission is to consider state reports[50] and deal with any pending communications. The Commission should also have enough time to formulate guidelines and general comments, along the lines of similar comments from the Human Rights Committee and the Committee on Economic, Social, and Cultural Rights.[51] The guidelines and comments would be useful in guiding states in reporting on their progress in promoting human rights. They would also play an interpretive role thus minimizing the inaction in this regard where states parties fail to request formal interpretation under Article 45(3).

Problems of funding have also denied the Commission a functional Secretariat. The Banjul office has only one professional staff member.[52] As such, the Secretariat cannot undertake studies or research; it cannot have Commission documents ready for meetings; and it cannot respond to correspondence from African non-governmental organizations interested in contributing to or benefiting from the Commission's work.[53] The situation was aptly put by Isaac Nguema, one of the Commissioners, that "the Commission has no Secretariat—just the idea of one."[54]

The implications of inadequate financial and institutional support for the promotion of women's access to land through the Commission are grave. The plausibility of arguments that invoke customary law and practice to deny women access to land need to be countered by scientific data showing that the tenets on which the customs were based are no longer valid. Research by the Commission in this area would be invaluable. The Commission also needs to guide states toward looking at this issue as part of their obligations under the Charter and therefore reporting on it periodically. The Committee on the Elimination of All Forms of Discrimination Against Women has adopted this strategy to bring the issue of violence against women into sharper focus and to encourage states to report on their progress toward its elimination.[55]

(d) National, regional, and international environment

Next to inadequate funding, the Commission's capacity to work effectively is affected most severely by the socioeconomic environment at national, regional, and international levels. It may not be grossly inaccurate to say that the perceived significance of the Commission as a human rights organization is to a large extent influenced by the politics, economics, and culture within and among African states and at an international level.

At the national level, there has been a high turnover in political leadership. Some of the "new" leadership used force of arms to come to power and continue to be paranoid about real and imaginary opponents. Such rulers are determined to stay in power at all costs, including individual human rights. Various, seemingly plausible excuses are then given to camouflage their personal political and economic ambition. Within communities, women's access to land, tied as it is to the principle of equality between sexes, raises questions that go to the root of traditional African social structures. The family, clan, and tribe were so structured that men, women, and children had defined roles, duties, and status. Property "ownership" and other subsidiary interests in the land also depended on the place of individuals within these structures.[56] Just as the eldest son in a family enjoyed certain privileges, so too did men in the family and clan. Women's status was low with no direct access to and control over land. Under the circumstances, attempts to guarantee women basic human rights and fundamental freedoms on an equal footing with men elicits emotional and hostile reactions.

In such a national environment, the African Commission needs to be very active and visible in ensuring that states comply with their obligations under the Charter. In particular, the obligation of states to educate the population on the protected rights and their individual obligations under the Charter needs to be emphasized. To change people's attitudes and practices, states would need to enforce nondiscriminatory laws systematically.

What the inaction by states means for efforts to promote women's access to land is that there is limited impetus at the national level for legislative reforms or for practical steps to reverse the trend. Whatever activities in this regard are taking place are by women's non-governmental organizations, which some governments dismiss as misguided elite women aping western concepts. The situation is compounded by a general lack of awareness of the law among women and the lack of opportunities for them to meet and discuss their legal status and map out strategies. The heavy workload for women in most African communities, and the lack of efficient and regular channels of communication to expose them to new ideas and involve them in a dialogue for change contribute to making national efforts to change the status quo a slow process. Traditional human rights groups in individual countries have also failed to promote women's right not to be discriminated against.

At the regional and international levels, possibilities for effective use of the African Commission are compromised by the nature of international human rights law and international politics. International human rights law, though imposing obligations on states to secure basic rights and freedoms for individuals, is characterized by a lack of reciprocity of interest among states. Save for abuse of rights of aliens, which might provoke protest and possible retaliation from the state of their nationality, the international community often fails to respond if the abuses are directed to a state's own citizenry.[57] Recent history has shown that there may be some verbal condemnation but seldom any tangible action sufficient to make a state act differently. The possibility of even a verbal condemnation from states parties to the African Charter directed against an African state government is indeed remote. In the many cases where it would have been called for, there was only general silence.[58] Even if some governments had explicitly condemned the violations, it would have been in vain due to the fact that retorsion or reprisals among African states is not possible.[59] There is little trade, economic aid, or other indispensable benefit accruing from one to the other. Of course there are special cases, like a state's being dependent on hydroelectricity from a neighboring state or where a landlocked country depends on another with a port for all its imports. The difficulty of using such arrangements to force another country to respect human rights is that both countries stand to make worse the current economic conditions. They cannot afford to do it. There is also some wisdom in the English adage that those who live in glass houses should not throw stones.

In direct contrast to the situation among African states, western or developed countries have been able to condemn and take action against a country they accuse of violating the human rights of its citizens. In the 1980s, the United States government was able to use its development aid to pressure the governments of the Sudan, Liberia, and Ethiopia to improve their human rights records.[60] More recently, the United States and several donor countries were able to pressurize the government of Kenya to allow multiparty politics and to allow greater freedoms to political opponents. There have been calls to Zaire's President Mobuto to resign, allegedly due to his bad human rights record.

The point here is that international human rights law, and international law generally, has reached a point where "enforcement" is largely dependent on those with economic and military muscle. The International Monetary Fund and World Bank's economic structural adjustment programs, have made it difficult for meaningful and significant bilateral relations among African states to develop. Such relations are crucial to developing a respect among the states, which respect is necessary for promoting human rights through the African Commission. The economic structural adjustment programs have also made the majority of the people in the implementing countries so poor that their major concern and occupation is sheer survival. Challenging the law or the practice of states is a luxury. Western governments under the leadership of the United States of America have taken on the role of "world policemen," as seen in the Gulf crisis and the current crisis in former Yugoslavia. The problem here is that these governments will only be moved to act where their individual national, economic, or military interests are directly or indirectly threatened. Although this aspect of developed countries' intervention is seldom explicitly acknowledged, a look around the world provides some insights.

(e) Women, non-governmental organizations, and the African commission

The next question that this chapter would like to highlight is the level of awareness and technical knowledge women and African NGOs have about the African Charter or Commission and its work. Most women in Africa are not aware of the rights they have under domestic law. They are unaware of the difference between custom and law, especially the fact that some customs are illegal under the laws of the country. Admittedly, there are some efforts by women's NGOs to reverse this situation but the process is just beginning. The NGOs themselves, spearheaded by women lawyers, though knowledgeable in domestic laws are not conversant with international human rights law. Specifically, many have only a cursory knowledge of the African Charter, the Commission, and their relevance and potential in the promotion of women's international human rights. It is not surprising, therefore, that the majority have not sought to include the Charter and the Commission in the legal rights awareness programs currently being implemented.

The Commission has not exploited this avenue of promoting human rights. Many NGOs that would be able to submit alternative reports when the Commission is considering a particular state report remain unaware of when their country's report is to be considered. The procedure for obtaining observer status or otherwise participating in the Commission's work is not widely publicized. Recently the International Commission of Jurists and the African Centre for Democracy and Human Rights Studies, have attempted to redress the situation by bringing African Human Rights organizations to a meeting parallel to the biannual Commission meetings. The NGOs have been able to make specific recommendations on how best the Commission can support them to support it. Most recommendations revolve around regular and efficient communication from the Commission and training in its procedures relating to communications from individuals and NGOs. The state of the Secretariat of the Commission, unless substantially refurbished, does not allow the Commission to put the proposals into effect.

(f) Domestic use of the African Charter

A final avenue of using the African Charter to secure women's right of access to land would be to use the Charter in domestic courts. Admittedly, the Charter, like other international instruments, does not become part of domestic law unless and until it is so incorporated by the national legislature. But this does not mean that an innovative lawyer or court cannot use it to make progressive decisions. In a recent case in the Supreme Court of Botswana, the Judge President put this aptly:

Botswana is a member of the community of civilized States which has undertaken to abide by certain standards of conduct, and, unless it is impossible to do otherwise, it would be wrong for its courts to interpret its legislation in a manner which conflicts with the international obligations which Botswana has undertaken.[61]

The learned judge went on to hold that the African Charter could be relied on as an aid to interpretation of national law in Botswana. The Tanzanian court used a similar argument to hold that Tanzanian customary rules, which prevented women from sharing in the inheritance of land, were not applicable as they were contrary to Tanzania's obligations under international law.[62]

Conclusion and the Way Forward

The chapter has attempted to show that the African Charter on Human and Peoples' Rights provides definite possibilities in securing the right of access to land. It provides the legal and institutional framework for this purpose. The African Commission, however, is not likely to be an effective tool in its present circumstances. Some of the impediments to the African Commission's effectiveness are more problematic than others. This section identifies some issues which can be corrected with relative success.

First is the question of publicity for the African Charter, the Commission, and its work. Women and women's and human rights NGOs will not use the Commission unless they understand what it stands for and the possibilities of using it to advance their work at the national level. The Commission needs to identify these African NGOs, communicate with them regularly and involve them in training activities relating to the Charter and how to access the Commission. Although the Commission is handicapped by finances, the possibility of its mounting this program with donor funds, and in conjunction with a reputable international human rights organization, is real. The fear is that African governments may see the Commission as controlled and financed by foreign governments. This fear is only justified if the operating costs of the Commission are subsidized from abroad. The advantage of visibility for the Commission is the possible workload from individuals and NGOs, which might force the OAU Secretary-General to increase the Commission budget.

Second is the Commission's taking time to streamline existing guidelines for state reports, which are confusing. These guidelines must not only cover procedural matters, but also clarify the substantive obligations of states under the Charter. Article 59 of the Charter only applies to action taken on communications. The Commission must be bold enough to publicly identify states that have failed to submit periodic reports or those whose reports make a mockery of the whole process. Such action would enable national and international NGOs and interested foreign states to take appropriate action to put pressure on the governments concerned.

Third is the initiative that women and human rights activists must take to "wake the Commission up." African NGOs have to take the initiative to learn about the Charter and how to access its institutions. Once this is achieved, they need to obtain observer status at the Commission and regularly attend its sessions. Since the Commission allows NGOs with observer states to propose items for its agenda,[63] women's concerns, including access to land, need to be addressed by the Commission. Some of the questions identified in this chapter as needing research can be undertaken by the NGOs and the reports submitted to the African Commission. The strategy here is to take the Commission seriously, give it a lot of work. That status may contribute to greater pressure on the OAU to improve the Commission's funding situation.

Fourth is corresponding activity and support for women's human rights at the international level. African governments have on many occasions shown great resistance to calls for change from their own citizenry but given in to international pressure. This is where the promotion of women's access to land in Africa may need significant support from what is going on at the international level. The more that women's rights are accepted as human rights by countries with economic, military, and political influence over Africa, the easier it will be to get them accepted in Africa. As long as there is resistance and inaction by those governments, or preoccupation with civil and political rights, African governments have little to fear from their own inaction. As long as the African governments are not interested in guaranteeing women's access to land, the African Commission is unlikely to ripple settled waters.

Notes

1. Fourth Advisory Opinion, Inter-Am. C.H.R., *Hum. Rts. L.J.* 5 (1984): 161 at 172.

2. *Abdulaziz, Cabales and Balkandali,* Eur. Ct. H.R. (ser. A), (1985) at 472.

3. See Land Ordinance Cap 113, Laws of Tanzania. See also Land Reform Decree, Decree No. 3 of 1975 (Uganda).

4. Margaret Schuler, ed., *WiLDAF: Origins and Issues* (Washington, DC: OEF International, 1990), 53.

5. Law of Marriage Act 1971, sec. 60.

6. Marriage Act, note 5 at sec. 114(2)(b).

7. [1977] L.R.T. 58. See also *Zawadi Abdalla v. Ibrahim Iddi,* H. Civ. App. 6/77.

8. Civ. App. 9/1983. See also *Pohoke v. Pohoke,* H.C.D. 184 (1971) and *Ciuari Konzi v. Abdulla Issa* (High Ct. Civ. App. 69/72).

9. Land Regulations 1948, sec. 3, made under the Land Ordinance, Cap. 113, Laws of Tanzania.

10. Cap. 139, Laws of Uganda.

11. Decree 22 of 1972.

12. Schuler, ed., *WiLDAF,* note 4 at 51.

13. Laws of Uganda, Cap. 139.

14. Barbara Rogers, *The Domestication of Women: Discrimination in Developing Societies* (New York: Tavistock Publications, 1981), chapter 6 at 132.

15. Nakazael L. Tenga, "The Laws of Succession in Tanzania: Women's Position Under the Customary Rules of Inheritance." Working Paper No. 15, Institute of Women's Law, University of Oslo, 1988 at 12.

16. Polygamy is very common in most societies in Tanzania.

17. Rule 19, Order No. 4 of 1963, General Notice 436/63 which codifies customary law.

18. *Ronadhan v. Miriam Ikunga,* H.C.D. 49 (1967). See also *Kamganya v. Ali Mpate,* H.C.D. 60 (1967); Rose Migiro, "Laws Relating to Marriage and Marital Property Relations," Guest Lectures, Women's Law Diploma Course, Institute of Women's Law, University of Oslo 1988, at 66.

19. H.C.D. 149 (1968).

20. Nakazael L. Tenga, "Women's Access to and Control of Land in Tanzania" in Schuler, ed., *WiLDAF,* note 4 at 188.

21. Tanzania High Ct. Civ. App. No. 70/1989, in which the judge relied on Tanzania's international obligation under the African Charter on Human and Peoples' Rights and other human rights treaties.

22. UN Charter, art. 1(3).

23. Political Covenant, art. 26.

24. African Charter, art. 3. For similar provisions see Art. 14 of the European Convention on Human Rights; art. 1 of the American Convention on Human Rights.

25. Anne Bayefsky, "The Principle of Equality or Nondiscrimination in International Law," *Hum. Rts. L.J.* 11 (1990): 1 at 3.

26. General Comment, CCPR/C/21/Rev.1/Add.1 of 1989.

27. Bayefsky, "Principle of Equality," note 25 at 9, 19.

28. Convention on the Elimination of All Forms of Discrimination Against Women, art. 1.

29. Bayefsky, "Principle of Equality," note 25 at 12; *Abdulaziz, Cabales, and Balkandali,* note 2.

30. African Charter, art. 1. Emphasis added.

31. Fifty countries are parties; see Appendix A, p. 585.

32. Art. 2(2). See also International Covenant on Economic, Social, and Cultural Rights; art. 2, Convention Against Torture and Other Inhuman or Degrading Treatment or Punishment, art. 2; American Convention on Human Rights, art. 1.

33. 32 Eur. Ct. H. R. (ser. A) (1979), para. 25.

34. Scott Leckie, "An Overview and Appraisal of the Fifth Session of the UN Committee on Economic, Social, and Cultural Rights," *Hum. Rts. Q.* 13 (1991): 545 at 546.

35. Ronald Thandabantu Nhlapo, "International Protection of Human Rights and the Family: African Variations on a Common Theme," *Int'l J. L. & Fam.* 3 (1989): 1, 9.

36. Ann Oakley, *Subject Women* (London: Fontana, 1981), 32; also Nhlapo, "African Variations," note 35 at 19–22.

37. African Charter, art. 30.

38. African Charter, art. 31.

39. African Charter, art. 33.

40. Isaac Nguema, "Legal and Infrastructural Constraints on the Commission," paper presented at the Fund for Peace Conference on the African Commission, June 24–26, 1991, *Conference Report* at 12.

41. Nguema, "Infrastructural Constraints," note 40 at 14.

42. African Charter, art. 53.

43. African Charter, art. 59.

44. Nguema, "Infrastructural Constraints," note 40.

45. Umozurike, "The African Charter on Human and Peoples' Rights," *Am. J. Int'l L.* 77 (1983): 902 at 909.

46. African Charter, art. 45(3).

47. Nguema, "Infrastructural Constraints," note 40 at 18.

48. African Charter, art. 45 (1) (a).

49. African Charter, art. 41.

50. The first and second reports have fallen due for most states. As of June 1991, only seven countries had submitted their first report. State reports should ideally be considered together with alternative reports submitted by non-governmental organizations.

51. Art. 40(5), International Covenant on Civil and Political Rights, and art. 19, International Covenant on Economic, Social, and Cultural Rights.

52. Nguema, "Infrastructural Constraints," note 40 at 14.

53. Makau wa Matua, "African Human Rights NGOs and the African Commission: Strategies for Mutual Support," paper presented at the Fund for Peace Conference, *Conference Report*, note 40 at 24.

54. Makau wa Matua, "Strategies," note 53 at 14.

55. CEDAW General Recommendation 12 (1989) and General Recommendation No. 19 (1992) CEDAW/1992/L.1/Add.15.

56. Nhlapo, "African Variations," note 35 at 9.

57. J. Shand Watson, "The Limited Utility of International Law in the Protection of Human Rights," *Proc. Am. Soc. Int'l L.*, 1–6 (1980): 1, 3.

58. Human rights abuses in Ethiopia, Somalia, Zaire, and Kenya and a host of other countries did not stir African governments.

59. Michael B. Akehurst, *A Modern Introduction to International Law*, 4th ed. (London: George Allen & Unwin, 1982), 6.

60. United States Ambassador James K. Bishop, at the Fund for Peace Conference on the African Commission on Human Rights. See note 40 at 1.

61. *Attorney General v. Unity Dow*, C.A. Civ. App. No.4/91 at 54.

62. *Ephrahim v. Pastory*, note 21.

63. Ambassador Ibrahim Ali Badawi El Sheikh, at the Fund for Peace Conference on the African Commission, *Conference Report*, note 40 at 16.

Chapter 22
Reproductive Rights as Human Rights: The Colombian Case

María Isabel Plata

Introduction

Over the past 15–20 years, women in different parts of the world have taken up issues of reproductive health. Their concern has been to empower women to control their own fertility and sexuality with maximum choice and minimum health problems by providing information and alternative services, and by campaigning for women's right to make informed choices about their fertility, for improved services and for more appropriate technologies.[1]

The Convention on the Elimination of All Forms of Discrimination Against Women (the Women's Convention)[2] is the major international treaty that protects the right of women to make their own decisions about their fertility and sexuality. Under the Women's Convention states are obligated to take all appropriate measures to eliminate all forms of discrimination against women, including those forms that result from the lack of reproductive health services and education. Under this Convention, policy-makers, governments, and service providers have to see fertility regulation and reproductive health services as a way to empower women, and not as a means to limit population growth, save the environment, and speed economic development.

Women's enjoyment and exercise of reproductive rights and fundamental freedoms will become a universal fact when women everywhere are allowed to make their own decisions about their fertility and sexuality. Women need appropriate information and services, but new reproductive health policies are also required. New policies should require family planning services to address other aspects of women's reproductive health, like pregnancy care, sexuality, and reproductive tract infections. These services will not succeed if they do not acknowledge that "choice" in the life of a woman is affected by many considerations. The choice of contraception is affected by personal circumstances such as her health, her sexual relationships, the stage she has reached in her reproductive life, her status in society, her risk of suffering violence, her possible exposure to infected partners, her prior experience with other contraceptive methods, and her access to education and information. For new policies to succeed, it is crucial to accept the facts that it will be some time before all women's and men's contraception needs are met and that all contraceptives have failure rates.[3] As a result, some women will always need safe abortions. It is also crucial to recognize that the need for education and information cannot be used as a smoke screen to shield the lack of or inadequate delivery of reproductive health and family planning services. Education and information without services, and services without education and information, infringe on women's rights to the liberty and security of their person and to be free from all forms of discrimination due to their status as women. Until recently in Colombia, government institutions would proudly say that they were educating families about reproductive welfare, but they left the provision of reproductive health services, especially those dealing with contraception, in the hands of private non-governmental organizations (NGOs). Thus the government did not have to confront society, politicians, or the Catholic Church, to which about 95 percent of the national population nominally belongs.

Profamilia is the leading private, nonprofit family planning association, affiliated since 1965 with the International Planned Parenthood Federation. The Colombian Ministry of Public Health has offered family planning services since 1969 as part of its health program, but because of severe constraints on the health care budget family planning services are not emphasized. Profamilia helps to fill the gap and currently provides more than 60 percent of all family planning services delivered in the country.[4] It runs 48 clinics located in all regions of Colombia, and directly markets contraceptives in pharmacies and small shops throughout the country. The role of the association continues to be "To promote and defend the basic human right of family planning in Colombia and work toward achieving better sexual and reproductive health by offering information and other services."

This chapter addresses the recent developments of reproductive rights in Colombia and the new programmatic initiatives taken by Profamilia to empower women to assert their rights.

The Development of Reproductive Rights in Colombia

The Importance of the Women's Convention

The Convention provides that states parties shall take all appropriate measures to ensure for women "The same rights to decide freely and responsibly on the number and spacing of their children and to have access to the information, education and means to enable them to exercise these rights" in all matters relating to marriage and family relations (Article 16). Therefore, the state must eliminate discrimination against women in the field of health care in order to ensure, "access to health care services, including those related to family planning" (Article 12). All states that are party to this Convention are obligated "to prevent discrimination against women on the grounds of marriage or maternity and . . . ensure their effective right to work" (Article 11(2)), and must prohibit dismissal on grounds of pregnancy or of maternity leave, introduce maternity leave with pay, and encourage the provision of the necessary supporting social services to enable parents to combine family obligations with work responsibilities and participation in public life. Consequently, the state must adopt measures to ensure that women have "[a]ccess to specific educational information to help to ensure the health and well-being of families, including information and advice on family planning" (Article 10), and that "family education includes a proper understanding of maternity as a social function" (Article 5).[5]

The Committee on the Elimination of Discrimination Against Women, established under the Women's Convention to monitor the progress made in its implementation, issued General Recommendation No. 19 on Violence Against Women.[6] This Recommendation explains that gender-based violence is "violence that is directed against a woman because she is a woman or that affects women disproportionately"[7] and it "impairs or nullifies the enjoyment by women of human rights and fundamental freedoms," including the right to be free from all forms of discrimination on account of their status as women.[8] The Committee found that violence against women in the form of coercion regarding fertility and reproduction places their health and lives at risk. It specifically explains that "compulsory sterilization or abortion adversely affects women's physical and mental health, and infringes the rights of women to choose the number and spacing of their children."[9] The Committee specifically recommends that

States parties should ensure that measures are taken to prevent coercion in regard to fertility and reproduction, and to ensure that women are not forced to seek unsafe medical procedures such as illegal abortion because of lack of appropriate services in regard to fertility control.[10]

The 1991 Colombian Constitution

It has been observed about Colombia's recent history that:

After the Supreme Court cleared the way for the constitutional process to begin, women joined with other groups and sectors in heeding President Gaviria's invitation (which explicitly included "feminist and women's organizations") to present their proposals for constitutional reform. . . . [Their] fundamental proposal was that the principles of the United Nations Convention on the Elimination of All Forms of Discrimination Against Women be elevated to constitutional rank.[11]

Women wanted the new Constitution not only to incorporate the Convention's prohibitions on all forms of discrimination against women but also to adopt concepts like that found in Article 4(1) of the Women's Convention requiring states to take "temporary special measures aimed at accelerating *de facto* equality between men and women," and other mechanisms that would ensure equal opportunities and not just formal equality for women.[12]

Although not all of our concerns were addressed, the new Constitution has incorporated many principles and rights that will help women in the country and reinforce, nationally and beyond, the Convention on the Elimination of All Forms of Discrimination Against Women. Article 13 of the Constitution, for instance, establishes that all persons are born free and equal before the law, will receive the same protection and treatment from governmental authorities and will enjoy the same rights, liberties and opportunities without any discrimination due to sex, race, national origin, family origin, language, religion, or political or philosophical opinions. The state will promote the conditions necessary for equality to be real and effective, and will adopt measures in favor of previously disadvantaged groups to remedy residual discrimination.

The new Constitution specifically addresses in article 40 the concerns of women by establishing that public authorities will guarantee the adequate and effective participation of women at the decision-making levels of government and in its administration. Article 43 adds that women and men are to have equal rights and opportunities, and that women cannot be subjected to any form of discrimination.

Article 42 of the new Constitution defines the family as the fundamental unit of society, which can be constituted by natural or legal bonds, meaning by the free decision of a man and a woman to marry or by their responsible mutual will to constitute a family. This article also stipulates that family relations are based on both partners' equality of rights and duties, mutual respect among all its members, and rejection of any form of domestic violence. It includes the right of the couple freely and responsibly to decide the number of their children and the right to a civil divorce for religiously celebrated marriages.

The Constitutional Right of Petition

Article 86 of the new national Constitution provides that:

Every individual may claim legal protection to claim before the judges, at any time or place, through a preferential and summary proceeding, for himself/herself or by whoever acts in his/her name, the immediate protection of his/her fundamental constitutional rights when the individual fears the latter may be jeopardized or threatened by the action or omission of any public authority.

The protection will consist of an order so that whoever solicits such protection may receive it by a judge enjoining others to act or refrain from acting. The order, which will have to be implemented immediately, may be challenged before the competent judge, and in any case the latter may send it to the Constitutional Court for possible revision.

This action will be followed only when the affected party does not dispose of other means of judicial defense, except when the former is used as a temporary device to avoid irreversible harm. In no case can more than 10 days elapse between the request for protection and its resolution.

The law will establish the cases in which the order of protection should apply to individuals entrusted with providing a public service or whose conduct may affect seriously and directly the collective interest or in respect of whom the applicant may find himself/herself in a state of subordination or vulnerability.

Under the new Constitution, women have the following fundamental rights that will protect their decisions about fertility and sexuality: the rights to life, liberty, equality and security of the person; to the unrestricted development of identity; to found a family; to decide freely and responsibly the number of children; of access to education and information; to the enjoyment of a healthy environment; and to health care.[13] Sex-related discrimination in any field, such as the political, economic, social, educational, cultural, or civil, constitutes an impediment to the recognition, enjoyment, and exercise by women of human rights and fundamental freedoms. An important goal is the interconnection of individual, specific rights with the overall right to health and to reproductive health. This will eventually be achieved through the jurisprudence the Constitutional Court will develop once women start using their right to petition.

Crucial to the enforcement of women's rights is the "order of protection" available when a woman applicant "may find herself in a state of subordination or vulnerability."[14] A very important petition has been won by a woman victim of domestic violence. The Constitutional Court decided, when her case was appealed, that the right to petition could be accepted because the national Penal Code did not consider the inhumane and degrading treatment to which her husband had subjected her to be an offense.[15] In order to protect the petitioner's constitutional rights to life and personal integrity, the police and the Institute of Family Welfare were required to take immediate measures to protect the woman.[16]

New Laws and Policies on Women's Health

The new political will, the incorporation of new groups in the government,[17] and the networking of feminist groups that started during the constitutional process and fortunately continues today, can all account for the recent public health policy issued by the Ministry of Public Health.

Evidence of this new political will is found in the *Guidelines for an Integrated Policy for Colombian Women* presented by the government on 8 March 1992. These identified the following issues that need special attention:

- *Health:* Basic problems relate to early pregnancies, child survival, and safe motherhood. Other concerns are health and safety in the workplace, mental health, and reproductive health.
- *The generation and improvement of income and employment:* The major problems are persistent manifestations of labor discrimination based on sex, sub-contracting of female labor, low standards of female training, high numbers of women working in the informal economic sector, low wages, women's low coverage by social security provisions, unlawful treatment of domestic servants, and the concentration of poverty in female-headed households.
- *The rural sector:* Basic problems refer to the almost nonexistent female ownership of land, the lack of infrastructure relevant to women's needs, difficulties that hamper women's access to agricultural credit and loans, destruction of the environment, illegal crops, and rural violence.
- *The family:* The main problems are the double workload faced by women, lack of housing and public services, and lack of title deeds.
- *Legislative and other measures:* These should address violence against women in the family, the lack of mechanisms to protect women, discrimination against women in specified areas, and the failure to

implement existing laws. Specific mention is made of the Convention on the Elimination of All Forms of Discrimination Against Women (Law 51 of 1981) to stress the political will to enforce and implement the Convention by reform of Decree 1878 of 1990, which gave responsibility to the Ministry of Labor. The Decree emphasizes the need and the government's intention to popularize the Convention.

- *The media:* The main problems are discriminatory concepts circulated by the mass media, and their sometimes astonishing lack of knowledge of women's legal rights.
- *Organization and participation of women in the public sphere:* Mass media campaigns have to be organized in order to stimulate and strengthen women's organizations in both the urban and rural sectors.
- *Recreation, culture, and sports:* Special efforts must be made to allow for a creative use of women's leisure time.
- *Family planning:* Official programs have to be strengthened in order to improve counseling and coverage of family planning services.
- *Research:* Attention must be given to improving women's issues and remedying the lack of information centers, and the poor indicators of the status of women in the country.

Resolution 1531, issued by the Ministry of Public Health on 6 March 1992 to celebrate the March 8 International Day of Women, warrants special attention. The Resolution is really a Bill of Rights concerning women and health issues, and sets the tone for forthcoming policy. The Resolution begins by empowering women. It enables women actively to participate in decision making on all issues in individual, community, and institutional spheres that affect their health, lives, bodies, and sexuality. The specific rights identified in the Resolution can be summarized as follows:

All women have the right:

- to a joyful maternity, meaning maternity that is desired, freely decided on, and without undue risk;
- to humanized medical treatment, including dignified and respectful care of their bodies, fears, intimacy, and privacy;
- to be treated by the health services as integral persons and not simply as biological reproducers;
- to integrated health services that respond to their specific needs based on age, activities, social class, race, and location;
- to an education that favors self-care and self-knowledge of a woman's body and benefits the self-esteem and empowerment of women;

- to information and counseling that guarantee the exercise of free, gratifying, and responsible sexuality not conditioned to pregnancy;
- to appropriate and sufficient information, counseling, and access concerning modern, safe contraception;
- to labor environments and living conditions that do not affect fertility or injure health;
- to non-rejection in employment settings or educational institutions because of pregnancy, responsibilities for children, or marital status;
- to have menstruation, pregnancy, birth, menopause, and old age treated as natural bodily events and not as illnesses;
- to have women's knowledge and cultural practices related to health that experience has shown to be sound, suitably considered, valued, and respected;
- to active, including protagonistic, participation in the health system at both community and government levels of decision-making;
- to access to public health services that take integral care of battered women and victims of all forms of violence.

Thus Resolution 1531 laid the foundation for the new governmental policy based on previous gender analysis, entitled, "Health for Women, Women for Health":

To consider social discrimination against women as an element explaining the cause of illness is what has been called gender perspective in the creation of health policy. And in the same terms, a woman does not end with her biological aspects, her reproductive system or with her body regarded only as related systems and functions. Women are bearers of that which is feminine. That is, they conduct roles and functions that make them service providers and functional intermediaries of the health system.[18]

This new women's health policy is an important contribution to the struggle for the advancement of women. If fully implemented, it should reduce the existing disparity of advantage between men and women, improve the quality of life of women and respond integrally to women's health problems. For instance, the maternal mortality rate in Colombia, estimated at one death per thousand live births, can be significantly lowered through a substantial improvement in the quality of health services. Factors associated with maternal mortality are age, short intervals between pregnancies, a high number of children born to a woman, malnutrition, lack of medical care during pregnancy and birth, and above all, unwanted pregnancies ending in unsafe abortions. Maternal mortality due to unsafe abortion accounts for 23 percent of the total of pregnancy-related deaths, and is the second highest cause of death among women between 15 and 44 years of age, second only to deaths related directly to obstetrical causes.[19]

The women's health policy is also a valuable instrument to strengthen women's roles within the health system, since it

> proposes to contribute towards the reduction of women's existing disadvantages as against men as a way to improve the quality of life of women and to respond to women in a comprehensive fashion that meets their health concerns. It is an instrument that will strengthen female initiative in the health-care system through the participation of women as subjects of the decisions that affect their lives, bodies, sexuality and health.[20]

The new women's health policy has identified four main groups of women whose economic, psychological, or social living conditions are precarious and demand special attention: (1) women who are the sole heads of families; (2) women between 15 and 49 years of age (reproductive age); (3) working women; and (4) women of an advanced age (over 60 years). It has also established five sub-programs:

- support and self-care in women's health issues;
- integrated services in reproductive health and sexuality;
- prevention of ill treatment of women and provision of services to women and minors who are victims of violence;
- mental health; and
- health and safety of working conditions.

The sub-program that focuses on integrated services in reproductive health and sexuality illustrates how the new governmental policy enhances and broadens the traditional concept of family planning as a health-care issue, as treated by the different UN international instruments. These instruments include the 1974 Plan of Action on Population, approved in the UN Bucharest Conference on Population, 1984 Plan for World Action on Population developed at the UN Mexico City Conference on Population, and the 1985 Forward Looking Strategies adopted at the UN Nairobi Conference on Women, which specify that "appropriate health facilities should be planned, designed, constructed and equipped to be readily accessible and acceptable. Services should be in harmony with the timing and patterns of women's work . . . and family planning services should be within easy reach of all women." The Nairobi Forward Looking Strategies also stressed that contraceptive methods have to comply with norms of quality, efficacy, and safety, and that family planning programs with incentives can be neither coercive nor discriminatory and must respect human rights and individual and cultural values.[21]

The new reproductive health policy does not make a direct reference to family planning implementing the rights to decide freely and responsibly the number and spacing of children and to have access to the information, education and means that permit the exercise of these rights. Instead, it focuses on fertility control as strengthening the self-esteem of women and guaranteeing their rights over their bodies, sexuality, health, and lives. The Ministry of Public Health considers that all fertility control programs must also help to create a collective conscience that accepts the right to a full and responsible exercise of sexuality, and that demands exercise of the right to a desired and planned pregnancy without undue health risks. The Ministry also acknowledges the necessity to increase coverage of services to the population of reproductive age (men and women), and to work on the prevention of unwanted pregnancies.

In addressing the right of individuals and/or couples to free and responsible reproduction, the policy includes the need for programs and services that deal with infertility as well as with contraception. It then considers the prevention of unwanted pregnancies, mentioning special programs for adolescents and an integrated treatment of incomplete abortions. Prevention is compelled by the estimates that 19 percent of all children born alive between 1985 and 1990 were from unwanted pregnancies, and another 15 percent of mothers would have preferred to have had their child(ren) later in life.[22] Adolescent women between 15 and 19 years of age who are pregnant or are mothers constitute 16 percent in rural areas and 11.8 percent in urban areas.[23] The program contemplates working with the community as an empowerment strategy for both men and women. It reaffirms the right to free and voluntary choice of contraceptive methods regardless of a person's marital status, and is strongly conscious of the fact that services must cover the population between fourteen and forty-nine, which of course includes adolescents.

Profamilia Programs to Empower Women

Despite wide-scale changes in constitutional and family law and in the status of women, public understanding of the implications and ramifications of these developments has not kept pace with the changing legal situation or the changing social environment. Notwithstanding women's progress regarding equal rights, their work in the home and in society is still undervalued. This has kept women from achieving authority within the family while assuming domestic and job responsibilities. Women in the middle and lower classes work to support the home and are obliged to handle domestic chores with little or no help from their spouses or companions. The woman who manages the home is also expected to fulfill a biological reproductive role (mother), to serve as a source of sexual satisfaction (wife or concubine), and to educate the children on the values, essence, and function of the social group.

Women are increasingly expected to compete with men in the production of goods and services. In recent decades there has been a notable increase in female participation in the labor market. In Latin America as a whole, the number of women in paid employment has grown 120 percent during the last thirty years. Colombia has one of the highest levels of women in the labor force among the Latin American countries. In 1985 the female labor participation rate reached 47 percent in the seven biggest cities, while the rate of global female participation was 31.6 percent.[24] The general labor situation of women has improved compared to that of men, but women's unemployment is higher than men's, the incorporation of women in the informal sector is still very high, and sexual discrimination remains in terms of salaries and job availability.

Unfortunately, and despite these changes in their participation in the labor force, women are still not expected to act independently of their fathers or husbands. The emphasis on male control and dominance of women creates situations that are sometimes no easier for the man than for the woman. As a result of the long tradition of female dependency and passivity, many Colombian women are ill-equipped psychologically and practically to take advantage of the opportunities and rights becoming available to them. A 1990 national study on violence against women[25] shows that, even though one-third of women had been assaulted, one out of five had been severely battered, and one out of ten had been forced to have sexual relations with her partner, only 11.2 percent of these victims went to the authorities. Of those battered, one-third did not look for any help nor talk to anyone. When asked why they did not go to the authorities, 31.3 percent answered that they thought they could solve the problem alone, 16.8 percent were afraid of retaliation, 14.1 percent thought the authorities would ridicule them, and 6.6 percent thought the battery would not happen again.

Profamilia has developed the following proactive strategies to redress the disadvantages that women suffer to their health, welfare and interests. In developing these strategies, Profamilia is well aware that

The transformation of the life of woman is a complex process where expectations of life that reaffirm female autonomy, independence and initiative are mixed up with persistent traditional forms based on a culture that holds women to discriminatory habits which are harmful to her human condition, her life, her sexuality and her body.[26]

The aim of these strategies is to reaffirm female autonomy and to eliminate the discriminatory habits.

The Legal Service for Women

Traditional social norms in the country regard women as different from men, resulting in the subordination of women in issues as delicate and private as rights to decide on contraceptive method. Women's problems are often made obvious to the staff working in Profamilia's clinics, for instance when a doctor or nurse notices bruises on a woman who has come in for contraceptive services. Upon questioning, she describes living in perpetual fear of a violent and abusive husband. Similarly, a patient urged to improve her diet complains that her husband's salary is too low to permit buying nutritional foods and that he has forbidden her to earn money of her own. A woman questioned about her general health may complain of permanent anxiety or fatigue, and reveal that she is fighting with her common-law partner for custody of a child or for child support. These daily dramas moved Profamilia to offer legal service in the family planning clinics to afford women information and services relevant to their reproductive health and rights.

Profamilia started the Legal Service for Women in 1987 and today has legal clinics in six family planning centers.[27] The purpose of the program is to educate women on their rights and offer them support in a society that proclaims legal equality while reinforcing women's inequality through custom, and to provide negotiation and legal services, including litigation.

Most recently, the Service has published a booklet on the constitutional right to petition.[28] If the new Constitutional right to petition is to become a major instrument to improve women's quality of life, women must know about that right and how it can be used to ensure the exercise of their rights. The Service has started to look for cases and to help women use the petition mechanism to seek redress for violations of their rights resulting from violence within the family, unequal sharing of household work, denial of reproductive rights, lack of sex education, and denial of other forms of equal opportunity.

The Legal Service for Women also aims to expand debate and raise consciousness in society about women's issues and reproductive rights. It has done this by developing a series of publications[29] and videos[30] to generate discussion about women's human rights.

The Legal Service also provides negotiation and mediating services. In one instance, the Legal Service in Bogotá had to counsel a 34-year-old woman with three children who obtained a tubal ligation but did not request her common-law partner's permission, which by law is not required. When he found out, he locked her in a room and forbade her to leave unless he gave permission "to show her who was the master of the household." He also told her that he would obtain legal custody of the children because "a good mother would never decide not to have more children." The Legal Service sent him a letter listing the internationally and nationally recognized rights he had violated and the criminal charges he might face if the woman decided to go to court. At the legal clinic, the lawyer explained to him in person why his actions were both socially wrong and illegal, and why his threat of taking the children would fail legally. When he learned that the law would not only protect his partner but also punish him, he recognized his ignorance of the law but offered the justification that he was only doing "what other men do." Since no direct physical violence had been used, and the woman strongly felt that she wanted to continue living with him, the lawyer did not press the issue of a separation. However, it was stressed that any act of psychological or physical violence on his part would give her all the legal and moral reasons required to end the common law marriage and keep her custody of the children.

Gender Training Workshops

Profamilia has held a series of workshops with its doctors and other health personnel at which gender issues were explored. These workshops have explained how the new national health policy for women proposes to reduce women's disadvantages in order to improve their quality of life and respond to their health concerns and have explored the implications for the work of Profamilia.[31] The analysis of men's and women's different perspectives on the services provided, as well as men's and women's differing reproductive health needs, allow the service providers to review these services from the client's point of view, resulting in better service to their clients.

These workshops have also explored how epidemiological, statistical, and fertility surveys and quality-of-care studies can be used to hold governments and institutions accountable for individuals' access to health care and how these surveys can be interpreted and analyzed from a gender perspective. The traditional indicators in the field of family planning (rates of acceptance of services, for example) could be expanded by a gender perspective to measure informed choice and user satisfaction. It has been observed that:

Access [to services] is not only a question of how distant her home is, or how much the transportation costs, or who will take care of the baby if she goes to the clinic. We have to ask what is the attitude of the husband, what is the attitude of the mother-in-law, what is the attitude of the neighbourhood, of the family, of the city, of the society at large with respect to that woman using that method? What are the sources of information? . . . Much more emphasis should be put on this field.[32]

Reproductive Health Services

Article 12(1) of the Women's Convention requires states parties to en-sure individual's access to health care services, including those related to family planning. Article 12(1) of the International Covenant on Eco-nomic, Social, and Cultural Rights, recognizes the right of everyone to the enjoyment of the highest attainable standard of physical and mental health. These rights will remain only theoretical unless epide-miological or statistical studies are used to indicate where and how women suffer limited access to care. In the case of family planning pro-grams, demographic and health surveys of countries or sub-regions, supply data on marriage and fertility, fertility preferences, contracep-tive knowledge and use, and maternal and child health. Governments could be held accountable under the Women's Convention and the International Covenant on Economic, Social, and Cultural Rights for not meeting the so-called "unmet need for family planning." The concept of unmet need is derived from the proportion of women in marriage who use no contraceptive method but want no more children or who wish to space their next pregnancy, or whose most recent birth or pregnancy was mis-timed or unwanted.[33]

These surveys can also be used to indicate where rights to reproduc-tive health might be in jeopardy and where reproductive health ser-vices might be provided to remedy or prevent alleged violations of this right. For example, based on the 1986 Demographic and Health Sur-vey, Profamilia decided in 1987 to organize a media campaign on the Atlantic Coast of the country to promote the use of temporary con-traceptive methods. The survey showed a high proportion of volun-tary surgical sterilization and low usage of temporary family planning methods, giving the region the lowest resort to birth control in the country. Profamilia, with support from the Futures Group/Somarc and Johns Hopkins University, organized a mass media campaign to pro-mote the use of temporary birth control, especially condoms. As a result of that campaign, sales of condoms by Profamilia increased by 60 percent.[34]

In order to guarantee rights to health, to free and informed choice, and to liberty and security to every woman who enters a health or family planning clinic, reproductive health services have to maximize options. Every woman must have the right to control not just her fertility but her sexuality, and for this purpose a variety of birth control methods and services related to her reproductive and sexual health must be provided. It has been observed that

The extent to which clients' needs can be met depends fundamentally on health and family planning infrastructure, including, among others, supply and logistics systems, service delivery points, staff skills, regulations and management capacity . . . the need to assess the skills, knowledge, attitudes, and practices of providers, including not simply medical skill and provision of technologies to clients, but also their ability to provide information and counselling.[35]

This requires that health personnel and clinic directors become familiar with gender issues and analysis. It is now known, for instance, that when a woman makes decisions concerning her fertility, all types of personal circumstances like her health, sex life, reproductive cycle, social status, previous experience with other birth control methods, access to information, level of empowerment, fears, contact with sexually transmitted diseases, and, for example, the legal status of abortion can become decisive factors. Health and family planning delivery systems must therefore be organized to support and endorse the right to health.

Conclusion

Women's rights can now be considered to belong in the category of fundamental legal rights that are based on international law. The conditions that block access to equal rights are in large part due to a lack of sincere political will to improve the social circumstances of women.

The new Colombian health policy "Health for Women, Women for Health" is an interesting official effort to incorporate women as active agents of public health policies and services in the country. The agency of women and women's groups can similarly become a useful instrument for other governments that are making serious efforts to comply with Article 12 of the Women's Convention but have had difficulty identifying the "appropriate measures to eliminate discrimination against women in the field of health care." New policies and strategies are greatly needed, since women in the twenty-first century will demand fertility control programs that strengthen their self-esteem and guarantee their rights over their bodies, sexuality, health, and lives.

The type of official policy that incorporates new interpretations of women's "health" and "family planning programs" and encompasses concepts like reproductive health has started to legitimize the work of women's health advocates. But unless international legal instruments and women's human rights are applied by women's advocates in practical ways to empower women in every corner of the world, the prevailing imbalance of power between men and women which cuts across social life, the family, the school, the workplace, the church, politics, science, legal rights, and emotional life, will continue to have a harmful impact on the health of women.

Notes

1. WHO and International Women's Health Coalition, *Creating Common Ground*, Report of a meeting between women's health advocates and scientists, WHO/HRP/ITT/91 (Geneva, 1991), 6.

2. G.A. Res. 34/180, U.N. GAOR, 34th Sess., Supp. No. 46 at 193, U.N. Doc. A/34/46 (1979).

3. Elise F. Jones and Jacqueline D. Forrest, "Contraceptive Failure Rates Based on the 1988 NSFG," *Family Planning Perspectives* 24 (1992): 12–19.

4. Digest, "Colombian Fertility Rates," *International Family Planning Perspectives* 18 (1992): 38, 39.

5. See generally Rebecca J. Cook, "International Protection of Women's Reproductive Rights," *N.Y.U.J. Int'l L. & Pol.* 24 (1992): 645; Rebecca J. Cook, "International Human Rights and Women's Reproductive Health," *Studies in Family Planning* 24 (1993): 73; Lynn P. Freedman and Stephen L. Isaacs, "Human Rights and Reproductive Choice," *Studies in Family Planning* 24 (1993): 18.

6. General Recommendation No. 19, U.N. Doc. CEDAW/C/1992/L.1/ Add.15 (1992); Arvonne Fraser and Miranda Kazantsis, CEDAW #11 (Minneapolis, MN: International Women's Rights Action Watch, 1992), 28–32.

7. CEDAW #11, note 6 at para. 6.

8. CEDAW #11, note 6 at para. 7.

9. CEDAW #11, note 6 at para. 22.

10. CEDAW #11, note 6 at para. 24(m).

11. Martha I. Morgan and Monica M. Alzate Buitrago, "Constitution Making in a Time of Cholera: Women and the 1991 Colombian Constitution," *Yale J. L. and Fem.* 4 (1992): 353–413, 375.

12. For a comprehensive study of Colombian women's efforts to make a better constitution, see generally Morgan and Buitrago, "Time of Cholera," note 11 at 353.

13. Profamilia Servicios Legales Para Mujeres, *Amparo de mis derechos fundamentales. La acción de tutela* (Safeguard My Fundamental Rights: The Right to Petition) (Bogotá: Profamilia, 1993), 3.

14. See generally Decreto 2591 of 1991 and Decreto 306 of 1992.

15. Constitutional Court Decision T-529 Sept. 18/92.

16. María Cristina Calderón, "La tutela, garantía para la mujer maltratada" (The Right to Petition: A Guarantee for the Battered Woman) *Profamilia* 9(21) (1993): 6.

17. The former guerrilla group, M-19, accepted peace offers and now forms part of the government. The current (summer, 1993) Minister or Secretary of Public Health is a member of M-19.

18. *Salud para las mujeres, mujeres para la salud* (Health for Women, Women for Health) (Ministerio de Salud, Bogotá, Colombia, May, 1992), 7.

19. *Salud para las mujeres,* note 18 at 17.

20. *Salud para las mujeres,* note 18 at 7.

21. See Rebecca J. Cook and Jeanne M. Haws, "The United Nations Convention on the Rights of Women: Opportunities for Family Planning Providers," *International Family Planning Perspectives* 12 (1986): 49–53.

22. *Salud para las mujeres,* note 18 at 13.

23. *Salud para las mujeres,* note 18 at 13.

24. Miguel Urrutia, *40 años de desarrollo: su impacto social* (40 Years of Development: Its Social Impact) (Bogotá: Biblioteca Banco Popular, 1990), 103.

25. "Encuesta de prevalencia, demografía y salud," *Profamilia and Demographic and Health Surveys* (Bogotá, 1990).

26. *Salud para las mujeres,* note 18 at 6.

27. María Isabel Plata, "Family Law and Family Planning in Colombia," *Int'l Family Planning Perspectives* 14 (1988): 109–111.

28. See note 13.

29. See, e.g., notes 13, 16, 27; Profamilia Servicios Legales Para Mujeres, *La violencia y los derechos humanos de la mujer* (Violence and the Human Rights of Women) (Bogotá: Printex Impresores, 1992); María Isabel Plata and María Yanusova, *Los derechos humanos y la convención sobre la eliminación de todas las formas de discriminación contra la mujer 1979* (Human Rights and the 1979 Convention on the Elimination of All Forms of Discrimination Against Women) (2nd ed., Bogotá: Printex Impresores, 1993), 193.

30. Erase una vez (Once Upon a Time) 1988; Cada día, cada instante (Every Day, Every Instant) 1989.

31. See María Cristina Calderón, *Talleres de género en 12 clínicas de Profamilia: Informe de actividades* (Gender Workshops in 12 Profamilia Clinics: Summary Report) (Bogotá: Profamilia, January 1993).

32. Anibal Faúndes, quoted in *Common Ground,* note 1 at 16.

33. *Digest,* note 4 at 39.

34. Juan Carlos Negrette, "Campaña promocional de métodos temporales en la Costa Atlántica" (Promotional Campaign of Temporary Methods in the Atlantic Coast) *Profamilia* 5(15) (1989): 14.

35. Anibal Faúndes, quoted in *Common Ground,* note 1 at 35.

Chapter 23
The Use of International Human Rights Norms to Combat Violence Against Women

Joan Fitzpatrick

Introduction

The variety of forms of violence against women is matched by an array of sources of international norms addressing that violence. However, none of these norms is sufficiently broad or focused to have more than a minimal impact in controlling or eradicating violence against women. The problem is illustrated by the existing text of the Convention on the Elimination of All Forms of Discrimination Against Women (the Women's Convention),[1] which does not specifically prohibit gender-based violence or place any explicit responsibilities on states parties to take action to reduce it. Instead, at least six articles of the Convention arguably bear some tangential relationship to forms of gender-based violence against women, though none actually mentions violence.[2] Whether this deficiency in the Convention is best remedied through interpretation[3] or through drafting a supplemental protocol or separate instrument[4] will be addressed in the section in "The Way Forward," this chapter.

At the risk of being labeled a "doctrinalist,"[5] I will devote major attention to cataloguing the myriad international norms that relate to gender-based violence against women. Critiquing what already exists will aid an informed determination whether and under what circumstances the elaboration of additional positive law is likely to have an actual effect upon these persistent violent practices.

Violence against women encompasses far more than the paradigm instances of battery or murder within the home and rape by acquaintances and strangers, though these are crucial issues. Different types of violence against women implicate a surprisingly diverse array of international law sources and international institutions. I have chosen to address seven areas, some, regrettably, in rather summary form:

(1) domestic violence (murder, rape, and battery by husbands or other male partners) and rape;
(2) genital mutilation ("female circumcision" or, even more euphemistically, "traditional practices");
(3) gender-based violence by police and security forces, including torture of detained women;
(4) gender-based violence against women during armed conflict;
(5) gender-based violence against women refugees and asylum-seekers;
(6) violence associated with prostitution and pornography;
(7) violence in the workplace, including sexual harassment.

Each of these forms of violence remains pervasive, yet each has been the subject of treaty provisions, resolutions of intergovernmental organizations (IGOs), studies, or debate at the international level. Thus, the rhetorical task of gaining initial recognition of these abuses as human rights issues of legitimate concern to the international community[6] has been accomplished. The remaining challenge is to explore why the existing norms and actions by IGOs have been ineffective and to devise more effective strategies for the future.

It is sobering to reflect that women are subject to the special threat of these forms of gender-based violence, while simultaneously being at risk of various types of non-gender-specific violence (crime, accidents, natural disasters, general risks from armed conflict). Women are also subject to gender-based life-threatening perils that are not so easily classified as "violence," such as deprivation of equal access to food and medical care. For the sake of coherence and the avoidance of superficiality, such practices will be excluded from this study.[7]

Three theoretical challenges must be confronted and resolved in order to move forward with effective strategies on violence against women: (1) considering when an equality paradigm is useful and when it is counterproductive in addressing the various forms of violence against women, and whether the focus of an equality rationale should be on equal treatment or on what is sometimes called "special treatment";[8] (2) overcoming the state-centered tradition of international law with revised notions of state responsibility and confronting the public/private distinction as a barrier to effective international action against gender-based violence; and (3) determining whether these problems are best addressed by elaborating binding international legal standards with formal systems of supervision or by promoting cooperation among governments through giving visibility to these issues as common problems of crime control and/or social policy.

Domestic Violence and Rape

These two aspects of violence against women are discussed together because they share a common characteristic of involving crimes against women by actors who are allegedly "private" rather than "public,"[9] and who may escape severe sanctions from the criminal justice system for reasons that appear linked to the gender-specific nature of their crimes. The category of domestic violence[10] itself has a variety of subparts, including battery, murder, and rape of women by their domestic partners (husbands and lovers). Both domestic violence and rape are gender-based, and are encouraged by cultural norms in all parts of the world, though these violence-stimulating norms vary from culture to culture. Domestic violence and rape reflect and reinforce the imbalance in power between the sexes and are selectively tolerated by state authorities. The key difference between these two forms of violence is the locus of domestic violence within a "family" setting. This factor must be taken into account because of potentially problematic international norms placing emphasis upon the family as the basic unit of society.[11]

These two forms of gender-based violence seriously affect the quality of women's lives, rape (and the threat of rape) in the case of every woman, and domestic violence in the case of many.[12] Yet no human rights treaty explicitly requires governments to take specific action against either practice. General human rights instruments such as the International Covenant on Civil and Political Rights (ICCPR) contain nondiscrimination provisions and dignitary guarantees that arguably pertain to these forms of violence, though the link may not be apparent to all.[13]

The Committee on the Elimination of Discrimination Against Women (CEDAW) is attempting to remedy this flaw through creative interpretation of the Convention on the Elimination of All Forms of Discrimination Against Women. General recommendation No. 19, adopted at CEDAW's eleventh session in January 1992, defined gender-based violence as "a form of discrimination which seriously inhibits women's ability to enjoy rights and freedoms on a basis of equality with men."[14] CEDAW noted that Article 1 of the Convention prohibits all gender-based discrimination that has the effect of impairing the enjoyment of fundamental rights and freedoms, and finds that gender-based violence (of all forms) has the effect of impairing enjoyment of the right to life, the prohibition on torture and cruel treatment, equal protection of humanitarian law, the right to liberty and security of the person, the equal protection of the law, the right to equality within the family, the right to physical and mental health, and the right to just and favorable conditions of work.[15]

General Recommendation No. 19 also drew on Article 2 of the Convention, which requires states to take necessary action to eliminate discrimination against women by "any person."[16] CEDAW read Article 2 as making states responsible for "private acts" if they fail "to act with due diligence to prevent violations of rights, or to investigate and punish acts of violence, and to provide compensation."[17]

Having adopted the strategy of attacking the problem of violence within an equality paradigm (almost inescapable, given the framework of the Convention)[18] and having surmounted the barrier of the public/private distinction, CEDAW then analyzed specific forms of violence in General Recommendation No. 19. With respect to domestic violence and rape, CEDAW asserted: (1) under Articles 2 and 3, laws on domestic violence and rape must give "adequate protection to all women" and "respect their integrity and dignity," and states must provide protective and support services to women and gender-sensitive training of judicial and law enforcement officers;[19] (2) states should conduct research on the extent and causes of gender-based violence;[20] (3) under Articles 2.f, 5, and 10.c, states must seek to eradicate attitudes toward women as limited to stereotyped roles, attitudes that justify the use of gender-based violence to perpetuate structures of subordination;[21] (4) under Article 12, states must establish support services for women whose health is damaged by domestic violence and rape;[22] (5) under Article 14, states must provide services to rural women at risk of gender-based violence and monitor the employment conditions of domestic workers, many of whom migrate to cities from rural areas;[23] and (6) under Article 16, states must impose criminal and civil penalties for domestic violence, remove the "defense of honor" in cases of assault or murder of female family members, create refuges and other services for victims of domestic violence, and provide rehabilitation to perpetrators and support services to victims of incest and intrafamily sexual abuse.[24] General Recommendation No. 19 also built on the reporting guidelines that had been set out in General Recommendation No. 12 in 1989.[25]

CEDAW's attention to issues of violence against women occurs in the context of sustained, though inconclusive, examination of these issues by various bodies within the UN framework. This activity can be traced back at least to the World Conference of the International Women's Year in Mexico City in 1975, which touched on the questions of dignity, equality, and conflict within the family.[26] These concerns were further addressed at the World Conference of the United Nations Decade for Women: Equality, Development and Peace in Copenhagen in 1980, which concluded that domestic violence had serious social consequences and perpetuated itself from one generation to the next, and that women must be protected from domestic violence and rape.[27]

These initial, somewhat offhand, initiatives were followed by consideration of domestic violence and rape in two different types of UN fora: (1) within the Commission on the Status of Women and its parent body, the Economic and Social Council (ECOSOC); and (2) within the crime control bodies, in particular the quinquennial Congresses on the Prevention of Crime and the Treatment of Offenders and the Committee on Crime Prevention and Control. ECOSOC adopted resolution 1982/22, at the urging of the Commission, labeling domestic violence and rape as offenses against the dignity of the person and calling for steps to combat these evils. ECOSOC further addressed violence in the family in resolution 1984/14. Parallel with this discussion within human rights bodies, the Crime Committee in 1982 noted special difficulties in eradicating domestic violence,[28] and a seminar was organized on the topic with non-governmental organizations (NGOs) and UN representatives involved in crime control issues.[29]

The year 1985 brought heightened attention with two developments: (1) the identification of violence against women as a major obstacle to peace in the Nairobi Forward-Looking Strategies for the Advancement of Women;[30] and (2) resolution by the Seventh Congress on Prevention of Crime and Treatment of Offenders that domestic violence and rape tend to be camouflaged abuses, that they occur worldwide, that they seriously jeopardize the personal and social development of women and are against the interests of society.[31] The General Assembly responded with Resolution 40/36, which invited member states to take urgent action to prevent domestic violence, to assist victims, and to make criminal justice systems more sensitive, and which requested the Secretary-General to undertake research on domestic violence from a criminological perspective. In 1986 an Expert Group Meeting on Violence in the Family with Special Emphasis on its Effect on Women was convened.

Three major social science studies of violence against women thereafter were issued under UN auspices: (1) a report of the Secretary-General to the Commission on the Status of Women on "Efforts to eradicate violence against women within the family and society," undertaken in response to ECOSOC resolution 1987/24 and decision 1987/121 which selected violence against women in the family and society as a priority theme in the area of peace;[32] (2) the more elaborate study *Violence Against Women in the Family* issued by the United Nations Centre for Social Development and Humanitarian Affairs in 1989;[33] and (3) the report of the Secretary-General on "domestic violence" prepared for the Eighth United Nations Congress on the Prevention of Crime and the Treatment of Offenders.[34]

The simultaneous activity within the past two decades among these various UN bodies to address the issues of domestic violence and rape highlights a strategic concern: should international activity to combat domestic violence and rape primarily take the form of conceptualizing these practices in normative human rights terms, as CEDAW is seeking to do, and then to place pressure on governments to reduce their occurrence through the usual mechanisms of implementing human rights norms, or is the criminological perspective likely to be more effective?[35] In the case of the latter, it is unnecessary to define domestic violence or rape, or government inactivity in the face of such practices, as violations of international human rights law. Rather, the UN bodies concerned with promoting good social policy or crime control can largely avoid the conceptual issues (though they cannot entirely finesse the cultural relativity questions), and focus on cooperation in research, education, and drafting of model penological standards, fostering interchange among governments to stimulate improvements in domestic institutions and policies.[36]

It is also possible to combine these approaches. The European Parliament's 1986 Resolution on Violence Against Women,[37] for example, adopts a normative approach in its preamble, citing various provisions of the Universal Declaration and various treaties, and describing violence as "an infringement of human rights," but also uses the term "social problem" to describe sexual violence.

One inquiry in constructing a strategy should be whether domestic violence and rape would be more vigorously addressed as a matter of high priority by human rights or by criminological bodies. As Laura Reanda remarked with respect to prostitution, there is little prospect that the UN crime control bodies will devote the resources and energy to battling prostitution that they have directed to eradicating drug abuse.[38] The same would certainly be true of domestic violence and rape, which have even fewer of the cross-boundary elements that help promote intergovernmental cooperation in matters of crime.

On the other hand, mainstream human rights bodies have shown a general lack of attention to domestic violence and rape.[39] And CEDAW, for all its creativity in interpreting the Convention, has yet to overcome its paucity of resources and lack of effective implementation powers.[40] The alternative of drafting an entirely new instrument has been criticized for creating a danger of confusion concerning existing instruments, the risk of limited ratification, and the expense of implementation.[41]

If a human rights/normative approach to domestic violence is favored, use of an equality paradigm has a certain logic and force. In many respects, the problem of domestic violence results from a failure of the legal system to treat the battery, murder, and rape of women by husbands or lovers as crimes, in the same manner and to the same degree as if they had occurred between strangers. Selective tolerance for domestic violence frequently stems from cultural norms that encourage men to abuse their wives.[42] Thus, victims of domestic violence are denied the equal protection of the criminal laws, contravening fundamental human rights principles of equality before the law.[43] At a deeper level, an equality paradigm might also address the root problem of domestic violence, the structures of subordination that the violence reinforces. As Catharine MacKinnon notes, what women really need and are denied is "a chance at productive lives of reasonable physical security, self-expression, individuation, and minimal respect and dignity."[44] These goods are, of course, what every human being deserves and what international human rights law supposedly aims to ensure.

The equality paradigm also appears to offer a solution to the problem of marital rape, which is often the subject of formal legal exemption from criminal liability. Under an equal treatment approach, all victims of forcible rape deserve to be treated alike, regardless of status.[45] The same principle of equal treatment would bar invidious practices such as selective failure to punish rapists of prostitutes[46] or members of vulnerable groups, such as disabled women.[47]

Formal or customary legal rules that permit men to murder their wives on suspicion of infidelity or because they do not otherwise conform to the husband's demands,[48] defenses not available to women who resort to violence against unfaithful husbands, would also logically be invalidated under an equality rationale mandating that spouses have equal rights in marriage.[49] CEDAW's General Recommendation No. 19 explicitly calls for the abolition of the "defense of honor."[50]

The acute problem of "bride burning" in India results from cultural practices that the state has prohibited but to which it shows selective indifference in practice. India has formally abolished the institution of dowry.[51] However, the tradition not only continues but reportedly is being exacerbated by growing consumerism on the part of husbands and mothers-in-law who kill or maim brides whose families will not or cannot meet their escalating demands.[52] The state undertakes few prosecutions, even though the law requires a special inquiry into suspicious deaths of women married fewer than seven years.[53] The scope of the problem was highlighted by the recent report that bride burning claimed more victims in recent years than the armed conflict in the Punjab.[54]

But a simple "equal treatment" approach to domestic violence leaves important issues unaddressed. As the UN studies on family violence note,[55] victims of domestic violence operate under pressures not felt by other crime victims. Socialization to define oneself primarily through relationships with men and lack of economic opportunity leave many women economically, socially, and emotionally dependent on their batterers.[56] An "equal treatment" approach (in the sense of equality of means) would provide victims of wife murder equality before the law, as it would serve the needs of women whose assault or rape had driven them to terminate their relationship to the attacker. But it does not so satisfactorily assist those victims of battery and marital rape who are not prepared to sever their ties to their assailants.

As the recommendations of CEDAW, the UN crime control bodies, the European Parliament and the draft Inter-American Convention all suggest,[57] forms of "special treatment" may be necessary to ameliorate the problem of domestic violence. Institutions such as battered women's shelters and special police units to handle domestic violence complaints are constructive, if inadequate, steps to redress the economic vulnerability of battered women[58] and the existing male-dominated police and prosecutorial apparatus which has historically been unresponsive to survivors of domestic violence. And even these forms of "special treatment" meet the needs only of those women who have decided to distance themselves from the batterers, sometimes temporarily.

Some women unable or afraid to sever their ties to the batterer might achieve a minimal level of safety and dignity only through "special treatment" of the batterer himself, in the form of rehabilitation programs that replace the imprisonment that would be meted out had he chosen a stranger as the target of his violence.[59] CEDAW proposes such rehabilitation measures in General Recommendation No. 19,[60] without any attempt to reconcile them with the equality principle that forms the textual basis for the recommendation. But such alternate dispositions are obviously at war with an equality paradigm, effectively decriminalizing the husband's conduct because of the identity and the dependency of his victim.[61]

Similar issues have been debated by feminists concerning legal aspects of pregnancy in the workplace.[62] As MacKinnon satirizes the strict equal treatment advocates, women actually have an ability men still lack, gestating children in utero. Pregnancy therefore is a difference. Difference doctrine says it is sex discrimination to give women what we need, because only women need it. It is not sex discrimination not to give women what we need because then only women will not get what we need.[63]

But determining what women "need" may be done within the structures of subordination. Many women "need" extended maternity leave because fathers do not share child-rearing and day care is unsatisfactory, both socially constructed "facts." The "needs" and "preferences" of battered women to remain with their batterers are equally socially constructed. In fact, they raise the sensitive issue of "false consciousness," which also figures in the debate over genital mutilation and prostitution.[64] Departing from the equal treatment paradigm to facilitate these "needs" appears humane and realistic, but carries the danger of reinforcing the same structures of subordination that promote the battering in the first place.

With respect to rape and other assault by non-family members, one could argue that all these acts are "political" in the broad sense because they manifest and reinforce patriarchal values. But sometimes the political element of this violence is especially strong. Beatings and acid attacks in order to force women to adopt Islamic dress are powerful examples of government-tolerated violence intended to deprive women of free opinion and expression, political, equal employment, and other rights.[65] Recent "power rapes" of politically active women in Pakistan appear motivated by government officials' desire to suppress their expressive activity.[66] Such acts violate not only equality norms but the basic civil and political rights guaranteed in instruments such as the ICCPR.

Genital Mutilation

While the appropriate terminology for this issue has been a matter of some debate,[67] I have chosen to follow the 1991 recommendation of the United Nations Seminar on Traditional Practices Affecting the Health of Women and Children[68] and use the term "genital mutilation" in order to convey the gravity of the practices, particularly infibulation. There are at least four types of practices, varying in severity, ranging from ceremonial cutting of the prepuce of the clitoris, to sunna involving the removal of the prepuce (thus analogous in some respects to male circumcision), to excision which involves removal of the clitoris and the labia minora, to infibulation which involves removal of all the outer female genitalia and sewing the remnants of the labia majora together so as to leave only a small opening for the passage of urine and menstrual blood.[69]

My task here is to examine genital mutilation as a form of gender-specific violence, to discuss whether adopting an equality paradigm is useful in attempting its eradication, to confront the public/private distinction as a potential barrier to the development of international norms, and to pose the choice between a focus on the practice as a human rights versus a social policy issue.

Female genital mutilation is arguably the most dramatic form of gender-specific violence. Female genital mutilation involves the use of dangerous and frightening weapons, causes permanent physical damage and sometimes death, and is targeted in the most gender-specific way possible at the female genitalia. Since the practice is increasingly performed on infants and small children, rather than as a puberty rite,[70] the issue of "consent"[71] does not mask the element of violence.

Female genital mutilation bears a powerful but complex relation to the principle of equality. The development and persistence of the practice of female genital mutilation seems deeply linked to the denigration of women as inferior beings and to a desire to subordinate women, especially to control their sexuality. CEDAW obliquely noted the linkage of genital mutilation to equality principles in General Recommendation No. 14 by calling upon states to report upon their efforts to eradicate the practice under the rubric not just of Article 12 (health) but also Article 10, whose subpart (c) requires the elimination of stereotyped conceptions of the roles of men and women.[72] This linkage was repeated in General Recommendation No. 19 by reference to Articles 2.f and 5 as well as Article 10(c), and by description of "female circumcision" as being the product of "[t]raditional attitudes under which women are regarded as subordinate or as having stereotyped roles."[73] Adherents of the practice often merely cite "tradition" as their explanation,[74] and while various myths are propounded about the practice being necessary for fertility or protection of newborns,[75] the pragmatic concern of many parents submitting their daughters for mutilation is to insure their marriageability. As Special Rapporteur Halima Embarek Warzazi notes, the "vulnerable social and economic status" of women perpetuates the practice; "marriage is the only social security for most women."[76] Thus, the thrust of education campaigns designed to demonstrate the actual physical harm caused by the practice may be ineffective so long as marriageability remains so crucial to women's survival.

As in the case of domestic violence and rape, the public/private distinction presents some theoretical difficulties in grappling with genital mutilation as a human rights issue. Especially troubling is the fact that the practitioners of the violence are frequently women.[77] The 1991 Seminar on Traditional Practices called upon NGOs and governments to cooperate in "retraining female circumcision practitioners to enable them to achieve financial self-sufficiency"[78] in a different line of work.

Because of the traditional state-oriented focus of human rights law, often the first step in battling the violence is a call for state officials to do nothing to encourage the practice. This may mean that the procedure will no longer be performed by medical personnel in state hospitals.[79] The effects of this strategy are difficult to assess: operations in hospitals may reduce the mortality and morbidity rate because of the greater cleanliness and skill, but they may lead to greater mutilation because the anesthetized girl puts up no resistance. The "private" practitioners of genital mutilation are addressed in recommendations calling for criminalization of the practice and public education campaigns to reduce acceptance among the public.[80]

The only codified prohibition on female genital mutilation in international human rights law is Article 24(3) of the Convention on the Rights of the Child,[81] which rather mildly requires states parties to take "all effective and appropriate measures with a view to abolishing traditional practices prejudicial to the health of children." This provision apparently includes female genital mutilation within its scope.[82] CEDAW in General Recommendation No. 14 also linked genital mutilation to the guarantee on health in Article 12 of the Women's Convention. The Sub-Commission, responding to the report of its Working Group on Traditional Practices, labeled genital mutilation as a violation of the rights of women without a specific textual basis.[83]

One factor that distinguishes genital mutilation from other forms of violence against women is its non-universality. The geographic limits on the extent of the practice,[84] and its prevalence in portions of the Third World, have meant that cultural relativity can be raised as a barrier to its discussion within UN fora.[85] Although Islam does not apparently command the practice,[86] religious elements are sometimes injected into the debate over the defensibility of the practice on cultural grounds.

As a matter of practical politics, the cultural specificity of genital mutilation may touch sensitive nerves regardless of whether a normative or social policy approach is adopted to combat it. Prohibitions such as those contained in Article 24(3) of the Convention on the Rights of the Child, while cast in universal terms, in reality impose burdens only on those states where the practice continues. And international cooperation may be more palatable where a social evil presents a problem for all societies (as in the case of domestic violence) than where the problem affects an isolated group of states. Patterns of immigration may be spreading the practice of genital mutilation, however.[87]

General Recommendation No. 14 is perhaps best described as taking a normative approach, its language tracking that of the Convention on the Rights of the Child. But the "appropriate and effective measures" that CEDAW urges upon states parties are essentially all educational in nature.[88] Reflecting the cultural delicacy of the issue, CEDAW urges that women's groups within the societies where genital mutilation is practiced take the lead in battling it, with support from UN and other sources. In contrast, the recommendations from the 1991 Seminar on Traditional Practices organized by the Sub-Commission go beyond educational suggestions to call upon states to draft legislation prohibiting female circumcision (though it is not explicit whether criminal penalties are intended), and to create a governmental body to implement an official policy against the practice.[89] The European Parliament likewise adopted a combined educational/prohibitionist stance.[90]

Gender-Based Violence by Police and Security Forces

Amnesty International's 1991 report *Women in the Front Line*[91] and its 1992 report *India: Torture, Rape, and Deaths in Custody*[92] have conferred a welcome prominence to the gender-based forms of violence that are inflicted upon women by police and security forces. Although there can be no genuine controversy about these practices being violations of fundamental human rights, mainstream human rights IGOs and NGOs have rarely devoted much attention to this issue.

In presenting his report to the 1992 session of the UN Commission on Human Rights, the Special Rapporteur on Torture laid great stress upon gender-specific forms of torture, responding to CEDAW's General Recommendation No. 19 which includes violence against detained women within its scope.[93] Although he indicated that he had brought a "number of cases" to the attention of governments involving gender-based violence and would seek further cooperation with CEDAW, his previous reports generally describe few female victims and do not probe the gender-based nature of the violence against them in any depth.[94]

Although it is perhaps reading too much into syntax, the Special Rapporteur's description of the torture of one Colombian woman illustrates the sometimes flawed approach of human rights institutions in addressing this problem:

Maria Elizabeth Suarez Giraldo [was] arrested on 2 March 1990 by members [of the army]. . . . During her detention, she was allegedly subjected to torture and ill-treatment, including being deprived of food and water, receiving death threats against herself and her seven-year-old daughter and being beaten, forced to stand for 8 or 10 hours and jabbed in the chest with pins. She was also allegedly raped by two men.[95]

The "also" in the final sentence might be taken to suggest that while the other harms inflicted on Ms. Suarez Giraldo were forms of torture or ill-treatment, the rape was something different.

Mainstream human rights institutions may have sometimes seen rape of women in detention as an act of personal gratification for the guard and thus "private" and beyond the scope of legitimate human rights concerns. Rape of women in detention can be either the deliberate policy of a repressive government or it can result from indifference and failure to take sufficient preventive measures. The public/private distinction thus stands as a potential obstacle to effective action against even this form of violence, committed by men bearing the emblems of the state and gaining the opportunity to harm women by exercising power conferred by the state. The relative neglect of this issue by mainstream human rights institutions has been countered to some degree by sustained attention since 1984 by the United Nations Commission on the Status of Women, which has induced ECOSOC to adopt several resolutions on "physical violence against detained women that is specific to their sex,"[96] and has requested the Secretary-General to compile several reports on the subject.[97]

Formal legal prohibitions in international and national law against violence and sexual abuse of detained women are not lacking.[98] The prohibitions on torture and cruel treatment and dignitary guarantees for detained persons, such as those contained in Articles 7 and 10 of the ICCPR and Articles 1 and 16 of the Convention Against Torture and Other Cruel, Inhuman, or Degrading Treatment or Punishment, reach gender-specific violence against detained women. Most governments providing information to the Commission on the Status of Women reported

that they do not have any special legal provisions that cover prevention against physical violence against detained women as such. They say that the offence is adequately covered by general legal provisions . . . designed to protect both male and female prisoners from ill treatment.[99]

Lack of reporting and a failure of treaty supervision bodies to focus on the issue in their scrutiny of state compliance are the real problems. For example, though forty-one states submitted information to the 1987 report of the Secretary-General, only two specific cases of sexual abuse of women prisoners were mentioned.[100] Yet the Working Group on Communications of the Commission on the Status of Women has identified violence against detained women as a major and recurrent issue in its work.[101] And Amnesty International reports pervasive gender-based violence by police and security forces in countries such as India[102] and El Salvador.[103] Andrew Byrnes has criticized the Committee Against Torture (CAT) for failing to give sufficient attention to gender-based forms of torture and ill-treatment.[104]

While existing norms prohibit gender-based violence by police and security forces and there is wide agreement that "such problems are under the Governments' control"[105] (that is, state responsibility is clear), strategies for eradicating this form of violence raise some intriguing issues of equality. Principle 5 of the Body of Principles for the Protection of All Persons Under Any Form of Detention or Imprisonment[106] neatly embodies the tension:

1. These Principles shall be applied to all persons within the territory of any given State, without distinction of any kind, such as . . . sex. . . .
2. Measures applied under the law and designed solely to protect the rights and special status of women, especially pregnant women and nursing mothers . . . shall not be deemed to be discriminatory. The need for, and the application of, such measures shall always be subject to review by a judicial or other authority.

Thus one strategy is to insure that women are treated the same as men (for example, not subjected to violence targeted at their gender, such as the rape and threats to her child inflicted on Ms. Suarez Giraldo) and benefit from general prohibitions on torture and cruel treatment. But a single-minded pursuit of this strategy runs the risk of burying gender-specific violence in general concerns for the rights of detainees. Since women comprise a very small minority of prisoners[107] and detained men are also subjected to violence, including sexual abuse, this strategy may fail as a practical matter. Torture of women detainees, including political prisoners, often takes distinct gender-based forms that deserve specific scrutiny.[108]

The alternate strategy is to assert the ultimate nondiscrimination goal but to impose preventive requirements on governments in order to reduce the incidence of gender-based violence, recognizing that women need special protection from special risks. Thus, segregation of female and male prisoners and restrictions on access to women prisoners by male guards, etc., may be required as violence-reduction steps. Such measures can create tension with nondiscrimination goals, such as by restricting employment opportunities or mobility for prison guards.

Tension with equality principles, at least those relating to equality of means and not equality of ends, may also arise when special attention is paid to the maternal role of women in devising penological policies. If a broad definition of violence is adopted, so as to include emotional violence,[109] then forced separation of mothers from their children could be seen as a gender-linked form of violence. Indeed, many states responding to the request for information on violence against detained women included information on their policies concerning reduction in prison terms for pregnant women and mothers or provisions for housing infants within women's prisons.[110] International norms exempting pregnant women and new mothers from the death penalty also come within the rubric of human rights standards concerning violence against detained women.[111] While such measures protect mothers and children from acute harms, they also obviously tend to reinforce traditionally defined parenting roles.

Gender-Based Violence Against Women During Armed Conflict

Gender-based violence against women during armed conflict raises many issues in common with violence against detained women: direct state responsibility (sometimes obscured by perceptions that sexual violence is inherently "private" in its motivation), and a tension between nondiscrimination norms and special preventive/protective measures in recognition of special risks faced by women because of gender and maternity. These elements are reflected in the highly codified terms of humanitarian law. In addition, general provisions of human rights treaties may prohibit gender-based violence during armed conflict.[112] As Françoise Krill notes, "If women in real life are not always protected as they should be, it is not due to the lack of a legal basis."[113]

Although women remain a small percentage of combatants,[114] their increased involvement in armed conflict beginning in the First World War has resulted in a number of gender-specific provisions in the key treaties. Of the roughly 560 articles of the four Geneva Conventions of 1949 and the two Additional Protocols of 1977, about 40 specifically concern women.[115] Humanitarian law addresses a number of distinct issues relating to gender-based violence against women: (1) humane treatment of female combatants, especially as prisoners of war; (2) protection of female internees and civilians accused of offenses against an occupying power; (3) protection of female civilians from sexual abuse and degrading treatment; and (4) provision for the special physical needs of pregnant women and mothers of young children. The Commission on the Status of Women has raised the additional issue of the exclusion of women from the decision-making process that leads to armed conflict.[116]

Women are entitled to the general protections of humanitarian law on a nondiscriminatory basis (either as combatants or as civilians), as well as to certain gender-specific protections. The four 1949 Conventions and the two Additional Protocols all contain an identical prohibition on "any adverse distinction founded on sex."[117] As Krill explains,

the prohibition of discrimination is not a prohibition of differentiation. . . . [D]istinctions are prohibited only to the extent that they are unfavorable. Equality could easily be transformed into injustice if it were to be applied to situations which are inherently unequal.[118]

Thus the nondiscrimination norm is frequently supplemented by provisions requiring that "women shall be treated with all the regard due to their sex."[119]

Specific provisions on the protection of women combatants were included in the 1929 Geneva Convention relative to the Treatment of Prisoners of War. Article 3 of the Convention mandated that "women shall be treated with all consideration due to their sex," while Article 4 prohibited differences in treatment of prisoners of war except on limited grounds, including the "sex of those who benefit from" the distinctions.

The Third Geneva Convention of 1949 includes provisions designed to deter gender-based violence and degrading treatment of women prisoners of war by requiring separate accommodations and sanitary conveniences[120] and prohibiting punishments in excess of those applicable to male prisoners of war.[121] Additional Protocol I provides that pregnant women and mothers of dependent infants who are prisoners of war should have their cases considered with "utmost priority";[122] the objective is their early release and repatriation.[123]

The greater likelihood for women to face dangers in armed conflict as civilians is reflected in numerous provisions. The Fourth Geneva Convention and the two Additional Protocols specifically forbid any attack upon the honor of non-combatant women, including "rape, enforced prostitution, or any form of indecent assault."[124] This concern is also addressed in rather vague language in the General Assembly's 1974 Declaration on the Protection of Women and Children in Emergency and Armed Conflict.[125] Yougindra Khushalani has asserted that outrages on the dignity and honor of women during armed conflict are grave breaches of humanitarian law, war crimes, and violations of a peremptory norm of international law.[126] Even before the exposure and international condemnation of policies of mass rape and forced pregnancy by Bosnian Serb forces in Bosnia-Herzegovina,[127]

mass rapes of women during the war for independence in Bangladesh,[128] the systematic rape of women suspected of complicity in the
insurgency in Kashmir,[129] and the belated but growing scandal concerning the "comfort women" who were abducted and forced into
prostitution by the Japanese army during the Second World War[130] had
revealed the dimensions of the problem.

Sexual assault against women civilians during armed conflict may be
part of an intentional strategy to suppress or punish the civilian population, or it may result from a failure by commanders to exercise
proper discipline over their troops. However, it is never a "private"
matter; humanitarian law requires occupying powers to protect the
civilian population, and soldiers who rape may be punished as war
criminals. This presents an interesting contrast to the rape of women in
peacetime, where the failure of governments to take adequate preventive and punitive efforts to combat the practice is only beginning to be
seen as creating state complicity in a human rights violation.[131] The
Japanese government has been unable to escape censure for its practice of forced prostitution by arguing that the brothels were a form of
private enterprise.[132]

Civilians may be interned or imprisoned by parties to armed conflict;
to prevent gender-based violence and degrading treatment humanitarian law provides that separate accommodations and female supervision
should be provided to women who are not interned with a family
group.[133] Article 76(3) of Protocol I urges states to the "maximum
extent feasible" to avoid pronouncing death sentences on pregnant
women or mothers of dependent infants. Article 6(4) of Protocol II for-
bids carrying out the death penalty on mothers of young children.[134]

This solicitude for the maternal role of women runs as a thread
throughout humanitarian law. While it might seem churlish to quarrel
with efforts to make the conduct of war more humane, the maternity-
oriented provisions of humanitarian law can be criticized for reflecting
rather Victorian views of women as being the equivalent of children in
their weakness and need for special care. During discussions leading to
the adoption of the Declaration on the Protection of Women and
Children in Emergency and Armed Conflict, participants observed
that women's "physical nature and dual role in society made them
more vulnerable in wartime."[135] The perceived special vulnerability of
pregnant women and mothers of small children to the consequences of
war (risks of being caught in the crossfire, deprivation of necessities)
has resulted in such provisions as prohibitions on the transfer of pregnant women except for imperative safety reasons,[136] their rapid release
from internment,[137] provision of additional food and medical care,[138]
their assimilation to the protected status of the sick and wounded,[139]

and their evacuation from besieged areas.[140] The violence from which these provisions protect pregnant women and mothers is gender-based in the sense that their physical condition and caregiving responsibilities can magnify the impact of the conflict on them. One possible consequence of special solicitude for maternity is the reinforcement of traditional role definitions.

Gender-based violence against women in armed conflict, as well as gender-based violence against detained women, are best addressed through a normative approach. State responsibility exists and the victims tend not to have the complex economic and social relationships with their attackers that confounds the problems of domestic violence and genital mutilation, often pushing IGOs toward a social policy approach.

Gender-Based Violence Against Women Refugees and Asylum-Seekers

Gender-based violence against refugee women has two distinct dimensions: (1) sexual and other assault facilitated by the refugees' vulnerable situation after flight; and (2) gender-based violence in the refugees' country of origin as a form of persecution qualifying the women for refugee status. Since 1988 the United Nations High Commissioner for Refugees (UNHCR) and the Executive Committee of the High Commissioner's Programme (the Ex. Comm.) have given increasing attention to the first set of issues, culminating in Guidelines on the Protection of Refugee Women.[141] The second issue is addressed in a 1985 policy statement of the Ex. Comm.,[142] in the new Guidelines with respect to interview processes for female asylum-seekers,[143] and in the case law of several asylum states.

Women who have fled from their countries of origin are frequently at special risk of sexual abuse. As High Commissioner Sadako Ogata noted in dedicating International Women's Day in 1991 to refugee women, "they are vulnerable to acts of violence and sexual harassment in exchange for their basic needs."[144] They may be raped while foraging for their families, during the course of their flight, in unsafe refugee camps, or by guards who demand sex in exchange for food or other necessities.[145] The Guidelines attempt to address these protection concerns by requiring protection officers and NGOs to restructure refugee assistance.[146] The resolution on refugee women adopted by the Commission on the Status of Women recommended that women be given individual identification and registration documents in order to reduce the dependency that makes them vulnerable to violence.[147]

Giving voice to the problems that led to these recommendations,

Central American women at a regional seminar in 1991 described how guards in refugee camps raped them in exchange for food, how development funds were channeled to men, how women were left out of repatriation decisions, and repatriation grants were made only to (and often squandered by) male relatives. Participants also reported increased incidence of domestic violence at the hands of idle refugee men.[148] The misogyny of rebel Afghans took the form of terrorizing women in camps in Pakistan in order to force refugee women to abandon training and education courses.[149]

The determination of refugee status in asylum states may require consideration of gender-specific violence against refugee women. This issue has two aspects: (1) whether women who have encountered gender-specific violence in their country of origin qualify as members of a "particular social group" and thus for refugee status within the definition of the 1951 Convention relating to the Status of Refugees;[150] and (2) whether adjudication procedures are adequate to glean the stories of women who have been raped in their countries of origin.

In 1985, the Ex. Comm. adopted Conclusion No. 39 (XXXVI), which provides:

States, in the exercise of their sovereignty, are free to adopt the interpretation that women asylum-seekers who face harsh or inhumane treatment due to their having transgressed the social mores of the society in which they live may be considered as a "particular social group" within the meaning of Article 1(A) (2) of the 1951 United Nations Refugee Convention.[151]

The force of this conclusion is obviously weakened by its optional nature, but it does partially fill the gap left by the absence of "sex" from the criteria of eligibility for refugee status. Adjudication of cases involving gender-specific violence against women has been uneven. In Canada, a Turkish widow who was subjected to rape and harassment by young men, and whose government was unwilling to protect her, qualified for refugee status as a member of the social group "single women living in a Moslem country without the protection of a male relative."[152] In contrast, an Indian woman who was physically attacked and threatened with stoning and arson by men in her community because she had married a man of lower caste, and was arrested by the police because she was active in a women's organization, was denied asylum in Germany because she was unable to prove that her predicament was due to governmental hostility to her activities.[153] In France the Solomonic decision was reached that while female genital mutilation is a form of persecution, the asylum claim of a woman from Mali would be denied because she had not yet been subjected to the procedure.[154] In the United States a Salvadoran woman obtained political asylum on grounds of imputed political opinion where she proved repeated rape and abuse by an army sergeant who threatened to accuse her falsely of subversion if she resisted him, but a dissenting judge argued that the sergeant's actions were purely personal.[155]

Women who have been sexually abused may be further traumatized by an asylum adjudication process that is insensitive to their suffering, and may fail to recount their experiences in a complete and convincing manner.[156] The Guidelines thus suggest "more careful handling of interviews with women applying for refugee status and the training of more female staff to conduct such interviews."[157]

Violence Associated with Prostitution and Pornography

Analysis of prostitution and associated violence as a human rights concern has the longest and most checkered history and poses perhaps the greatest theoretical difficulties for devising a strategy forward. Feminists disagree profoundly whether all prostitution is inherently coerced and what the focus of international norms concerning prostitution should be. Feminists also disagree on normative approaches to pornography.

A complex social history lies behind Article 6 of the CEDAW Convention and its elaboration in General Recommendation No. 19.[158] The earliest feminist efforts to raise human rights concerns in relation to prostitution attempted to repeal national laws that subjected prostitutes to invasive inspection procedures.[159] The aim of these feminists was to empower and to protect the dignity of prostitutes, many of whom were working-class women engaged in casual prostitution in order to supplement their earnings. The effect of governmental regulation of prostitution was often to increase the marginalization of prostitutes in society and to expose them to vastly increased violence:

Control of prostitution shifted from madams and prostitutes themselves to pimps and organized crime syndicates. . . . In addition, [the prostitute] faced increased brutality, not only from the police, but also from her new "employers."[160]

International attention to prostitution, however, was first directed at the phenomenon called "white slavery," in which women and girls were coerced or tricked into prostitution in colonial territories and foreign countries. A series of conventions beginning in 1904 culminated in the Convention for the Suppression of the Traffic in Persons and of the Exploitation of the Prostitution of Others in 1949.[161] The 1949 Convention does not draw an explicit distinction between coerced and voluntary prostitution[162] and represents the then-current consensus on an "abolitionist" model. States have varied among "prohibitionist" approaches, under which prostitution is forcefully suppressed, often by heavy penalties against the prostitute, including execution;[163] "regulationist" systems under which prostitutes are channeled into licensed brothels or "red light" districts, taxed and subjected to inspections;[164] and "abolitionist" systems under which the prostitute is supposedly not penalized but procuring, pimping, and brothel-keeping are penalized.[165]

Unfortunately, violence against prostitutes occurs under all these systems at the hands of customers, pimps, and the police, who exploit the prostitutes' fear of the authorities, low social status, and economic vulnerability. Even abolitionist systems can feed violence by exposing prostitutes to more dangerous working conditions. Sometimes law itself fosters violence against prostitutes, as where the rape of prostitutes is decriminalized or trivialized.[166] And extreme state violence can be directed at prostitutes, as in the case of approximately twenty-five Burmese prostitutes deported from Thailand who were reportedly executed by the Burmese military because they had been infected with the AIDS virus.[167]

Arguably the 1949 Convention reflects an assumption that all prostitution is inherently coerced, although some critics assert that it implicitly distinguishes between free and forced prostitution.[168] By eradicating pimps and procurers, the hope may have been that prostitution itself would disappear because women left to themselves would not freely choose prostitution. The fact that discussions of prostitution within the United Nations Sub-Commission on Prevention of Discrimination and Protection of Minorities have occurred under the rubric of "slavery and slavery-like practices" likewise suggests inherent coercion.[169] The 1983 report of the Special Rapporteur on the Suppression of the Traffic in Persons and the Exploitation of the Prostitution of Others emphasizes prostitution's alienation of intimacy and inherent inconsistency with human dignity,[170] but also agrees that "even when prostitution seems to have been chosen freely, it is actually the result of coercion."[171] Article 6 of the CEDAW Convention, with its emphasis on traffic in women and exploitation of prostitution of women, duplicates the approach of the 1949 Convention. But the Draft Declaration on Violence against Women includes only "trafficking in women and forced prostitution," despite notice that the 1949 Convention considers all prostitution to have been compelled.[172] The Draft Declaration fails to define when prostitution is "forced."

The 1949 Convention is vulnerable to attack from two sides. Radical feminists argue that prostitution is another manifestation of the subor-

dination of women, similar to rape, domestic violence, and sexual harassment, and constitutes a human rights abuse whether or not pimps,
traffickers, or overt violence are involved. The Coalition Against Trafficking in Women, with the cooperation of UNESCO, organized a
group of experts who drafted a convention broadly prohibiting sexual
exploitation, defined as

a practice by which person(s) achieve sexual gratification or financial gain or
advancement through the abuse of a person's sexuality by abrogating that
person's human rights to dignity, equality, autonomy and physical and mental
well-being.[173]

The draft convention calls on states to suppress all prostitution, including "casual, brothel, military, pornographic prostitution and sex tourism, mail order bride markets, and trafficking in women."[174] The rationale of the drafters is that:

When prostitution is accepted and normalized, what is legitimized is the sale of
body and sex. . . . By reducing women to a commodity to be bought, sold,
appropriated, exchanged, or acquired, prostitution affects women as a group.
It reinforces the societal equation of women to sex which reduces women to
being less than human, and contributes to sustaining women's second class
status throughout the world.[175]

Thus prostitution is identified as incompatible with equality principles,
whether or not physical violence is directly involved. A focus on violence associated with prostitution might mask the basic clash with
principles of human dignity and equality.[176]

On the other hand, prostitutes' rights organizations and some states,
such as the Netherlands,[177] argue that prohibition and regulation of
prostitution aggravate the risks of violence and impair women's self-
determination to decide whether prostitution is their best economic
alternative.[178] This position raises the familiar problem of "choice"
constrained by structures of subordination. While prostitutes' rights
groups might see as coercive only those situations "in which the use of
force is extremely obvious,"[179] the Netherlands suggests that prostitution is involuntary if "physical or psychological coercion is used or if
one person has *de facto* influence or authority over another. . . . Economic coercion also represents a violation of human rights."[180]

Additional dilemmas surround the issue of pornography, which
often depicts extreme forms of violence against women. Not only are
the women involved in the production of this pornography physically
and emotionally harmed,[181] but many feminists assert that all women
are harmed by dissemination of the idea that violence against women is
desirable and by constructs of female sexuality that are unauthentic,

defined in terms of male demands.[182] CEDAW's General Recommendation No. 19 reflects this view: "the propagation of pornography . . .
contributes to gender-based violence."[183] On the other hand, workers
in the pornography industry may be making the same type of "choice"
as prostitutes to obtain the most remunerative work available to them.
Suppression of pornography also clashes with principles of free expression, much as in the case of racist speech.[184] Opposition to pornography may bring feminists into alliance with groups attached to
traditional moral values that subjugate women,[185] but a civil liberties
approach creates an uneasy alliance with pornographers. The 1991
Draft Declaration on Violence against Women included a prohibition
on "degrading representation of women in the media," noting that
"when rights to freedom of expression conflicted with women's rights,
it was all too often that women's rights were compromised."[186]

Violence in the Workplace, Including Sexual Harassment

The prohibition on employment discrimination in Article 11 of the
CEDAW Convention is helpfully explicated in General Recommendation No. 19 in relation to sexual harassment:

> Equality in employment can be seriously impaired when women are sub-
> jected to gender specific violence, such as sexual harassment in the workplace.
> Sexual harassment includes such unwelcome sexually determined behavior
> as physical contacts and advances, sexually coloured remarks, showing por-
> nography, and sexual demands, whether by words or actions. Such conduct can
> be humiliating and may constitute a health and safety problem; it is discrimina-
> tory when the woman has reasonable grounds to believe that her objection
> would disadvantage her in connection with her employment . . . or when it
> creates a hostile working environment.[187]

This approach of analyzing sexual harassment as a form of discrimination follows the pattern that has developed in some national laws[188] and
in the recent Code of Practice on Measures to Combat Sexual Harassment of the European Community.[189]

One of the advantages of approaching sexual harassment from an
anti-discrimination perspective is that the offending conduct can be
broadly defined. Emphasizing sexual harassment as a form of "violence" might lead to a narrowing of its definition. For example, the
European Community's Code of Conduct includes "unwanted conduct
of a sexual nature, or other conduct based on sex affecting the dignity
of women and men at work," including "unwelcome physical, verbal or
non-verbal conduct."[190] But France's new criminal prohibition on sex-

ual harassment applies only to constraint or pressure against a subordinate (quid pro quo harassment), not harassment by peers (which often creates a hostile work environment).[191]

Some commentators still question whether sexual harassment is properly seen as a matter of discrimination rather than, for example, tortious conduct.[192] On the other hand, Catharine MacKinnon sees sexual harassment as a manifestation of the pervasive structures of subordination within which women live, thus raising broad equality issues.[193] MacKinnon's view consciously seeks to avoid labeling sexual harassment as a problem of individuals, which might facilitate its submergence into the "private" sphere and risk placing the blame on the subjectivity of the offended woman rather than on the harasser.[194]

Approaching sexual harassment as a form of violence against women requires a broad definition of violence in order to encompass all harassing behavior. The 1991 Draft Declaration on Violence Against Women defined violence in its Article 1 as "any act, omission, controlling behaviour or threat, in any sphere, that results in, or is likely to result in, physical, sexual or psychological injury to women."[195] Article 2(b) prohibited "[p]hysical, sexual and psychological violence occurring within the general community, including . . . sexual harassment and intimidation in the workplace."[196] The draft OAS Convention likewise adopted a very broad definition of violence, reaching that inflicted by public officials or private persons in the context, inter alia, of work, "such as sexual harassment, either imposed as a condition, or which undermines participation, effectiveness or self-esteem."[197]

The Way Forward

Recent developments within CEDAW, the United Nations Commission on the Status of Women, and the Inter-American Commission of Women have generated some concrete proposals that helpfully frame debate about the best way forward to combat violence against women in its many manifestations. The key issues are: (1) whether new normative instruments are desirable; (2) if so, whether these should take the form of a declaration or a treaty, and if a treaty form is preferred, should it be a protocol to the CEDAW Convention, a separate instrument, a regional convention, or more than one of these; (3) whether new implementation measures should be adopted, and whether these should include: (a) enhanced authority for CEDAW, including longer periods to meet and the capacity to review cases from individuals, either on violence or on all the provisions of the Convention, (b) enhanced authority for the Commission on the Status of Women to review communications, (c) a Special Rapporteur on Violence Against

Women, reporting to the Commission on the Status of Women, the Commission on Human Rights, or both.

Need for a New Instrument

CEDAW adopted General Recommendation No. 19 shortly after the Expert Group Meeting on Violence Against Women had drawn up the 1991 Draft Declaration on Violence Against Women and the Meeting of Experts within the OAS system had formulated its draft convention in August 1991. While there is much commonality among these three documents, there are noteworthy differences. They adopt different points of departure, with CEDAW identifying gender-based violence as a form of discrimination[198] and subdividing its various forms on the basis of the different articles of the CEDAW Convention. In contrast, the 1991 Draft Declaration emphasized gender-based violence as "a violation of human rights" first and secondarily as a form of discrimination,[199] attempting to provide a unified definition applicable to all forms of gender-based violence. The 1993 Draft Declaration added pre-ambular language that strongly emphasized the equality aspect of violence against women.[200] The OAS draft convention describes violence equivalently as a deprivation of human dignity and a form of discrimination,[201] and adopts the comprehensive definition approach in its Articles 1 and 2.[202]

These different frameworks lead to subtle differences in content. For example, CEDAW provides a clearer definition of sexual harassment than that contained in the Draft Declaration.[203] CEDAW specifically addresses violence against rural women[204] and forced sterilization and abortion,[205] and the OAS draft convention requires states to take special account in their remedial measures of the needs of women who are especially vulnerable for reasons of race, ethnicity, migrant or refugee status, pregnancy, handicap, age, poverty, or exposure to armed conflict.[206] The more unified approach of the Draft Declaration leaves such matters largely to implication.

Thus there are a variety of possible reasons to favor one of these documents over the others. One advantage of General Recommendation No. 19 is that it has been authoritatively issued by CEDAW, in its capacity to provide interpretive guidance to the states parties to the CEDAW Convention. The risk of confusion raised by the divergent approaches of these instruments is troublesome. But, as Andrew Byrnes notes, such concerns have not deterred the drafting of useful instruments such as the Body of Principles for the Protection of All Persons under Any Form of Detention or Imprisonment.[207] And the fact that

General Recommendation No. 19 has already been issued diminishes the risk that a new instrument might suggest that violence is not covered by the CEDAW Convention.

Declaration or Treaty?

The Draft Declaration has the advantage of being universal in its coverage, and the disadvantage of being hortatory rather than legally binding. Its adoption by the UN General Assembly would give additional prominence to gender-based violence as a human rights issue. Moreover, it could serve as the precursor of a UN treaty on the subject, if consensus later built on the need for a specific treaty on violence against women.

General Recommendation No. 19 binds only the states parties to the Women's Convention, though this is a large group. Support may be waning for the idea of a substantive protocol on violence to the Convention,[208] but may revive if state compliance and reporting do not improve in response to General Recommendation No. 19. A substantive protocol carries the risk of attracting only a small number of ratifications and thus casting doubt on the scope of the existing terms of the Convention.

The OAS draft convention would be open only to OAS member states, but a regional focus on issues such as torture has been found useful.[209] The OAS draft convention proposes innovative enforcement mechanisms, with reporting to the Inter-American Commission of Women and individual complaints to the Inter-American Commission of Human Rights, as well as the prospect of advisory opinions and optional contentious jurisdiction in the Inter-American Court of Human Rights.[210] Completion and implementation of the OAS draft convention on violence against women could provide an instructive precedent for standard-setting at the regional level as well as for further development of implementation measures by UN bodies.

Improvements in Implementation

The idea of a Special Rapporteur on Violence against Women has a great deal of merit. The advantages of such a "theme" mechanism, following the precedents of the Working Group on Enforced and Involuntary Disappearances and previous special rapporteurs, are multiple. Questions of state responsibility for the abuses need not be addressed in a judgmental way, as the role of the Special Rapporteur is to stop the abuses without necessarily casting blame. The Special Rapporteur can combine a humanitarian role of seeking redress for individual victims with an analytic exploration of the nature of the phenomenon and an examination of country situations through on-site visits. The appointment of a theme rapporteur or working group has come to signal an awareness of the need to deal vigorously with a particular human rights problem, and it would add welcome visibility to the previously neglected question of violence against women.

One important question is the parent body of the Special Rapporteur. The bureaucratic implications of reporting to both the Commission on the Status of Women and the Commission on Human Rights may prove daunting.[211] Reporting to the Commission on the Status of Women arguably is appropriate because that body has attempted to highlight the issue of violence against women and might be expected to give it continuing prominence in their work. Reporting to the Commission on Human Rights offers the advantages of drawing on that body's experience with other theme mechanisms and of providing an ongoing, formal mechanism to inject concerns for women's human rights into the work of the key political human rights body within the UN system.[212] Some care would have to be taken in any case to avoid a confusing overlap with the mandates of existing theme mechanisms, particularly the Special Rapporteur on Torture.

Other promising fronts include improvement in the communications procedures of the Commission on the Status of Women,[213] amendment or an optional protocol to the Women's Convention to confer authority to consider individual complaints or situations of pervasive gross violations,[214] and increased time for CEDAW meetings. The last might require amendment to Article 20 of the Women's Convention, which limits CEDAW meetings "normally" to an annual period of two weeks, inadequate for reviewing reports and likely to become even more inadequate if an individual complaint mechanism were adopted.[215]

Efforts could also be made by advocates for women to pressure the Human Rights Committee to revise its general comments on provisions of the ICCPR to highlight particular gender dimensions of some violations, and to bring complaints of gender-based violence under the Optional Protocol procedures. The Committee on Economic, Social and Cultural Rights could also be urged to address issues of violence against women within its mandate, such as sexual harassment in the workplace. Similar efforts could be made with respect to regional bodies such as the European Commission and Court of Human Rights and the Inter-American Commission and Court of Human Rights, on issues within their scope of reference.

Notes

1. Adopted Dec. 18, 1979, entered into force Sept. 3, 1981, G.A. Res. 34/180, U.N. GAOR, Supp. No. 46 at 193, U.N. Doc. A/RES/34/180 (1980).

2. CEDAW identified five articles relevant to violence (2, 5, 11, 12, 16) in its General Recommendation No. 12, which called on states to include information on gender-based violence in their reports. *Report of the Committee on the Elimination of Discrimination Against Women*, U.N. GAOR CEDAW, 44th Sess., Supp. No. 38, U.N. Doc. A/44/38 at 81 (1989). CEDAW failed to include art. 6, concerning prostitution, among the relevant articles.

3. A major breakthrough occurred in January 1992 when CEDAW adopted General Recommendation No. 19 on violence against women. U.N. Doc. CEDAW/C/1992/L.1/Add.15 (1992).

4. See discussion of a draft OAS convention, proposals for a protocol to CEDAW or separate UN convention, and the Draft Declaration on Violence Against Women, "The Way Forward," last section of this chapter.

5. Karen Engle categorizes feminist analysts of international human rights law into doctrinalists, institutionalists and external critics. Engle criticizes doctrinalists for their tendency to pile up citations to international norms as part of a strategy to establish that human rights violations against women already contravene international law. Karen Engle, "International Human Rights and Feminism: When Discourses Meet," *Mich. J. Int'l L.* 13 (1992): 517.

6. The most recent rhetorical recognition of violence against women as a human rights concern has come in the Final Document of the 1993 United Nations World Conference on Human Rights. U.N. Doc. A/CONF.157/DC/1/Add.1 at 22–23 (1993):

> [T]he World Conference stresses the importance of working towards the elimination of violence against women in public and private life, the elimination of all forms of sexual harassment, exploitation and trafficking in women, the elimination of gender bias in the administration of justice and the eradication of any conflicts which may arise between the rights of women and the harmful effects of certain traditional or customary practices, cultural prejudices and religious extremism.

7. Also excluded for reasons of space are incest (raising issues of the rights of the child) and forced sterilization and abortion (raising issues of reproductive rights).

8. Anne F. Bayefsky, "The Principle of Equality or Non-Discrimination in International Law," *Hum. Rts. L.J.* 11 (1990): 1.

9. Rape by "public" actors is addressed in the sections on "Gender-Based Violence by Police and Armed Forces," "Gender-Based Violence Against Women During Armed Conflict," and "Gender-Based Violence Against Women Refugees and Asylum-Seekers."

10. Terminology is loaded in the case of "domestic violence," as it is with "genital mutilation." A 1989 UN study on violence against women in the family correctly observed that the term "domestic violence" has the unfortunate effect of seeming to spread blame for the violence evenly among family members, shifting attention away from the batterers (or killers or rapists). Terms such as "battered wives" erroneously place the spotlight on the victim, suggesting that

she is the person with the problem and the guilt. The absurdity of this terminology was pointed out by English researcher Jan M. Pahl, who doubted that terrorist hijackings of airplanes would come to be labeled "the problem of hostages." *Violence Against Women in the Family,* U.N. Doc. ST/CSDHA/2, Sales No. E.89.IV.5 at 16 (1989). The UN study favors the terms "wife assault" or "wife abuse," but I did not find them satisfactory because of the assumption of a marital relationship. "Domestic violence" is used to suggest that the women victims of this practice become targets by virtue of their domestic relationship to the male assailant. The violence is often but not exclusively inflicted within the confines of the home.

11. For example, Article 23(1) of the International Covenant on Civil and Political Rights, G.A. Res. 2200 (XXI), 21 U.N. GAOR 21st Sess., Supp. No. 16 at 52, U.N. Doc. A/6316 (1966), describes the family as "the natural and fundamental group unit of society . . . entitled to protection by society and the State," and Article 17 prohibits interference with privacy and family. The Expert Group Meeting on Violence against Women suggested this be reconceptualized as the right to "violence-free private and family life" (U.N. Doc. E/CN.6/1992/4 para. 34 (1991)).

12. Empirical studies of the extent of domestic violence are inadequate and tend to provide more complete information concerning Western nations than for Eastern Europe or developing states. *Domestic Violence,* U.N. Doc. A/CONF.144/17 paras. 10–16 (1990). Even within Western nations, information is often more available concerning violence against poorer women whose lives are more open to scrutiny by state agencies (e.g., social workers, public hospitals). Statistics on rape are also seriously flawed by underreporting.

13. Article 6 of the ICCPR guarantees the right to life; art. 7 prohibits torture and cruel, inhuman, and degrading treatment or punishment; art. 23(4) guarantees equal rights in marriage; arts. 2(1), 3, and 26 contain guarantees of equality.

14. CEDAW, Recommendation 19, note 3.

15. CEDAW, note 3 at 2–3.

16. This expansive provision has been criticized by mainstream human rights scholars but is vital for insuring that human rights reach the reality of women's lives and the locus of their oppression. See Theodor Meron, *Human Rights Law-Making in the United Nations* (Oxford: Clarendon Press, 1986), 57–73.

17. Recommendation 19, note 3 at 3.

18. CEDAW member Justice Elizabeth Evatt of Australia cautioned in an article written shortly before the adoption of General Recommendation No. 19 that "Clearly there is a need to lift the issue of violence out of the sphere of discrimination and private rights and to put it squarely on the mainstream human rights agenda." Elizabeth Evatt, "Eliminating Discrimination against Women: The Impact of the UN Convention," *Melbourne U. L.R.* 18 (1991): 435, 444.

19. CEDAW, Recommendation 19, note 3 at 3.

20. CEDAW, note 3 at 4.

21. CEDAW, note 3.

22. CEDAW, note 3 at 5.

23. CEDAW, note 3 at 6.

24. CEDAW, note 3 at 6–7.

25. See CEDAW, Recommendation 12, note 2.

26. Report of the World Conference on the International Women's Year, Mexico City, 19 June–2 July 1975, UN Publication Sales No. E.76.IV.1, chap. II, s. A, paras. 124 and 131.

27. Report of the World Conference of the United Nations Decade for Women: Equality, Development and Peace, Copenhagen, 14–30 July 1980, U.N. Publication Sales No. E.80.IV.3, chap. 1, s. A, para. 141(f), and s. B, res. 5.

28. Report of the Committee on Crime Prevention and Control on its Seventh Session, U.N. Doc. E/CN.5/1983/2, chap. IV, sec. B, paras. 106 and 138.

29. See U.N. Doc. E/CN.6/1988/6, para. 6 (1987).

30. Report of the World Conference to Review and Appraise the Achievements of the United Nations Decade for Women: Equality, Development and Peace, Nairobi, 15–26 July 1985, U.N. Publication Sales No. E.85.IV.10, chap. I, sec. A. The Nairobi Conference also called for preventive measures and assistance to victims of domestic violence (chap. III, sec. B, para. 258; chap. IV, sec. E, para. 288).

31. Seventh United Nations Conference on the Prevention of Crime and the Treatment of Offenders, Milan, 25 August to 6 September 1985: Report prepared by the Secretariat, U.N. Publication Sales No. E.86.IV.1, chap. IV, sec. C, paras. 230, 232, 233.

32. U.N. Doc. E/CN.6/1988/6 (1987).

33. U.N. Publication Sales No. E.89.IV.5 (1989).

34. U.N. Doc. A/CONF.144/17 (1990).

35. The report on domestic violence in Brazil by Americas Watch and the Women's Rights Project of Human Rights Watch prefaces the results of its investigation with an explanation that Brazil was selected because of the visibility of the issue there and the "problem of impunity" that contravenes Brazil's international obligations. The report cites Articles 3 and 26 of the ICCPR (equal rights and nondiscrimination) and Article 2 of the CEDAW Convention, concluding that "Brazil is failing to meet its international obligations to guarantee to its female citizens the equal enjoyment of their civil and political rights and the equal protection of the law," *Criminal Injustice: Violence Against Women in Brazil*, vol. 2 (Washington, DC: Americas Watch, 1991), 4–5.

36. For example, the Council of Europe Steering Committee on Social Policy (CDPS) held a Colloquy on Violence within the Family: Measures in the Social Field" on 25–27 November 1987, which called on member states of the Council of Europe "to recognize violence in the family as a policy question which should be tackled jointly by member States." Council of Europe Doc. No. CDPS-VF(87) 14 Revised at 2 (1987). The Colloquy further noted that:

Laws, in particular criminal laws and administrative laws, cannot solve the whole range of problems of violence in the family. Legal provisions however cannot be seen separately from social situations and attitudes; thus some suggestions were made for legal measures although they might be considered as falling outside the primarily social scope of the Colloquy. (p. 3)

37. Resolution on Violence Against Women of 11 June, 1986, O.J. (C 176/73).

38. Laura Reanda, "Prostitution as a Human Rights Question: Problems and Prospects of United Nations Action," *Hum. Rts. Q.* 13 (1991): 202, 226–27.

39. See generally Andrew Byrnes, "Women, Feminism and International

Human Rights Law—Methodological Myopia, Fundamental Flaws or Meaningful Marginalisation?" *Austl. Y.B. Int'l L.* 12 (1992): 205, 217 (noting, for example, that the Human Rights Committee in its general comments on the right to bodily integrity (general comment 7(16)) and the right to life (general comment 6(16)) gave "not the faintest intimation that women face major, different threats to their enjoyment of these rights").

40. CEDAW meets for only two weeks per year and has no capacity to review individual complaints. Evatt, "Eliminating Discrimination," note 18 at 442, 446–49.

41. Such drawbacks led the Expert Group Meeting on Violence against Women in November 1991 to adopt the approach of drafting a Declaration on Violence Against Women rather than a separate treaty, though the group reserved the possibility of a new treaty if other approaches prove unsuccessful. U.N. Doc. E/CN.6/1992/4 paras. 25–27 (1991). See also Evatt, "Eliminating Discrimination," note 18; Andrew Byrnes, "Observations on the Background Paper Prepared by the Government of Canada on Issues in the Development of an International Instrument on Violence Against Women," paper presented to the Expert Group Meeting, 11–19; Government of Canada, "Issues in the Development of an International Instrument on Violence Against Women," prepared for the Expert Group Meeting, 11–12. During the discussion surrounding adoption of General Recommendation No. 19, members of CEDAW expressed opposition to either a substantive or procedural optional protocol to the Convention dealing solely with issues of violence. U.N. Doc. CEDAW/C/1992/L.1/Add.15, note 3 at 9–10 (1992).

42. This encouragement may result from socially constructed views of women as flawed and wayward creatures who require chastisement for their own and society's good. Or the encouragement may stem from a dominant focus on male self-identity, using violence against women to define and differentiate men from the inferior "other" (a dynamic that also underlies many racial bias crimes against strangers). Or the encouragement may result from society's excessive solicitude for the husband's feelings of inadequacy, weakness of character or lack of self-control (resulting from causes such as unemployment, low social status, violent childhood, drug addiction, or alcoholism), which forgives the man for inflicting violence and terror on his wife, even though she is also likely to be suffering from the same social deprivations.

43. Article 2 of the ICCPR guarantees nondiscriminatory access to remedies for violations of the rights recognized in the Covenant, and Article 14 guarantees equality before courts.

44. In MacKinnon's view mainstream sex equality law "has been . . . utterly ineffective" at getting these values for women. Catharine MacKinnon, *Feminism Unmodified: Discourses on Life and Law* (Cambridge, MA: Harvard University Press, 1987), 32.

45. The Draft Declaration on Violence against Women provides in its art. 2(a) that states must prohibit marital rape, note 41. Criminalization of marital rape is specifically called for by General Consideration 10 of the European Parliament's 11 June 1986 resolution on violence against women. See Resolution on Violence Against Women, note 37.

46. Evatt, "Eliminating Discrimination," note 18 at 440.

47. The European Court of Human Rights based the Netherlands' obligation to provide a remedy for the rape of an institutionalized retarded girl on the right to privacy under Article 8 of the European Convention on Human

Rights and Fundamental Freedoms. *X and Y v. The Netherlands,* 91 Eur. Ct. H.R. (ser. A), (1985).

48. See Americas Watch, *Criminal Injustice,* note 35.

49. See art. 16 of the CEDAW Convention, Article 23(4) of ICCPR, and art. 17(4) of American Convention on Human Rights.

50. CEDAW, Recommendation 19, note 3 at 6–7.

51. *Violence Against Women,* note 10 at 30, 67.

52. *Violence Against Women,* note 10 at 30.

53. See "Bride Burning Increasing in India," *WIN News* 10(4) (1984): 68; "Bride Burning on Rise in India: Few Convictions in Court," *WIN News* 12 (4) (1986): 40.

54. "Dowry Deaths," *Globe and Mail,* Mar. 12, 1992 (15,891 dowry deaths between 1988 and 1991, compared to 14,500 deaths in armed conflict).

55. *Violence Against Women,* note 10 at 67–74.

56. Even targets of failed bride burning attempts are reported to be reluctant to press charges because their options outside marriage are so limited.

57. General Recommendation No. 19, CEDAW, Recommendation 19, note 3 at 6–7; U.N. Doc. A/CONF. 144/17, note 34 at 24–25; O.A.S. Doc. OEA/ Ser.L/II.7.4, CIM/ Doc.1/91 at art. 8(b–d) (1991); European Parliament Resolution on Violence Against Women, note 37 at paras. 20–31.

58. The Draft Inter-American Convention, note 57, draws an explicit link between eradication of gender-based violence and measures to provide women with a "right of access to a fair distribution of economic, social and cultural resources to enable them to fully participate in the public, private and social life of the nation" (art. 7.i.).

59. The effectiveness of a counseling approach remains controversial, as do mandatory arrest and incarceration schemes. See *Violence Against Women,* note 10 at 59–61, 79.

60. CEDAW, note 3 at 7.

61. A far more cautious approach is evidenced in the draft OAS treaty, which contains a bracketed clause (indicating lack of consensus) providing that batterer rehabilitation programs could be adopted "where appropriate." O.A.S. Doc., note 57 at art. 8(d).

62. See, e.g., MacKinnon, *Feminism Unmodified,* note 44; Wendy W. Williams, "The Equality Crisis: Some Reflections on Culture, Courts, and Feminism," *Women's Rts. L. Rep.* 7 (1982): 175.

63. MacKinnon, *Feminism Unmodified,* note 44 at 36.

64. See sections on "Genital Mutilation" and "Violence Associated with Prostitution and Pornography" in this chapter. Similar issues surfaced during debates in the United States over regulation of silicone breast implants. The "need" for cosmetic implants is obviously socially constructed. Yet strict prohibitions might tend to reinforce stereotypes about women being unable to make rational choices. The worst-offending surgeons thus were enabled to take the high road in public debate as the champions of women's freedom. See, e.g., Philip J. Hilts, "Under Pressure, U.S. Weighs Ban on Use of Breast Implants," *N.Y. Times,* Oct. 21, 1991 at A1 (describing 400 women recruited by plastic surgeons to travel to Washington to lobby officials not to restrict implants, quoting one woman with cosmetic implants asserting the right to a choice not to be "disfigured" by small breasts).

65. Recent developments in the Sudan are described in "Dossier: Women's Rights Eroding in Sudan," *Africa News,* May 25, 1992 (NEXIS). Acid attacks in

Algeria are noted in Faika Medgahed, "Algeria: Fundamental Betrayals," *Ms.*, March/April 1992 at 13. Violence and legal changes to drive women out of public life in Afghanistan are recounted by Deborah Scroggins, "The Force of Law," *Atlanta Const.*, June 28, 1992 at P1.

66. Melissa Robinson, "Unveiled: Rape in Pakistan," *New Republic* 206 (10) (9 March 1992): 11.

67. The Sub-Commission placed the issue under the rubric of "traditional practices affecting the health of women and children" (see the *Report of the Working Group on Traditional Practices Affecting the Health of Women and Children*, U.N. Doc. E/CN.4/1986/42 (1986), and the Study on Traditional Practices Affecting the Health of Women and Children by Special Rapporteur Halima Embarek Warzazi, U.N. Doc. E/CN.4/Sub.2/1991/6). CEDAW adopted the terminology "female circumcision," as do some commentators, in its General Recommendation No. 14 of 1 February 1990, *Report of the Committee on the Elimination of Discrimination Against Women*, 45 U.N. GAOR Supp. (No. 38), U.N. Doc. A/45/38 para. 438 (1990).

68. U.N. Doc. E/CN.4/Sub.2/1991/48 para. 136(5) (1991).

69. See Alison Slack, "Female Circumcision: A Critical Appraisal," *Hum. Rts. Q.* 10 (1988): 437, 440–43.

70. Slack, "Female Circumcision," note 69 at 442–43; Katherine Brennan, "The Influence of Cultural Relativism on International Human Rights Law: Female Circumcision as a Case Study," *L. & Inequality* 7 (1989): 367, 389.

71. Where adult women submit to genital mutilation, human rights issues similar to those involved in domestic violence against women dependent on their batterers are raised.

72. CEDAW, Recommendation 14, note 67 at (d).

73. CEDAW, note 3 at para. 15.

74. U.N. Doc., note 68 at para. 28.

75. U.N. Doc. E/CN.4/Sub.2/1991/6, note 67 at para. 16; Slack, "Female Circumcision," note 69 at 447–48.

76. U.N. Doc. E/CN.4/Sub.2/1991/6, note 67 at para. 18.

77. U.N. Doc., note 67 at para. 10.

78. U.N. Doc. E/CN.4/Sub.2/1991/48, note 68 at paras. 34, 37, 136(3) (d).

79. U.N. Doc., note 68 at para. 19.

80. U.N. Doc., note 68 at paras. 136(1) (c), (f)–(m).

81. G.A. Res. 44/25 of 20 Nov. 1989, U.N. Doc. A/RES/44/25 (1989).

82. Brennan, "Influence of Cultural Relativism," note 70 at 394.

83. Brennan, "Influence of Cultural Relativism," note 70 at 388–93 (citing Sub-Comm'n Res. 1988/34, which expressed concern about "harmful traditional practices which violate the rights of women and children").

84. Slack states that genital mutilation occurs in over forty countries, primarily in Africa, the Arabian peninsula, and the Persian Gulf. The highest incidence is in Somalia, Sudan, and Ethiopia. "Female Circumcision," note 69 at 443.

85. See Brennan, "Influence of Cultural Relativism," note 70.

86. Slack, "Female Circumcision," note 69 at 446–47.

87. See note 90.

88. These range from classroom curricula to discourage the practice to retraining of traditional birth attendants in the hope that they will discourage mothers from circumcising their infants.

89. U.N. Doc. E/CN.4/Sub.2/1991/48, note 68 at 29.

90. The Resolution calls on member states to prohibit the practice among immigrant groups in their territory and also to launch educational campaigns among those groups, Council of Europe Doc., note 36 at para. 47. *WIN News* reports cases arising among immigrant groups in countries such as France. See, e.g., *WIN News* 12 (3) (1986): 42–43.

91. AI Index: ACT 77/01/91 (1991).

92. AI Index: ASA 20/06/92 (1992).

93. The Special Rapporteur stated that "it was clear that rape or other forms of sexual assault against women held in detention were a particularly ignominious violation of the inherent dignity and right to physical integrity of the human being [and] accordingly constituted an act of torture," U.N. Doc. E/CN.4/1992/SR.21 para. 35 (1992).

94. For example, his report to the forty-sixth session of the Commission notes a pattern of women from the scheduled castes in the Indian state of Bihar being the targets of police violence. He briefly describes an instance of one 18-year-old woman being stripped naked and beaten unconscious by seven policemen. But the other two illustrative incidents involve a male political party worker hung from a tree and beaten over several days, and eleven children, both boys and girls, being subjected to electric shocks and beatings by police suspecting them of theft. U.N. Doc. E/CN.4/1990/17 para. 88 (1989). It is thus rather difficult to tell why women are the usual targets of police violence in Bihar.

95. U.N. Doc., note 94 at para. 49(e) (1991).

96. See *Report of the Commission on the Status of Women on Its Thirty-fourth Session,* U.N. Doc. E/1990/25, E/CN.6/1990/1 at 9 (1990) (noting ECOSOC resolutions 76(v) of 5 August 1947, 304 I (XI) of 14 and 17 July 1950, 1984/19 of 24 May 1984 and 1986/29 of 23 May 1986). ECOSOC adopted resolution 1990/5 on 24 May 1990, noting the persistence of violence against detained women and placing the issue on the agenda of the Commission's thirty-sixth session in 1992.

97. See U.N. Doc. E/CN.6/1992/5 (1992), U.N. Doc. E/CN.6/1988/9 (1987), U.N. Doc. E/CN.6/1986/11 (1986). The number of replies has been disappointing, with only seventeen states providing information to the report for the Commission's Thirty-first session, forty-one to the report for the Thirty-second session, and thirty-six to the report to the Thirty-sixth session. U.N. Doc. E/CN.6/1992/5 paras. 1, 4. The 1991 report cautions that "Due to the limited number of responses, the survey cannot be considered a representative sample of the actual situation confronting detained women in all countries." U.N. Doc. E/CN.6/1991/10, para. 4.

98. CEDAW's General Recommendation No. 19 does not contain a specific provision on violence against detained women, though it notes that "violence perpetrated by public authorities" violates both the CEDAW Convention and "general international human rights law" and other treaties (note 3 at 3).

99. U.N. Doc. E/CN.6/1992/5, note 97 at para. 5.

100. U.N. Doc. E/CN.4/1988/9, note 97 at para. 61.

101. U.N. Doc. E/CN.6/1991/10 paras. 22–24.

102. See AI Index, note 92.

103. *Front Line,* AI Index, note 91 at 19. See also Adrianne Aron, Shawn Corne, Anthea Fursland, and Barbara Zelwer, "The Gender-Specific Terror of El Salvador and Guatemala," *Women's Stud. Int'l F.* 14 (1991): 37.

104. Andrew Byrnes, "The Committee Against Torture," in *The Human Rights Organs of the United Nations,* ed. Philip Alston (Oxford: Clarendon Press, 1991).

105. U.N. Doc. E/CN.6/1988/9, note 97 at para. 14.

106. G.A. Res. 43/173 of 9 December 1988.

107. For example, in 1987 2.4 percent of federal prisoners in Canada were women; 4.2 percent of prisoners in France were women; and Senegal reported fewer than 100 women prisoners. U.N. Doc. E/CN.6/1988/9, note 97 at paras. 18–19.

108. See Ximena Bunster, "The Torture of Women Political Prisoners: A Case Study in Female Sexual Slavery," in *International Feminism: Networking Against Female Sexual Slavery,* ed. Kathleen Barry, Shirley Castley, and Charlotte Bunch (New York: International Women's Tribune Center, 1984), 94–102.

109. The OAS draft convention, note 57 at art. 1, defines violence so as to include, *inter alia,* mental suffering resulting from threats and deceit.

110. See, e.g., U.N. Doc. E/CN.6/1992/5, note 97 at paras. 34–41.

111. For example, ICCPR art. 6(5) (death penalty not to be carried out on pregnant women), American Convention Article 4(5) (death penalty not to be applied to pregnant women).

112. For example, the non-derogable prohibition on torture in art. 3 of the European Convention on Human Rights and Fundamental Freedoms was violated when Turkish troops raped women during the invasion of Cyprus. *Cyprus v. Turkey,* 4 Eur. Comm'n H.R. Dec.& Rep. 482 (1976).

113. Françoise Krill, "The Protection of Women in International Humanitarian Law," *Int'l Rev. Red Cross* (Nov.–Dec. 1985): 337.

114. For example, female military units of the United Kingdom in the Second World War constituted approximately 9.37 percent of the UK's armed forces. Krill, "Protection of Women," note 113 at 350.

115. Krill, "Protection of Women," note 113 at 359.

116. U.N. Doc. E/CN.6/1990/4 paras. 3–5 (1990). See also Barbara Stark, "Nurturing Rights: An Essay on Women, Peace and International Human Rights," *Mich. J. Int'l L.* 13 (1991): 144.

117. See Article 12 of the First Geneva Convention (C.I), Article 12 of the Second Geneva Convention (C.II), Article 16 of the Third Geneva Convention (C.III, which also provides in its Article 14 that women "shall in all cases benefit by treatment as favorable as that granted to men"), Article 27 of the Fourth Geneva Convention (C.IV), Article 75 of Additional Protocol I (P.I), and Article 4 of Additional Protocol II (P.II).

118. Krill, "Protection of Women," note 113 at 339.

119. Art. 12 of C.I, art. 12 of C.II, art. 14 of C.III.

120. Art. 14(2) of C.III requires separate accommodations for women prisoners of war, and arts. 97 and 108 require separate accommodation and female supervision for women prisoners of war undergoing disciplinary or penal punishments; art. 29(2) requires separate sanitary conveniences; arts. 75(5) and 5(2) (a) of P.I require separate accommodation and female supervision of women whose liberty has been restricted for reasons related to the armed conflict.

121. Article 88(3) of C.III. Article 88(2) prohibits punishments more severe than those that would be imposed on a female member of the detaining power's armed forces.

122. Article 76(2) of P.I.

123. Krill, "Protection of Women," note 113 at 353–54.

124. Art. 27(2) of C.IV, arts. 75 and 76 of P.I, art. 4 of P.II.

125. G.A. Res. 3318 U.N. GAOR (XXIX), 14 December 1974. Operative paragraph 4 requires states to make "[a]ll efforts" to spare women from the ravages of war, including torture and degrading treatment and violence."

126. Yougindra Khushalani, *Dignity and Honour of Women as Basic and Fundamental Human Rights* (Dordrecht: Martinus Nijhoff, 1982), 153. Khushalani's book includes an extensive discussion of the relevant sources of humanitarian and human rights law concerning rape and indecent assault during armed conflict.

127. See Amnesty International, *Bosnia-Herzegovina: Rape and Sexual Abuse by Armed Forces,* AI Index: EUR 63/01/93 (1993); *Interim Report of the Commission of Experts Established Pursuant to Security Council Resolution 780* (1992), UN Doc. S/25274 Annex I (1993); Julia Preston, "Balkan War Crimes Tribunal Established," *Washington Post,* May 25, 1993 at A25.

128. Khushalani, *Dignity and Honour,* note 126 at 109.

129. *India,* note 92 at 21–22 (describing rape of more than twenty women by soldiers in the village of Kunan Poshpora).

130. "Japan: Small Comfort for Comfort Women," *Ms.,* March–April 1992 at 11; David E. Sanger, "Japan Admits It Ran Army Brothels During War," *N.Y. Times,* July 7, 1992, A1.

131. See section in this chapter on "Domestic Violence and Rape." This difference is neatly illustrated by the fact that women who are raped in their own country "under circumstances that have no relation to the armed conflict" are not protected by the prohibition on rape in Additional Protocol I. Krill, "Protection of Women," note 113 at 342.

132. Sanger, "Japan Admits," note 130.

133. Arts. 76, 85, 124 of C.IV; art. 75(5) of P.I; and art. 5(2) (a) of P.II.

134. Krill notes that an absolute prohibition on death sentences for pregnant women and mothers of young children was not politically possible. "Protection of Women," note 113 at 347.

135. Khushalani, *Dignity and Honour,* note 126 at 110 (quoting U.N. Doc. E/CN.6/546 para. 145 (1970)).

136. Art. 127 of C.IV.

137. Art. 132 of C.IV, art. 76(2) of P.I.

138. Arts. 16, 23, 89 and 91 of C.IV.

139. Art. 8 of P.I.

140. Art. 17 of C.IV.

141. See U.N. Doc. A/46/12/Add.1 at 11–12 (1991); Jan Burgess, "New UNHCR Guidelines for Protection of Women," *Refugees* 87 (October 1991): 40–41.

142. U.N. Doc. HCR/IP/1/Rev. 1986, at Conclusion No. 39 (XXXVI), para. k. (1985).

143. Burgess, "New UNHCR Guidelines," note 141 at 40.

144. Christiane Berthiaume, "Principles and Practice," *Refugees* 84 (April 1991): 10.

145. Burgess, "New UNHCR Guidelines," note 141 at 40.

146. Burgess, "New UNHCR Guidelines," note 141 at 41.

147. U.N. Doc. E/1991/28, E/CN.6/1991/14 at 20 (1991).

148. Kyra Nunez, "Women Speak Out in Central America," *Refugees* 89 (May 1992): 39–40.

149. Nancy Hatch Dupree, "Observations on Afghan Women Refugees in Pakistan: 1990," *World Refugee Survey 1991* (U.S. Committee for Refugees, 1991), 28.

150. See generally David L. Neal, "Women as a Social Group: Recognizing Sex-Based Persecution as Grounds for Asylum," *Colum. H.R. L. Rev.* 20 (1988): 203; Karen Bower, "Recognizing Violence Against Women as Persecution on the Basis of Membership in a Particular Social Group," *Geo. Immigr. L.J.* 7 (1993): 173.

151. See James C. Hathaway, *The Law of Refugee Status* (Toronto and Salem, NH: Butterworths, 1991), 162.

152. Zekiye Incirciyan, Immigration Appeal Board Decision M87–1541X, 10 August 1987, discussed by Hathaway, *Refugee Status*, note 151 at 162.

153. Maryellen Fullerton, "Persecution Due to Membership in a Particular Social Group: Jurisprudence in the Federal Republic of Germany," *Geo. Immigr. L.J.* 4 (1990): 381, 403–8. The significance of the arrest was dismissed because her association with the women's group was actually legal.

154. Jana Meredyth Talton, "Asylum for Genital Mutilation Fugitives: Building a Precedent," *Ms.* (Jan./Feb. 1992): 17.

155. *Lazo-Majano v. I.N.S.*, 813 F.2d 1432 (9th Cir. 1987).

156. See Aron et al., "Gender-Specific Terror," note 103; Stefan Teloken, "Doubly Punished," *Refugees* 71 (Dec. 1989): 38–39.

157. Burgess, "New UNHCR Guidelines," note 141 at 40.

158. Art. 6 requires states to "suppress all forms of traffic in women and exploitation of prostitution of women."

159. The efforts of Josephine Butler and others were successful in obtaining repeal of the United Kingdom's Contagious Disease Act. Judith R. Walkowitz, "Male Vice and Female Virtue: Feminism and the Politics of Prostitution in Nineteenth-Century Britain," in *Powers of Desire: The Politics of Sexuality,* ed. Ann B. Snitow, Christine Stansell, and Sharon Thompson (New York: Monthly Review Press, 1983), 419–38.

160. Ruth Rosen, *The Lost Sisterhood* (Baltimore: Johns Hopkins University Press, 1982), xii, quoted in Michael Musheno and Kathryn Seeley, "Prostitution Policy and the Women's Movement," *Contemporary Crises* 10 (1986): 237, 238.

161. G.A. Res. 317(IV) U.N. GAOR, 2 December 1949, U.N. Doc. A/1251 at 33–35 (1949). Laura Reanda describes this history in "Prostitution," note 38 at 207–11.

162. Art. 1(1), for example, requires states to punish procurers who act "even with the consent of" the prostitute.

163. Reanda, "Prostitution," note 38 at 203; Ralph Joseph, "Iran Hangs Five Women to Prove Its Islamic Zeal," *Daily Telegraph*, Feb. 1, 1989 at 10.

164. Reanda, "Prostitution," note 38 at 203.

165. Reanda, "Prostitution," note 38.

166. The short sentence of an armed rapist and the pronouncement that "Prostitutes suffer little or no sense of shame or defilement when raped" by the Supreme Court of Victoria led to an international outcry. Michael Perry, "Australian Court Rules Prostitutes Suffer Little From Rape," *Reuters Library Report,* Jan. 15, 1992 (NEXIS). CEDAW's General Recommendation No. 19 provides that prostitutes are entitled to "the equal protection of laws against rape and other forms of violence" (CEDAW, note 3 para. 20).

167. "AIDS-Infected Burmese Prostitutes Injected with Cyanide," *UPI,*

Apr. 2, 1992 (NEXIS, BC cycle). The murdered women had probably been kidnapped or sold into prostitution.

168. *The Penn State Report, Report of an International Meeting of Experts on Sexual Exploitation, Violence and Prostitution,* State College, Pennsylvania, April 1991 (New York: UNESCO and Coalition Against Trafficking in Women, 1992), 1.

169. See, e.g., U.N. Doc. E/CN.4/Sub.2/AC.2/1991/4/Add.1 (1991).

170. The Special Rapporteur regards the "underlying ethic" of human rights and anti-slavery instruments to reflect a principle that "sexual relations should always be associated with affection and never debased by the desire for power or greed for profit," and that the alienation suffered by prostitutes may be greater than that experienced by slaves because their intimacy and not just their labor is alienated. UN Doc. E/1983/7 at paras. 7, 18 (1983).

171. U.N. Doc., note 170 at para. 23.

172. U.N. Doc. E/CN.6/1992/4 para. 36, Annex at art. 2 (b) (1991); UN Doc. E/CN.6/1993/12, Annex at art. 2(b).

173. *Penn State Report,* note 168 at 7–8.

174. *Penn State Report,* note 168 at 7.

175. *Penn State Report,* note 168.

176. See CEDAW, Recommendation 19, note 3 at para. 19 states that all forms of prostitution "are incompatible with the equal enjoyment of rights by women and with respect for their rights and dignity," but also notes that they "put women at special risk of violence and abuse."

177. See information provided by the Netherlands to the Economic and Social Council in U.N. Doc. E/1990/33 paras. 18–60 (1990) (para. 20 states, "It follows from the right of self-determination . . . that [men and women are] at liberty to decide to act as a prostitute and allow another person to profit from his or her earnings"). See also Johannes C.J. Boutellier, "Prostitution, Criminal Law, and Morality in the Netherlands," *Crime, Law and Social Change* 15 (1991): 201.

178. See Jody Freeman, "The Feminist Debate over Prostitution Reform: Prostitutes' Rights Groups, Radical Feminists, and the (Im)possibility of Consent," *Berkeley Women's L.J.* 5 (1989–90): 75; Pasqua Scibelli, "Empowering Prostitutes: A Proposal for International Legal Reform," *Harv. Women's L.J.* 10 (1987): 117.

179. Freeman, "Feminist Debate," note 178 at 91.

180. U.N. Doc. E/1990/33, note 177 at para. 34.

181. Catharine MacKinnon has written extensively on this subject. See "On Torture: A Feminist Perspective on Human Rights," paper presented at the International Conference on Human Rights, Banff, Alberta, November 11, 1990.

182. Freeman, "Feminist Debate," note 178 at 95–97 (discussing theories of Catharine MacKinnon).

183. CEDAW, Recommendation 19, note 3 at para. 16.

184. See generally Sandra Coliver, ed., *Striking a Balance: Hate Speech, Freedom of Expression and Non-Discrimination* (Colcheski Human Rights Centre, University of Essex, 1992).

185. Freeman, "Feminist Debate," note 178 at 76 (quoting Robin West).

186. U.N. Doc. E/CN.6/1992/4 para. 35, annex at art. 2(b) (1991). No similar provision was included in the Draft Declaration presented to the Commission on the Status of Women in 1993. U.N. Doc. E/CN.6/1993/12 (1992).

187. CEDAW, Recommendation 19, note 3 at paras. 22–24.

188. For example, under Title VII of the Civil Rights Act of 1964 in the United States.

189. The Code of Practice was developed as an elaboration of the 1976 Equal Treatment Directive. Nicolle R. Lipper, "Sexual Harassment in the Workplace: A Comparative Study of Great Britain and the United States," *Comp. Lab. L. J.* 13 (1992): 293, 338–42; Abbie Jones, "Priority Code: Europeans Seek Unity Against Harassment," *Chi. Trib.,* Dec. 1, 1991, at 1. The Code was preceded by a 1987 study by Michael Rubenstein entitled *The Dignity of Women at Work: A Report on the Problem of Sexual Harassment in the Member States of the European Communities,* cited in Lipper, "Sexual Harassment," note 189 at 216.

190. Jones, "Priority Code," note 189.

191. Gloria Gordon, "A Worldwide Look at Sexual Harassment," *Communication World* 8(12) (Dec. 1991): 15 (NEXIS).

192. Ellen Frankel Paul, "Sexual Harassment as Sex Discrimination: A Defective Paradigm," *Yale L. & Pol'y Rev.* 8 (1990): 333, 346–53 (arguing that sexual harassment is most often a "sex-plus" phenomenon rather than directed at all women in the workplace).

193. MacKinnon wrote an early and highly influential treatise on sexual harassment which also served as a starting point for her more comprehensive theories of feminism and law, Catharine MacKinnon, *Sexual Harassment of Working Women: A Case of Sex Discrimination* (New Haven, CT: Yale University Press, 1979).

194. MacKinnon, *Sexual Harassment of Working Women,* note 193 at 88.

195. U.N. Doc. E/CN.6/1992/4, note 11 at 12 (1991). This was later revised to "any act of gender-based violence that results in, or is likely to result in, physical, sexual or psychological harm or suffering to women, including threats of such acts, coercion or arbitrary deprivation of liberty, whether occurring in public or private life." U.N. Doc. E/CN.6/1993/12, note 186 at 7.

196. U.N. Doc. E/CN.6/1992/4, note 11 at 12. This is essentially unchanged in the 1993 draft. U.N. Doc., note 186 at 7–8.

197. O.A.S. Doc., note 57 at art. 1, 2A.

198. CEDAW, Recommendation 19, note 3 at paras. 1, 7. The draft resolution on violence against women adopted by the Commission on the Status of Women in 1991 also stated that "violence against women is an equality rights issue that derives from a power imbalance between women and men in society." U.N. Doc. E/1991/28, E/CN.6/1991/14 at 55 (1991).

199. The Preamble states that gender-based violence is "also a manifestation of . . . discrimination." U.N. Doc., note 11 at 11.

200. "[V]iolence against women is a manifestation of historically unequal power relations between men and women, which have led to domination over and discrimination against women by men . . . violence against women is one of the crucial social mechanisms by which women are forced into a subordinate position compared to men." U.N. Doc. E/CN.6/1993/12, note 186 at 6.

201. O.A.S. Doc., note 57 at para. 4.

202. Art. 7 at 19, requires states to condemn, prevent, punish and eradicate "all forms of violence inflicted on women."

203. CEDAW, Recommendation 19, note 3 at para. 23, describes sexual harassment as "unwelcome sexually determined behaviour [including] physical contacts and advances, sexually coloured remarks, showing pornography and sexual demands, whether by words or actions. . . . [I]t is discriminatory

when the woman has reasonable grounds to believe that her objection would disadvantage her in connection with her employment, including recruiting or promotion, or when it creates a hostile working environment." Art. 2(b) of the Draft Declaration, note 11, simply lists "sexual harassment and intimidation in the workplace" (qualified by the Article 1 definition of violence as "any act, omission, controlling behaviour or threat . . . that results in, or is likely to result in, physical, sexual or psychological injury to women"). The OAS draft convention adopts a very broad definition of violence in its Article 1 ("any act, omission or conduct by means of which physical, sexual or mental suffering is inflicted, directly or indirectly, through deceit, seduction, threat, [harassment], coercion, or any other means, on any woman . . . [whether or not it causes physical or mental injury or suffering.]" One version of art. 2 goes on to proscribe violence by public officials or private persons in the workplace, including "sexual harassment, either imposed as a condition, or which undermines participation, effectiveness or self-esteem." O.A.S. Doc., note 57 at 17–18.

204. CEDAW, Recommendation 19, note 3 at paras. 29 and 30 (explicating art. 14 of the CEDAW Convention).
Convention).

205. CEDAW, note 3 at para. 27.

206. O.A.S. Doc., note 57 at art. 9.

207. Byrnes, "Observations," note 41 at 10–11.

208. Suggested by the Commission on the Status of Women at its thirty-fifth session (U.N. Doc. E/1991/28, E/CN.6/1991/14 at 55 (1991)) and favored in the submission by the Government of Canada to the November 1991 Expert Group Meeting in Vienna. U.N. Doc., note 41 at 13. But it was not accepted by CEDAW at its January 1992 meeting (Evatt, "Eliminating Discrimination," note 18 at 449) or by the Expert Group Meeting as an immediate strategy, U.N. Doc., note 11 at paras. 25 and 26.

209. See, e.g., the Inter-American Convention to Prevent and Punish Torture of 1985, and the European Convention on the Protection of Detainees from Torture and from Cruel, Inhuman or Degrading Treatment or Punishment of 1987.

210. O.A.S. Doc., note 57 at art. 10–16.

211. The Expert Group Meeting noted this, U.N. Doc., note 11 at paras. 21–23.

212. The World Conference on Human Rights welcomed the decision of the Commission on Human Rights at its Fiftieth session in 1993 to "consider the appointment of a special rapporteur on violence against women." U.N. Doc. A/CONF.157/DC/1/Add.1, U.N. Doc., note 6 at 24.

213. See *Report of the Commission on the Status of Women*, U.N. Doc. E/1991/28, E/CN.6/1991/14 at 37–39 (1991).

214. See Evatt, "Eliminating Discrimination," note 18 at 447–48. Amendment would be a complex procedure with many potential pitfalls. The optional procedural protocol carries the risk of a small number of ratifications but is arguably the preferable route.

215. Evatt, "Eliminating Discrimination," note 18 at 446–47.

Appendix A: Ratifications of Selected Human Rights Instruments

Ratifications as of 21 January 1994

States	International Covenant on Economic, Social and Cultural Rights	International Covenant on Civil and Political Rights	Optional Protocol to the International Covenant on Civil and Political Rights	Convention on the Right of the Child	Convention on the Elimination of All Forms of Discrimination against Women	Convention on the Political Rights of Women	Convention on the Nationality of Married Women	Convention on Consent to Marriage, Minimum Age for Marriage and Registration of Marriages	Convention against Torture and other Cruel, Inhuman or Degrading Treatment or Punishment	Convention for the Suppression of the Traffic in Persons and the Exploitation of the Prostitution of Others	European Convention for the Protection of Human Rights and Fundamental Freedoms	American Convention on Human Rights	African Charter on Human and Peoples' Rights
Afghanistan	X	X		s	s	X			X	X			
Albania	X	X	X	X		X	X			X			
Algeria	X	X^a	X	X					X^c	X			X
Angola	X	X	X	X	X	X							X
Antigua and Barbuda				X	X	X	X	X	X				
Argentina	X	X^a	X	X	X	X	X	X	X	X		X	
Armenia	X	X		X	X	X	X						
Australia	X	X^a	X	X	X	X	X		X^c				
Austria	X	X^a	X	X	X	X	X	X	X^c		X		
Azerbaijan	X	X											
Bahamas				X	X	X	X						
Bahrain				X									

Country	1	2	3	4	5	6	7	8	9	10	11	12	13	14
Bangladesh				X		X						X		
Barbados	X	X[a]	X	X	X	X		X				X	X	
Belarus	X	X[a]	X	X	X	X		X				X		X
Belgium	X		X	X	s	s		s		X		X	X	X
Belize			X	X		X		X						
Benin	X	X	X	X		X		X		X				
Bhutan			X	X										
Bolivia	X	X	X	X	X	X		s				X	X	
Bosnia & Herzegovina	X	X	X	X	X	X		X		X		X		
Botswana														X
Brazil	X	X	X	X	X	X		X		X		X	X	
Brunei Darussalam														
Bulgaria	X	X[a]	X	X	X	X		X[c]		X		X	X	
Burkina Faso			X			X				X		X		X
Burundi	X	X	X	X	X	X		X		X				X
Cambodia	X	X	X	X		X		X		X		X		
Cameroon	X	X	s	X		X		X		X		X		X
Canada	X	X[a]	X	X	X	X		X[c]			s			X
Cape Verde	X	X	X	X		X		X						X
Central Africa Republic	X	X	X	X		X		X				X		X
Chad			X											X

Ratifications as of 21 January 1994 (Continued)

States	International Covenant on Economic, Social and Cultural Rights	International Covenant on Civil and Political Rights	Optional Protocol to the International Covenant on Civil and Political Rights	Convention on the Right of the Child	Convention on the Elimination of All Forms of Discrimination against Women	Convention on the Political Rights of Women	Convention on the Nationality of Married Women	Convention on Consent to Marriage, Minimum Age for Marriage and Registration of Marriages	Convention against Torture and other Cruel, Inhuman or Degrading Treatment or Punishment	Convention for the Suppression of the Traffic in Persons and the Exploitation of the Prostitution of Others	European Convention for the Protection of Human Rights and Fundamental Freedoms	American Convention on Human Rights	African Charter on Human and Peoples' Rights
Chile	X	X[a]	X	X	X	X	s	s	X			X	
China				X	X				X				
Colombia	X	X	X	X	X	X	s		X			X	
Comoros				X									X
Congo	X	X[a]	X	X	X	X				X			X
Costa Rica	X	X	X	X	X	X		X				X	
Côte d'Ivoire	X	X		X	s				s				X
Croatia	X	X	X	X	X	X	X	X	X[c]	X			
Cuba				X	X	X	X	X	s	X			
Cyprus	X	X	X	X	X	X	X		X[c]	X	X		
Czech Republic	X	X		X	X	X		X	X		X		
Dem. People's Rep. of Korea	X	X		X									

Country											
Denmark	X	Xᵃ	X	X	X	X	X	Xᶜ	s		X
Djibouti				X	X				X	X	X
Dominica	X	X	X	X	X					X	
Dominican Republic	X	X	X	X	X	X	X	s			X
Ecuador	X	Xᵃ	X	X	X	X		Xᶜ	X	X	
Egypt	X	X	X	X	X	X		X	X		X
El Salvador	X	X	s	X	X	s					
Equatorial Guinea	X	X	X	X	X						X
Eritrea				X							
Estonia	X	X	X	X	X			X		s	
Ethiopia	X	X		X	X	X		X			
Fiji				X	X	X	X		X	X	
Finland	X	Xᵃ	X	X	X	X	X	Xᶜ	X	X	X
France	X	X	X	X	X	X	s	Xᶜ	X	X	X
Gabon	X	X		s	X	X		s			
Gambia	X	Xᵃ	X	X	X			s			X
Germany	X	X		X	X	X	X	X	X*	X	
Ghana				X	X	X	X		s		
Greece	X			X	X	X		Xᶜ		X	

Ratifications as of 21 January 1994 (Continued)

States	International Covenant on Economic, Social and Cultural Rights	International Covenant on Civil and Political Rights	Optional Protocol to the International Covenant on Civil and Political Rights	Convention on the Right of the Child	Convention on the Elimination of All Forms of Discrimination against Women	Convention on the Political Rights of Women	Convention on the Nationality of Married Women	Convention on Consent to Marriage, Minimum Age for Marriage and Registration of Marriages	Convention against Torture and other Cruel, Inhuman or Degrading Treatment or Punishment	Convention for the Suppression of the Traffic in Persons and the Exploitation of the Prostitution of Others	European Convention for the Protection of Human Rights and Fundamental Freedoms	American Convention on Human Rights	African Charter on Human and Peoples' Rights
Grenada	X	X		X	X							X	
Guatemala	X	X	s	X	X	X	X	X	X			X	
Guinea	X	X		X	X	X	s	X	X	X			X
Guinea-Bissau	X	X[a]		X	X								X
Guyana	X	X[a]	X	X	X	X			X				
Haiti		X		s	X	X	X			X		X	
Holy See				X									
Honduras	X	s	s	X	X	X	X	X		X		X	
Hungary	X	X[a]	X	X	X	X	X	X	X[c]	X	X		
Iceland	X	X[a]	X	X	X	X	X	X	s		X		
India	X	X		X	X	X	s	X		X			

Indonesia						X	X	X		s		s			
Iran	X	X				s									
Iraq	X	X			X		X				X				
Ireland	X	Xa	X		X	X	X		X	s	X			
Israel	X	X		X	X	X		s	X	X	X			
Italy	X	Xa	X	X	X	X		s	X	Xc	X	X			
Jamaica	X		X	X	X	X							X		
Japan	X	X		X	X	s					X				
Jordan	X	X		X	X	X	X		X	X	X				
Kenya	X			X	X									X	
Kiribati															
Kuwait				X							X				
Lao People's Dem. Republic				X	X	X				X	X				
Latvia	X			X	X	X			X					
Lebanon	X			X	X	X									
Lesotho	X			X	s	X	X							X	
Liberia	s	s		X	X	s					s			X	
Libyan Arab Jamahiriya	X	X	X	X	X	X	X		X	X	X			X	
Liechtenstein				s					Xc	Xc		X			

Ratifications as of 21 January 1994 (Continued)

States	International Covenant on Economic, Social and Cultural Rights	International Covenant on Civil and Political Rights	Optional Protocol to the International Covenant on Civil and Political Rights	Convention on the Rights of the Child	Convention on the Elimination of All Forms of Discrimination against Women	Convention on the Political Rights of Women	Convention on the Nationality of Married Women	Convention on Consent to Marriage, Minimum Age for Marriage and Registration of Marriages	Convention against Torture and other Cruel, Inhuman or Degrading Treatment or Punishment	Convention for the Suppression of the Traffic in Persons and the Exploitation of the Prostitution of Others	European Convention for the Protection of Human Rights and Fundamental Freedoms	American Convention on Human Rights	African Charter on Human and Peoples' Rights
Lithuania	X	X	X	X	X				X[c]		s		
Luxembourg	X	X[a]	X	s	X	X	X			X	X		
Madagascar	X	X	X	X	X	X							X
Malawi	X	X		X	X	X	X			X			X
Malaysia				X	X		X						
Maldives				X	X								
Mali	X	X	X	X	X	X	X	X		X			X
Malta	X	X[a]	X	X	X	X	X		X[c]		X		
Marshall Islands				X									
Mauritania				X		X				X			X
Mauritius	X	X		X	X	X	X	X	X	X			X
Mexico	X	X		X	X	X	X	X	X	X		X	

Country										
Micronesia					X					
Monaco					X		X[c]			
Mongolia	X	X	X	X	X	X	X			
Morocco	X	X	X	X	X	X		X		X
Mozambique		X		s				s		X
Myanmar (Burma)				s	X	s		s		
Namibia				X	X					X
Nauru										
Nepal	X	X	X	X	X	X	X			
Netherlands	X	X[a]	X	s	X	X	X[c]	X		
New Zealand	X	X[a]	X	X	X	X	X[c]	X		
Nicaragua	X	X	X	X	X	X	s	X		
Niger	X	X	X	X	X	X		X		X
Nigeria	X	X		X	X		s			X
Norway	X	X[a]	X	X	X	X	X[c]	X	X	
Oman										
Pakistan				X	X	s		X		
Panama	X	X	X	X	X		X			
Papua New Guinea				X	X					

Ratifications as of 21 January 1994 (Continued)

States	International Covenant on Economic, Social and Cultural Rights	International Covenant on Civil and Political Rights	Optional Protocol to the International Covenant on Civil and Political Rights	Convention on the Right of the Child	Convention on the Elimination of All Forms of Discrimination against Women	Convention on the Political Rights of Women	Convention on the Nationality of Married Women	Convention on Consent to Marriage, Minimum Age for Marriage and Registration of Marriages	Convention against Torture and other Cruel, Inhuman or Degrading Treatment or Punishment	Convention for the Suppression of the Traffic in Persons and the Exploitation of the Prostitution of Others	European Convention for the Protection of Human Rights and Fundamental Freedoms	American Convention on Human Rights	African Charter on Human and Peoples' Rights
Paraguay	X	X		X	X	X			X			X	
Peru	X	X[a]	X	X	X	X			X	s		X	
Philippines	X	X[a]	X	X	X	X		X	X	X			
Poland	X	X[a]	X	X	X	X	X	X	X[c]	X	X		
Portugal	X	X	X	X	X	X	s		X[c]	X	X		
Qatar				s									
Republic of Korea	X	X[a]	X	X	X	X				X			
Republic of Moldova	X	X		X		X							
Romania	X	X		X	X	X	X	X	X	X	X		
Russian Federation	X	X[a]	X	X	X	X	X		X[c]	X			
Rwanda	X	X		X	X								X

Country	1	2	3	4	5	6	7	8	9	10	11	12	13
Sahrawi Arab Dem. Rep.													X
Saint Kitts and Nevis			X										
Saint Lucia			X	X									
Saint Vincent & Grenadines	X	X	X	X	X								
Samoa		s	s						X				
San Marino	X	X	X	X					X			X	
Sao Tome & Principe			X				X		X				X
Saudi Arabia													
Senegal	X[a]	X	X	X	X			X		X	X		X
Seychelles	X	X	X	X				X		X	X		X
Sierra Leone	X		X	X	X			s		s			X
Singapore					X	X			X		X		
Slovakia	X	X	X	X	X		X	X	X	X	X	X	X
Slovenia	X[a]	X	X		X					X[c]		s	s
Solomon Islands	X				X								
Somalia	X	s	s				X	X		X			X
South Africa		s		s	s	s	X	s	X	s	X		X
Spain	X[a]	X	X	X	X	s	X	X[c]	X		X		
Sri Lanka	X[a]	X	X	X	X	s	s		X		X		
Sudan	X	X	X	X				s		s			X
Suriname	X	X	X									X	
Swaziland	s		s	X	X								

Ratifications as of 21 January 1994 (Continued)

States	International Covenant on Economic, Social and Cultural Rights	International Covenant on Civil and Political Rights	Optional Protocol to the International Covenant on Civil and Political Rights	Convention on the Right of the Child	Convention on the Elimination of All Forms of Discrimination against Women	Convention on the Political Rights of Women	Convention on the Nationality of Married Women	Convention on Consent to Marriage, Minimum Age for Marriage and Registration of Marriages	Convention against Torture and other Cruel, Inhuman or Degrading Treatment or Punishment	Convention for the Suppression of the Traffic in Persons and the Exploitation of the Prostitution of Others	European Convention for the Protection of Human Rights and Fundamental Freedoms	American Convention on Human Rights	African Charter on Human and Peoples' Rights
Sweden	X	X[a]	X	X	X	X	X	X	X[c]		X		
Switzerland	X	X[a]		s	s				X[c]		X		
Syrian Arab Rep.	X	X		X						X			
Tajikhistan				X	X								
Thailand				X	X	X							
Togo	X	X	X	X	X			X	X[c]	X			X
Tonga													
Trinidad & Tobago	X	X	X	X	X	X	X	X	X[c]			X	
Tunisia	X	X[a]		X	X	X	X	X	X[c]				X
Turkey				s	X	X			X[c]		X		
Turkmenistan				X									
Tuvalu													

Uganda	X			X	X	X	X		X				X
Ukraine	X	X^a	X	X	X	X	X		X	X			
United Arab Emirates													
United Kingdom of Great Britain and Northern Ireland	X	X^a	X^a	X	X	X		X	X^d		X		
United Republic of Tanzania	X	X		X	X	X	X						X
United States of America	s	X^a			s	X		s	s			s	
Uruguay	X	X	X	X	X	s	s	X	X^c			X	
Vanuatu				X									
Venezuela	X	X	X	X	X	X	X	X	X	X		X	
Viet Nam	X	X		X	X								
Yemen	X	X		X	X	X		X	X	X**			
Yugoslavia		X	s	X	X	X	X	X	X^c	X			
Zaire	X	X	X	X	X	X							X
Zambia	X	X	X	X	X	X	X						X
Zimbabwe	X	X^a	X	X	X								X
Total Number of States Parties	126	125	68	152	131	106	61	48	77	67	29	25	50
Total signatures not followed by ratification	2	2	4	17	7	4	9	7	16	5	3	2	0

(*Continued*)

X Ratification, accession, approval, notification or succession, acceptance or definitive signature.

s Signature not yet followed by ratification

* Ratification, accession, approval, notification or succession, acceptance or definitive signature which have been given only by the former German Democratic Republic before the reunification

** Ratification, accession, approval, notification or succession, acceptance or definitive signature which have been given only by the former Republic of Yemen

a Declaration recognizing the competence of the Human Rights Committee under article 41 of the International Covenant on Civil and Political Rights

b Declaration recognizing the competence of the Committee on the Elimination of Racial Discrimination under article 14 of the International Convention on the Elimination of All Forms of Racial Discrimination

c Declarations recognizing the competence of the Committee against Torture under Articles 21 and 22 of the Convention against Torture and Other Cruel, Inhuman or Degrading Treatment or Punishment

d Declaration under article 21 only

All parties to the European Convention have accepted Article 25 allowing for individual petitions. All parties to the American Convention automatically accept the right of individual petition under Articles 41–47, and all parties to the African Charter automatically permit individual communications under Articles 55–59.

Sources: Status of International Instruments, U.N. Doc. ST/HR/5 31 Jan. 1993, Personal Communications with the U.N. Treaty Office, Human Rights Directorate, Council of Europe, Organization of American States and Organization of African Unity, Sept. 1993

Appendix B: Model Communication Form

Date: _____

Communication to:

The Commission on the Status of Women c/o Division for the Advancement of Women Department for Policy Coordination & Sustainable Development RM. DC2-1128 P.O. Box 20 United Nations New York, 10017 NY U.S.A.	The Human Rights Committee c/o Centre for Human Rights United Nations Office 8–14 Avenue de la Paix 1211 Geneva 10, Switzerland	The Committee against Torture c/o Centre for Human Rights United Nations Office 8–14 Avenue de la Paix 1211 Geneva 10, Switzerland
Submitted for consideration under resolution 76 (V) of the Economic and Social Council, as amended by its resolutions 304 (XI) and 1983/27, all regarding "Communications concerning the status of women."	*Submitted for consideration under the Optional Protocol to the International Covenant on Civil and Political Rights*	*Submitted for consideration under the Convention Against Torture and other Cruel, Inhuman or Degrading Treatment or Punishment*

I. Information Concerning the Author of the Communication

Name: _____ First name(s): _____

Nationality: _____ Profession: _____

Present address: _____

Address for exchange of confidential correspondence (if other than present address) _____

Submitting the communication as:

a) Victim of the violation or violations set forth below   ☐
b) Appointed representative (legal counsel) of the alleged victim(s)   ☐
c) Other _____   ☐

If box (c) is indicated, the author should explain:

(i)   in what capacity he is acting on behalf of the victim(s) (e.g., family relationship or other personal links with the alleged victim: _____
_____

(ii) Why the victim(s) is (are) unable to submit the communication himself (themselves): _____

II. Information Concerning the Alleged Victim(s) (if other than author)

Name: _____ First Name(s) _____
Nationality: _____ Profession: _____
Present address or whereabouts:

III. State Concerned/Domestic Remedies

Name of the State against which the Communication is directed (in the case of the Commission on the Status of Women): _____
_____

Name of the State Party (country) to the International Covenant on Civil and Political Rights and the Optional Protocol against which the Communication is directed: _____
_____

Name of the State Party (country) to the Convention against Torture and other Cruel, Inhuman or Degrading Treatment or Punishment against which the Communication is directed: _____
_____

Articles of the International Covenant on Civil and Political Rights or the Convention against Torture allegedly violated: _____
_____

Steps taken by or on behalf of the alleged victim(s) to exhaust domestic remedies (recourse to the courts or other public authorities, whom and with what results and, if possible, enclose copies of all relevant judicial or administrative decisions): _____
_____
_____

If domestic remedies have not been exhausted, explain why: _____
_____

IV. Other International Procedures

Has the same matter been submitted for examination under another procedure of international investigation or settlement (for example, the Inter-

American Commission on Human Rights, the European Commission on Human Rights)? If so, when and with what results? _____

_____

_____

V. The Facts of the Claim (add as many pages as necessary for this
   description)

Detailed description of the facts of the alleged reliably attested injustice, and
discriminatory practices against women (in the case of the Commission), or the
alleged violation(s) (in the case of the Covenant and the Convention) (including relevant dates): _____

_____

_____

_____

Author's Signature

Appendix C: Organizational Resources

The following is an incomplete listing of organizations that work toward the development and application of international human rights law for women. Where possible, organization reports or periodicals are indicated.

A. International and Regional Governmental Organizations

Commonwealth Secretariat. Legal and Constitutional Division, Marlborough House, Pall Mall, London SW14 5HX, United Kingdom. Tel: 44-1-839-3411; Fax: 44-1-930-0827.

Council of Europe. Directorate of Human Rights, B.P. 431 R6, F 67006 Strasbourg, France.

European Community. Women's Information Office, 200 Rue de la Loi, B-1049 Brussels, Belgium. Tel: 32-2-299-411/416; Fax: 32-2-299-9283.

International Labour Office (ILO). Adviser on Women Workers, 4, Route des Morillons, CH 1211 Geneva 22, Switzerland. Tel: 41-22-799-6111; Fax: 41-22-798-8685.

Organization of American States. Inter-American Commission of Women (*CIM*), 1889 F Street NW, Washington, DC 20006 U.S.A. Tel: 202-458-6084; Fax: 202-458-6094.

United Nations Crime Prevention and Criminal Justice Branch. Vienna International Centre, P.O. Box 500, A-1400 Vienna, Austria. Tel: 43-1-21131-4269; Fax: 43-1-2192-599.

United Nations Centre for Human Rights. Palais des Nations, 1211 Geneva 10, Switzerland. Tel: 41-22-734-6011; Fax: 41-22-917-0123.

United Nations Division for the Advancement of Women (DAW). DC-2 Bldg., 12th Floor, 2 United Nations Plaza, New York, NY 10017 U.S.A. DAW has developed the Women's Information System, a computerized bibliographic data system and publishes *Women 2000.* Tel: 212-963-4668; Fax: 212-963-3463.

United Nations Development Fund for Women (UNIFEM). 304 East 45th Street, New York, NY 10017, U.S.A. Tel: 212-906-6454; Fax: 212-906-6705.

United Nations Educational, Scientific and Cultural Organization (UNESCO). Adviser on Women, 7 Place de Fontenoy, Paris 75700, France. Tel: 33-1-4568-3814; Fax: 33-1-4065-9871.

United Nations Food and Agricultural Organization (FAO). Adviser on Women and Agriculture, Via delle Terme di Caracalla, 00100 Rome, Italy.

United Nations High Commission for Refugees (UNHCR). Centre William Rappard, 154 Rue de Lausanne, 1202 Geneva, Switzerland.

United Nations International Children's Emergency Fund (UNICEF). Adviser on Women, 3 United Nations Plaza, UNICEF House, New York, NY 10017, U.S.A. Tel: 212-326-7000; Fax: 212-888-7465.

United Nations International Research and Training Institute for the Advancement of Women (INSTRAW). P.O. Box 21747, Calle Cesar Nicolas, Penson No. 102-A, Santo Domingo, Dominican Republic.

United Nations Population Fund (UNFPA). Adviser on Women, Population, and Development, 220 East 42nd Street, New York, NY 10017, U.S.A. Tel: 212-297-5141; Fax: 212-297-4907.

World Health Organization (WHO). Adviser on Women, Health, and Development, CH 1211 Geneva 27, Switzerland. Tel: 41-22-791-2111; Fax: 41-22-791-0746.

B. Non-Governmental Organizations

African Centre for Democracy and Human Rights Studies. Kairaba Avenue, K.S.M.D., Banjul, The Gambia.

Amnesty International. International Secretariat, 1 Easton Street, London WC1X 8DJ, U.K. Tel: 44-71-413-5500; Fax: 44-71-965-1157. Or 322 Eighth Avenue, New York, NY 10001, U.S.A. Tel: 212-807-8400; Fax: 212-463-9193.

Anti-Slavery Society for the Protection of Human Rights. 180 Brixton Road, London SW9 6AT, U.K. Tel: 44-71-582-4040.

Annual Review of Population Law. Harvard Law School Library, Cambridge, MA 02138 U.S.A. Publishes the *Annual Review.* Tel: 617-495-9623; Fax: 617-495-4449.

Arab Women's Solidarity Association (AWSA). 25 Murad Street, Giza 12211, Egypt. Tel: 202-723-976.

Asia Pacific Forum on Women, Law and Development. Asia Pacific Development Centre, Pesiaran Duta, P.O. Box 12224, 50770 Kuala Lumpur, Malaysia. Tel: 603-255-0648/255-0649; Fax: 603-254-1371.

Asia Pacific International Women's Rights Action Watch. 2nd floor, Block F, Anjung FELDA, Jalan Maktab, 54000 Kuala Lumpur, Malaysia. Tel: 603-291-3292; Fax: 603-292-9958.

Asian Women's Human Rights Council. P.O. Box 190, 1099 Manila, Philippines. TeleFax: 632-921-5571/999-437; Fax: 632-911-0513/0535.

Asian Womennews. AWHRC, P.O. Box 190, 1099 Manila, Philippines. TeleFax: 632-921-5571/999-437; Fax: 632-911-0513/0535.

Association of African Women for Research and Development. B.P. 3304, Dakar, Senegal. Publishes *Echo* in French and English.

Association for Women in Development. Women's Program Office, Virginia Tech, 1060 Litton Reaves Hall, Blacksburg, VA 24061-0334 U.S.A. Publishes a newsletter. Tel: 703-231-3765; Fax: 703-231-6741.

Caribbean Association for Feminist Research and Action (CAFRA). P.O. Box 422, Tunapuna, Trinidad and Tobago. Publishes *CAFRA News* quarterly in English and *Novedades CAFRA* in Spanish. Tel: 809-663-8670; Fax: 809-663-9684.

Center for Reproductive Law and Policy. 120 Wall Street, New York, NY 10005, U.S.A. Tel: 212-514-5534/5; Fax: 212-514-5538.

Centre for Women's Global Leadership. Douglas College, 27 Clifton Avenue, New Brunswick, NJ 08903, U.S.A. Tel: 908-932-8782; Fax: 908-932-1180.

Change. P.O. Box 824, London SE24 9JS, U.K. Tel/Fax: 44-71-277-6187.

Comisión para la Defensa de los Derechos Humanos en Centroamérica (CODEHUCA) (Commission for the Defense of Human Rights in Central America). Apartado Postal 189, Paseo de los Estudiantes, San José, Costa Rica. Tel: 506-34-59-70; Fax: 506-34-29-35.

Comité Latinamericano para la Defensa de los Derechos de la Mujer (CLADEM) (Latin American Committee for Defense of Women's Rights). Apartado Postal 11-0470, Lima, 11 Peru.

Equality Now. P.O. Box 20646, Columbus Circle Station, New York, NY 10023, U.S.A. Tel/Fax: 212-586-0906.

Human Rights Internet. University of Ottawa, 57 Louis Pasteur, Ottawa, Ontario, K1N 6N5, Canada. Publishes *Internet Reporter* and *The Tribune.* Tel: 613-564-3492; Fax: 613-564-4054.

Human Rights Watch. Women's Rights Project, 1922 K Street NW, Washington, DC 20005-1202, U.S.A. Publishes reports on fact-finding missions in state violations of women's rights. Tel: 202-371-6592; Fax: 202-371-0124.

Institute of Women's Law. Department of Public and International Law, University of Oslo, Karl Johans gt. 47, 0162 Oslo, Norway. Tel: 47-22-859-465; Fax: 47-22-859-466.

Institute for Women, Law and Development. 733 15th Street NW, Suite 700, Washington, DC 20005, U.S.A. Tel: 202-393-3663; Fax: 202-393-3664.

Instituto Latinoamericano de Servicios Legales Alternativos (ILSA) (Inter-American Legal Services Association). A.A. 077844, Calle 38 #16-45, Bogotá, Colombia. Publishes *Human Rights Working Paper* in English. Tel: 571-288-4772/245-5995; Fax: 571-288-4854.

Inter-African Committee on Traditional Practices Affecting the Health of Women and Children. 147 Rue de Lausanne, 1202 Geneva, Switzerland. Tel: 41-22-731-2420/732-0821; Fax: 41-22-738-1823.

Inter-American Institute of Human Rights. Women's Program, Apartado Postal 10.081, 1000 San José, Costa Rica. Tel: 506-340-404; Fax: 506-34-09-55.

International Alliance of Women. 1 Lycavittou Street, Athens, 106 72 Greece.

International Centre for Ethnic Studies. 8 Kynsey Terrace, Colombo 8, Sri Lanka. Publishes *Thatched Patio.* Tel: 94-1-698-048/685-085/694-664; Fax: 94-1-696-618/449-875.

International Centre for the Legal Protection of Human Rights (Interights). 5-15 Cromer Street, London WC1H 8LS, U.K. Publishes *Interights Bulletin.* Tel: 44-71-278-3230; Fax: 44-71-278-4334.

International Commission of Jurists (ICJ). P.O. Box 160, CH-1216, Countrin, Geneva, Switzerland. Publishes reports on fact-finding missions into state violations of women's rights and the *ICJ Review.* Tel: 41-22-788-4747; Fax: 41-22-788-4880.

International Council of Women. Avenue Louise 183, B-1050 Brussels, Belgium. Tel: 32-2-647-0905.

International Human Rights Law Group. 1601 Connecticut Avenue, NW, Suite 700, Washington, DC 20005 U.S.A. Publishes *The Docket,* and periodic reports on UN protection of women's human rights. Tel: 202-659-5023; Fax: 202-232-6731.

International League of Human Rights. 432 Park Avenue South, Suite 1103, New York, NY 10016 U.S.A. Tel: 212-684-1221; Fax: 212-684-1696.

International Service for Human Rights. Case postale 16, 1 Rue de Varembé, CH 1211 Geneva 20, Switzerland. Publishes *Human Rights Monitor* in English and French. Tel: 41-22-647-0905.

International Women's Rights Action Watch (IWRAW). Humphrey Institute, University of Minnesota, 301-19th Avenue South, Minneapolis MN 55455, U.S.A. Publishes *Women's Watch* and an annual report on the Committee on the Elimination of Discrimination against Women. Tel: 612-625-2505; Fax: 612-625-6351.

International Women's Human Rights Law Clinic. City University of New York, School of Law, 65-21 Main Street, Flushing, NY 11367, U.S.A. Tel: 718-575-4329; Fax: 718-575-4482.

International Women's Tribune Centre (IWTC). 777 United Nations Plaza, New York, NY 10017 U.S.A. Publishes *Tribune* in English, French, and Spanish. Tel: 212-687-8633; Fax: 212-661-2704.

ISIS International. Casilla 2067—Correo Centra, Santiago, Chile. Publishes the *Women's Health Journal* in English and *Revista de Salud* in Spanish. Tel: 562-633-4582; Fax: 562-638-3142; E-mail: isis@ax.apc.org.

Japanese Association of International Women's Rights. Bunkyo Women's College, 1196 Kamekubo, Oimachi, Iruma-gun, Saitama, 356 Japan. Publishes *International Women* in Japanese. Tel: 81-0492-61-6488; Fax: 81-0492-64-1150.

Latin American Institute for the Prevention of Crime and Delinquency (ILANUD). Program on Justice and Gender, O.I.J., San José, Costa Rica. Tel: 506-21-38-86; Fax: 506-33-71-75.

Lawyers Collective. Jalaram Jyot, 4th floor, 63 Janmabhoomi Marg (Ghoga Street), Fort, Bombay 400 001 India. Publishes *The Lawyers Collective* Tel: 91-22-283-0957; Fax: 91-22-287-5033.

Match International Centre. 1102-200 Elgin Street, Ottawa, Ontario K2P 1L5 Canada. Publishes *Match,* in English and French. Tel: 613-238-1312; Fax: 613-238-6867.

Netherlands Institute of Human Rights (Studie en Informatie-centrum Mensen-rechten-SIM). Domplein 24, 3512 JE Utrecht, Netherlands. Publishes *SIM Newsletter* in English. Tel: 31-30-39-40-33.

Physicians for Human Rights. Women's Rights Program, 100 Boylston Street, Boston, MA 02116, U.S.A. Publishes *The Record.* Tel: 617-695-0041; Fax: 617-695-0307.

Profamilia Servicios Legales Para Mujeres (Profamilia Legal Services for Women). Profamilia, Calle 34, No. 14-52, Bogotá, Colombia. Publishes *Profamilia* and *Mujeres en Accion* (Women in Action) in Spanish. Tel: 57-1-287-2100; Fax: 57-1-287-5530.

Reproductive Rights Project. Development Law and Policy Program, Columbia University, School of Public Health, 60 Haven Avenue, B-3, New York, NY 10032 U.S.A. Tel: 212-781-8831; Fax: 212-305-7024.

Response Directory of International Networking Resources on Violence Against Women and Children. 4136 Leland Street, Chevy Chase, MD 20815 U.S.A. Publishes *Response.*

Sociedad Mexicana pro Derechos de la Mujer. Alpina, 37, Tizapan, San Angel, 01090 México, DF, Mexico. Tel/Fax: 52-5-50-76-71.

Urban Morgan Institute for Human Rights. College of Law, University of Cincinnati, Cincinnati, OH 45221-0040 U.S.A. Tel: 513-556-0093; Fax: 513-556-6265.

Women and Law in Southern Africa Research Project. Suite 204, Stemar House, P.O. Box UA 171, Union Avenue, Harare, Zimbabwe. Publishes a newsletter. Tel: 263-4-729-151; Fax: 263-4-731-901/2.

Women in Law and Development in Africa. Suite 204, Stemar House, P.O. Box UA 171, Union Avenue, Harare, Zimbabwe. Publishes a newsletter. Tel: 263-4-729-151; Fax: 263-4-731-901/2.

Women Living Under Muslim Laws. International Solidarity Network, Bolle Postal 23-34790 Grabels (Montpellier) France. Fax: 33-67-45-25-47. Co-ordination office/Asia, 18-A Mian Mir Rd., Po Moghalpura, Lahore 54860, Pakistan; Shirkat Gah, 14/300 (27-A), Nisar Road, Lahore, Cantt., Pakistan. Tel: 92-42-372-414; Fax: 92-42-874-914. Sends out urgent action notices on violations of women's rights and publishes *Newsheet.*

Women's Exchange Programme International. Mathenesserlaan 177, 3014 HA or P.O. Box 25096, 3001 HB Rotterdam, Netherlands. Tel: 31-10-436-0166; Fax: 31-10-436-0043.

Women's Forum '95. NGO Planning Committee, 777 United Nations Plaza, 8th Floor, New York, NY 10017. Tel: 212-986-0987; Fax: 212-986-0821; E-mail: ngoforum95@igc.apc.org.

Women's International Network (WIN), 187 Grant Street, Lexington, MA 02173, U.S.A. Publishes *WIN News.* Tel: 617-862-9431.

Contributors

Abdullahi Ahmed An-Naʿim, LL.B. (Khartoum), Ph.D. (Edinburgh), is Executive Director, Human Rights Watch/Africa Watch, Washington, DC and President of the International Third World Legal Studies Association. (Human Rights Watch/Africa Watch, 1522 K Street, NW, Suite 910, Washington, DC 20005-1202, U.S.A. Tel: 202-371-6592; Fax: 202-371-0124.)

Anne Bayefsky, M.A. (Toronto), LL.B. (Toronto), M. Litt., (Oxford), is Associate Professor at the Faculty of Law, Common Law Section, University of Ottawa. She was awarded the 1992 Bora Laskin National Fellowship in Human Rights Research. (Faculty of Law, Common Law Section, University of Ottawa, Ottawa, Ontario, K1N 6N5, Canada. Tel: 613-564-4060; Fax: 613-564-9800.)

Chaloka Beyani, LL.B., LL.M. (Zam.), M.A., D. Phil. (Oxford), Fellow (Research) of Wolfson College, Faculty of Law, Oxford University. (Wolfson College, Linton Road, Oxford 2 6UD, United Kingdom. Tel: 44-865-274-100; Fax: 44-865-274-125.)

Andrew Byrnes, B.A. (Hons), LL.B. (Hons) (Australian National University), LL.M. (Harvard), LL.M. (Columbia), is a Lecturer in the Faculty of Law, University of Hong Kong. He has previously worked for the Australian Attorney-General's Department and the Australian Human Rights Commission, and has taught at the University of Sydney. He has worked with a number of international and local organizations in the area of human rights, including women's rights. (University of Hong Kong, Faculty of Law, Pokfulam Road, Hong Kong. Tel: 852-859-2942; Fax: 852-559-3543.)

Florence Butegwa, LL.B., LL.M., is the regional coordinator (Chief Executive) of Women in Law and Development in Africa (WiLDAF) a pan-African network of organizations and individuals working to promote women's rights in sixteen African countries. (Women in Law and Development in Africa, P.O. Box 4622, Lenbern House,

Union Avenue, Harare, Zimbabwe. Tel: 263-4-752-105; Fax: 263-4-731-901/2.)

Hilary Charlesworth, B.A. (Melbourne), LL.B. (Melbourne), S.J.D. (Harvard), is Professor of Law, Faculty of Law, University of Adelaide. (Faculty of Law, University of Adelaide, GPO Box 498, Adelaide, South Australia 5001. Tel: 61-8-303-4448; Fax: 61-8-303-4344.)

Rebecca J. Cook, J.D. (Georgetown), J.S.D. (Columbia), is Associate Professor (Research) and Director of the International Human Rights Programme, Faculty of Law, University of Toronto, and a member of the Washington, DC Bar. (Faculty of Law, University of Toronto, 78 Queen's Park Crescent, Toronto, Ontario, M5S 2C5, Canada. Tel: 416-978-4446; Fax: 416-978-7899.)

Radhika Coomaraswamy, B.A. (Yale), J.D. (Columbia), LL.M. (Harvard), is Director of the International Centre for Ethnic Studies, Colombo, Sri Lanka. She is a member of the UNESCO Panel of Jurists for the awarding of the Teaching of Human Rights Prize, the U.N. Special Rapporteur on Violence Against Women, and a Board member of the Asian and Pacific Forum on Women, Law, and Development. (International Centre for Ethnic Studies, 8 Kynsey Terrace, Colombo 8, Sri Lanka. Tel: 94-1-698-048, 94-1-685-085, 94-1-694-664; Fax: 94-1-696-618, 94-1-449-875.)

Rhonda Copelon, LL.B. (Yale), is Professor of Law at the City University of New York Law School and Co-Director of its International Women's Human Rights Law Clinic. She is Vice-President of the Center for Constitutional Rights in New York City and a consultant to the women's programs of the Inter-American Institute of Human Rights and the UN Latin American Institute for the Prevention of Crime and Treatment of Delinquency (ILANUD) in Costa Rica. (City University of New York, Law School at Queen's College, 65-21 Main St., Flushing, NY 11367, U.S.A. Tel: 718-575-4329; Fax: 718-575-4482.)

Joan Fitzpatrick, J.D., Diploma of Law (Oxford), is Professor of Law and Associate Dean at the University of Washington School of Law in Seattle. She presently serves on Amnesty International's U.S. Section Steering Committee on Women's Rights. She is the author of *Human Rights in Crisis: The International System for Protecting Human Rights During States of Emergency* (Philadelphia: University of Pennsylvania Press, 1993). (University of Washington, School of Law JB-20, Seattle, WA 98105, U.S.A. Tel: 206-543-9368; Fax: 206-543-5671.)

Asma Abdel Halim, LL.B., LL.M. (Khartoum), is a Research Associate at the Institute for Women, Law and Development in Washington, DC, a member of the Executive Committee of Women in Law and Development in Africa, and a member of Mutawinat (Women Working

Together), in the Sudan. (Institute for Women, Law, and Development, 733 15th St. NW, Suite 700, Washington, DC 20005, U.S.A. Tel: 202-393-3663; Fax: 202-393-3664.)

Sara Hossain, LL.B. (Oxford), graduated in law from Oxford University in 1988 and is currently practicing law in Dhaka, Bangladesh. (Dr. K. Hossain & Assocs., Chamber Bldg., Third Fl., 122-124 Motijheel C.A., Dhaka, Bangladesh. Tel: 880-2-864-966; Fax: 880-2-863-409.)

Adetoun O. Ilumoka, B.A. (Kent), LL.M. (Warwick), is a partner in A.O. Ilumoka and Associates, Lagos, Nigeria, and has held several consultancies in the field of reproductive health, most particularly on legal and ethical issues. She is also currently the Executive Director of the Empowerment and Action Research Centre (EMPARC), Lagos, Nigeria, a not-for-profit NGO involved in research and advocacy on health and human rights. (Empowerment and Action Research Centre, P.O. Box 9823, Somolu, Lagos, Nigeria. Tel: 234-1-864-656; Fax: 234-1-862-425.)

Karen Knop, B.Sc., LL.B., LL.M., is Assistant Professor at the Faculty of Law, University of Toronto. She is a member of the Team of Minority Rights Experts to Hungary and Slovakia under the Conference on Security and Cooperation in Europe, High Commissioner on National Minorities. (Faculty of Law, University of Toronto, 78 Queen's Park Cr., Toronto, Ontario M5S 2C5, Canada. Tel: 416-978-4035; Fax: 416-978-7899.)

Akua Kuenyehia, LL.B. (Gh.), B.C.L. (Oxford), is Senior Lecturer at the Faculty of Law, University of Ghana in Legon. Actively involved in the International Federation of Women Lawyers (FIDA) (President 1986–1989), she promotes women's rights and has written on legal aid services to women in Ghana. (Faculty of Law, University of Ghana, Legon, Ghana. Tel: 233-21-775-304; Fax: 233-21-223-024.)

Kathleen E. Mahoney, LL.B. (University of British Columbia), LL.M. (Cambridge), Diploma (Strasbourg), is Professor of Law at the Faculty of Law, University of Calgary. She has appeared as advocate in the Supreme Court of Canada in cases relating to freedom of speech and pornography. (Faculty of Law, University of Calgary, 2500 University Drive NW, Calgary, Alberta, T2N 1N4, Canada. Tel: 403-220-7254; Fax: 403-282-8325.)

Cecilia Medina-Quiroga, LL.M. (Chile), LL.D. (Utrecht), is Professor of International Human Rights Law at the University Diego Portales and the University of Chile, and Researcher at the Netherlands Institute of Human Rights, University of Utrecht. She was the co-director of human rights training courses for South American judges and lawyers at the Peace Palace, the Netherlands. (Facultad de Derecho, Universidad Diego Portales, Republica 105, Santiago, Chile. Tel: 56-2-697-1089; Fax: 56-2-698-6403.)

María Isabel Plata, LL.B., M.C.L., an attorney, is Deputy Director of Profamilia, the family planning association of Colombia, and a member of the International Women's Rights Action Watch and the Women's Advisory Panel of International Planned Parenthood Federation. (Profamilia, Calle 34, No. 14-52, Bogotá, Colombia. Tel: 571-287-2100; Fax: 571-287-5530.)

Mona Rishmawi, LL.M. (Columbia), Lic.D. (Ain Shams), is the Director of the Centre for the Independence of Judges and Lawyers, a component of the International Commission of Jurists. (International Commission of Jurists, P.O. Box 160, 1216 Cointrin, 26 Chemin de Joinville, Geneva, Switzerland. Tel: 41-22-788-4747; Fax: 41-22-788-4880.)

Celina Romany, J.D., LL.M., is Professor of Law at City University of New York Law School. (City University of New York, Law School at Queen's College, 65-21 Main St., Flushing, NY 11367, U.S.A. Tel: 718-575-4326; Fax: 718-575-4275.)

Kenneth Roth, B.A. (Brown), J.D. (Yale), is Executive Director, Human Rights Watch, New York City. He has conducted human rights investigations to Albania, Cambodia, Cuba, Czechoslovakia, El Salvador, Guatemala, Haiti, Kuwait, Malaysia, Poland, and Singapore. (Human Rights Watch, 485 Fifth Ave., New York, NY 10017-6104, U.S.A. Tel: 212-972-8400; Fax: 212-972-0905.)

Kirti Singh, B.A. (Hons.) (Delhi), M.A. (Delhi), LL.B., practices law in the courts in Delhi and heads the legal cell for women of the Janvadi Mahila Samiti, Delhi. As a member of the Samiti she has been advocating legal reform for women since 1980. (H32 Jangpura Extension, New Delhi 110014, India. Tel: 91-11-462-7958.)

Sonia Picado Sotela, LL.B., is Executive Director of the Inter-American Institute of Human Rights and a judge of the Inter-American Court of Human Rights. (Inter-American Institute of Human Rights, Apartado Postal 10061, San José, Costa Rica. Tel: 506-34-0404; Fax: 506-34-0955.)

Table of Cases

International Court of Justice

Human Rights Committee

Committee on the Elimination of Racial Discrimination

European Court of Human Rights and European Human Rights Commission

Inter-American Court of Human Rights and Inter-American Commission of Human Rights

Colombia

India

United States

Index

University of Pennsylvania Press
Pennsylvania Studies in Human Rights

Bert B. Lockwood, Jr., Series Editor

Professor and Director, Urban Morgan Institute for Human Rights, University of Cincinnati College of Law

Advisory Board

Marjorie Agosin
Philip Alston
Kevin Boyle
Richard P. Claude
David Weissbrodt

This book was set in Baskerville and Eras typefaces. Baskerville was designed by John Baskerville at his private press in Birmingham, England, in the eighteenth century. The first typeface to depart from oldstyle typeface design, Baskerville has more variation between thick and thin strokes. In an effort to insure that the thick and thin strokes of his typeface reproduced well on paper, John Baskerville developed the first wove paper, the surface of which was much smoother than the laid paper of the time. The development of wove paper was partly responsible for the introduction of typefaces classified as modern, which have even more contrast between thick and thin strokes.

Eras was designed in 1969 by Studio Hollenstein in Paris for the Wagner Typefoundry. A contemporary script-like version of a sans-serif typeface, the letters of Eras have a monotone stroke and are slightly inclined.

Printed on acid-free paper.